Praise for *Prayer in A[merica]*

D0769568

"*Prayer in America* will become the most tal[ked about]
Given that nothing like it has ever been written, it surely will become an overnight sensation. Readers will find it hard to put down, as I did. No one should miss it."

—Father Benedict Groeschel, C.F.R., author and television personality

"*Prayer in America* may well outsell *Gone With the Wind* and with a superior message. This book is a great idea, beautifully written and executed."

—Hugh Sidey, former *Time* columnist

"My husband [General Omar N. Bradley] would have loved this book and in particular its treatment of prayer during wartime. *Prayer in America* is nothing less than a national treasure for all Americans to appreciate now and in the future."

—Mrs. Omar "Kitty" Bradley (1922–2004)

"*Prayer in America* is a fascinating pageant of conscience, urgency, pious pleading, and faithful prayer. Jim Moore has done a truly extraordinary job in telling this nation's history through prayer, reminding us not only of the turbulent events of our history, but of our dreams and our sacred hopes."

—Rabbi David Wolpe, author and Chief Rabbi, Temple Sinai, Los Angeles, California

"Jim Moore has been prodigious in composing an exceptional, all-encompassing look into the prayer life of the country that is destined to become a national best-seller."

—Reza Aslan, author of *No God But God*

"This is a staggeringly important book from an important person. It should be read by all who hope and pray for the best in America. I am happy to recommend it highly."

—Father Theodore M. Hesburgh, C.S.C., President Emeritus, Notre Dame University

PRAYER IN AMERICA

A Spiritual History of Our Nation

JAMES P. MOORE, JR.

[Previously titled *One Nation Under God*]

IMAGE BOOKS

Doubleday
New York London Toronto
Sydney Auckland

This book is dedicated to my mother and father

Dr. and Mrs. James P. Moore

Who first taught my brothers and me how to pray

AN IMAGE BOOK
PUBLISHED BY DOUBLEDAY
Copyright © 2005 by James P. Moore, Jr.

All Rights Reserved

A hardcover edition of this book was originally published in 2005
by Doubleday under the title *One Nation Under God*.

Published in the United States by Doubleday, an imprint of The Doubleday Broadway
Publishing Group, a division of Random House, Inc., New York.
www.doubleday.com

IMAGE, DOUBLEDAY, and the portrayal of a deer drinking from a stream
are registered trademarks of Random House, Inc.

Book design by rlf Design

Library of Congress Cataloging-in-Publication Data
Moore, James P.
[One nation under God]
Prayer in America : a spiritual history of our nation / James P. Moore, Jr.
p. cm.
Originally published: One nation under God. New York : Doubleday, 2005.
ISBN-13: 978-0-385-50404-1
1. Prayer—United States—History. 2. United States—Religious life and customs. I. Title.
BV207.M66 2007
248.3'20973—dc22
2007023362

PRINTED IN THE UNITED STATES OF AMERICA

1 3 5 7 9 10 8 6 4 2

First Paperback Edition

CONTENTS

Exactly how *Prayer in America* was conceived and developed over time remains a mystery to me. I do remember, however, when I first thought about the project, during the fall of 1997.

It was early in the morning on Columbus Day that my brother called to tell me that our father had died unexpectedly in the middle of the night. It was a heart attack, and he had gone peacefully. As anyone who has ever experienced the news of that kind of sudden death can attest, the initial shock and the hours that followed became vivid memories frozen in time.

In the coming weeks and months, which would quickly turn into years, I traveled between Washington, D.C., and Ford City, Pennsylvania, to provide support to my mother, a strong and fiercely independent woman, who within weeks of my father's death was diagnosed with Parkinson's disease. During those first few car trips, as I drove along the ridges and over the crests of the spectacular Allegheny Mountains, I began to think about prayer and the part it played in my life and in the life of the country. I thought about America's earliest settlers, their heirs, and the role that prayer had played in their lives. I remembered some of the country's most prominent figures and the crucial moments in history when prayer had provided meaning and given strength when comfort and hope were hard to come by. It also struck me that if prayer represents the most private, innermost thoughts of an individual or of a people, then it must convey something rather special about us as Americans and the times in which we have lived. It was then that I began to search for some kind of book that captured the significance of prayer in American history.

I was soon spending my evenings at the Bishop Payne Library at the Virginia Theological Seminary, the largest and oldest Episcopal seminary in the United States, located a few miles from my home. Night after night and during weekends I tried to find a book that spoke comprehensively to the importance of prayer throughout American history. To my amazement, none existed. Intrigued by the possibilities, I started to put the pieces of the puzzle together myself.

Being neither a professional historian nor a clergyman, I realized that I was at a bit of a disadvantage. Nonetheless, I had a lifelong interest for everything American—history, religion, politics, literature, music, culture, sports, and so much more. Given that my initial research only fired my passions further, I thought that I could bring a fresh perspective to the subject matter. By the time I had completed the manuscript, after more than seven years, I knew I had unearthed a marvelous, hidden treasure chest. Although I knew that religious historians and even the general public were familiar with many of these riches, I also realized that the trove never before had been viewed so comprehensively. Rather excitedly, I now find myself in the position of lifting the chest's lid for others to see, hoping they will share the fascination I have felt during this incredible odyssey.

In many ways, what I refer to as "American prayer" has been a difficult subject to tackle. Most people consider prayer so private that they shy away from discussing it. After dogged probing, however, I have managed to find fascinating anecdotes, long-forgotten diary entries, and other archived material related to the importance of prayer in people's lives. Reading the prayers left behind by a fallen soldier on the battlefield or by a person long gone, whose attic treasures hold intimate details of a spiritual life never fully known by others, seems to be terribly intrusive at times. And yet the legacy discovered after piecing together their lives and peering through their special lenses to understand more fully what they encountered and how they endured can offer precious, intimate insights. The intensely private world of one individual in prayer can unlock critical portals that would otherwise remain closed to another.

Having literally combed through thousands of books, periodicals, manuscripts, letters, and documents spanning several hundred years, I have been extremely careful to verify the accuracy of the material contained in this book. Since the beginning of the republic, several writers have attempted to embellish facts surrounding the spiritual nature or public religious acts of our most beloved figures, from Washington to Lincoln and beyond. In some instances they have recorded events that never happened. In their drive to create a pious aura around a particular individual or event in U.S. history, they have let their imagination get in the way of what truly happened. Consequently, their absorbing but inaccurate accounts have been accepted as authentic by others and have ended up as gospel in subsequent writings, some two centuries later.

Quite frankly, the story of American prayer is so powerful that it does not need to rely on anything but historic fact and reasonable interpretation. To create or perpetuate myths can only take away from that compelling story. I have tried at every turn to make sure that *Prayer in America* does not fall into that trap.

AFTER SO MUCH RESEARCH and considerable reflection, I find it sadly odd that so many extensive biographies have been written about famous Americans in which the author barely, if at all, has touched upon the spiritual life of the subject. Far from being merely sentimental, prayer is an integral, vibrant influence, particularly for Americans and within the context of the American experience. If someone has devoted even a limited amount of time to things spiritual—whether as a child in Sunday school, or even in confronting the death of a parent or spouse, or even in listening respectfully to the heartfelt prayers of others—prayer can affect that individual significantly. A person's spiritual life becomes part of his or her human composite, and by its very nature should be examined. At times the search is difficult given its private nature or the biographer's preoccupation with material more titillating. Not to try to probe the character of an individual to the fullest, unlocking in some way that person's spiritual dimensions, however, forfeits a more complete and often critical story from being told.

By examining the past and present of America's prayer life, the book also provides insight into how the country and its leaders are approaching the future in an increasingly volatile and independent world, a tinderbox far different from the one our forefathers faced.

While *Prayer in America* attempts to be comprehensive, it can only touch upon a few of the figures and events in American history in which prayer has played an important role. Furthermore, it does not pretend to delve fully into such richly evocative perspectives on prayer as congregational rituals, varieties of personal expression, or theological debates on its efficacy. Rather, *Prayer in America* was written as a sweeping commentary describing how prayer has affected the country and its people over several centuries.

*　*　*

THIS BOOK WOULD NEVER have materialized without the unqualified support of a steadfast and loving family and helpful friends, including my brothers Terry and Gregory Moore, Father Benedict Groeschel, the late Diane Sherwood, Carlos Rosales-Coronado Jr., Christopher Brueningsen, Michael and Karen Yukevich, Russ and Ellen Swank, Louise and Bob Parsley, Eva and Alma Saloum, Peter Allen, Suzette Perkins, Patty Ostermick, Bob Huck, Zachary Vlahos, Alfred and Jacqueline Kingon, Wendy Smith, Jesse A. Meman, Terence and Laurence Flannery, Chip Duncan and the Duncan Group, the John Stiners, Jeffery Wieser, Vinoda Basnayake, and Holly Peppe. I also must give particular thanks to James L. Bayless, who provided unflinching support and spent countless hours reviewing the manuscript, serving as a confidant, along with Elizabeth Bayless, throughout much of the project.

I also benefited from the fine team at Doubleday that shared my vision for the book and worked with me over a long period of time, superb individuals who have included Stephen Rubin, Eric Major, Michelle Rapkin, and Kendra Harpster as well as Sean Mills, Ingrid Sterner, Frances Jones, and Frances O'Connor. My thanks also go to my literary agent, Peter Rubie, who helped me launch this effort.

I want to express my gratitude to individuals who offered invaluable support, insights, or critiques of the manuscript while it was being written. They include the late Stephen Ambrose, Martin Marty, the late Mrs. Omar Bradley, Elie Wiesel, Father William Byron, James McPherson, Father John McCloskey, and James Hutson. I am also enormously appreciative for the support of the librarians and staffs at the Library of Congress, the Landauer Library of Georgetown University, the New York Public Library, the Woodstock Theological Center, the Martin Luther King, Jr., Library of Washington, D.C., the Southern Baptist Seminary, the library of the National Museum of the American Indian, and the Washington Theological Union. The bulk of the research, however, could not have been conducted without the generous assistance of Mitzi Budde and her associates at the Bishop Payne Library at the Virginia Theological Seminary in Alexandria.

Given the intensity of the project and the need to concentrate on the manuscript, I had to find a way to escape from distractions on more than a dozen occasions and turned to several retreat centers on the East Coast. Consequently, I would like to extend my sincere thanks to Abbot

Benedict McDermott and the Benedictine priests and brothers of Mary Mother of the Church Abbey in Richmond, Virginia; the Community of Franciscan Friars of the Renewal Trinity Retreat in Larchmont, New York; the Dominican Sisters at the Dominican Retreat House in McLean, Virginia; the Sisters of Bon Secours at the Bon Secours Spiritual Center in Marriottsville, Maryland; and the Jesuit priests of the Loyola Retreat House in Faulkner, Maryland.

IN THE END *Prayer in America* has become a love story. It stands as an extraordinarily intimate portrait of our people, our relationship with God, and our entire way of life. These are the prayers of Quakers and Shakers, Sikhs and Muslims, the prayers of saints and sinners, the victorious and the downcast, the newly arrived and the born and bred. Take away the very real, palpable presence of prayer throughout the American experience, and we would be nothing more than a shadow of ourselves today. These pages stand as proof of that fact and, more important, attest to the promise of what we still may become.

—*James P. Moore, Jr.*
Washington, D.C.
October 1, 2005

Nothing in human experience compares to prayer. By any objective measure it has remained one of the most critical and indisputable influences on the course of American history and on the lives of individual Americans. Without prayer, the political, cultural, religious, social, and even economic and military annals of the nation would have been far different from what they are today. Furthermore, given the influence that the United States has wielded around the world for so many generations, even global history would have taken a far different path in the absence of American prayer.

In its purest form, prayer is the elevated communication of human beings with their God. Whether in praise, contrition, petition, or thanksgiving, prayer can be expressed in rich, elaborate rituals or in the hushed tones of complete solitude. It can also provide individuals with a vital means to cultivate a deeper understanding of themselves and those around them. Like grains of sand, however, no two individuals pray or perceive God exactly alike. Even men and women who have joined one another in religious communities over many years, worshipping at the same hours of the day, in the same manner, and under the same doctrines and traditions, recognize that there exist different understandings brought about by individual experience. In short, the act of prayer is a personal, transcendent force in the lives of men and women.

The United States, of course, does not hold a monopoly on prayer but has developed its own prayer culture, in part born from the faith traditions of other lands but also nurtured by its unique historical experience. Never having been reduced to a sentimental anachronism, as it has for other developed countries, prayer is as palpable an influence on the country today as it was on early America. Not unlike the observation of Alexis de Tocqueville made more than a hundred years earlier, British writer and critic G. K. Chesterton also was struck by the vibrant spirituality and prayer life of the country when he wrote, "America is a nation with the soul of a church."[1]

For the razor-thin minority of Americans who do not believe in prayer or who regard it with suspicion, it must be understood that prayer is not inconsequential. Rather, it is a very real presence in the lives of most Americans, individuals who are affecting the welfare of others and appreciably influencing the interests of the country every minute of every day.

Unlike many other peoples, Americans have embraced prayer individually and collectively from the beginning of the country's history. While it is true that the United States has developed a strong secular culture, it has not done so to the exclusion of its deeply rooted spirituality. Some element of prayer winds its way through almost every aspect of American life, and has forevermore become a part of the country's DNA. It may be in the simple recitation of grace at the family table or in the invocation of God in opening sessions of the U.S. House, Senate, Supreme Court, or presidential Cabinet meetings. It may be in the incorporation of prayer in the creative arts or in the millions of "prayer hits" made by Americans every day on the Internet.

THE STORY OF AMERICAN PRAYER, of course, began long before the age of European discovery and even before the earliest settlements of Native Americans. To be sure, the prayer tradition in America, much like that in the rest of the world, is part of a continuum that has existed for as long as time itself. Modern geneticists have even gone so far as to claim that the human brain has been "hardwired" for prayer, arguing that although religion has given prayer its context over the millennia, prayer has far predated organized religion. While one can hardly imagine structured religion in today's world without prayer, prayer can exist, and has done so, without the benefit of established churches.

As important, as ennobling, and as divisive as religion has been in human history, prayer stands as the great common denominator among human beings. Long before Moses parted the Red Sea, before Buddha described the path toward nirvana, before Christ died on the cross, and before Muhammad revealed the message of the Koran, there was prayer. The earliest recorded prayers and hymns were among the first writings ever discovered by archaeologists, found on stone tablets from the middle of the third millennium B.C.[2] It was prayer that became the significant

We did not think of the great open plains, the beautiful rolling hills, and the winding streams with tangled growth, as "wild." Only to the white man was nature "wilderness," and only to him was the land "infested" with "wild" animals and "savage" people. To us it was tame. Earth was bountiful, and we were surrounded with the blessings of the Great Mystery.[3]

To the first European settlers, America represented divine intervention, God's giving humanity a second chance to fulfill a sacred destiny. Not unlike the people in Exodus, early settlers saw the Almighty's hand guiding them to a land that promised new life. Through prayer they hoped to lead an inspired existence of disciplined spirituality and personal rigor that would in turn cement their relationship with God, who had granted them such blessings.

Prayer gave enslaved African-Americans, who would be denied the true promise of America for generations, the faith, hope, and love to prevail under the most horrific circumstances. For other immigrants arriving on the country's shores, America represented a refuge from harm of every kind, and for most of them the practice of prayer only became more engrained into their lives once they arrived.

AMERICAN PRAYER has been behind a number of firsts in the cultural realm. The first book printed in America, for example, was a prayer book, and the first songbook published was a hymnal. The first poems and symphonies; the first authentically American opera, *Porgy and Bess;* and the first talking movie, *The Jazz Singer,* the story about a Jewish cantor, all were steeped in prayer. The great African-American spirituals, infused with prayer and the rhythms of another continent, spawned such American musical idioms as jazz, the blues, and gospel. The first successful self-help program, Alcoholics Anonymous, was principally founded on the notion that prayer could transfer human weakness away from the power of addiction. Every one of the country's major anthems, including "The Star-Spangled Banner," "America," and "My Country 'Tis of Thee," speaks in some way of prayer.

Everyday life also holds continuous reminders of the institution of prayer and the country's spiritual heritage, from a skyline of church steeples to makeshift altars along highways and city streets memorializing those who have died. Even government has done its part to personalize the importance of God and prayer to the country. The national mottoes "In God We Trust" and "Annuit Coeptis," translated as "Providence has favored our undertakings," a clause incorporated into the Great Seal of the United States by the Founding Fathers, have been imprinted on the nation's currency. The officially recognized National Day of Prayer, and the inclusion of the words "under God" in the Pledge of Allegiance, more recent developments, have become part of the national cadence. Even individual states have developed their own defining mottoes like Arizona's "God Enriches," South Dakota's "Under God the People Rule," Ohio's "With God All Things Are Possible," and Colorado's "Nothing Without Providence."

The continuum of God and prayer in the nation's heritage can be found in the monuments the United States has built to remind future generations of their legacy. Standing in the Rotunda of the U.S. Capitol, that central axis where the House of Representatives and the Senate come together structurally and symbolically, a person can view several massive paintings that attest to America's spiritual past—Columbus and his men kneeling in prayer after landing in the New World, Pocahontas in prayer as she is about to be baptized, Pilgrim families praying with wonder and trepidation as their ship the *Speedwell* embarks for America. The belted mural that surrounds the great dome, with George Washington looking down from above, depicts the prayerful solemnity of the first settlers in New England and the somber burial of the Spanish explorer Hernando de Soto along the Mississippi River.

Other reminders of American prayer lie beyond Capitol Hill. Visiting the Washington Monument, few tourists realize that engraved on the brass cap of the obelisk 555 feet above the ground are the words "Praise be to God." Other visitors miss the quotation chiseled into the rotunda of the Jefferson Memorial, taken from a letter Thomas Jefferson wrote to John Adams, which begins with the words "The God who gave us life gave us liberty at the same time." Not far away, carved into the granite of the Lincoln Memorial, is the entire text of Lincoln's second inaugural address, a prayer unto itself and the greatest speech of its kind in American history. If a person looks for it, evidence of American prayer can be found everywhere in the nation's capital.

Ever since the first oath of office was administered to George Washington in 1789, every President of the United States has invoked the name of God and prayer, either directly or indirectly, in his inaugural address. Even presidents whose religious piety was questionable at best felt compelled to set the tone for their administrations and agendas for the nation by acknowledging the hand of God in the business of the country. Indeed, most remarks delivered by presidents from the Oval Office end with the signature "and may God bless America." The line is so expected that without it, most individuals would notice consciously or subconsciously and question why it had been omitted.

Although Americans may recoil at public displays of religious devotion that seem either affected or to exceed undefined boundaries of taste, they still want their national politicians to show the pious humility that comes with prayer and the recognition of a higher power. That is why presidents, joined by justices of the Supreme Court and members of Congress, have welcomed the chance to attend annual prayer breakfasts on the National Day of Prayer, an observance instituted over fifty years ago, and why elected officials publicly bristle when judges try to eliminate words like "under God" from the Pledge of Allegiance.

While national memorials and customs tell one story, the lives of individual Americans who have been deeply influenced by prayer and have made a difference in the life of the country reveal another. Without prayer, the "kitchen conversion" of Martin Luther King, Jr., at a critical point in his ministry, might not have carried on his leadership of the modern civil rights movement; Woody Guthrie, Elvis Presley, and Johnny Cash might not have continued to compose songs or perform onstage after confronting personal setbacks; Abraham Lincoln might not have endured the enormous pressures of war and family tragedy; Anne Bradstreet and Harriet Beecher Stowe might not have written their seminal works at pivotal moments; and such very different men as Woodrow Wilson, Jimmy Carter, and George W. Bush might not have entered public life, let alone become President.

While prayer has remained such a decisive, uplifting force for individual Americans and for the country as a whole, it has become the subject of divisive legal battles. In the twists of modern-day life, the country's courts have interpreted the U.S. Constitution, and the motives of the Founding Fathers, as largely confining prayer to the narrower context of established religion. Decisions handed down over the past several decades have only guaranteed that the subject of prayer, particularly in public places, will be debated for generations.

At the same time, it would be remiss to ignore the fact that prayer has been abused throughout American history. The Civil War, for example, not only tested the superiority of one military force over another but also became a contest in the minds of many as to which petitioner could summon God's favor more. Most egregiously, prayer has been conjured up to condone evil acts of all kinds. From recitations by members of the Ku Klux Klan before a lynching to the spiritual entreaties of suicide bombers before an attack, prayer has been used in heinously corrupt ways. Its powerful symbolism and ages-long practice are so entrenched in the human psyche that it has become a vehicle for justifications of every kind.

Wherever the spiritual compass lies for each individual, certain aspects of modern American life intrude on the practice of prayer, at times denying individuals the solitude of those spiritual "rests." In his autobiography J. C. Penney, the founder of the retail chain, recalled a letter he had read from an unnamed Trappist monk in the 1950s, most probably Thomas Merton, who succinctly captured the quandary of many Americans in praying in the modern world and his prescription for dealing with it:

> We Americans want everything in a hurry. Yet an interior life, dedicated to the practice of prayer, is not the work of a year, or even ten. We of the high-strung western world seek the natural outlet of nervous energy in action. It takes us a long time to discover the fact that mental activity can become the best and most satisfying kind of action, that is interaction, which takes place between God and the Praying Soul . . . There are two main pitfalls on the road to mastery of the art of prayer. If a person gets what he asks for, his humility is in danger. If he fails to get what he asks for, he is apt to lose confidence. Indeed no matter whether prayer seems to be succeeding or failing, humility and confidence are two virtues, which are absolutely essential.[4]

And yet prayer has remained a critical anchor in the lives of most Americans, and even for those with the most profound faith its practice is the very act of passionate uncertainty.

DESPITE THE ROLE of prayer in American life, historians, even religious historians, have neglected this important part of the country's past, as well as the spirituality and even patriotism to which it is so often joined.

There have been moments when, together as a people, the nation has been seriously shaken by catastrophic events and has turned to prayer as a bulwark, uniting Americans against serious division and chaos. Prayer has even become a critical refuge, the place to turn to in the face of human failure or the fallibility of human institutions.

In a word, then, prayer is dynamic. It is not simply a static force in a person's life or in the life of the nation. If a person utters the same prayer as a child and then again as an adult, its meaning intrinsically changes. Growth and endurance make it so, altering its meaning and even its tonal inflection. For someone saying the Prayer of Saint Francis or singing "God Bless America" on the day before September 11, 2001, and then again forty-eight hours later, the entire meaning changed. Certain phrases take on a nuance that did not exist earlier. In a short time, those same invocations will take on a different connotation yet again. Prayer does not sit still.

If American history can be likened to a great musical composition, prayer must be seen as an integral and powerful theme throughout the piece. At times it is softer; louder at others. It has its own rhythm, its own pulse. It is always there, fundamentally contributing to whatever melody may be playing. Most important, it is an integral component to the arrangement. To remove it is to take away the depth, the breadth, and the richness of what gives the work, at least in part, its special character.

To dismiss prayer in the life of America is to embark on a fool's errand. Prayer has been and always will be an integral part of the national character. It is clearly a subject that must be explored in far greater depth if anyone is to understand the people who have made the United States what it is today and what it will be tomorrow.

CHAPTER 1

THE INHABITANTS, EXPLORERS, AND SETTLERS

God created this Indian country and it was like He spread out a big blanket. He put the Indians on it. They were created here in this country, and that was the time this river started to run. Then God created fish in this river and put deer in these mountains and made laws through which has come the increase of game and fish . . . Whenever the seasons open I raise my heart in thanks to the Creator for his bounty that this food has come.

—Meninock, Yakima chief, 1915

*T*HE HISTORY OF PRAYER in America began unfolding long before the golden age of exploration, a fact often missed by modern Americans. Nonetheless, when European settlers arrived in the New World, they did not at first recognize the unique spiritual heritage of Native Americans. Religious, cultural, and language barriers too often obfuscated the fact that these various tribes and nations had developed their own prayers and devotional rituals over generations. While Native Americans' conception of a higher power had been formed in isolation of revelations experienced by other civilizations, their desire to express themselves spiritually was every bit as intense and as devout. In time both groups would come to recognize their common spirituality.

On the eve of Christopher Columbus's arrival in the New World, more than 250 languages, largely unintelligible to one another, were spoken throughout the territory that now makes up the United States.[1] From the Inuits of the Arctic, whom the English voyager Martin

Frobisher first encountered, to the Seminoles of Florida, who greeted the Spanish explorer Ponce de León in his quest for the fountain of youth, entire Indian nations had developed independent cultures. For Native Americans, prayer stood as a channel to some guiding force that they did not clearly understand but that, they believed, contributed in some important way to their existence. Central to all of them was a profound sense of a higher power, who had a critical impact on their welfare.

AMERICAN INDIANS THRIVED in a daily rhythm in which the word "religion" did not exist, simply because no distinct creed of faith could be separated from existence itself. No churches were built; no weekdays were set aside for worship. Life and prayer were practically seamless. In effect, God cast no shadow because Native Americans integrated the divine into all things. An etched panel at the Jemez State Monument in New Mexico, written by an anonymous member of the Jemez tribe, captures the basic Indian approach to spirituality: "We have no word that translates what is meant by 'religion.' We have a spiritual life that is part of us twenty-four hours a day. It determines our relationship with the natural world of our fellow man. Our religious practices are the same as in the time of our ancestors."[2]

Through the power, wisdom, and genuine love of the Great Creator, all living things by extension were sacred. Indeed the word "sacred" was interwoven into the languages and pervaded the thoughts of all Native Americans. Its very notion sustained a reverence that reminded them always of their obligations as inheritors of the earth and vanguards of their people—past, present, and future. In many ways Native Americans were more attuned to prayer than most newly arrived Europeans and Africans. They often built doors to their tepees and huts to the East, allowing them to wake up in the morning, face the sun, and pray as their first act of the day. "Each soul must meet the morning sun, the new sweet earth, and the Great Silence alone," was how Ohiyesa put it.[3] One Indian chief, in what today is Oklahoma, put it another way more than a century ago: "When you arise in the morning, give thanks for the morning light. Give thanks for your life and strength. Give thanks for your food and give thanks for the joy of living. And if per chance you see no reason for giving thanks, rest assured the fault is in yourself."[4]

Few early Native Americans took their lives for granted. In prayer they thanked all living things. Only in practice did prayer differ from nation to nation, defined by geography, climate, harvests, hunting, and other circumstances. The Hupas of northwestern California held an annual acorn feast, normally celebrated in November, to express their gratitude for the latest acorn harvest. After the elaborate sacred invocations were finished, the tribe would eat the first acorns that had fallen from the tan oak trees nearby, jubilant that for another season the Creator had blessed them. "All plants are our brothers and sisters," they believed. "They talk to us and if we listen, we can hear them." A Choctaw hunter in modern Louisiana would always whisper before killing his prey, "Deer, I am sorry to hurt you. But the people are hungry."[5] America's flora and fauna were sacred, integral members of the Indian life cycle.

The environment played an important part in the life of Native Americans, contributing to a peaceful spiritual existence for the Navajos of the southwest deserts or the more ambitious Algonquins in the woodlands of the Northeast. The Inuits of the Arctic, better known as Eskimos, were a case in point. Never numbering more than 100,000 and spread over a territory that extended from Alaska to Greenland, they were greatly influenced by climate and their immediate surroundings. The water and the sky were the focus of their needs for survival and, in turn, of their prayers. The aurora borealis, those great northern lights, constantly reminded them of the wonders of the universe.

In the midst of the long, dark winter and the seemingly endless daylight of summer, the Inuits conjured up fascinating tales that gave rise to their prayers. Some stories told of the old woman who lived under the sea and interacted with the waters and the great spirits of the earth where the Inuits gathered most of their food. Prayer was such a potent force for the Inuit people that it was used as an independent, powerful commodity to be traded. These prayers, known as *serrats,* originated from the visions of blessed people and were thought to have the power to either heal or impart good fortune. Seen as independent forces in their own right, *serrats* would be bartered, allowing the owner to receive something of great value in return.[6]

While each person would commune with the spirit world throughout the day, their prayers as second nature to them as breathing, they would also join one another in offering special invocations. Within a group, prayer could be spoken, chanted, whispered, or sung, almost always through one individual on behalf of everyone else. The words, rhythms, and melodies were carefully chosen to convey the images and the proper setting of a particular petition. Special ceremonial dances were performed to provide meaning to a prayer, each step and bodily movement holding special significance. Together penitents worked toward achieving "one thought," a collective mindfulness in reaching out to a higher power.

At critical moments in their lives, Native Americans relied on the skills of the shaman. The shaman, either a man or a woman, could possess various levels of spiritual potency and perform certain rituals that varied widely from tribe to tribe. Despite the differences, however, shamans shared one vital purpose: they served as a medium to the spiritual world.

A tribe would determine whether a person was destined to become a shaman during his or her childhood and adolescence. At a tender age, a future shaman would undergo some spiritual experience, not always comprehensible to others but confirmed and blessed by the elders. From that transforming moment, the tribe would formally recognize the chosen one's calling and ability to help effect change in the future life of the tribe.

The novice shaman would then face an initiation rite in which he or she would attest to out-of-body experiences. Whether soaring to the heavens or plunging to the depths of the underworld, a shaman would meet the spirits with whom a lifetime relationship would be formed. These gods and other supernatural forces would provide the shaman with the wherewithal to perform everything from curing sickness to ensuring that the fall harvest or the upcoming buffalo hunt would yield enough food for the tribe.

In their vision quests and supplications to the supernatural, Native Americans used objects and natural substances to enhance their rituals. Prayer sticks, prayer bowls, and prayer feathers were integral to their ceremonies, as were animal skulls and bones. Colorful attire was worn to project a particular mood and carry special petitions to the Creator. Special drums, bells, and wind instruments were played only in sacred settings. Tobacco, corn husks, and even hallucinatory peyote from western cactus were used to heighten the human senses in spiritual encounters.

One of the more endearing prayer ceremonies involved the use of the sacred pipe, a tradition among tribes in the West and Midwest. Finding a special, holy spot, a shaman or elder would pack a long ornamental pipe with some natural substance and turn the bowl of the pipe in the direction of the heavens, as if to offer the Almighty a smoke from his pipe.

Like the practitioners of many world religions, Native Americans showed their reverence by both fasting and praying, cleansing their bodies and souls in the process. Not unlike Muslims who wash their feet and hands before entering a mosque, many Indians built sweat lodges, the equivalent of saunas, to cleanse themselves before praying on important occasions. The Iroquois nation in today's upstate New York even conducted "thanksgiving addresses" every time a tribal ceremony was held to show gratitude to their Creator. More regularly, they would chant a series of spiritual "gratitudes" similar to the litanies of Catholics or the mantras of Asian religions. To lend their prayer of thanks the greatest piety possible, they would add some eighteen different expressions of gratitude.

Indians also took pilgrimages to sacred sites that reinforced their ties to ancient traditions. These holy places could be the edge of a village boundary or some destination several days away. Each year, for example, the men of the Papago tribe in modern-day Arizona would travel by foot for several days to the Gulf of California, where they would gather salt for their village. Taking a carefully charted route, the pilgrims, the youngest being no more than sixteen years old, would pray at designated stops along the way. During one leg of the journey and for a twenty-four-hour period, the men would neither eat nor drink, each receiving a personal vision from the spiritual world. Once they reached the salt deposits along the shore, they would pray far more intensely, offering cornmeal and prayer sticks, which they had prayed over before leaving their village, to show their devotion. When they returned home with their sacks of salt, intended to be used for everything from food preparation to ceremonial rituals, they would pray again in gratitude for the gifts they had been given and for having been able to endure the journey.

MOST NATIVE AMERICANS lacked a written language, so their prayers were passed down verbally from one generation to the next. Fascinated by the lore and richness of Indian culture, Europeans and their early American descendants recorded many of the prayers and spiritual practices of the tribes and nations on the continent.

One prayer, documented by John Heckewelder, a prominent Moravian missionary from eastern Pennsylvania, was titled "The Song of the Lenape Warriors Going against the Enemy." As the Lenape invocation shows, a warrior preparing for battle experienced much of the same anxieties and emotions that any modern American GI would face. In the end prayer provided a spiritual shield to what might lie ahead:

> *O poor me!*
> *Who am going out to fight the enemy*
> *And know not whether I shall return again,*
> *To enjoy the embraces of my children*
> *And my wife.*
> *O poor creature!*
> *Whose life is not in his own hands,*
> *Who has no power over his own body,*
> *But tries to do his duty*
> *For the welfare of his nation.*
> *O! thou Great Spirit above!*
> *Take pity on my children*
> *And on my wife!*
> *Prevent their mourning on my account!*
> *Grant that I may be successful in this attempt—*
> *That I may slay my enemy,*
> *And bring home the trophies of war*
> *To my dear family and friends,*
> *That we may rejoice together.*
> *O! Take pity on me!*
> *Give me strength and courage to meet my enemy,*
> *Suffer me to return again to my children,*
> *To my wife*
> *And to my relations!*
> *Take pity on me and preserve my life*
> *And I will make to thee a sacrifice.*[7]

There were less stressful prayer rites, invocations joyously offered at seminal moments in a person's life. The Zunis of the Southwest developed some of the most elaborate prayer rituals of any of the ancient American civilizations, the sun being the focus of their attention.

In one of the most important Zuni rites, each infant, eight days after birth, was made ready for presentation to the sun, the equivalent of a Christian baptism. His "aunts," the women of his father's clan, would wash his head and begin a strict, time-honored rite. Cornmeal was then fixed to the baby's hand as he was taken outside at sunrise and gently cradled. In facing the sun to the east, the paternal grandmother would sprinkle cornmeal around the baby's body while invoking the prayer:

> *Now this is the day,*
> *Our child,*
> *Into the daylight*
> *You will go out standing . . .*
> *Our child,*
> *It is your day.*
> *This day,*
> *The flesh of white corn,*
> *Prayer meal,*
> *To our sun father*
> *This prayer meal we offer.*
> *May your road be fulfilled*
> *Reaching to the road of your sun father,*
> *When your road is fulfilled*
> *In your thoughts (may we live).*
> *May we be the ones whom your thoughts will embrace,*
> *For this, on this day*
> *To our sun father.*
> *We offer prayer meal.*
> *To this end:*
> *May you help us all to finish our roads.*[8]

Later events in the child's life, from the first laugh to the advent of adolescence, would be commemorated with special prayer rituals as well. Every Indian mother, Zuni or otherwise, considered her first duty to teach her child about the sacredness of life and death, and the importance of prayer.

MODERN AMERICANS may have difficulty differentiating between the great Native American nations and identifying their leaders, but the distinctions are enormous. There was the Shawnee prophet Tenskwatawa, from modern-day Ohio, who underwent an extraordinary mystical experience through his prayers. In his visions, he spoke of how he saw the heaven and the hell that awaited his kinsmen after earthly life. He also summoned in his mind the distant past and the future, mesmerizing the Shawnees with his riveting tales. There were the prophets Wodziwob and Wovoka of the northern Paiutes in the area of today's Nevada, who initiated two different movements to promote the Ghost Dance, a prayer ritual that rapidly spread across American tribes in the late nineteenth century, to implore the Creator to help them confront the realities of living alongside the white man.

No single figure, however, provided as many insights into the spirituality of Native America as Black Elk, a member of the Oglala Sioux. Black Elk's history came fully to light when Nebraska's poet laureate John G. Neihardt first recorded his story in 1931. Born during the Civil War, Black Elk had a dramatic vision on his eighteenth birthday, when his prayers sparked a new awareness of his universe. Grandfathers, representing north, south, east, and west, told him that he had been given special powers to become "the center of the nation's hoop," intended to "make it live." He spent the rest of his life trying to discover exactly what the vision meant. Joining Buffalo Bill's circus and ultimately traveling to New York and Europe to learn the ways of non-Indians, he came to understand more than most the spiritual ties that bind individuals to their God.

Although he converted to Catholicism after a near-death experience in 1904 and never again practiced his Indian rituals, Black Elk continued to return to his roots, both in prayer and in thought, providing invaluable accounts of the prayer life of his tribe. He also recorded for posterity a series of prayers that he had learned during childhood and others that he had composed. One of his more endearing prayers he wrote spoke to God, as so many Indian prayers did, as the great Creator, the first among all ancestors:

I am sending a voice, Great Spirit, my Grandfather, forgetting nothing you have made, the stars of the universe and the grasses of the earth. You have said to me, when I was still young and could hope, that in difficulty I should send a voice four times, once for each quarter of the earth, and you would hear me. Today I send a voice for people in despair . . . Hear me, not for myself, but for my people; I am old. Hear me that they once more go back into the sacred hoop and find the good red road, the shielding tree![9]

Black Elk's legacy allowed people of all faiths to understand that when it came to the practice of prayer, they had far more in common with one another than not. For most Europeans, Native American spirituality was far too exotic and impenetrable to comprehend. More important, there was an overriding desire to convert them to the tenets of Christianity.

Ministers like John Eliot spent their entire adult lives trying to convert Indians to Christianity, translating the Bible and prayer books into native languages, preaching and praying in their newly learned exotic tongues. They even created "praying towns," villages constructed solely for the purpose of containing and immersing Native Americans in Scripture, prayer, and the ways of Europeans. By 1674, fourteen praying towns in the Massachusetts Bay Colony would be formed through the effort of Eliot and others with 2,200 Indians confined to the mainland and as many as 2,600 moved to the island of Martha's Vineyard. It was an experiment doomed to failure given such an ill-conceived notion, not to mention the logistics, and within a few years they would cease to exist.

Nevertheless, the praying towns would become one of the many early indicators of problems to come. Eventually the strife between Native Americans and the European settlers and their descendants would evolve into peaceful coexistence and support, but the years ahead would be tumultuous ones.

FOR THE ELITE OF EUROPE, restless and consumed by conquests of all kinds, the notion of reaching, exploring, and finally settling new lands to the west proved irresistible. Gaining new fortunes, extending territorial empires, and converting fresh souls to Christianity provided the high stakes. With each new voyage across the Atlantic followed by tales and evidence of extraordinary discoveries, the draw of the New World became more seductive.

Sailing across the ocean in the late fifteenth and the sixteenth century was as daunting for these European explorers as it had been for the Vikings five hundred years earlier. Royal investment in men, ships, and provisions, not to mention the soaring and unpredictable costs associated with extended voyages, was a chancy proposition at best. Even the notion that the world was round was far too theoretical for most people, a fact that would not be conclusively proven until the explorer Ferdinand Magellan and his men circled the globe almost twenty years later.

For sailors and their captains it was critical that Divine Providence be on their side to help them surmount overwhelming odds on the high seas. Consequently, prayer was structured to become part of their daily lives. From the time they were woken by the call to prayer before morning watch to the moment they fell back to sleep, they were continually reminded of their relationship to the "Master of the Universe." For some of these sailors prayer was a short-term life-insurance policy. For others it was an inextricable part of their being, a lifetime link with God.

Often christened with a variation on the name of God, the Virgin Mary, or a saint, ships became another means for solidifying a spiritual bond with the Almighty. Although the construction of ships vastly improved over time, ocean vessels needed constant attending, particularly from seawater seeping or pouring into ship bilges. Vigilance and a quick response to the fickle temperament of both sea and weather were required at all times.

Thanks to his meticulous diary, letters, and notes, Christopher Columbus left behind rich details of his voyages. In his historic first letter to his sponsors King Ferdinand and Queen Isabella of Spain, announcing his discovery, he wrote, "I went into the ocean where many islands inhabited by innumerable people I found."[10] With this opening line scripted in Latin, the written history of the Americas had begun.

For all of his virtues and failings, Columbus was a devout and religious man. Like his patrons King Ferdinand and Queen Isabella, he belonged to the Secular Franciscan Order, a lay group of Catholics committed to an intense daily prayer life, among other things. "I am a most unworthy sinner, but I have cried out to the Lord for grace and mercy, and they have covered me completely," he confessed.[11] Ironically, Columbus's deeply held faith made him a bold visionary for fifteenth-century Europe, combining science with religious belief. While many Europeans continued to doubt the theory of a round earth, Columbus put himself at great personal risk to prove reality by reaching the trading routes of the East. After all, it would be more than a hundred years before Galileo refined the work of Copernicus on the dynamics of a revolving earth, ultimately incurring the wrath of the Holy See.

Ready to embark on his journey with a crew of 120 men aboard his flagship, the *Santa María,* and the smaller caravels, the *Niña* and *Pinta,* Columbus did not order the ships to set sail until he had pleaded before his men in Latin, "Jesus through Mary, Be with us on our way."[12] Columbus and his men took off from Palos, Spain, with provisions to last them a year, their white sails painted with red crosses, the sign of their Christian faith.

During the voyage, whether in his private cabin or with his men on deck, Columbus prayed three times a day—sometime between 8 and 9 a.m. (terce), between noon and sunset (vespers), and between 6 and 9 p.m. (compline)—the same discipline followed by religious orders throughout Europe. Although many of his men had long strayed from their religious roots, Columbus expected them to be as diligent in their prayers as they were in their onboard duties. There were no exceptions. Despite slight variances from one ship to another, all the crews shared the same daily routine, often hearing one another's prayers across the lapping of the waves.

Consequently, the custom on these long and arduous voyages called for one of the youngest mates aboard to awaken the men each morning by chanting:

> *Blessed be the light of day*
> *And the Holy Cross, we say;*
> *And the Lord of the Verite*
> *And the Holy Trinity*
> *Blessed be th' immortal soul*
> *And the Lord who keeps it whole,*
> *Blessed be the light of day*
> *And He who sends the night away.*[13]

Roused from their sleep, the sailors would then gather on deck in loose formation, reciting the Our Father, the Hail Mary, and their signature prayer:

> *God give us good days, good voyage, good passage to the ship,*
> *sir captain and master and good company,*
> *so let there be a good voyage;*
> *many good days may God grant your graces, gentlemen of the afterguard*
> *and gentlemen forward.*[14]

At sunset all hands would assemble while the ship's mate lit a lamp and led the men once again in reciting the same set of prayers. As the ship sailed into the darkness, fixed firmly on the stars above to stay its course, the boy on duty would pierce the silence and the steady beat of the waves, chanting each half hour:

> *One glass is gone*
> *and now the second floweth;*
> *more shall run down*
> *if my God willeth.*
> *To my God let's pray*
> *to give us a good voyage.*

While prayer served to secure divine protection, it also created discipline. What the men needed more than physical sustenance was the psychological wherewithal to confront the unknown. False landfall sightings, real and imagined fears, and sheer boredom had taken their toll by October 10, when the sailors on the *Santa María* openly revolted.[15] The next day, however, circumstances changed dramatically. Although they still could not see land, there was no mistaking the signs of life everywhere, from floating branches to circling birds. That evening after vespers, Columbus stood on the sterncastle of the *Santa María* and addressed his crew. First he delivered a prayer of thanksgiving, and then reminded them how their lack of faith only twenty-four hours earlier had almost led to their defeat.[16] Their prayers, after all, had been answered.

A few hours later, under the light of a past-full moon, the lookout on the *Pinta* finally sighted the eastern coastline of one of the Bahamas. By midday, Columbus and his men had shipped ashore, and in a scene that would be repeated from site to site, they dropped to their knees to offer thanks and invoke God's continued favor:

> *O Lord, Almighty and everlasting God,*
> *by Thy holy Word Thou hast created the heaven,*
> *and the earth, and the sea;*
> *blessed and glorified be Thy name, and praised be Thy Majesty,*
> *which hath deigned to use us, Thy humble servants,*
> *that Thy holy Name may be proclaimed in this second part of the earth.*[17]

At his first landing on the island of San Salvador (Holy Savior), and at every landing thereafter, Columbus erected a wooden cross and recited a brief prayer on his knees, thanking God and taking "possession" of the new lands on behalf of the Christian faith and the King and Queen of Spain.[18]

Although Columbus had not yet found the direct trade route to the East Indies, he was vindicated in the eyes of his patrons by his astonishing discoveries and by the enormous potential to convert so many Indians to Christianity, buying time and more investment for future voyages. Once his exploits became known, the major European powers tripped over one another to finance expeditions to the New World. To varying degrees, the prayer regimen that had been such a fixture during Columbus's voyages remained an integral part of the age of discovery. For the sailors of Renaissance Europe on their way across the Atlantic, prayer was so much a part of daily life that it even entered many of the sea chanteys they sang as they went about their duties. Even in play, pleas for fair weather and calm seas were not far from their minds.

WHILE A SECULAR CREW held religious observances on these early trips, it was not long before priests and ministers accompanied the voyages, supporting their captains on board while bringing Christianity to the natives of the Western Hemisphere. Sebastian Cabot, the son of the famous explorer John Cabot, who had discovered and claimed the North American continent for England, followed in his father's footsteps as a captain. Forever haunted by the inexplicable disappearance of his father and a crew of four ships, Cabot, who sailed at different times under the flags of England, Spain, and the emperor Charles V, was particularly conscientious in seeking the support of Divine Providence. He insisted "that morning and evening prayer, with the common services appointed by the king's Majestie be read dayly by the chaplain or some other person learned," and that "the Bible or paraphrases be read devoutly and Christianly to God's honour, and for His grace to be obtained."[19] He would allow nothing to be taken for granted.

Jacques Cartier, the French explorer who discovered the St. Lawrence Seaway and laid claim to other Canadian territories for the French, also was devoutly committed to seeking God's protection, convinced that the true and absolute mark of "a good and perfect navigator" was to make sure that the men under his command were "careful to have prayers said morning and evening."[20] Martin Frobisher, who surveyed the northern shores of North America and was a favorite courtier of Queen Elizabeth I, was an even more intense spiritual taskmaster, requiring his men to participate in longer and more elaborate prayer services twice a day according to "the standards of the Church of England." On one occasion, when a delegation of Eskimos visited his ship, he "chased" them away, later writing in his diary that he did so "since we were going to prayer."[21]

Promoting prayer and other religious practices as well as banning all blasphemy aboard ship became so important to captains and to their investors back in Europe that sailors were required to sign contracts stating that they would abide by the spiritual dictates of their captain. In later years Captain John Smith, who led the British expedition that settled Virginia, went so far as to prescribe standard prayers and religious practices aboard transatlantic voyages, putting pen to paper in his widely read and accepted *Sea Grammar* of 1627.[22] The indefatigable Smith stipulated not only what psalms and prayers should be recited but also where and when they should be invoked: "They may first goe to prayer, then to supper, and at six a-clocke sing a Psalme, say a Prayer, and the master with his side begins the watch, then all the rest may doe what they will till midnight; and then his Mate with his Larboord men with a Psalme and a prayer releeves them until foure in the morning."[23]

Some mariners took these acts of devotion a step further by composing their own prayers to befit their circumstances. The formidable Sir Francis Drake, who had helped lead England's victory over the Spanish Armada in 1588, was one of them. Nearly eighty years after Columbus's final voyage to the Americas, Drake became the first Englishman to circumnavigate the globe. Exploring the northwest coast from San Francisco to Vancouver and vanquishing the Spaniards at Florida's St. Augustine, he emerged as one of the most celebrated navigators in British history and may even have sailed as far as Alaska.[24]

It was under the Queen's commission in 1587 that Drake helped lead the British fleet to the Spanish harbor of Cádiz, destroying or capturing twenty-four ships of King Philip's Armada as well as significant supplies and armaments. On his way to Cádiz, realizing that the upcoming battle would be the opening salvo to England's long and excruciating quest for supremacy on the high seas, Drake showed a piety that belied his image, even in England. The prayer, recited by many in the Episcopalian community today, shored up his tenacity:

> *O Lord God, when Thou givest to Thy servants any great matter,*
> *grant us to know that it is not the beginning,*
> *but the continuing of the same unto the end,*
> *until it be thoroughly finished, which yieldeth the true glory:*
> *through Him who for the finishing of Thy work laid down His life,*
> *our Redeemer Jesus Christ. Amen.*[25]

Drake's contemporary the flamboyant Sir Walter Raleigh was equally devout and as fiercely Protestant. Although he sailed to Trinidad, Raleigh never set foot on the North American mainland. Nevertheless, he was the driving force in the colonization of America's east coast once he had received the Queen's patent to proceed. His considerable influence and contributions in helping to introduce Europe to the potato and to Virginia tobacco became the stuff of legends. And yet the rest of his life was one of intense personal trial, leading to trumped-up charges against him by the court of James I. Sentenced to be executed in the Tower of London, Raleigh spent his remaining days writing entries in his diary and finding solace in composing prayers. None was more beloved than his "Rise, O My Soul," which later became a standard invocation in the Book of Common Prayer of America's Episcopal Church:

> *Rise, O my soul, with thy desires to heaven . . .*
> *To thee, O Jesu, I direct my eyes;*
> *To thee my hands, to thee my humble knees;*
> *To thee my heart shall offer sacrifice;*
> *To thee my thoughts, who my thoughts only sees;*
> *To thee my self—my self and all I give;*
> *To thee I die; to thee I only live.*[26]

As settlements began to spring up, prayer remained as essential to colonial life as it had been to the voyages that carried Europeans across the Atlantic. In Jamestown, Virginia, for example, the colonial leadership instituted laws in 1610 that required all residents to attend morning and evening prayers. Any colonist's absence from prayer services incurred punishment. Those guilty of one absence would lose a day's provisions, while another would lead to a whipping. Miss prayer services a third time and a colonist would be condemned to the oceangoing alleys for no less than six months.[27] Everyone was obliged to follow the same rules.

For the military platoons of the Virginia Colony, captains of the guard were required twice a day to lead their men in a prayer that historian Perry Miller would describe as "in length and substance the equal of any Puritan supplication."[28] It laid bare their failings to God by acknowledging their "blindness of mind, profanity of spirit, hardness of heart, self-love, carnal lusts, hypocrisy, pride, vanity, unthankfulness, infidelity, and other native corruptions."[29] It was a hard prayer that reminded the soldiers of every possible transgression known to man.

In America's northern wilderness, prayer became a major focus for a small Protestant sect of immigrants known to history simply as the Pilgrims. After escaping religious persecution in England by traveling to Holland, this largely poor and underprivileged group of spiritual wayfarers decided to take their chances and resettle in the New World, becoming "pilgrims" in their search for God's perfection and eternal life. Confirmed Calvinists, with their belief in predetermination, they took enormous pride in being labeled "unrepentant rebels" as they challenged the rituals and doctrines of the traditional churches of the day.[30]

Before making a decision of any consequence, the Pilgrims would pray both privately and as a group, reflecting on how God might be directing them to proceed. As William Bradford, effectively the first governor of the Pilgrim colony, explained, "Prayer is the Christian's vital breath, the Christian's native air."[31] And so it was only natural that en route to the New World in 1620, the Pilgrims signed a compact while on board the *Mayflower,* pledging themselves and their mission "for the glory of God, and the advancement of the Christian faith."[32]

Throughout their journey and in the years that followed, the Pilgrims prayed incessantly. Although they left no detailed account of their thanksgiving celebration during their first fall of 1621, historians have recorded that they invited their neighbors and allies, the Wampanoag tribe, to their three-day feast. In commemorating this rite of passage through prayer and celebration, they set the stage for the later American observance of Thanksgiving.

The Pilgrims were keen to do away with written prayer texts. Instead, they turned to spontaneous prayer, which they believed to be a purer way of conversing with the Almighty because it flowed naturally from the mind, heart, and soul. They even believed that the Lord's Prayer was merely a guideline passed down from Christ and did not need to be recited in exact iteration. The one exception to their rule was their use of the *Ainsworth Psalter,* a devotional of psalms set to verse that they brought with them from Europe. The Psalter, named after Henry Ainsworth, a renowned clergyman who had fled England for the Netherlands with his fellow Puritans, was a very strict translation of the Psalms and was seen as an acceptable extension of the Bible.

In their public worship, the men wore tall, buckled hats and, like the rest of the congregation, stood throughout the service, never kneeling. The only time they would remove their hats was when prayers were being recited.[33] The Pilgrims saw their devotional rites as an important way to distinguish themselves from the Catholic and Anglican churches, both of which they viewed as the antithesis of their political, cultural, and religious beliefs.

ENGLAND AND THE REST OF EUROPE were soon galvanized over the unlimited potential of the Americas, both temporally and spiritually. Creating new beginnings, tackling the unknown, and devoting one's life totally to God in a structured, isolated environment captured the imagination. No one articulated the vision more compellingly than the wealthy and erudite John Winthrop. Gathering four hundred settlers in eleven ships, he embarked from Southampton, England, for the newly formed Massachusetts Bay Colony in 1630, just ten years after the Pilgrims had arrived at Plymouth Rock. Launching what later became known as "the Great Migration," Winthrop, already in his forties and having survived the deaths of two wives, was elected the colony's first governor. By the time he relinquished his position, after being reelected twelve times, the Puritan population had reached more than twenty thousand "souls."[34]

On board the ship *Arbella* with his family and fellow Puritans, Winthrop began to compose a remarkable diary, later renamed *The History of New England.* Infused throughout with prayer, it spanned the early beginnings of the new settlement to his last days in 1649. Winthrop quite literally saw the founding of a permanent settlement in the New World as part of God's great plan, truly believing that he and his fellow settlers were God's new chosen people. "God's candlesticks" was the description he used.[35]

It was on the voyage that he wrote and delivered to those on board one of the most remarkable treatises in American colonial history, "A Model of Christian Charity," a work that would be required reading for school children well into the twentieth century. In it he spoke to the Christian ideal of selfless love, the critical ingredient to success in the New World. He stressed that their community could succeed in their quest for eternal salvation through the grace of the Holy Ghost found through continual prayer and meditation. In this way, he argued, Christ could be "formed in them and they in him, all in each other, knit together by this bond of love."[36] In his most unforgettable line, adapted from Matthew 5:14, he saw the Puritans, those indefatigable Calvinists who believed in predestination, as establishing nothing less than a "shining city upon a hill," in which "the eyes of all people are upon us."[37] It was an image that both Presidents John F. Kennedy and Ronald Reagan would brandish more than three hundred years later to describe their own visions for America.

The imprint of Cambridge-educated John Winthrop on both the civil and the ecclesiastical governance of Puritan New England became all-encompassing. A lawyer by training, Winthrop spent considerable time trying to manage the delicate balance between competing interests among the settlers. At various times he sacrificed civil and religious tolerance to maintain political stability within the fractious colony. Anne Hutchinson and Roger Williams, whose prayer lives were as intense as their political convictions, were two of the most celebrated figures banished from the colony by Winthrop and his tribunal.

Winthrop ended each entry in his diary with a prayer or an introspective reference to prayer. One of the more fascinating revelations came during a period of spiritual restlessness when he was moved to convey graphically his deepest intimacy with God. To read the passage carefully is to realize how closely Winthrop mirrored the spiritual intensity and even the phrasing that one finds in the prayers of Catholic mystics such as Saint Teresa of Ávila and Saint John of the Cross—though of course any comparison to such Catholic religious figures, antithetical to any good Puritan as they were, would have horrified Winthrop:

O my Lord, my love, how wholly delectable thou art! Let him [Jesus] kiss me with the kisses of his mouth, for his love is sweeter than wine: how lovely is thy countenance! How pleasant are thy embraces! My heart leaps for joy when I hear the voice of thee my Lord, my love, when thou sayest to my soul, thou art her salvation. O my God, my king, what am I but dust! A worm, a rebel, and thine enemy was I, wallowing in the blood and filth of my sins, when thou didst cast the light of Countenance upon me, when thou spread over me the lap of thy love, and saidest that I should live.[38]

Winthrop's influence grew steadily throughout the colony, helping to establish Puritanism in America, but the true eloquence of the age belonged not to him, not to a churchman, not to any educated gentleman. It rested with a tough yet sensitive wife and mother, a firsthand witness to the struggles of early Puritan New England: Anne Bradstreet, who composed some of the richest prose and poetry of the colonial period. She would become America's first poet, inspired by the three Puritan tenets of hard work, sacrifice, and, most important, prayer.

Born in Northampton, England, around 1612 to a young clerk and his wife, Thomas and Dorothy Dudley, Bradstreet grew up in a Puritan household. Her father served as a close and favored steward to a prominent Puritan intellectual, Theophilus Clinton, earl of Lincolnshire.

Given his elevated position in the earl's service, Dudley hired a recent graduate of Cambridge University as his apprentice, the bright and ambitious Simon Bradstreet. By 1628 it had become clear that Simon was deeply in love with Dudley's sixteen-year-old daughter, Anne, nine years his junior. He soon proposed marriage, and the two were wed later that year. Shortly thereafter, intrigued by the prospects of the new Massachusetts Bay Colony being formed and financed by the earl, both the Bradstreets and the Dudleys decided to stake their spiritual fortunes in the New World. Together with John Winthrop, just appointed the first governor of the colony, they joined their fellow Puritans on that historic first voyage of the *Arbella*.

In describing Anne Bradstreet at the time, Winthrop remarked that she was "a godly young woman" but prone to a kind of madness given her penchant for reading so many books and even writing poetry and prose.[39] And yet Bradstreet's literary talent might have gone unnoticed if her brother-in-law had not decided to take her manuscript with him to England. Unbeknownst to her, he had it published in 1650 under the title *The Tenth Muse Lately Sprung up in America*. London's tough critics pored over the spiritual musings and trials of colonial life. They found Bradstreet's prayers and poetry refreshingly original and pronounced her an eloquent eyewitness to the great Puritan adventure on the other side of the Atlantic. In 1678, six years after her death, her poetry would be published in a second edition from the presses of New England.

Bradstreet's poetry, drawn from her native England but inspired by everyday life in the New World, became even more popular toward the end of her life, when she wrote some of her most exquisite works, such as "Verses upon the Burning of Our House" and "To My Dear and Loving Husband," a piece that Leonard Bernstein set to music in the twentieth century.[40]

One of the great frustrations early in Anne Bradstreet's marriage was her seeming inability to bear a child. In her despair she fervently prayed for the chance to become a mother, setting pen to paper after overcoming a fainting spell:

> *Worthy art Thou, O Lord, of praise,*
> *But ah! It's not in me.*
> *My sinking heart I pray Thee raise*
> *So shall I give it Thee.*
>
> *My life as spider's web's cut off,*
> *Thus fainting have I said,*
> *And living man no more shall see*
> *But be in silence laid.*
>
> *My feeble spirit Thou didst revive,*
> *My doubting Thou didst chide,*
> *And though as dead mad'st me alive,*
> *I here a while might 'bide.*
>
> *Why should I live but to Thy praise?*
> *My life is hid with Thee.*
> *O Lord, no longer be my days*
> *Than I may fruitful be.*[41]

She finally gave birth to Samuel, the first of her eight children, in 1633, naming him after the first of the great prophets of the Old Testament, translated from the Hebrew as "asked of God."

Anne Bradstreet's contribution in sharing such intense personal introspection about life and spirituality within Puritan culture was enormous. Her prayers seemed to be religious acts in themselves, as the words and cadence of her prayer "From Another Sore Fit" show:

> *In my distress I sought the Lord,*
> *When nought on Earth could comfort give;*
> *And when my Soul these things abhor'd*
> *Then, Lord, thou said'st unto me, Live . . .*
>
> *What shall I render to my God*
> *For all his Bounty shew'd to me,*
> *Even for his mercyes in his rod,*
> *Where pitty most of all I see?*
>
> *My heart I wholly give to Thee:*
> *O make it fruitfull, faithfull Lord!*
> *My life shall dedicated bee*
> *To praise in thought, in Deed, in Word . . .*[42]

A product of two distinct cultures, Anne Bradstreet's poetry seemed to be a religious act in itself but ultimately provided an eloquent, historic window into the hard realities and spirituality of early New England. Her poems bore witness to the maturing and deepening spirituality of a unique literary talent who somehow blossomed under the most difficult of conditions.

AS SETTLERS WERE CREATING their notion of the ideal society in New England, a different kind of commonwealth was being formed farther south under the defiant, visionary leadership of William Penn. Granted a charter in 1681 by King Charles II to found a colony north of Maryland in payment for services and loans provided to the Crown by his father, Admiral Sir William Penn, the young William Penn became consumed with the idea of establishing a new kind of colony. A recent Quaker convert, he dreamed of founding a colony, named after his father, where Quakers and individuals of other religious faiths could live in relative freedom and certain self-rule.

On arriving in the New World with one hundred settlers in 1682, Penn moved quickly to ensure that the Pennsylvania colony would unconditionally guarantee religious and cultural tolerance as well as be committed to the separation of church and state—for all settlers. He even included Native Americans in his plan, purchasing lands from them to enlarge his holdings rather than confiscating their territory, as many other European settlers had done before him.

Through paid advertisements, Penn launched a coordinated publicity campaign in Europe to promote his "Holy Experiment."[43] The colony rapidly became the home of Quakers, Mennonites, Moravians, Schwenkfelders, and Dunkards (Church of the Brethren). Settlers came from England, Ireland, France, Wales, Scotland, Germany, Bohemia, and Sweden. So many diverse denominations and sects had settled in Pennsylvania by the turn of the eighteenth century that one observer referred to the colony as "an asylum for banished sects."[44]

At a time when the Puritans of the Massachusetts Bay Colony were quarreling over divergent views within their own church, Penn competed for settlers by showing little patience for bigotry of any kind, admonishing, "O God, help us not to despise or oppose what we do not understand."[45] When it came to personal prayer, however, Penn was very much the product of his deeply help Quaker faith, as envisioned by its founder, George Fox. Quietude, reflection through mental and spiritual immersion, and a deep reverence for God were the underpinnings of eternal salvation. As in traditional Quaker meetings, Penn and his followers sat with one another in prayer, never speaking unless the "inner light" moved them to do so. Only by constructing this kind of meditative environment, they believed, could true, unadorned prayer be perfected. On the surface it seemed almost contradictory to refer to members of the Society of Friends as "Quakers," a moniker that conveyed the physical and mental trembling they experienced when they heard the word of God.

In his writings, Penn, sounding more like an Eastern mystic than a European settler, once noted that *"how to pray is still greater than to pray; it is not the request but the frame of the petitioner's spirit."*[46] Perhaps his most striking piece of advice for finding true spiritual repose through prayer came when he wrote, "In the rush and noise of life, as you have intervals, step within yourselves and be still. Wait upon God and feel his good presence; this will carry you through your day's business."[47]

Toward the end of his life, Penn was imprisoned three times in the Tower of London for his religious convictions, adhering to strict, disciplined prayer throughout his ordeal. He credited his endurance to his religious faith. Those convictions and his steadfast belief in individual freedoms produced a thriving colony and a body of work that continues to have great meaning to this day. In his "Prayer for Philadelphia," which hangs in Philadelphia's City Hall, Penn wrote his greatest memorial to the New World:

> *And thou, Philadelphia, the Virgin settlement of this province named before thou wert born, what love, what care. What service and what traveil have there been to bring thee forth and preserve thee from such as would abuse and defile thee.*
>
> *O that thou mayest be kept from the evil that would overwhelm thee. That faithful to God of thy mercies, in the Life of Righteousness, thou mayest be preserved to the end. My soul prays to God for thee, that thou mayest stand in the day of trial, that thy children may be blest of the Lord and thy people saved by His Power.*[48]

ELSEWHERE ON THE CONTINENT, a very different prayer culture was developing. Unlike England, which had established largely Protestant and family-oriented colonies along the east coast, Catholic Spain and France sent their male explorers and priests to areas north, south, and west of the British-held territory along the Atlantic corridor. France concentrated its exploration along the vast lands on either side of the Mississippi River, achieving its most lasting impact in the region surrounding the river's basin, an area that would ultimately be named Louisiana after King Louis XIV. Spain, on the other hand, set out to claim territory that would ultimately run from Tierra del Fuego in southern Argentina all the way to northern California.

Each new wave of European explorers brought a different order of Catholic priests. Having distinct identities, these orders competed with one another for souls and for religious influence in the New World.

Although major religious orders were not necessarily confined to strict geographic regions, each one exerted special influence in specific areas. The Dominicans made their mark primarily in Florida, the Gulf Coast, and Texas. The Jesuits, through their leaders Fathers Jacques Marquette and Isaac Jogues, settled in lands along the Mississippi River from Canada to the Gulf Coast. The Franciscans under Father Louis Hennepin established a presence west of the Mississippi in areas like Missouri, Iowa, and Minnesota, while Father Junípero Serra extended Franciscan control throughout most of modern-day California. It was estimated that in the first two decades of the settlement of "New Spain" alone, as many as ten million Native Americans may have been baptized.[49]

While these priests and monks were often successful in their mission, they faced extraordinary perils in the American wilderness, ill prepared as they were for hostile natives and difficult climates and terrain. The Jesuits in particular suffered enormously, experiencing devastating casualties due to disease, starvation, and attacks by Indians. Ignorant of the customs of the tribes and nations they encountered, they unknowingly broke cultural taboos. On one occasion the priests prayed the Our Father in front of members of the Huron nation, not realizing that the Hurons found prayer to human spirits unconscionable.[50] They quickly learned to explain themselves first.

Unlike the Puritans, who eschewed set, formatted prayers, the Catholic missionaries relied heavily on memorized and written texts of time-honored prayers for two reasons. First, the prayers helped to unite a flock that was geographically widespread and diverse. Second, they aided the missionaries in educating the newly converted and instilling in them both devotion and understanding of the Old and New Testaments.

Catholic prayer traditions also sustained Spanish settlers at crucial moments. Father Junípero Serra, for example, led his fellow priests in reciting a nine-day novena to ensure that critical rations and supplies arrived by ship at their outpost in San Diego. To everyone's relief the Spanish ship finally arrived on the ninth day. Had another day passed without provisions, the Franciscans would have been forced to return to Mexico City, cutting off for the near future any future colonization of America's west coast.[51]

The first major effort by the Spanish to penetrate the North American mainland, however, came with the arrival of Juan Ponce de León in 1513, when he landed somewhere between modern day St. Augustine and Cape Canaveral. A member of Columbus's second voyage, Ponce de

León had become fixated on stories of a fountain of youth and untold deposits of gold and set out to discover their source. Returning to Florida in 1521, he brought with him several priests, who became the first clergymen to celebrate Mass on the American mainland. Within the next few years Spain became the first country to introduce a written European language in the New World, while its explorers and priests began to produce meticulously logged diaries and accounts of their civil, military, and ecclesiastical exploits. Undoubtedly the first Thanksgiving by Europeans on America's shores was actually celebrated by Ponce de León and his men a hundred years before the Pilgrims in New England.

One of the most gripping diary entries and fantastic tales in those early years came not from a priest but from a Spanish officer named Álvar Núñez Cabeza de Vaca. His journal, titled *La relación (The Account)*, described in excruciating detail the tortuous odyssey he and his men faced from 1528 to 1536 as they set out on foot to search for gold and to explore the southern regions of North America from Florida to Mexico. Cabeza de Vaca's account of the eight-year journey was the first description Europe ever received of the land extending from Florida to Arizona and is the oldest written history of Native Americans. It also became the basis for Spain's decision to launch its conquest of the New World more aggressively. Remarkably, prayer was the linchpin to Cabeza de Vaca's survival and return to Spain to present in person his discoveries to the royal court.

The Spanish expedition had set off with three hundred men, but with shipwrecks, disease, and attacks by Indians their number had plummeted to four by the time they reached Texas. Surviving were Cabeza de Vaca, who had originally been appointed second in command; Alonso del Castillo Maldonado and Andrés Dorantes, two white Spaniards; and Estevánico, a black slave who had accompanied them from Spain.

No matter what he and his men experienced during their most difficult days, Cabeza de Vaca credited prayer as their greatest source of strength. On one leg of his trip he could barely write about what he and his men faced during a particularly cold November. "We looked the picture of death," he wrote, "closer to death than to life." Able to find a way to make a fire, each man thanked God in his own way, entreating the Lord's mercy and forgiveness by "shedding many tears" for what they now were forced to undergo.[52]

Throughout his diary Cabeza de Vaca alternated between horror and affection for the Indians he encountered. For a period of time the men were even held as slaves by two different tribes until they were given the chance to escape.

No sooner had they escaped, emaciated and with nothing to wear but loincloths, than they encountered the Avavares tribe in a place they would forever name the "Village of Misfortune," near modern-day Galveston. Upon their arrival, Cabeza de Vaca and his men realized the local natives had been overcome by a variety of illnesses. With nowhere to turn, the Indians asked the Spaniards to heal their sick by "blowing" on them to cast out the illness, believing the four men were healers from another world. As Cabeza de Vaca would recount, he and his men "laughed at the idea" that they could heal anyone, but after the Indians refused to give them any more of the meager food supplies they had until they did, the men went to work.

As he neared a group of huts, Cabeza de Vaca found a man with his eyes rolled up, no pulse, and every bit "the appearance of death." Kneeling next to him, he and Dorantes prayed as fervently as they could not only for the man but also for the other ailing villagers. After walking away from the man's litter, having recited the Our Father and Hail Mary and blessing him with the sign of the cross, they accepted the fact that the man was indeed dead. Not more than a few hours later, however, the man suddenly arose and began to talk and eat. For Cabeza de Vaca, the entire episode created "profound wonder and fear." Soon word spread, and "people talked of nothing else" as they came from great distances to be cured by the men and have them bless their children.[53]

As Cabeza de Vaca noted in his journal, he soon found that "God, our Lord, in his mercy desired to heal all those for whom we prayed," while the tribe showered the men with gifts and a generous portion of what little food they had.[54]

Spanish explorers had little success in setting up entire colonies. Indeed, it was only through Spanish priests bent on Christian conversion that a more permanent presence was felt in North America. There would be no greater example of this phenomenon than with the Franciscan priests and their missions in the northern Rio Grande. In an area comprising modern-day Arizona, Colorado, and New Mexico, missionaries set up communities in which the native peoples developed a prayer regimen that blended the traditions of the Catholic Church, European culture, and their strong local culture. These missions were far removed from the larger population centers and were primarily inhabited by an unassuming, nonviolent people who welcomed the foreign missionaries, enthusiastically opening themselves to their religious teachings.

Through prayer, the priests were able both to educate and to provide a spiritual outlet for Christian devotion. While the roots of these prayers, known as *alabados,* emanated from seventeenth-century Spain, their inspiration also came from the native culture itself. Some were sung without musical accompaniment, while others were composed for voice and a single instrument.

There were prayers called "I Am a Slave of Jesus," "Have Pity, My God," and "Along the Trail of Blood." One prayer reflecting on the Passion and crucifixion of Christ conveyed both haunting torment and intense personal piety:

My Dios y mi Redentor	My God and my Redeemer
en quien espero y confio	in whom I hope and confide,
por tu pasión, Dios mío,	through your passion, my God,
abrázame en vuestro amor.	Embrace me in your love.
Escuchan con atención	Listen with attention
lo que padeció Jesús,	what Jesus suffered
desde el huerto hasta la cruz	from the garden to the cross
en su sagrada pasión,	in his sacred passion,
lágrimas de devoción	tears of devotion
nos dé a todos el Señor.	The Lord gave us all.
Por tu pasión, Dios mío,	Through your passion, my God,
abrázame en vuestro amor.	Embrace me in your love.[55]

These early American prayers and hymns were not completely devoid of joy and grace, however. There were compositions titled "Good Morning, White Dove," "Sweet Husband of My Soul," and "With Docility and Tenderness." One *alabado,* a morning prayer of thanksgiving, expressed refreshing optimism at the beginning of a new day:

En este nuevo día,	On this new day,
gracias te tributamos,	thanks we pay in tribute,
oh, Dios omnipotente,	oh, omnipotent God,
Señor de todo lo creado . . .	Lord of all creation . . .

Por ti nacen las flores	For you the flowers grow
y reverdece el campo,	and the countryside turns green,
los árboles dan fruta	and trees give fruit
y el sol nos da sus rayos . . .	and the sun gives us your rays . . .
Dirige Dios immenso	Immense God, direct
y guía nuestros pasos	and guide our steps
para que eternamente	so that eternally
tu santa ley sigamos.	We follow your holy law.[56]

While these prayers were steeped in the centuries-old theology of Roman Catholicism, they also were shaped by the culture of a simple people who wanted nothing more than to express spiritual devotion in their own way.

BY THE SECOND HALF of the seventeenth century, new traditions in American prayer had begun to take root across the New World. Europeans brought to the continent a prayer life steeped in centuries of Christianity and Judaism, while Africans, caught in the grip of the burgeoning slave trade, brought to America their own unique piety. In the midst of their diversity, prayer became the great common denominator among Native Americans, European Americans, and later African-Americans. In the words of the seventeenth-century British poet Owen Felltham, prayer for all of America's settlers had become "the key of the morning and the lock of the night."[57]

CHAPTER 2

THE PREACHERS

1640–1750

Such prayer will gradually spread and increase more and more, ushering in a revival of religion. This would be characterized by greater worship and service to God among believers. Others will be awakened to their need for God, motivating them to earnestly cry out to God for mercy. They will be led to join with God's people in that extraordinary seeking and serving of God which they see around them. In this way the revival will grow to be ten times larger than it was before. Indeed, at length, all nations of the world will be converted unto God.

—Jonathan Edwards (1747)

*I*F THE EXPLORERS AND SETTLERS brought new ideas, culture, and religion to America, a group of zealous preachers infused the New World with its sense of Puritan spirituality and its work ethic as the proper prescription for true Christian living. They unquestionably believed Divine Providence had reserved this vast, unspoiled land to allow them, as God's instruments, to make good mankind's spiritual destiny. Certainly, they could find no greater example of John Calvin's doctrine of preordination than in the bounty of the American continent.

Although other colonies and territories were being settled in the New World to varying degrees, the single-mindedness, speed, and completeness of the Puritans in establishing a largely stable and thriving community distinguished them from other Europeans. Dogmatic, disciplined, and passionate, they were ardent evangelists who set God and prayer at the center of their universe.

Not only were the churches of the day centers of Puritan zeal, but so were the colleges. Every college established before the Revolutionary War was founded and headed by successive ministers who extolled the virtues of Puritan doctrine and promoted prayer as an inseparable part of a student's educational curriculum.

Flowing largely from the Protestant churches of Great Britain, Puritanism called for a religious simplicity based on the literal translation of the Bible, regular private and communal worship, and strict church organization. It was critical that congregations "purify" themselves from the elaborate rituals so prevalent in Catholic Europe and in the High Church of England. While the Puritans counted themselves among the Anglican faithful, they also saw themselves as the true adherents to the Church of England's proper teachings.

One minister, the Reverend Samuel Danforth, went so far as to call the Puritan presence in America, freed from the trappings of the Old World, "New England's Errand into the Wilderness."[1] As the twentieth-century scholar on early America Perry Miller argued, religion, not economics, was the driving force behind the Puritans' coming to America. Rather than being some crazed, dour bunch of European misfits, they exuded refinement, intelligence, and theological purpose for their overall mission and their individual lives.

When it came to prayer, Puritans felt continuous spiritual dialogue was the indispensable medium for creating a one-on-one relationship with God. Effectively, they believed that there was no need for middlemen, such as Catholic saints or the Virgin Mary, in their relationship with God. Furthermore, unobstructed prayer helped to affirm the "covenant" between God and those he created in "His Likeness." This approach to prayer and worship extended to their architecture as well; in constructing their houses of worship, the Puritans built meetinghouses, not churches. While these barnlike buildings were also intended to serve the Puritan community in secular ways, their primary purpose was to allow direct interaction with God. Public prayer was to be offered in a simple, straightforward, and completely unadorned setting. From the exterior structure to the interior seating design, the Puritans built unique spiritual edifices for themselves.

By stripping their meetinghouses of any hint of the cuneiform structure of Anglican or Roman Catholic churches in Europe and what they considered the ostentatious trappings of stained-glass windows and sculpture-mad sanctuaries, they intended for their congregations to be entirely "absorbed in prayer or sermon."[2] Even in developing their interior designs from an oblong to a foursquare floor plan by mid-century, the Puritans used unvarnished practicality to break new ground in architecture.

For most colonists, Sunday worship began in the morning and resumed in the afternoon, when they would return for more prayer services that could include everything from baptisms to welcoming new members recently arrived from England.[3] The morning program remained essentially the same throughout the first decades of the colonial period:

Opening prayer
Scripture reading
Exposition of Scripture
Psalm singing
Sermon
Prayer
Psalm singing
Blessing

In the early days, one individual, normally a deacon, or what the Puritans called a precentor, took the only Psalter owned within the congregation and directed everyone in psalm singing. He would sing one line, and the congregation would echo it back. Called "lining-out," this method of psalm singing made for unusually long services.[4] Spoken prayers could last as long as the sermon, well over an hour, and most of the time they were delivered while the congregation stood uncomfortably in their pews. If members wanted to submit individual prayer petitions or intercessions, they could write them down on what were called "prayer bills" and hand them to the minister to read during the service.

The Reverend Thomas Clapp, a Harvard graduate, gave some idea of the lengths to which a minister would go to write out just one prayer. In his 1725 diary he wrote that he employed a "Scheme of Prayer" to prepare himself for Sunday service. His six-page outline consisted of the following:

Part I.   Adoration of God—thirty-one subheads
Part II.   Confession—forty-nine subheads, in five classes
Part III.   Petitions—ninety subheads, in five classes
Part IV.   Thanksgiving—forty-two subheads, in seven classes
Part V.   Intercession—twenty-eight subheads, in four classes
              Total, two hundred and forty subheads.[5]

Further testing the stamina of a congregation, kneeling, let alone sitting, was strictly forbidden. Considered "noxious," kneeling, like so many other customs, was seen as a throwback to Catholicism and the Church of England. Although the early Puritans withstood such discomforts, sympathetic architects of later Puritan churches did their part to ease the situation by hinging the pew seats. In this way the pews could be tipped up, allowing worshippers to lean against the rail.[6] While this design breakthrough may have provided some welcome relief, it often encouraged ministers to preach and pray even longer. One Puritan congregant, Nathaniel Ward, bemoaned the propensity for ministers to pray almost ad infinitum, "We have a strong weakness in New England that when we are speaking we know not how to conclude: We make many ends before we can end."[7]

As if the endurance test were not difficult enough, most churches had a "tithingman," an officer of the parish appointed annually to preserve strict order during services. Specifically, the tithingman would sit at a desk near the front of the church and carefully watch the moves of every worshipper. While the minister conducted the service, the tithingman would take firm hold of a long staff, heavily knobbed on one end, and rap the heads of glassy-eyed men and inattentive boys. On the other end of the "wand of office" hung a foxtail or rabbit's foot, which the tithingman would thrust into the faces of errant women. Unlike the men, who could be bruised by the experience, the ladies were tickled into submission.[8] With no watches or timepieces to determine the length of services, the tithingman was also responsible for turning over an hourglass on his desk.[9] To many congregants, particularly children, the very thought that an hourglass could be turned over three or fours times during a single service was staggering.

THE MINISTERS OF THE DAY had very clear ideas of what was acceptable in their communion with God. Prescribed prayers in the Anglican

Book of Common Prayer were denounced as contrived and shallow at best. At worst they were viewed as violating the second commandment, "Thou shalt not take the name of the Lord, thy God, in vain." Puritans believed that God had forbidden them from bowing down before the efforts of their own hands.[10] Spontaneous prayer, they contended, was far more pleasing in the eyes of God. The expanse, the beauty, and the unpredictability of the American continent fed into the development of their spontaneous prayers.

At the same time, the Puritans were inspired in their prayer by the Psalms of Scripture. They took issue, however, with the Church of England's "imperfect" translations of those ageless prayers of David. It was no accident, then, that the first book published in the United States was *The Whole Booke of Psalmes Faithfully Translated into English Metre*, better known as *The Bay Psalm Book*. The technical ability to produce copies came during the summer of 1638, when the Reverend Jose Glover, his assistant Stephen Daye, and their families set sail for Cambridge, Massachusetts, with a newly built printing press.[11] With the recent founding of Harvard College, a desire to proselytize American Indians to Christianity by translating prayer tracts and the Bible into native languages, and the need simply to meet the religious demands of the Puritan settlers, the introduction of a printing press on New World soil had great appeal both spiritually and financially. Although the costs of importing raw paper, ink, bindings, and other materials continued to make buying books from England more practical in the short term, local ministers salivated at the prospect of publishing a book of psalms under their own control.

Once the printing press was ready for production, the Reverend John Cotton and three other prominent ministers established a committee to publish their personal translation of the "songs of David." The clergymen had two purposes in mind. First, being fluent in Hebrew and Latin, they believed they could do a far better job of translating sacred Scripture. Second, they recognized that by definition the Psalms had to be set to music. Concerned that the devil not make his way into a congregation through its choir or that musical instruments not create excessive "merriment," the clergymen made sure that their translated psalms were set to no more than a handful of tunes.

The differences between the Psalms of the Church of England and those of America's Puritans were striking, as a comparison of the opening lines of Psalm 23 shows. In reading the two versions side by side, one clearly sees that the King James Version is far more readable, if not more grammatically correct:

King James Version (1629 edition)	Bay Psalm Version (1651 edition)

The Lord is my Shepard;
   I shall not want.
He maketh me to lie down
   in green pastures;
	The Lord to me a shepard is
	   Want therefore shall not I
	He in the folds of tender grass
	   Doth make me down to lie.

He leadeth me beside the
   still waters;
He restoreth my soul.
He leadeth me in the paths of
   righteousness
for his name's sake.
	He leads me to the waters
	   still;
	Restore my soul doth he;
	In paths of righteousness,
	   he will
	For his name's sake lead me.[12]

Some seventeen hundred copies of the book, of which only ten survive, were produced from a printing press shipped over from London and set up in Cambridge, Massachusetts.[13] Although the typesetting and final printing of *The Bay Psalm Book* were less than perfect, the book's publication was an incredible achievement, coming just ten years after the Puritans had landed in Massachusetts Bay. By 1744 the book was in its twenty-sixth edition, reaffirming with each new printing that Puritan congregations would no longer be wholly dependent on England for religious books or even interpretations of sacred text. With this one publication the colonists had made a dramatic statement in developing their own culture of prayer and spirituality in the New World.

For the next twenty years the Cambridge Press remained the only publishing company in the New World as it continued to provide colonists with prayer tracts and other spiritual as well as secular materials.

As the years passed, the Puritans began singing hymns besides the Psalms. Despite those few religious zealots who still believed that prayer should only be spoken, it was clear that the singing of prayers would only flourish over time. Particularly within a congregational setting, hymns could be both intimately personal and deeply communal, all at once. As this musical side of prayerful worship began to take greater root, however, it became clear that the task stretched their limits, and the quality of their singing declined precipitously. The situation became so serious that ministers from around New England gathered to discuss their common dilemma and to come up with easy melodies. Unfortunately, the outcome proved too difficult for most people to handle. One elder noted that his congregation sounded "like five hundred different tunes roared out at the same time," with everyone singing at least one or two words out of sync.[14] Thomas Walter, another elder, bemoaned in 1721 that "the tunes are now miserably tortured, and twisted, and quavered into a horrid Medley of confused and disorderly Noises."[15] Incredibly, some churchgoers believed that discordant singing was the single most devout way that a person could show spiritual devotion to God.

In the end, communal, harmonious singing became the norm after a series of travails. One story was told about an elderly seventeenth-century deacon who suffered from both failing eyesight and failing hearing. In the tradition of lining-out, the church's newly formed choir anxiously anticipated their first Sunday singing together. When the moment finally arrived, they looked to the deacon for direction, because he was the only one in the church with the new hymnal. Unable to read the first line, he exclaimed in a loud voice, "My eyes, indeed, are blind." The choir listened carefully and took his words as their cue, singing out, "My eyes, indeed, are blind." Astonished, the deacon responded, "[No, no], I cannot see at all!" Convinced that he was speaking metaphorically, they promptly echoed his words even more loudly: "I cannot see at all." At this point, the frustration became too much for the old man, and he turned to the choir, crying, "I really believe you are bewitched!" With that, they sang out once again. Finally, out of sheer exhaustion, he shouted, "The mischief's in you all." Hearing his words come back to him one final time, he fell back in his pew, shook his head, and never uttered another word.[16]

The challenges of incorporating more music into worship services and having uniform singing would lead to the first singing schools and societies in New England.[17]

THE EARLY COLONIAL PERIOD was a time for "digging in" by religious zealots and well-intentioned ministers, who effectively set in motion the culture, attitudes, and mores that would leave a permanent impression on America. One of the more remarkable figures, who poured his heart into his ministry but was not widely known in his time, was the Reverend Edward Taylor. A graduate of Harvard Divinity School, Taylor was both a physician and the pastor of the Congregational Church in Westfield, Connecticut, in what is now Massachusetts, from 1671 to 1729. Prior to the twentieth century only one or two of his writings had ever been published, given his belief that the publication of a person's prayers was unseemly—not to mention that he knew he would be open to charges of blasphemy from other Puritan clergymen. What he produced in those prayers, however, was a set of devotional writings that combined a deep spirituality with exquisite artistry.

For all of his remarkable prayer poems, full knowledge of Edward Taylor's works only came to light by accident. Ezra Stiles, Taylor's grandson and the highly renowned president of Yale College during the Revolutionary War, was highly protective of his grandfather's wishes, making sure that all of his writings were stored away for safekeeping. A later nineteenth-century descendant of both men discovered the writings and, not knowing of Taylor's instructions, had them donated to the college. Yale's archivist at the time was unaware of what he had in his possession and filed the manuscript deep in the recesses of the library. Not for another fifty years, just before the outbreak of World War II, did Yale professor Thomas Johnson, working on a separate project, accidentally discover Taylor's great literary contribution.[18] His discovery helped to put to rest the debate over whether the most ardent Puritans, particularly clergymen, were capable of serious poetic art. More than two hundred years after his death, Edward Taylor attained a place along with Anne Bradstreet as one of the great writers of colonial America.

One of the quintessential prayers he wrote in English meter was a devotion in which he reduced himself to "Dust" before the eyes of God:

> Lord, Can a Crumb of Dust the Earth outweigh,
> Outmatch all mountains, nay, the Crystall Sky?
> Imbosom in't designs that shall Display
> And trace into the Boundless Deity?
> Yea hand a Pen whose moysture doth guild o'er
> Eternall Glory with a glorious glore . . .
> I am this Crumb of Dust which is design'd
> To make my Pen unto thy Praise alone,

And my dull Phancy I would gladly grinde
Unto an edge on Zion's pretious Stone,
And write in Liquid Gold upon thy Name
My Letters till thy glory forth doth flame.[19]

The inspiration for almost all of Taylor's prayers came from the spiritual fervor he felt when preparing for Eucharistic services at his church. He poured his soul into finding the right words to express his deepest piety.

In a ministry that spanned fifty-eight years and the composition of hundreds of prayers, Taylor's most famous work was a poem called "Huswifery," a prayer invoking his endless desire to be "spun" to the Almighty as God's junior partner. In his meditation he placed himself in the role of a spinning wheel and cast God as an authoritative, but also maternal, figure. In turn, Taylor submitted himself to God to help him weave his character and allow him to forge a lifetime of good works in the quest to achieve ultimate redemption:

Make me, O Lord, Thy spinning wheel complete,
Thy holy word my distaff make for me.
Make mine affections Thy swift flyers neat
And make my soul Thy holy spoole to be.
My conversation make to be Thy reel
And reel the yarn thereon spun of Thy wheel.

Make me Thy loom then, knit therein this twine:
And make Thy holy spirit, Lord, wind quills.
Then weave the web Thyself. The yarn is fine,
Thin ordinances make my fulling mills.
Then dye the same in heavenly colors choice.
All pinked with varnished flowers of paradise.

Then clothe therewith mine understanding, will.
Affections, judgment, conscience, memory,
My words, and actions, that their shine may fill
My ways with glory and Thee glorify.
Then mine apparel shall display before Ye
That I am clothed in holy robes for glory.[20]

Other ministers, however, extolled a darker, sterner side of Christianity. They felt compelled to emphasize the fire and damnation that awaited sinners, and few clergymen took the challenge more seriously than the legendary Increase Mather.

Increase Mather served as the Congregationalist minister of the Second Church of Boston, the Old North Church of later Revolutionary War fame, and was gifted with a sharp intellect. It was said by his contemporaries that he could spend as many as sixteen hours a day in his study without surfacing and committed to memory each of his sermons and congregational prayers. In addition, he wrote over a hundred books, theological tomes, and scientific treatises. His scholarship and considerable reputation led his alma mater, Harvard College, to ask him to serve as its president in 1685, a post he held for the next sixteen years.

Throughout his ministry Mather firmly believed that sermons were the single most effective way to instill in his congregation unvarnished Puritan theology and to promote prayer as critical to a person's salvation. Practicing what he preached, he began each week by preparing for his upcoming sermon with a prayer:

Dear Lord, Jesus! Thou that knowest my works! Help! Help! Help a poor creature, I earnestly beseech thee, so to improve his time as shall be most for thy glory, the good of thy people, and the rejoicing of his own soul, in that day when I shall see, my Lord, and speak with thee face to face! Amen! Amen! Amen![21]

Tough as Increase Mather may have been at the pulpit and with himself, he secured an honored place in history by ultimately condemning the Salem witch trials. It was not a popular position to take at the time, but he was direct: "It were better that ten suspected witches should escape than one innocent person should be condemned."[22] Suffering a stroke in 1722 at the age of eighty-three, he was confined to bed for the next eleven months until his death. His oldest son, Cotton, in whose arms he died, wrote about his father's last days, recounting how he spent hour upon hour praying, spiritually emboldened by "sufferings from the Lord" as he faced the infirmities of old age.

Committed to the notion that the promise of America could lead to the path of eternal salvation, Cotton Mather carried on his family's ministry. Named after his mother Mariah's famous father, the Reverend John Cotton, he was a brilliant, at times controversial, theologian. A stammerer from birth, he had such intensity and spiritual fervor that he could easily deliver four-hour sermons accompanied by extensive prayers each Sunday. Like his father, Mather became a highly disciplined and prodigious writer, producing over 450 books and pamphlets. Being the staunch Puritan that he was, one of his more interesting works was entitled "The Lord's Prayer: Or, A New Attempt to Recover the Right Version, and Genuine Meaning of That Prayer."

In February 1684, when he was just twenty years old, Cotton Mather wrote one of his more unusual journal entries as he described in detail his custom of praying under his breath for various people he encountered each day. Referring to these prayers as "blessings" or "ejaculations," he was dogged in what he saw as his private spiritual mission:

When I have been sitting in a Room full of people, at a Funeral, where they take not much Liberty for Talk, and where yet much Time is most reasonably lost, I have unusually set my wits to work, to contrive agreeable Benedictions, for each Person in the Company.

In passing along the Street, I have set myself to bless thousands of persons, who never knew that I did it; with secret Wishes, after this manner sent unto Heaven for them.

Upon the Sight of	Ejaculations
A *tall* Man.	*Lord*, give that Man, *High Attainments* in Christianity: Let him fear God, *above many*.
A *lame* Man.	*Lord*, help that Man, to *walk uprightly*.
A *Negro*.	*Lord*, wash that poor Soul *white* in the *Blood* of thy Son.
A Man, who going by me took *no Notice* of me.	*Lord*, help that Man, to take a *due Notice* of the Lord Jesus Christ. I pray thee.[23]

At critical moments in his spiritual life, he choreographed elaborate prayer rituals, lasting from dawn to dusk, in striving to become one with God through prayer. In time his sure-footed theology and enthusiasm, however, would be seriously challenged.

Breaking with his father, Cotton Mather lost much of his considerable reputation when he promoted the trials and executions of the condemned women and men at the Salem witch trials. He became convinced that the devil was trying to destroy their great religious experiment by possessing the young women and men of the colony. By the end of this bizarre, tragic chapter, the Puritan community had become numb over the extent of the trials and their individual culpability in them. As Cotton Mather would later echo, "Great hardships were brought upon innocent persons and (we fear) guilt incurred which all have cause to bewail."[24] Continuous days of fasting and prayer did little to salve guilty consciences.

Arguably the pivotal figure in the Salem witch trials of 1692 was Samuel Sewall, the chief justice of Massachusetts. Highly educated and trained originally to be a minister, Sewall chose instead to become a jurist, a merchant, and a landowner. Appointed to preside over many of the trials, he helped to keep the fervor alive as the wildest of tales led to nineteen individuals being hanged and another being stoned to death.

Five years after the executions, Sewall made one of the great acts of public contrition when he stood before his church's congregation as the Reverend Samuel Willard read aloud his confession. His prayer bill made clear to the congregation that he must "take the Blame and shame of it. Asking pardon of men, and especially desiring prayers that God, who has an unlimited Authority, would pardon that sin and all other sins."[25] For the rest of his life Sewall regularly set aside whole days for prayer and fasting, lost at times in the thoughts of those difficult days and his own incomprehensible actions.

HOW TO TEACH CHRISTIANITY and convey proper moral values to children was a particular challenge for the Puritans of New England. Parents genuinely feared that children would die before adolescence and, worse yet, without the benefit of being in the state of divine grace.

Believing that a person's inability to read was the design of Satan to keep people from reading the Scriptures, America's Puritan leaders decided they needed a guide that could educate children and instruct them on the need for prayer and strong morals. The answer came in the publication of *The New England Primer*, a version of which had been wildly popular in London. With its first printing in Boston in 1690, the primer covered a mere sixty-five pages; it was so small that it could almost be hidden in the praying hands of an adult.

The textbook caught on immediately. After the Bible, no other book was more popular in the New World. Combining the study of the alphabet with the Bible, a basic catechism, and a prayer book, *The New England Primer* sold over five million copies. An integral tool in educating youth well into the nineteenth century, it had a profound impact on the character of early America.

The one prayer from the primer that stood out and became its most quoted passage generation after generation was the "Evening Prayer for a Child":

> *Now I lay me down to sleep,*
> *I pray the Lord, my soul to keep;*
> *If I should die before I wake,*
> *I pray thee, Lord, my soul to take.*[26]

Although less familiar today, "Morning Prayer for a Child" was recited by children at the beginning of the day:

> *Now I wake and see the light:*
> *'Tis God who kept me through the night.*
> *To him I lift my voice and pray*
> *That he would keep me through the day:*
> *If I should die before 'tis done,*
> *O God, accept me through thy Son.*[27]

In its closing, the primer offered "A Prayer for Children in Imitation of Our Lord's Prayer," a decidedly more positive note to end its life lessons and prayers:

> *O Lord, my God, though thou art in heaven and I on earth, yet thou seest*
> *me and observest all I do and say . . . Wilt thou O Lord, bless me, and keep*
> *me in the right way? Make my duty plain, and assist me to do all that is*
> *good and virtuous. Give me food and raiment while I live in Thy world.*

*Forgive all my offenses against thee, and help me to forgive my enemies, and
to wish them well . . . May I walk in all virtue and honesty in this world,
so that I may be prepared to dwell in thy heavenly kingdom when thou shalt
close my eyes in death; all which I would ask in the name and for the sake
of my divine Redeemer.*[28]

Some of the Puritans who had crossed the Atlantic were not formally
educated, and they wanted to make sure their children did not suffer the
same fate. Integrating prayer and spirituality with practical learning
became the perfect formula.

DESPITE THESE EFFORTS to educate the colony's children, by the early
eighteenth century some religious leaders had come to believe that the
spiritual fire among adults had grown lax. Even spontaneous prayer, in
which the early Puritans had taken such enormous pride, seemed to be
lost in growing apathy. Although church attendance remained steady,
public devotion had become just a rote exercise.

Religious complacency, however, was turned on its head when the
brilliant Jonathan Edwards, a Congregationalist minister from East
Windsor, Connecticut, launched the First Great Awakening. By sheer
physical and intellectual force, Edwards became the single greatest
theologian America ever produced. His cutting-edge theological finesse
regarding church teachings and the sheer volume of his output influenced, challenged, and cajoled seminarians and intellectuals for generations to come.

Greatly influenced by his father, Timothy, a powerful preacher in his
own right, Jonathan showed a penchant for spiritual revivalism practically from birth. He later recollected that by the age of seven or eight, "I
used to pray five times a day in secret, and to spend much time in religious conversation with other boys; and used to meet with them to pray
together." Yet by his early teenage years he had lost sight of the efficacy
of prayer and the importance of righteous living, claiming to have
"returned like a dog to his vomit, and went on in ways of sin."[29] Entering Yale College at the age of twelve, he later regained his faith after
being struck by pleurisy months before his graduation.[30]

The new era of religious consciousness that Edwards helped spur in
the 1730s and 1740s forcefully reminded colonists of their religious roots

and why they and their parents had immigrated to America in the first place. The Great Awakening forced Americans to reconsider their spiritual convictions, recognizing that prayers must never be invoked as "heat without light."[31] The roots of modern Evangelicalism in America had taken hold.

With unusual clarity Edwards set the framework for the revival by delivering a series of electrifying sermons and writing thought-provoking treatises. There were such works as "Hypocrites Deficient in the Duty of Prayer," *A Faithful Narrative of the Surprising Work of God,* and his most famous oration, *Sinners in the Hands of an Angry God.*[32] Although his contributions to Puritan religious life centered on the composition of sermons rather than prayers, Edwards spoke of prayer continually and wrote a detailed guide in September 1747 that he titled, with little appetite for abridgment, *An Humble Attempt to Promote Explicit Agreement and Visible Union of God's People throughout the World in Extraordinary Prayer for the Revival of Religion and the Advancement of Christ's Kingdom on Earth, pursuant to Scripture Promises and Prophecies concerning the Last Time.*[33] Edwards believed that the revival of religious life in America could only be achieved through prayer. "There is no way that Christians, in a private capacity, can do so much to promote the work of God and advance the Kingdom of Christ as by prayer," he admonished.[34]

In *An Humble Attempt,* which was immensely influential across the colonies as well as in Scotland, he pleaded for Christian society to accept the reality of the Second Coming of Christ and to prepare for it through prayer. He also promoted a blueprint that would lead to a massive prayer chain of the faithful extending to both sides of the Atlantic. Calling it a "Concert of Prayer," Edwards advocated that Puritan congregations in the colonies and in the British Isles commit themselves, by international agreements if possible, to use prayer, "the engagement of the heart," as a means to stir spiritual passions.[35]

After serving for almost twenty-five years as minister of the First Christian Church in Northampton, Massachusetts, Edwards resigned in 1750 following a struggle with the church's board over his exacting theology and regimen. Working among the Native Americans of Stockbridge, Massachusetts, while continuing to write, he was asked in the fall of 1757 to head up the new College of New Jersey, now Princeton, as its third president. In office for only three months, he unexpectedly died due

to complications from a smallpox inoculation. Had he lived just a few years longer, he could well have taught James Madison and his own grandson Aaron Burr, the impact of which can only be imagined.

In a very practical way Edwards left one final mark to his legacy by bringing to the public's attention the life of David Brainerd, one of the most striking religious figures of the colonial period. Brainerd, who would become the patron saint for Protestant missionaries in America, persevered under extraordinary odds to bring Christianity to Native Americans and to promote prayer as indispensable to human existence. Through the posthumous publication of his diary and the direct efforts of Edwards, Brainerd's reputation resonated far more in death than it did in life.

Born in Connecticut in 1718, Brainerd defied a series of early setbacks, including the death of his father in 1727 and that of his mother five years later. Moving in with his older sister and her family, he seemed to pick up every malady, from measles to tuberculosis. Nonetheless, he developed an extraordinarily intense prayer life.

He later recounted the experience of his conversion to Christianity just after turning twenty-one. Forging his way through a dark grove of trees near his home one afternoon, "endeavoring to pray" as he walked, he heard the voice of God as "light dawning." From that day on, he knew he had no choice but to become totally immersed in the calling of a Christian ministry, ultimately finding his home with the Presbyterian Church.

Inspired by the religious zealotry of Jonathan Edwards and George Whitefield, Brainerd decided after studying at Yale to take the message of the Great Awakening to Native Americans throughout the Northeast, to tribes such as the Mohegans, the Mahicans, the Delawares, and the Susquehannas. In little more than six years he logged thousands of miles on horseback, reaching remote areas never seen by men of European descent. From the outset he prayed, "Here I am, Lord, send me; send me to the ends of the earth . . . send me from all that is called comfort in earth, or earthly comfort; send me even to death itself, if it be but in Thy service and to promote Thy Kingdom."[36]

Praying several times a day, Brainerd would intensify his efforts whenever he felt depressed, believing that it was the only way for him to escape from "being under great darkness." In describing his prayer life, he used such phrases as "my soul wrapt up in divine love" and "my long-

ing desires after God." He was utterly transfixed by prayer, convinced that it allowed him to achieve "progressive sanctification," the ultimate path to salvation.[37]

With Brainerd's tuberculosis becoming more severe, Jonathan Edwards's daughter Jerusha, to whom Brainerd had proposed marriage, joined him in his ministry, serving as both companion and nurse. In the end, however, he became too ill, and the two of them returned to her parents' home in Northampton. In the remaining days of Brainerd's life, Edwards came to realize the full extent of his young protégé's self-effacement and his all-consuming spirituality. Edwards's biographer George Marsden observed that Jonathan Edwards found Brainerd's prayers "stunning." His invocation of grace at the table even as he faced death was "awe-inspiring."[38] John and Charles Wesley, the Anglican founders of the Methodist Church, considered Brainerd the epitome of Christian piety, weaving the example of his life into their sermons, essays, and even hymns.

IF JONATHAN EDWARDS was the intellectual catalyst for the Great Awakening, the Reverend George Whitefield was its greatest, most mesmerizing messenger. Arguably, Whitefield became the most significant and influential preacher in American history.

The son of an innkeeper, Whitefield was born in Gloucester, England, in 1714. Accepted to Oxford University, he became close friends with John and Charles Wesley, and by his early twenties he had begun to preach in his hometown and in the surrounding areas. His complete conversion, however, came in 1735 while he was praying and fasting during Lent. Collapsing from hunger and the onset of what he believed to be a serious illness, he later recalled, he had thrown himself on his bed, crying, "I thirst, I thirst," imitating Christ's last minutes on the cross. At that single moment, he believed, he had been "born again," convinced that God had called on him to spread the revivalist message of "dynamic Christianity."[39]

With a gift for extemporaneous oratory and a voice that could carry across huge throngs of people, this pale, pudgy preacher from a modest English background was spellbinding, admonishing his audiences to "be much in prayer." Next to the King of England, he was the most famous figure in the English-speaking world, reportedly delivering eighteen thousand sermons in his lifetime and seen and heard by more people than any other individual in the eighteenth century.[40]

While continuing to preach and make a name for himself in England, Whitefield eagerly waited for reports from John and Charles Wesley, who were spreading the Gospel in the Georgia colony. He soon learned that they had become seriously disillusioned by their missionary work in America. The culmination of their despair soon came in 1737 when a grand jury in Savannah served John Wesley with papers, accusing him and his brother of grievously undermining the religious tranquility of the colony through their prayers. Both the civil and religious establishment were outraged that the Wesleys had been "introducing into the church and service at the Altar compositions of psalms and hymns not inspected or authorized by any proper judication."[41] In reality, they were upset over any changes the brothers wanted to make in the traditional composition and singing of hymns, and in turn the authority of the clerical establishment.

In exasperation, John Wesley wrote to George Whitefield how "the harvest is so great and the labourers are so few,"[42] trying to coax his friend into coming to the New World. For the Wesleys, however, the die was cast. After a scant eighteen months in 1735–37, the Wesley brothers concluded that their efforts in winning converts with their message of Methodism had failed. In departing for England, they had no idea that they had launched a religious movement that would number tens of millions by the twenty-first century.

Despite the Wesleys' disillusionment, Whitefield would not be dissuaded from sailing to America two years later and returning on six other occasions. Throughout his ministry in the American colonies, he received the same kind of reception he had in England: the clergy loathed him, and the people revered him. When church doors were closed to him, he simply preached outdoors. He had a carpenter build a collapsible, portable pulpit from which he could deliver his sermons and offer spontaneous prayers. Over time, Whitefield's audiences ranged in number from the hundreds to the tens of thousands, with people traveling vast distances to see and hear him. Throughout his ministry, his message on prayer was always the same, paraphrased from the New Testament: "Pray, pray, pray without ceasing" (1 Thessalonians 5:17).

As Jonathan Edwards's wife, Sarah, marveled, "It is wonderful to see what a spell he casts over an audience by proclaiming the simplest truths of the Bible. I have seen . . . people hang on his words with breathless silence, broken only by an occasional half-suppressed sob . . . Our mechanics shut up their shops, and the day laborers throw down their tools to go and hear him preach, and few return unaffected."[43]

When a young man, John Adams heard Whitefield speak and described him as "that great model of theatrical grace."[44] George Washington remarked that "upon his lips the Gospel appears even to the coarsest of men as sweet and as true as, in fact, it is."[45] Benjamin Franklin took to him instantly and brokered an arrangement where he held exclusive rights to publish all of Whitefield's writings throughout the colonies. Revenues from the sales of Whitefield's enormously popular works greatly enriched Franklin's personal wealth, helping to sustain him financially after he entered public service.

As much as overflow crowds loved Whitefield, he clearly drew spiritual breath from them, particularly when he could successfully exhort them to pray. On one occasion when he got together with friends in Philadelphia and suggested that they kneel together to pray, he was delighted, almost impishly so, by the scene, remarking, "I was greatly rejoiced to look round them, because there were some who had been marvelous offenders against God."[46]

In speaking to audiences throughout America, however, Whitefield came to personify the growing unity being felt among the separate colonies. Some historians even credit him with helping to coalesce the colonies toward eventual revolution. As James H. Hutson of the Library of Congress framed the relevance of George Whitefield for today's world:

> To make Whitefield comprehensible to a modern audience, a scholar has compared his revivals to "the civil rights demonstrations, the campus disturbances, and the urban riots of the 1960's combined." Another comparison is also possible: a captivating young Britisher from a modest background, rebelling against authority, performing in a new style with a new voice. Using clever self-promotion to draw huge, emotionally charged crowds in one city after another—Whitefield and his entourage might, without doing too much violence to the facts, be called the Beatles with Bibles.[47]

George Whitefield delivered his last sermon to an audience in Exeter, New Hampshire. At the end of his remarks he looked out at his audience and prayed:

Lord Jesus, I am weary in thy work, but not of thy work. If I have not yet finished my course, let me go and speak for thee once more in the fields, seal thy truth, and come home and die.[48]

He then retreated to the parsonage of a local minister and died early the next morning. Hearing the news of his death, thousands of mourners traveled enormous distances to attend the funeral.

GEORGE WHITEFIELD, like the Wesley brothers, believed that prayer could be enhanced exponentially through the singing of hymns. Isaac Watts and the Wesleys, who were composing hymns prolifically back in England, had a profound influence on a new generation of American composers and lyricists. Among them was the first American to compose original hymns, the Reverend Samuel Davies, Jonathan Edwards's successor as president of the College of New Jersey. Tall, good-looking, and eloquent, Davies stood out from the crowd. Always impeccably dressed, it was said that he could easily have been mistaken for an ambassador of some great European king. Indeed, he became so respected for his oratorical skills that on a visit to London he was invited to officiate at Sunday services for George II.

Born in New Castle County, Delaware, in 1723, Davies liked to say that his parents had named him "Samuel" to remind him always that he was the "son of prayer," harking back to the Old Testament prophet. Known for his patriotic service during the French and Indian Wars, he was ordained as a "New Light" Presbyterian minister, committed to serving as an evangelical preacher in spreading the word of God. In his early career, he was particularly active as an itinerant preacher throughout the middle colonies, earning him the title the "Apostle of Virginia." During these extensive travels he often paid for his room and board by holding prayer services for the family and their servants who hosted him.

Like Edward Taylor before him, Davies spent considerable time composing prayers and hymns to accompany his Sunday services. Criticized by some of his detractors for writing hymns outside the traditional texts of the Psalms, he reveled in providing spiritual relevance for the benefit of others. In his prayers, he would approach God by likening himself to "a piece of clay" or "an atom sporting in Thy ray."[49] Unlike Taylor, who eschewed publication of his prayers, Davies had no problem with his works being published in Thomas Gibbons's *Hymns Adapted to Divine*

Worship. In doing so, he effectively became America's first official composer of hymns.

Although his output was not prodigious or of the quality of Taylor's, he did compose over a hundred religious poems and prayers, many of which he appended to his sermons. Perhaps his most famous hymn is "Great God of Wonders," a piece sung in churches to this day:

> *Great God of wonders! all Thy ways*
> *Are worthy of thyself—divine;*
> *But the bright glories of Thy grace*
> *Among thine other wonders shine;*
> *Who is pard'ning God like thee?*
> *Or who has grace so rich and free?*[50]

Like his predecessor Jonathan Edwards, Davies was president of the College of New Jersey for only a short time, eighteen months to be exact, due to a serious bout of pneumonia. On New Year's Day, 1761, addressing his students in a chapel prayer service, he foreshadowed the end of his life: "Death may meet some of us within the compass of a year. Perhaps I may die this year . . . It is of little importance to me whether I die this year or not, but the only important point is, that I make good use of my future time, whether it be longer or shorter." He then sternly admonished the young men before him, "Pray frequently, pray fervently!" as the only way to live one's life in union with God. Within little more than a month after delivering his sermon, Samuel Davies was dead.[51]

WHILE MOST OF THE prominent clergymen of the seventeenth and eighteenth centuries were associated with colleges throughout the colonies, thousands of others carried out their ministries in smaller communities or as itinerant preachers. In offering up communal prayer and worship week after week, they became the focal point for the colonists, providing most people with the only intellectual and moral guidance they received outside the home. Many colonists idolized these men as they helped them to confirm their religious convictions and to reinforce the need for a one-on-one relationship with God through prayer.

By the eighteenth century every city and major town in colonial America had built an impressive skyline of white church spires. They stood as monuments to the religious convictions of a people committed to God and to their divine destiny. Whereas prayer had an almost desperate quality to it for America's earliest settlers, it was a staple to everyday living for subsequent generations. With the growing legion of ministers and evangelists preaching up and down the eastern seaboard, God and prayer were becoming exciting and integral elements in the lives of ordinary people. This virtual explosion of religious revivalism, not to mention the solace that the colonists found in turning to prayer, would help bring the colonies closer together at the dawn of the American Revolution.

CHAPTER 3

THE VISIONARIES

1750–1800

The Continental Congress having ordered, Friday the 17th. Instant to be observed as a day of "fasting, humiliation and prayer, humbly to supplicate the mercy of Almighty God, that it would please him to pardon all our manifold sins and transgressions, and to prosper the Arms of the United Colonies, and finally, establish the peace and freedom of America, upon a solid and lasting foundation"—The General [Washington] commands all officers, and soldiers, to pay strict obedience to the Orders of the Continental Congress, and by their unfeigned, and pious observance of their religious duties, incline the Lord, and Giver of Victory, to prosper our arms.

—General Orders, May 15, 1776

"THESE ARE THE TIMES that try men's souls,"[1] Thomas Paine wrote during some of the darkest days of the Revolutionary War. Other Americans could not help but echo the same anxiousness. For colonists who had committed themselves to this new land or whose ancestors had abandoned Europe for a variety of reasons, the long arm of the British Crown and its thirst for greater control were reaching a breaking point.

As important as prayer was to the early colonists, it was indispensable in coalescing the country into a unified force. Prayer was used by the Founding Fathers as a coalescing tool to bring together widely disparate colonies, communities, and churches.

As with most rebellions, the causes of the American Revolution developed over many years and intensified exponentially when the delegates from the thirteen colonies convened in Philadelphia in 1774 for the first time. When they gathered for that initial meeting, the delegates were still searching for ways to force the British to accept America's liberties, not to declare independence. As the crescendo of grievances against the Crown grew to a fevered pitch, however, there was no turning back from outright insurrection.

Excessive taxation on everything from sugar to paper had been imposed on the colonists to pay for the presence of British troops on American soil; to compensate England's past war debts, including the French and Indian Wars that had ended eleven years earlier; and to cover the exorbitant costs of British colonial administration. Jonathan Mayhew, a prominent Massachusetts clergyman who served as pastor of West Church in Boston, delivered a scathing sermon in defiance of the Stamp Act of 1765. In his *Discourse concerning Unlimited Submission*, the Congregationalist minister called on all Christians to view resistance to tyranny as a "glorious" Christian duty, urging his congregation to pray for enlightenment to find the most effective means to confront the Crown's "insidious tyranny."[2] By 1770 tensions had become so raw that British troops fired into a crowd of protesting townspeople in what Samuel Adams, the colony's most recognizable brewer, quickly dubbed "the Boston Massacre," an incident in which five were killed and six injured but which had a far greater impact than the immediate number of casualties suggested.

The stubborn George III and his easily cowed Prime Minister, Frederick, Lord North, swiftly rebuffed any petition from representatives of the American colonists. The long and extensive ties that had patched over past problems were now severely strained. Something had to give.

A war was about to be waged over the next eight years against the homeland of most colonists, many of whom still had family in England. Ties were not just threatened; they were being torn to shreds. By John Adams's reckoning, Americans were seriously split over the subject: "We were about one third Tories, and [one] third timid, and one third true blue Americans."[3]

It was difficult to fathom that just thirteen years before the breaking point, Americans like George Washington had fought under British command during the French and Indian Wars, helping to secure for the British extensive lands to the north and to the west. Men like Benjamin Franklin had lived in London for long periods and had served the British

Crown both as government officials and as liaisons of the King to the colonies. Some colonists like Benjamin Rush, the handsome, popular physician and delegate from Pennsylvania, had studied medicine in Edinburgh and London. Others like the Reverend George Whitefield, his followers, and dozens of other ministers had pursued their preaching on both sides of the Atlantic, maintaining strong ties to both the New and the Old World. Childhood friends and entire families were sharply divided in their loyalties.

Given the early history of the colonies and the religious revival taking hold in the late 1760s, it is little wonder that the restless, apprehensive colonists found enormous comfort in turning to God. Thomas Paine became a catalyst for the Revolution in his much-celebrated *Common Sense*, a pamphlet that legitimized the uprising by arguing that the colonists were exercising their rights under the same covenant that the Israelites had pursued in the Old Testament. Agnostic at best, the hot-tempered and at times erratic Paine, whom Theodore Roosevelt later called "that filthy little atheist,"[4] persuasively argued that "the cause of America is, in great measure, the cause of all mankind. Many circumstances have, and will arise, which are not local, but universal, and through which the principles of all lovers of mankind are affected."[5] Defending his position further, Paine used rich citations from both the Old and the New Testament to illustrate the natural tendency to prayer:

So Samuel called unto the Lord, and the Lord sent thunder and rain that day, and all the people greatly feared the Lord and Samuel. And all the people said unto Samuel, Pray for thy servants unto the Lord thy God that we die not for WE HAVE ADDED UNTO OUR SINS THIS EVIL, TO ASK A KING.[6]

The son of a bankrupt Quaker corset maker had changed the terms of the political debate overnight. Paine's *Common Sense* riveted the colonies and Great Britain alike by clearly laying out the merits of the revolutionary cause by denouncing the oppression of the monarchy, if not the very foundations of hereditary rule. As disingenuous as it may have been coming from Paine, his invoking God and prayer, in effect trumping the authority of the King of England, was a brilliant strategic move. Turning to God in overcoming human oppression had been an age-old entreaty. To bolster his case even further, Thomas Paine added an appendix to *Common Sense* that included another essay addressed specifically to the pacifist Quakers of the New World to defend the "act of bearing arms" as well as the "American Patriot's Prayer." The prayer intertwined a petition to God as well as a philosophical treatise on behalf of revolution.

> *Parent of all, omnipotent*
> *In heav'n and earth below,*
> *Thro' all creation's bounds unspent*
> *Whole streams of goodness flow.*
>
> *But chief to hear my country's voice,*
> *May all my thoughts incline,*
> *'Tis reason's law, 'tis virtue's choice,*
> *'Tis nature's call and thine.*[7]

By the end of 1776, *Common Sense* had been circulated by more than a dozen printers from Philadelphia to Boston, and to the astonishment of even the most ardent patriots one hundred fifty thousand readers had bought the pamphlet at two shillings apiece and had pored over every word.

Another great personality who stirred colonial passions to the cause through his oratory was the Virginia lawyer Patrick Henry, whose deep religious convictions were equaled only by his unshaken belief in individual liberties. Early in his career, Henry's reputation as a champion of free speech and religion was forever secured when he learned that a group of Baptist preachers had just been jailed in Spotsylvania, Virginia, for holding prayer services and preaching in the countryside. Clergymen from more established churches were outraged that these Baptist "rabble rousers" were making inroads by attracting adherents to their religious faith. Jumping on his horse, Henry, a devout Anglican, rode some fifty miles to take up their cause and defend them.[8]

The future governor of Virginia used God's name in the most significant speeches of his career. Before Virginia's colonial convention held in Richmond's Henrico Parish Church on March 23, 1775, Henry, like a bubbling cauldron, erupted in indignation over British arrogance and the Crown's disregard for the grievances of its American subjects. Standing before the colony's delegates, who included Thomas Jefferson and members of Virginia's influential Lee family, Henry roared:

I repeat it, sir, we must fight! An appeal to arms and to the God of Hosts is all that is left us! . . . Besides, sir, we shall not fight our battles alone. There is a just God who presides over the destinies of nations; and who will raise up friends to fight our cause. The battle, sir, is not to the strong alone; it is to the vigilant, the active, the brave . . . Gentlemen may cry peace, peace—but there is no peace. The war is actually begun! The next gale that sweeps from the north will bring to our ears the clash of resounding arms! Our brethren are already in the field! Why stand we here idle? What is it that gentlemen wish? What would they have? Is life so dear, or peace so sweet, as to be purchased at the price of chains and slavery? Forbid it, Almighty God! I know not what course others may take; but as for me, give me liberty, or give me death![9]

As he began to enunciate those last words for rhetorical effect, Henry raised his right hand as if to pierce his heart with a dagger. After he was finished, more than a hundred delegates sat in place in complete, stunned silence for what seemed an eternity. One young man, newly enlisted in the militia, had perched himself on the ledge of an open window outside the church. Positioned only a few feet away from the pew where Henry stood, he turned to a friend standing next to him and remarked just above a whisper, "Let me be buried on this spot!"[10]

Those colonists ready to go to war believed that if God was on their side, as surely he must be, they would triumph. To this "glorious end," they believed, there were no greater centers to engage the debate or to make their case before God than the pulpits of the colonies. A diverse group of churches now dotted America's landscape: 749 Congregationalist, 485 Presbyterian, 457 Baptist, 406 Anglican (including Methodist), 240 Lutheran, 328 Dutch or German Reformed, and 56 Roman Catholic. In addition, Quakers now had 200 meetinghouses, and the infant Jewish community had 5 synagogues, extending from New York to South Carolina.[11] The colonists were clearly an eclectic group of people, and they were now being asked to pull together and forge a common cause.

When the representatives of the colonies finally gathered to chart their future course in Philadelphia on September 5, 1774, at the first of two continental conventions, many of them came from towns and cities hundreds of miles away. Most of them had never been to Philadelphia and were meeting one another for the first time.

While the first two days of meetings were largely focused on organizing the Congress, the first real substance came on September 7. To begin the process of bonding strangers and to harness their cause to a larger purpose, several leading delegates quickly concluded that the first order of business should be to seek divine guidance, thereby integrating both God and prayer in their public, organized cause. It was a catalytic moment. No one better described the setting or the events that first morning than John Adams in a letter to his wife, Abigail:

> When the Congress met, Mr. Cushing [of Massachusetts] made a motion that it should be opened with Prayer. It was opposed by Mr. Jay of New York and Mr. Rutledge of South Carolina, because we were so divided in religious sentiments, some Episcopalians, some Quakers, some Anabaptists, some Presbyterians, and some Congregationalists, so that we could not join in the same act of worship.
>
> Mr. Samuel Adams arose and said that he was no bigot, and could hear a Prayer from any gentleman of Piety and Virtue, who was at the same time a friend to his Country. He was a stranger in Philadelphia, but had heard that Mr. Duché deserved that character, and therefore he moved that Mr. Duché, an Episcopal clergyman, might be desired, to read Prayers to Congress, tomorrow morning. The Motion was seconded, and passed in the affirmative. Mr. Randolph, our President, waited on Mr. Duché, and received for answer, that if his health would permit, he certainly would. Accordingly, the next morning [the Reverend Mr. Duché] appeared with his clerk and in his pontificals, and read several Prayers in the established form; and then read the Collect for the seventh day of September, which was the Thirty-fifth Psalm.
>
> You must remember this was the next morning after we heard the horrible rumor of the cannonade of Boston.
>
> I never saw a greater effect upon an audience. It seemed as if Heaven had ordained that Psalm to be read on that morning.[12]

The psalm read by the Reverend Jacob Duché for that seventh day of September under the Anglican calendar was known as David's Prayer for Help against Unjust Enemies. Few psalms could have affected the delegates with a greater sense of what they were facing or the role that

Divine Providence could play in their cause. Overnight, news of a British incursion in and around Boston had been circulating throughout Philadelphia. Several delegates had every reason to believe that their homes and families were in harm's way. The British had already made clear that they were ready to use any force necessary to put down dissent. Psalm 35 hit a chord:

> Plead my case, O Lord, with them that strive with me, fight against them that fight against me. Take hold of buckler and shield, and rise up for my help. Draw also the spear and the battle-axe to meet those who pursue me; Say to my soul, "I am your salvation." Let those be ashamed and dishonored who seek my life; let those be turned back and humiliated who devise evil against me.[13]

After he finished, Duché spontaneously added, "Be Thou present O God of Wisdom and direct the counsel of this Honorable Assembly; enable them to settle all things on the best and surest foundations; that the scene of blood may be speedily closed; that order, Harmony, and peace may be effectually restored, and Truth and Justice, Religion and Piety, prevail and flourish among the people."

The importance of the moment at the outset of the convention cannot be overestimated. Present that day were George Washington, Patrick Henry, and Peyton Randolph. As the delegates prayed "for America, for Congress, for the Province of Massachusetts Bay, and especially the town of Boston," John Adams wrote in his diary, the prayer and the emotions that erupted were "as permanent, as affectionate, as sublime, as devout, as I have ever heard offered up to Heaven."[14] The diplomat Silas Deane remarked that Duché "prayed with such fervency, purity, and sublimity of style and sentiment . . . that even Quakers shed tears."[15] Joseph Reed of Pennsylvania thought the prayer was a "masterful stroke of policy," while Samuel Ward of Rhode Island called it "one of the most sublime, catholic, well adapted prayers I have ever heard."[16]

Although John Jay of New York and John Rutledge of South Carolina had initially expressed concern about having a chaplain offer a daily invocation, arguing that the religious diversity of the delegates would prevent any one prayer from being all-inclusive, even they came to realize that their fears had been misplaced. Men of dissimilar origins had found common ground in reasoned, timely prayer. That first public prayer set an important precedent, one continued by both houses of Congress into the twenty-first century.

ON JUNE 12, 1775, the delegates in Philadelphia called for a day of fasting and prayer across the colonies on July 20. By the time the day arrived, the Battle of Bunker Hill had already taken place, Washington had assumed formal command of the Revolutionary armies, and the second Continental Congress had been in session for more than a month. As John Adams wrote with some pride to Abigail, "Millions will be upon their knees at once before their great Creator, imploring his forgiveness and blessing, his smiles on American Councils and arms."[17] The day of prayer and fasting was widely publicized in newspapers and handbills, much to the annoyance of the British, but then again, the British could hardly deny the colonists access to churches or the chance to pray even ostensibly for peace.

When July 20 finally arrived, the delegates gathered at their regular meeting place, Pennsylvania's State House, later renamed Independence Hall, and walked as a group to Duché's Christ Church, attending prayer services throughout the morning, and then proceeding to the First Presbyterian Church to continue praying for the rest of the afternoon. When it was all over, Adams wrote to his wife, noting in amazement that the day "was observed here with a Decorum and solemnity, never before seen ever on a Sabbath. The Clergy of all Denominations, here preach Politicks and War in a manner that I never heard in N. England. They are a Flame of Fire."[18]

On July 9, 1776, shortly after the signing of the Declaration of Independence and one day after the first public reading of the document, the delegates elected the Reverend Mr. Duché as the first chaplain of Congress.[19] After the unanimous vote, Duché took to the floor and prayed:

> Look down in mercy, we beseech Thee, on these our American States who have fled to Thee from the rod of the oppressor, who have thrown themselves on thy gracious protection, desiring to be henceforth dependent only on Thee . . . defeat the malicious designs of our cruel adversaries.

Duché, however, was far more complicated than his prayers might indicate. Wrestling with the implications of the newly signed declaration, he turned to the elders of Christ Church to decide whether it was advisable "for the peace and welfare of the congregation, to shut up the churches or to continue the service without using the prayers for the Royal Family."[20] With little debate the vestry closed ranks and agreed to keep the doors of the church open, making clear that all prayers for the King were to be replaced by prayers for the new Congress. Before his congregation, he opened the *Book of Common Prayer* and with his pen struck out all references to King George and his parliament. He inserted instead "the representatives of the American people," and from that day forward the prayer petitions of Christ Church would be used to bolster the revolutionary cause. It was a scene repeated across the colonies.

In the fall of 1776, however, Duché astounded his congregation and Congress when he abruptly resigned his position as chaplain. Soon all of Philadelphia was abuzz, learning of how Duché was now in sympathy with the British, questioning the judgment of the colonial delegates, and bemoaning the role that America's churches had played in inciting rebellion. Infuriated by Duché's hubris, the delegates promptly accepted his resignation and appointed two ministers to serve simultaneously as chaplains: the Reverend George Duffield, pastor of the Third Presbyterian Church of Philadelphia and former minister to the Pennsylvania militia; and the Reverend William White, who would succeed Duché at Christ Church and later be named an Episcopal Bishop. With little debate the delegates agreed that in the future chaplains would be rotated among different religious denominations.[21]

In one of the great misjudgments, if not betrayals, in American history, Jacob Duché ultimately defected unconditionally to the British, believing that the war had turned against the colonists. He provided General William Howe and his men with as much intelligence about the leaders of the Revolution and their troop movements as he could. In a further show of loyalty to the Crown, Duché wrote to George Washington urging him to negotiate at once for immediate surrender. With the help of the British the letter was posted throughout Philadelphia. The delegates were incredulous. "Judas," "fop," and "ass" were some of the kinder words used to describe Duché.[22] His brother-in-law Francis Hopkinson, the distinguished and talented statesman and signer of the Declaration of Independence, wrote to Duché in absolute bewilderment: "Words cannot express the grief and consternation that wounded my Soul at sight of this fatal performance . . . I am perfectly disposed to attribute this unfortunate step to the timidity of your temper, the weakness of your nerves, and the undue influence of those about you. But will the world hold you excused?"[23]

WITH THE Declaration of Independence, the delegates forged through uncharted territory in beginning the document with such metaphors as "Nature's God" and "Our Creator." They used God to frame their arguments against the King while invoking God's divine righteousness to their cause. The last lines of the document in particular bound the delegates to one another and to the people they represented: "As for the support of this Declaration, with a firm reliance on the Protection of Divine Providence, we mutually pledge to each other our Lives, our Fortunes, and our sacred Honor."[24]

More than half of all ministers throughout the colonies soon came forward to offer their services to the war effort. They enlisted as members of state legislatures and Congress, became army chaplains and regular military recruits, and served as recording secretaries to correspond with officials and the public. The first chaplains of the war had been created by Congress on July 29, 1775, with one chaplain assigned to each regiment. By 1777 the financial strains had become so onerous that Congress tried to reduce the number of chaplains, but George Washington intervened, and for a while the number remained the same.[25] With the chaplains' help, the Continental Congress endorsed publication of a new American Bible,[26] created national days of thanksgiving, and called for days of "humiliation, fasting, and prayer" at least twice a year throughout the war.[27]

From pulpit to battlefield, ministers across the colonies called on their congregations to pray continuously for the Revolutionary cause. Ministers strongly encouraged their congregations to examine their consciences, to understand that this was "a just cause sinless," and to review their "saving acquaintance with God through prayer."[28] Peter Muhlenberg, known to his contemporaries as the "fighting parson," became an overnight sensation for one particularly noteworthy episode played out in front of his Lutheran congregation in Woodstock, Virginia. The son of a founder of the Lutheran Church in America, Henry Melchior Muhlenberg, Peter had an innate flair for the dramatic. At the conclusion of one of his vintage, fiery sermons, and after reciting a series of inflammatory prayers, all of which spoke to the cause of freedom, he ripped off his black clerical robe to the gasps of his parishioners, revealing the uniform of a Virginia militia officer.[29]

In another display of patriotic fervor, the Reverend James Caldwell of New Jersey used a local church's prayer books in a rather creative, unorthodox way. Just as they were about to engage the British, the troops he was assigned to as chaplain discovered that they had no paper wadding for their muskets. Without wadding to secure the musket balls, the muskets would be worthless.

Realizing there was no other solution, Caldwell galloped at full speed to the nearest church and gathered every copy of *Psalms of David, Hymns, and Spiritual Songs* he could find to carry back to his men. The hymnal, compiled by Isaac Watts, the most famous British hymnist of the eighteenth century, was a staple of every church throughout the colonies. Returning to camp, Caldwell tore the pages out of their bindings and eagerly handed the freshly minted wadding to each of his men, admonishing them, "Put Watts into them, boys!"[30]

Arguably the most famous American clergyman of the Revolution was John Witherspoon. Lured to the presidency of the College of New Jersey from his native Scotland, the ordained Presbyterian minister became known as much for his piety and intellectual brilliance as for his lilting brogue and ability to forge political compromise. Chosen to represent New Jersey in the Continental Congress days before the Declaration of Independence became official, Witherspoon, who had been in America for less than eight years but had become an unabashed patriot, signed the document. Serving as president of the College of New Jersey from 1768 to 1794, he was known as a superb administrator and greatly influenced his students and the surrounding community of Princeton. It was only a matter of time before he was accused by British loyalists of turning the college into a "seminary of sedition." His lasting influence could be seen in the lives and careers of the students he taught. They included one Vice President, twelve members of the Continental Congress, five delegates to the Constitutional Convention, forty-nine U.S. representatives, and twenty-eight U.S. senators; three Supreme Court justices, eight U.S. district judges, three attorneys general, and one Secretary of State.[31]

Relatively unknown in the modern world as one of America's Founding Fathers, Witherspoon was a palpable force behind the scenes. While a member of the convention, he became the resident expert on drafting official declarations about prayer and fasting. Through his efforts the famous proclamation of June 1775 was written, calling on delegates and colonists alike to spend an entire day in church in the faint hope that reconciliation with Great Britain might still be possible.

Witherspoon continued to write the official prayer decrees of Congress, and on December 18, 1777, he drafted its first proclamation calling for a day of thanksgiving throughout the colonies, having argued that the delegates could hardly continue to make entreaties to God for success on the battlefield without expressing some measure of gratitude for past favors. "To adore the Superintending Providence of Almighty God" for the "innumerable bounties of His Common Providence" had to be part of the prayer equation for the delegates.[32] While Witherspoon's quiet influence would always be felt, Congress's preoccupation in turning to prayer at critical moments in the war effort remained steadfast. Over and over again the delegates and future representatives of the citizens of the United States continued to rededicate themselves and their cause to Divine Providence, "our shield in the day of battle, our comforter in the hour of death and our kind parent and merciful judge through time and through eternity."[33]

WITH THE WAR BUILDING to a fever pitch, budding American composers began to write patriotic tunes and set prayers to music, capturing the revolutionary spirit of the moment. William Billings, a poor Boston tanner who had to overcome serious physical disfigurements, became America's unofficial composer laureate, writing both popular hymns and secular anthems. In publishing the first American book of music with the help of Boston's Paul Revere, a collection of hymns called *The New-England Psalm-Singer,* Billings set into motion America's first formal foray into composing serious, original music. Idiosyncratic, often dissonant, and lacking traditional European refinement, the songs he wrote had an edgy quality. Although his music seemed to some listeners nothing more than a form of howling, the structure of his choral hymns became a standard in America for years with such pieces as "Hear My Pray'r" and "Let Tyrants Shake Their Iron Rods."[34]

Despite the patriotic ditties and prayers for victory, idealism gave way to the reality of desperation. Horrendous stories of hardship were being reported from one colony to the next. The saga of Valley Forge, where George Washington commanded a ragtag group of farmers, merchants, boys, and other amateur soldiers who were unprepared, ill equipped, and half starved, became the stuff of legends. By the brutal winter of 1777–78, it had become clear that without some kind of financial support for the most basic provisions, many of the soldiers could not physically, let alone mentally, survive. Fifty thousand dollars were needed to tide the troops over. The entire Revolutionary cause hung in the balance, but the Continental Congress simply could not raise the funds in time.

Facing overwhelming odds and with several months of rough weather ahead, Washington and Congress had no one to turn to but the Philadelphia financier Robert Morris. Having immigrated to America as a teenager from Liverpool, Morris had become the most successful merchant in America, utilizing the Port of Philadelphia to great advantage in moving goods between the colonies and Great Britain. Having already stretched his financial resources to the breaking point to keep the war afloat, Morris had few options left. On New Year's Eve he decided to attend St. George's Methodist Church in Philadelphia, which was holding an all-night prayer vigil to ask God's help to sustain the troops at Valley Forge just a few miles away. After spending considerable time in prayer, he realized what he needed to do. Walking out of the church in the middle of the night, he went from door to door, rousing wealthy friends and acquaintances from their sleep and asking for their help. By the end of the first day of the New Year, he had convinced merchants and real-estate owners to help him secure the necessary funds. Within hours Washington was told that his troops would have the provisions, equipment, guns, and ammunition they so badly needed.[35]

It would be nearly three years from that winter in Valley Forge before Washington and his men routed the British at Yorktown, effectively ending the war. Prayer had played an integral role in the hard-fought and decisive defeat of the British, as it would in the formation of the new republic.

On July 4, 1783, the first recorded celebration of American independence took place in the Moravian community of Salem, North Carolina, where the entire day was spent in prayerful thanksgiving. As they gathered at dawn in their local church, 160 townspeople were greeted to the blaring sound of trombones. For the rest of the day, they prayed, they sang hymns, and they feasted on sweet cakes, blended wine, and other treats until it was time to go to bed.[36]

Several hundred miles to the north in Newburgh, New York, William

Billings had prepared an effusive anthem, steeped in both prayer and patriotism, to celebrate victory and independence. The message was simple. Americans now only had one king, and that was God Almighty.

> The States, O Lord, with Songs of Praise
> Shall in they Strength rejoice . . .
> A covenant of Peace thou mad'st with us and confirmed by thy word,
> A covenant thou mad'st with us and seal'd it with thy Blood.
> To the King they shall sing Halleluiah.
> And all the Continent shall sing: Down with this earthly King,
> No King, but God . . .
> May his reign be Glorious, America victorious and may the earth
>   acknowledge
> God is the King. Amen, Amen, Amen.[37]

TO APPRECIATE THE DEPTH and pervasiveness of American prayer in the eighteenth century, particularly among the country's leaders, one need only look at the institutions of higher learning throughout the colonies. By the conclusion of the war almost two dozen colleges had come into existence. Already these institutions had served as springboards for colonial politicians, lawyers, doctors, clergymen, and merchants. In turn, they cast a wide net in their influence on the affairs of the budding United States. There were John Adams and John Hancock (Harvard), Alexander Hamilton and Gouverneur Morris (King's College, now Columbia), James Madison and Benjamin Rush (College of New Jersey, now Princeton), Thomas Jefferson and Edmund Randolph (William and Mary), and William Livingston (Yale), to name a few. Each college had been founded by a specific church or group of ministers whose intent was to nourish both mind and soul, providing, in their words, "a truly Christian education."[38] Even Benjamin Franklin felt it important in 1751 to declare in the case of the College of Philadelphia (University of Pennsylvania), a school he helped to found, that a rigorous morning and evening regimen of worship had been instituted to provide short, spiritually charged prayers for regular recitation by students and faculty alike.[39]

The schools covered a wide swath of geographic territory and represented all of the major Protestant denominations. Founded either before or during the Revolutionary War, these colleges grew into formidable institutions, all of which exist today:

COLLEGE	FOUNDED	RELIGIOUS ORIGINS
Harvard Cambridge, Massachusetts	1636	Congregationalist (Puritan)
William and Mary Williamsburg, Virginia	1693	Anglican
Yale New Haven, Connecticut	1701	Congregationalist (Puritan)
College of Philadelphia (University of Pennsylvania) Philadelphia, Pennsylvania	1740	Presbyterian (New Light)
College of New Jersey (Princeton) Princeton, New Jersey	1746	Presbyterian
King's College (Columbia) New York, New York	1754	Anglican
Brown Providence, Rhode Island	1764	Baptist
Queen's College (Rutgers) New Brunswick, New Jersey	1766	Dutch Reformed
Dartmouth Hanover, New Hampshire	1769	Congregationalist
College of Charleston Charleston, South Carolina	1770	Anglican

For these all-male institutions, the spiritual regimen was as difficult as the curriculum. Almost uniformly, all the students arose between four and five o'clock in the morning, got dressed, and proceeded to the college's assembly room or chapel to pray and listen to a brief sermon by one of their tutors. After prayer services the students sat down to breakfast in the dining hall, where grace was said by one of the professors. If any young man missed grace without proper excuse, he forfeited his next meal. Once the day's courses and studies were finished, students would attend another mandatory prayer service to put the day's activities in perspective and seek God's guidance for the next. If a student missed a service without "sufficient cause," a set of stiff financial penalties, depending on the circumstances, would be assessed.[40]

On Sundays the routine was even more intense. Longer services and invocations were held, with the president of the college in most instances delivering the sermon. Of his experience as a student at the College of New Jersey years earlier, a graduate recounted:

> At five in the morning, when it was still quite dark, he woke with a start at the blowing outside his door a horn which sounded like the last trumpet. It was the servant whose duty it was to rouse the students for morning prayers . . . At its summons the student hustled out of bed, lit his candle, washed his face and hands, got into his clothes and joined the stream of boys on the way to the Prayer Hall. On the opening day it was the president who conducted morning prayers. He mounted the pulpit in the south end of the room, the roll was called, and all united in singing a psalm. After which he made a brief talk, expressing the hope that the students would improve their time by hard study, observe all the laws of the college, and open their hearts to the influence of religion. It was only on special occasions that the president graced either morning or evening prayers, for it usually fell to the lot of the tutors to conduct these services. The students as a rule preserved order in the Prayer Hall, because they realized that any disrespect to religion would bring speedy and severe punishment.[41]

At the same time, errant students would try to test the limits of school administrators. On one occasion one or more students at the College of New Jersey sneaked into the Prayer Hall before morning services and strategically placed a stuffed raccoon behind the chapel's Bible. As students and faculty filed into their assigned seats, still trying to adjust themselves to the early morning hour, the raccoon sat, staring out at them.

There were no records as to whether the individual or individuals responsible were ever caught.[42]

The president of King's College (Columbia) presided over each morning's prayer service. After dinner he again officiated at evening services, allowing each young man to reflect on the day's activities, thinking about where he may have succeeded or needed improvement. He would then dismiss the students for the night, urging them to pray silently in their rooms, reminding them of the pledge they made upon entering the school to avoid "passions and youthful lusts and all temptations." Together, the president and the students beseeched God to instill in them diligence in their studies and good moral character in their lives, affirming through prayer that only "by truly exemplary lives [may we] be creditable to our family and friends, ornaments to our country, and useful in our generation to promote Thy glory and the good of mankind."[43]

As a student at King's College, Alexander Hamilton took the missives of college president Myles Cooper to heart. Abandoned by his father at the age of ten, Hamilton lost his mother to fever two years later. His cousin, who promptly adopted the young Alexander as his own, committed suicide not long after, while his grandmother, aunt, and uncle died within a few months of each other. Through the remarkable kindness and mentorship of the Reverend Hugh Knox, an ordained Presbyterian minister who had graduated from the College of New Jersey (Princeton), the precocious, seventeen-year-old Hamilton found his way to King's College, and his life gained a stability that he had not known for years. He faithfully followed the school's admonitions to pray often, not only publicly with his classmates but also in the privacy of his dorm room. His roommate and lifelong friend Robert Troup recalled how Hamilton "was attentive to public worship and in the habit of praying upon his knees both night and morning." So impressed was Troup with Hamilton's piety that he wrote in his diary, "I have lived in the same room with him for some time, and I have often been powerfully affected by the fervor and eloquence of his prayers."[44]

WITH THE REVOLUTIONARY WAR now behind them, the colonial delegates came together once again in Philadelphia to see if they could form a confederation. A constitutional convention was set for May 1787 to agree on the character, nature, and logistics of such a union.

Anyone attending both the Continental Congress and the Constitutional Convention would have noticed significant differences between the two gatherings, from the agendas to the new faces. Unlike the Continental Congress, the Constitutional Convention did not begin each day with a prayer. The Declaration of Independence had been drafted under extraordinary duress, but the Constitution was approached as a working, albeit monumental, document.

With George Washington chairing the proceedings as president of the convention from late May to the middle of September 1789, delegates and others poured into Philadelphia. Before the gavel called the first session to order, however, it had become clear that many delegates had arrived with their own agendas. Debates and backroom maneuvering were providing fertile ground for a variety of ideas, as well as launching future careers.

As tempers frayed after a few weeks of deliberations, the eighty-three-year-old Benjamin Franklin, a veteran of the two continental congresses, decided to intervene. Not only did he recall how prayer had become such a catalyst during the war against Great Britain, but he even harkened back to 1747 when he strongly advocated public prayer and fasting when the colonists of Pennsylvania were facing Indian wars.[45] Realizing that the debates were only becoming more heated and susceptible to political impasse, Franklin took to the floor out of frustration and addressed the delegates on the importance of their turning to prayer:

Mr. President: The small progress we have made after four or five weeks' close attendance and continual reasonings with each other—our different sentiments on almost every question, several of the last producing as many noes as ayes—is, methinks, a melancholy proof of the imperfection of the human understanding. We indeed seem to feel our own want of political wisdom, since we have been running about in search of it. We have gone back to ancient history for models of government, and examined the different forms of those republics which, having been formed with the seeds of their own dissolution, now no longer exist. And we have viewed modern states all round Europe, but find none of their constitutions suitable to our circumstances.

In this situation of this assembly, groping, as it were, in the dark, to find political truth, and scarce able to distinguish it when presented to us, how has it happened, Sir, that we have not hitherto once thought of humbly applying to the Father of lights to illuminate our understandings? In the beginning of the contest with Great Britain, when we were sensible of dangers, we had daily prayer in this room for divine protection. Our prayers, Sir, were heard, and they were graciously answered. All of us who were engaged in the struggle must have observed frequent instances of a superintending Providence in our favor. To that kind Providence, we owe this happy opportunity of consulting in peace on the means of establishing our future national felicity. And have we now forgotten that powerful Friend? Or do we imagine that we no longer need His assistance?

I have lived, Sir, a long time, and the longer I live, the more convincing proofs I see of this truth—that God governs in the affairs of men. And if a sparrow cannot fall to the ground without his notice, is it probable that an empire can rise without his aid? We have been assured, Sir, in the sacred writings, that "Except the Lord build the house, they labor in vain that build it."

I firmly believe this: and I also believe that without His concurring aid we shall succeed, in this political building, no better than the builders of the Tower of Babel. We shall be divided by our partial local interests; our projects will be confounded; and we ourselves shall become a reproach and by-word down to future ages. And what is worse, mankind may hereafter, from this unfortunate instance, despair of establishing governments by human wisdom, and leave it to chance, war, and conquest.

I therefore beg leave to move that henceforth, prayers imploring the assistance of Heaven, and its blessings on our deliberations, be held in this assembly every morning before we proceed to business, and that one or more of the clergy of this city be requested to officiate at this service.[46]

Roger Sherman of Connecticut, who had fought in the political trenches with Franklin since the signing of the Declaration of Independence, seconded the motion, but the delegates were either embarrassed over the matter or unconvinced that in drafting a constitution there was need for prayer. Given that it was Franklin who intervened, however, the matter had to be addressed in some form.

The first to speak was Alexander Hamilton of New York. Although he agreed that prayers should have been said from the first day of the convention, he expressed concern that because of the "embarrassments and dissensions within the Convention,"[47] the public might conclude that the delegates had become desperate.

Edmund Randolph of Virginia, later the country's first attorney general, offered a solution. Given that the Fourth of July was in six days, the delegates could commemorate the occasion with an officially sanctioned sermon delivered from the floor by a local Protestant minister, followed by a series of prayers for the ongoing deliberations. From that point forward, each session of the convention could begin with a prayer, and the transition from having no prayer to offering a daily prayer would appear almost seamless. Franklin liked the idea and quickly seconded the motion.

Randolph's solution made many delegates uncomfortable, however. While it covered the delinquency matter, it opened the door to extending prayer into a religious sermon. At a time when the delegates were debating the delicate issue of separation of church and state, Randolph's proposal might create even more problems.

The official minutes of that day conveyed the unease of the delegates and their disposition to adjourn without taking up the matter. In the end, that is exactly what happened, and no vote was taken. Most of the delegates attended private prayer services on the Fourth, but Franklin considered the underwhelming response shortsighted, noting in his diary with clear annoyance, "The convention, except three or four persons, thought prayer unnecessary!"[48]

What has been lost in interpretations of the First Amendment to the Constitution, "Congress shall make no law respecting an establishment of religion, or prohibiting the free exercise thereof," is that religion, not prayer, was the object of the framers' concerns. While the subject of daily prayer was deferred during the four months of the Constitutional Convention, the larger issue of prayer in the new republic was not relegated to the sidelines. The prudent approach for this new republic was to allow religion and the tenets of different faiths to flourish on their own and compete for the hearts, minds, and souls of Americans. That had become clear on that first day in 1774 when interfaith prayer was invoked, creating an environment conducive to the moment but reminding the participants of their larger purpose and their accountability to a higher power.

DESPITE FRANKLIN'S FAILURE to institute prayer in the remaining weeks of the Constitutional Convention, his influence on the formation of the new republic was enormous, fortified by a spirituality that only grew over the years. What is extraordinary about Benjamin Franklin is how he bridged the span of American history that extended from his accepting advice as a teenager from that Puritan divine the Reverend Cotton Mather to his becoming only one of three signers of the Declaration of Independence, the Constitution, and the Articles of Confederation. Having long pursued avocations as an entrepreneur, printer, writer, and scientist, Franklin was an outspoken and integral part of America's new dynamic. In his wildly popular *Poor Richard's Almanack*, which made him a household name in colonial America, he wrote, "God helps those who help themselves," and in another proverb admonished, "Work as if you were to live a hundred years, pray as if you were to die tomorrow."[49] By the time of his death, Franklin had composed a more extensive introspection on prayer than any other Founding Father.

When he was all of twenty-two, he wrote a piece called *Articles of Belief and Acts of Religion*. In it he related to God as "my friend" as he pondered the role of prayer in a person's life. In a straightforward account, Franklin confirmed his belief in God, and then wrote a series of prayers that he felt expressed his spiritual sentiments and should be recited as a guide to virtuous living. Divided into three sections, his invocations included adoration (Praise Be Thy Name Forever), petition (Help Me, O Father), and thanksgiving (Good God, I Thank Thee). As a prelude to the passage, he shared his thoughts on how to optimize the prayer experience: "Being mindful that before I address the Deity, my soul ought to be calm and serene, free from passion and perturbation, or otherwise elevated with rational joy and pleasure, I ought to use a countenance that expresses a filial respect, mixed with a kind of smiling that signifies inward joy and satisfaction and admiration."[50]

He also rewrote the Lord's Prayer in 1768 to make it "more concise, equally expressive, and better modern English,"[51] believing that it contained the most important formula to self-fulfillment:

Heavenly Father, May all revere Thee, And become Thy dutiful children
and faithful subjects. May thy Laws be obeyed on earth as perfectly as
they are in Heaven. Provide for us this day as Thou hast hitherto daily
done. Forgive us our trespasses, and enable us likewise to forgive
those that offend us. Keep us out of temptation and deliver us from Evil.[52]

The fact that Franklin was not a member of the Church of England
did not stop him from revising the *Book of Common Prayer* in the fall of
1775 in collaboration with Great Britain's Lord Le Despencer, better
known as Sir Francis Dashwood. In setting to work, he and Dashwood,
a rather colorful and somewhat scandalous figure, decided to abridge the
work rather dramatically, hoping to give the rites and prayers of the
Anglican Church greater meaning.

Franklin had always eschewed long prayers, writing to Yale's Ezra
Stiles in 1772 that he had even studied the prayers of Eastern Religions,
finding them to be overly complicated. In the end, he believed that Jesus
had set the right tone in offering "short prayer as an example."[53] Otherwise, he argued, "true prayer becomes impracticable, the mind wanders,
and the fervency of devotion is slackened."[54] In the end, the drastic
abridgement of the *Book of Common Prayer* never caught on, and Franklin
would candidly admit that "some were given away, very few sold, and I
suppose the bulk became waste paper."[55] It was not his first or last failure
in the publishing business.

In his *Autobiography*, published posthumously and certainly the finest
work of its kind to come out of America up to that time, Franklin also
let it be known that there was one special prayer that he held dear, one
that he recited almost daily throughout most of his adult life. He
explained, "Conceiving God to be the fountain of wisdom, I thought it
right and necessary to solicit his assistance for obtaining it; to this end I
formed the following little prayer which was prefixed to my tables of
examination for daily use":

O powerful goodness! Bountiful Father! Merciful Guide! Increase in me
that wisdom which discovers my truest interest. Strengthen my resolution
to perform what that wisdom dictates. Accept my kind offices to thy
other children as the only return in my power for thy continual favours
to me.[56]

Like his younger contemporaries Thomas Jefferson, Thomas Paine, and Ethan Allen, Franklin was often cast as a deist, someone who believes that God is nothing more than a retired clockmaker, intervening rarely in human affairs. As his writings would ultimately show, however, he was far more complex theologically. Despite his lifelong discomfort with orthodox theology and church membership, Franklin clearly showed his belief in the efficacy of prayer. By lifting the human spirit in deference, if not supplication, to the "Father of Lights," one of his favorite and most fanciful metaphors, individuals and whole communities could be lifted beyond their greatest aspirations.[57]

When Benjamin Franklin passed away at the remarkable age of eighty-four in 1790, he was buried at Christ Church in Philadelphia. Before a crowd estimated to exceed twenty thousand, he was lavishly eulogized. Nothing like it had ever been seen before in America. Clergymen from all of the city's major denominations led the procession of mourners, while muffled requiem bells tolled throughout Philadelphia.

No individual, of course, possessed the extraordinary personal attributes or was more critical in setting the political tone in the early days of the Republic than George Washington. Religiously Washington was as enigmatic to his contemporaries as he would be to his later chroniclers. While he regularly attended Episcopal services at both Truro Parish and Christ Church, near his estate at Mount Vernon, as well as in various churches when he temporarily resided in Philadelphia and New York, he simply did not speak openly on issues of ecclesiastical doctrine, leading many historians to label him, fairly or unfairly, a deist.

In trying to bolster the spiritual credentials of Washington, some of his biographers have helped to perpetuate myths that, over many generations, are now hard to shake off. Certain prayers and pious acts that have been attributed to the country's first president simply never took place. What he did reveal throughout his life, however, was his absolute devotion to God and an unwavering belief in the need for and efficacy of prayer.

While precious little is known of Washington's early childhood, his jottings as a thirteen-year-old were interspersed with reflections of his observant religious upbringing. In a series of verses he recorded in his notebook entitled "On Christmas Day," he wrote one brief entry that read,

Assist me, Muse divine, to sing the morn
On which the Saviour of mankind was born.[58]

By the time Washington entered the military, his notion of the worth of prayer had become so deeply engrained that he was convinced that no soldier was worth his salt without being spiritually vigilant at all times. From promoting the hiring of chaplains in the army to conducting prayer services in camp, he instilled spiritual discipline. As a colonel in the British army during the French and Indian War, he saw to it that prayer exercises were held daily.[59] Later when the Continental Congress called for days of prayer and fasting, Washington not only reinforced those directives with his men, but he also noted in his diaries how he personally had followed them.[60] At every turn during the war, he promoted prayer in all its forms, urging the troops to "implore the Lord, and Giver of all victory to pardon our manifold sins and wickedness" on one occasion while stressing the need "to approach the throne of Almighty God, with gratitude and praise" on another.[61]

More than three years into the war, Washington became more convinced than ever that prayer had been critical to his success and to the cause of the colonists. In a letter to one of his generals he wrote, "The hand of Providence has been so conspicuous in all this, that he must be worse than an infidel that lacks faith, and more than wicked, that has not gratitude enough to acknowledge his obligations, but it will be time enough for me to turn preacher, when my present appointment ceases."[62] In the end he believed that God had played a central part in the outcome of the war.

Grateful for the chance to fade into retirement, George Washington returned to Mount Vernon where he intended to live out his days overseeing his working farm. Before doing so, however, he felt compelled to write a letter to all of the governors of the newly freed states invoking God's continued blessings upon them. It was one of the most heartfelt and moving set of remarks he would ever make. The last paragraph would become known to many as "Washington's Prayer."[63]

I now make it my earnest prayer, that God would have you, and the State over which you preside, in his holy protection, that he would incline the hearts of the Citizens to cultivate a spirit of subordination and obedience to Government, to entertain a brotherly affection and love for one another, for their fellow Citizens of the United

States at large, and particularly for their brethren who have served in the Field, and finally, that he would most graciously be pleased to dispose us all, to do Justice, to love mercy, and to demean ourselves that Charity, humility and pacific temper of mind, which are the Characteristics of the Divine Author of our blessed Religion, and without an humble imitation of whose example in these things, we can never hope to be a happy Nation.[64]

Washington's plans to return to his beloved Virginia, of course, were short-lived, and soon he was called upon to preside over the Constitutional Convention in Philadelphia, and in turn to serve as the country's first President. By the time he was sworn into office, a reluctant George Washington comprehended more fully than most the hard road that soon would face him and the country.

On April 30, 1789, at his inauguration on the balcony of Federal Hall in New York City, the country's first seat of government, chancellor of the State of New York Robert Livingston administered the oath of office. Washington recited the prescribed oath under the Constitution, spontaneously adding the words "so help me God" as he leaned down to kiss the Bible. Those two acts—"so help me God" and kissing the Bible— would launch a tradition, if not set an overall spiritual tenor, which would be followed by his successors for generations to come.

Once the oath of office was administered to cheers to "Long live George Washington, President of the United States!," Washington delivered an address replete with direct and indirect references to God invoking "the Invisible Hand which conducts the affairs of men" and "tendering this homage to the Great Author of every public and private good." It was the last lines of his speech, however, that seemed to capture the essence of his personal theology, "resorting once more to the Parent of the Human Race in supplication," imploring the nation never to forget "His divine blessing . . . on which the success of this government must depend."[65]

Once the ceremony was over, and at the direction of the U.S. Congress, the President, members of the Senate and House, foreign dignitaries, heads of newly formed departments, and other invited guests walked the seven hundred yards from Federal Hall to St. Paul's Episcopal Church en masse in what was described by Pennsylvania Senator William Maclay as a "grand procession" with the colorful militia lined up in a double column the entire way.

Arriving at St. Paul's, the assembled congregation was led in a prayer service by Samuel Provoost, New York's Episcopal bishop, a prelate who would be named the U.S. Senate's first chaplain five days later. With George Washington sitting in the front pew, the new leaders joined one another in singing the Te Deum and reciting a set of prayers specially chosen for the occasion.[66] For the next two years the seat of the new government would remain in New York City where Washington would issue his first official Thanksgiving message, again reinforcing his position on prayer, ". . . it is the duty of all nations to acknowledge the providence of Almighty God, to obey his will, to be grateful for his benefits, and humbly to implore his protection and favor."[67]

THE SPIRITUAL HUMILITY that George Washington showed in public only made him more endearing. The country loved its new President, and ministers and laypeople alike composed intercessory prayers as a way to show it. John Carroll, the country's first Catholic Bishop and later Archbishop, and the founder of Georgetown University, offered one of those tributes.

What was particularly significant about Carroll was his unrelenting embrace of a country whose citizens were largely suspicious of Roman Catholics. While the Catholic Church also held on to its own prejudices about the correctness of Protestantism, Carroll did not let doctrine stand in the way of ensuring that the Church's followers were fully integrated into the country's mainstream. Rather, he deftly used prayer to demonstrate the Church's civic loyalty by directing parishioners in every American Catholic church to remain in their pews at the conclusion of Sunday Mass to pray for their leaders. He even composed a prayer on the occasion of Washington's birthday in 1794 that was read from every pulpit.

Carroll's use of prayer for civil authority became a significant, symbolic signal to the country's leaders, to his Catholic flock, and to the country in general in trying to break down religious barriers. In an attempt to integrate the great diversity of Catholic immigrants, he even went so far as to petition the Vatican to allow the Catholic Church of America to recite the Mass and all its prayers in English rather than Latin.

ON DECEMBER 7, 1796, the nation took another step in its development when John Adams was elected the second President of the United States after a brief but grueling campaign.

Adams fully appreciated the mantle of the office he had inherited, although it was a difficult one for him to carry. Born into a Congregationalist family, he felt most comfortable as an adult identifying himself as a Unitarian, believing that God did intervene in human affairs, that a hereafter did exist, and that Christ was a paragon of virtue, but not divine. He certainly shared the sentiments of his wife, Abigail, herself the daughter of a Congregationalist minister, when she wrote to their daughter-in-law Louisa, the wife of John Quincy, and declared that "true religion is from the Heart, between Man and his Creator, and not the imposition of man or creeds and tests."[68]

Throughout most of his administration, John Adams resided in Philadelphia while the President's House was being built in the country's new capital, Washington, D.C. With the house almost completed and without fanfare, Adams rode from Philadelphia to Washington on November 1, 1800, becoming the first President to occupy the White House. The Executive Mansion, as it was then called, was still under heavy construction. Nonetheless, Adams was pleased to be there. On the second night after his arrival, he carefully walked around the scaffolding and building materials strewn everywhere, climbing up to the second floor to go to bed. He awoke the next morning, took out a plain piece of paper, and scribbled at the top of the page for the first time, "President's House, Washington City." In a memorable letter to his wife, and there were many, he spoke of his awe for the office he now held on behalf of the nation, and wrote the following prayer: "I pray Heaven to bestow THE BEST OF BLESSINGS ON THIS HOUSE and All that shall hereafter Inhabit it, May none but honest and Wise Men ever rule."[69]

His invocation was later engraved on a plaque by President Franklin Roosevelt and placed on the mantel of the grand fireplace in the State Room of the White House, where it hangs today.

ADAMS, LIKE WASHINGTON, issued several national days of fasting and prayer while he was President. It was his fourth and last proclamation, for Thursday, April 25, 1799, calling on all Americans to "abstain as far as may be from their secular occupations, [to] devote the time to the sacred duties of religion, in public and private," and to "call to mind our numerous offences with the sincerest penitence" that later became problematical for him, even though it was in keeping with past declarations. It read in part: "And I do, also, recommend that, with these acts of humiliation, penitence, and prayer, fervent thanksgiving to the author of all good be united, for the countless favors which he is still continuing to the people of the United States, and which render their condition as a nation eminently happy, when compared with the lot of others."[70]

The problem arose when the Presbyterian Church, which had been gaining strength in both numbers and influence, helped promote the proclamation. Deeply resented by other Protestant denominations, the General Assembly of the Presbyterian Church was seen in some quarters as aggressively trying to establish itself as America's national church. Although Adams was not Presbyterian, their endorsement turned into a political nightmare for him.

While serving as Adams's Vice President, Thomas Jefferson fanned the flames, along with Alexander Hamilton, Aaron Burr, and James Madison, to see that the Presbyterian connection stuck to the President, using it to argue that Adams should not be reelected in 1800. Although there were a variety of reasons why he was turned out of office, losing to Jefferson by only eight electoral votes, Adams was still stung, twelve years later, by the unfair criticism that his proclamation on prayer had generated. As Adams's biographer David McCullough put it, that particular election "became a contest of personal vilification surpassing any presidential election in American history."[71] In retirement, Adams would write to the unabashedly pious Benjamin Rush in exasperation:

> The national fast recommended by me turned me out of office . . .
> A general suspicion prevailed that the Presbyterian Church was ambitious . . . I was represented as a Presbyterian and at the head of this political and ecclesiastical project. The secret whisper ran through all the sects, "Let us have Jefferson, Madison, Burr, anybody, whether they be philosophers, Deists, or even atheists, rather than a Presbyterian President." This principle is at the bottom of the unpopularity of national fasts and thanksgivings.[72]

Despite his expressed frustrations, Adams may well have been trying to rationalize his defeat for a second term. The fact remained that prayer had played and continued to play a vital role in the life of America. To examine the personal backgrounds of more than a hundred men who debated, as well as signed, the Declaration of Independence, the Constitution, and the Articles of Confederation is to appreciate their unusual spiritual mettle.

ATTEMPTS TO UNDERSTAND the intentions and deliberations of the Founding Fathers, particularly related to matters of the divine, have often been based on the extensive writings of a handful of individuals like Thomas Jefferson and James Madison, men who were not particularly religious. However, the vast majority of delegates came from established churches, were genuinely spiritual by all objective measures, and showed real sensitivity to the religious diversity of the colonists.

Prayer served to bind, to inspire, and to acknowledge the existence of a higher power. That is why Jefferson, when drafting the Declaration of Independence, included so many allusions to God. To a diverse assembly of colonial representatives, who had agreed to pray as their first order of business under the pressures they faced in 1774, such references could bring everyone together. To the Founding Fathers spiritual matters counted. Turning to God for guidance, wisdom, and support during those formative, difficult days was natural and had a catalytic effect that could have been achieved in no other way.

Prayer would continue to be a source of introspection, vision, and support in launching and sustaining the new republic. Although its use under certain circumstances would be debated for years to come, it would always hold sway and relevance in the life of the country and its people.

CHAPTER 4

THE DEVELOPERS

1800–1840

The religious atmosphere of the country was the first thing that struck me on arrival in the United States. The longer I stayed in the country, the more conscious I became of the important political consequences resulting from this novel situation.

In France I had seen the spirits of religion and of freedom almost always marching in opposite directions. In America I found them intimately linked together in joint reign over the same land.

My longing to understand this phenomenon increased daily.

—Alexis de Tocqueville (1835)

With the Republic firmly established, it was left to a new group of civic, cultural, and religious builders to take the country to the next step. Although Americans had inherited a formidable Constitution and Bill of Rights, they had done so largely from the vantage of America's male gentry. Women were disenfranchised from voting, Native Americans were barred from becoming citizens, and most African-Americans were held in bondage. Confronting the issue of slavery, expanding westward, and developing self-expression became hallmarks of the early nineteenth century.

With freedom came an implicit understanding for most people of the need to turn to God through prayer. Americans quickly concluded that to secure their future they needed to set parameters in their lives, determining what was right and wrong, acceptable and not acceptable in a civilized society. In that journey, prayer helped Americans to cope with one another, to bond with a higher power, and to forge their own prescriptions for a fulfilling life.

One person who balanced his public duties with a deep, private belief in God was Chief Justice John Marshall, indisputably the most important influence in the formation of the Supreme Court of the United States and the judicial branch. Born in rural Virginia, Marshall, together with his father, Thomas, fought in the Revolutionary War. Having come to admire George Washington greatly during those years, he would be the President's first great biographer, helping to reinforce the idea of Washington's piety. Marshall's landmark decision as chief justice in *Marbury* v. *Madison* forever established the right of judicial review over acts of the U.S. Congress. That single pronouncement became his crowning achievement.

In trying to capture the unusual character of his predecessor, Chief Justice Melville Fuller, who served on the Court at the turn of the twentieth century, expressed awe at Marshall's simplicity and extraordinary influence on the daily life of Court. In particular Fuller marveled at Marshall's strength of character and personal piety, making the point that there was nothing "more striking than the fact that the head of the most powerful tribunal on earth never retired to rest without repeating the Lord's Prayer and lines commencing with 'Now I lay me down to sleep.' "[1] Intensely devoted to his wife, Martha, who was an invalid for most of their forty-two-year marriage, Marshall often knelt at her bedside while he prayed.[2]

Most Americans followed prayer practices similar to Marshall's, with the vast number of prayers recited and concentrating on the individual. Hell, death, and the perfection of a person's earthly existence and eternal soul were singular preoccupations.

Perhaps no figure was more elusive or complex in this regard than the enigmatic Thomas Jefferson. Choosing to define God by the limits of his five senses, he believed that most of human existence could be explained away through cool, dispassionate reason. His religious apathy became an object of attack for his political enemies and a genuine concern for his friends. Few people, if any, could pin down the full tenor of Jefferson's deistic beliefs.

At the same time, Jefferson was a political pragmatist to the core, readily accepting that the large majority of Americans believed in God's role in their everyday life. Consequently, as he was being sworn into office as President, Jefferson turned to the Providence of God when ending his inaugural address: "And may that Infinite Power which rules the destinies of the universe lead our councils to what is best, and give them a favorable issue for your peace and prosperity."[3] The speech he delivered for his second inauguration was even longer and more profuse on the subject of prayer, turning to "the favor of that Being in whose hands we are" and imploring Americans "to join in supplications with me that He will so enlighten the minds of your servants, guide their councils, and prosper their measures."[4]

Although Jefferson never issued any presidential proclamations calling for fasting and prayer, as both Washington and Adams had done, he suddenly and inexplicably began to attend prayer services in the U.S. Capitol in 1802, often accompanied by his daughters Martha and Maria as well as his two grandchildren. His Sunday appearances, in which he stood shoulder to shoulder with members of Congress in prayer, caused a minor sensation, in large part because of reports circulating that he had fathered several children with his slave Sally Hemings. The conservative weekly *Port Folio* referred sarcastically to his demonstrated piety as "one of the most remarkable events of the present time."[5]

Exactly what Jefferson's religious views were became one of the most contentious issues of a political career that spanned well over fifty years. His authorship of Virginia's Act for Establishing Religious Freedom, enacted in 1785, was one of his proudest and greatest achievements. In retirement he responded to his critics by writing what became known as *The Jefferson Bible,* his version of the New Testament, a book that would be published posthumously. Giving new meaning to the word "abridged," he highlighted what he found legitimate, discarding the rest. He admitted somewhat audaciously that doing so was as easy as finding "diamonds in a dunghill."[6] When he died almost seven years later, leaving behind a series of writings on various subjects, Jefferson's views on prayer, religion, and basic spirituality remained as enigmatic as ever.

Jefferson's two immediate successors were also creatures of the Enlightenment and not given to open discussions of personal religious views. James Madison had seriously considered becoming a minister while under the tutelage of the Reverend John Witherspoon at the College of New Jersey. To brush up on the Old Testament and the classical languages, including Hebrew, he spent an extra year at the college and continued to immerse himself in its rigorous prayer regimen. Yet after deciding that the ministry was not for him, Madison rarely attested to his religious beliefs privately or publicly.

Like Jefferson, he was filled with contradictions when it came to public prayer. The last of the Founding Fathers to be elected President and the major architect of the U.S. Constitution, he wrote more on the subject of religion and the need for the strict separation of church and state than anyone at the dawn of the new republic. In his first inaugural address he spoke of "the guardianship and guidance of the Almighty whose power regulates the destiny of nations, whose blessings have been so conspicuously disposed to the rising of this Republic, and to whom we are bound to address our devout gratitude for the past, as well as our fervent supplications and best hopes for the future."[7]

In the early months of his administration, the construction of St. John's Episcopal Church was completed across the street from the Executive Mansion. While the Madison family had attended prayer services in the Capitol, much as Jefferson had done, they decided to become members of St. John's and chose pew 54 from which to worship, paying annual dues for its rental. After Madison's presidency the pastor and church elders decided that pew 54 would be reserved for all future presidents.[8]

During the War of 1812, which the President's detractors liked to call "Madison's dirty little war," Madison felt compelled to call on the country to fast and pray on several occasions. Although Congress somewhat pressured him to do so, he also remembered the catalytic effect prayer had had on the American people during the Revolutionary War some three decades earlier. This prayer did not just ask for divine intervention, however. Rather, it stressed the need for Americans to acknowledge fully their sins and to ask for God's divine redemption to absolve the country's past "transgressions." In one of those presidential proclamations Madison wrote:

I do therefore recommend the third Thursday in August next as a convenient day to be set apart for the devout purposes of rendering the Sovereign of the Universe and the Benefactor of Mankind the public homage due to His holy attributes; of acknowledging the transgressions which might justly provoke the manifestations of His divine displeasure; of seeking His merciful forgiveness and

His assistance in the great duties of repentance and amendment, and especially of offering fervent supplications that in the present season of calamity and war He would take the American people under His peculiar care and protection; that He would guide their public councils, animate their patriotism, and bestow His blessing on their arms; that He would inspire all nations with a love of justice and of concord with reverence for the unerring precept of our holy religion to do to others as they would require that others should do to them; and finally, that turning the hearts of our enemies from the violence and injustice which sway their councils against us, He would hasten a restoration of the blessings of peace.[9]

In seeming contradiction, however, Madison wrote in the last years of his life how sorely he felt tried by those who advocated public prayer, believing that such invocations opened the door to religious sectarian bickering. His critics would charge that he had easily forgotten how the nation's practice of prayer had provided a unifying balm during two wars, helping to overcome the gulfs that divided Americans.

James Monroe, Madison's Secretary of State and immediate successor, limited his public sentiment on prayer to his two swearing-in ceremonies. In one of the longest inaugural addresses on record he declared, "I enter on the trust to which I have been called by the suffrages of my fellow citizens with my fervent prayers to the Almighty that He will be graciously pleased to continue to us that protection which He has already so conspicuously displayed in our favor."[10] References to God in the inaugural addresses of Madison and Monroe practically mirrored each other in tone, if not words. While they both generally kept almost anything that could be perceived as public religious display at arm's length, they nonetheless solidified the practice, begun by Washington, of invoking God's blessings upon them and the country during their inaugurations.

WHEREAS PROPONENTS OF PRAYER may have found presidential interest wanting, grassroots America was beginning to show a religious fervor in peacetime not known since long before the Revolutionary War. The Second Great Awakening was being born, a thundering crescendo as tens of thousands of Americans publicly displayed their devotion, atoned for their sins, and found a way to renew themselves spiritually.[11]

Charles G. Finney, a lawyer, minister, theology professor, and president of Oberlin College, became the very embodiment of the revival and arguably its greatest preacher and chronicler. No American-born minister had affected so many people up to that time. Bemoaning the spiritual state of the country, he cried out such admonitions as "Backslidden Christians will be brought to repentance" and "Christians will have their faith renewed." The fire of his own devotion had come through his rather spectacular conversion, when, as he later wrote:

> [The] Holy Spirit descended upon me in a manner that seemed to go through me, body and soul . . . I literally bellowed out the unutterable gushings of my heart. These waves came over me, and over me, and over me, one after the other, until I recollect I called out, "I shall die if these waves continue to pass over me." I said, "Lord, I cannot bear any more"; yet I had no fear of death.[12]

From that moment to the end of his life, Finney zealously pursued his revival ministry. His penetrating eyes, his bodily gestures, and his booming voice made him spellbinding. It was said that when he spoke "an assembly often quivers under him."[13] His reputation extended far beyond North America as his books and published lectures became enormously popular in Europe.

Throughout his ministry, Finney spoke extensively on the subject of prayer, defining the essence of effectual, or, as he called it, "prevailing," prayer. In one of his many sermons on the subject, he laid out eleven essential attributes that he believed God "required" in order for prayer to make its mark. They included perseverance, frequency, "praying from right motives," and having the proper mind-set to submit ultimately to the will of God. He believed fervently, as so many clergymen did after him, that the very act of prayer could change the character and ultimate fortunes of the penitent. While the Almighty might indeed be the intended recipient of a person's prayer, the Holy Spirit could change the aspirations of the individual for the better.[14]

This rather amazing spiritual revival, spurred on by Finney, lasted for several decades and was particularly visible in the camp and prayer meetings that spread rapidly across the country. Beginning in Cane Ridge, Kentucky, in 1801, fields, groves, farms, and even ocean beach-fronts became settings for Christians of all denominations to gather and pray while listening to the exhortations of clerics and lay preachers alike on God's "relationship to His people." As the Reverend Barton Stone, a Presbyterian minister who participated in that first gathering, later recounted:

> The roads were literally crowded with wagons, carriages, horse-men, and footmen moving to the solemn camp. The sight was affecting. It was judged by military men on the ground that there were between twenty and thirty thousand collected. Four or five preachers were frequently speaking at the same time in different parts of the encampment without confusion . . . We all engaged in singing the same songs of praise—all united in prayer . . . A partic-ular description of this meeting would fill a large volume, and then the half would not be told. The numbers converted will only be known in eternity.[15]

With dozens and sometimes hundreds of tents being erected to accommodate the massive crowds for several days, entire families would arrive, having traveled long distances to be with other like-minded indi-viduals. For some of the camp participants, the prayer revivals were the only "vacation" they would ever know. Places like Rehoboth Beach, Delaware, and Ocean Grove, New Jersey, first gained prominence by hosting these prayer revivals.

The organizers of the camps awoke the faithful before dawn each day with a blare of trumpets, signaling that private prayer should begin and that breakfast would soon be served. After the first meal of the day, the trumpets would sound again, announcing the beginning of public prayer, followed by two hours of preaching. After lunch, which was normally served in each tent, the afternoon would be consumed by more prayer and sermonizing until early supper. Organizers scheduled another four hours, from six to ten, mainly for prayer, so that at ten o'clock everyone could retire after a long day. For those diehards who needed even more prayer time, informal groups continued well into the wee hours of the morning.

Prayer camp meetings in the early nineteenth century could last a week or more. As the great finale to each event, everyone would come together for the "solemn love feast" as tents were taken down, and a farewell hymn would be sung by all of the participants. Exhausted but in most instances exhilarated by the experience, everyone would break for home, only to look forward to the next revival. In later years, tents were replaced by more permanent cabins along rivers, creeks, and other rural areas to host returning participants and welcome new ones.[16] For many Americans in the early nineteenth century, these annual meetings would be the only "vacations" they would know in their lives.

Most of the camp meetings were sponsored by Presbyterians, Baptists, and Methodists, but some church leaders who originally gave their blessing to the gatherings began to grow concerned over the wild restiveness of some participants as they prayed, particularly their "bodily agitations," as Stone described them. These physical demonstrations were known by a variety of names, such as "the falling exercise," "the jerks," "the dancing exercise," "the barking exercise," and "the laughing and singing exercise."[17] After a few choice experiences, the Presbyterians and Baptists distanced themselves from the camp meetings for a time, while the Methodists continued to organize the assemblies, a decision that dramatically added to their membership ranks.

Throughout the Second Great Awakening, religious leaders prodded their followers toward social reform by imploring the Almighty for guidance in choosing their politicians, a development not lost on the nation's capital. One of the most important voices of the era came from the Reverend Lyman Beecher, a Congregationalist and later Presbyterian minister and the father of two of the most prominent figures of nineteenth-century America, Harriet Beecher Stowe and the Reverend Henry Ward Beecher. Known for his relentless spiritual admonitions to all Americans to pray and conduct themselves as a moral people, he was outraged when he learned about the fatal duel between Alexander Hamilton and Aaron Burr in 1804. The tragedy haunted the nation like no other. It was an event that Henry Adams described as "the most dramatic moment in the early politics of the Union."[18]

Hamilton, the country's first Secretary of the Treasury, and Burr, the sitting Vice President, grandson of the Reverend Jonathan Edwards, and son of the College of New Jersey's second president, had started out their legal careers together in New York as law partners. Over a period of twenty years, however, they grew to detest each other, often vying for political prominence. When Burr lost the election for governor of New York in 1804, he blamed Hamilton for his defeat, believing he was responsible for spreading malicious half-truths across the state. It had been the proverbial last straw.

The death of the illustrious Hamilton, particularly under such circumstances, brought anger, tears, and sheer bewilderment. Throughout a rich career that extended from serving as an aide-de-camp to George Washington and becoming a hero during the war to being appointed to the first president's cabinet, Hamilton was a nominal Episcopalian, drifting away from the piety he had displayed during his days at King's College. His devoted marriage to Elizabeth, a regular churchgoer and mother to his seven surviving children, as well as his growing aversion to those he perceived as challenging the foundations of Christianity, everyone from his nemesis, Thomas Jefferson, to the leaders of the French Revolution, had its effect in the last years of his life. He even went so far in 1797 as to advocate to John Adams's Secretary of State, Thomas Pickering, a close friend and political ally, that a day of prayer be declared in the midst of international tensions to allow Americans to take up the cause "against atheism, conquest, and anarchy" in withstanding a sinful, chaotic world.[19] His son John Church Hamilton would later reveal how his father had returned to his private daily prayers as well. Clearly, his spiritual life came to preoccupy him as it had never done throughout most of his adulthood.

While dueling was considered a mortal sin among churches of all denominations, Hamilton believed that he had little choice but to go through with it. Resolved to shoot above Burr's head when the moment came, he gambled that Burr would do the same. Having lost his son Philip to the cult of dueling in the late fall of 1801, Hamilton appeared uncommonly tranquil. Not telling his wife of the duel, he gathered the family together to pray the morning service of the Episcopalian Church on the Sunday before he was to meet Burr on a rocky ledge overlooking the Hudson River in Weehawken, New Jersey.

On the dawn of July 11, 1804, the two men finally faced off as they drew .56 caliber flintlock pistols at ten paces. In the end Hamilton was wrong. Burr aimed directly at him, mortally wounding him in the lower part of his torso. In little more than twenty-four hours, Hamilton would be dead.[20]

As he lay dying on the bed in a friend's home, he asked for the Episcopal Bishop of New York and president of his alma mater, King's College, renamed Columbia in 1784, to administer last rites. Given that Hamilton was not considered an Episcopalian in good standing, not to mention his having entered into a duel, Bishop Benjamin Moore at first refused to give him Communion. A few hours later, however, Moore returned to the house and accepted his private confession and prayers as sufficient contrition. Moore would later write that after receiving communion "with great devotion," Hamilton "appeared to be perfectly at rest."[21] Within minutes one of the country's most illustrious founding fathers was dead.

Charged with two counts of murder, Aaron Burr, the grandson of the illustrious Jonathan Edwards, was indicted but never tried and convicted. Although he remained Vice President until his term expired, he never again served in elected office, shunned for his deed that fateful summer morning. To the Reverend Lyman Beecher the incident was an abomination, a capital offense against all moral sensibilities. He roared his disapproval from the pulpit as he urged his followers to avoid the hypocrisy of invoking God's blessings for "good rulers" of moral character and then voting for such miscreants.

THE UNITED STATES faced its first great test during the War of 1812, the last invasion on its soil for almost two hundred years. A complicated affair between the United States and its old foe Great Britain, the conflict extended from Canada to the coast of Brazil, from the interior of the American continent to the Mediterranean Sea, and would last for more than three years.

The causes of the war arose when the British confronted the ambitious Napoleon on one front while enforcing naval embargoes on the other to ensure their dominance on the high seas. Adding to the tensions, the British were forcibly boarding American ships searching for AWOL British sailors. The burning of Washington by British troops came in direct retaliation for the torching of British facilities in Canada by American troops.

Prayer in churches and homes across the country intensified greatly during the war. Despite partisan divisions over the conflict, patriotism too was in full bloom, bringing to the fore Francis Scott Key, whose legacy would be wrapped in a few lines of poetry. A lawyer from a privileged background who had argued more cases before the U.S. Supreme Court than anyone else up to that time, Key had expressed serious reservations about the war, believing that it could not be justified on rational, let alone moral, grounds.

While trying to determine the fate of a close friend who had ended up behind enemy lines, Key briefly became a British prisoner in 1814 and was held on a ship off the coast of Baltimore as the British bombarded nearby Fort McHenry. Standing on the deck of the ship in the thick of the worst shelling, Key was mesmerized as he watched the men of the fort holding their own against the relentless barrage. As the smoke cleared, he could barely make out the American flag with its fifteen stars and fifteen stripes, but soon he could clearly see it, flapping in the wind, remaining at full mast.

Moved by the moment, he jotted down the lyrics to what he first called "The Defence of Fort McHenry." Once the piece was publicized in two Baltimore newspapers, however, Key's patriotic ode was renamed "The Star-Spangled Banner." In addition to penning its familiar, spirited first verse, "Oh, say, can you see . . . and the home of the brave," Key wrote a fourth verse, bringing God directly into play:

> Oh, thus be it ever when freemen shall stand,
> Between their lov'd homes and the war's desolation;
> Blest with vict'ry and peace, may the heav'n-rescued land
> Praise the pow'r that hath made and preserv'd us a nation!
> Then conquer we must, when our cause it is just,
> And this be our motto: "In God is our trust."
> And the star-spangled banner in triumph shall wave
> O'er the land of the free and the home of the brave![22]

For the first time a variation on the phrase "In God We Trust" was memorialized in an American context, and the entire piece was set to the music of a favorite old English tavern melody titled "To Anacreon in Heaven," a tune originating from the Anacreontic Society in London, whose "patron saint" was the Greek bard Anacreon from the sixth century B.C. Key's "Star-Spangled Banner" became an overnight sensation, but it was not until March 3, 1931, that the U.S. Congress officially designated it the country's national anthem.[23]

LESSER KNOWN to Americans today but a figure who had enormous influence on the society of his time was the Reverend Timothy Dwight. No single individual wielded greater influence in higher education than

Dwight, both in his writings and in his role as president of Yale University for more than twenty years.

A longtime friend of George Washington's from his days as a chaplain in the Revolutionary army, Dwight received his doctorate of divinity from the College of New Jersey and became the driving force in establishing New England's first seminary in Andover, Massachusetts. Gifted with a strong, facile mind like his grandfather Jonathan Edwards and a skill for academic administration, Dwight wrote a series of powerful sermons, prayers, and hymns that were delivered to Yale undergraduates and published in the United States and Europe. One prayer that was set to music, believed to be the oldest hymn written by an American still in common use, sang out:

> *I love Thy kingdom, Lord,*
> *The house of Thine abode,*
> *The church our blessed Redeemer saved*
> *With His own precious blood.*

> *I love Thy church, O God.*
> *Her walls before Thee stand*
> *Dear as the apple of Thine eye,*
> *And written on Thy hand.*

> *Should I wish coffers join*
> *Her altars to abuse?*
> *No! Better far my tongue were dumb,*
> *My hand its skill should lose.*[24]

Dwight also was passionate about the spiritual durability of the family in the new republic. He wrote a series of essays in which he pressed parents to encourage their children to pray regularly:

All the duties of religion are eminently solemn and venerable in the eyes of children. But none will so strongly prove the sincerity of the parent; none so powerfully awaken the reverence of the child; none so happily recommend the instruction he receives as family devotions, particularly those in which petitions for the children occupy a distinguished place.[25]

Leading by example, Timothy Dwight and his family gathered together each day to pray. His grandson and namesake followed in his footsteps later in the century by being named president of Yale.

As AMERICANS BECAME more preoccupied with their children's schooling both in academics and in the instruction of prayer and religion, *The New England Primer* evolved into *The New England Primer Improved; or, An Easy and Pleasant Guide to the Art of Reading; to which is added, The Assembly's Shorter Catechism*. The book now highlighted what were known as the "three choice sentences" that every child was made to memorize:

1. Praying will make us leave sinning, or sinning will make us leave praying.
2. Our weakness and inabilities break not the bond of our duties.
3. What we are afraid to speak before men, we should be afraid to think before God.[26]

While *The New England Primer* continued to be popular, many other prayer books were in circulation, such as *Juvenile Devotion*. Printed in New York, the book was widely circulated for schoolteachers to distribute to their students. No more than four inches in length and width, the paperback book had space on the front page where a teacher could inscribe his or her name and that of the student to treasure as a keepsake. The introduction read:

The writer of the following, having been long impressed with the sentiment, that a concise treatise, calculated to instruct children in the duty of prayer, is much needed; and having sought in vain for one of the kind for use of schools, offers this consideration as an apology for his adding the following humble production to the already swelled list of juvenile books.

Parents and teachers, conscientiously engaged in training up youth in the ways of PIETY, will reflect, that prayer is the *first* and *last* duty of the sinner; that children must be taught not only diligently, but *early*, a sense of obligation to God for all his mercies, and likewise the duty of asking them from him by prayer: and that in the *morning* the wise husbandman sows his seed, and in the *evening* withholds not his hand, leaving the issue of his labour to the divine disposal.[27]

Like *The New England Primer, Juvenile Devotion,* much of it written in English meter, was preoccupied with death. For morning prayer there were such dark spiritual intimacies as:

> *While many younger far than I,*
> *Last night by death were snatch'd away,*
> *The angel of the Lord hath kept*
> *My health in safety while I slept.*[28]

Evening prayer completed the day's theme:

> *While many younger far than I,*
> *This day by death were snatch'd away,*
> *My wand'ring steps have been his care,*
> *To guard from death and every snare.*[29]

Prayers that might be considered "positive bonding" in a child's devotion to God were practically nonexistent. Instant death, the fires of hell, and original sin were the major preoccupations, keeping with the spiritual cast of the Second Great Awakening.

The desire and need to educate children in religion and prayer were not confined to the relationship between teacher and pupil. Another widely circulated book, *Family Prayers,* focused on the family's devotional life. In particular, it stressed the need for fathers, not mothers, to take the lead in ensuring that their children became constant in their prayers as the sure path to a virtuous life:

The utility of books of this description in a Christian country, can be questioned by none. There is not a Christian Father of a Family, who is not ready to acknowledge his obligations to the author, by whom he is furnished with the means of guiding the devotions of his household, and of teaching those, whose spiritual as well as temporal interests, are committed to his care, how, suitably, to address themselves to the Father of their spirits, the preserver of their lives, the Bestower of their blessings, and the redeemer of their souls.[30]

The authors clearly believed that only through prayer could the family be properly bound together, gaining a fuller, more grounded sense of God and morality.

PRAYER BOOKS SOON PROLIFERATED in unprecedented numbers. With printing presses now an integral part of the new country, religious leaders lost no time circulating Bibles, prayer books, and other religious publications on a massive scale. With continued growth in the West, many Americans found themselves and their families isolated by distance and time from churches and larger communities. Consequently, Bibles and prayer books served an important function in helping many Americans maintain some kind of spiritual devotion. The American Bible Society, founded in 1816, became the most formidable of all the publishers and by the dawn of the new millennium, almost two hundred years later, could lay claim to having distributed more than three billion copies of religious texts.[31]

The Episcopal Church, which continued to maintain ties to the Anglican Church in England without the trappings of allegiance to the British monarch, was particularly aggressive in reaching out to its members and gaining new adherents in the aftermath of the War of 1812. After a general convention of Episcopal leaders in 1789, the *Book of Common Prayer* had been revised to accommodate the nascent American church, and became a devotional that would be used for the next hundred years.[32] Beyond the *Book of Common Prayer*, the Episcopal Church published a series of prayer books that were widely circulated and found in the homes of Episcopalians and non-Episcopalians alike.

One of these devotionals, sponsored by the Episcopal Diocese of North Carolina and published in New York, was the *New Manual of Private Devotions*. This prayer book, like so many others, offered personal invocations for every occasion. There were prayers titled "A Prayer for a Person Engaged in a Law-Suit, or Like to Be So," "A Prayer for a Person Troubled in Mind (Including Suicide)," "A Prayer in Stormy and Tempestuous Weather, as Great Thunder and Lightning," "A Prayer for a Prisoner for Debt," and "A Thanksgiving to Be Used by a Woman in Private, before Her Going Abroad."[33] Anachronistic as these prayers may now sound, they spoke to the real-life concerns of the day.

Two prayers at mealtime, "A Grace before Meat" and "A Grace after Meat," recalled David's cry in Psalm 145, "The eyes of all wait upon thee;

and thou givest them meat in due season." The prayers also pointed to the plentiful bounty that immigrants found in their new country and their gratitude for the abundance. "A Grace before Meat" has an intriguing twist as the supplicant asks God to strengthen the dead animals that have already been cooked:

> *Bless to us, O Lord, these thy good creatures, which we are now about to receive. Give them strength to nourish us, and us grace to serve thee, through Jesus Christ our Lord.*[34]

The most curious and perhaps charming of all the devotional prayers were those written to provide comfort to a mother during and after the delivery of her infant. In the midst of delivery, the mother was urged to pray a sequence of ejaculations with the support of her husband or a female friend:

> *Save, Lord, and hear me, O King of heaven! Now I call upon thee in this time of my trouble.*

> *Thou art my helper and Redeemer, make no long tarrying, O my God, nor suffer me to sink under the burdens of my pain.*

> *Oh! Be thou my help in this time of my trouble; for without thee, vain is the help of man.*

> *O Lord, let it be thy pleasure to deliver me; make haste, O Lord, to help me.*[35]

The petitioner was then instructed to read other prayers in the devotional in the event that "the child is living," a not too subtle reminder of the high infant-mortality rate during those difficult years.

NOT ONLY PROTESTANTS reached for the high ground in evangelizing and providing prayer guides for the faithful. Of all the Europeans who came to America, none was more enterprising or more despised in certain quarters than Roman Catholics. The religious conflicts, both real and imagined, that had pitted Catholic against Protestant in Europe since the Reformation were still fresh in many minds, and the Pope was still seen as the Antichrist by many Protestants.

Few people in the early nineteenth century faced the kind of prejudice that Catholic affiliation brought more than Elizabeth Bayley Seton. The daughter of Dr. Richard Bayley, the first health officer for the Port of New York, she was raised in a privileged Episcopalian family. In 1794 she married William Seton, the son of a wealthy shipping merchant and confidant of Alexander Hamilton's, and eventually bore five children. A seemingly idyllic life gave way to tragedy after her husband suffered severe business losses, declared bankruptcy, and soon died of tuberculosis.

Facing such overwhelming problems, Elizabeth found solace in Roman Catholicism, to which she had been introduced by friends in Italy. In deciding to convert, she was shunned by almost all her family and friends. With her children in tow, she began a remarkable journey from New York to Maryland to supervise the construction and operation of a Catholic school in Baltimore. Deciding to take her vows as a nun, she ultimately founded the order of the Sisters of Charity and soon established the first viable parochial school system in the United States.

Confronting interminable struggles with the Catholic hierarchy in establishing her various institutions, Mother Seton turned to prayer as her bulwark. "O, let our souls praise You . . . These storms which now obstruct our path, these shades which obscure the light of Your heavenly truth," she would confide. However, her anchor each day was a rather gentle and loving prayer:

> *Adored, Lord, increase my Faith, perfect it,*
> *crown it Your own,*
> *Your choicest, dearest gift.*
> *Keep me in your fold and lead me to eternal life.*[36]

Throughout her life as a nun she would compose dozens of short prayers both in English and in French, which she had learned as a girl. Canonized in 1975, Elizabeth Seton was the first American-born saint of the Catholic Church. By the time of her death in 1821, she had established twenty different religious communities throughout the eastern United States and left a prayer legacy that continued to serve her Sisters and others for generations.

Another remarkable trailblazer from a very different world was Sarah Josepha Hale. Widowed at thirty-four, left with five small children, and having no formal education, Hale nonetheless decided to pursue a career in writing and publishing. Gifted with a hard-nosed business sense and writing ability, she quickly became America's first female editor. By the time she was forty in 1828, she had acquired *Ladies' Magazine,* the first successful women's periodical to be published in the United States. Her merging *Ladies' Magazine* with *Godey's Lady's Book* was a major accomplishment in the first half of the nineteenth century, creating one of the most formidable publications of the day. The combined periodicals allowed her to advance prayers, spiritual articles, and topical opinions to a highly diverse mass readership. Deeply religious and committed to improving rights for women, Hale helped to finance and organize the fledgling all-female Vassar College. In addition, she strongly promoted the role of women as teachers in public schools and founded the country's first nursery school.

To millions of children then and now, Sarah Josepha Hale's best-known work is the nursery rhyme "Mary Had a Little Lamb," taken from her 1830 book *Poems for Our Children.* Less familiar to Americans, however, is the role she played late in her life in persuading President Abraham Lincoln to declare Thanksgiving a national holiday. Hale had been trying for many years to convince the public of the importance of such a gesture. For example, in an 1858 editorial she wrote, "Would it not be more noble, more truly American, to become national in unity when we offer God our tribute of joy and gratitude for the blessings of the year?"[37] While Lincoln in 1863 needed little prompting to institute Thanksgiving, he found Hale to be an inspiration, remembering how the widow with five children had turned tragedy into such an accomplished life.

DURING ITS FORMATIVE YEARS, the United States began to produce a cadre of distinguished artists. Several gifted painters had made a great impression not only in America but in the Old World as well.

The very talented Benjamin West was the dean of those early artists, ultimately becoming president of the Royal Academy of Arts and official court painter to King George III. Growing up in a simple Quaker community in modern-day Swarthmore, Pennsylvania, West began to draw the flowers, birds, and insects near his home in amazing detail. With crayons given to him by his Indian playmates, he produced first-class etchings almost effortlessly. By the time he was a teenager, he had completely overwhelmed his family and neighbors, who had no idea how to handle, let alone nurture, his gifts. Although the West family had never officially registered as Quakers, they were welcomed by the elders of the local Friends church. The elders soon offered to help resolve the important question of what to do with young Benjamin by holding a special service with the entire congregation in their meetinghouse.

John Williamson, one of the church's respected elders, took the lead and addressed the assembly, declaring, "It is true that our tenets deny the utility of that art to mankind. But God has bestowed on the youth a genius for the art, and can we believe that Omniscience bestows his gifts but for great purposes?"[38] For the simple Quakers, who considered most decorative arts as unnecessary worldly trappings, Benjamin West's talent turned their spiritual world upside down. As West's biographer John Galt wrote in 1816, after the Quakers interviewed West extensively that evening, the most remarkable scene took place: "The women rose and kissed the young artist, and the men, one by one, laid their hands on his head and prayed that the Lord might verify in his life the value of the gift which had induced them, in spite of their religious tenets, to allow him to cultivate the faculties of his genius."[39] From that point forward, West believed, his destiny had been set, and soon a series of opportunities led him to the great art galleries and studios of Europe. His lifelike portraits; battle scenes, including one of his most memorable paintings, *Penn's Treaty with the Indians*; and religious depictions from the Old and New Testaments made him America's first internationally recognized painter.

Edward Hicks, a younger contemporary of West's, had a far different impact on his native country. Born in eastern Pennsylvania as well, Hicks converted to the Quaker faith after his family had sampled the services of different churches in and around modern-day Langhorne, Pennsylvania. Arguably the finest and certainly the most influential folk painter America ever produced, Hicks became so inspired by the church that he decided to become a Quaker minister. Unlike West, whose Quaker community encouraged his talent, Hicks found enormous resistance in some quarters to his artistic abilities. This, combined with his notion that all of God's children could find the inner light of the Almighty through prayer, whether or not they were Christians, caused him to splinter from the orthodox of his church. "Under the influence of the blessed spirit," he wrote, "my soul finds sweet union with all God's children in their devotional exercises, whether it is performed in a Protestant meetinghouse, a Roman cathedral, a Jewish synagogue, a Hindu temple, an

Indian wigwam, or by the wild Arab of the great desert with his face towards Mecca."[40]

Although he rendered several paintings of William Penn and his treaty with the Indians, as Benjamin West had done before him, Hicks became best known for painting more than one hundred depictions of "the lion and the lamb." He saw his paintings as reflecting the goodness of God, the bond between God and humanity, and the promise of America. As he admonished in one of his sermons, "American citizens, of all inhabitants of this globe, are under the strongest obligation to render thanks to their Heavenly Father that God has preserved in this land an asylum for the bodies and souls of the children of men . . . protecting civil and religious rights."[41] He keenly hoped that his primitive paintings would lead individuals to reflection, leading in turn to heartfelt prayer and righteous living. Indeed, his artwork so captivated the public that printers fiercely competed with one another to use his illustrations for their Bibles, prayer books, and penny spiritual pamphlets.

WHILE AMERICAN PAINTERS were beginning to develop their own individual styles, a new school of art sprang up in the early part of the century that was nothing less than breathtaking. Dozens of painters began to capture on canvas the beauty of the American landscape, underscoring the country's deep spirituality and divine destiny. One of the more significant cultural developments emerged in the advent of the Hudson River school of art.

Influenced in part by European romanticism, the flourishing cadre of artists associated with this school tried to capture the country's underlying spirituality and the beauty of its natural, unspoiled landscapes on sweeping, massive canvases. Whether representing wilderness scenes from the Catskills or the Rockies, they painted spectacular mountains and waterfalls, lush plains and forests, and dazzling skies. Instinctively, the inspiration for prayer lay just beneath the surface, at times overtly so; the country's focus on the doctrine of Manifest Destiny and God's divine plan for America was reinforced by the Hudson River paintings. Spiritual beauty was being depicted as unfathomable, well beyond human capacity for genuine understanding.

From the outset, Thomas Cole, the founder of the Hudson River school, defined the new phenomenon as nothing less than "divine visual language." Realizing that the Protestant roots of the nation viscerally rejected artistic representation of religious subjects, Cole and his fellow artists bridged the theological divide by showing that God could be found in nature and that through their art they could unlock that reality without turning to religious icons.

Through publication of *The Crayon,* the most important art journal of the day, theologians and artists alike could debate the interconnection of God, nature, art, and each human being. To capture the essence of his paintings, Cole wrote prayers for the journal with such lines as:

> *Thou art the dawn to my blessed sight*
> *That o'er the mountain breaks*
> *Already by thy holy light*
> *My soul triumphant wakes.*[42]

Following Cole, dozens of landscape painters spread out over three generations would be part of the Hudson River school and its transcendent world of art, artists such as Frederick Church, Jasper Cropsey, Albert Bierstadt, and Asher Durand. In the end, as with all artistic movements, the last generation of Hudson River painters began to stray from the school's roots, responding to a changing America. Although later art critics and historians looked on the productions of the Hudson River school as naive, treating the works with indifference if not outright disdain, the movement left an indelible mark on the American public and became an integral part of the country's cultural heritage.

AS AMERICA DEVELOPED its institutions and expanded its boundaries, it became fertile ground for cultivating a variety of hybrid churches and Christian denominations. One of the more fascinating denominations to emerge was the community of Ephrata, Pennsylvania. The Ephrata commune, now extinct but with many of its original buildings still intact, fused Jewish, Roman Catholic, and Protestant beliefs and traditions.

Enticed by the religious tolerance promised by William Penn, these German immigrants committed themselves to long, hard days of work and prayer. Surviving well into the nineteenth century, the Ephrata cloister believed in a life of intense asceticism and celibacy. Although their numbers were always small, no more than a few hundred at any one time, their reputation for spiritual rigor and mysticism was admired greatly by European intellectuals, including France's Voltaire. Always seeking to engage in a variety of intellectual pursuits, the Ephrata community produced the first comprehensive hymnal in the colonies, *The Turtle Dove*.[43]

Another noteworthy religious group, who had first made their way to America about the same time the Ephrata cloister was established, was the Moravians. Emigrating from Germany, they became distinguished for prostrating their bodies facedown in prayer and for embodying the promise of America's spiritual destiny in their one-line vow, repeated over and over again, "I will make an everlasting covenant with you."[44]

There also was the Church of the New Jerusalem, known as the Swedenborgians, who had come to America from Stockholm, elevating prayer to a special "correspondence" between the natural world and the spiritual world. To other parts of the country came the Huguenots, who emigrated from France, bringing with them their Calvinist traditions of adhering to a strict daily prayer regimen and promoting moral athleticism in their spiritual life.

No church or religious group, however, created as much of a stir as the United Society of Believers in Christ's Second Appearance, better known as "Shakers" for the violent, prescribed body gyrations they made while praying during worship services. Although they ultimately reached a population of just several thousand, spread among eighteen communities from Maine to Kentucky, their influence lasted for years.

The major force behind their success was the spiritual charisma of a British émigré, Ann Lee, later known as Mother Ann. Unable to read or write, she suffered a miserable early life that included the death of her four children and an abusive husband. Looking for somewhere to turn, she found comfort in the spiritual message of the Shakers, founded by Jane and James Wardley, with their practice of sexual equality and their belief that Christ's Second Coming would arrive in female form.

In a dream, as she later told her followers, she clearly saw Adam and Eve in the act of sexual intercourse and felt she had discovered the root of original sin. Ann Lee became convinced that human redemption could be found only through complete sexual abstinence. Believing she had been chosen specially by God as the second appearance of "the Christ spirit," she viewed herself as the feminine side of the divine. The secret to life, she believed, was to become absorbed in continuous spiritual contemplation with "the latent living Christ."[45] Ready to advance her cause to the fullest, she and eight followers departed England to set up their first community near Albany, New York. Within a few years the Shakers who surrounded Mother Ann began to believe that she was the actual Second Coming.

Similar in some ways to the Ephrata cloister, the Shakers were a complete religious community searching for divine perfection by living a life of poverty and hard labor, committing themselves to full equality and chastity. "Hands to work and hearts to God" was their creed. By refraining from sexual intimacy, they believed that untapped human energy could be redirected toward prayer and moral living. From architecture and furniture making to daily chores, they were singularly focused. Symmetry, order, and function became their hallmarks. Their craftsmanship, known for its elegant, unstudied simplicity, became a statement of belief, a "religion in wood," as it was later described.[46] One Shaker elder referred to it as "surrounding [the] spiritual world in daily living," while another admonished, "Let every breath be a continual prayer to God."[47] More to the point, the Shakers, like the Puritans and even the Catholic monastic orders before them, believed that prayer could not be compartmentalized. To pray at one hour while neglecting devotional sentiments throughout the rest of the day was a spiritual non sequitur. The act of prayer had to be part of life's never-ending constant.

When it came to praying, the Shakers were unique among America's religious congregations. Mainly unspoken, prayer was considered so weighty that if a Shaker farmer in the middle of the day dropped to his knees, other members of the community within sight of him or her would stand or kneel in silence out of respect. At the same time, prayer was formally intertwined throughout daily life. Beginning their day at exactly 5:00 a.m. in the summer, 5:50 a.m. in the winter, the Shakers would pray both individually and as a group at prescribed hours. From Saturday night through Sunday they would consecrate almost every waking hour to prayer. Particularly striking was the manner in which they worshipped. Believing that devotion to God could be expressed through bodily movements in addition to thought and recitation, the Shakers would move every part of their bodies. This was not a free-form practice but part of a carefully choreographed set of movements to give praise to the Almighty. The Shakers in 1813 described the ritual as "a gift in which Believers can best unite their feelings of joy and thanksgiving for the gospel—in which they can lift their voices together in praise to God."[48]

On a typical Sunday evening the Shakers would gather in their plain, functional hall and kneel in silence until one voice began to sing. Immediately the congregation would follow suit, extending their hands at right angles with elbows and palms turned downward. Gripped by the moment, many of them would quietly weep. Once the hymn was over, the congregation would drop their arms to their sides, fold them, and get to their feet, almost in perfect synchronization. They then would dance, making the same kind of prescribed motions over and over again, a ritual that could be seen dramatically in the singing of "O Lord Protect Thy Chosen Flock."

Witnessing a Shaker service would have been an unusual experience. Chroniclers of the day, including many of the great American writers coming into prominence, were driven to observe the phenomenon firsthand, and most of them had plenty to say about their impressions. James Fenimore Cooper, although admiring their outward appearance of order and cleanliness, described them as "deluded fanatics."[49] Ralph Waldo Emerson was convinced that the "protestant monastery" had created "a set of clean, well disposed, dull and incapable animals."[50] Nathaniel Hawthorne went so far as to write, "On the whole they lead a good and comfortable life, and if it were not for their ridiculous ceremonies, a man could not do a wiser thing than to join them."[51]

Even foreigners had their opinions. Friedrich Engles, the German socialist who helped provide the ideological underpinnings to the Communist movement, found the religious practices harmless and spoke of the Shakers admiringly for having been the "first people to set up a society on the basis of community goods in America, indeed in the whole world." Charles Dickens, after his much-publicized trip to the United States later in the century, wrote rather extensively about the Shakers. Visiting their community in New Lebanon, New York, he was disappointed when he was turned away from watching them in the middle of prayer. Nevertheless, based on the firsthand accounts of others, Dickens described their services as "unspeakably absurd" and "infinitely grotesque."[52] No one seemed to be without an opinion.

Despite the growth of the Shakers in the first half of the nineteenth century, by the end of the twentieth century, only one community, at Sabbathday Lake, Maine, still existed, with six followers managing the farm and making various handicrafts. Despite the dwindling numbers and practical extinction of a vibrant community, Mother Ann Lee and her Shakers had great influence on American thought, culture, and spirituality. One prayer known to many Americans, later enshrined in Aaron Copland's symphonic work for Martha Graham and her dance troupe, *Appalachian Spring,* was the Shaker invocation "Simple Gifts":

> 'Tis the gift to be simple,
> 'Tis the gift to be free;
> 'Tis the gift to come down where we ought to be;
> And when we find ourselves in the place just right,
> 'Twill be in the valley of love and delight . . .
> Amen.[53]

While some communities, like the Shakers and the cloister at Ephrata, thrived on communal living, the Amish, who had arrived in America in 1685, managed to combine the family with the larger Amish society. At home, adults and children would pray silently in the morning and at night before going to bed. They only said prayers aloud at mealtimes, never varying from their prescribed words:

> O Lord God, heavenly Father, bless us and these Thy gifts, which we shall accept from Thy tender goodness. Give us food and drink also for our souls unto life eternal, and make us partake of Thy heavenly table through Jesus Christ. Amen.[54]

The ceremonial richness of prayer, like that of their Mennonite cousins, was reserved for communal gatherings held not in some church or meetinghouse but in the home of each Amish family. It was not uncommon for two hundred people to gather at a neighbor's home for a three-hour service. With few variations the service followed a regulated pattern:

Fellowship upon arrival
Silence in worship areas
Congregational singing (forty minutes)
Ministers meet in a separate room
Opening sermon (twenty to thirty minutes)
Silent kneeling prayer
Scripture reading by a deacon (members standing)

Main sermon (fifty to seventy minutes)
Affirmations from other ministers and elders
Kneeling prayer is read from a prayer book
Benediction (members standing)
Closing hymn[55]

Although having several Amish families in the close confines of another family's home tested the patience of even the most faithful stalwart, there was something endearing to have such a community, young and old, worshipping together in such a setting.

WHILE FOR MOST Americans prayer was a highly personal exercise or one best practiced within religious communities, the role of prayer and the maturing spirituality of the American people were readily apparent, even to foreign observers. One such individual was the great political scientist and sociologist of the century, Alexis de Tocqueville. Traveling to the United States from his native France in 1831, originally intending to study the country's prison system, he expanded the scope of his work dramatically after he arrived. Fascinated by what he saw, he recorded his experiences and observations as he toured the new republic. Publishing those findings in his eight-hundred-page *Democracy in America,* he took a sharp, unvarnished look into what America had become during its first years in existence. The book became an immediate best seller, solidifying Tocqueville's reputation forever.

In it, Tocqueville claimed that nothing impressed him more than "the equality of conditions" he found throughout the country.[56] One area of particular interest was the deep religious devotion he saw almost everywhere he looked: "One can say that there is not a single religious doctrine in the United States hostile to democratic and republic institutions. All the clergy there speak the same language; opinions are in harmony with the laws, and there is, so to say, only one mental current."[57]

In one of his most striking findings, Tocqueville confirmed that religion flourished in the United States due to the separation of church and state. In Europe, where church and state were often indistinguishable, religion and spirituality languished. America, however, was different.

As an outsider, Tocqueville brought an objectivity to his observations of the country's virtues and weaknesses, effectively holding up a mirror for the country to view itself and for Europeans to gain some understanding

of their cousins an ocean away. His unfolding tales attested to the prayerful vitality of the American people. In one account he elaborated:

> In the United States, when the seventh day comes, trade and indus-
> try seem suspended throughout the nation. All noise stops. A deep
> repose, or rather solemn contemplation takes its place. At last the
> soul comes into its own and meditates upon itself . . .
>
> Thus it is that the American in some degree from time to time
> escapes from himself, and for a moment free from the petty passions
> that trouble his life and the passing interests that fill it, he suddenly
> breaks into an ideal world where all is great, pure, and eternal."[58]

Tocqueville's observations would resound well into the twenty-first
century.

ONE OF THE TRULY GREAT MEN of the day, who bridged the country's generations and took the challenges of the new republic seriously,
was the oldest son of President John Adams, John Quincy Adams, who
would become the sixth President of the United States. Although the
exceptionally precocious Adams disliked the rough-and-tumble of politics, he had an abiding commitment to public service from representing
the United States as minister to the Netherlands at the age of twenty-
nine to being named Secretary of State under President James Monroe.

Adams's marriage to Louisa Catherine Johnson, the English-born
daughter of an American merchant in London, was a distant one during
his years in the diplomatic corps and in the White House. Louisa found
the entire Adams family unusually cold, and soon suffered from depression and migraine headaches. It was only after the death of their two
sons—George, a mentally unstable lawyer who jumped off a steamer in
Providence, Rhode Island, when he began to hear voices, and John II,
who died from a sudden illness—that their marriage coalesced in any
kind of loving way. In sharing their grief, they began to pray together,
and although John Quincy Adams eschewed the Episcopal faith, they
turned to the *Book of Common Prayer* as a guide to mourn their dead sons.
As it was, Adams had always been prayerful, reciting daily the prayers he
had learned when a child from *The New England Primer*. As President, he
often attended Sunday services at the Unitarian church in the morning
and the Presbyterian church in the afternoon.[59]

In 1853, five years after Adams's death, two former colleagues in Congress, Senators Thomas Hart Benton of Missouri and John Davis of Massachusetts, compiled a number of his poems and prayers from among his papers. Collectively, these works showed a spiritual side to Adams that was as moving as it was revealing of the man himself. The prayers had such titles as "O God, with Goodness All Thy Own," "My Soul, before Thy Maker Kneel," and "O Heal Me Lord, for I Am Weak." His invocation "O Lord, Thy All-Discerning Eyes" made clear he understood and welcomed God's watchful eye both day and night.

In perhaps his most striking prayer, Adams revealed his unwavering belief in God and the sure condemnation of those who had no faith. It was a personal testament called "Lord of All Worlds," and it put into question his disbelief in the divinity of Christ:

> *Lord of all worlds, let thanks and praise*
> *To Thee forever fill my soul;*
> *With blessings Thou has crowned my days,*
> *My heart, my head, my hand control:*
> *O, let no vain presumptions rise,*
> *No impious murmur in my heart,*
> *To crave the boon Thy will denies,*
> *Or shrink from ill Thy hands impart.*
>
> *Thy child am I, and not an hour,*
> *Revolving in the orbs above,*
> *But brings some token of Thy power,*
> *But brings some token of Thy love;*
> *And shall this bosom dare repine,*
> *In darkness dare deny the dawn,*
> *Or spurn the treasures of the mine,*
> *Because one diamond is withdrawn?*
>
> *The fool denies, the fool alone,*
> *Thy being, Lord, and boundless might;*
> *Denies the firmament, Thy throne,*
> *Denies the sun's meridian light,*
> *Denies the fashion of his frame.*
> *The voice he hears, the breath he draws:*

O idiot atheist! To proclaim
Effects unnumbered without cause!

Matter and mind, mysterious one,
Are man's for threesome years and ten;
Where, ere the thread of life was spun?
Where, when reduced to dust again?
All-seeing God, the doubt suppress;
The doubt Thou only canst relieve;
My soul Thy Saviour-Son shall bless,
Fly to Thy Gospel, and believe.[60]

In the same House chamber where he had written many of those prayers and delivered numerous impassioned remarks on subjects as diverse as the ills of slavery and American territorial expansion in the West, John Quincy Adams collapsed from a stroke and soon died, leaving behind one of the fullest and richest public lives in American history.

ADAMS'S IMMEDIATE SUCCESSOR, Andrew Jackson, not particularly known by his contemporaries for his piety, in reality grew deeply religious with age. For Jackson prayer was best kept a private affair, away from any endorsement by the federal government. While he was particularly eloquent in his 1829 inaugural address in offering up "my ardent supplications that He will continue to make our beloved country the object of His divine care and gracious benediction," he, like Jefferson, refused to call for any national days of prayer while President.[61] For Jackson prayer was a matter within the purview of states' rights and church pulpits, not Washington.

In the summer of 1832, toward the end of Jackson's first term, as cholera was spreading across Europe, killing tens of thousands of people, and beginning to work its way across the United States, the synod of the Reformed Church of America petitioned him to invoke his powers as President to call for "a day of fasting, humiliation, and prayer" to protect the American people from the disease. Without hesitation, Jackson denied the request on the grounds that it was not up to the President of the United States "to disturb the security which religion now enjoys in this country in its complete separation from the political concerns of the Central Government."[62]

Henry Clay, the Senate majority leader, had other ideas, however, and soon sponsored a resolution calling on the President to declare a national day of prayer. As the legislation headed to the House of Representatives after passing the Senate, Jackson announced that he would veto the measure should it be sent to his desk for signature. The President and his supporters were livid at what they perceived as Clay's posturing over prayer, one ally of the President's remarking, "Could he gain votes by it, he would kiss the toe of the Pope and prostrate himself before the grand lama." In the end Clay found that the battle was not worth the fight.[63]

"Old Hickory," as Jackson was known after the Battle of New Orleans, won the sympathy of the country when his wife, Rachel, died days before he was to be first sworn into office. Rachel Jackson had endured a grueling presidential campaign with her husband. Having been married before, she wed Jackson, not realizing that the divorce from her first husband had not been officially completed. Charges of adultery and loose morals abounded from Jackson's opponents, and the false innuendos took their toll on her. Dying, some speculated of a heart attack, she was laid to rest in the dress she would have worn to the presidential inaugural. Despite a wild inauguration, in which Jackson's fellow southerners and frontiersmen partied for several days in the presidential mansion, Jackson remained grief stricken by his wife's death. He soon found prayer the most endearing consolation.

Retiring each evening from the Oval Office to the family quarters, Jackson would unclasp the locket containing the portrait of his wife, hanging from a thick black cord around his neck, and place it on the table in front of him. He would then open her prayer book and spend as long as an hour reading from it. On more than one occasion aides coming to see the President after hours found him immersed in prayer, always following the same routine "to read in that book with that picture under his eyes."

To no one's surprise Jackson ran for and won a second term, once again beseeching at his swearing-in God's "hands" to "overrule all my intentions and actions and inspire the hearts of my fellow-citizens that we may be preserved from dangers of all kinds and continue forever a united and a happy people."[64]

In the months to come he would dodge the bullets of a would-be assassin while attending a funeral in the capitol, becoming the first U.S. President to have his life threatened in office. His spirituality only became stronger as the months wore on. In an unusually open letter to

Andrew Jackson, Jr., a nephew whom he and Rachel had adopted as their own, Jackson wrote, "I nightly offer up my prayers to the throne of grace for the health and safety of you all, and that we ought all to rely with confidence on the promises of our dear redeemer, and give our hearts. This is all he requires and all that we can do, and if we sincerely do this, we are sure of salvation through atonement."[65]

BY THE TIME HIS SECOND TERM was coming to an end, age had clearly caught up with Jackson. After ensuring the election of his Vice President, Martin Van Buren, as his successor, Jackson retired to his much-loved Hermitage outside Nashville, holding prayer services every evening with his entire family.

While Jackson had officially become a member of the Presbyterian Church in his retirement years, Martin Van Buren had been a lifelong member of the Dutch Reformed Church. Given that no such church existed in Washington at the time, he regularly worshipped across the street from the President's House at St. John's. Van Buren let everyone know that public praying and citing Scripture were not his style, but he nonetheless loved to belt out hymns every Sunday in church, much to the annoyed distraction of those around him. Although Van Buren, like his predecessors, kept his own spiritual counsel, he drew a direct connection to God in his inaugural address, declaring, "I only look to the gracious protection of the Divine Being whose strengthening support I humbly solicit, and whom I fervently pray to look down upon us all."[66]

Within the first half century of the country's existence, the presidents of the United States set in motion a tradition of invoking Divine Providence as they were sworn into office, integrating into some of the most important speeches of their careers the link between America and the Almighty. Whatever the presidents' motivations in doing so, the American people were clearly coming to expect from their leaders a certain respectful humility and deference to a higher power. This practice would become an almost inviolable part of every inaugural address and observance from those early days to the present.

DURING THIS SAME PERIOD, one of the country's most treasured patriotic anthems was born at the hand of Samuel F. Smith when he penned the words to "America." The genesis of the piece came after Smith entered Andover Theological Seminary in Massachusetts in 1832 as a student, the institution co-founded by Timothy Dwight just a few years earlier, and was trying to make ends meet. A gifted linguist, he was hired by Lowell Mason, the music editor, composer, and founder of the Boston Academy of Music, to translate a collection of German songs brought back from Europe by a friend. As he pored over the voluminous material, he found one tune, "God Bless Our Native Land," particularly appealing. The melody had been used throughout Europe and had served as the accompaniment to Britain's "God Save the King." Beethoven and Haydn had even used the music to compose several striking variations in their own compositions. Smith soon found that the tune had been used in early America for such patriotic anthems as "God Save the President" and "God Save George Washington."

Convinced that the United States needed a national hymn and not able to rid his mind of the piece of music, Smith went to work composing lyrics to the melody, doing so, as he later noted, "in a brief period of time at the close of a dismal afternoon."[67] While underscoring national pride in his first three verses, he reserved his last one as a direct invocation for God's continued protection of America:

> *My country 'tis of thee,*
> *Sweet land of liberty,*
> *Of thee I sing.*
> *Land where my fathers died!*
> *Land of the Pilgrims' pride!*
> *From every mountainside,*
> *Let freedom ring!*
>
> *My native country, thee,*
> *Land of the noble free,*
> *Thy name I love.*
> *I love thy rocks and rills,*
> *Thy woods and templed hills;*
> *My heart with rapture fills*
> *Like that above.*
>
> *Let music swell the breeze*
> *And ring from all the trees*
> *Sweet freedom's song.*
> *Let mortal tongues awake;*

> *Let all that breathe partake;*
> *Let rocks their silence break,*
> *The sound prolong.*
>
> *Our fathers' God to Thee,*
> *Author of Liberty,*
> *To Thee we sing.*
> *Long may our land be bright*
> *With freedom's holy light*
> *Protect us by Thy might,*
> *Great God, our King!*[68]

The voices of five hundred children premiered the piece during a Sunday-school celebration at the Park Street Church in Boston on July 4, 1832, and within months it was being performed throughout the country.

For the rest of his life the Reverend Samuel Smith traveled the world over as a Baptist missionary, putting to use more than a dozen languages he knew. Living to a ripe eighty-six years of age, he composed well over 150 hymns. Together with his friend the Reverend Baron Stow, the diarist of the historic Cane Ridge, Kentucky, revival, he wrote *The Psalmist*, the most widely used Baptist hymnal of the nineteenth century. In the end, however, he knew that his single most remembered contribution would always be "America," the hymn he dashed off as a seminary student on one memorably dreary day.

FROM THE OUTSET of the nineteenth century the country was clearly experiencing growing pains. With the backdrop of the Second Great Awakening, however, a profound sense of the Almighty was solidified on the grassroots level. America was evolving into a society in which prayer was an integral part of the national fabric. Despite mounting optimism, however, nothing could hide the underlying tremors the nation now felt. Its deep faith in God was being sorely tried by mounting pressures over the issue of slavery. The seeds that had long been sown were leading to civil war.

CHAPTER 5

THE DREAMERS

The Legacy of Slavery

It's me, it's me,
It's me, O Lord,
Standin' in the need of prayer
'Taint my mother or my father.
But it's me, O Lord,
Standin' in the need of prayer.

—Unknown African-American slave

SAINT AUGUSTINE WROTE that when a person sings praise to God, he prays twice. Had he observed the worship of African-Americans, particularly during the days of slavery, he would have redefined his notion of prayer. The spiritual expression of enslaved African-Americans is one of the most significant influences in the culture of American prayer. African-Americans, much like Native Americans, were firmly rooted in what the cultural historian Lawrence Levine referred to as "the intimate relationship between the world of sound and the world of sacred time and space in which there were no lines between the past and the present, between the sacred and the secular."[1]

It is one of the great ironies and dark, defining moments in American history that the early colonists and their immediate heirs, who themselves had escaped persecution and prejudice in Europe, forced African men, women, and children into total, and in most instances permanent, bondage—ten million people over four centuries.[2]

The plight of the country's enslaved was most strikingly depicted in the tens of thousands of plaques that abolitionists had engraved showing a male slave on his knees, in chains, and with his hands folded. Locked somewhere between prayer to God and a plea to the white man for his freedom, the figure was framed with the words "Am I not a man and a brother?"

That cruel irony served as a backdrop as African-Americans were forced to learn the tenets of Christianity from those individuals who seemed most incapable of practicing its basic principles. As Daniel Payne, Bishop of the African Methodist Episcopal Church, wrote in 1852:

> The slaves are sensible of the oppression exercised by their masters, and they see these masters on the Lord's day worshipping in his holy Sanctuary. They hear their masters professing Christianity; they see their masters preaching the gospel; they hear these masters praying with their families; and they know that oppression and slavery are inconsistent with the Christian religion; therefore they scoff at religion itself—mock their masters, and distrust both the goodness and justice of God.[3]

The renowned orator and former slave Frederick Douglass was even more direct. After moving to Great Britain to escape the clutches of slave catchers, he was asked on numerous occasions to speak before British audiences about his experiences as a slave and his insights on the institution of slavery. On September 14, 1846, in the weeks just before he was able to buy his freedom, he spoke before the Evangelical Alliance of Britain, an event anxiously anticipated by the British public and covered by London's *Inquirer* and *Patriot*. Douglass focused his remarks on the defense of slavery by certain members of the religious establishment in the United States, noting, "The slave system in America finds no stronger ally in any quarter than in the American church." He then pointed to the vile hypocrisy of slave owners:

> I have all my days been accustomed to prayer, in connection with slavery: my master was a praying man; the man who claims to own these hands, and who has bound himself almost with the solemnity of an oath, that if ever again I set my feet on the American soil I

shall be a slave, that man prays, at morning, noon, and nights; and I have seen him tie up by the hands a female cousin of my own, and lash her with a cow-skin, till the warm blood trickled at her feet, and all the while say, "the slave that knoweth his master's will, and doeth it not, shall be beaten with many stripes."

The audience, swept up in the moment, yelled out, "Shame!" Once they had quieted, he continued:

I have seen my master's brother trample my own brother to the ground, and stamp on him with his boot, till the blood gushed from his nose. I have seen these things in the midst of prayer . . .

I know the prayers of slaveholders. I have been the slave of religious and irreligious slaveholders, and I bear my testimony, that next to being a slave at all, I regard the greatest calamity to be that of belonging to a religious slaveholder.

The audience erupted into applause and cries of "Hear! Hear!"[4] Douglass had made his point.

Douglass's *Narrative of the Life of Frederick Douglass*, written in 1845, became an eloquent contribution to American literature and a vital part of the historical record. From North America to Europe, readers were spellbound by his firsthand accounts of life as a Maryland slave. For a world not fully familiar with the horrors of slavery, Douglass's accounts were devastating. He described his master's "fiendish barbarity" toward both him and his mother in the most vivid terms.

From his master's estate on the Chesapeake, Douglass pondered his plight as he sat on the banks of the bay, "with no audience but the Almighty," as he watched sailboats glide effortlessly across the water out of sight, most of them bound for the free states of the North:

You are loosed from your moorings, and are free; I am fast in my chains and am a slave! You move merrily before the gentle gale and I sadly before the bloody whip! You are freedom's swift-winged angels that fly round the world; I am confined in bands of iron! Oh that I were free! . . . O God, save me! God deliver me! Let me be free! Is there any God? Why am I a slave? I will run away. I will not stand it . . . I have only one life to lose. I had as well be killed running as die standing. Only think of it; one hundred miles straight north, and I am free! Yes! God helping me, I will.[5]

With the help of British friends, Douglass received the necessary financial support to buy his freedom and return to the United States a free man. Throughout the rest of his life Douglass was tireless in his efforts to give voice to defenseless slaves while lending his moral support and counsel to Abraham Lincoln in the thick of the Civil War.

DESPITE THE SPIRITUAL DUPLICITY, the overwhelming number of African-Americans embraced their newfound religion, hanging on to it tightly during the worst days of slavery, looking forward to the time when there would be "a rebalancing of the moral scales."[6] For some, the prayer meeting was a cherished opportunity to come together to pray at least once a week. As one slave later explained, prayer meetings gave slaves the chance to realize how much "everybody's heart was in tune" and to see that "when they called on God they made heaven ring."[7] The prayer meetings could be joyous occasions without fear of interruption, or they could be quiet gatherings in which collective prayer was barely said above a whisper to avoid detection.

Some slaves were so determined to pray together that they would deprive themselves of much-needed sleep, stealing off into the night to a familiar hollow or a field where they had worked earlier in the day. They called these rendezvous points "hush harbors." Here they would recount the stories of the Old Testament and how God's "chosen people" were delivered from bondage. Like their historic ancestors, the Israelites, they hoped, they dreamed, and they prayed that their faith would sustain and ultimately deliver them to the land foretold by God.

There was no need to have a preacher present at these gatherings because each person had more than enough to say. This precious time together, before God and with one another, allowed pent-up emotions to be released in a variety of ways for one very special moment during the week.

Given the frequent need to change prayer meeting sites to avoid detection, the first person to forge a path to the appointed spot would break twigs and boughs along the way, laying the trail to the service. While waiting for others to arrive, each person would catch up on any personal news since their last gathering. Once everyone was finally together, they would pray, sing, preach, and give testimony to their faith. As a runaway slave, Peter Randolph, remembered, "The slave forgets all his sufferings, except to remind others of the trials during the past week, exclaiming 'Thank God, I shall not live here always!' "[8] At the end of the service they would shake hands, wishing one another well until their next meeting, and then softly sing a spiritual as they returned to their cabins.

For others like Tom Robinson, who had been sold at the age of eleven, the importance of prayer weighed heavily and became the only true memory he ever had of his mother:

> I can just barely remember her. But I do remember how she used to take us children and kneel down in front of the fireplace and pray. She'd pray that the time would come when everybody could worship the Lord under their own vine and fig tree—all of them free. It's come to me lots of times since. There she was a'praying. All over the country the same prayer was being prayed. Guess the Lord done heard the prayer and answered it.[9]

Many white masters, fearful of slaves' congregating in one spot, would get suspicious and try to cajole children into tattling on their parents about secret prayer meetings. The children, however, were sworn to secrecy and taught to reply convincingly, "No, sir." Other masters had no problem allowing their slaves to attend public worship services, but they forbade them to pray for freedom.

MORE THAN FEAR OF THEIR MASTERS, many slaves lived in fear of the barbarity of night riders, or patrollers, who galloped throughout the countryside, sometimes without the permission of individual slave owners, punishing slaves who were not meeting curfews or respecting the strictures of plantation society. One slave, W. B. Allen, who was subsequently ordained a minister, noted many years later what it was like to deal with the mix of prayer and the ever-present threat of the menacing, despised night riders:

> They [the slaves] had a hard time trying to serve God. The patrollers would break up their prayer meetings and whip all caught in attendance—unless, of course, a nigger saved himself in flight. My father

was once attending a prayer meeting in a house, which had only one door. The slaves had turned a large pot down in the center of the floor to hold the sounds of their voices within. (No sounds can escape from a closed room, if a big pot be turned down in the middle of it.) But, despite their precaution, the patrollers found them and broke in. Of course, every Nigger present was "in" for a severe whipping, but the Lord must have spoken to my father. Thinking fast and acting quickly (as if he were inspired), my father stuck a big shovel in the fireplace, drew out a peck or more of hot ashes and cinders and flung them broadcast into the faces of them patrollers. The room was soon filled with smoke and the smell of burning clothes and white flesh and, in the confusion and general hubbub that followed, every Negro escaped.[10]

Allen's father was luckier than most.

How africans came to america in the first place is a sordid, twisted tale. The first arrivals, twenty of them, disembarked in Jamestown, Virginia, in 1619. They boarded ships in West Africa from lands known in the modern world as Senegal, Gambia, and Gabon. To put their numbers in perspective: By the time of the Civil War, the United States had a population of a little more than thirty-one million. Of this number almost five million were African-American, most were slaves, and the vast majority were American born.[11]

The slave trade prospered by effectively setting up a commercial triangle. First, a ship would set sail from England, practically empty but for a cache of weapons and ammunition, liquor, cloth, and various trinkets to use as barter in paying African chieftains for men, women, and children. Often the human merchandise traded for cheap Western goods had been captured through the spoils of war with other tribes. Once the deals were made, the slaves were boarded on ships headed for the American continent or the West Indies in a voyage that became known as the Middle Passage. The ship's captain would try to ensure that the mortality rate among the Africans was no more than 20 percent. If someone contracted dysentery or smallpox, he or she was simply thrown overboard. Once the slaves arrived at port, they were exchanged for sugar and molasses to manufacture rum for sale in England. The ship would then return to England, and the process would begin all over again.

Out of this setting, one of the world's most endearing prayers was written. Born in London and motherless by the age of two, John Newton went off to sea while still a young boy, accompanying his father, who commanded a British merchant ship. After his father's retirement, Newton began to serve aboard slave ships. Assigned to the *Greyhound* in the spring of 1748, he was returning home to England after selling a large cargo of slaves in America. Having some free time, he began to read a copy of Thomas à Kempis's *Imitation of Christ* that he found in the captain's library. Transfixed from the opening page, he pored over every word of the devotional, with its theme of freeing oneself from earthly temptations and its in-depth treatment of the efficacy of prayer. He realized he was facing an epiphany.

Only a few weeks later, his increased faith was put to the test. While the *Greyhound* was sailing off the coast of Newfoundland, a severe storm arose. Although Newton had experienced storms before, he had never faced anything quite like the hurricane-force winds and waves of this one. Over the next twenty-four hours he alternated between manning the pumps and steering the ship.

During the worst of the storm and with *Imitation of Christ* still fresh in his mind, Newton screamed, "Lord, have mercy on us." As he later wrote in his diary, it was on that night of May 10 that he promised to dedicate the rest of his life to Christ. The next day, the storm having passed, he began to compose the words to "Amazing Grace":

> *Amazing grace! (how sweet the sound)*
> *That sav'd a wretch like me!*
> *I once was lost but now am found,*
> *Was blind, but now I see.*
>
> *'Twas grace that taught my heart to fear,*
> *And grace my fears reliev'd;*
> *How precious did that grace appear*
> *The hour I first believ'd!*
>
> *Thro' many dangers, toils and snares*
> *I have already come;*
> *'Tis grace has brought me safe thus far,*
> *And grace will lead me home.*

The Lord has promised good to me,
His word my hope secures;
He will my shield and portion be,
As long as life endures.

Yes, when this flesh and heart shall fail,
And mortal life shall cease;
I shall possess, within the veil,
A life of joy and peace.

The earth shall soon dissolve like snow,
The sun forbear to shine;
But God, who call'd me here below,
Will be forever mine.[12]

Where the tune "Amazing Grace" originated continues to be debated. Some believe it came from an American folk melody called "Virginia Harmony." Others are convinced that it emanated from the plantations of the South or even directly from Africa. What is clear is that the stirring combination of words and melody had a powerful effect on its listeners. In retrospect it even seemed to presage the blues many decades later. As the Vanderbilt musicologist Dale Cockrell noted in making the connection, "The song [is] a blues resonance—a blending of Saturday night and Sunday morning . . . victory over sorrow."[13]

Newton's conversion is hard to mistake for anything but a life-altering redemption. Although he continued to run slave ships for several more years, his conscience gnawed at him until he finally broke down and turned his life around. An ardent admirer of George Whitefield, he became an Anglican minister after nine years of study. Soon emerging as one of England's most articulate spokesman for the abolition of slavery, Newton spent the rest of his life writing 348 religious songs and chronicling in graphic detail the horrors of the slave trade for eighteenth-century England. In writing other popular hymns such as "How Sweet the Name of Jesus Sounds" and "Glorious Things of Thee Are Spoken," he produced an impressive spiritual repertoire that he published in *Olney Hymns*, a devotional named after his home in Buckinghamshire. "Amazing Grace," however, would become Newton's greatest legacy. By the turn of the twenty-first century, the Library of Congress had confirmed that "Amazing Grace" had been recorded more often and by more American artists than any other piece of its kind.[14]

ALTHOUGH SOME AFRICANS bound for the Americas had already been converted to Christianity or to Islam in their native land, they were in the minority. Most of them came from animist or other spiritual traditions. Arriving on America's shores, they were largely prohibited from following their old religious practices while being introduced to the basic tenets of Christianity. As a result, long-ingrained African customs often found their way in some form into their prayer practices, which included ancestor veneration, a belief in the use of magic for good or ill, and devotion to a pantheon of gods while still focusing on one god.

Many Africans began their American odyssey after landing in Virginia. In most instances they would be handcuffed and then chained to a mobile bar that forced them to form two rows. Men on horseback would hover over them with whips, while slave fiddlers were forced to play their instruments along the route to take everyone's mind off the journey. This was a form of antebellum slave control. With or without the fiddlers the slaves would sing their songs and prayers of woe:

> *See these poor souls from Africa*
> *Transported to America:*
> *We are stolen and sold to Georgia, will you go along with me?*
> *We are stolen and sold to Georgia, go sound the jubilee.*
>
> *See wives and husbands sold apart,*
> *The children's screams!—it breaks my heart;*
> *There's a better day a-coming, will you go along with me?*
> *There's a better day a-coming, go sound the jubilee.*
>
> *O gracious Lord! When shall it be*
> *That we poor souls shall all be free?*
> *Lord, break them Slavery powers—will you go along with me?*
> *Lord, break them Slavery powers, go sound the jubilee.*[15]

Spirituals were a powerful release, providing both personal and communal prayer to God through song, giving voice to the dreams and aspirations of those enslaved. They were sung in fields and around campfires;

mothers sang them just above a whisper as they nursed their children or the children of their masters to sleep. Spirituals were sung wherever people gathered.

As the spiritual "Ev'ry Time I Feel de Spirit" proclaimed:

> Ev'ry time I feel de spirit, movin' in my heart, I will pray.
> O, ev'ry time I feel de spirit, movin' in my heart, I will pray.
> Upon de mountain my Lord spoke,
> Out of his mouth came fire and smoke.
> An' all roun' me look so fine,
> Aska my Lord, if all was mine.
> Jordan river chilly, cold,
> Chilla de body but not de soul.

> O, ev'ry time I feel de spirit, movin' in my heart, I will pray.[16]

Here was prayer at its most eloquent, an almost out-of-body experience to help them confront their burdens, their sorrows, their joys, and their hopes. It is no wonder that American slaves found some solace in hearing and repeating the stories of the captive Israelites of the Old Testament through such spirituals as "Ride on, Moses," "Didn't Old Pharro Get Los'?," and "Joshua Fit de Battle of Jericho." The spiritual provided what Albert Raboteau of Princeton University has referred to as a "sense of sacred time operated," in which the here and now for slaves was extended backward and scenes, characters, and events from the Old and New Testaments felt vividly alive.[17]

For future generations, the spiritual provided critical documentation in understanding how African-Americans, individually and as a community, survived and how they viewed God within their world. In the words of Frederick Douglass:

They told a tale which was then altogether beyond my feeble comprehension; they were tones, loud, long and deep, the bitterest anguish. Every tone was a testimony against slavery, and a prayer to God for deliverance from chains . . . The mere recurrence, even now, afflicts my spirit, and while I am writing these lines, my tears are falling. To those songs I trace my first glimmering conceptions of the dehumanizing character of slavery. I can never get rid of that conception. Those songs still follow me, to deepen my hatred of slavery, and quicken my sympathies for my brethren in bonds.[18]

That slaves could withstand their own trials by relating them to the sufferings of Christ was central in such spirituals as "Were You There When They Crucified My Lord," "The Blood Came Twinklin' Down," and "He Never Said a Mumblin' Word." To face a world of slavery and to confront the reality that your own children would be sentenced to the same fate were indescribable. The spiritual provided a salve that made daily existence somewhat more bearable. At the same time, many of the prayer messages within the spirituals gave voice to an unmistakable defiance. Double-entendre songs like "Go Down Moses," "Joshua Fit de Battle of Jericho," and "Didn't My Lord Deliver Daniel?" allowed many men and women to challenge their enslavers under spiritual cover.

After the Civil War, Harris Barrett, a professor at the Hampton Institute in Virginia, tried to capture the spiritual in its original context:

Those who have never heard these songs in their native setting can have no conception of the influence they exert upon the people. I have sat in a gathering where everything was as quiet and placid as a lake on a summer day, where the preacher strove in vain to awaken an interest; I have heard a brother or a sister start one of these spirituals, slowly and monotonously; I have seen the congregation irresistibly drawn to take up the refrain; I have seen the entire body gradually worked up from one degree of emotion to another until, like a turbulent, angry sea, men and women, to the accompaniment of the singing, and with shouting, moaning, and clapping of hands, surged and swayed to and fro. I have seen men and women at these times look and express themselves as if they were conversing with their Lord and Master, with their hands in His.[19]

Realizing the significance of this unique heritage, a handful of individuals just after the Civil War began to catalog and publicize the spiritual. In 1871 the Jubilee Singers of Fisk University, in an effort to raise money for their school in Nashville, Tennessee, took the spirituals on the road. For the first time audiences in major cities of the United States and Europe were exposed to the haunting echoes of America's slave legacy.

Musically, the spirituals were exotic to the ears of most people. The harmonies, the rhythms, and the lack of instrumental accompaniment exuded both joy and heartbreak.

The response from audiences everywhere was overwhelming. Not only did the singers raise considerable sums for the university over the next four years, but they also helped to export the first major American cultural phenomenon.[20] Soon the very popular college glee clubs of the day were embracing spirituals as well, performing them as an integral part of their repertoire. African-American churches soon accepted the sacred heritage of slavery as something to be embraced, rather than scorned, and began to integrate spirituals as musical prayers in their liturgy. After listening to the Fisk Jubilee Singers for the first time, the respected Reverend William H. Goodrich of Binghamton, New York, tried to put the spiritual in perspective:

> The slaves of the South came to begin a totally new history . . . Born of ignorant emotion, uncorrected by any reading of Scripture, they are confused in language, broken in connection, wild and odd in suggestion, but inconceivably touching, and sometimes grand. At first you smile or laugh out at the queer association of ideas, but before you know it your eyes fill and your heart is heaving with a true devotional feeling. You see clearly that these songs have been, in their untaught years, a real liturgy, a cry of the soul.[21]

While the Fisk singers provided the world with a taste of spirituals, they had only a few works to perform. The vast number of spirituals that had been sung for decades were simply not known across the South, because most of them had developed regionally. It was left to two remarkable brothers, James Weldon Johnson and J. Rosamond Johnson, leaders in the Harlem Renaissance of the early twentieth century, to catalog and arrange every spiritual they could find, allowing even wider audiences to appreciate the diversity of the hymns.

Some of the most heart-wrenching spirituals, known as "sorrow songs," captured the desolation and sheer loneliness of slavery in turning to God for consolation. "A City Called Heaven," for example, reaffirmed that true peace, freedom, and personal fulfillment were to be found not on earth but in the promise of heaven:

I am a poor pilgrim of sorrow,
I'm tossed in this wild world alone.
No hope have I for tomorrow;
I've started to make Heaven my home.

Sometimes I am tossed and driven, Lord,
Sometimes I don't know where to roam.
I've heard of a city called Heaven;
I've started to make it my home.[22]

One of the most devastating and gut-wrenching spirituals of them all was "Lord, How Come Me Here?" Its cry could not have been more simple or more piercing:

Lord, how come me here?
I wish I never was born.

There ain't no freedom here, Lord.
I wish I never was born.

They treat me so mean here, Lord.
I wish I never was born.

They sold my children away, Lord.
I wish I never was born.

Lord, how come me here?
I wish I never was born.[23]

There was a spiritual expressing complete desolation when even prayer was difficult to invoke:

I couldn't hear nobody pray,
Oh, I couldn't hear nobody pray.
Oh, way down yonder by myself,
And I couldn't hear nobody pray.[24]

Familiar to millions of people, "Nobody Knows de Trouble I See" may well have been written by a slave while he helplessly watched his wife and children being sold away to another master. Although accounts of its origin vary, the spiritual conveyed the depth of such despair:

> *Nobody knows de trouble I see,*
> *Nobody knows but Jesus;*
> *Nobody knows de trouble I see,*
> *Glory, hallelujah!*

> *Sometimes I'm up, Sometimes I'm down*
> *Oh, yes, Lord;*
> *Sometimes I'm almos' to de groun'*
> *Oh, yes, Lord,*
> *Altho' you see me goin' 'long so,*
> *Oh, yes, Lord, I have my trials here below,*
> *Oh, yes, Lord.*

> *Nobody knows de trouble I see,*
> *Nobody knows but Jesus;*
> *Nobody knows de trouble I see,*
> *Glory, hallelujah!*[25]

For the newly arrived slaves, English, of course, was a second language, and in most instances their masters had no desire to teach them either grammar or diction, making the composition of the earliest spirituals even more remarkable. In some cases it took years to reproduce accurately on paper what was being sung, because the chronicler was unable to discern the words.

What also made the spirituals so difficult for many people to comprehend was their reliance on rhythm rather than melody, which was so much a part of European hymns. This unique hybrid had developed into spirituals like "Lord, I Got a Right," a call for some human dignity:

> *Lord, I got a right,*
> *Lord, I got a right,*
> *Lord, I got a right,*
> *I got a right to the tree of life.*[26]

This is not to say that spirituals lacked strong lines of melody. They simply blended it together with rhythms that were uncommon for the day. "Michael, Row the Boat Ashore" and "Come by Here, My Lord" ("Kumbaya") are only two such examples.

"Let Us Break Bread Togedder" serves as a particularly strong example of forging a common bond with one another and with God. Originally written as a secret call to gather African-Americans for clandestine religious prayer meetings, it evolved as a piece to be said before meals or during liturgical Communions. The phrase "with my face to the rising sun" may well have been rooted in the African Islamic tradition of facing east during daily prayer:

> *Let us break bread togedder on our knees,*
> *Yes, on our knees*
> *Let us break bread togedder on our knees,*
> *When I fall on my knees, Wid my face to de risin' sun;*
> *Oh, Lord have mercy on me.*
>
> *Let us drink wine togedder on our knees,*
> *Yes, on our knees*
> *Let us drink wine togedder on our knees,*
> *When I fall on my knees, Wid my face to de risin' sun;*
> *Oh, Lord have mercy on me.*
>
> *Let us praise God togedder on our knees,*
> *Yes, on our knees*
> *Let us praise God togedder on our knees,*
> *When I fall on my knees, Wid my face to de risin' sun;*
> *Oh, Lord have mercy on me.*[27]

These sorrow songs, however, were offset in part by the great jubilee spirituals. These were hymns about which the music biographer Andrew Ward, in writing about these great prayers, has said, "They not only declared faith but carried news, raised protests, expressed grief, asked questions, made jokes, lubricated a slave's never ending toil."[28]

Bringing together vibrant rhythms, a memorable tune, and uplifting lyrics, "When the Saints Go Marchin' In" became one of the most beloved of them all. Popularized in the 1890s in the traditions of New Orleans ragtime and later in the jazz intonations of Louis Armstrong, the song showed a pulsating renewal of faith in God and salvation. Its blatant sentimental vigor, particularly in its chorus, conveyed pure elation:

> *When the saints go marchin' in,*
> *When the saints go marchin' in,*
> *Lord, I want to be in that number*
> *When the saints go marchin' in.*[29]

From the inspiration of songs like "When the Saints Go Marchin' In," a unique venue for spiritual expression developed in the form of the New Orleans jazz funeral. "Rejoice when you die" became the theme of this late-eighteenth-century phenomenon, in which slaves transplanted from Africa wanted to make sure that their loved ones, who had sacrificed so much in life, would not be forgotten in death. A band would play dirges as it accompanied mourners to a burial site, and then joyously go into an up tempo once the body had been interred. It was now time for jubilation. "Lord, Lord, Lord, You been so good to me. You saved my soul from sin and shame," went one of the more popular funeral spirituals.

The spiritual that stands out as perhaps the grandest is "Deep River." H. L. Mencken, the famous Baltimore journalist, remarked that whoever composed "Deep River" had to be "one of the greatest poets we have ever produced."[30] The work reflected the barrier between the here and now and the assurances of heaven and deliverance enshrined in the metaphor "campground." In addition, it conjured up the freedom of the North, giving the spiritual an unmistakably regal air in both its character and its meaning:

> *Deep river, my home is over Jordan;*
> *Deep river, Lord, I want to cross over into campground,*
> *Lord, I want to cross over into campground,*
> *Lord, I want to cross over into campground,*
> *Lord, I want to cross over into campground.*
>
> *Oh, chillun,*
> *Oh, don't you want to go to that gospel feast,*
> *That promised land, where all is peace?*

Walk into heaven and take my seat,
And cast my crown at Jesus' feet;
Lord, I want to cross over into campground,
Lord, I want to cross over into campground,
Lord, I want to cross over into campground.

Deep river, my home is over Jordan;
Deep river, Lord, I want to cross over into campground.[31]

Another form of prayer for the slaves, steeped in the traditions of Africa, was the "ring shout." At the end of Sunday services, capping off their devotion to God, congregants would push their benches to the sides of the meeting room. A few individuals, both young and old, would gather in the middle of the room, while the rest of the people sat or stood along the walls and began to sing spirituals especially composed for the shouts. Those in the center of the room would then start to dance, trying not to cross their feet or lift them from the floor, a ritual that could go on for as long as five hours as everyone moved continuously in a circle. The dancers and shouters would eventually be transformed into a state of frenzy, often falling to the ground in complete exhaustion. They saw the shout ritual as a way to communicate with God, welcoming the Holy Spirit to enter their bodies and take possession of their souls.

In one firsthand account, Vinnie Brunson described, some sixty years after being freed from slavery, what the shout ritual was all about:

De Bible tells how de angels shouted in heaven, so dat is where dey get de scriptures fer de dance dat is called de "Shout." De ones dat do dis does not sing, dey jes dance, dey songs are sung by de congregashun. In most cases de "shout" is done at de end of de services . . .

De folks in de congregashun jine de singin' an keepin' de time by pattin' de hands an feet an' hit makes a big noise an praise service.

As one crowd gits tired an quits, another starts up 'till dey all has a chance to take part in de praise service of de dance shout. De spiritual songs I sing fast an if hit is a funeral hit is sung slow. Dey sing "Swing Low Sweet Chariot" a heap at de praise song, an' at de funerals bof.

(Praise song fast)
Swing low, Sweet chariot, Comin' fer ter carry me home.
Swing low, sweet chariot, comin' fer ter carry me home.
I looked over Jordan an' what did I see,
'Comin' fer to carry me home?
A band of angels comin' after me,
Comin' fer to carry me home.

(Funeral slow)
Swing low, sweet chariot, comin' fer to carry me home,
Swing l-o-w, s-w-e-e-t-char-iot, C'omin' fer to carry me home.[32]

Most dispossessed Africans used every fiber of their being in their devotional prayers to God. While slaves would try to dull their senses to their daily hardships, they desperately wanted, and in fact needed, to release their pent-up raw emotions and pressures through profound and passionate prayer to the Almighty.

PRAYER FOR SOME African-Americans was a perceptible influence in defying their enslavement, and no case was more striking than that of Nat Turner. Precocious, literate, and fearless, Turner became a favorite of his white master and was taken regularly to Methodist prayer meetings before he reached the age of ten. To those who met him even then, his intellectual gifts were obvious, and very soon he could recite practically every passage of the Bible. Before Turner became an adolescent, however, his master died, leaving him without a mentor. The master's son, who took over his father's estate, had little time for intellectual pursuits or for the young Turner, and soon he was picking cotton with the other slaves.

Despite his new situation, Turner never lost his faith and was soon conducting Sunday "praise meetings" for local blacks with the permission of their masters. By all accounts, he had an uncanny ability to mesmerize almost any gathering through the cadence of his voice and the charisma of his personality. When he reached his early twenties, however, he had a series of apocalyptic visions of blacks in mortal combat with whites. Not knowing what the signs meant, he began to pray even more fervently and soon believed he was engaged in continuous dialogue with God, much like the figures of the Old Testament.

On May 12, 1828, the voice became most direct. "I heard a loud noise in the heavens," he later recalled, and was given the order that "I should arise and prepare myself and slay my enemies with their own weapons."[33] Told to wait for further signs as to when to strike, Turner witnessed a solar eclipse in February 1831, followed by other natural phenomena, and he believed the time had come.

Having prayed for guidance, Turner convinced seven other slaves to join him in killing his master, Joseph Travis, and the Travis family while they slept in their beds. Soon other slaves joined Turner, stalking plantations and, in the end, murdering five dozen white people with knives and hatchets, the bloodiest slave revolt in U.S. history. Ultimately Turner was captured, tried, and executed, his actions sending a chilling signal throughout the South. While he awaited his hanging, he spent several hours in his jail cell with his court-appointed attorney, Thomas R. Gray, sharing some of his most intimate thoughts. With the permission of the jailer, Gray took extensive notes for what became known as *The Confessions of Nat Turner*. By the time Gray was finished, he would have a composite of the motives that consumed Turner and the actions he took, all triggered, as he told Gray, by the word of God.

OTHER ENSLAVED AFRICAN-AMERICANS used their ingenuity to find personal freedom in nonviolent ways, turning to prayer as a guiding force. Harriet Tubman, that nineteenth-century "Moses" who found inspiration in the stories of Exodus, led dozens of slaves to freedom through the obstacle course of the Underground Railroad. Her success in delivering slaves to the freedom of the North was nothing less than remarkable. "I never run my train off the track, and I never lost a passenger," Tubman liked to say.[34]

Having escaped from slavery in 1849, the frail-looking Tubman lived into her nineties, dying just before World War I. The seminal moment in her life occurred when she was a teenager. Working on a Maryland plantation, she tried to shield a slave who was about to be whipped by their master. In the middle of the fracas, she was struck by a large rock intended for the other slave. Knocked unconscious, she hovered between life and death. During her long convalescence, she turned to God, talking aloud to him almost incessantly. After many months, she began to believe that God was telling her to escape to freedom and in turn show others that they, too, could break their chains of bondage.

From the moment she began her mission, leading men, women, and children to their freedom—nineteen harrowing trips in all—she prayed daily. Fueled by an intense faith, she later told friends, "I always told God, 'I'm going to hold steady on You, an' You've got to see me through.'" One of the prayers she often sang to her own melody spoke of her journey north of the U.S. border:

> *I'm on my way to Canada,*
> *That cold but happy land;*
> *The dire effects of slavery*
> *I can no longer stand*
> *O righteous Father*
> *Do look down on me,*
> *And help me on to Canada,*
> *Where colored folks are free!*[35]

She normally targeted the long, dark winter months to hatch an escape, finding ways to send messages to the men and women she would soon be helping, telling them to meet her, often as far away as ten miles from their plantations. Saturday nights seem to have been the most opportune time to avoid detection, because slave owners and their families were preoccupied with their Sabbath activities of the next day. In most instances the owner would not realize anyone was missing until Monday morning.

Her task became more difficult, however, after Congress passed the Fugitive Slave Act of 1850, forcing all escaped slaves, north or south, to be returned to their masters. The act meant that Tubman would have to forge an escape route all the way to the Canadian border. With the help of abolitionists in the North, men like William Henry Rosensteel of Johnstown, Pennsylvania, who sheltered runaways in specially designed rooms in his house and then drove them by carriage to their next rendezvous point, she was able to succeed.

Every trip, of course, was different from the last, and anything could go wrong. On one occasion, Tubman and a black woman named Tilly were carrying forged passes, trying to cross a river, when a boatman turned to them and sternly said that he would deal with them in a moment. Believing that they had been found out, Harriet Tubman began to tremble but prayed as she did so, staring into the water below, saying under her breath, "Oh, Lord, You've been with me in six troubles, don't desert me in the seventh!" The boatman finally returned to the back of the boat and simply told the women he would now issue their tickets. Once again, Tubman believed that Divine Providence had been in her corner.[36] As the northern abolitionist Thomas Garrett later remarked, "I never met a person of any color who had more confidence in the voice of God."[37]

Other slaves also found their way to freedom through the use of cunning, fortitude, and prayer. One of the most remarkable, riveting stories of the era involved the escape of William and Ellen Craft from Georgia in 1848. Ellen Craft, the daughter of a biracial mother and a white father, had been able to pass as Caucasian since she was a little girl. She and the distinguished-looking William Craft had met, fallen in love, and gotten married, but they ended up living a hundred miles apart. Over two years, however, they meticulously planned their escape. Ellen would disguise herself as a man, and William would serve as her slave. The scheme, if it worked, would allow them unfettered passage to freedom in the North. Throughout their daring journey, they never made a move without turning to God for help. As William Craft later recounted:

> When the time had arrived for us to start, we blew out the lights, knelt down, and prayed to our Heavenly Father mercifully to assist us, as he did his people of old, to escape from cruel bondage; and we shall ever feel that God heard and answered our prayer. Had we not been sustained by a kind, and I sometimes think special, providence, we could never have overcome the mountainous difficulties which I am now about to describe.[38]

Off they went, with Ellen wearing a face scarf to hide her lack of a beard and a hand bandage to avoid signing anything that would give away her illiteracy. What was so remarkable about their journey was that unlike the slaves who found their way to freedom through rivers, thickets, and woods, the Crafts used public transportation and stayed in hotels all the way to Philadelphia. On the last leg of their trip, taken by train, William looked out the window as Ellen slept next to him, seeing lights in the distance but not quite knowing what to make of them. Soon he overheard another passenger announce that they were about to pull into the Philadelphia train station. "As the train speeded on, I rejoiced and thanked God with all my heart and soul for his great kindness and tender mercy, in watching over us, and bringing us safely through," William recalled. After disembarking, they took a carriage to a boardinghouse recommended to them by an abolitionist. While in the carriage, Ellen collapsed in sobs, saying, "Thank God, William, we are safe." As they were shown to their room, she could barely hold herself together. No sooner had the door closed behind them than they dropped to their knees to pray. It was Sunday, Christmas Day, and, as William wrote, we "poured out our heartfeld gratitude to God."[39]

Their story was electrifying, and soon prominent abolitionists like William Lloyd Garrison were publicizing their account across the country. The passage of the Fugitive Slave Act, however, made Garrison's hopes for change short-lived. With its enactment, making it illegal for escaped slaves to remain free in the North, William and Ellen Craft fled to England, where they shared their experience in William's autobiography, *Running a Thousand Miles for Freedom*. The Crafts and two of their five children returned to the United States after the Civil War, settling on a farm in their native Georgia.

OTHER EARLY AFRICAN-AMERICANS contributed to the prayer culture of America through both their preaching and their writings. They brought to their worship and to their zeal for God a prose that hid nothing and was clearly committed to the search for divine intimacy and ultimate salvation.

In 1760, Jupiter Hammon, a slave born in 1711 on the Lloyd Estate, now Lloyd's Neck, New York, became the first published black poet. In a work titled *An Evening Thought: Salvation by Christ, with Penitential Cries* he defined his faith in the precepts of Christ's teachings. Excerpts from one of his prayers rang with Christian and spiritual fidelity:

> *Salvation comes by Jesus Christ alone,*
> *The only Son of God;*
> *Redemption now to every one,*
> *That love his holy Word . . .*

> *Now is the Day, excepted Time;*
> *The Day of Salvation;*
> *Increase your Faith, do not repine:*
> *Awake ye, every Nation.*[40]

Even more noteworthy in showing extraordinary literary talent around the time of the Revolutionary War was the gifted Phillis Wheatley, a woman forty years younger than Jupiter Hammon. Soon after reading her first published works, Hammon became one of her most stalwart supporters.

Born in what today is Senegal around 1753, Wheatley, like so many others, was abducted and brought to America, where she was sold to a modest family in Boston. The family wanted her to provide them with little more than companionship, and when they learned that she had a genuine desire and aptitude for learning, they did everything possible to help. Soon she mastered English, Latin, and Greek, reading many of the classics, including John Milton and Alexander Pope.

She was captivated by the eloquence and intellectual depth of the Reverend George Whitefield and soon became one of his most staunch followers. Her first published poetry, written when she learned of his death, was a memorial to him. As a result, her name came to the attention of readers not only in America but also in England. For abolitionists and many whites, Phillis Wheatley's works single-handedly dispelled the notion that transplanted Africans were intellectually inferior or lacked genuine spirituality. George Washington even wrote to her to express his great admiration.

Phillis Wheatley's introspective devotion was enshrined in a prayer found in her Bible after her death. "A Mother's Prayer for the Child in Her Womb" was probably written in anticipation of the birth of her son Johnny. It was certainly reminiscent of a similar prayer written by Anne Bradstreet more than a century earlier:

> Oh my gracious Preserver! Hitherto Thou hast brought me,
> Be pleased when Thou bringest to the birth to give me strength
> To bring forth living and perfect a being who shall be greatly instrumental
>   in promoting Thy glory.
> Though conceived in sin and brought forth in iniquity,
> Thy infinite wisdom can bring a clean thing out of an unclean vessel of
>   Honor filled for Thy glory.
> Grant me to live a life of gratitude to Thee for the innumerable benefits.[41]

Wheatley's work became an important milestone in giving literary form to the spiritual devotion of early African-Americans. More than fifty years later, a preacher came on the scene whose charming earnestness made her a celebrity in her own day. Born a slave at the turn of the nineteenth century, Sojourner Truth had originally been known as Isabella. During her time in bondage she was sold from one master to the next. Every time she gave birth, her infant was taken away and sold to another owner. By the time she was in her twenties, she had escaped from her slave owners with the help of Quaker abolitionists and soon became a streetcorner evangelist, ultimately founding a shelter for homeless women.

With her new freedom, she decided to put as much of her past behind her as possible. Consequently, she took a new name for herself, choosing "Sojourner" to fit her new image as "a citizen of heaven" and "Truth" to signify her intention to remain true to God and to herself.

Sojourner Truth possessed a number of remarkable qualities. Tall and distinguished in her wire-rimmed glasses, she was gracious and intellectually curious despite her illiteracy. After hearing her sing, people often remarked that she left a lasting impression with the unusual timbre of her voice and the way she conveyed the feeling of each word and phrase.

Prayer was as much a part of her as breathing. In her widely read memoirs, *Narrative of Sojourner Truth*, dictated to a neighbor, the abolitionist Olive Gilbert, she made clear where she stood. "Let others say what they will about the efficacy of prayer, I believe in it, and I shall pray. Thank God! Yes, I *shall always pray*."[42] Her approach to prayer, however, was unique. As Gilbert would write about her early years, she "talked with God as familiarly as if he had been a creature like herself; and a thousand times more so, than if she had been in the presence of some earthly potentate. She demanded, with little expenditure of reverence or fear, a supply of all her more pressing wants, and at times her demands approached very near to commands. She felt as if God was under obligation to her, much more than she was to him. He seemed to her a benighted vision in some manner bound to do her bidding."[43]

When she felt she had been wronged, she would ask without hesitation, "Do you think that's right, God?," knowing full well that she had already answered her own question. When her son was ill, she exclaimed, "If you were in trouble, as I am, and I could help you, as you can me, think I wouldn't do it? Yes, God, you know I would do it!" She could cajole, even nag, the Almighty at times, adding after one of her many petitions. "I will never give you peace till you do, God!"[44]

Gilbert noted, however, that in time Sojourner Truth cringed at the thought of how she once had approached God. "Her heart recoils now, with very dread, when she recalls these shocking, almost blasphemous conversations with the great Jehovah."[45] As her *Narrative* would show, the passage of time allowed her to develop a more mature, and in turn, loving, relationship with God.

IN ADDITION to these colorful personalities, two men arose who, after being freed from bondage, decided to join the religious establishment. In their own separate ways the two close friends, Richard Allen and Absalom Jones, contributed enormously to the prayer life of African-Americans and to the early republic as a whole. They not only helped to shape American religious culture but also defined the struggles and aspirations of African-Americans in the larger context of American society.

Born a slave in 1760, Richard Allen was sold from a family in Philadelphia to Stockley Sturgis, a plantation owner near Dover, Delaware. Impressed by the precocious Allen, Sturgis allowed him to join the local Methodist Society, where Allen learned to read and write and showed a talent for preaching. Growing more confident in his God-given talents, Allen asked Sturgis for permission to hold a prayer service in Sturgis's home. Attending the service, Sturgis was so taken with Allen's religious convictions that he joined the Methodist Church and set about having Richard Allen buy his freedom and that of his brother. Working double jobs as a wagoner and woodcutter, Allen raised the necessary two thousand dollars over five years and immediately turned his attention to the work of the Church.

Concerned that many northern blacks were not being given proper access to the teachings of Christianity, Allen took his preaching and his message of prayer into fields, town squares, and any other place where he might be heard. As he later wrote, "I frequently preached twice a day, at 5:00 o'clock in the morning and evening, and it was not uncommon for me to preach from four to five times a day."[46]

The crystallizing moment for Allen came in Philadelphia in 1787. While watching his friend and fellow parishioner Absalom Jones kneeling in prayer in the sanctuary of the newly built St. George's Methodist Church, he was horrified to see white trustees of the parish physically force Jones to his feet. He later recounted the moment:

When the colored people began to get numerous in attending the church, they moved us from the seats we usually sat on . . . on Sabbath morning we went to church and the sexton stood at the door, and told us to go in the gallery . . . Meeting had begun, and they were nearly done singing, and just as we got to the seats, the elder said, "Let us pray." We had not been long upon our knees before I heard considerable scuffling and low talking. I raised my head up and saw one of the trustees . . . having hold of the Rev. Absalom Jones, pulling him up off of his knees, and saying, "You must get up—you must not kneel here." Mr. Jones replied, "Wait until prayer is over." [The trustee then] said, "No, you must get up now, or I will call for aid and force you away." Mr. Jones said, "Wait until prayer is over, and I will get up and trouble you no more." With that he beckoned to one of the other trustees . . . to come to his assistance . . . By this time prayer was over, and we all went out of the church in a body, and they were no more plagued with us in the church.[47]

Ironically, the black parishioners of St. George's, which today stands as the oldest Methodist church in the United States in continuous service, had built its gallery, laid its flooring, and even contributed financially to its construction. That single incident of forced segregation, even more striking in that it occurred during the saying of prayers, turned out to be a mighty catalyst. Allen and Jones, as well as hundreds of black parishioners, left St. George's that Sunday never to return. With the support of Benjamin Rush, who would soon be leaving his imprint in the founding of the United States, Richard Allen united sixteen independent Methodist congregations into the African Methodist Episcopal (AME) Church, becoming its first Bishop. By the end of the eighteenth century the Church had a membership of almost half a million people.[48] By 1784 the elders of St. George's had asked Allen to return, this time as the first black ever to preach before the Methodist Society of America.

One of Allen's first acts as minister was to collect a series of prayers and hymns, some of which he composed himself, that he knew would appeal to his congregation. He then had them bound into the first published African-American hymnal. His religious innovations and personal dynamism made him a legend to his parishioners and to non-parishioners.

★   ★   ★

LIKE HIS FRIEND RICHARD ALLEN, Absalom Jones was born into slavery in Delaware in 1746. At age sixteen he was sold to a store owner in Philadelphia who allowed him to attend night classes at a school operated by the Quakers. At the age of twenty he fell in love with another slave and was married by the Reverend Jacob Duché, the same Anglican minister who would serve as the first congressional chaplain. Committed to securing his freedom and that of his wife, Jones worked long and hard during the Revolutionary War with one goal in mind, to pay for his wife's freedom. He understood that under Pennsylvania law his wife's freedom, more than his own, would allow for his children to be born free. Through the donations of others, which he ultimately paid back, and with his own earnings, he was able to secure her freedom in 1778. His master, however, would not allow him to buy his release for another seven years.

After working with Richard Allen to set up churches and to organize the Free African Society, the first African-American organization to reach out to the needy and unite African-Americans across the country, Jones set out on a different course from Allen. Choosing to remain an Episcopalian, he was received into the Episcopal Church of Pennsylvania and ordained a priest in 1802. Named the first pastor of Philadelphia's St. Thomas Church, the Reverend Absalom Jones signed up over five hundred African-American members in his first year.

By all accounts, Jones was a mild-mannered figure, gifted with a magnetic personality. Dedicated to the tenets of the Episcopal Church, he amicably split with Richard Allen, and between the two of them, each in his own way, they worked tirelessly toward change and dignity for all African-Americans.

Highly patriotic in the early days of the new republic despite the continued scourge of slavery, Jones delivered a widely published and moving thanksgiving sermon on New Year's Day, 1808. In it he expressed his gratitude to Congress and to President Thomas Jefferson for signing into law the act permanently abolishing any further trafficking of slaves from Africa. In ending the sermon, he offered the following prayer:

Oh thou God of all the nations upon the earth! . . . We thank thee, that the sun of righteousness has at last shed his morning beams upon them . . . We implore thy blessing, O God, upon the President, and all who are in

authority in the United States. Direct them by thy wisdom, in all their
deliberations and O save thy people from the calamities of war. Give peace
in our day, we beseech thee, O thou God of peace! And grant that this
highly favoured country may continue to afford a safe and peaceful retreat
from the calamities of war and slavery, for ages to come.[49]

The actions of Allen and Jones and the depth of their devotion served
Christianity and their country at a critical time in its infancy. Both men
made clear in their ministries that prayer not only was a personal matter
but had to exist as a force within the community itself, as a bulwark
against slavery, and as a constant source of hope for the future.

FOR THE COUNTRY'S EARLY African-Americans prayer was catharsis.
It provided spiritual sustenance in the face of America's original sin. If
white Americans were unprepared to acknowledge the human dignity
enshrined in their Constitution, then African-Americans would find
strength in their Maker. Without prayer, slavery would have been even
more unbearable. One can only wonder how individual men, women,
and children in bondage would have fared without it.

These expressions of prayer also served as omens of what lay ahead
for America. It is difficult to read these spiritual discourses, the dreams of
an enslaved people, and not recognize that the outbreak of war would
soon be at hand.

CHAPTER 6

THE PATHFINDERS

1840–1860

Tell me not, in mournful numbers,
Life is but an empty dream!—
For the soul is dead that slumbers,
And things are not what they seem.

Life is real! Life is earnest!
And the grave is not its goal;
Dust thou art, to dust returnest,
Was not spoken of the soul . . .

Trust no Future, howe'er pleasant!
Let the dead Past bury its dead!
Act,—act in the living Present!
Heart within, and God o'erhead!

Lives of great men all remind us
We can make our lives sublime,
And, departing, leave behind us
Footprints on the sands of time.

—Henry Wadsworth Longfellow,
"A Psalm of Life" (1838)

IN THE MID-NINETEENTH CENTURY, a growing restlessness marked America's intellectual, military, political, and religious pursuits. Attempts to confront these national anxieties and challenges were played out time and again in the halls of Congress and among the country's influential literary elite. Slavery, a variety of reform movements, and the prospect of all-out war moved American prayer into a more comprehensive realm where Christianity's Golden Rule became a still more integral part of a person's salvation.

One prevailing force affecting America centered on exploring, conquering, and settling the West. John L. O'Sullivan, editor of the influential *United States Democratic Review,* coined the term "Manifest Destiny" to describe "the far-reaching, the boundless future [that] will be the era of American greatness . . . the noblest temple ever dedicated to the worship of the Most High—the Sacred and the True."[1] The doctrine of Manifest Destiny came to represent the spiritual wanderlust that so many Americans from all walks of life seemed to possess.

Sam Houston, Stephen Austin, Jim Bowie, and Davy Crockett had already made their mark in settling Texas, with the republic becoming a state in 1845. Soldiers were making their fame and fortune in the Mexican War, a conflict lasting from 1846 to 1848 that would cede California, Nevada, Utah, most of New Mexico and Arizona, and parts of Colorado and Wyoming to the United States. At the same time, the West was becoming a magnet for missionaries from the east coast as well as a draw for recent immigrants and other Americans who wanted to launch new communities, none more formidable than the Mormon exodus to Salt Lake City, Utah. The western push also came at a time when European, mainly Catholic, immigration flooded the harbors of America, particularly in the aftermath of Ireland's great famine.

In addition, American institutions and culture were flourishing at a pace uniquely their own. The country as a whole was fostering an identity distinctly different from its European roots. By 1840 it had already elected nine presidents and twenty-six Congresses, strengthening the foundations of government put into place by the Founding Fathers.

On the cultural front American writers were emerging as a new dynamic. Spiritual self-discovery was central to the creativity of these men and women, an integral theme in their most important works. At the same time, however, a disconnect existed between many of them and their fellow Americans as to how they viewed and ultimately related to God. While most Americans remained rooted in the Second Great Awakening, with its calls for personal salvation, others, particularly the intellectual elite of New England, were finding a far different means to convey spiritual expression.

Most important of all, the United States was facing the untenable status quo of slavery, confronting not just regional and ideological factionalism but the irreversible path to war. No single event had as profound an effect on the country or its people than the outbreak of what came to be known as America's Civil War.

THE PRESIDENTS OF THE PERIOD reflected the diversity of prayer and religious observance within the country. William Henry Harrison, who followed Van Buren, was a bona fide war hero and a devout Episcopalian who read the Bible and recited a set group of prayers daily, a practice he had begun after serving in the army. Brimming with optimism after his election, he celebrated the occasion by purchasing a new Bible for his swearing in and showing off his vigor for office at the age of sixty-eight by enduring the outdoor inaugural ceremonies without an overcoat in the middle of a rainy, unforgiving March day.[2] Delivering the longest inaugural address in history on the eastern portico of the U.S. Capitol, he contracted pneumonia, and less than a month later he was dead. It was the first time that the American people had experienced the shock of a President dying in office. The unusual circumstances made his death all the more surreal, as audiences packed churches across the States to pray and make sense of what had happened to their war hero "Tippacanoe."

Harrison's Vice President, John Tyler, assumed the Oval Office immediately, issuing the first presidential "recommendation" of its kind, calling on the American people to observe a day of fasting and prayer to remember Harrison. The declaration urged all Americans to turn to their "Heavenly Parent":

> When a Christian people feel themselves to be overtaken by a great public calamity, it becomes them to humble themselves under the dispensation of Divine Providence . . . The death of William Henry Harrison, late President of the United States, so soon after his elevation to that high office, is a bereavement peculiarly calculated to be regarded as a heavy affliction and to impress all minds with a sense of the uncertainty of human things and of the dependence of nations, as well as individuals, upon our Heavenly Parent.[3]

Possessed of a shy, dignified charm emanating from his privileged upbringing, Tyler never quite fit in with the hard politics of Washington and soon alienated many politicians within his own party. Known to historians more for having sired fourteen children than for almost anything else, he tried to catch his breath after being sworn in to office just a few weeks after he had taken the oath of office as Vice President.

Happily married to Letitia Christian for twenty-nine years, Tyler faced a difficult time when she was confined to a wheelchair following a stroke. After her husband became President, Letitia largely remained at the family quarters of the Executive Mansion, where she read the Bible and recited prayers from the *Book of Common Prayer* for several hours every day. Two years after her death in 1842 and while still President, Tyler married Julia Gardiner, a devout Episcopalian who later converted to Catholicism. Choosing not to run for election in his own right given his lack of party support, Tyler wrote a rather revealing letter while President. In it he declared his pride in the "great and noble experiment" of the United States, emphasizing the extraordinary notion that men and women of all religious creeds, even non-Christians, could worship and pray freely on American soil and acknowledging that "our system of government would be imperfect without it."[4]

No President since Jackson or before Lincoln would have such an impact on the future of the United States as James Knox Polk. Born in North Carolina but moving to rural Tennessee with his parents at the age of ten, Polk grew up in a household where his mother, Jane, took enormous pride in being an ancestor of John Knox, the founder of the Presbyterian Church. Despite being named after the Scottish Protestant reformer, Polk was never baptized a Presbyterian due to an altercation between his father, Samuel, and the local minister over Church doctrine.

After graduating with honors from the University of North Carolina in 1818, Polk went back to Tennessee, where he studied and worked as a lawyer in Nashville, and then returned to his home near Columbia to run for public office. While campaigning for the U.S. House, he attended a Methodist prayer camp meeting in Columbia in the summer of 1833. As any seasoned politician could attest, even county fairs did not provide an opportunity to meet so many people at one time. Although Polk was only there to expand his political base, he was awed by the Reverend John B. McFerrin, a minister who was later named a Bishop of the Methodist Church. McFerrin was mesmerizing and had already brought hundreds of white and black converts into the Church by his spellbinding oratory and emphasis on the influence of prayer in people's lives.[5]

Impressed with one another, the two became lifelong friends, with Polk promising that should he ever decide to be baptized, he would do so as a Methodist.

Despite his new affinity for Methodism, Polk continued to attend Presbyterian services to appease his mother and his wife, Sarah, whom he had married in 1824. Being elected to Congress in 1825, Speaker of the House ten years later, governor of Tennessee in 1838, and President in 1844, Polk made a steady political climb. Dubbed "Young Hickory" by Andrew Jackson, his longtime mentor, Polk faced an ominous agenda, from declaring war on Mexico over the U.S. annexation of Texas to overseeing the largest expansion of American territory since Jefferson.

Sarah Polk was very mindful of the burdens of office her husband faced and allowed affairs of state to supersede all else—except attending Sunday services. With Cabinet members, congressional leaders, and others pressing her husband on a variety of matters, she would wait until she heard the local church bells chime, and then waltz into a usually full room, cheerily announcing that it was time for everyone to get ready for church.[6] Her bubbly piety and cunning approach to taking her husband away from the nation's business made for many an awkward situation, but her attentiveness ensured that Polk attended services almost every Sunday while in office.

By the time Polk was well into his first term, with war, domestic politics, and the issue of slavery hanging over him and the country, he had begun to face growing opposition in Congress and to experience failing health. Deciding to retire, he returned to Tennessee and within three months was dead from the effects of cholera, most likely contracted on his way home via New Orleans. Attended by his elderly mother and his wife, Polk finally confronted his mortality, confiding that it was time for him to prepare "to meet the great event."[7] While his mother called for a Presbyterian minister to baptize him, she was gently told that he wanted his old friend John McFerrin, now a Methodist Bishop, to perform the rites. McFerrin soon arrived, baptizing Polk and praying with him in his last hours, much to the disappointment of his mother and his wife.

Polk's successor and great adversary, General Zachary Taylor, came into office in the election of 1848 after distinguishing himself as the nation's most famous Mexican War hero. As President, he was an irregular churchgoer at St. John's Episcopal Church next to the Executive Mansion, while his semi-invalid wife, Margaret, attended services at St.

John's daily.[8] An extremely pious woman, Margaret Taylor, who had been born into great wealth, organized her prayer life around her husband's career. During his time away from home, she offered daily intentions that he might return safely from the battlefield, promising God that if he did come back to her, she would forgo social pleasures as a sign of gratitude. Consequently, when she arrived in Washington, rumors abounded that her reclusive ways were directly related to her prayer petitions. Her retreating from Washington society may also have been linked to her depression over Taylor's becoming President. After following her husband around from fort to fort for almost thirty years, she had pleaded with him over and over again not to run for office, concerned that the job would take its toll on their family, health, and ultimate happiness. She prayed day and night that he would be defeated, to no avail.

Unlike his wife, Taylor showed little outward piety but felt strongly enough to issue an extraordinary presidential proclamation in the summer of 1849 calling for prayer and fasting after a serious epidemic of cholera had broken out, spreading to every state across the country. Within months over five thousand people had died, and many thousands more had been stricken with the disease. Despite being criticized by some pundits for "political religious canting" inconsistent with the separation of church and state, "Old Rough and Ready" paid little attention to their carping. Most businesses closed that August 3, and churches and synagogues of every denomination opened their doors for a day of prayer.[9]

On July 4, 1850, just a little more than a year into his presidency and while celebrating Independence Day, Taylor drank a glass of milk while eating a bowl of cherries on the lawn of the Executive Mansion. Soon he experienced serious cramps brought on by the heat and lack of sanitary conditions. Contracting cholera, he died within five days, and his wife, Margaret, followed two years later.

Millard Fillmore, who became a Unitarian late in life, was then sworn in to office, and is perhaps best known more for installing the first bathtub in the Executive Mansion. Despite marrying Abigail Powers, the daughter of a Baptist minister, Fillmore showed little outward piety. Nevertheless, like John Tyler before him, he was consumed by the responsibilities now thrust upon him. In a special message to Congress on July 10, asking the House and Senate to make the necessary arrangements for Taylor's funeral, Fillmore asked for their support "under the trying circumstances which surround me." He then went on to write, "I rely upon

Him who holds in His hands the destinies of nations to endow me with the requisite strength for the task and to avert from our country the evils apprehended from the heavy calamity which has befallen us."[10]

Following Fillmore in the election of 1852 was the equally forgettable Franklin Pierce, an ancestor of future First Lady Barbara Bush. A Bowdoin College classmate of Henry Wadsworth Longfellow as well as Nathaniel Hawthorne, who volunteered to write his official campaign biography, Pierce had a certain magnetic charm. Deeply religious, he would kneel next to his bed each night as did his college roommate Zenas Caldwell, and they would say their prayers aloud together. Although Pierce, an Episcopalian, continued to pray daily, he never felt comfortable avowing his religious faith publicly.

Barely two months before the presidential inauguration, Pierce and his wife, Jane, were traveling by train with their only living son, eleven-year-old Bennie, to attend the funeral of a longtime family friend. Two earlier boys had died in childhood. As the train was making its way from Amherst, Massachusetts, to Concord, New Hampshire, a freak accident occurred, and the passenger car where the Pierces were sitting broke loose and rolled down an embankment. Franklin and Jane Pierce watched in horror as Bennie was killed before their eyes. The two became inconsolable, and during the first two years of Pierce's administration Jane, who had been physically delicate to begin with, secluded herself in the family quarters of the Executive Mansion, writing maudlin letters to her dead son.[11]

Believing that the tragedy had been caused by a lack of religious piety, Pierce became more devout than ever. He took to reading the Bible more frequently and praying in private every chance he had. After he took the oath of office, he and Jane would begin their day by bringing together the mansion's servants to offer thanks to God. The Pierces would start every meal with an elaborate grace, and every Sunday they would follow church services with more prayer throughout the afternoon and evening. Barring some extraordinary circumstance, they would not even read mail or other secular literature on the Sabbath. In the end, however, Pierce's one-term presidency was deemed a failure due to his continued vacillation over the issue of slavery, which helped to ignite the Civil War.

WHILE AMERICA'S PRESIDENTS showed their religious devotion to various degrees, the country's churches continued to grow, some, like the Methodists, in greater numbers than others. Even a budding Jewish community was gaining footing in the United States. Jewish émigrés, particularly from Germany, were escaping European prejudices and arriving on America's shores to tie their fortunes to the New World. Through the sheer drive and tenacity of figures like Isaac Leeser and Rebecca Gratz, a reformed Judaism developed that was more in keeping with the diverse American religious landscape than anchored to the Jewish cultural heritage of Europe.

In the midst of continental expansion, Protestant churches met in religious conferences and assemblies to discuss and agree on the wording of prayer books and hymnals. In addition to various standardized editions of the Bible, these approved prayer texts were a unifying force and allowed churches to provide a canon of faith for their followers.

Outside of churches and formal worship services, there was a growing interest in singing hymns in group sing-alongs. Two composers from Georgia, B. F. White and E. J. King, composed a "tune book" known as *The Sacred Harp*, a collection of some one hundred odes, hymns, and anthems drawn from every Protestant denomination. With its title evoking the image of David in the Old Testament offering up psalms to God with his harp, *The Sacred Harp* was first published in 1849 and contained largely religious works but also some patriotic tunes. Unlike church hymnals, which were organized by subject matter with complete prayers as lyrics, the songbook was structured according to participants particular tunes that were then followed by an abbreviated text.

Hundreds of people would travel great distances to join other devotees of *Sacred Harp* music. Gathering mainly in civic halls rather than churches, they could spend entire days together in song, breaking only for lavish buffets prepared by the women participants. Sitting in carefully arranged rows of chairs, the singers would face each other by voice part—sopranos, altos, tenors, and basses—forming a hollow square. Each tune would then be sung in three or four parts by using only the four syllables fa, sol, la, mi, written in what were called "shape notes." The sounds that emanated from this kind of singing were a striking contrast to the full seven notes of the musical scale used in most songs. This structural difference projected a distinctively somber, pulse-driven intensity, lending an exotic sound to the music and lyrics. Some even likened it to a cross between bluegrass and Gregorian chant.

The popularity of *Sacred Harp* singing clearly showed that American prayer was being integrated into popular culture. Stephen Collins Foster, the most popular American songwriter of the nineteenth century, for example, was swept up in writing music to accompany prayers for both children and adults. His musical gifts were unequaled as he composed such songs as "Jeanie with the Light Brown Hair," "My Old Kentucky Home," "Camptown Races," "Swanee River," and "Oh! Susanna." Given the ready market for new hymns, however, he often found that he could make money faster by combining prayer and music than by writing secular tunes.

WHILE TRADITIONAL CHURCHES were intent on reaching out to as many followers and potential converts as possible, a segment of the population questioned whether established churches were meeting their individual spiritual needs. No group voiced this sentiment more loudly than Joseph Smith and his followers.

The story of Joseph Smith, the founder of the Church of Jesus Christ of Latter-Day Saints, better known as the Mormons, is an extraordinary one. Uniquely American, the Church emerged in 1820 from the experience of fourteen-year-old Joseph Smith, who related to his family and friends how he had been transformed in the woods adjacent to his parents' farm in Palmyra, New York. He vividly recounted being visited by both God the Father and his son Jesus Christ who told him not to join any existing Protestant denomination because the churches of the day had lost the true meaning of Christ's teachings.

Three years after the encounter, Smith was visited again, this time by the prophet Moroni, who had been resurrected from his former life by God as an angel of light. This new messenger told Smith that he could find the true and complete holy Scriptures to accompany the Bible encoded on a set of golden plates and stone tablets buried not far from the farm. On the tablets Smith would find writings key to divine revelation that had been left by Moroni's father, Mormon, several centuries earlier.

From the very beginning of his ministry Joseph Smith let it be known that his primary inspiration had come from the admonition found in the Epistle of James, "If any of you lack wisdom, let him ask of God, that giveth to all men liberally, and upbraideth not; and it shall be given to him." That single missive had struck a chord with him like no other.[12]

Consequently, for the rest of his life Smith would stress the central creed of Mormonism: that "salvation cannot come without revelation" and that revelation can be found only through sacred Scripture (the Book of Mormon and other sacred texts), the Bible, and prayer.[13] Prayer had to be the centering of his church. "Communion with the Infinite" was how he put it.[14]

Most of Smith's life, however, was consumed by serious personal trial as he faced the fury of those who found his beliefs bizarre, if not completely sacrilegious. Certainly the most visible target for Smith's detractors was his belief in polygamy, which he considered critical to his ministry in the formation of the Mormon Church. Although at the age of twenty-two he married Emma Hale, who became his lifelong pillar but expressed her early disapproval of his having more than one wife, Smith argued that conjugal pluralism was sanctioned by holy Scripture. Estimates as to how many women Smith married vary from 26 to 149.[15]

One of his wives was the remarkable Eliza Roxey Snow, perhaps the most prominent literary figure of the early Mormon Church. Lionized as "the Poetess of Zion," she wrote the lyrics to such popular hymns as "O My Father" and "Truth Reflects upon Our Senses." Her faith in Joseph Smith and the Mormon Church drove her to write prayers that evoked both praise to God and an affirmation of Church doctrine. After Smith's assassination in Illinois at the hands of an unruly mob in 1844, Snow became "joined" to Brigham Young as one of his wives and continued to write some of the richest prayers and religious poetry of the early Church, living to the ripe age of eighty-two.

While the Mormons were building the foundations of their Church, they had begun their final push to the Great Salt Lake in Utah by 1847. Throughout the arduous crossing of the West under the leadership of Brigham Young, the elders of the Church recorded over and over again that prayer had been critical in sustaining them. At the end of their transcontinental journey, discovering the Great Salt Lake and believing they had been led to that very spot, they thanked God for delivering them to the promised land. Their prayers had brought them to a spiritual harbor not unlike the odyssey of the Israelites of the Old Testament and of America's Puritan forefathers two centuries earlier.

BY MID-CENTURY the United States had produced a generation of writers, largely northerners, who were bringing to life their unique American experiences. With few exceptions, the great novels, essays, and poems of this period had a profound religious grounding. In one variation or another authors believed that a spiritual understanding of God could only be attained by probing the full nature of the material world.

Among the poets of the day were a group of devout traditionalists who exuded the tone of their Puritan forefathers when it came to prayer but who broadened their notions of God as well. The prayers of this newest generation were not those of solitary figures unconcerned about those around them. These writers saw themselves in many ways as spiritual reformers, concerned about others, particularly when it came to the issue of slavery.

An influential writer who endeared himself to the American people, someone who possessed an extraordinary pedigree, was Oliver Wendell Holmes. The son of a prominent Congregationalist minister and a direct descendant of Simon and Anne Bradstreet on his mother's side, he was also the father of the future U.S. Supreme Court justice Oliver Wendell Holmes, Jr. Trained as a physician at Harvard, where he also taught and conducted cutting-edge research in medical science, Holmes showed a true gift for writing poems and essays that his readers found to be fresh, humorous, and completely captivating.

It was in 1830 that Holmes, barely out of his teens, won overnight acclaim. Through a combination of New England pluck and sheer eloquence, he single-handedly took up the cause of the frigate the USS *Constitution*. The ship, which had been built just after the Revolutionary War and had seen combat during the War of 1812, was about to be decommissioned and effectively put into mothballs. Championing the cause of the vessel, Holmes wrote the poem "Old Ironsides," bemoaning the scrapping of such a symbol of the country's proud past. After the piece appeared in the *Boston Daily Advertiser,* the reaction was overwhelming. The ship was saved and finally moored in Boston Harbor, where it stands today.

As Holmes matured, he wrote a series of lush, charming prayers. One of them was a mere two lines long, but it became so popular that Americans, young and old alike, would repeat it to each other by heart. Titled "Unto Thy Care," it read simply, "Our families in Thine arms enfold, As Thou didst keep Thy folk of old." His "O Love Divine" showed the passion of his spiritual writings and helped to solidify his reputation as one of the country's best-loved poets:

> *O Love Divine, that stooped to share*
> *Our sharpest pang, our bitterest tear,*

> *On Thee are cast each earth-born care,*
> *We smile at pain while Thou art near!* . . .

> *On Thee we fling our burdening woe,*
> *O Love Divine, forever dear,*
> *Content to suffer while we know,*
> *Living and dying, Thou art near!*[16]

Unquestionably the most popular American poet during the century was Henry Wadsworth Longfellow. Like his friend Oliver Wendell Holmes, he built his reputation at a young age with the publication of a single poem that appealed to the country's growing patriotism, *The Midnight Ride of Paul Revere*. There was a gentleness and a simplicity in the way Longfellow brought history alive with the iteration of each verse. In such narrative works as *Hiawatha*, with its shaman-like rhythms, and *The Courtship of Miles Standish*, with its adept use of hexameters to convey the story of requited love, Longfellow reveled in conveying the tales of an earlier America.

Initially Longfellow showed little interest in religion despite his affiliation with the Unitarian Church. His faith, however, evolved more rapidly after he confronted the horror of watching his wife die, consumed in flames. The incident occurred during the summer of 1861 after a piece of hot wax fell on her dress as she was sealing the lockets of her children's hair for keepsakes. Desperately trying to put out the flames, he badly scarred his hands and face and for the rest of his life wore a beard to cover his disfigurement. His poem "The Cross of Snow," steeped in spirituality, memorialized the wife he had lost.

In old age, Longfellow wrote poetry that was more overtly spiritual, and for the first time he made direct references to Jesus Christ. *Christus: A Mystery*, his last major work, conveyed his fascination with the holy Trinity. It laid out the life of Christ through different historical viewpoints, revealing unique perspectives.

In addition to writing great epic poems, Longfellow contributed to the country's patriotic heritage by appending a fifth stanza to Samuel Smith's "America," an addition that has become a permanent part of the hymn:

> *Lord, let war's tempest cease,*
> *Fold the whole world in peace*

Under Thy wings.
Make all the nations one,
All hearts beneath the sun,
Till Thou shalt reign alone,
Great King of Kings.[17]

DURING THE ANTEBELLUM years a group of writers emerged whose theology, if they had one, was difficult to define or characterize. They seemed to enjoy flaunting convention and were generally indifferent to the debate on slavery. Writers like James Fenimore Cooper and Washington Irving led the way in publishing gripping tales of God-fearing heroes who confronted the challenges of early America. There were others like Nathaniel Hawthorne, masterfully defined by his morality tale in *The Scarlet Letter,* who remained seductively drawn to America's Puritan past while at the same time being repelled by its no-nonsense rigidity. As Emily Dickinson in later life was quoted as saying, "We thank Thee, Father, for these strange minds that enamor us against Thee."[18] These were chroniclers of not only their age but also beyond. Religious apathies aside, they drew literary inspiration from America's Puritan tradition. These roots were so ingrained that they could not escape constructing in their literary works the all-encompassing human relationship with God.

Arguably the most seminal work in all of American literature, *Moby-Dick* was published during this period. In telling the story of an elusive whale and his pursuer, Herman Melville wrote one of Western civilization's greatest and most spiritually laced novels, using over a thousand scriptural references to spin his tale. Here is the cosmic, contortioned tug and pull between God and man played out on the open sea. On one side is the irresistible, unrelenting, and in the end, crushing whale; on the other is the maddeningly obsessed Ahab, consumed with harpooning the whale that has bedeviled him for so long. Just as Ahab and his men get ready to weigh anchor, they listen with rapt attention to Father Mapple who stood before them and "offered a prayer so deeply devout that he seemed kneeling and praying at the bottom of the sea." The men then join him in singing a hymn with the haunting lyrics:

In black distress, I called my God,
When I could scarce believe Him mine,

> *He bowed his ear to my complaints—*
> *No more the whale did me confine.*[19]

The piece was adapted from an old Dutch Reformed Church hymn that Melville had first heard as a child.[20] Like many of his contemporaries, he used his creativity to embellish traditional sacred poetry of the day to fit the needs of his characters and story lines. It was an approach that would be perfected to an even greater art form in the later poetry of Emily Dickinson.

Moby-Dick forever ranked Melville as the quintessential agnostic of American literature, a man driven to search for universal answers that only faith could have provided. Melville's own spiritual quest would later take him to to the Holy Land, almost like his character Ahab, searching for answers. In the end he would acknowledge, as he wrote in his philosophical allegory *Mardi and a Voyage Thither,* that "prayer draws us near to our own souls."[21]

A contemporary of Melville's in this literary-rich era, a man whom James Russell Lowell referred to as "three-fifths . . . genius, and two-fifths sheer fudge," was the enigmatic Edgar Allan Poe.[22] Writing both prose and poetry, Poe could be eerie and foreboding at one moment, and exude boundless idealism the next. "The Tell-Tale Heart," "Annabel Lee," and "The Raven" all stand as testaments to his complexity. His sense of God was equally enigmatic. In his "Mesmeric Revelation," he set up a dialogue between two men attempting to resolve once and for all the character and nature of the Almighty but coming to no successful conclusion. He struggled for definition, using at times amorphous labels such as "God is mind," "God is matter," and "God is motion." At the same time, Poe proved to have great facility at composing a prayer, not to God, but to the Blessed Mother. The poem he wrote focused on Mary as the perfect conduit to the mysteries of the divine. In the end it seemed easier for Poe to approach Christ's mother than to speak directly to God:

> *At morn,—at noon,—at twilight dim,*
> *Maria! Thou hast heard my hymn!*
> *In joy and woe,—in good and ill,*
> *Mother of God, be with me still!*
> *When the hours flew brightly by,*
> *And not a cloud obscured the sky,*

My soul, lest it should truant be,
Thy grace did guide to thine and thee;
Now, when storms of fate o'ercast
Darkly my present and my past.
Let my future radiant shine
With sweet hopes of thee and thine![23]

On Sunday morning, October 7, 1849, Poe lay on his deathbed in Washington College Hospital of Baltimore, suffering either from the effects of alcoholism or from rabies that he may have contracted from one of his house pets. His difficult life seemed at times to mirror his bizarre, brilliantly told stories. All of forty years of age, he reportedly whispered his last words as he slipped away, "Lord, help my poor soul!"[24]

The final figure in this group of peripatetic writers was the elusive Walt Whitman. During his day no writer generated so much debate. Notwithstanding works dealing with slavery, his landmark work, *Leaves of Grass*, published in 1855, created more controversy than any other book written during the century.

Sensuous and self-absorbed, Whitman immersed himself in things spiritual without elevating his sights to the Supreme Being. Quite simply, he found it much easier to view God through the eyes of others, a literary device he employed in his "Prayer of Columbus." Presenting Christopher Columbus as a sympathetic, tragic figure, destined "to die, unrecognized, neglected, and in want," Whitman vicariously spoke his piece through Spain's most famous explorer:

I am too full of woe!
Haply I may not live another day;
I cannot rest, O God—I cannot eat or drink or sleep,
Till I put forth myself, my prayer, once more to Thee,
Breathe, bathe myself once more in Thee—commune with Thee,
Report myself once more to Thee.[25]

Whitman's appeal, then as now, related to the way in which he took his reader to a very different level of consciousness, ironically suffused with religion, spirituality, and continuous prayer but refusing to acknowledge the supreme deity known to most Americans in the nineteenth century. As each poem unfolds in *Leaves of Grass*, a work that Whitman later referred to as "the new Bible," the case is made almost in the form of a modern-day psalm.[26] In a poem titled "To Him That Was Crucified," Whitman reached out to bond with Christ, his "comrade":

My spirit to yours, dear brother;
Do not mind because many, sounding your name, do not understand you;
I do not sound your name, but I understand you, (there are others also;)
I specify you with joy, O my comrade, to salute you, and to salute those who
are with you before and since—and those to come also.[27]

Whitman's unique belief system and form of prayer created its own dynamic, while generating controversy among his contemporaries, and helped to set him apart from other poets of his day. If prayer had a purpose for Whitman, and it did, it was to commune with God in human form. Prayer in its purest form allowed a person to explore the cosmos, to be in touch more fully with the character and limitlessness of human nature and in turn the reality of God himself.

WHITMAN'S APPROACH to his spiritual life surfaced at a time when a small, influential group of America's intellectuals was seeking new answers to age-old questions. Unsatisfied with the country's Puritan theological heritage, these men and women developed a new perspective, quirky as it was, to take into account a new school of thought. Labeled "transcendentalism," a term first used by the German philosopher Immanuel Kant, this burgeoning philosophy had originally developed in Europe. Its direct appeal to most Americans as a substitute for the religion of their forefathers, however, was rather limited. Historian Perry Miller would later refer to the movement as a "sort of mid-summer madness that overtook a few intellectuals in or around Boston about the year 1840."[28] Although the philosophy never gained widespread popularity, it did take root in the intellectual psyche of the country.

In addressing spirituality, transcendentalists cobbled together a set of philosophical beliefs challenging human beings to rise above society's traditional understanding of morality, achieving absolute truth and goodness by using their own intuition. Spirituality, and in turn prayer, were to be approached through the senses rather than through rigid church doctrines. Although transcendentalists did not deny the existence of God, they saw in themselves, as well as in all things, part of the divine.

Through a sort of twinning with God, a person could find individual enlightenment.

The intellectual high priest who gave some form to transcendentalism's credo was Ralph Waldo Emerson. By background, temperament, and demeanor, Emerson remained in a class by himself, certainly the country's most prominent intellectual during the period. Born into a family that counted nine generations of ministers, Emerson, with his facile mind, his unique outlook, and his penchant for exuding a certain smugness and egotism, changed American literature and philosophy in profound ways. To Emerson the Puritanism of his forefathers was effectively dying, and he intended to find new answers to the mysteries of the universe. Subjective spontaneity, not rote convention, he believed, should rule the hearts and minds of men and women.

Emerson's personal theology was formed from the roots of Unitarianism, which espoused the belief that men and women actually reflected divinity. "As soon as the man is at one with God, he will not beg. He will then see prayer in all action," was the way he put it in his famous essay "Self-Reliance."[29]

In his first sermon, "Pray without Ceasing," he championed the notion that every hope, secret, and desire of the mind should be considered a prayer. Prayer could only be invoked effectively by coming to grips with one's inner being and connecting that higher understanding with one's surroundings.[30] In "Self-Reliance," Emerson spoke of prayer in vivid terms: "The prayer of the farmer kneeling in his field to weed it, the prayer of the rower kneeling with the stroke of his oar, are true prayers heard throughout nature." In the same essay, he scorned those who would use prayer as a means to seek greater material enrichment: "Prayer that craves a particular commodity, anything less than all good, is vicious . . . Prayer as means to a private end is meanness and theft."[31] In the end, he believed, prayer should be one continuous, integral, and catalyzing force of life.

Emerson's contributions to transcendentalism were only the tip of the iceberg. Although relatively few individuals called themselves transcendentalists, those that did came to have a profound impact on nineteenth-century American thought and on the country's spiritual life. For all the inherent drawbacks to this at times quirky philosophy, its adherents stretched the boundaries of logic, imagination, and mysticism.

The movement's gentle heart was Henry David Thoreau, who, after graduating from Harvard, moved into Emerson's household in 1841 to work as the family's handyman. From the beginning Thoreau and Emerson were fast friends, and soon Thoreau was writing essays for *The Dial*, the transcendental periodical Emerson edited and published. Acknowledging the talents of his young protégé, Emerson offered Thoreau the opportunity to live on property he owned two miles from Concord, Massachusetts, a site known as Walden Pond.

Moving to Walden Pond, Thoreau built a crude hut for himself and carved out a solitary existence, growing his own food, fishing for his dinner, and recording in great detail the flora and fauna around him. It was in this setting that he looked for inspiration in organizing his thoughts on the larger issues of human existence within the universe. Communing with nature in this way had taken him to new levels of consciousness, and from these experiences between 1845 and 1847 he wrote *Walden*. The work established Thoreau as an original thinker and an extraordinary literary talent, securing for him a place within the transcendental movement second only to that of Emerson.

"We need to pray for no higher heaven than the pure senses can furnish, a purely sensuous life," he wrote. "Our present senses are but the rudiments of what they are destined to become. We are comparatively deaf and dumb and blind, and without smell or taste or feeling. Every generation makes the discovery that its divine vigor has been dissipated, and each sense and faculty misapplied and debauched."[32] Prayer became a searching tool in a person's spiritual evolution toward understanding the divine in all things, including his and her own being. For Thoreau the pond itself came to symbolize the ultimate expression of a person's oneness with the divine, "deepened and clarified" by the mind of God.[33]

And yet, in "My Prayer," Thoreau could write a prayer that aspired to engage God almost like an older brother:

> Great God, I ask thee for no meaner pelf,
> Than that I may not disappoint myself;
> That in my action I may soar as high
> As I can now discern with this clear eye.
> And next in value, which Thy kindness lends,
> That I may greatly disappoint my friends,

Howe'er they think or hope that it may be,
They may not dream how Thou'st distinguished me.

That my weak hand may equal my firm faith,
And my life practice more than my tongue saith;
That my low conduct may not show,
Nor my relenting lines,
That I Thy purpose did not know,
Or overrated Thy designs.[34]

It is no wonder, then, that prayer came to have a special significance for Emerson, Thoreau, and their fellow transcendentalists. Prayers were conceived not simply as two-way dialogues but, more important, as ways of communicating with one's self. As Jones Very, one of the major forces of the movement, wrote in poetic verse, "His way is hidden that thine eye may seek, And in the seeking thou thyself may find."[35] The individual soul was one with "God" and, in turn, one with everything else.

In the end, transcendentalism lost its steam; it could not be sustained beyond a small group of men and women in mid-nineteenth-century America. Nevertheless, the influence of the transcendentalists upon the culture of American prayer cannot be underestimated. For generations to come, the movement's philosophy on God and nature, personal independence, and the spiritual links among human beings would continue to resound in the spiritual life of Americans.

WHILE THE COUNTRY'S INTELLECTUAL elite was engaged in esoteric religious and spiritual debate, a far more fundamental and onerous development was unfolding in the streets of America. The trouble began as the latest wave of Irish immigration was beginning to hit its peak in the 1840s, a dramatic development that permanently transformed the country's social demographics. Escaping the devastating famine arising in large part from Ireland's potato blight, hundreds of thousands of Irish Catholic immigrants found their way to American shores. Poor, uneducated, but full of hope, they settled mainly in the country's major cities, choosing to live in neighborhoods where they could attend church and be among fellow immigrants. What they did not count on were the suspicions, if not outright hostility, of segments of the country's Protestant majority who believed that the true loyalties of these new Americans rested with Rome, not Washington.

Despite the conflicts, the Irish slowly began to integrate into American society. Irish parents in particular took great pride in seeing their children educated in the country's burgeoning public school system.

Serious trouble erupted, however, after Pennsylvania's state legislature mandated in 1838 that all schoolchildren recite the Lord's Prayer and passages from the Bible each day in their classrooms. Soon all schoolchildren were required to invoke the King James Version of the Bible for praying and instruction. Teachers were even leading their classes in singing Protestant hymns. For Irish Catholics who found the King James Bible heretical, the situation became untenable. To add to the furor, some public school textbooks were even referring to the Pope as the "Antichrist," and some newspapers claimed that the Vatican was hatching a secret plan to seize control of all public schools. It was only a matter of time before full-scale rioting broke out.

Although Philadelphia's Bishop Francis Kenrick, who had been born in Dublin, tried to work with civil authorities to quell the growing tensions, his efforts were to no avail. After Catholics openly protested against the mandate, hundreds and then thousands of Protestants took matters into their own hands, marching into Catholic neighborhoods, brandishing pistols, and firing cannons. Despite the state militia's being called out to restore order, St. Augustine's Church and the convent of the Sisters of Charity, founded by Mother Elizabeth Seton to care for the sick and educate the young, were burned to the ground. Kenrick soon closed churches throughout the city and had valuable chalices, statues, and other religious articles taken from churches in the middle of the night and shipped to private homes, well out of harm's way. With stricter enforcement of martial law and the state militia's being reinforced to patrol city streets, the riots finally came to an end. By the time casualties were counted on both sides, eighteen people had been killed, scores of others injured.

Although the Philadelphia Bible riots became little more than a footnote for most Americans, historical memory of the episode hung over the Supreme Court more than a century later as it tackled the issue of school prayer. Rather than seeing nonsectarian prayer as the answer to the divisiveness created in Philadelphia and other parts of the country, the Warren Court would see the riots as clear evidence that prayer mandated by government had the potential to divide. Given that the First

Amendment of the Constitution prohibited the establishment of religion, the Court would place prayer squarely within the rubric of religion and as such forbid its exercise in the public classroom.

WHILE RELIGIOUS TENSIONS simmered just below the surface, the one issue gathering steam was slavery. As Frederick Douglass was riveting audiences in the North, abolitionists such as William Lloyd Garrison and the Reverend Henry Ward Beecher were inflaming antebellum America, helping to turn the country through their rhetoric into a bubbling cauldron. Sermons and public speeches related to the issue of slavery grew in number and intensity, constant reminders of the country's unfinished business.

During this period, Congress took a far larger role in setting the national debates and in leading the country than it had in the past, offering a visible counterpoint to weaker and weaker presidencies. Senator Henry Clay of Kentucky, known as "the Great Compromiser," worked tirelessly to keep the country from splitting apart. When told that his antislavery stance would cost him the presidency, he remarked, "I would rather be right than President."[36] In one of the most dramatic speeches of his career, as the Senate debated a series of compromise resolutions in 1850 on the issues of slavery and secession, he addressed his colleagues from the well of the chamber: "I implore, as the best blessing which Heaven can bestow upon me upon earth, that if the direful and sad event of the dissolution of the Union shall happen, I may not survive to behold the sad and heart-rending spectacle."[37]

From Massachusetts came another legislative giant in Daniel Webster, whose soaring oratory, arguably the most eloquent in the history of the U.S. Senate, could mesmerize his listeners, including most of his adversaries. Throughout a public life committed to preserving the Union, he continually invoked God's name, often challenging Americans to find spiritual rapport with their Maker. He created his own daily discipline that included morning and evening prayer. When his own death approached in 1852, Webster remained determined to the end: "Hold me up; I do not wish to pray with a fainting voice."[38] And with that he died. Two weeks prior to his death, he asked George Ticknor Curtis, the executor of his will, to see that his tombstone in Marshfield, Massachusetts, was chiseled with a prayer and testament to his faith. It was an epitaph that began, "Lord, I believe. Help Thou mine unbelief."

★ ★ ★

THE VOICES OF THESE national figures were only echoing the hardening mind-set of the American people. Divergent and at times strained translations of the Bible were being presented, justifying the causes of both north and south. In turn, prayers were being invoked from two completely different perspectives, appealing to the same God. For both sides, prayer would become a major preoccupation, lending credibility to their cause and sustaining them in their struggle.

Prior to the first shots of the war being fired, however, one book and one tragic incident captured for most Americans the high stakes involved. The publication of *Uncle Tom's Cabin* was a seminal moment in American literary and political history. Its author, Harriet Beecher Stowe, the daughter of the Reverend Lyman Beecher, whose voice was so much a part of the Second Great Awakening, spun out a story of the indescribable horrors of slavery, focusing on such characters as the kindly Uncle Tom, the innocent Little Eva, and the despicable Simon Legree. In one of the most tension-filled moments of the book, the villain Legree is about to pounce on Uncle Tom and his fellow slaves, but before he does, he hears a tenor voice in the distance sing out:

> *When I can read my title clear*
> *To mansions in the skies,*
> *I'll bid farewell to every fear,*
> *And wipe my weeping eyes.*
>
> *Should earth against my soul engage,*
> *And hellish darts be hurled,*
> *Then I can smile at Satan's rage,*
> *And face a frowning world.*
>
> *Let cares like a wild deluge come,*
> *And storms of sorrow fall,*
> *May I but safely reach my home,*
> *My God, my heaven, my All!*[39]

Infuriated by "these accursed Methodist hymns," Legree picks up his riding whip and beats Tom mercilessly. "Mansions in the Sky" vividly conjured up visions of both heaven and earthly freedom.

Written initially for serial publication in *National Era*, an abolitionist newspaper, in 1850 and 1851, the book was published in 1852 by a reluctant printing house, concerned over the public's reaction to its antislavery treatise. Within forty-eight hours, however, all 5,000 copies of the first printing had been swept up. By the end of the first year, over 300,000 books had been sold in America and another 200,000 in England. One contemporary critic of Stowe later admitted that *Uncle Tom's Cabin* had become "perhaps the most influential novel ever published. A verbal earthquake, an ink-and-paper tidal wave."[40] It is no wonder that Abraham Lincoln, in finally meeting Stowe at the White House, greeted her with the welcome "So you're the little lady who started the big war."[41] For the rest of her life she continued to write essays and dozens of short prayers.

UNCLE TOM'S CABIN had a profound impact on the simmering issue of slavery, but the polarizing figure of John Brown, a descendant of the Pilgrims, and the events of October 16, 1859, jolted the national consciousness overnight. Only two years earlier, the Supreme Court of the United States had delivered its notorious *Dred Scott* decision. With words that would resound forever, the Court handed down its decision in a case involving the self-educated slave: "We think they [slaves] are not . . . to be included under the word 'citizens' in the Constitution." Underscoring their rationale, the justices ruled that those of African origin must be "considered as a subordinate and inferior class of beings, who had been subjugated by the dominant race."[42]

For people like Brown, this fateful decision was a declaration of war. In quick succession Brown had been a tanner, land surveyor, shepherd, and farmer, and, having been married twice, he had fathered twenty children. He would write in his diary that after the *Dred Scott* decision he began to immerse himself in prayer as never before, asking for divine guidance to determine what to do next. He even met with Harriet Tubman to pray for guidance and to discuss what he could do to stem the tide of slavery and free those still in the hands of white owners. Moving with his sons to Kansas, a pivotal state in the slavery debate, he led an attack in which five pro-slavery advocates were murdered in Pottawatomie Creek in May 1856. Immediately thereafter he and his growing band of followers went into hiding as they plotted to carry out the next strike.

Few people remained indifferent to John Brown or to his cause. His detractors saw him as nothing less than a satanic madman, while his sympathizers viewed him as a latter-day John the Baptist, the glorious precursor of things to come. After carefully considering what to do next, Brown decided to target Harpers Ferry at the confluence of the Shenandoah and Potomac Rivers in modern-day West Virginia. By using the arms already in his possession to seize the large cache of weapons stored in the local federal arsenal, he could supply his followers to help him free the slaves in the area and then escape into the thick of the Appalachian Mountains. The rugged terrain would hide him between raids on other outposts. With "instructions" from God, he was convinced that his actions would create terror among slave owners, breaking their will and putting an end to slavery itself. With a band of twenty-one men, including five former slaves, he carried out his attack, instigating one of the most momentous events in U.S. history.

Meanwhile, back in Washington, James Buchanan, a particularly weak President, continued to show indifference to the brewing storm over slavery. The only bachelor President in U.S. history, Buchanan awoke each morning, read a passage from the Bible, and then turned to a popular spiritual devotional published in London known as *Jay's Exercises* to help inspire him to pray.

On taking the oath of office, he seemed oblivious to a country coming apart at the seams. The raid at Harpers Ferry and the challenge it posed to the federal government, however, had serious consequences. To the delight of southern sympathizers, Buchanan ordered Colonel Robert E. Lee and his federal troops to deal forcefully with the rebellion.

Brown's twenty-one men were no match for Lee's soldiers, and soon ten of the men were shot dead, including two of Brown's sons, with Brown himself severely wounded. Within hours Brown and the remaining survivors were put into cuffs and carted off to federal prison, where they were tried and quickly sentenced to death by hanging. In the days before he was executed, Brown wrote to his lawyer that he attributed the "calm" he had experienced in jail to prayer, calling it a "delightful *dream,* until I come to know those realities, which 'eyes have not seen, and ears have not heard.' "[43]

The tale of John Brown's execution and of the events surrounding his raid on Harpers Ferry was retold over and over again throughout the United States and Europe. Songs were composed in his honor, and essays were written condemning his wild-eyed fanaticism. Even into the twentieth century, tributes were given to his memory. In 1928 Stephen Vincent Benét won the Pulitzer Prize for his book-length poem about the Civil War called *John Brown's Body*. In the very popular work he imagined the kind of prayer that Brown would have uttered to God, keeping in mind the rampages at both Pottawatomie Creek and Harpers Ferry. "Omnipotent and steadfast God . . . Destruction from my hand . . . It was at Thy command," the poem reads.[44]

No matter where one came out on the subject of John Brown, the crusader turned terrorist had knocked America off its balance beam. He claimed that prayer had led him to undertake the cause of enslaved African-Americans. It was a legacy that would long reverberate within the conscience of the country.

AT NO TIME IN AMERICAN HISTORY had the promise or the stakes of "these united states" seemed greater while the signs of upheaval appeared so ominous. Self-inflicted wounds began to take their toll, drawing the country closer to outright civil war. Ironically, the prayer culture of the United States had never been more intense or flourishing. With the thick pall of likely war hanging over the country, Americans took to their knees to make sense of it all and to pray for the future. Few could have predicted what would come next.

CHAPTER 7

THE SOLDIERS

1860–1870

We have been the recipients of the choicest bounties of Heaven. We have been preserved, these many years, in peace and prosperity. We have grown in numbers, wealth, and power as no other nation has ever grown; but we have forgotten God. We have forgotten the gracious hand, which preserved us in peace, and multiplied and enriched and strengthened us; and we have vainly imagined, in the deceitfulness of our hearts, that all these blessings were produced by some superior wisdom and virtue of our own. Intoxicated with unbroken success, we have become too self-sufficient to feel the necessity of redeeming and reserving grace, too proud to pray to the God that made us.

—Abraham Lincoln (1863)

OMENS WERE EVERYWHERE; it was only a matter of time. When it came to slavery, couched by some as an issue solely in the defense of states' rights, compromise was nothing more than a temporary remedy. The only questions that remained were when and where hostilities would begin, and with whom God would side.

Notwithstanding the horror of slavery, this was a time of spiritual innocence for Americans that would never again return. For most, God was not a multidimensional figure. An understanding of God could be achieved exclusively through the Scriptures of the Old and New Testaments—literal, straightforward, wrathful, and loving.

No prayer evoked this spiritual state of mind on the eve of the war more than "Jesus Loves Me," the 1860 composition of two sisters, Anna and Susan Warner, who lived in West Point, New York. Both women taught Sunday-school classes to the cadets of the United States Military Academy nearby. Most of their students would end up in the war; many would end up fighting each other on the battlefield. "Jesus Loves Me" represented an innocence destined to dissipate in the coming months:

> *Jesus loves me! This I know,*
> *For the Bible tells me so;*
> *Little ones to Him belong,*
> *They are weak but He is strong.*
>
> *Yes, Jesus loves me!*
> *Yes, Jesus loves me!*
> *Yes, Jesus loves me!*
> *The Bible tells me so . . .*
>
> *Jesus loves me! He will stay*
> *Close beside me all the way;*
> *Thou hast bled and died for me,*
> *I will henceforth live for Thee.*
>
> *Yes, Jesus loves me!*
> *Yes, Jesus loves me!*
> *Yes, Jesus loves me!*
> *The Bible tells me so.*[1]

While described as "mawkish" by some critics, "Jesus Loves Me" nonetheless became a much beloved and powerful tool, later used by American Christian missionaries in such far-flung lands as India and China.[2]

At no time did prayer ever seem more important, more needed, or more misunderstood. The very real fears of many Americans could only be quelled by the conviction that God was joined to their struggle and that they would prevail. God was effectively being set up in an absurd way, pitted between two diametrically opposed forces and positions. For the Confederacy, God donned a gray uniform, while for the Union he served in dress blues. For many, notwithstanding the merits of their cause, winning could occur only through divine intervention, and that meant prayer and lots of it. The Civil War had become nothing less than a religious event in the minds of many Americans and in turn stood as a virtual laboratory in probing the depths of American spirituality.

Attention in the months and days preceding the outbreak of war was focused on Congress, as it had been for some time. Here, a microcosm of the country was able to come together to discuss differences and resolve whether the Union would fracture or continue to stand as it had since the founding of the country.

One of the strangest and most ominous episodes paving the way to war was Jefferson Davis's farewell address to the U.S. Senate. A graduate of West Point, a hero of the Mexican War, Secretary of War for four years under Franklin Pierce, and senator from Mississippi, Davis was by far the best politically positioned person to head up the secessionist forces. On January 21, 1861, he spoke to a hushed chamber:

> I rise, Mr. President, for the purpose of announcing to the Senate that I have satisfactory evidence that the State of Mississippi, by a solemn ordinance of her people, in convention assembled, has declared her separation from the United States. Under these circumstances, of course, my functions are terminated here . . . I am sure I feel no hostility towards you, Senators of the North . . . I hope for peaceable relations with you . . . The reverse may bring disaster on every portion of the country, and if you will have it thus, we will invoke the God of our fathers, who delivered them from the power of the lion, to protect us from the ravages of the bear; and thus putting our trust in God and in our firm hearts and strong arms, we will vindicate the right as best we may . . . I bid you a final adieu.[3]

The drama and the unfolding nightmares were taking shape. South Carolina, Mississippi, Florida, Alabama, and Georgia had already officially declared their common confederacy. Louisiana, Texas, Virginia, Arkansas, North Carolina, and Tennessee would soon follow. Day after day there came news, some event, some signal of what lay ahead. The sheer apprehension of what tomorrow would bring grew more palpable. It became clear in Davis's swearing in as President of the Confederacy that both sides in this conflict would be praying to the same God, believing that the Almighty had a vested interest in responding to their immediate needs and cause. "It will but remain for us, with firm resolve, to appeal to arms and invoke the blessings of Providence on a just cause."

was how Davis put it in his first inaugural address.[4] In the preamble to the new constitution of the Confederacy were written the South's fondest hopes for "the favor and guidance of Almighty God."

On April 12, 1861, the mounting tension ruptured. Southern secessionists opened fire on the federal site of Fort Sumter in the bay of Charleston, South Carolina. A well-known advocate of the secessionist movement, Edmund Ruffin, was given the "honor" of firing the first shot. No words in the American lexicon then or now could describe the dimensions of death and destruction that followed over the next four years. Prayers both old and new were rolled out in an instant, almost a weapon deployment in itself. The American Bible Society and other religious organizations began to print enough Bibles, prayer books, and religious tracts for every Union soldier. Sixteen power presses were printing and binding books around the clock, providing hundreds of thousands of pieces of religious material within a few months.[5] Confederate soldiers were not so lucky given that printing presses were far more rare in the South. Often several men in camp would share the same Bible or prayer book with one another. Ironically, the situation was alleviated somewhat when the American Bible Society in the North shipped thousands of publications through religious groups in Tennessee for distribution to Confederate lines.[6] Nonetheless, Southern printers did try.

From the now-Confederate Fort Sumter came *Prayers Suitable for the Times in Which We Live*, a thirty-page hymnal and prayer book geared to soldiers and the churchgoing public alike. The introductory prayer clearly conveyed the manual's intent:

> *We humbly beseech Thee be present with us in all the course and passages of our lives, but especially in the Secession we have undertaken, and the hostilities in which it has involved us . . . Defeat, we implore Thee, the designs and confound the machinations of our enemies; abate their pride and assuage their fury; soften their hearts and change their unnatural hatred into Christian love, and forgive them all their sins against Thee and against us. Grant that their ships may find no way in our seas, nor any path in our floods; may their spies be speedily detected and effectually banished from our midst; preserve us from war and tumult; from battle, murder, and sudden death; guard us from sedition, conspiracy, and rebellion; defend our soil from invasion, our ports from blockade—that we may glorify Thee for these deliverances.[7]*

The prayer book then offered "A Prayer for Our Enemies," "A Prayer for Our Armies," and "Washington's Prayer." The last prayer tried to reaffirm for the Confederate states that they were the historical, if not moral, descendants of George Washington and the Founding Fathers and that their cause was just.

In addition to prayer books, sheet music was coming off the presses in quantities and in a variety never known before in the United States. Patriotic songs and hymns were meeting the demand of a population starved for continuous spiritual and patriotic outlet, and in turn the American songwriting industry was born. This new sheet music was being sent to churches and assembly halls as well as to regimental bands on the war front. Some of the same sheet music wound up in the hands of both Union and Confederate bands, who at times played hymns and patriotic tunes together across battle lines as they waited to fight each other.

In confronting this kind of suffering and trial, most soldiers, if not most Americans, could maintain their sanity only by putting the entire matter into a cosmic framework. Not only did Americans need to consider the designs of the Almighty, seeking at the very least divine assurance, but also they needed to construct for themselves their own role and purpose. Consequently, many Americans were forced to create an even stronger relationship with God. For the first time "In God We Trust" was recognized by the federal government as the country's official motto. The holiday Thanksgiving was institutionalized by the President and Congress. In ways never seen before, the country, though divided, was formalizing a spiritual, if not religious, observance for America.

Throughout the war, men and women on both sides glorified the struggle by writing prayers, hymns, and spiritual ballads. One of the most inspired hymns composed during this era came at the height of the war in 1864. As the weary nation questioned how much longer the war could go on, northern cities were being hard hit by a typhoid epidemic killing thousands. On what he described as an "oppressively hot" July afternoon, Robert Lowry, a professor of rhetoric and the pastor of the Hanson Place Baptist Church in Brooklyn, was "in a state of physical exhaustion"[8] as he rested on a lounge sofa. Having just read the latest casualty figures of the war in the newspaper, he also dwelled on how many parishioners and friends had contracted typhoid. Although the numbers of victims succumbing to the disease were not known at the time, he knew instinctively that it had taken a particularly hard toll in New York.

It was at that moment that his "imagination began to take itself wings," he would remember, as he began to think of how to lift everyone's spirits. He wondered why it was that "hymn writers say so much about the river of death and so little about the pure river of the water of life." With the country facing such enormous human devastation, there had to be a way to convey the positive message of God's promise of salvation. In fifteen minutes he sketched out the hymn "Shall We Gather at the River?" and then sat down to the parsonage organ and began to add the melody:

> *Shall we gather at the river*
> *Where bright angel feet have trod,*
> *With its crystal tide forever*
> *Flowing by the throne of God?*

> *Yes, we'll gather at the river,*
> *The beautiful, the beautiful river;*
> *Gather with the saints at the river*
> *That flows by the throne of God.*

> *Soon we'll reach the shining river,*
> *Soon our pilgrimage will cease;*
> *Soon our happy hearts will quiver*
> *With the melody of peace.*[9]

The hymn had an immediate impact. Years later, long after the war had ended, Lowry was riding on the train between Harrisburg and Lewisburg in Pennsylvania when he heard a group of half-drunk lumbermen singing his hymn, reciting by heart every word. Although he squirmed a bit in his seat, he realized that he had written a work that would endure long after he was gone.[10]

THE WAR OUT IN THE FIELD, away from city centers and miles from the comfort of the family hearth, created its own prayer dynamic. Soldiers were confronting their mortality and what their futures might hold. Rural settings with strange names, never before known to most

Americans and spread out across the country's vast landscape, became the backdrop for some of the bloodiest and most horrendous battles of the war. There were Gettysburg, Pennsylvania (51,112 casualties); Chicka-mauga, Georgia (34,624 casualties); Chancellorsville, Virginia (30,099 casualties); and Antietam, Maryland (26,134 casualties).[11] This human toll, mostly concentrated on the male population, was enormous for a country of little more than thirty million people.

Many men wrote ballads that attempted to capture the times and the circumstances they faced. From the war experience in Shiloh, Tennessee, a battle that claimed 23,741 casualties in 1862, came the story of a drum-mer boy. Although his identity would never be known, he became the subject of one of the most famous ballads of the war, written by Will "Shakespeare" Hays, which read in part:

> On Shiloh's dark and bloody ground,
> The dead and wounded lay.
> Amongst them was a drummer boy,
> Who beat the drum that day.
> A wounded soldier held him up,
> His drum was by his side.
> He clasped his hands, then raised his eyes,
> And prayed before he died . . .
> "Look down upon the battlefield,
> Oh Thou, our heavenly friend!
> Have mercy on our sinful souls!"
> The soldiers cried "Amen!"
> For gather'd round a little group,
> Each brave man knelt and cried.
> They listened to the drummer boy,
> Who prayed before he died.[12]

Some prayers were written to commemorate great victories. George Herbert Sass, who came from a distinguished family in Charleston, gloried in the routing of the Union troops in Richmond, Kentucky, as he wrote:

> Now blessed be the Lord of Hosts through all our Southern land,
> And blessed be His holy name, in whose great might we stand;
> For He who loves the voice of prayer hath heard His people's cry . . .

> *'Tis done! the gory field is ours; we've conquered the fight!*
> *And yet once more our tongues can tell the triumph of the right;*
> *And humbled is the haughty foe, who our destruction sought,*
> *For God's right hand and holy arm have great deliverance wrought.*
> *Oh, then, unto His holy name ring out the joyful song—*
> *The race has not been to the swift, the battle to the strong.*[13]

Hymns emanating from across the Atlantic, such as "Onward, Christian Soldiers," "Stand Up, Stand Up for Jesus," and "Rock of Ages," were soon being adapted to the American consciousness and wartime culture. The single most electric hymn of the Civil War, however, emerged not from Europe or from the South but from the pen of Julia Ward Howe, the daughter of a wealthy New York banker. "The Battle Hymn of the Republic" would become the American hymn of hymns, soaring above all others.

A poet and writer from New England, Howe was frustrated, as she later confided to her daughter, by those who believed that a woman could not contribute to the war effort in some meaningful way. She intended to do something about it.

The inspiration for her writing "The Battle Hymn of the Republic" came in 1861, when she and her husband, Samuel Gridley Howe, a physician and social reformer, traveled to Washington, D.C., to attend a wartime meeting of the President's Sanitary Commission, of which Samuel Howe was a member. Staying at the Willard Hotel a block from the White House, they ventured out into Virginia with their minister from New York, the Reverend James Clark. From their carriage the three of them watched precision drills and formations among Union troops in northern Virginia, all of which left an indelible impression.

As they returned to Washington later that day, they sang songs along the way, including the familiar "John Brown's Body," with its popular tune memorializing the abolitionist. After singing one round, Clark suggested to Howe that with her gift for words she ought to consider writing new lyrics to the melody. In her hotel room that evening, she turned and tossed throughout the night. By dawn, the words had finally come to her:

> *Mine eyes have seen the glory of the coming of the Lord:*
> *He is trampling out the vintage where the grapes of wrath are stored;*

He hath loosed the fateful lightning of His terrible swift sword:
His truth is marching on.

I have seen Him in the watch-fires of a hundred circling camps,
They have builded Him an altar in the evening dews and damps;
I can read His righteous sentence by the dim and flaring lamps:
His day is marching on.

I have read a fiery gospel writ in burnish'd rows of steel,
"As ye deal with my contemners, so with you my grace shall deal;"
Let the Hero, born of woman, crush the serpent with his heel
Since God is marching on.

He has sounded forth the trumpet that shall never call retreat;
He is sifting out the hearts of men before His judgment-seat:
Oh, be swift, my soul, to answer Him! Be jubilant, my feet!
Our God is marching on.

In the beauty of the lilies Christ was born across the sea;
With a glory in his bosom that transfigures you and me:
As he died to make men holy, let us die to make men free,
While God is marching on.[14]

On returning to New York, Julia Ward Howe showed the hymn to her next-door neighbor, James T. Fields, the editor of *The Atlantic Monthly*, the same periodical that had made Oliver Wendell Holmes and James Russell Lowell such household names. Fields, recognizing the piece for what it was, convinced Howe to let him publish it and paid her five dollars. Within days "The Battle Hymn of the Republic" was reprinted in dozens of newspapers across the North and even found its way into publications in the South.[15]

Julia Ward Howe got her wish. "The Battle Hymn of the Republic," binding patriotism and God together as practically indistinguishable, struck an important chord for the northern war effort, becoming a treasured piece of America's heritage.

ANOTHER LEGACY of the Civil War is the haunting but simple bugle melody of "Taps." Although it is not a prayer in a traditional sense, there is no greater American call to prayer or meditation than "Taps." Every bit as powerful as the chanting atop a Muslim minaret, the blowing of a Jewish shofar, or the clanging of a Buddhist gong, "Taps" immediately conjures up the spiritual seriousness of the moment. It has allowed soldiers and civilians alike, as it did during the Civil War, to immerse themselves in solitary thought at a particularly poignant moment, whether it is at the end of the day or in remembrance of a fallen soldier.

The story of "Taps" began in the hot, steamy summer of 1862 at Harrison's Landing in southern Virginia, not far from Richmond. The Seven Days battles raged on as some 130,000 Union troops, who had intended under General George McClellan to take over the southern capital, were holed up by the Confederate Army's counterattack. The casualties had been heavy: sixteen thousand for the North, twenty thousand for the South. One of the Union officers, Brigadier General Daniel Adams Butterfield, had been in the thick of the fighting, commanding the Third Brigade of the Fifth Army Corps. A former law student, he was only thirty but had won the admiration of his men because of his constant vigilance over their safety and general well-being.

For some time he had been annoyed by the harsh sound of bugle taps sounded each evening. Somewhat of an amateur musician, General Butterfield sent for his bugler, twenty-three-year-old Private Oliver Wilcox Norton, and showed him notes he had drawn on the back of an envelope. Norton played the melody and worked with the general to fine-tune the length of the notes until he captured exactly what Butterfield had in mind.[16]

That night "Taps" was played for the first time, with its haunting cadence as each note seemed to hang heavy in the air. The impression on the general's men was immediate, as it is for anyone who hears it for the first time. Soon "Butterfield's Lullaby," as some in the company called it, was being imitated by other brigades in the area. A few days later, when a Union cannoneer was mortally wounded by a Confederate shell, Battery Captain John Tidball decided to have "Taps" played at the soldier's funeral.[17] Once the army chaplain had finished reciting prayers at the burial site, Tidball commanded his men to fire rounds of gunfire overhead, slowly but steadily, followed by the playing of "Taps." A new military tradition had been born. Within months "Taps" was being played by the armies of both sides, creating an eerie bond between the North and the South.

* * *

GIVEN THE INTENSITY OF THE WAR, it is no surprise that a wealth of prayers were written by soldiers as they waited, interminably it seemed, for the next battle to begin. For example, a soldier from North Carolina wrote in his diary: "Lord, we have a mighty big fight down here, and a sight of trouble; and we hope Lord, that you give us the victory."[18] Other prayers, spiritual letters of sorts, seemed to reach into the inner recesses of self-awareness. Perhaps no prayer written on the Civil War battlefield had such lasting resonance as the one recovered from the body of a dead Confederate soldier, found in Devil's Den after the Battle of Gettysburg:

> *I asked You, God, for strength that I might achieve,*
> *I was made weak that I might learn humbly to obey;*
> *I asked for health that I might do greater things,*
> *I was given infirmity that I might do better things;*
> *I asked for riches that I might be happy,*
> *I was given poverty that I might be wise;*
> *I asked for power that I might have the praise of men,*
> *I was given weakness that I might feel the need of God;*
> *I got nothing that I asked for,*
> *But everything I hoped for;*
> *I am among all men most richly blessed.*[19]

As soldiers sought some kind of spiritual rationale for the war, they were drawn to the prayer revivals taking hold among the armies. One minister with the Army of Tennessee near Dalton, Georgia, wrote in April 1864, "This revival spirit is not confined to a part only, but pervades the whole army . . . Many presented themselves [for baptism], and I could hear many among them, with sobs and groans, imploring God to have mercy upon them."[20] The bloodier and more desperate the war became, the more soldiers wrestled to find divine recourse. Army chaplains and ministers assigned to local churches along battle routes were astounded by the conversions they were witnessing and the baptisms they were performing, sometimes hundreds a week. This fervor even extended to the sailors from both sides who patrolled and fought along the Atlantic coast.

Appreciation for prayer on the battlefield was not confined to rank-and-file soldiers. Although commanders like Generals Ulysses S. Grant and William T. Sherman were not religious in any traditional sense, they understood the power of prayer. Grant once remarked, thinking of his own pious mother, "How much American soldiers are indebted to good American mothers. When they go to the front, what prayers go with them!"[21]

One of the stories that entered into popular northern folklore focused on Sherman's decisive offensive in the South. During his sixty-mile "March to the Sea" through Georgia, Sherman led a force of well over sixty thousand men. Interspersed throughout the two massive columns marched several regimental bands. As the troops continued their push to the coast during that winter of 1864, one of the bands began to play "Praise God from Whom All Blessings Flow." Band after band picked up the lead, while the men sang a hymn that so many of them had first learned in their churches back home. Within minutes thousands of troops, those "creatures here below," were singing the doxology in unison. Having seen the effect on his men, Sherman, who popularized the phrase "war is hell," later wrote in his diary that with such visible devotion among these "noble fellows," surely "God will take care of them."[22]

In the South, General Robert E. Lee took every opportunity to encourage his men to pray. It was not uncommon for him to dismount from his horse when he saw his men praying, joining them with little fanfare. During the Mexican War more than a decade earlier, he traded his leather-bound prayer book to a dealer in fine books in return for twelve new devotionals. Lee thought he had struck a terrific bargain as he held on to one of them and gave the rest to his men.[23] In the weeks after the Battle of Gettysburg, when Jefferson Davis, as he had on so many other occasions, called on the Confederacy to observe a day of "fasting, humiliation, and prayer," General Lee sent out orders to his men that "all military duties, except those absolutely necessary, be suspended" on that day.[24]

No general, however, was more assured of the worth of prayer than the Confederacy's Thomas J. "Stonewall" Jackson, who earned his nickname after the First Battle of Bull Run when a fellow general cried out, "Look at Jackson, he stands there like a stone wall!"[25] Arguably the most gifted tactician and military ground commander America ever produced, Jackson took only one thing more seriously during the war and that was his relationship with God.

Not unlike the country's religious forefathers who took to heart Paul's admonishment to the Thessalonians to "pray without ceasing," Stonewall Jackson remained steadfast in a prayer regimen that included invoking a continuous stream of spiritual ejaculations. As he confided to his West Point classmate D. H. Maury before the war, "I can no more forget it (prayer) than to forget to drink when I am thirsty. The habit has become as delightful as regular." He continued to explain to his old friend:

> When we take our meals, there is grace. When I take a draught of water, I always pause, as my palate receives the refreshment, to lift up my heart to God in thanks and prayer . . . Whenever I drop a letter into the box at the post office I send a petition along with it for God's blessing upon its mission, and upon the person to whom it is sent. When I break the seal upon a letter, I stop to pray to God that he might prepare me for its contents, and make it a messenger of good. When I go to the classroom, and wait for the arrangement of the cadets in their places, that is my time to intercede with God for them. And so of every familiar act of the day.[26]

Early in the war the Reverend William Brown, editor of *The Central Presbyterian*, recounted how he visited Jackson's camp and came across an old friend and soldier in Jackson's army: "The truth is, sir, that 'old Jack' is *crazy*. I can account for his conduct in no other way. Why, I frequently meet him out in the woods, walking back and forth, muttering to himself incoherent sentences and gesticulating wildly, and at such times he seems utterly oblivious of my presence and everything else."

That night Brown ended up sleeping next to Jackson in his tent and asked him about his practice. Jackson became quietly introspective as he explained:

> I find it greatly helps me in fixing my mind and quickening my devotions to give articulate utterances to my prayers, and hence I am in the habit of going off into the woods, where I can be alone and speak audibly to myself in the prayers I would pour out to my God. I was at first annoyed that I was compelled to keep my eyes open to avoid running against the trees and stumps; but upon investigating the matter I do not find that the Scriptures require us to close our eyes in prayer, and the exercise has proven to me very delightful and profitable.[27]

The end for Stonewall Jackson ironically came in the Battle of Chancellorsville in Virginia, site of such a great victory for the Confederacy that historians to this day speculate how the South's fortunes might have changed had he lived.

At the outset of the campaign, Jackson's chief signal officer, Captain Richard E. Wilbourn, remembered, the general would "stop, raise his hand, and turn his eyes toward Heaven, as if praying for a blessing on our arms. When he came across any of his men who had died or had been injured, he would ask a blessing upon them, and pray to God to save their souls."[28] Only hours later, Jackson was shot by his own men, who mistook him for the enemy. Within days he was dead of pneumonia, his injured arm having been amputated by the army's surgeon.

Accounts of Stonewall Jackson's last hours tell of his incredible calm in the face of death. Jackson was one of over 620,000 fatalities in this war, but his single death turned into a spiritual crisis for the Confederacy. Many southerners could not understand how such a pious, prayerful individual could be taken from them when they needed him most. Those attending the burial service heard "Taps" played that morning, some for the first time. Most of the mourners had no idea that the haunting salute had been written by a Union general and his bugler just ten months earlier.

WITH THE EXCEPTION of Christ, no one has been more scrutinized or more written about than Abraham Lincoln. While the trauma of his assassination continues to color his place in history, the sixteenth President of the United States left behind a collection of writings, decisions, and impressions that have only grown more extraordinary over time.

Born in Kentucky in 1809, just a few miles away from the famous religious revival meeting of 1801 that had helped to propel the Second Great Awakening, Lincoln was steeped at a young age in the Old and New Testaments. In the years just preceding his death, he showed an unconditional dependence on and surrender to "the will of God." What is remarkable is that he was so open about it, confiding at one point, "I have been driven many times to my knees by the overwhelming conviction that I had nowhere else to go."[29]

He was elected President despite continuous setbacks. The only office he had held on the national level was as a one-term congressman, losing his bid for reelection. In 1832 he was defeated for a seat in the state legislature and a year later was forced to declare bankruptcy, a financial pall that hung over his head for the next thirteen years. By 1835 his sweetheart died, which helped lead to his nervous breakdown just months later. He lost more quests for office than he won, including the U.S. Senate and vice presidency. By the time he was elected president and assumed office, he would continue to face personal trials with the death of his two sons and the increasingly erratic actions and unbalanced condition of his wife, Mary Todd Lincoln.

No set of remarks made by Lincoln ever quite captured the man, the desolation of leadership, the magnitude of his new responsibilities, or the reasons for his growing dependence on the Almighty more than his farewell to the people of Illinois as he set off for Washington after being elected President. It would be the last time he saw his home state:

> My friends: No one, not in my situation, can appreciate my feeling of sadness at this parting. To this place, and the kindness of these people, I owe everything. Here I have lived a quarter of a century, and have passed from a young to an old man. Here my children have been born, and one is buried. I now leave, not knowing when or whether ever I may return, with a task before me greater than that which rested upon Washington. Without the assistance of that Divine Being who ever attended him, I cannot succeed. With that assistance, I cannot fail. Trusting in Him who can go with me, and remain with you, and be everywhere for good, let us confidently hope that all will yet be well. To His care commending you, as I hope in your prayers you will commend me, I bid you an affectionate farewell.[30]

The pressure of the war was a constant, tightening vise, but Lincoln was still able to compartmentalize his daily existence. Never did he become wholly self-absorbed. Over and over again he showed concern for others, both known and unknown to him. Nothing had quite prepared him, however, for the tale of a mother and widow.

One cold fall morning, Lincoln learned from an aide that Mrs. Lydia Bixby of Boston had lost all five of her sons to the war. Dumbfounded by the report, Lincoln sent off a letter that conveyed his compassion as well as his deep spirituality:

Executive Mansion
Washington, Nov. 21, 1864

To Mrs. Bixby, Boston, Mass.

Dear Madam,

> *I have been shown in the files of the War Department a statement of the Adjutant General of Massachusetts, that you are the mother of five sons who have died gloriously on the field of battle.*
> *I feel how weak and fruitless must be any words of mine which should attempt to beguile you from the grief of a loss so overwhelming. But I cannot refrain from rendering to you the consolation that may be found in the thanks of the Republic they died to save.*
> *I pray that our Heavenly Father may assuage the anguish of your bereavement, and leave you only the cherished memory of the loved and lost, and the solemn pride that must be yours, to have laid so costly a sacrifice upon the altar of Freedom.*
> *Yours very sincerely and respectfully*

> *A. Lincoln*[31]

Information on exact casualties and circumstances was tough to come by during the war, and much later it would be reported that three of her boys had made it back home alive. Nonetheless, the episode revealed once again the exceptional dimensions of Lincoln's character.

At no time, even in the depths of the war, did Lincoln ever question the motives, the wisdom, or the goodness of God. His prayers were those of wonderment, entreaty, and resignation. His only musings about God were confined to conjecturing what his Maker must think of the way America's Christians justified their actions and purposes, particularly in regard to slavery. But at the same time, Lincoln would not be pushed. Met in the Oval Office by a group of ministers from Chicago who announced that through their prayers they had been summoned by God to obtain immediate emancipation for all slaves, Lincoln rejoined, "If it is probable that God would reveal his will to others, on a point so connected with my duty, it might be supposed he would reveal it directly to me."[32]

Throughout his career, people often underestimated the unaffected and peculiar-looking Lincoln. When he boarded a train for Gettysburg to deliver his historic address in November 1863, a little more than four months after the bloody three-day battle, few people expected greatness of any kind. Gettysburg had been a watershed moment for Lincoln and for the war. It was the farthest Lee had made it into the North, and success or defeat held enormous consequences for everyone. As Lincoln confided to General Daniel E. Sickles after the northern victory, "I knew that defeat in a great battle on Northern soil involved the loss of Washington. I went to my room and got down on my knees in prayer. Never before had I prayed with as much earnestness. I wish I could repeat my prayer. I felt I must put all my trust in Almighty God . . . the burden was more than I could bear . . . I asked him to help us and give us victory now. I was sure my prayer was answered. I had no misgivings about the result at Gettysburg."[33]

While the Gettysburg Address was to become one of the most revered speeches in American history, it was followed by an even greater oration, one that jolted the illusions of human folly and placed in perspective the condition in which America now found itself. Speaking less than six weeks before his assassination, Lincoln stood before the largest crowd ever brought together in Washington for what would amount to the crowning achievement to an exceptional life, his second inaugural address:

Fellow Countrymen:
  At this second appearing to take the oath of the presidential office, there is less occasion for an extended address than there was at the first. Then a statement, somewhat in detail, of a course to be pursued, seemed fitting and proper. Now, at the expiration of four years, during which public declarations have been constantly called forth on every point and phase of the great contest which still absorbs the attention and engrosses the energies of the nation, little that is new could be presented. The progress of our arms, upon which all else chiefly depends, is as well known to the public as to myself; and it is, I trust, reasonably satisfactory and encouraging to all. With high hope for the future, no prediction in regard to it is ventured.
  On the occasion corresponding to this four years ago, all thoughts were anxiously directed to an impending civil war. All dreaded it—all sought to avert it. While the inaugural address was

being delivered from this place, devoted altogether to saving the Union without war, insurgent agents were in the city seeking to destroy it without war—seeking to dissolve the Union, and divide effects, by negotiation. Both parties deprecated war; but one of them would make war rather than let the nation survive; and the other would accept war rather than let it perish. And the war came.

One-eighth of the whole population were colored slaves, not distributed generally over the Union, but localized in the Southern part of it. These slaves constituted a peculiar and powerful interest. All knew that this interest was, somehow, the cause of the war. To strengthen, perpetuate, and extend this interest was the object for which the insurgents would rend the Union, even by war; while the government claimed no right to do more than to restrict the territorial enlargement of it.

Neither party expected for the war the magnitude or the duration, which it has already attained. Neither anticipated that the cause of the conflict might cease with, or even before, the conflict itself should cease. Each looked for an easier triumph, and a result less fundamental and astounding. Both read the same Bible, and pray to the same God; and each invokes his aid against the other. It may seem strange that any men should dare to ask a just God's assistance in wringing their bread from the sweat of other men's faces; but let us not judge, that we be judged. The answers of both could not be answered—that of neither has been answered fully.

The Almighty has his own purposes. "Woe unto the world because of offenses! For it must needs be that offenses come; but woe to that man by whom offenses cometh." If we shall suppose that American slavery is one of those offenses which, in the providence of God, must needs come, but which, having continued through his appointed time, he now wills to remove, and that he gives to both North and South this terrible war, as the woe to those by whom the offense came, shall we discern any departure from those divine attributes which the believers in a loving God always ascribe to him? Fondly do we hope—fervently do we pray—that this mighty scourge of war may speedily pass away. Yet, if God wills that it continue until all the wealth piled up by the bondsman's two hundred and fifty years of unrequited toil shall be sunk, and until every drop of blood drawn with the lash shall be paid by another drawn with the sword, as was said three thousand years ago, so still it must be said, "The judgments of the Lord are true and righteous altogether."

With malice toward none; with charity for all; with firmness in the right, as God gives us to see the right, let us strive on to finish the work we are in: to bind up the nation's wounds; to care for him who shall have borne the battle, and for his widow, and his orphan—to do all which may achieve and cherish a just and lasting peace among ourselves, and with all nations.[34]

In reverential tones Frederick Douglass, who visited Lincoln that evening at the White House, declared that the President's address sounded "more like a sermon than a state paper."[35]

Although Lincoln had long understood and maneuvered through the rough-and-tumble of politics, he was far more private than his public introspections would have indicated. That is why it is remarkable that he answered the question of Noah Brooks, a young reporter covering the nation's capital for California's Sacramento Bee, on whether he prayed. Responding rather softly without elaboration, Lincoln admitted that from the moment he had become President he said at least one prayer a day. Maybe that prayer would consist of as few as "ten words," but "those ten words he had."[36] To a synod of Presbyterian clergymen in Baltimore, he confided, "I sincerely wish that I was a more devoted man than I am. Sometimes in my difficulties I have been driven to the last resort to say God is still my only hope. It [turning to God in prayer] is still all the world to me."[37]

What he did not share with Brooks or the ministers, however, was that he kept with him at all times a prayer book that he could easily tuck in his pocket. Most probably a gift from his wife, The Believer's Daily Treasure was a spiritual guide for every day of the year. Each day's entry first would list a brief verse from Scripture, followed by an equally succinct prayer. It was easily digestible for Lincoln, as it was for anyone who wanted to reflect on a single spiritual theme for the day.

Lincoln had the devotional with him on Good Friday, April 14, 1865. The entry for that day read:

Search the Scriptures; for in them ye think ye have eternal life: and they are they, which testify of me. John 5:39

> *Lord, Thy teaching grace impart,*
> *That we may not read in vain;*
> *Write Thy precepts on our heart,*
> *Make Thy truths and doctrines plain,*
> *Let the message of Thy love*
> *Guide us to Thy rest above.*[38]

Lincoln's assassination at the hand of the actor John Wilkes Booth came six days after Lee's surrender to Grant at Appomattox, Virginia. The North and even pockets of the South went into deep mourning. On Easter Sunday, the day after his death, so full of reminders of the crucifixion and resurrection of Jesus Christ, the pulpits of the country were filled with sermons and prayers that overflowed with grief.

Between 10:00 p.m., when Lincoln was shot, and 7:30 the next morning, when he died; his friend and pastor at the New York Avenue Presbyterian Church in Washington, D.C., the Reverend Phineas D. Gurley, sat next to his bedside with Mary Todd Lincoln, praying for the President. During his vigil, Gurley no doubt remembered the highly personal talks he had had with the President and the many Sunday mornings the President had attended services. He could even recount how Lincoln had attended so many Wednesday evening prayer services, trying to sit inconspicuously in the church office with the door ajar while Gurley led the congregation in prayer in the main lecture room. He would never forget the counseling sessions he had with him after his son Willie died or how his prayer life had become more intense in the midst of what the President called the "process of crystallization."[39]

After the surgeon general announced that the President was dead, the Reverend Mr. Gurley began to prepare for the funeral service, which was held four days later in the East Room of the Executive Mansion. A relatively brief ceremony, it was charged with an emotion never known in that building since John Adams had taken possession of it on behalf of the American people sixty-five years earlier. The funeral party soon made its way to Union Station to board the train that would take the slain President to his final resting place.

The journey between Washington, D.C., and Springfield, Illinois, took over two weeks and was planned to allow as many people as possible to pay their respects. Accompanying Lincoln's body, Dr. Gurley watched in awe as hundreds of thousands of people came out to view the passing

train, bowing their heads in prayer, attempting to pay some small tribute. Throughout the seventeen-hundred-mile trip, Gurley continued to
refine the lyrics he had set to music to be sung at Lincoln's grave site. The
hymn became a fitting tribute:

> *Rest, noble Martyr! Rest in peace:*
> *Rest with the true and brave,*
> *Who, like thee, fell in Freedom's cause,*
> *The nation's life to save.*

> *Thy name shall live while time endures,*
> *And men shall say of thee,*
> *"He saved his country from its foes,*
> *And bade the slave be free"* . . .

> *O God! Before whom we, in tears,*
> *Our fallen Chief deplore;*
> *Grant that the cause, for which he died,*
> *May live forevermore.*[40]

WITH THE PASSING OF Abraham Lincoln and the national trauma of
the Civil War, America's immediate future was anything but certain. At
times it seemed as though Lincoln's successor, Andrew Johnson, his Tennessee roots notwithstanding, was the wrong man in the wrong place at
the wrong time. Few people who had seen him when he was sworn in as
Vice President could ever forget what happened that day. Having been
under the weather for several days, he proceeded to the Capitol for the
inaugural ceremonies, walked into his new office, and immediately
asked for some whiskey. Someone quickly came up with a bottle and a
shot glass, and Johnson downed one drink after the next. By the time Lincoln's soon-to-be Vice President showed up for the ceremonies, he could
barely stand. After taking the oath of office, he cried out in a strong
voice, "I kiss this book in the face of my nation of the United States," and
then leaned over and kissed the Bible in front of him, almost falling over.
After Johnson had rambled on for seventeen minutes, Hannibal Hamlin,
his immediate predecessor, tugged at his coattail to make him sit down.
When it was all over, *The New York Herald* reported on its front page that
Johnson had delivered "a speech remarkable for its incoherence which

brought a blush to the cheek of every senator and official of the government."[41]

Few people had ever expected Johnson to become President. Lincoln had chosen him to balance his ticket at a critical time, but then the unthinkable happened. Having the dubious distinction of being America's first President to be impeached, escaping removal as president by only a single vote in the U.S. Senate, the often-scowling Johnson was strangely impolitic after Lincoln's death. Clearly incapable of leading the country through Reconstruction, he would step aside and not stand for election in his own right in 1868 but return to Washington to serve as a senator again in 1875.

During his administration he issued four proclamations for national days of prayer, beginning with one in memory of Abraham Lincoln. A month before he died of a stroke in 1875, brought on by the lasting effects of cholera, Johnson clearly knew he was on death's doorstep and wrote in his journal, "I have performed my duty to my God, my country, and my family. I have nothing to fear in approaching death. To me it is the mere shadow of God's protecting way."[42] They were the last words he would write.

With the end of the Civil War, the United States had to confront the stark reality of the cost of human folly. Lives had been lost and destroyed, a President had senselessly been killed, and freed African-Americans were coming warily out of the shadows of slavery. For a mostly Christian country, the shedding of so much blood stood as a reminder of Christ's Passion, crucifixion, and redemption for the sinfulness of man. America, it seemed, had gone through its own ablution before God. It would be left to the next generation to make greater sense of the war, pull together the remnants of the nations's great heritage, and forge its future.

One hymn that captured the subdued mood of the country just after the war with its lyrics and soft, lilting melody was "Sweet By and By." Written by Sanford Bennett, the owner of a drugstore in Elkhorn, Wisconsin, who had just returned from the war, the hymn was put to music by his friend Joseph Webster, a formally trained, gifted musician. In the slower pace of small-town America, Webster visited Bennett and other people at the drugstore each day to catch up on the local gossip and occasionally play chess. Bennett would always gauge Webster's mood when he walked into the store, knowing that he could be quite sullen at times:

He came into my place of business, walked down to the stove, and turned his back on me without speaking. I was at my desk writing. Turning to him I said, "Webster, what is the matter now?"

"It's no matter," he replied, "it will be alright by and by."

The idea came to me like a flash of sunlight, and I replied, "The Sweet By and By! Why would not that make a good hymn?"

"Maybe it would," said he indifferently. Turning to my desk, I penned the words as fast as I could write. I handed the words to Webster. As he read, his eyes kindled, and stepping to the desk, he began writing the notes of the chorus. It was not over thirty minutes from the time I took my pen to write the words before two friends with Webster and myself were singing the hymn.[43]

The hymn became one of the most beloved songs in churches and civic halls across America:

> There's a land that is fairer than day,
> And by faith we can see it afar,
> For the Father waits over the way
> To prepare us a dwelling place there.
>
> In the sweet by and by,
> We shall meet on that beautiful shore;
> In the sweet by and by,
> We shall meet on that beautiful shore.[44]

Bennett continued to manage his drugstore while Webster pursued a composer's career, writing over a thousand musical compositions and compiling the very popular Sunday school hymnal *The Signet Ring*. But nothing would quite match the success of "Sweet By and By." The hymn conveyed pathos with its mix of comforting warmth and post–Civil War reality. It came to typify the virtues of spiritual hope. The question for Americans everywhere, however, was what lay ahead.

CHAPTER 8

THE HEALERS

1865–1885

I never saw a moor,
I never saw the sea—
 Yet know I how the heather looks,
And what a wave must be—

I never spoke with God,
Nor visited in heaven—
Yet certain am I of the spot
As if the chart were given—

—Emily Dickinson

𝐵Y THE LATE 1860s the country had become battle weary. Reconstruction had not gone smoothly, and deep-seated resentments from the war remained. General Ulysses S. Grant had been elected President, but his successes on the battlefield had become a distant memory while his administration became mired in scandal and lethargy. A Methodist in name only, he showed little visible interest in matters pertaining to religion, attending Sunday services only to please his wife, Julia. Never did he display the outward piety of the men he commanded on the battlefield, the Confederate generals he fought against in the war, or his former commander in chief Abraham Lincoln. Still, he believed in God and the divine destiny of the United States, a fact he highlighted in his second inaugural address when he declared, "I believe our Great

Maker is preparing the world, in His own good time, to become one nation, speaking one language, and when armies and navies will no longer be required."[1] Throughout his presidency, he peppered his public remarks with admonitions to the American people to pray for him and for the country.[2] Grant did help to institutionalize Thanksgiving, however, in keeping with the precedent Lincoln had established. In his first Thanksgiving proclamation in 1869 he presented a long list of blessings, from the abundance of crops and "liberal yields" of mines and forests to "harmony and fraternal intercourse obliterating the marks of past conflict and estrangement." In asking the American people to set aside November 18 "to render praise and thanksgiving," he also asked them "to implore a continuance of God's mercies."[3]

In retirement, Grant became a silent partner in a banking house ultimately bankrupted by two partners who swindled the firm. From there he plunged into writing his autobiography, the finest presidential memoirs ever written, completing them hours before he fell into semiconsciousness stemming from his battle with throat cancer. Nowhere in his chronicles did he mention God or become spiritually introspective in any way.

When Grant's end came, Methodist Bishop John Philip Newman was asked by Julia Grant to attend to the spiritual needs of her husband. Realizing Grant's significance in the consciousness of the country and wanting to shore up the reputation of the hard-drinking hero of the Civil War, Newman announced to the press that he personally witnessed Grant's last hours as he recited prayers and came into full communion with the Methodist Church. Disconcerted by the Bishop's public account, one of Grant's four children let journalists know that their father had never shown that kind of piety, simply because he had been too sick to acknowledge much of anything. The press had a field day trying to figure out what exactly had transpired. Wherever the truth lay, the Methodist funeral for Grant turned out to be an elaborate affair of national mourning. Fanny Crosby's newly composed "Safe in the Arms of Jesus" was sung, and the nation openly mourned Grant and the passing of an era.

Grant's successor, Rutherford B. Hayes, was baptized a Presbyterian but was more fascinated by transcendentalism and the works of Ralph Waldo Emerson than by the tenets of any one church. His wife, Lucy, a graduate of Wesleyan Women's College, had other ideas, however.

When she learned that the inauguration was scheduled for a Sunday, she had her husband reschedule the ceremony for the preceding Saturday. The Sabbath, she insisted, was for the Lord and prayer, not for secular affairs, no matter how important.

Once her husband was in office and much to the dismay of social Washington, "Lemonade Lucy" Hayes, an active member of the Woman's Christian Temperance Union, announced that the first family would not be serving alcohol at Executive Mansion functions. When Secretary of State William Evarts was asked after a reception whether he had enjoyed himself, he responded, "Splendid! Water flowed like champagne."[4]

Forgoing traditional social gatherings, Lucy and her husband hosted prayer services that included hymn sing-alongs on Sunday evenings for members of the Cabinet, the Congress, and their families. These services were the first of their kind at the Executive Mansion, and an invitation to them carried considerable prestige.[5] Even more special was the celebration in the Executive Mansion of the Hayes' twenty-fifth wedding anniversary, when they renewed their vows before a Methodist minister and many of the people who had attended their original wedding in Cincinnati. The event was the buzz of Washington society for months.[6]

While Hayes did call "for the guidance of that Divine Hand by which the destinies of nations and individuals are shaped" in his 1877 inaugural address, a time when Reconstruction was finally coming to an end, he said privately, "The mystery of our existence—I have no faith in any attempted explanation of it. It is all a dark, unfathomed profound."[7] At the end of his life he confided that he had remained "a Christian according to my conscience," which included saying prayers, but the principles of Christianity had never held great import for him.[8] Nevertheless, Christian tenets guided many of his presidential proclamations, including his calling for six national days of prayer and thanksgiving during four years as President, a record-breaking number in peacetime.

The spiritual malaise of Grant and Hayes, offset in part by their devout wives, reflected demographic pockets of America in those years after the war. The population of the United States had now reached over forty million. Five million were African-American; another 2.5 million were recent European immigrants. The face of the reunited states was changing in striking ways—socially, ethnically, geographically, and religiously.

With Civil War casualties having taken a dramatic toll, questions lingered as to why God could have allowed such devastation to occur. Where was Divine Providence in controlling the destinies of men and women when it counted most? Where was the God of America's Puritan forefathers? As the nineteenth-century transcendental writer Octavius Brooks Frothingham saw it, "Organizations are splitting asunder, institutions are falling into decay, customs are becoming uncustomary, usages are perishing from neglect, sacraments are decried by the multitude, creeds are decomposing under the action of liberal studies and independent thought."[9]

This new era evolved into America's "Gilded Age," a term used by historians to evoke the less than admirable qualities of the period extending from the Civil War to World War I. It was a time of healing and of adventure. In one of the most remarkable achievements and milestones in history, the transcontinental railroad was built and finally completed on May 10, 1869, at Promontory Point, Utah, when a golden spike was hammered into the rails with the engines of the Union Pacific and the Central Pacific meeting face-to-face. Two great oceans were now joined together by human ingenuity through the American continent. Prayers were in abundance that late morning as the Reverend John Todd of Boston, serving both as officiating minister and correspondent for two east coast religious magazines, thanked and implored God to bless the human feat as a "gentle stream" in bringing together "the Atlantic of Thy strength and the Pacific of Thy love."[10] Other clergymen prayed at the site as well. Finally out of exasperation, the telegraph operator tapped out to both ends of the country, "We have got done praying. The spike is about to be presented."[11] And so it was. Engraved next to the historic spike were the words "May God continue the unity of our Country as this Railroad unites the two great Oceans of the World."[12]

At no time before or since, however, had the United States experienced such social tensions and a growing sense of being adrift. The rigid religious values that had dominated prior to the war and the assumptions of only a generation earlier were being transformed. No longer were certain spiritual truths of the Bible or Protestant tenets of faith accepted literally or completely by such large segments of the population. With the Industrial Revolution taking hold, new influences competed with traditional religion. Education, a growing economic and cultural affluence, and a seemingly different world altogether were having a profound effect on Americans and their religious culture.

Of dramatic consequence in the decades following the Civil War were the startling findings underlying the theory of evolution. Although Charles Darwin's *Origin of Species,* espousing the evolution hypothesis, had been published in late 1859, it was not fully understood and integrated into American thinking until after the Civil War.

Spiritual truths and doctrines that had been unquestioned for centuries were shaken to the core. Rather than attempt to convert these new understandings to religion at the outset, however, two conflicting schools of thought emerged: evolutionists, who saw creation as a continuous natural development with no divine intervention whatsoever; and creationists, who saw God's seven-day formation of the world, culminating with the conception of Adam and Eve, as the one and only truth. Any attempt to bring these polar positions together made for explosive debate. This fundamental shift in the understanding of human creation effected one of the most seminal intellectual transformations in the Western world. In turn, American perceptions of spirituality and even prayer were being redefined.

This is not to say that spirituality was fading away. To the contrary, it remained a powerful force in the country, and by 1880 a new great awakening, the third in American history, had begun to blossom. What evolved during this period, and lasted well into the next century, was a combination of spiritual romanticism and the conviction that in the midst of rapid social and economic change the Golden Rule applied to American Christianity more than ever. Rather than simply pray to a distant God, Americans looked to probe, to understand, and to make their protector more accessible.

Two poets who demonstrated this great generational divide when it came to prayer and spirituality were the gifted John Greenleaf Whittier and Emily Dickinson. Both had a profound impact on American culture—Whittier during his lifetime, the reclusive Dickinson well after her death.

No American poet during the nineteenth century composed traditional religious verse as prolifically and with such artistry as John Greenleaf Whittier. Very much a product of his Quaker background, Whittier believed that the ability to experience the presence of God firsthand was central to spirituality. As George Fox, the founder of the Society of Friends, explained, "Worship . . . is not the performance of a dead ritual, but genuine waiting on the Lord to hear His voice and to know His power at firsthand."[13]

Whittier used in his everyday speech such pronouns as "thee," "thine," and "thou," reflecting the language of the Bible and the norm of strict Quakers. Even to his contemporaries, his quaint way of addressing others was strangely anachronistic, but no one could deny his mastery of the English language. When it came to prayer, he revealed in his long poem *Andrew Rykman's Prayer,* "I am groping for the heavenly harmonies."[14] Throughout an exceptional literary career he wrote such classic works as "My Soul and I," "The Eternal Goodness," and "My Psalm," all conveying how prayer had become an integral part of his life. For Whittier there could be no doubt as to the efficacy of prayer. As he wrote in "Our Master":

> *O Lord and Master of us all,*
> *Whate'er our name or sign,*
> *We own Thy sway, we hear Thy call,*
> *We test our lives by Thine.*[15]

Although Whittier used his creativity to defend the spiritual traditions of his Quaker heritage, he wrote an intriguing poem called "The Brewing of Soma." Composed in 1872, the poem referred to an intoxicating drink called soma, a concoction made from a fungus found in Asia and fermented over a fire. The Vedic Hindus of India used the mold fly agaric, or *Amanita muscaria,* in their religious rituals. When stirred with milk and passed through the bladder, it produced a "soma," a strong hallucinogenic effect, and for the Hindu sect a state of religious frenzy. Although Whittier had never been to India, he learned of the practice from friends who had traveled to the Indian Subcontinent and witnessed the practice firsthand.

Inducing religious fervor through artificial, sensual means was nothing less than sacrilege to Whittier. God's greatness and special nature could be found only in prayer through spiritual silence. Whittier, of course, was targeting a specific audience when he wrote "The Brewing of Soma," those evangelical Christians whose prayer and worship practices were distasteful to him.

"Dear Lord and Father of Mankind," the prayer contained within the poem, speaks of the need for tranquillity in God's presence and asks God for forgiveness from "foolish ways." Ironically, the prayer was later set to music by several composers and has become one of the most popular hymns in the English language. Given Whittier's intense dislike for singing during religious services, he would have been aghast at the use of his prayer in this way. No matter what tune has accompanied this prayer, it is sung today with great zeal and remains an integral part of Christian worship:

> *Dear Lord and father of mankind,*
> *Forgive our foolish ways!*
> *Re-clothe us in our rightful mind,*
> *In purer lives Thy service find,*
> *In deeper reverence, praise . . .*

> *Drop Thy still dews of quietness,*
> *Till all our strivings cease;*
> *Take from our souls the strain and stress,*
> *And let our ordered lives confess*
> *The beauty of Thy peace.*

> *Breathe through the heats of our desire*
> *Thy coolness and Thy balm;*
> *Let sense be dumb, let flesh retire;*
> *Speak through the earthquake, wind, and fire,*
> *O still small voice of calm!*[16]

By the time Whittier reached the age of seventy, he had become one of America's most beloved literary figures. To commemorate the country's centennial in 1876, he was commissioned to write a hymn. Set to music and performed by a full orchestra and choir of a thousand voices in Philadelphia, "Centennial Hymn" was one of the highlights of the nation's anniversary celebration:

> *Our fathers' God! From out whose hand*
> *The centuries fall like grains of sand,*
> *We meet today, united free,*
> *And loyal to our land and Thee,*
> *To thank Thee for the era done,*
> *And trust Thee for the opening one . . .*

Be with us while the New World greets
The Old World thronging all its streets,
Unveiling all the triumphs won
By art or toil beneath the sun;
And unto common good ordain
This rivalship of hand and brain . . .

Oh make Thou us, through centuries long,
In peace secure, in justice strong;
Around our gift of freedom draw
The safeguards of Thy righteous law:
And, cast in some diviner mould,
Let the new cycle shame the old![17]

The counterpoint to Whittier was the withdrawn, quirky, but intellectually brilliant Emily Dickinson. Born to an orthodox Congregationalist family in Amherst, Massachusetts, Dickinson was intimately familiar with the prayers and hymns of New England. A product of her age as she chronicled the country's changing image of the divine, she evolved into what her biographer Roger Lundin referred to as the "art of belief."[18] Growing more and more a restless agnostic, she actively searched for clues to the existence and nature of God. While no one can be sure how far Dickinson had come in her quest by the end of her life, the prayerful introspections of her poetry provide unique insights. Furthermore, the evolution of that journey, so eloquently expressed through her mind's eye and pen, has afforded others a means to measure and enhance their own spirituality.

Early in her life, Dickinson experienced what she thought at the time was a sudden religious conversion. She later wrote in her journal, "It was then my greatest pleasure to commune alone with the great God and to feel that he would listen to my prayers." Ultimately concluding that her experience had been a figment of her overactive imagination, she realized that her spiritual journey was far from over.[19]

While New England's Puritans had emphasized extemporaneous prayer, Dickinson found that most of the ministers of her day were scripted and showed little sign of the spiritual restlessness that consumed her more and more. While a student at Mount Holyoke Female Seminary, she joined a small prayer group, one of many on campuses across the country. She refused, however, to be force-fed religious belief. Mysterious, strong-willed, and free-spirited, Dickinson was a continuous challenge and was visited on numerous occasions by the school's spiritual monitors. She would not be pinned down by them or anyone else, however, and poured herself into her literary passions, her only way to express herself fully. Writing some seventeen hundred poems over her fifty-six years, she would see only seven of them published in her lifetime.

In the end, Emily Dickinson, who took to wearing only all-white dresses, resolved to continue her search for personal spiritual discovery, seeing prayer as "the little implement through which men reach where presence is denied them."[20] One of the great ironies in her life is that while she became a virtual recluse, closing herself off to only her most intimate friends and family, she showed an unquenchable thirst for knowledge and for understanding God and the universe. For Dickinson, God was a distant and unfeeling stranger and yet remained a curiosity who might indeed be the ultimate power and authority. In her search for spiritual reality, she described herself as "a soul at the white heat."[21] For a restless poet who found little definition in either her life or her spirituality, prayer became a precious friend.

Like her contemporaries—Melville, Russia's Dostoyevsky, and Germany's Nietzsche—Dickinson bemoaned her generation's perceived inability to understand God with the kind of clarity and exactitude that earlier generations had done. The intellectual movement of the transcendentalists, the lingering psychological scars of the war, and Darwin's work on evolution made prior notions of God seem dated and out of focus for Dickinson. She appeared to swim in the recesses of her mind as she searched for a higher, spiritual truth, saddened that she was not more firmly anchored spiritually:

> *Savior! I've no one else to tell—*
> *And so I trouble thee.*
> *I am the one forgot thee so—*
> *Dost thou remember me?*
> *Nor, for myself, I came so far—*
> *That were the little load—*
> *I brought thee the imperial Heart*
> *I had not strength to hold.*
> *The Heart I carried in my own—*

Till mine too heavy grew—
Yet—strangest—heavier since it went—
Is it too large for you?[22]

While Dickinson's musings about God and prayer have been open to interpretation over the years, her use of the English language and her walk through new corridors of intuition and personal exploration were exceptional achievements. Purposely vague at times, surgically precise at others, Dickinson used the English language to profound effect. Her spiritual struggles challenged some while solidifying the faith of others. By finding novel ways to perceive God, even when the exact nature of God's existence was in question, she allowed others to examine more deeply and thoughtfully their own prayer life.

WHILE THE COUNTRY'S WRITERS were exploring approaches to spirituality and prayer that differed from those of earlier generations, a transformation was also taking place in the education of children. Whereas *The New England Primer* had been an important influence from the colonial period into the nineteenth century, another series of books was now becoming the educational core for millions of schoolchildren. First published as *McGuffey's Readers* in 1836, these textbooks were geared to teach students through each grade of elementary school. Seven million copies had been sold by 1850, and within the next forty years the books became the basis for all public education in the country's thirty-seven states.

The readers were the brainchild of William Holmes McGuffey, an ordained Presbyterian minister, educator, and president of Ohio University and several other colleges. Part of the McGuffey legend told to thousands of children, apocryphal though it might be, centered on how McGuffey launched his own formal education. Born to a poor farming family in western Pennsylvania in 1800, he learned to read and write with the help of his mother, Anna. Realizing that her son was gifted beyond his years and with few resources at her disposal, she was overcome with worry one afternoon while working outside and fell to her knees to pray with William at her side. Totally immersed in her prayers, seeking God's help, she suddenly found the Reverend Thomas Hughes, a stranger, standing next to her. Hughes, walking down the road and seeing her so intensely engaged in prayer, introduced himself and soon found out about young William and Anna's predicament. Letting her know that he was headmaster of the local Greersburg Academy, he enrolled young William on the spot, and with his mother's prayers answered, the legend of William Holmes McGuffey began.[23]

Whatever the veracity of the story, McGuffey was a truly gifted individual. Realizing that the country sorely needed a more relevant sequel to *The New England Primer,* he championed an educational model that taught students moral lessons through the popular literature of the day as well as through his personal insights on how to lead a proper Christian life, including plenty of prayer. Over the next few years, six readers would be published, the first four entirely written by McGuffey. Children could read selections of poetry from Longfellow, Whittier, and Thoreau while learning practical lessons at the same time. *McGuffey's Fourth Reader* emphasized punctuation marks, articulation, and accent, for example, while the *Fifth Reader* highlighted modulation, poetic pauses, and voice inflection.

McGuffey continuously edited his readers in their early years of publication. As he updated his material, he made direct references to God and to prayer, stating in his *First Reader:*

At the close of day before you go to sleep, you should not fail to pray to God to keep you from sin and from harm.

You ask your friends for food, and drink, and books, and clothes; and when they give you these things you thank them, and love them for the good they do you.

So should you ask your God for those things, which He can give you, which no one else can give you.

You should ask Him for life and strength and health; and you should pray to Him to keep your feet from the ways of sin and shame.

You should thank Him for all his good gifts; and learn, while young, to put your trust in Him; and the kind care of God will be with you, both in your youth and in your old age.[24]

After McGuffey's death in 1873 subsequent editions removed some of the stronger references to God and prayer, reflecting changes in the perception of God, Puritan values, and modern-day education. Even educational traditions were feeling the seismic shift of the times.

★ ★ ★

WHILE THE COUNTRY was in the throes of spiritual and social conflict, several religious voices, steeped in the traditions of America's past,
arose to provide religious gravity and common sense. Surprisingly, this
was one of the most fertile periods in the country's history for writing
hymns and focusing more vigorously than ever on the importance of
prayer.

The most credible individual confronting the spiritual turmoil of the
Gilded Age was the Reverend Henry Ward Beecher, an extraordinarily
eloquent man who possessed a brilliant mind. Son of the strict, doctri-
naire Reverend Lyman Beecher and brother of Harriet Beecher Stowe,
Henry Ward Beecher seemed to be the embodiment of the country's
spiritual journey in the second half of the nineteenth century and
spanned very disparate generations of Americans. He was a strong supporter of the abolitionist movement before the Civil War and a powerful voice in healing the country's lingering wounds. Even on the
question of evolution, Beecher was critical in trying to bring two clash-
ing worlds together. Finding common ground in his famous sermon
"Evolution and the Church," he enunciated clearly, *"Evolution will affect
the Church,* BUT for its greater health and power among men."[25]

Beecher wrote extensively and eloquently on the subject of prayer,
seeing in it the chance for individuals to search for God in their own way
without fear of being turned away. "The soul without imagination is
what an observatory would be without a telescope."[26] Prayer by its very
nature had to be the fulcrum of a person's existence. From sermon to
admonition, prayer became a calling card for Beecher in trying to fathom
the divinity of the Almighty. It is said that on his deathbed, after a lifetime of prayer, his last words were "Now comes the mystery."[27]

Despite the spiritual morass of some segments of the country, ministers like Beecher continued to proliferate. One of the most riveting
preachers in American history, who was seen and heard by more people
than any other human being in the second half of the nineteenth century, was Dwight Lyman Moody. Originally a very savvy and successful
shoe salesman in Chicago, Moody underwent a conversion and began to
preach about his experience as an example to others. With his three-
hundred-pound frame and booming voice, he was spellbinding as he
talked about prayer and its relation to "the three R's"—ruin by sin,
redemption by Christ, and regeneration by the Holy Spirit. Audiences
flocked to hear him preach, mesmerized by his down-to-earth style.

Chopping his hands in midair for emphasis as he spoke in almost staccato fashion, Moody converted thousands on the spot.

During his lay ministry, Moody wrote perhaps the most popular spiritual book of his generation, *Prevailing Prayer*, in 1884. In it he discussed chapter by chapter the different forms of prayer, from thanksgiving to petition. He began his work by stating, "Those who have left the deepest impression on this sin-cursed earth have been men and women of prayer. You will find that prayer has been a mighty power that has moved not only God, but man."[28] He would tell his audiences time and again that "every great movement of God can be traced to a kneeling figure."[29]

Helping him to deliver his message of salvation across the country was his friend and partner Ira Sankey, one of the great hymnists and religious musicologists in American history, whom he had met at one of his revival prayer meetings. With Moody's encouragement, Sankey single-handedly popularized such classics as "Onward, Christian Soldiers," "Rock of Ages," and "What a Friend We Have in Jesus." Moody would work his audience into a frenzy with his rhetoric while Sankey provided the emotional release through musical religious expression. With Moody's charisma and Sankey's savvy, the men obtained financing not only from their audiences but also from the growing industrialist class, who could relate more closely to Moody, the former shoe salesman, than to traditional ministers. The two men became the most successful team in American religious history.

Another great spiritual writer and preacher was Phillips Brooks, known in his day as "Prince of the Pulpit." Reputed to speak at a rate of 250 words per minute, the imposing six-foot six-inch Brooks arguably became the most influential Episcopalian Bishop in the nineteenth century. While his most-recognized work today is the Christmas carol "O Little Town of Bethlehem," which he wrote after spending a memorable Christmas Eve in the Holy Land, he was known in his own day for, among other things, his one-line admonitions such as "Pray not for crutches but for wings." His pronouncement "I do not pray for a lighter load, but for a stronger back"[30] was later used by both Theodore Roosevelt and John Kennedy on the political stump. He was a seminal force in the life of the blind and deaf Helen Keller, who when a little girl sat on his lap as he taught her to reach out to God and to find ways in which to connect with her fellow men and women. Keller later credited his influence with giving her the spiritual fortitude to make Bibles and prayer books more accessible to the physically challenged through Braille, large print, and audio.

Another Episcopal priest, the Reverend Daniel C. Roberts, made one of the great contributions to American hymnody when he wrote a piece for the country's centennial celebration in Brandon, Vermont, a prayer called "God of Our Fathers." Later set to the music of George Warren, one of the country's greatest organists, from St. Thomas Church in New York City, it became an instant sensation. Not long after its premiere, the Episcopal Church of the United States published it as the "National Hymn":

God of our fathers, whose almighty hand
Leads forth in beauty all the starry band
Of shining worlds in splendor through the skies,
Our grateful songs before Thy throne arise.

Thy love divine hath led us in the past,
In this free land by Thee our lot is cast;
By Thou our ruler, guardian, guide, and stay,
Thy word our law, Thy paths our chosen way.[31]

When it came to pure hymn writing, however, no one was more prodigious in lyrical religious verse than Fanny Crosby. Struck by a rare eye inflammation, which was poorly treated by a local physician, she was blinded permanently at six weeks of age. Taught by both family and friends, she showed unusual literary promise at a young age, and by the time she was a teenager she had become something of a celebrity. Horace Greeley asked her to compose poetry for his *New-York Tribune*. Presidents Martin Van Buren and James K. Polk met with her on several occasions and were struck by her infectious enthusiasm despite her blindness. President Grover Cleveland fondly remembered her influence on him when he worked as a young man as a secretarial clerk at the New York Institute for the Blind, where she was a teacher.[32]

At the age of thirty-eight, Crosby married Alexander Van Alstyne, a gifted organist and composer who also was blind and who wrote the music to many of her lyrics. Crosby chose to live in poverty for most of her adult life while writing over nine thousand hymns. Her first major success came in 1864 with the publication of "Pass Me Not, O Gentle Savior," a hymn that captured the essence of her life's work:

Pass me not, O Gentle Savior,
Hear my humble cry;
While on others Thou art smiling,
Do not pass me by.

Let me at a throne of mercy
Find a sweet relief;
Kneeling there in deep contrition
Help my unbelief.[33]

One of her most treasured verses, memorized by children and adults alike, was found in four simple lines:

Thou, My Everlasting Portion,
More than friend or life to me,
All along my pilgrim journey,
Savior, let me walk with Thee.[34]

While women had long been the country's champions of prayer, ensuring that children were properly taught to turn to God, their voices in the latter part of the nineteenth century became louder and more creative than ever. The longtime friend and neighbor of Emily Dickinson, Helen Hunt Jackson, wrote one of the most heartrending prayers of the period, "A Last Prayer," as she too came to the end of her life. Movingly, she bemoaned that she had not done more for others during her lifetime, touching on the message of the Beatitudes:

Father, I scarcely dare to pray,
So clear I see, now it is done,
How I have wasted half my day,
And left my work but just begun.

So clear I see that things I thought
Were right or harmless were a sin
So clear I see that I have sought,
Unconscious, selfish aims to win;
So clear I see that I have hurt
The souls I might have helped to save,

That I have slothful been, inert,
Deaf to the calls thy leaders gave.

In outskirts of thy kingdoms vast,
Father, the humblest spot give me;
Set me the lowliest task thou hast:
Let me repentant work for thee![35]

Once published, the prayer was circulated widely and read from church pulpits across the country. Among her other achievements was a book called *Ramona,* written while she lived in Colorado Springs, the first major work to call attention to the plight of Native Americans.

HAVING MOVED TO COLORADO, Helen Hunt Jackson, like so many Americans, was awed by the beauty and genuine possibilities of the West, so stunningly captured for easterners in the paintings of the Hudson River school and the prose of America's writers. Tens of thousands of Americans were now homesteading on frontier lands, building new communities at a faster pace than ever. Prayer became the steadfast companion to settlers confronting the unknown.

Indeed, American-bred men and women from the east coast were being joined in this western movement by newly arrived immigrants with their own prayer practices. Eastern Orthodox immigrants, men and women who settled in such far reaches as Alaska, for example, brought some unique prayer customs from the Old World. To ward off the austere environment and the threat of disease, for instance, many mothers treated their babies with "brauching," a practice combining prayer with massage to provide remedy to a sickly infant.[36] At the moment the mother believed her child was coming down with something, she would coat the child's arms and legs with a mixture of vinegar and fat. She would then rub the homemade salve into the skin while rocking the child back and forth on her lap. All the time, with each rhythmic motion, she would recite a prayer, sometimes the same one over and over again, ultimately sliding into deep meditation. If the baby became too fussy, she would fill a sock with heated oats, lay it on the child's stomach like a hot-water bottle, and continue to pray as she applied her massage.

While immigrants and other Americans resettling in regions west of the Mississippi were sustained by the traditions of Old World and New

World prayer, they also longed to build their own houses of worship. Indeed, for many of them the first community project was to build a church, one that could double as a meeting hall for the town, not unlike what the early Puritans did. Given the mix of faiths, finding one minister to tend to the entire community was difficult but important. A one-room schoolhouse would often be built not far from the church, with the words "In God We Trust" embedded prominently in front of the classroom to remind children of their heritage as they opened and closed daily classes in prayer.

One prayer, written in the early part of the next century by Badger Clark, the son of a minister and also the first poet laureate of South Dakota, captured the spirit of the cowboy in America's burgeoning West. He wrote the piece to his mother, expressing his heartfelt approach to God. Ultimately it became one of the country's most beloved poems, capturing the feel of the wide-open American West:

> *O Lord, I've never lived where churches grow,*
> *I've always loved Creation better as it stood*
> *That day you finished it so long ago*
> *And looked upon your work and called it good.*
> *I know that others find You in the light*
> *That's sifted down through tinted window panes,*
> *And yet I seem to feel You near tonight.*
> *In this dim, quiet starlight on the plains.*
>
> *I thank you, Lord, that I am placed so well,*
> *That you made my freedom so complete;*
> *That I'm no slave of whistle, clock or bell,*
> *Nor weak-eyed prisoner of wall and street.*
> *Just let me live my life as I've begun*
> *And give me work that is open to the sky;*
> *Make me a pardner of the wind and sun,*
> *And I won't ask for a life that's soft or high.*
>
> *Let me be easy on the man that's down*
> *And make me square and generous with all.*
> *I'm careless sometimes, Lord, when I'm in town,*
> *But never let them call me mean or small!*

Make me as big and open as the plains,
As honest as the hawse between my knees,
Clean as the wind that blows behind the rains,
Free as the hawk that circles down the breeze!

Forgive me, Lord, if sometimes I forget.
You know about the reasons that are hid.
You understand the things that gall and fret;
You know me better than my mother did.
Just keep an eye on all that's done and said
And right me, sometimes, when I turn aside,
And guide me on the long, dim trail ahead
That stretches upward toward the Great Divide.[37]

For solitary figures with few personal ties out on the fringes of civilization, life could be terribly lonely. It paid not to think too hard or too long about being so isolated. They found escape and excitement in mining for gold in California, tilling soil in Kansas, or rustling cattle in Texas. Prayer was practically nonexistent. Prostitution, liquor, and a host of other vices, rather than spirituality, were the ready choices when it came to comforting a tired soul. In fact, the closest that some of these men and women ever came to a prayer book was using wrappers they called "prayer books" to roll tobacco for their cigarettes.

This "irresolute behavior," as some ministers referred to it, did not go unnoticed by transplanted easterners who were prepared to do something about it. One of the most colorful figures to become a crusader in turning the country into a "liquor-free, tobacco-empty, sex-abstaining, decadence-rejecting America" was the indomitable Carry Nation.[38] Having put up with an alcoholic husband who died at an early age, she was ready to wage a national fight. Convinced that she was God's stalwart, avenging angel, Nation claimed that she had received visions from God instructing her to take matters into her own hands.

Wielding an ax and a Bible, she barreled her way into saloons to "preach, pray, and smash."[39] Small and big towns alike from Texas to Kansas felt her wrath. No one would stand in her way. When she learned that her friends were horrified by her growing fanaticism, she proudly responded through a reporter, "I like to go just as far as the farthest. I like my religion like my oysters and beef steak—piping hot!"[40]

Some saw Carry Nation's divine revelations in launching her "morals campaign" as virtuous martyrdom, nothing less than God's empowerment of her on behalf of America's women to strike out against social ills of all kinds. Others, of course, saw her example as false prayer run amok. To them she was just "a holy crone on a broomstick."[41] Even Thomas Alva Edison could not resist social commentary and produced two pointed movies with his newly patented kinescope camera. The first, *Kansas Saloon Smashers,* was a sarcastic portrayal of Nation's demolishing saloons, places depicted more as family gathering spots than as "dens of iniquity." She and her followers were livid about the film but became even more outraged when *Why Mr. Nation Wants a Divorce* was released, an account of how Carry Nation's second husband had suffered from marital neglect, all of this coming just as he was in the process of filing divorce papers.[42]

At times newspapers were filled almost weekly with the latest accounts of Carry Nation's actions and her arrests by local authorities. Basking in the exposure she was generating, she would only consent to a reporter's taking her photograph behind bars if she was pictured on her knees in prayer. Nation had become an American celebrity like no other.

While Carry Nation certainly had her detractors, thousands of other individuals had also taken up the cause of Prohibition. In the aftermath of the Civil War, social movements of all kinds had taken root and were flourishing, from giving women the right to vote to organizing labor unions. Taking on alcoholism had an appeal across the board for many Americans. From Eliza Davison Rockefeller, the mother of John D. Rockefeller, to poor, abused wives in the inner city, women would walk into local bars and proceed to kneel and pray for everyone present. They would then accuse the store owner and any patrons on the premises of being guilty of "the sin of liquor indulgence." Recognizing that they would have far greater strength in numbers, they formed such organizations as the Woman's Christian Temperance Union; the Anti-Saloon League, funded largely with Rockefeller money; and the Catholic Total Abstinence Society.

The second president of the Woman's Christian Temperance Union, Frances Willard was a particularly potent force. Through the efforts of Willard and her officers, rallies, local organizational brainstorming sessions, and parades were held across the country, sending the one-note message that many of the nation's problems were tied to the evils of liquor. The WCTU was helped enormously by a sympathetic press that buttressed the cause by publishing riveting stories about real cases of individuals and their families confronting alcohol abuse.

In launching the WCTU at its initial convention in November 1873, the delegates quickly adopted Willard's approach to the scourge of alcoholism by "meeting argument with argument, misjudgment with patience, and all difficulties and dangers with prayer."[43]

Willard then perfected the tactics of the organization by arguing that the most effective means to attack the "scourge" was to bring prayer and music together on America's streets and in its saloons. Consequently, people soon became familiar with the WCTU anthem, "The Crusade Hymn," and its lines "God hears thy sighs and counts thy tears. God shall lift up thy head." The country also heard the stirring lyrics of songs like "Saloons Must Go!" and "Prohibition." Although women had not yet gained the right to vote, they maintained that prayer had to be accompanied by action at the election polls. Consequently, they sang "Vote As You Pray" throughout local and national political campaigns, often facing voters at the polling booth.

The most gut-wrenching hymn of all was "An Incident True," which argued that society was at the heart of the problem, countering God's will. The work began:

> If you'll listen I'll tell you an incident true,
> Which occurred in a high license place,
> Where five thousand saloons pay a large revenue,
> For the right to breed crime and disgrace.[44]

From there the gripping story unfolds of "a poor drunken man" in Chicago who beat his dying wife after confronting the loss of his infant. "Licensed rum made him frantic and wild." And then comes the hard-hitting line "But who sold him the drink? Who enacted the laws?" Verse after verse condemned the "saloonist" and the system that helped turn the man into a raging alcoholic.

ALTHOUGH PROHIBITION became the law of the land by amending the Constitution in January 1919, it would be repealed in 1933. In the end, the rate of alcoholism during Prohibition never abated; it grew worse.

In their focus on prayer as key to saving both the body and the soul from alcoholism, these social prohibitionists were not alone. One of the seminal movements of the era, leading to the creation of Church of Christ, Scientist, better known as the Christian Science Church, emanated from the pen and organizational leadership of Mary Baker Eddy.

Born into a traditional Congregationalist family, Mary Baker Eddy suffered from continual health problems from early childhood. Not finding relief from doctors or medications, she experimented with everything from séances to alternative methods of healing. After reading and rereading passages of Christ's miracles in curing the sick, Eddy began to believe that prayer could have an extraordinary effect in restoring a person's health. Soon she set out to convert people to her cause and ultimately to her faith.

By 1875 Mary Baker Eddy had written her groundbreaking publication *Science and Health with Key to the Scriptures,* in which she laid out her religious prescriptions for living a healthy, spiritual life. Alcoholism and all other physical and psychological illnesses could be resisted through faith and prayer. Bringing heart, mind, and soul together would provide the recipe for a spiritually fulfilled, vigorous life.

For Eddy personal prayer was central to anyone's redemption. "The highest prayer is not one of faith merely; it is demonstration. Such prayer heals sickness, and must destroy sin and death."[45] And yet her notion of how best to voice prayer was very different from that of traditional faiths:

> Audible prayer can never do the works of spiritual understanding, which regenerates; but silent prayer, watchfulness, and devout obedience enable us to follow Jesus' example. Long prayers, superstition, and creeds clip the strong pinions of love, and clothe religion in human forms. Whatever materializes worship hinders man's spiritual growth and keeps him from demonstrating his power over error.[46]

Not only did the visionary Eddy argue for the need to find solace in the intimacy of prayer; she also believed that God spoke continuously to her as she organized her mother church in Boston.

Willa Cather, the Pulitzer Prize–winning novelist and composer of her own prayers, was so fascinated by the story of Mary Baker Eddy that she wrote an extensive biography of her. In it she underscored that for Eddy prayer was quite different from what it was for most Christians:

> Prayer, as commonly practiced, had no place in [Eddy's] religion, in which God is Principle and not a Person. "To address Deity as a Person," she said, impedes spiritual progress and hides Truth. Prayer is sometimes employed, like a Catholic confession, to cancel sin, and this impedes Christianity. Sin is not forgiven; we cannot escape its penalty . . . Suffering for sin is all that destroys it. When we pray aright, we shall . . . shut the door of the lips, and in the silent sanctuary of earnest longings, deny sin and sense, and take up the cross, while we go forth with honest hearts, labouring to reach Wisdom, Love and Truth."[47]

Mary Baker Eddy annotated the Lord's Prayer to reflect what she saw as a deeper meaning in the Gospel. Like Mother Ann Lee, the founder of the Shakers, and Eliza Snow of the Mormon Church, she perceived God as both masculine and feminine:

> *Our Father which art in heaven,*
> Our Father-Mother God, all-harmonious,
>
> *Hallowed be thy name.*
> Adorable One.[48]

Beyond her religious faith, Eddy's genius lay in effectively organizing her religious movement from the ground up and in promoting her beliefs like few others could have done. While controversial, she became quite successful in drawing to her church a very devout following, and by 1895 she had inspired the creation of some 250 Christian Science congregations throughout the United States. By the time of her death in 1910, that number had increased to over 1,200.

THE ERA WAS ALSO PRODUCING a very vocal, active core of women intent on influencing the national agenda, largely by seeking to empower women to hold a public stake in the life of the country. The Women's National League, with the support of Senator Charles Sumner of Massachusetts in 1864, delivered to the U.S. Congress "The Prayer of One Hundred Thousand." The petition, signed by over 100,000 men and women from states across the North, called for a permanent end to slavery, an effort that ultimately helped to ratify the Thirteenth Amendment to the Constitution in December 1865, abolishing all "involuntary servitude."

Arguably the three most prominent leaders of the women's movement were an organizer, a preacher, and a writer. Susan B. Anthony, Lucretia C. Mott, and Elizabeth Cady Stanton first gained national attention in the launching of the women's movement at the historic Seneca Falls Convention in New York in 1848. At times the three women would seriously diverge in their approach to the movement, becoming estranged from one another. Their passion for achieving equality, however, remained their common hallmark.

Susan B. Anthony, the most prominent of the three, was a gifted organizer. Influenced by her Quaker roots, she had been a fierce opponent of slavery and a strong champion of the temperance movement, bringing to her work the same passion as she addressed the equality of women. In her stump speeches, largely in the Northeast, she often recounted how Frederick Douglass had once told her that his prayers to God to escape the bonds of slavery were left unanswered until the day he decided "to pray with his heels." For Anthony, the women's movement was no different. Interviewed by the pioneering journalist Nellie Bly, who asked whether she prayed, Anthony did not pull any punches: "I pray every single second of my life; not on my knees, but with my work. My prayer is to lift women to equality with men. Work and worship are one with me. I cannot imagine a God of the universe made happy by my getting down on my knees and calling him 'great.'"[49]

The oldest and most religious of the three was the resilient Lucretia Mott. Consecrated a Quaker minister, she delighted in challenging her listeners to expand their spiritual horizons. God recognized the equality of men and women, she would tell them. It was man who had taken untoward liberties in subjugating the female segment of the population. Unlike her colleagues, she devoutly practiced her faith, using her sermons to combine spirituality with the women's movement. On one occasion she delivered a highly publicized and much anticipated sermon at the Second Unitarian Church in Brooklyn, New York, on the subject of prayer. She began her remarks by saying, "When the heart is attuned to prayer, by the melody of sweet sounds, or, it may be, by silent introversion, it seems sometimes almost as if words were a desecration."[50] She did not believe that genuine results could ever be achieved without seeking God's intervention first.

Elizabeth Cady Stanton, on the other hand, immersed herself in the Scriptures to illustrate how men had manipulated both the Old and the New Testament to vanquish women over the ages. The daughter of a popular New York congressman, she believed that even prayer books had been written to exclude women from equal standing in the eyes of God. In response to the perceived inequities, she coordinated a committee of women in 1895 to compile *The Woman's Bible,* which focused primarily on the Old Testament and tried to show that even the prayers of prophets were sexist and that women had been relegated to second-class status. Such an approach to social ills did not appeal to the larger female population. Nevertheless, the work of Stanton, Anthony, and Mott would resound into the next century.

THE COUNTRY'S POLITICAL LEADERS reflected these times of social and spiritual turbulence. One of the sadder chapters in American history was the four-month presidency of James Garfield in 1881, cut short by an assassin. Frustrated by his rejection from the government's civil service, the young man claimed to have heard voices from the beyond telling him to shoot America's twentieth President.

Garfield attributed his success in large part to his deeply religious, widowed mother who had raised him and his brother alone. Fascinated by the teachings of Alexander Campbell in the first half of the nineteenth century, Garfield joined the Disciples of Christ, eventually becoming a preacher, the only President ever to do so.

As a zealous preacher, Garfield immersed himself in organizing prayer meetings throughout Ohio and in neighboring states, converting new souls to the "Campbellites" and stressing the need for prayer to a loving God, rather than the wrathful God of the "fire and damnation" circuit preachers. Even after his election to the Ohio state senate, Garfield continued his missionary work.

Elected in 1863 to Congress, where he would serve for the next seventeen years, Garfield was visiting New York City on personal business when word came that Abraham Lincoln had been assassinated. When he learned that some fifty thousand people were gathering on Wall Street, reacting to the news by seeking out suspected southern sympathizers in order to lynch them, he moved into action. As the crowd began to careen out of control, Garfield walked out onto the balcony of the imposing Custom House, the center of New York politics, waving a small American flag. Reporters from the *New-York Tribune* and the *Herald* were spellbound by the moment, busily jotting down in their notepads how Garfield took control of the unruly crowd, crying out in a booming voice: "Fellow citizens! Clouds and darkness are around Him! His pavilion is dark waters and thick clouds of the skies! Justice and judgment are the establishment of His throne! Mercy and truth shall go before His face! Fellow citizens! God reigns, and the Government of Washington still lives!"[51]

The crowd soon calmed, and the story was splashed in newspapers across the country the next day. No matter what the facts may have been to the headline story "Garfield Stills Mob," the incident created a mythology about Garfield that helped propel his future candidacy for President.

While Garfield made only one reference in his inaugural address to "the support and blessing of Almighty God," he clearly took his faith seriously in assuming office. Never did he lose his belief that the only way to become close to God was through private prayer, a practice that remained constant until his death. While he set about the nation's business, criticized by his detractors for being a shady politician at times, he had no idea what was transpiring in the mind of Charles Guiteau.

Having tried to sell insurance policies and religious prayer tracts on the streets of Boston, Guiteau found politics far more appealing. After working as a campaign volunteer for Garfield in the close election of 1880, he believed he was entitled to a position in the Garfield administration, in particular an appointment as consul to the U.S. Embassy in Paris. When no job materialized, the psychotic forty-year-old Guiteau began to imagine that Garfield was being politically duplicitous in not helping a faithful supporter, and he started to stalk the President. In particular he took enormous delight in following the former preacher and his family to Sunday services. Seeing himself as God's messenger, he believed that the small wood-framed church the Garfields attended would be the perfect place for the assassination. He later confided to a reporter with *The New York Herald* that to "remove" the President "at his devotions" would show poetic justice. On the Sunday that he planned to execute his plot, however, Guiteau learned that the President would not be in church. At the last minute Garfield had decided to spend the weekend on the New Jersey shore to be with his wife, Lucretia, who was convalescing from an illness diagnosed as everything from malaria to meningitis.

Altering his plans, Guiteau decided to meet the train carrying the President back to Washington on the morning of July 2, 1881. As the train pulled into Washington's Baltimore and Potomac Station on Sixth Street and the President emerged onto the platform, Guiteau fired two bullets, striking Garfield not far from where Robert Todd Lincoln, the late President's son, stood watching.

Garfield fought hard for his life, lingering for more than two months. Even Alexander Graham Bell was called in to use his newly invented metal detector to try to find one of the bullets lodged in the President's body. Garfield's doctor later recalled how fervently he had prayed aloud to be spared death until he could see his wife just one more time. When Lucretia Garfield finally did arrive, she dropped to her knees next to her unconscious husband, and within minutes he slipped away.[52] Although the country had only known Garfield for a few months, the outpouring of grief and offering of prayers were genuine.

Charles Guiteau was hanged for his crime on June 30, 1882. Before his execution he wrote the makings of a hymn that he took to the gallows, surreally recommending to the journalists and invited guests that the lyrics, "if set to music . . . may be rendered very effective." He then recited what he had written in a rather rambling, ranting last statement:

> *I am going to the Lordy; I'm so glad . . .*
> *I saved my party and my land,*
> *Glory hallelujah!*
> *But they have murdered me for it.*
> *And that is the reason I am going to the Lordy,*
> *Glory hallelujah! Glory hallelujah!*
> *I am going to the Lordy!*[53]

When he was finished, Guiteau held on to the piece of paper while the executioner fixed the black hood over his head, tying the rope, and then opened the trapdoor. As Guiteau took his last breath, his prayer floated to the ground before the assembled crowd.[54]

Within hours of Garfield's death, around two in the morning on September 20, 1881, the rather dignified Vice President Chester Arthur was sworn in to office. Looking very much the part of the country's chief executive, always dressed in his Brooks Brothers best, Arthur would only serve out the remaining years of Garfield's term. Although his tenure was not remarkable, he brought back to the presidency the prestige that had been missing under Johnson and Grant. Christened in the Episcopal Church as a baby, Arthur had never been a strong churchgoer or man of prayer until he became President.

While much of his newfound devotion was due to his new responsibilities, he also continued to mourn the death of his wife, Ellen, the previous year. Although their marriage had been both loving and difficult, he was devastated when, at the age of forty-two, she suddenly died of pneumonia, brought on two days earlier while she was waiting for a carriage in the cold after attending a New York concert.

Confronting his grief at the pinnacle of his career, Arthur donated a window in Ellen's memory at St. John's Episcopal Church, requesting that it be installed on the south side so he could see it from the second story of the Executive Mansion when he said his prayers. Recounting how his wife had grown up in and around Washington and had sung in the choir at St. John's, Arthur took enormous comfort in that one window.[55] On leaving office, having issued four national days of thanksgiving and prayer while President, he retired to his home in New York and died the next year of kidney failure at the age of fifty-seven.

WHILE THE GILDED AGE produced social and spiritual turmoil in the United States, it also strengthened the prayer culture. Trying both to explore and ultimately to discover answers to age-old questions was a natural outcome of the post–Civil War period. The country continued to wrangle over its future—politically, economically, socially, and spiritually. The Industrial Revolution in the United States had become an incontrovertible fact, making daily life more challenging than ever. For most Americans, these modern realities had the effect of infusing their prayers with greater resolve in confronting and living with an even greater unknown.

CHAPTER 9

THE OPPORTUNISTS

1885–1900

The livid lightnings flashed in the clouds;
The leaden thunders crashed.
A worshipper raised his arm.
"Hearken! Hearken! The voice of God!"

"Not so," said a man.
"The voice of God whispers in the heart
So softly
That the soul pauses,
Making no noise,
And strives for these melodies,
Distant, sighing, like faintest breath,
And all the being is still to hear."

—Stephen Crane (1895)

A GENERATION HAD NOW PASSED since the end of the Civil War, and an unfettered optimism seemed to define many Americans. Industry boomed, in part due to the technological breakthroughs and manufacturing needs that stemmed from the war itself. Factories seemed to spring up overnight in cities up and down the east coast. Agrarian America was giving way to a different world, one dominated by manufacturing, oil and gas production, banking, and retail business. To feed the demands of this new industrial age, the country had little choice but to turn to immigrants, predominantly from Europe but also from Asia and Latin America, millions of them, to support the labor pool. The economic heartbeat of the United States was changing and with it the prayer culture. Bishop John Neumann of Philadelphia, a Bohemian immigrant and the first American male to be declared a saint, had long since instituted the Church's Forty Hours Prayer Devotion, a practice continued to this day.

This period gave life to what some historians identify as the country's Third Great Awakening, a time when a new religious revival took hold and more Americans than ever seemed to be tuning in to their spiritual lives. It was an era that lasted well into the next century, the product of a number of social factors, much like the earlier awakenings.

Industrialists of the era were an unusual group of entrepreneurs whose drive to make money and expand their commercial empires earned them the title "robber barons." While many of these pioneers were ruthless in their business dealings, they also took enormous risks expanding the country's limits geographically and commercially, in ways that even the U.S. government could never have conceived, let alone managed. Once they had reached a certain critical mass, there was little to stop their vast reach until the government stepped in to break up their monopolies.

Despite their hard-nosed tactics, some of these business giants, belonging to different but almost entirely Protestant denominations, showed remarkable religious devotion and with their great wealth helped to fuel the country's religious resurgence. They contributed tens of millions of dollars to the building of churches, seminaries, hospitals, and foundations. At times, their support seemed to be as intense as their business dealings, some critics even arguing that their spiritual devotion was a convenient publicity tool to cover their commercial practices. While there may well have been a conscious or subconscious desire to justify boardroom actions, many industrialists genuinely believed that they reflected the spiritual values of their parents.

Many of the most formidable businessmen of the period were Episcopalians—men like John Pierpont Morgan, Andrew Mellon, Eugene DuPont, Henry Clay Frick, Cornelius Vanderbilt, and Edward Henry Harriman. With its roots in England and America's past, the Episcopal Church brought Protestant credibility, pomp and ceremony, and clear identification with the country's establishment. Other industrial figures represented the growing diversity of the country's other thriving

Protestant denominations, men such as John D. Rockefeller (Baptist), Cyrus McCormick (Presbyterian), Milton Hershey (Mennonite), John Wanamaker (Disciples of Christ), Andrew Carnegie (Presbyterian), and W. K. Kellogg (Seventh-Day Adventist). No matter to which Protestant denomination these commercial titans belonged, however, they did have several common characteristics. First, they had a moral stake in connecting the accumulation of wealth with the Puritan work ethic, which in turn was tied to spirituality. Second, they had little time for what they saw as the fuzzy intellectualism of transcendentalism or the denial of the divinity of Christ as practiced by the Unitarian Church. Finally, they were more interested in finding a bottom line to religious devotion, much as they were doing in business.

These characteristics were not simply ingrained in the business elite but reached deeply into the country's entire commercial community, dating back to the great panic of 1857, when almost five thousand businesses were driven into bankruptcy.[1] Although economic conditions had improved by 1859, a reinvigorated religious devotion emerged, the likes of which had never been seen before, a phenomenon that became known as the Businessmen's Revival.

In every major city across the United States, shopkeepers, factory managers, bankers, and other middle-class executives were gathering at lunchtime to conduct prayer meetings. They crowded into churches, theaters, and town halls, where they held their prayer services as though they had an appointment with God. While the hour of the prayer meetings could vary, there was a set format that could best be described as a business agenda. Commencing in most instances at noon, the meetings had a tightly scripted service that began with a hymn, a Bible reading, and the leader's prayer. At exactly 12:30 p.m., individual businessmen would stand up for no more than thirty seconds to offer a prayer or "exhortation," with no "controverted" points being permitted to keep them on schedule. By 12:55 p.m., individual prayers would end, and the final hymn was sung. Everyone returned to work, prepared to repeat the service the next day.[2]

Led on most occasions by laymen rather than clerics, these daily services brought the world of business together with prayer and spirituality, away from traditional churches as well as the faddish religious musings of eastern intellectuals.

One hymn that became wildly popular and was identified with the

Businessmen's Revival was "Stand Up, Stand Up for Jesus." The prayer reaffirmed the strong convictions of the country's commercial class, making it a no-nonsense, unapologetic affirmation of biblical revelation:

> *Stand Up, stand up for Jesus, ye soldiers of the cross;*
> *Lift high His royal banner, it must not suffer loss.*
> *From victory unto victory His army shall he lead,*
> *Till every foe is vanquished, and Christ is Lord indeed.*[3]

The prayer, written by the Reverend George Duffield of Philadelphia, came to the Presbyterian minister as he listened to the dying words of his young friend the Reverend Dudley Tyng.[4] The son of the Reverend Stephen Tyng, a charismatic rival to Henry Ward Beecher and the spiritual mentor to J. P. Morgan and the Episcopal elite of the time, Dudley Tyng rejected what he believed to be his father's unyielding tenets of faith.[5] Leaving the Episcopal priesthood to launch his own Church of the Covenant, he rallied businessmen across Philadelphia with his evangelical fervor, preaching and praying before massive crowds. After preaching before an assembly of five thousand, still dressed in his clerical robes, he returned to his farm and decided to walk around his farm. As he patted one of his mules, the sleeve of his gown, which he had not yet taken off, got caught in a corn thresher, tearing away his arm. Passing out almost immediately from the loss of blood, Tyng was found by Duffield and several other friends, who lifted his almost lifeless body and carried it into the house. Realizing that he was about to die and desperately wanting to ensure that his ministry would not be forgotten, Tyng reached for Duffield's hand and whispered, "Tell them . . . tell them to stand up for Jesus," and with that he died.[6]

Duffield was stunned and at the same time profoundly moved by the last words of his friend. Incorporating "stand up for Jesus" into lyrics he was now inspired to write, he put them together with a tune written by George Webb, the organist at Boston's Old South Church. Within weeks of its publication "Stand Up, Stand Up for Jesus" was being sung in practically every Protestant church across the country and became the unofficial anthem of the Businessmen's Revival movement.

WHILE RANK-AND-FILE businessmen became engrossed in a spiritual dynamic all their own, few occupied center stage quite the way John D.

Rockefeller did throughout his long career. Born in 1839 in upstate New York, Rockefeller was raised in a devout Baptist household. Although his father's escapades with women and continued absences made home life difficult, his religious, doting mother made life bearable for Rockefeller and his siblings.

While building Standard Oil into a massive energy monopoly, John D. Rockefeller held fast to his religious beliefs, contributing millions of dollars to Baptist causes in addition to medical research and universities. Living in Cleveland for more than forty years, he and his wife, Laura "Cettie" Spelman, seldom missed Sunday and Friday evening prayer services at the Euclid Avenue Baptist Church, a practice they would continue after moving to New York City and becoming members of the Fifth Avenue Baptist Church. From 1872 to 1905 he actually served as superintendent of the Sunday school in Cleveland, promoting prayer as paramount in any religious teaching.[7] As with most dutiful Baptists, Rockefeller believed the Bible to be the most important inspirational tool in stimulating prayer. He would first concentrate on a particular passage of the Bible, and then sit back in silence to reflect for a moment on the verse he had just read. Only then would he be ready to pray.

Although he had his critics, most of them agreed that Rockefeller's prayerful devotions were not hypocritical. Indeed, that is what helped make him such an enigma. As his biographer Ron Chernow noted, Rockefeller saw God as "an ally, a sort of honorary shareholder of Standard Oil, who had richly blessed his fortunes."[8] Prayer was integral to the life of the business and the family.

While Rockefeller dominated the energy sector, the colorful John Wanamaker of Philadelphia was revolutionary in helping to transform the nation's retail industry. Experiencing a religious conversion during a prayer service in 1856, when he was only eighteen, he told his Presbyterian minister, the prominent Reverend John Chambers, that he had felt overwhelmed by the presence of God that night and had committed himself to strive from that day forward "that I might be more like Christ."[9] In time he would become the best-known Christian layman of his generation as a member of the Disciples of Christ.

With an eye for anticipating consumer tastes, understanding the dynamics of modern retail management, and instinctively knowing how to generate publicity, Wanamaker brought together his two passions, business and religion. Erecting one of the great department stores of the twentieth century in Philadelphia, he constructed within the design a "Grand Court" as its centerpiece, finishing it off with an intricate dome surrounded by massive Ionic and Corinthian columns. Positioned high above the court's massive floor space, which could hold more than fourteen thousand people at a time, the world's largest organ was installed, ultimately with 28,482 pipes, producing a sound that visitor after visitor called "glorious."[10] While organ recitals were being held, usually at noon, salespeople would hand out prayer tracts to customers, intended to enrich their spiritual life. In addition to supporting Wanamaker's retail trade, the Grand Court had ample room to accommodate religious services, creating the largest indoor space of its kind in the country for such gatherings. Although Wanamaker insisted that his efforts to proselytize through organ music and prayer admonishments had nothing to do with increasing his business, he also realized that the effect helped to make him one of the world's great mercantilists.

Like Rockefeller, Wanamaker served as a Sunday-school superintendent, holding the same position for sixty-five years. As a member of the Bethany Presbyterian Church, he was sometimes asked to take to the pulpit, and on one such occasion he delivered a prayer that showed the character of an unaffected, deeply devout person: "Oh, Lord, Thou hast told us how to pray. Help us to shut the door, shutting out the world, and the enemy and any fear or doubt, which spoils prayer. May there be no distance between our souls and Thee."[11]

While Wanamaker was breaking new ground in the retail business and Rockefeller was building his empire, John Pierpont Morgan was providing critical economic lifelines to a country in desperate need of his support. Arguably the most powerful figure in American financial history, Morgan was both revered and reviled by his contemporaries. Regardless, he had gained the reputation of being a man of his word, a standing in the business world in which he took much pride. During critical moments for a country experiencing the birth pains of industrialization, he took responsibility for preventing the transcontinental railroad system from falling into total collapse; structuring the incorporation of General Electric, International Harvester, and United States Steel; and ensuring that a run on U.S. gold in 1895 was averted. As a one-man Federal Reserve Board before such an agency existed, Morgan held a position in America's economic life like no private figure before or since.

Effectively estranged from his wife and a legendary womanizer, Morgan nonetheless kept strong ties to the Episcopal Church. When he was a child, his parents had required him and his sisters to memorize three hymns each Sunday evening to sing to family and friends. As an adult, Morgan continued the practice of having people gather on a Sunday evening to pray and sing his favorite hymns, all this after attending public services that morning.[12]

Throughout his life Morgan strongly supported the tenets of his faith and the traditions of the Church and believed that prayer was central to anyone's gaining salvation. Consequently, it was no surprise when he agreed to take part in 1886 in revising the *Book of Common Prayer*, the devotional mainstay of the Episcopal Church that Morgan seemed to know by heart. Once the final revision was approved by liturgical committee, he paid for richly bound copies to be sent to all of the country's Episcopal dioceses and saw to it that hundreds more were made available for laypeople as well as for libraries throughout the United States and Britain.[13]

Another dominant force, who contributed to the prayer life of millions of Americans before and after his death, was Andrew Carnegie. By the end of the nineteenth century, Carnegie had effectively come to control the entire U.S. steel industry, amassing one of the great fortunes in U.S. history. A confirmed agnostic despite attending Presbyterian church services throughout his life, he believed that religion and spiritual piety could unlock and help ease much of the strife in the world.

In 1873 Carnegie received a seemingly routine request. A Presbyterian minister in Scotland wrote to him, asking if he would contribute money to purchase an organ for his church. With such a grand instrument, the minister argued, his parishioners could hold Sunday and weekday prayer services that would appreciably enhance their worship. The amount was insignificant for Carnegie, and so with little hesitation he had his secretary write a check and send it to the minister. After the check arrived, the press picked up the story, and within days articles in every leading newspaper in Europe and the United States detailed his generosity. Dozens of churches, particularly in the United States, were soon making requests, presenting much the same argument as the Scottish minister. Over the next forty years Carnegie helped to purchase and build over seven thousand organs for churches and schools, becoming the largest organ philanthropist in history, most of which continue to be played to this day.[14] Realizing what he had unleashed, Carnegie later wrote that "music is religion," convinced that his philanthropy would increase the faith of others exponentially.

Another millionaire businessman who was not in the financial league of the great tycoons, but who became one of the most recognized personalities of his day, was the inimitable P. T. Barnum. Obsessed by self-promotion, Barnum seemed to advance the three-ring extravaganza both inside and outside his circus tents, and yet he sustained a deep faith and sincere belief in the value of prayer.

Born in 1810 in Bethel, Connecticut, Barnum was deeply affected by the "literal fire and brimstone" preachers he encountered as a young boy during the Second Great Awakening. He seemed to relive the absolute terror of the experience later in his life when he wrote:

> When I was from ten to fourteen years of age, I attended prayer meetings where I could almost feel the burning waves and smell the sulphurous fumes. I remember the shrieks and groans of suffering children and parents and even aged grandparents . . .
>
> Many and many a time have I returned home from an evening prayer meeting frightened . . . with my eyes streaming with tears, and every fiber of my body trembling with fear, I have dropped upon my bended knees and fervently prayed this cold, stern God to let me die immediately, if thereby it was possible to save my soul and body from His endless wrath.[15]

Given his innate optimism and his desire to see the Almighty primarily as a loving God, Barnum was drawn to the faith of the Universalist Church. Brought to America from England in the eighteenth century, Universalism was built on the fundamental belief that God's great purpose in the world was to ensure that every human being be saved from sin, no exceptions. Universalism, combined with prayer, was perfect for Barnum, who saw in his new faith an important psychological anchor to a fulfilling life.

Once, when returning to America from London on a British ocean liner, Barnum approached the captain with a simple request. Could he and several of the ship's passengers conduct a prayer service with the famous preacher Robert Baird officiating? Without hesitation, the captain said he could not grant the request, given that an Anglican service had already been held that morning. "Captain, do you pretend to say you

will not allow a respectable clergyman to offer a prayer and hold religious services on board your ship at the request of your passengers?"[16]
Barnum responded. With that the two men locked horns, with the captain finally threatening to place Barnum in the ship's brig, shackled in
irons.

Barnum, of course, reveled in the notion of pulling into Manhattan's
harbor in handcuffs and leg irons for all the press to see, particularly over
a matter of religious freedom. Realizing what was about to be unleashed, the captain relented and apologized for his rash behavior. Once
on shore, Barnum told the press the full details, and soon the story had
hit most of America's major daily newspapers.

It was not until he turned sixty-one that he opened his first circus.
Publicizing his entertainment showcase from opening night as "the
greatest show on earth," Barnum delighted in being called everything
from a shameless huckster to a visionary, so long as his name was spelled
correctly.

At the age of eighty, Barnum suffered a stroke, and his wife, family,
friends, and employees knew he would die in a matter of weeks. As he
had done since his conversion to Universalism, he awoke each morning
and recited prayers in the Church's devotional *Manna: A Book of Daily
Worship.* Nancy Barnum later wrote that every night before her husband
fell asleep, he would utter the words "Thy will be done."[17] Within a few
months of his stroke, he peacefully died in bed, but not before asking the
New York Evening Sun to publish his obituary on its front page so that he
could see it in print. The *Sun* gladly obliged with the headline "Great and
Only Barnum—He Wanted to Read His Obituary—Here It Is."[18] He also
choreographed his own funeral, choosing each of the hymns and
prayers.

THROUGH THE FINANCIAL SUPPORT of many of America's industrialists, major charities and educational institutions began to spring up
across the country, many of which exist to this day. Prominent among
them was the Tuskegee Normal and Industrial Institute in Tuskegee,
Alabama. Chartered by the state of Alabama during Reconstruction, the
institute opened its doors in 1881 with a mission to educate black students to become teachers while training others to work in various trades
of agriculture and industry. Men like Andrew Carnegie and John D.
Rockefeller were soon contributing to the institute's upkeep, paying for

construction of buildings and scholarships. Although their support was certainly important during those early days, Tuskegee's initial success was due in large measure to the moral certitude, work ethic, and vision of Booker T. Washington and George Washington Carver. While both were enormously gifted in their own way, they shared the common bond of having been born into the cradle of slavery.

Appointed Tuskegee's first principal, Booker T. Washington became legendary for pushing his students to strive for their personal best and for the riveting tales in his best-selling autobiography, *Up from Slavery*. While visiting the Grand Central Palace in New York in March 1898 to hear Dwight Lyman Moody preach, he was unexpectedly asked by the evangelist to speak before the standing-room-only crowd. Washington ascended the stage and began to speak frankly about his faith:

> I well remember the first prayer I heard from my mother's lips. I was a slave. As I look back now, I can see my mother bending over me as I lay on my pallet in the poor little cabin in which we lived. She is about to leave me for a day of hard labor, and she bends over me and her lips move in prayer. I hear her as she prays that Mr. Lincoln will succeed, and set us free. She prayed that at least her child might be free.
>
> I remember also the second prayer I heard from her lips. Mr. Lincoln had triumphed, and we were free American citizens. She prayed then that her child might be educated. Both prayers were answered. If there is one thing the Negro race can teach the white race, it is simple faith.[19]

As *The New York Times* reported in the next day's edition, the response was tumultuous. Although Washington was criticized for not advocating a more militant approach to race relations, he took the criticism in stride, believing that he could advance the cause of African-Americans more effectively in his own way. He made sure that every one of his students at Tuskegee attended prayer services in the college chapel on Tuesdays and Thursdays as well as shorter prayer gatherings every other night except Saturday. If he was not traveling to raise money for the school or to address various audiences, he would speak and offer prayers at the services personally.

During his tenure he made by far his most prudent hiring decision when he appointed the brilliant George Washington Carver to head up the agriculture department at Tuskegee. The move not only helped to enhance the prestige of the institute but also contributed to significant scientific breakthroughs.

The true nature of Carver's genius came to light when he tackled the dilemma of revitalizing Alabama's soil to produce more vibrant crops, particularly peanuts, pecans, and sweet potatoes. In the aftermath of his success, crop yields soon began to exceed demand, so Carver turned his Tuskegee laboratory into both a lab and a kitchen, coming up with hundreds of new uses for crops, from peanut butter to sweet-potato pie. By the time he died in 1943, Carver not only had helped the economies of southern farmers but also had registered dozens of patents for such products as instant coffee, shaving cream, axle grease, milk flakes, talcum powder, synthetic rubber, and shampoo.

Considered a genius by his contemporaries, Carver profoundly believed that prayer had contributed directly to his scientific insights. He always believed that his experience at the age of ten, while shucking corn, sparked his lifelong commitment to prayer:

> One of our neighbors, about my age, came by one Saturday morning and in talking and playing he told me he was going to Sunday school tomorrow morning. I was eager to know what a Sunday school was. He said they sang hymns and prayed. I asked him what prayer was and what they said. I do not remember what he said; I only recall that as soon as he left, I climbed into the loft, knelt down by the barrel of corn and prayed as best I could. I do not remember what I said. I only recall that I felt so good that I prayed several times before I quit.[20]

From that moment Carver prayed constantly—when he arose in the morning, when he went to bed, and, at times, hourly throughout the day. He readily let people know that he talked to God in his laboratory all the time, and whenever he had the chance, he urged his students to do likewise. Once, after witnessing a rather spectacular sunset alone, he remarked in a letter to a friend how he had undergone yet another religious experience, and how he had cried out, "O God, I thank Thee for such direct manifestation of Thy goodness, majesty, and power."[21] Science and Divine Providence were one and the same for Carver.

* * *

IMMIGRANTS WERE NOW FLEEING EUROPE in greater numbers than ever to escape economic hardships and political unrest. In the decade before the Civil War, 1.7 million immigrants had arrived on the country's shores; in the decade following the war, the number rose to 2.8 million. Between 1881 and the outbreak of World War I, another 23 million European immigrants would come to the United States, helping to triple the overall population of the country.[22] By the time of the 1886 dedication of the Statue of Liberty, France's remarkable gift to the United States, America's leaders were acutely aware of the dramatic transformation taking place. Emma Lazarus's poem "The New Colossus," with its line, "Give me your tired, your poor," etched a few years later at the base of the statue, poignantly captured the country's message of welcome. At the dedication ceremony on an unusually foggy morning, President Grover Cleveland delivered the keynote address as two of America's foremost clergymen, Presbyterian minister Richard Storrs of Brooklyn and Episcopal Bishop Henry Potter, the force behind the construction of the Cathedral of St. John the Divine, offered prayers of welcome to America's latest immigrants.[23]

As these new immigrants settled in the United States, they tipped the traditional balance of the white Anglo-Saxon Protestant establishment that had dominated for so long. By sheer numbers, the Catholics and Jews who arrived on American soil energized their new country with a prayer culture born from centuries of ritual and practice, complementing rather than duplicating earlier Protestant traditions. Socially, economically, and religiously, lines were being drawn, and with such dramatic transformations taking place, deep-seated prejudices were forming.

While prayers continued to be recited in classrooms, the strong emphasis on prayer that had been so much a part of *The New England Primer* and *McGuffey's Readers* had begun to ebb by the late nineteenth century. Parochial schools with their own prayer traditions began to spring up among Catholic, Jewish, and some Protestant, mainly Episcopalian, congregations.

WHILE THE IMPACT OF MILLIONS of immigrants was altering the country's spiritual landscape forever, the established religious and intellectual elite of the United States was also being influenced. Throughout the closing decades of the nineteenth century, more native-born Americans than ever were leaving the country to travel, work, and study abroad. American students from well-to-do families were enticed to acquire college degrees in England and France, and their parents, siblings, and friends often joined them for extended vacations. More adventurous souls, like Christian missionaries and journalists, expanded their horizons far beyond Europe to Asia, Africa, the Middle East, and Latin America.

Returning to the United States, these individuals could not help but be changed by their unusual experiences. Visiting cathedrals and ancient ruins; encountering new peoples, languages, and religious faiths; and generally discovering venues beyond the virtual parameters of the United States had a profound impact.

Against this backdrop, one of the extraordinary events in the religious history of America and the world took place in Chicago during the 1893 World's Fair. From May until September 1893 the Columbian Exposition became a spectacular showcase for the city of Chicago and the United States as the country commemorated the four hundredth anniversary of Christopher Columbus's arrival in the New World and showed the enormous progress it had made since the settlement of the first Europeans.

George W. Ferris, a Pittsburgh bridge builder, debuted his Ferris wheel. The Czech composer Antonín Dvořák premiered his *New World Symphony*, after spending months immersing himself in the spiritual expressions of Native Americans and African-Americans, while John Philip Sousa played his marches and Scott Joplin performed his ragtime music. Products like Shredded Wheat, Pabst beer, Aunt Jemima syrup, carbonated soda, hamburgers, and Juicy Fruit gum were introduced to the public for the first time. Hundreds of thousands of people attended the exposition each day, transfixed by America's technological advances and the promise they held for the future.

Meanwhile, several civic and religious leaders believed that the time was ripe to bring together representatives from the world's religions to conduct an interfaith dialogue. For the organizers it was a daring move. Nonetheless, the World Parliament of Religions became a reality in September 1893 as delegates representing Protestant denominations, Roman Catholicism, Orthodox Christianity, and Judaism joined representatives of such exotic faiths to nineteenth-century America as Islam, Buddhism, Hinduism, Jainism, Shintoism, Zoroastrianism, and the newly established Bahaism, which brought together within one creed a variety of religious traditions. Only the Baptists refused to send a delegate, to protest against the fair's being open on Sundays, while the Mormons were refused entry because of their practice of polygamy. It was an amazing gathering. In the words of the American religious scholar Martin E. Marty, it turned out to be "the most elaborate display of religious cosmopolitanism yet seen on the continent."[24]

While individuals like Julia Ward Howe spoke eloquently at the parliament and American clergymen offered moving ecumenical prayers, the clerics from Asia created the greatest stir. For the first time, American audiences were learning about the fundamentals of Eastern religions. Anagarika Dharmapala, who had traveled from Sri Lanka, then known as Ceylon, fascinated everyone as he spoke of the beginnings of a faith that had existed, as he put it, "six centuries before Jesus of Nazareth walked over the plains of Galilee."[25] He then introduced the meditation practices of Zen Buddhism, a truly unique experience for his American audience.

The spiritual figure who left the most lasting impression, however, was Swami Vivekananda, who had traveled for almost two months from his native Calcutta, India. In a speech that began "Sisters and Brothers of America" to thunderous applause, Vivekananda placed Hinduism in a context readily understood by his American audience. He spoke of the origins of Hinduism, always respectful of his largely Christian listeners. His references to God and to divine love, however, hit the greatest chord. In speaking of Krishna, whom the Hindus believe to have been God incarnate on earth, he explained that each person must entrust "his heart to God and his hands to work."[26] It was not unlike the creed of America's Shakers.

He then spoke about the love of God by admonishing his audience, "It is good to love God for hope of reward in this or the next world, but it is better to love God for love's sake." He illustrated his point by offering the prayer: "Lord, I do not want wealth, nor children, nor learning. If it be thy will I will go to a hundred hells, but grant me this, that I may love thee without hope of reward—unselfishly love for love's sake." To the seven thousand people assembled, he ended his remarks with an invocation. It was a prayer that he had repeated every day of his life, as indeed millions of other Hindus continued to do as well. It read simply, "As the different streams having their sources in different places all mingle their water in the sea, Oh, Lord, so the different paths which men take through different tendencies, various though they appear, crooked or straight, all lead to Thee."[27]

His remarks reverberated well beyond Chicago and became the single greatest catalyst in laying the roots for Hinduism in the United States. The World Parliament of Religions had opened doors to the prayers of other religious cultures, doors that would remain open forever.

THE GROWING FASCINATION for things foreign and the evangelical desire to spread Christianity to remote regions around the globe inspired several thousand men and women to missionary work. In the same way that the Wesley brothers, George Whitefield, and other clergymen had traveled from Europe to the New World to preach their faith to the colonists and to Native Americans, Christian Americans now believed it was their duty, if not their destiny, to bring the Gospel to cultures that had never heard of Jesus Christ or the God of Jacob.

The U.S. government helped pave the way for those American missionaries by exerting its influence on the high seas. As each new ship was commissioned before gathered dignitaries, servicemen, and invited guests, an officiating clergyman would invoke a prayer. First recited in the Philadelphia Shipyard in 1843, the same prayer with slight variations would be said to commission all new ships up to the modern day:

> O Eternal God . . . may the vessels of our Navy be guarded by Thy gracious Providence and care. May they not bear the sword in vain, but as the minister of God, be a terror to those who do evil and a defense to those who do well. Graciously bless the officers and men of our Navy. May love of country be engraven on their hearts and may their adventurous spirits and severe toils be duly appreciated by a grateful nation. May their lives be precious in Thy sight, and if ever our ships of war should be engaged in battle, grant that their struggles may be only an enforced necessity for the defense of what is right. Bless all nations and kindreds on the face of the earth and hasten the time when the principles of holy religion shall so prevail that none shall wage war any more for the purpose of aggression, and none shall need it as a means of defense. All of which blessings we ask through the merits of Jesus Christ our Lord. Amen.[28]

Under direct orders from President Millard Fillmore in the summer of 1853, Commodore Matthew C. Perry had led a fleet of four U.S. ships to open diplomatic and trade relations between the United States and the Tokugawa shogunate of Japan. As a consequence, Japan's self-imposed isolation quickly came to an end. Soon the tales of Perry's voyage were published throughout the United States and Europe, stirring the imaginations of missionaries, business entrepreneurs, and just plain adventurers.

Thanks to the financial support of wealthy businessmen such as Rockefeller, Wanamaker, and McCormick, American missionaries were able to take their message to Japan, China, India, and Africa. The Lord's Prayer and other prayer tracts were now being printed in the thousands for potential foreign converts. Both the conduct of the missionaries' work overseas and the impact these experiences had on them after they returned to the United States are important in understanding the political, social, and spiritual dynamics that evolved.

No tale is more revealing of the times or more intertwined with both the Christian faith and the culture of American prayer than the history of Hawaii. Discovered by England's Captain James Cook in 1778 and visited by U.S. trading vessels on their way to the Far East a few years later, the islands, originally called the Sandwich Islands, were united by King Kamehameha in 1810. Nine years later his son succeeded him, abolished the native religion of Hawaii, and encouraged American Protestant missionaries to settle and convert his subjects to Christianity, drawing his country even closer to the outside world.

The Protestant faith, Congregationalism in particular, soon dominated Hawaii. Its influence had become so strong by the late 1820s that newly arriving Catholics were either imprisoned or forced to leave the islands, a situation that changed only after France threatened to invade Hawaii over the issue. By the mid-nineteenth century, American businessmen had followed the missionaries across the Pacific, settling and working the Hawaiian plantations. To offset the growing influence of American expatriates, the urbane King Kamehameha IV, who had traveled extensively throughout Europe in his youth with his brother, invited the Church of England to establish a presence on the islands, and he and his wife became devout Anglicans.

Both the King and his wife, Queen Emma, took great pride in practicing and promoting their Christian faith. While the Queen spent much of her time involved in charitable efforts, the King personally translated the entire *Book of Common Prayer* and many devotional hymns from English to Hawaiian, an extraordinary achievement.

With the King's death in 1863 at the age of twenty-nine, months after his only child, Prince Albert, had died of infant meningitis, Hawaii was plunged into turmoil for almost three decades. Short-lived as it was, some sense of tranquillity returned when Hawaii's last monarch, the dignified and religious Queen Liliuokalani, ascended the throne in 1891. Educated as a girl by U.S. missionaries and fluent in English like her predecessors from a young age, the fifty-two-year-old Queen faced her own personal trials after her husband, John Owen Dominis, the son of a Boston sea captain, died within months of her coming to power. Fiercely proud of her Hawaiian roots, she set out to find ways to return her country to its unique heritage, minimizing the influence of the powerful American interests that had come to dominate the islands.

Not long after her consort's death, the Queen was used as a pawn by different interest groups in a complicated, volatile game that by 1893 had led to her being imprisoned in her palace. During her eight-month imprisonment, Queen Liliuokalani occupied herself largely by reading and praying, but she also passed time by knitting an intricate quilt made from the fabric of her ball gowns, and composing lyrics that she put to music. The Hawaiian anthem "Aloha Oe" (Farewell to Thee) was her most famous composition, a work that she embroidered and sent to Grover Cleveland as a present for his second inaugural. An equally enduring composition was her heartfelt prayer set to music that spoke to her captors, to her Hawaii, and to her God. She also composed this invocation during her captivity:

O! kou aloha no,	Lord, thy loving mercy,
Aiaika lani,	Is high as the heavens,
Ao kou oiaia	It tells us of thy truth,
He hemolele hoi.	And 'tis filled with holiness.
Kou noho mihi ana	Whilst humbly meditating
A paahao ia	Within these walls imprisoned
Ooe kuu lama	Thou art my light, my haven
Kou nani kou koo.	Thy glory my support.
Mai nana ino ino.	Oh! Look not on their failings
Na hewa o kanaka	Nor on the sins of men
Aka e huikala	Forgive with loving kindness
A maemae no.	That we might be made pure.

No laila e ka Haku	For thy grace I beseech thee
Malalo kou eheu	Bring us neath thy protection
Ko makou maluhia	And peace will be our portion
A mau loa aku no. Amene.	Now and forever more. Amen.[29]

Queen Liliuokalani, who died in 1917 at the age of seventy-nine, forgave those settlers who had wronged her, and was a staunch supporter of the United States in its entry into World War I. Her influence among Hawaiians lasted for generations.

While most missionaries to Hawaii had conversion on their minds, some wanted to serve both the spiritual and the temporal needs of the Hawaiian people. No one was more selfless than Father Joseph De Veuster, known as Father Damien. Born and raised in Belgium, he told friends after learning about the Pacific islands that he believed his destiny was tied to performing missionary work in the far-off land. After some resistance, Damien's Bishop gave him permission to settle in Hawaii after his ordination in 1864. From the day he arrived, Damien was drawn to the stories he heard about the colony of several hundred lepers, victims of Hansen's disease, who lived on the island of Molokai. An indescribable death for all of them was only a matter of time.

After persistent requests to Hawaii's Catholic Bishop Louis Désiré Maigret, Father Damien was finally given permission in 1873, after turning thirty-three, to live out the rest of his life by ministering to the colony. Upon his arrival, he was overwhelmed by the conditions of the people, most of whom had never seen a medical doctor. His greatest struggle, and in the end his greatest success, would come in removing the fear of death from these dispossessed lepers. As he wrote in his journal: "From morning till night I am in the midst of physical and moral miseries which rend my heart. Nevertheless, I endeavor to show myself always cheerful, that I may raise the courage of the weak. I place death before their eyes as the end of all their evil."[30] Believing that prayer was fundamental to their spiritual and mental health, Father Damien worked with members of the colony to form prayer groups and choirs. Soon Bishop Maigret and the nuns of the diocese provided him with dozens of musical instruments and reams of sheet music for various hymns.

Predictably, Father Damien eventually contracted the disease, an affliction that instilled in him an even greater faith in God, a more intense prayer life, and a spiritual intimacy with his fellow lepers. Within five years he was dead.

The Scottish novelist Robert Louis Stevenson, who first brought Father Damien's story to the outside world, learned of his deeds during his South Seas travels. Ten years after it became the fiftieth state, Hawaii gave a statue of Father Damien to be erected in the U.S. Capitol to remind other Americans of his personal sacrifice.

THE EVENTS IN HAWAII and the onset of the Spanish-American War in 1898 that led to the annexation of the Philippines troubled some Americans. William Randolph Hearst, the formidable newspaper publisher, was a major instigator in fanning the flames of war to sell his newspapers from coast to coast. Ruthless in many ways, Hearst nonetheless believed in God. While he was recovering from an illness at his massive estate, San Simeon, in California, a friend came to visit and found an embossed prayer on Hearst's nightstand that read, "No one should die without a prayer on his lips." When the friend approvingly pointed it out to him, Hearst rejoined, "No one should live without a prayer on his lips."[31]

The thrill of the publishing hunt, however, meant the most to Hearst. Having been sent to Cuba in 1897 to find and etch a few "war drawings" for Hearst's newspapers, the famous illustrator and sculptor Frederic Remington cabled from Havana: "Everything is quiet <STOP> There is no trouble here <STOP> There will be no war <STOP> I wish to return <STOP>." In response Hearst wrote, "Please remain <STOP> You furnish the pictures and I'll furnish the war <STOP>."[32]

Hearst had successfully tapped into the country's growing appetite for war with Spain, culminating in the mysterious explosion of the U.S. battleship *Maine* in Havana harbor on February 15, 1898. Although the Spanish-American War officially lasted only from April until December 1898, it established the United States as a growing military presence in a world long dominated by European powers. The tales that emerged from the conflict would become part of American folklore.

A U.S. commander who had served in Cuba during the war, General Curtis Guild, Jr., described an incident that occurred when the Seventh Army Corps was dug into the hills surrounding Havana on Christmas Eve, 1898. An eerie silence filled the air until a sentinel from Iowa's Forty-ninth called out the traditional "Number ten: twelve o'clock and all is well!" It was then that an unexpected voice rang out from another direction, singing the familiar "How Firm a Foundation." Soon American soldiers from the Sixth Missouri and the Fourth Virginia joined the troops from Iowa, literally hundreds of men, singing the hymn as though they were part of some massive military choir.[33]

"How Firm a Foundation" had long been an American favorite. While the lyrics have been attributed to three different men, they first appeared in John Rippon's *A Selection of Hymns from the Best Authors* in 1787 in London. The melody was an early American folk tune most likely from the South. Friends of Andrew Jackson remembered the former President's genuine affection for the hymn and how in retirement he asked that it be played daily at the Hermitage. It was the last hymn he heard the day he died. General Robert E. Lee left instructions that it be performed at his funeral, while President Theodore Roosevelt, the hero of San Juan Hill during the Spanish-American War, considered it "just about my favorite hymn of all."[34] For a country in the midst of war, the hymn exuded spiritual rigor from beginning to end:

> *How firm a foundation, ye saints of the Lord,*
> *Is laid for your faith in his excellent word!*
> *What more can he say than to you he hath said?*
> *To you who for refuge to Jesus have fled?*
>
> *Fear not I am with thee, O be not dismayed,*
> *For I am thy God, and will give thee aid;*
> *I'll strengthen thee, help thee, and cause thee to stand,*
> *Upheld by my righteous, omnipotent hand.*[35]

With Admiral George Dewey soundly defeating the Spanish fleet at the Battle of Manila Bay in the Philippines on May 1, 1898, the war was officially over by Christmas. After the decisive victory, President William McKinley addressed a meeting of fellow Methodists, taking the opportunity to share his motivations for leading the country into war and rationalizing the conflict as an extension of America's desire to spread the foundations of Western civilization, democracy, and Christianity to people everywhere:

I am not ashamed to tell you, gentlemen, that I went down on my knees and prayed Almighty God for light and guidance more than one night. And one night late it came to me this way . . . There was nothing left for us to do but to take them all and to educate the Filipinos and uplift and civilize and Christianize them and by God's grace do the very best we could by them, as our fellow men for whom Christ also died. And then I went to bed and went to sleep and slept soundly.[36]

Despite the brevity of the war, the impact on the United States was profound, prompting Americans to view their country in ways they had never imagined. No one had a more vitriolic reaction to what he saw as the uncontrolled appetite for American expansion than Samuel Clemens, better known as Mark Twain. Long an icon in American letters, Twain had never been deeply religious. In fact, he wrote more prose skewering religion, churches, and zealots than praising them—even though he believed that his greatest work was his novel about a fifteenth-century French saint, *Personal Recollections of Joan of Arc.*[37] But he reserved his greatest disdain for the extraterritorial ambitions of the country's leaders, readily tweaking those "corrupt" forces through the power of his pen.

Twain held special contempt for William McKinley, whom he viewed as a "sleazy political manipulator."[38] To vent his mounting frustration, he wrote a short story, dripping with sarcasm, called "The War Prayer." It is the tale of a town preparing to send its young men to war. While patriotic fervor is at its most frenzied, the townspeople gather at their church to pray for a decisive victory. As the officiating minister is about to end the service, he and the congregation are startled when an "aged man" appears dramatically in the vestibule of the church. Slowly walking down the aisle, the stranger announces that he is a messenger from God. Turning to face his spellbound audience, the man asks them whether they fully understand what they are asking of God. With the congregation frozen in their pews, he then delivers his own prayer, underscoring the consequences and serious, unintended impact that would follow victory.

Immediately after reciting his prayer, the stranger departs as mysteriously as he has appeared. In the end the congregation agrees that the old man "was a lunatic because there was no sense in what he said."[39] For Twain, however, the message was clear: the American people did not fully comprehend the actions of their leaders.

Finding the work to be cathartic, Mark Twain filed away "The War

Prayer." In the spring of 1905, however, almost a decade after the Spanish-American War had ended, he had a change of heart. Consequently, he submitted the piece to *Harper's Bazaar,* the magazine owned by Harper and Brothers, the publishing house with which he had an exclusive contract. After reading the short story, the editors immediately rejected it, explaining that it was inappropriate for a woman's magazine. Privately, the editors believed that if they published Twain's biting attack on U.S. foreign policy, his public image would be tarnished and his other literary works would languish on bookstore shelves.

Mark Twain's friends had similar concerns about "The War Prayer," and finally Twain locked it away for good in a back desk drawer. Even those who had known of the story forgot about it until after his death in 1910, when it was found among his personal possessions. With World War I raging in Europe and with debate at a heated frenzy in the United States over whether the country should get involved, *Harper's Weekly* finally published the short story in 1916. "The War Prayer" became Mark Twain's emotional commentary from beyond the grave and was used decades later by American critics of other wars.

AS ENORMOUS DEMOGRAPHIC SHIFTS were taking place and the country's intellectuals were displaying a spiritual restlessness, political leaders held steady in advancing prayer as a vital part of America's future. Grover Cleveland, the only President to serve two nonconsecutive terms, was a case in point. The son of a Presbyterian minister, he was named after his father's predecessor at a church in Caldwell, New Jersey, the Reverend Stephen Grover. Obliged as a boy to attend not only two services on Sundays when his father preached but also Wednesday evening prayer services, Cleveland had a strong appreciation for prayer. The Cleveland household was so devout, in fact, that his oldest sister, Anna, became a missionary in Ceylon, modern-day Sri Lanka, and his brother William, an ordained Presbyterian minister, married Cleveland and his fiancée, Frances Folsom, in the only presidential wedding ever held in the Executive Mansion.

At the age of thirty-five, Cleveland faced the most serious personal and political crisis of his career. As a bachelor, he had begun dating Maria Halpin, a thirty-three-year-old widow who had moved to Buffalo, New York, where Cleveland was practicing law. A little more than a year after they met, Halpin delivered a baby boy, naming Cleveland as the father.

Realizing that she had enjoyed several intimate relationships with other men, he questioned the paternity of the child but in the end accepted responsibility and paid for the child's care. After Halpin was institutionalized for mental instability and the young boy had to be placed in an orphanage, the *Buffalo Evening Telegraph* ran the entire story on its front page, with the headline "A Terrible Tale—Dark Chapter in Public Man's History," just as Cleveland was running for President in 1884.

His opponents reveled in the scandal, chanting, "Ma, Ma, Where's My Pa? Gone to the White House, Ha, Ha, Ha!," and Cleveland decided to be as open as possible about the entire affair. Astonished by his candor, the electorate narrowly voted him into office. Shaken to the core by the incident, Cleveland later confided in his memoirs that prayer had been a life-altering force for him, particularly in those difficult days.[40] Continuing the tradition of his predecessors in calling for the observance of Thanksgiving, Cleveland went one step further. Rather than suggesting that Americans offer their gratitude to God for the blessings of the past year, he directed, "On that day let all secular business be suspended, and let people assemble in their usual places of worship and with prayer and songs of praise devoutly testify their gratitude to the Giver of Every Good and Perfect Gift." His presidential proclamation was replete with references to the need for setting aside one day of the year to give thanks to God and to find ways for families to reunite." It was a directive that came as close as any to capturing the essence of the holiday.[41]

Cleveland's immediate successor and political adversary, whom he would later defeat in 1892, was the pious Benjamin Harrison, grandson of President William Henry Harrison. Like Cleveland, Harrison belonged to the Presbyterian Church and from his earliest days had supported the activities of his local church. He practically grew up on prayer meetings, and his mother reinforced in all of her five children the need to pray throughout the day, always ending with a silent prayer. On being elected President, he issued an executive order that no government business would be conducted on Sundays unless an emergency arose.

When Harrison moved into the Executive Mansion, so did his father-in-law, the Reverend John Scott, a Presbyterian minister, who held morning prayer services for the First Family after breakfast each day. Completely absorbed in his faith, Harrison issued a record eight presidential proclamations for national days of thanksgiving and prayer between 1889 and 1891. As his first term was coming to an end, however, he was beset by policy setbacks and refrained from issuing any further declarations, blunting criticism that his prayer proclamations were made for political advantage.

In the midst of a bruising reelection battle, Harrison was also dealing with his wife, Caroline's, tuberculosis, which took her life just two weeks before the election. Facing the double blows of his wife's death and his subsequent defeat at the polls, he would later credit prayer with having kept him afloat both spiritually and psychologically.[42]

William McKinley, the man whom Mark Twain vilified, seemed to personify the country's mood in the latter part of the nineteenth century. In reality, McKinley was not quite the villain Twain made him out to be. Born a Methodist, he first professed his faith at the age of ten in a prayer revival in Poland, Ohio, and was known to his friends and adversaries alike as a genuinely pious man.

On the evening of his election in 1896, when it appeared he would win handily over William Jennings Bryan, giddy supporters tracked him down at the home of his elderly mother, Nancy McKinley. There they found the President and his wife, Ida, kneeling in prayer next to his mother. Dressed in white lace and a black dress not unlike Whistler's mother, Nancy McKinley was heard to pray, "Oh, God, keep him humble!"[43] McKinley did not disappoint his mother, choosing at his swearing-in to place his hand on the passage of the Bible that read, "Give me now wisdom and knowledge, that I may go out and come in before this people: for who can judge this Thy people, that is so great?"[44]

Determined to carry his religious devotion into the Executive Mansion to offset the pressures of office, McKinley invited friends and special guests to the Blue Room on Sunday evenings, where he or a visiting clergyman would lead everyone in singing hymns, followed by a light supper. No matter what program had been planned, the President always included his two favorite hymns, "Nearer, My God, to Thee" and "Lead, Kindly Light," in the service.

Reelected with ease in 1900, the President had long intended to attend the Pan-American Exposition in Buffalo, New York, the plans for which had been in the making for several years. A spectacular success from its opening day, the exposition attracted more than eight million visitors as it displayed the latest technology and scientific advances of the country. Arriving at the fair on September 5, 1901, McKinley addressed an enthusiastic, standing-room-only crowd in the newly constructed hall known as the Temple of Music. In his speech, coming at the dawn of the new century, McKinley ended his remarks with an allusion to the hand of Divine Providence: "Our earnest prayer is that God will graciously vouchsafe prosperity, happiness, and peace to all our neighbors, and like blessings to all the peoples and powers of earth."[45]

Those would be his last public words.

As he left the stage, McKinley greeted the well-wishers who mobbed him. One of the individuals who rushed the President was the twenty-eight-year-old son of Polish immigrants, Leon F. Czolgosz. An unemployed mill worker from Michigan, Czolgosz was an avowed anarchist who had long suffered from clinical depression. His local Polish priest in Detroit had tried to work with him, even joining him in prayer to overcome his demons, but in the end he would have none of it. Incorrectly believing that he had contracted syphilis and had only a few months to live, he decided to take the President of the United States with him.[46] Although he misfired his first shot, the second hit the President at point-blank range. Falling backward, and with hysterical confusion all around him, McKinley called out for the people around him not to harm his assailant.

For more than a week McKinley lingered between life and death, undergoing two operations to remove the fatal bullet that had torn into several of his organs. His physicians worked around the clock to save his life, noting that each time the President regained consciousness he would recite the Lord's Prayer over and over again. As he edged into his final relapse, McKinley spoke out softly but firmly, "It is God's way. His will, not ours, be done."[47] With that, one of the attending physicians checked his pulse and officially pronounced the death of the nation's twenty-fifth President. Theodore Roosevelt, McKinley's forty-two-year-old Vice President, who had rushed to be with him at his bedside, was then sworn in to office as the youngest President in the nation's history.

BY THE END OF THE NINETEENTH CENTURY, America's unfettered sense of optimism seemed to have no bounds, and the prayer culture reflected those times. Even as prayer continued to mature in content and purpose, it grew even more deeply embedded, becoming an inextricable part of the country's increasing presence on the world stage.

CHAPTER 10

THE IDEALISTS

1900–1920

Where our fathers went into their closets to pray, we go into our laboratories to experiment and into our factories to create. When the drought came they prayed for rain. We replant the denuded mountain slopes, and the rain comes. When pestilence threatened, they cried to God for healing. We diagnose the cause of the disease and apply the appropriate remedy. Thus slowly but surely man's control over nature is increasing, and his need for prayer, in the older sense of that term, has grown correspondingly less.

—William Adams Brown, *The Life of Prayer in a World of Science*, 1927

*B*Y THE TURN OF THE TWENTIETH CENTURY, which historians later referred to as the "American century," the United States had become a transforming global force. Unabashed confidence and idealism were in the air. Due partly to American invention, creativity, and entrepreneurship, a whole new world was born. Electric lights, the telephone, the automobile, electric locomotives, the radio, and modern photography had come into popular use in little more than a generation. German émigré Emile Berliner had helped to perfect commercial production of the phonograph record after his historic recitation in 1888 of the Lord's Prayer on the first flat disc of its kind ever. The two sons of a Bishop of the United Brethren in Christ Church in Dayton, Ohio, Wilbur and Orville Wright, successfully flew for the first time a plane heavier than air at Kitty Hawk, North Carolina, in 1903, defying the notion that human beings were not meant to fly.

The impact of such advances was affecting American prayer as well, particularly as it was practiced by the country's mainline Protestants. Having solved some of the mysteries of the cosmos that had eluded human capacity for millennia, the country's intellectuals brimmed with confidence. If advances in science and technology had revealed so much in such little time, it only seemed to follow that humans could ultimately surmount any obstacle. These increasingly voluble voices believed that their forefathers' intense devotion to Divine Providence was anachronistic, simplistic, and, in the end, misplaced. L. Frank Baum, the author of the wildly successful *The Wonderful Wizard of Oz*, referred to the period as "the Age of Unbelief," contending that many Americans were turning away from the tenets of organized religion to probe for themselves the true essence of universal spirituality.[1] Only 40 percent of the population identified themselves with an established church, but that figure would later climb dramatically.[2]

While those who had lost faith in traditional religion saw prayer as their sole spiritual outlet, others found even prayer to be tough going. As George Coe, the eminent theologian from Northwestern University, reflected at the time:

> Nothing more clearly shows the drift of religion in our days than the differences between the way we pray and the way our father's prayed. The contrast is not a slight one. They agonized in prayer. They wrestled with God. They stormed the gates of heaven, and by sheer violence of desire seized upon the promises and made them a personal possession. We pray for far less assertiveness, with far less confidence in the power of prayer to work specific, tangible effects in the world about us. We question and hesitate where they simply believed . . . There is something in our modern modes of thought, our modern attitudes toward religious problems, that involves hesitance and confusion with respect to prayer.[3]

No individual grappled more with this new dynamic than William James. A year older than his brother the great novelist Henry James, William grew up in a wealthy household, where his father, Henry senior, had the reputation for being a rather brilliant but eccentric theologian. Adhering to the Swedenborgian philosophy of "the law of correspondences," devised by the eighteenth-century Swedish mystic and scientist

Emanual Swedenborg, Henry senior firmly believed that there was a visible and an invisible dimension to the universe. Only through prayer could men and women experience the essence of the great unseen, what Swedenborg called the "divine realm," and in turn find their destined path toward full union with God.

Like the sons and daughters of so many ministers and educators who came of age during and after the Civil War, William James attempted to define universal truths in his own unique way. Originally trained as a physician, he was drawn to philosophy while a student at Harvard. An ardent believer in the theory of evolution, he became his generation's foremost proponent of pragmatism, the theory that there is no absolute in people's lives as they tackle day-to-day existence. Rather, James argued, the individual's unique perceptions and experiences allowed him or her to succeed. Human existence is in essence a subjective proposition, each person finding his or her own path to happiness. Organized religion was effectively being superseded by a kind of expressive individualism.

Arguably his greatest contribution came in the 1902 publication of *The Varieties of Religious Experience*. In this groundbreaking work, he edited a series of lectures he had delivered in Edinburgh, Scotland, to explore what he called the "psychology of religion." He wanted to show how individual religious experience, not the tenets of traditional religion, became the basis for all spiritual life. By extension, he believed that prayer in its broadest sense was "the very soul and essence of religion." "We hear, in these days of scientific enlightenment, a great deal of discussion about the efficacy of prayer; and many reasons are given us why we should not pray, whilst others are given us why we should. But in all this very little is said of the reason why we *do* pray, which is simply that we cannot *help* praying. It seems probable that, in spite of all that 'science' may do to the contrary, men will continue to pray to the end of time."[4]

If belief in the Almighty and in prayer benefits an individual, James argued, then he or she should pursue that relationship. "The exercise of prayer in those who habitually exert it, must be regarded by us doctors as the most adequate and normal of all pacifiers of the mind and calmer of the nerves," he wrote.[5]

James was trying to analyze prayer, religion, and human beings on the proverbial psychiatrist's couch in a way no one had ever done. At a time when many Americans were spiritually adrift, experiencing a loss of faith in the maturing industrial age, he helped to make religion and even mystical experiences more acceptable by mingling science and religion in profoundly novel ways.

IF ONE WERE TO READ only the writings of James and his followers during this period, one might conclude that organized religion was on a slippery slope to oblivion and that prayer seemed to hold more questions than answers. Indeed, orthodoxy on America's campuses was being transformed in part due to this increasing religious pragmatism. With so many scholars in academia exploring new theoretical worlds, it seemed as though religion had taken a permanent backseat to other academic endeavors. That was not quite the case, however, as religious devotion continued to hold sway on college campuses.

Hymn books and sheet music that spoke to the unique religious traditions of each school were now being specially printed for colleges. Almost every institution of higher learning that had opened its doors by the turn of the century was having students memorize some hymn or prayer distinctive to the school. Although attendance at daily chapel services was no longer mandatory in most cases, as it had been for America's Founding Fathers, "chapel" remained the spiritual heartbeat of most college campuses. Consequently, college hymns and prayers would be sung or recited for vespers or Sunday morning services as well as at larger commencement ceremonies. Like the cheers and songs for alma mater and the gridiron, prayer helped classmates to forge lifelong bonds.

In the case of Harvard, the Latin professor James Bradstreet wrote the words to the school's hymn "Deus Omnium Creator" in 1894.[6] Rather than write English lyrics to the equivalent of "O God, Omnipotent Creator," he wanted to embody the college's classical traditions. By combining his lyrics with an 1862 melody composed by John Knowles Pain, Harvard's first appointed music professor, Bradstreet was bringing together the traditions of Harvard since its founding by the Puritans.

The "Rutgers Prayer" was a bit more accessible to the community, and more representative of college hymns generally, as it emotively asked for God's daily help. Written around the same time as the Harvard hymn and memorably arranged later by the Rutgers professor F. Austin Walter, the piece held a special place in campus life:

We, men of Rutgers, bow in prayer, to ask Thy blessing, loving care,
provision for our many needs, Thy guidance in our daily deeds.
Protect us, God, as we go on to meet the challenge of the dawn.

We, men of Rutgers, turn to Thee to make our hearts beat pure and free,
To see the glimmer of the Light that leads men into paths of right.
As we trudge old Rutgers sod, keep us ever near Thee God.[7]

Traditional colleges were not the only educational institutions to develop their own hymns and prayers. The country's military academies at West Point and Annapolis had long instilled a sense of both national and religious destiny through their songs and prayers. At the U.S. Military Academy at West Point, founded on the banks of the Hudson River in 1802 during the Jefferson administration, prayer had always played an important role in a cadet's life. "God of Our Fathers," known to many as the "National Hymn" when it was composed for the country's centennial celebration, was adopted by the academy as its own.

By 1920 the Reverend Clayton Wheat, the head chaplain and chairman of the academy's English department, had written a prayer for cadets that he hoped would have staying power and meaning, as though it had "come naturally from the lips of young men." Approved by West Point's Commandant Douglas MacArthur, it became a prayer that future army men and women would learn by heart and take with them into battlefields overseas. It was even recited as the last words of dying soldiers:

> *O God, our Father, Thou Searcher of men's hearts,*
> *help us to draw near to Thee in sincerity and truth.*
> *May our religion be filled with gladness and*
> *may our worship of Thee be natural.*
>
> *Strengthen and increase our admiration*
> *for honest dealing and clean thinking,*
> *and suffer not our hatred of hypocrisy*
> *and pretense ever to diminish . . .*
>
> *Make us to choose the harder right*
> *instead of the easier wrong, and never to*

be content with a half truth when the
whole truth can be won . . .

Help us to maintain the honor of the
Corps untarnished and unsullied and to
show forth in our lives the ideals of West
Point in doing our duty to Thee and to our Country.

All of which we ask in the name of the
great Friend and Master of Men.[8]

Many of the hymns and prayers adopted by the academies became a part of the tradition of the larger armed services as well. A case in point was "Eternal Father," chosen by the United States Naval Academy at Annapolis as its official hymn and in turn adopted by the U.S. Navy. The words had been written by William Whiting, an Englishman, for a young man about to embark for America on the eve of the Civil War. With a tune composed by the Reverend John Bacchus Dykes, a prolific composer and Anglican priest from Cambridge University, "Eternal Father" is one of the most hauntingly beautiful hymns every written:

Eternal Father, Strong to Save
Whose arm hath bound the restless wave,
Who bid'st the mighty Ocean deep
Its own appointed limits keep;
O hear us when we cry to Thee,
For those in peril on the sea . . .

O Trinity of love and power!
Our brethren shield in danger's hour;
From rock and tempest, fire and foe,
Protect them wheresoe'er they go;
Thus evermore shall rise to Thee,
Glad hymns of praise from land and sea.[9]

"Eternal Father" was played at the funerals of President Franklin Roosevelt, a former Assistant Secretary of the Navy, and President John Kennedy, the World War II hero and commander of PT 109.

* * *

WHILE THE DEBATE AMONG the country's intelligentsia over the depth of spirituality in America became fodder for the lecture circuit, in reality a profound transformation was well under way. By 1900 the country's third great religious awakening already had taken root for more than a generation. A variety of forces had been converging. Not only was the largest influx of Catholic and Jewish immigrants from Europe leaving its imprint on the country, but also there was a defining Protestant grassroots movement erupting in rural and in some pockets of urban America, forcefully standing up for the fundamental truths of the Bible.

Auspiciously, the Pentecostal movement was born on January 1, 1901, when Agnes Ozman, a student at the Bethel Bible College in Topeka, Kansas, began to speak in an unknown language that her fellow students thought to be some Chinese dialect. Soon both students and professors concluded that Ozman had been shown God's favor, like Christ's apostles, in receiving the "gift of tongues" from the Holy Spirit to be able to preach the Gospel of Christ. While it was not clear why twentieth-century Christians in America were being chosen to speak in tongues when almost everyone spoke English, the effect was mesmerizing, and the movement spread like wildfire across the country.

Perhaps Pentecostalism's most noteworthy immediate offshoot was the Azusa Street Revival in Los Angeles, which was launched by an African-American named William J. Seymour, who believed he was "God's instrument" chosen to evangelize the city's dispossessed and spiritually needy.[10] Los Angeles, a city of just over 100,000 people—compared with New York City's 3.4 million inhabitants—at the turn of the century, was growing rapidly.[11] Seymour and his Azusa Street Revival were soon breaking down all racial, ethnic, and sexual barriers as people gathered for prayer meetings, raising their arms to God and speaking in tongues. The scene evoked the camp meetings of rural Kentucky and elsewhere more than a hundred years earlier. The newspaper of the revival, *The Apostolic Faith*, reported on its front page, "All over this city, God has been setting homes on fire and coming down and melting and saving and sanctifying and baptizing with the Holy Spirit."[12] This was only one of several religious movements forming at the time, which included the Jehovah's Witnesses, a millennialist sectarian group founded by Charles Taze Russell, who preached, among other things, that only through the

Bible and prayer could men and women be saved in time for the coming of God's Kingdom.

Of all the individuals who commanded center stage during this new religious awakening, none was more colorful or devout than the fundamentalist William Ashley "Billy" Sunday. Born in Ames, Iowa, and launching a career as a pitcher with the Chicago White Stockings, Sunday underwent a religious conversion after his retirement from baseball in 1891. While working with the Young Men's Christian Association in Chicago, he was ordained a minister and found that the more he preached, the larger his audiences grew. Railing against liberalism, alcohol, and humanism, Sunday would contort his body and project a voice that soared across vast halls and churches. His charisma made him a phenomenon, and his audiences loved him. From tent meetings and urban civic halls to the corridors of Congress and World War I army camps, Billy Sunday's message of fire and wrath left an indelible mark on his followers and on future generations of twentieth-century preachers. Often he would admonish his listeners to pray from the heart rather than recite stale prescriptions that held little personal meaning. "Yank some of the groans out of your prayers, and shove in some shouts," he liked to say.[13]

Sunday's signature photograph showed him winding his entire body as if ready to throw a strike over home plate. It was "Billy's way" of "pitching the gospel of Christ and His message on the power of prayer," just as one of his more famous prayers conveyed:

> O Lord,
> give us some coaching
> out at this tabernacle
> so that people
> can be brought home to You.
> Some of them are dying, Lord,
> and we don't want that.
> Lord, have the people play the game of life
> right up to the limit
> so that home runs
> may be scored.[14]

Billy Sunday would be remembered as a genuine American original.

* * *

THE THIRD GREAT AWAKENING was very different from the previous two. With the backdrop of the Industrial Revolution, massive immigration, and cities bulging at the seams, the emphasis shifted from personal to social sin. The ills of modern society—poverty, crime, ignorance, and prejudice—were erupting rapidly.

On the one hand, there were the sins that had been targeted by the Woman's Christian Temperance Union—drinking, gambling, and prostitution. On the other, there were the sins of human neglect during a period when the robber barons provided a striking contrast to the rest of the population, amassing great wealth and privilege with limited scrutiny by anyone. Given the disease, squalor, and hunger of the day, male babies born in 1900 could expect to live an average of 46 years. Traditional institutions were cracking under the social pressures flooding urban centers and rural areas alike. If God's children were to be cared for, they could be helped in the immediate term only by men and women of faith committed to living out their religious principles.

Out of this setting one very simple question for the reform-minded to ask themselves was "What would Jesus do?" A Congregationalist minister, the Reverend Charles Sheldon from Topeka, Kansas, where the Pentecostal movement was born, greatly popularized the spiritual proposition in his 1896 best-selling book, *In His Steps.* During Sheldon's lifetime the book had the second-largest circulation of any book outside the Bible, and it became one of the most published works, translated into more than two dozen languages, of all time.[15]

In its most poignant passage, much like Mark Twain's "War Prayer," a stranger interrupts the Sunday services at a local church, questioning the honesty of the congregation's prayers and hymns:

> What do you Christians mean by following the steps of Jesus? I've tramped through this city for three days trying to find a job, and in all that time I've not had a word of sympathy or comfort except from your minister here, who said he was sorry for me and hoped I would find a job somewhere . . . but what I feel puzzled about is, what is meant by following Jesus? What do you mean when you sing, "I'll go with him all the way"? . . . It seems to me there's an awful lot of trouble in the world that somehow wouldn't exist if all people who sing such songs went and lived them out.[16]

Sheldon's book shook up conservatives and liberals alike by challenging readers to think of prayer as one seamless invocation both inside and outside of church.

Translating lofty thoughts into action became the hallmark of the Reverend Walter Rauschenbusch, one of the most forceful activists of the day, who gave expression and face to the spiritual void created by the Gilded Age. Formidable in advancing this Social Gospel movement, Rauschenbusch confronted every facet of urban plight in the United States. Ordained a Baptist minister, he was the son of a German minister who had immigrated to America a few decades earlier. Having studied in Europe and graduated from the Rochester Theological Seminary, Rauschenbusch had grown into an intellectual of a different sort, committed as much to working in soup kitchens as to writing spiritual treatises.

In his *Prayers of the Social Awakening*, Rauschenbusch categorized his invocations according to social groups, classes, and causes. To read through them is to see the social problems of his time, many of which remain to this day. There are prayers called "Children of the Street" and "Women Who Toil." Others are called "Discoverers and Inventors" and "Artists and Musicians." There is even one titled "On the Harm We Have Done." It was a book that was published to critical acclaim.

The most touching prayer was one Rauschenbusch wrote on behalf of underage children forced to work in sweatshops:

> *Thou great Father of the weak, lay thy hand tenderly on all the little children of the earth and bless them . . . But bless with a sevenfold blessing the young lives whose slender shoulders are already bowed beneath the yoke of toil, and whose glad growth is being stunted forever. Suffer not their little bodies to be sapped, and their minds to be given over to stupidity and the vices of an empty soul. We have all jointly deserved the millstone of thy wrath for making these little ones to stumble and fall. Grant all employers of labor stout hearts to refuse enrichment at such a price. Grant to all the citizens and officers of states, which now permit this wrong the grace of holy anger. Help us to realize that every child of our nation is in very truth our child, a member of our great family. By the Holy Child that nestled in Mary's bosom; by the memories of our own childhood joys and sorrows; by the sacred possibilities that slumber in every child, we beseech thee to save us from killing the sweetness of young life by the greed of gain.* [17]

Through his sharp mind and by example, Rauschenbusch brought to the country a consciousness of urban plight as both a religious and a social responsibility that could not be ignored. Indeed, the salvation of human souls depended on it.

Rauschenbusch's efforts were given greater voice by organizations like the Salvation Army. Through its corps of volunteer soldiers, aided by contributions from thousands of Americans, "God's Army" prayed and preached the Gospel of Jesus while meeting the needs of the less fortunate no matter what their race or creed. One member of the Salvation Army who left a mark beyond the inner city was George Bennard. His work on the streets of America's cities inspired him to compose a hymn that arguably became the most popular gospel song written in the twentieth century. With its publication in 1913, "The Old Rugged Cross" became an instant classic:

> *On a hill far away stood an old rugged cross.*
> *The emblem of suffering and shame;*
> *And I love that old cross where the dearest and best*
> *For a world of lost sinners was slain.*

> *So I'll cherish the old rugged cross*
> *Till my trophies at last I lay down;*
> *I will cling to the old rugged cross*
> *And exchange it some day for a crown.*[18]

"The Old Rugged Cross" soon became the unofficial anthem for the country's social reform movement.

Complementing the Social Gospel of the Protestant establishment was a vigorous advocacy of workers and their rights by the Catholic Church. In his encyclical *Rerum novarum*, Pope Leo XIII strongly rejected socialism while at the same time speaking to the interdependence of capital and labor and calling for social justice among the less fortunate. For such American Catholic social pioneers as Mother Frances Cabrini and Mother Katharine Drexel, both of whom would be named saints of the Church, the message of the encyclical, combined with steadfast, daily prayer, became life's most important prescription.

★ ★ ★

WHILE SOCIAL CHANGE churned forward, an event occurred that was stunning in both detail and scope. There was perhaps no greater symbol of the era or challenge to the notion of human invulnerability than the wrenching saga of the RMS *Titanic*. This single story captured the imagination as few others could.

Built by the British in Belfast to be the flagship of the White Star Line, the *Titanic* was spectacular in design and size. Nothing like it had ever been conceived, let alone built. The forty-six-thousand-ton vessel was launched with great fanfare before a crowd of over 100,000 and immediately billed by the press as nothing less than "unsinkable" and "invincible." Embarking on its maiden voyage to New York City in April 1912, the ship carried passengers from all social and economic classes, a microcosm of America itself. For those passengers traveling third class, the voyage had begun on the docks of Europe, where they attended Mass before boarding, praying for both a safe voyage and a fresh start in America.

From the outset, the crew of the *Titanic* ran on adrenaline, awed by the cutting-edge technology of their floating city and the special and historic role they were playing. Private prayer services were held daily for passengers. Every possible convenience, it seemed, had been made available.

As the ship reached the open seas, however, ominous signs began to appear as radio operators received wires from other ships cautioning the *Titanic* about heavy ice, but, inexplicably, the warnings were ignored. None of the lookouts even had binoculars. When the unthinkable happened and the ship struck the fatal iceberg in the last hour of Sunday, April 14, 1912, all of the assumptions about the ship's structural integrity were shattered.

While some survivors have given contradictory accounts of that fateful night, one of the most vivid descriptions of the liner's last moments entered into the permanent folklore of the *Titanic*. As passengers ran for the all-too-few lifeboats on board, the seven-man orchestra, still dressed in the tuxedos they had worn earlier to entertain the first-class passengers, played light dance music to calm everyone. It was a surreal backdrop to what was taking place. Finally, when it was clear that all hope was now lost, the men began to play the familiar hymn "Nearer, My God, to Thee."

Written by Sarah Flower Adams, a Unitarian, in 1841, "Nearer, My

God, to Thee" was considered one of the finest sets of lyrics from the nineteenth century.[19] It was so popular that it had been set to the music of several composers, including America's Lowell Mason and England's Sir Arthur Sullivan and John Bacchus Dykes. While there is some debate as to which tune was used, those who heard the melody that night knew what they were hearing. Said to have been recited by President McKinley several times in his dying hours, "Nearer, My God, to Thee" had become a mainstay in churches across America, with its brimming optimism of a life hereafter:

> *Nearer, my God, to Thee.*
> *Nearer to Thee!*
> *E'en though it be a cross*
> *That raiseth me;*
> *Still all my song shall be,*
> *Nearer, my God, to Thee,*
> *Nearer to Thee! . . .*
>
> *There let the way appear*
> *Steps unto Heaven;*
> *All that Thou sendest to me*
> *In mercy given;*
> *Angels to beckon me*
> *Nearer, my God, to Thee,*
> *Nearer to Thee!*[20]

After the sinking of the *Titanic*, the hymn gained a special significance for future generations, joined forever, as it was, to one of history's greatest disasters.

WHILE THE COUNTRY'S URBAN CENTERS bulged at the seams with new immigrants and the social ills of a newly industrialized society, Americans spread out across the prairies of the Midwest and over the Rockies to the West. Across the plains, churches were being built at a rapid pace. In the late nineteenth and early twentieth centuries, more than twenty-two hundred prairie churches were built in North Dakota alone.[21] Nevertheless, established churches still needed to find a way to reach out to their American followers.

Through the help of America's philanthropists, major churches were able to tackle the changing demographics of America with chapel cars, also known as prayer or cathedral cars. The Russian Orthodox Church inspired the use of the first chapel cars in America. Priests and laypeople in tsarist Russia found that the only way to reach and administer the sacraments to the Church's followers in the Siberian frontier was to travel directly to them in specially designed railcars.[22] With the transcontinental railroad being completed in 1849 and expanding dramatically in the following years, enterprising ministers and priests pursued this creative way of reaching out to sparsely populated American communities. With names like Herald of Hope, Messenger of Peace, and Emmanuel, thirteen cars were built that could be hooked to other trains and travel to remote areas that lacked churches. Once they reached their destination, they could be detached and serve a community indefinitely.

Although some cars were retrofitted from older models, most were newly built in grand style. The main cabin of the car was designed to serve as the sanctuary. Pews, a pulpit, an altar, and an organ were built in an interior filled with richly engraved mahogany or oak, brass fixtures, and a stove; even stained-glass windows were installed in some cabins. The rest of the car was designed as living quarters for the clergyman and his associates or family. Seeing these spectacular cars for the first time while listening to hymns being played on the organ, people in desolate sawmill and mining towns were in awe.

Boston W. Smith, a Baptist missionary, was primarily responsible for making the chapel car popular in the United States. Known to thousands of children and adults as "Uncle Boston," Smith was unflagging in his determination to launch one of the first cars, Evangel. The prayer composed for the christening of the chapel car succinctly captured Smith's mission:

> Roll on, thou Bright Evangel,
> Go like the flying wind
> Till all shall know of Jesus
> The savior of mankind.[23]

Another Baptist, the Reverend Charles Rust, was the force behind the building of Glad Tidings, a prayer car that toured mainly in the Dakotas, Wisconsin, and Minnesota. On one occasion he found that several young boys had heard about the Lord's Prayer but did not know the words to it. When one of them asked if the minister would write out the Our Father, Rust decided to gather the boys together and with his pen highlighted the prayer in thirty-five Bibles he had on board. After handing them out, he later recounted, "We went through the prayer carefully, word by word. They learned it readily, and in two or three days were able to repeat it from memory."[24] Such experiences only underscored for Rust and others the vital importance of the chapel cars.

The Catholic Church built the most elaborate of the cars and the first steel car of its kind, known as the St. Peter. The Catholic cars were particularly well traveled across the country, and for many Catholic children they offered the only opportunity to receive first Holy Communion.[25]

By the late 1930s, the chapel cars had long proven their worth but were beginning to show their age, soon becoming vestiges of America's past. Today several of these cars still exist, the most famous of them, the Evangel, now integrated into the construction of the First Baptist Church of Rawlins, Wyoming.[26]

WHEREAS AMERICA'S early colonists had taken enormous pride in building plain meetinghouses that served as civic and religious halls, established churches began building magnificent houses of prayer and worship in the Old World tradition to increase their visible presence in the country. The Episcopal Church's Cathedral of St. John the Divine, with the help of John Pierpont Morgan, had long broken ground, becoming second in size only to St. Peter's Basilica in Rome. The magnificent St. Patrick's Cathedral, the seat of the Roman Catholic Archdiocese of New York, had been in operation since the 1890s. The building of Washington National Cathedral, however, captured the ecumenical imagination of the nation.

Referred to as America's "House of Prayer" by its spiritual architects, a national church had originally been conceived by Major Pierre Charles L'Enfant, the chief designer of Washington, D.C., to stand on the space where the Patent Office was ultimately built, equidistantly placed between the Capitol and the White House. In his diary L'Enfant envisioned a church to be built "for national purposes, such as public prayer, thanksgiving, and funeral orations; and be assigned to the special use of no particular denomination or sect, but be equally open to all. It will be likewise a proper shelter for such monuments as were voted by the last

Continental Congress for those heroes who fell in the causes of liberty, and for such others as may hereafter be decreed by the voice of a grateful nation."[27]

With the government cash-strapped after the Revolutionary War and with churches cropping up across the country, the plans to build a house of prayer took a backseat to the construction of basic government facilities. At first, the Capitol and the White House were used for public prayer and religious observances.[28]

In 1891, however, a serious effort was launched to integrate the desire for a national house of worship with the need to erect a cathedral for the newly created Episcopal Diocese of Washington. On January 6, 1893, Congress granted and President Benjamin Harrison signed into law a charter for the Protestant Episcopal Cathedral Foundation of the District of Columbia to build the cathedral.

Five years later, as the Spanish-American War was winding down, contracts for the land, located at the highest point in the upper northwest quadrant of the city, were signed, and the private fund-raising began. The first Episcopal Bishop of Washington, the Reverend Henry Yates Satterlee, was the major force behind the cathedral. He refined L'Enfant's original intent by envisioning Washington's National Cathedral in the following way: "A House of Prayer for all people means not only a house of God where all people are welcome, but where all people can join in a service, in which while they pray with spirit, they pray with understanding also; not only a church where all the congregation sing praises with understanding, but a church which unites every congregation in every place, with people of God of all ages."[29]

When he learned that the Spanish-American War had ended, Satterlee announced that even though the cathedral was not yet built, a thanksgiving service would be held on the open grounds. To commemorate the historic moment, he dedicated a "Cross for Peace" inscribed with the words "That it may please Thee to give all nations unity, peace, and concord; we beseech Thee to hear us, Good Lord!"[30] With the laying of the cornerstone by President Theodore Roosevelt in 1907, construction of the cathedral, known also as the Cathedral Church of St. Peter and St. Paul, began, taking more than eighty years to complete.

When finished, it stood as the sixth-largest cathedral in the world, with its soaring ten-story structure flanked on either side by massive flying buttresses. The artisans of the cathedral installed 215 jewellike stained-glass windows of every imaginable color and mounted some 110 gargoyles along the building's exterior with figures of grotesque monsters and depictions of the famous and the not so famous. Like London's Westminster Abbey and St. Paul's, the cathedral provided a final resting place for some 150 of the country's most famous citizens, including the Spanish-American War hero Admiral George Dewey, President Woodrow Wilson, Secretary of State Cordell Hull, and Helen Keller.

It was at the cathedral that the Reverend Martin Luther King, Jr., gave his last sermon, that clergy and laypeople alike prayed for the souls of America's departed leaders and invoked God's name in times of crisis with the President and his Cabinet, the Supreme Court, and Congress in attendance. It was there that many sacred instrumental and choral works premiered, providing spiritual inspiration for the nation. Indeed, in a tradition that continued into the twenty-first century, annual prayer days were set aside for each of the states and territories, honoring them with individually crafted prayers.

WHILE AMERICA'S CHURCHES were reaching out to both members and prospective members, a trend toward "muscular Christianity" developed. The term had first been used in the mid-nineteenth century by two British novelists, Thomas Hughes and Charles Kingsley, who were concerned that the Anglican Church was becoming too effeminate and tolerant of physical flabbiness. Projecting a strong British presence at home and abroad and building robust physical specimens "to house the holy temples of God" were paramount to salvation, they argued. They believed that men strong in body, mind, and spirit could overcome the world's ills and forge a promising future. This was a man's club; no women were allowed.

Helping to ingrain this philosophy into the fabric of the country was the Young Men's Christian Association, founded by Sir George Williams in London in 1844. Originally intended to engage young men in the pursuit of healthy living, turning them away from drinking and gambling, the YMCA offered athletics, Bible studies, and prayer meetings. It even helped to sponsor several of America's chapel cars.

There simply was no more fertile ground for the YMCA in fostering an environment of muscular Christianity than the United States. Launched in Boston with the aid of the Reverend Lyman Beecher and later financially supported by Philadelphia's John Wanamaker, the association promoted "God in the gym." Through the initiative of the American chapter of the YMCA, the international organization institutionalized an annual week of prayer observance, beginning on the second Sunday of November. By the mid-twentieth century, the YMCA had begun to issue thousands of prayer books each year to commemorate the event.

Throughout the life of the larger movement, prayer remained the nucleus of muscular Christianity, intended to dispel weakness in the American character before God and man. Admiral Alfred Thayer Mahan, arguably the finest naval tactician in American history, saw prayer within muscular Christianity as "inherently a force, demanding energy for its development and manifesting energy in its operation."[31] Indeed, it was even suggested that the country had relied for too long on the overly sentimental prayers and hymns of Ira Sanicey, Fanny Crosby, and others, losing sight of the need to reinforce spiritual mettle through prayer. Even John Philip Sousa wrote stirring, robust compositions like "Power and Glory" and "Songs of Grace and Songs of Glory" in his familiar march time, musical pieces that virtually set prayers on parade.

No one, however, promoted the virtues of spiritual as well as physical vigor more than President Theodore Roosevelt. As the first-elected American President of the twentieth century, he personified "the strenuous life," writing in his autobiography, "I do not like to see young Christians with shoulders that slope like a champagne bottle."[32] Born to a Dutch Reformed father and a Presbyterian mother in 1858, Roosevelt grew up in a religiously vibrant household. While the Roosevelt family attended Sunday services regularly, usually at the Dutch Reformed Church, they also co-hosted weekly prayer meetings with their close friends and neighbors, the Dodges, always singing their favorite hymn, "Shall We Gather at the River?" Roosevelt's father, known to his friends as "Thee," was particularly close with William E. Dodge, scion of a family fortune and a future member of Congress from New York. The two men were fanatical on the subject of muscular Christianity and together helped to finance the growth of the YMCA in New York City and throughout the country.[33]

To help promote the need for greater spiritual vigor, the future President's father even hosted a series of prayer breakfasts for Dwight Lyman Moody. Some people who knew the young Theodore Roosevelt believed that his admiration for Moody, whom he watched closely at those prayer breakfasts, led him to use many of the same arm gestures and the public speaking style that had made Moody so popular. In the end, this kind of home life led Roosevelt to see Christ as a "strong man physically, muscular, sinewy, enduring."[34] Bibles, prayer, and barbells were the perfect formula for a healthy, spiritual life.

Although Roosevelt fervently believed in personal spirituality, he wanted it kept as far away from the government as possible.

While Roosevelt had no problem issuing executive orders for national days of prayer, he did have concerns over the words "In God We Trust" being printed on the country's currency. He even went so far as to have new coins designed that did not include the motto, but Congress would have none of it.

Roosevelt's successor and later adversary, William Howard Taft, was a strong advocate of muscular Christianity as well, despite tipping the scales at almost 350 pounds. Attending All Souls Unitarian Church while serving as President and later chief justice of the Supreme Court, Taft was unable to fit in the pews. Consequently, the church's minister had to find a large enough chair to place in the center aisle for the President's use. What kind of prayer life Taft may have had is open to question, but, like Roosevelt, he issued several proclamations calling for thanksgiving and prayer during his tenure as President.

By THE TIME WORLD WAR I ARRIVED, muscular Christianity had come to be considered a godsend for many Christians. As war clouds in Europe grew darker, the YMCA and other fraternal organizations became even more aggressive in promoting their "religion of the trenches" and portraying the Almighty as "God with guts."[35] Religion and prayer were advanced as instruments of spiritual empowerment in a world gone mad.

As war broke out in Europe, triggered by the assassination in Sarajevo of Archduke Francis Ferdinand, the Crown Prince of Austria, voices bemoaned that the United States would be forced into a conflict thousands of miles away. The distinguished John Haynes Holmes, an ordained Unitarian minister and a founder of both the NAACP and the American Civil Liberties Union, was one of the most outspoken antiwar voices. Having long been an active participant in spreading the Social Gospel, he passionately defended his often unpopular stands and did so in part through his hymns, prayers, and essays.

One of his prayers was written for Peace Sunday, a day organized by

Protestants, Catholics, and Jews across the country to pray for international understanding, with one eye to keeping the United States out of the war. Holmes's composition was one of the first modern prayers written for an interfaith gathering and was later added to the standard *Unitarian Hymn and Tune Book:*

> God of the nations, near and far,
> Ruler of all mankind,
> Bless thou thy peoples as they strive
> The paths of peace to find.
>
> The clash of arms still shakes the sky,
> King battles still with king;
> Wild through the frighted air of night
> The bloody tocsins ring.
>
> But clearer far the friendly speech
> Of scientists and seers,
> The wise debate of statesmen, and
> The shouts of pioneers.
>
> And stronger far the clasped hands
> Of labor's teeming throngs
> Who, in a hundred tongues, repeat
> Their common creeds and songs.
>
> From shore to shore the peoples call
> In loud and sweet acclaim;
> The gloom of land and sea is lit
> With pentecostal flame.
>
> O Father from the curse of war
> We pray thee give release;
> And speed, O speed thy blessed day
> Of justice, love, and peace.[36]

The entire country, which had been split between those who wanted to intervene and those who did not, pulled together once the decision was made to enter the war. Reflecting American solidarity came Irving Berlin's popular song of the time, "Let's All Be Americans Now", with its lyrics "we'll fight if we must," remaining resolute that "still, in God we trust."[37]

WITH THE REALITY OF WAR, America's churches and synagogues banded together to support the country and particularly the boys being shipped overseas. Besides providing chaplains to serve on the high seas and in army trenches, each major church and Jewish denomination published tailor-made devotionals consisting of prayers, Bible readings, and hymns. With tough, durable covers, the prayer books were produced in the thousands, each having a title page that could be inscribed personally for each serviceman by his local minister, priest, or rabbi.

The Lutheran Church printed a prayer book that compiled sixty-five specific devotions with such titles as "For the Success of Our Arms," "Against the Enemies of Our Nation," "Before Battle," and "After Battle."[38] The Chaplain's Aid Association of the Catholic Church published military missals for use at Mass and a separate prayer book that prescribed "A Rule of Life" for servicemen to follow.[39]

The Episcopalians did likewise through the Bishop White Prayer Book Society, their outreach organization that had been founded in Philadelphia in 1833 to distribute the *Book of Common Prayer* and Bibles to poor parishes and missions. Each serviceman was asked to sign a pledge that he would read a portion of the prayer book daily. Like the Lutheran devotional, it was filled with prayers designed to effect a special purpose: "A Prayer in Case of Sudden Surprise and Immediate Danger," "For a Safe Return from the Sea," and "For Those in Training."[40] Every one of the prayer books included a petition to God "for a happy death."

The prayer effort extended even to funding the war as the U.S. Treasury Department urged Americans to buy savings stamps, thrift stamps, and bonds. Posters were plastered on the walls of public and private buildings. One especially popular poster, titled "My Soldier," showed a mother and child just before bedtime with an American banner in red, white, and blue framing the scene. Kneeling, with her head bowed against her mother's lap, the child reverently prays:

> *Now I lay me down to sleep*
> *I pray the Lord my soul to keep.*

> God bless my brother gone to war
> Across the seas, in France, so far.
> Oh, may his fight for Liberty,
> Save millions more than little me
> From cruel fates or ruthless blast,
> And bring him safely home at last.[41]

At the bottom of the poster Americans were urged to buy war savings and thrift stamps, with a reminder that the stamps had a quarterly compound rate of 4 percent.

Popular patriotic and religious songs also were being written to bolster the war effort, sheet music coming off the presses in record numbers. One composition was titled "Let Us Say a Prayer for Daddy":

> In a humble home
> Two hearts alone
> Mother holding babe tenderly
> Tears in mother's eyes
> Babe don't realize
> Daddy's far across the sea . . .
>
> Then with a goodnight kiss
> To baby she'll say this . . .
>
> Let us say a prayer for Daddy
> He is across the sea . . .
> You have never seen him little baby
> Of us he is thinking constantly . . .
>
> Pray that soon he will be with us
> Pray protection for him dear . . .
> Tho' you have your mother with you baby
> Pray that dad will soon be here.[42]

The heartrending story of one of America's most promising writers and poets, Joyce Kilmer, portrayed all too well the utter waste and lasting legacy of the war. Born in New Brunswick, New Jersey, in 1886, Kilmer showed a passion for writing while studying at Rutgers College and Columbia University. At the age of twenty-six, he published what became his most famous poem, "Trees," by far the most widely quoted verse among schoolchildren in the first half of the twentieth century:

> *I think that I shall never see*
> *A poem as lovely as a tree.*
>
> *A tree whose hungry mouth is prest*
> *Against the earth's sweet flowing breast;*
>
> *A tree that looks at God all day,*
> *And lifts her leafy arms to pray;*
>
> *A tree that may in Summer wear*
> *A nest of robins in her hair;*
>
> *Upon whose bosom snow has lain;*
> *Who intimately lives with rain.*
>
> *Poems are made by fools like me,*
> *But only God can make a tree.*[43]

Kilmer and his wife, the poet Aline Murray, became devout converts to Catholicism, and Kilmer struck up close relationships with priests and nuns who shared his passion for prayer and for discussing their individual spiritual experiences.

With America entering the war in Europe, Kilmer felt he had no choice but to sign up for duty in 1917. After training in New Jersey at a facility that was later designated "Camp Kilmer," he was assigned to the famous Fighting Sixty-ninth. Posted less than a hundred miles east of Paris, Kilmer had little opportunity to write, but he did compose one significant poem, which he enclosed in a letter to his wife. Titled "Prayer of a Soldier in France," the poem is written much in the tradition of the great Catholic mystics, alternating between Kilmer's personal struggles and the Passion of Christ:

> *My shoulders ache beneath my pack*
> *(Lie easier, Cross, upon His back).*

> I march with feet that burn and smart
> (Tread, Holy Feet, upon my heart).
>
> Men shout at me who may not speak
> (They scourged Thy back and smote Thy cheek).
>
> I may not lift a hand to clear
> My eyes of salty drops that sear.
>
> (Then shall my fickle soul forget
> Thy Agony of Bloody Sweat?)
>
> My rifle hand is stiff and numb
> (From Thy pierced palm red rivers come).
>
> Lord, Thou didst suffer more for me
> Than all the hosts of land and sea.
>
> So let me render back again
> This millionth of Thy gift. Amen.[44]

This poem was Joyce Kilmer's last literary work. Volunteering to scout behind enemy lines to find a machine-gun nest that had pinned down his men in the Battle of Ourcq, Kilmer, who had recently been promoted to sergeant, was killed instantly by a single sniper's bullet. In the last letter he ever wrote, he described to his friend Sister Emerentia of St. Joseph's College in Toronto why he was so consumed by prayer:

> Pray that I may love God more. It seems to me that if I can learn to love God more passionately, more constantly, without distractions, that absolutely nothing else can matter. Except while we are in the trenches I receive Holy Communion every morning, so it ought to be all the easier for me to attain this object of my prayers. I got Faith, you know, by praying for it. I hope to get Love the same way.[45]

Joyce Kilmer was only thirty-one years old.

★　★　★

TECHNICALLY, the war for America began on April 2, 1917, and lasted until the armistice was signed on November 11, 1918, a period of little more than eighteen months, but its repercussions were more far-reaching than its relatively short duration might suggest. Idealism, which had been so much in fashion before the war, came crashing down around America, and it hit no one harder than President Woodrow Wilson. Despite the jubilation in America's streets, the mood in the Oval Office was anything but triumphal.

Few people who occupied the White House had been as infused with religious zeal or their own sense of destiny as Woodrow Wilson. While many in the academic community seemed little concerned with things spiritual, this history scholar and former president of Princeton University was totally consumed with things spiritual. Indeed, Wilson believed that God had chosen him to lead the United States for purposes that would be revealed to him over time. As he told his campaign chairman, William F. McCombs, after winning the election, "Whether you did little or much, remember that God ordained that I should be the next President of the United States. Neither you nor any mortal or mortals could have prevented it."[46] When he realized that his inauguration was to fall on a Sunday, Wilson broke precedent and agreed to be sworn in on "the Lord's Day." It seemed like the perfect omen.

Growing up in a household that required morning and evening prayers, grace before meals, Sunday school followed by two Sunday services, and plenty of group Bible readings and singing of hymns, Wilson came to believe that prayer was the linchpin of human existence.[47] Consequently, he put into practice a lifetime of disciplined prayer, kneeling beside his bed each morning and each evening, saying grace before all meals, and reading the Bible for devotional inspiration when he faced particularly difficult challenges. That is why he could say with absolute sincerity just before taking office, "I do not feel exuberant or cheerful. I feel exceedingly solemn. I have no inclination to jump up and crack my heels together. A weight of seriousness and responsibility seems to be pressing down upon me. I feel more like kneeling down and praying for strength to do what is expected of me."[48]

Wilson was such a fascinating figure not only to Americans but also to Europeans that Sigmund Freud, the father of psychoanalysis, offered his own observations on the President's psychological profile in a study published after Freud's death. Over some three hundred pages, Freud analyzed his subject's libido, superego, Oedipus complex, and relationship with his father. He probed and scrutinized Wilson's subliminal character, targeting in particular the President's prayer life, noting that without prayer Wilson may never have made it to the White House:

> So great was his need to submit to his God that never in his life could he allow himself to entertain religious doubt . . . "God is the source of strength to every man and only by prayer can he keep himself close to the Father of his spirit," he said. Twice, at least, he remarked: "I believe in Divine Providence. If I did not I would go crazy" . . . If he had not been able to make his daily submissions to God, he might indeed have taken refuge in paranoia and developed a "persecution mania"; he might have become not the occupant of the White House but the inmate of an asylum.[49]

With the war having come to a formal close in November 1918, Wilson tried to comprehend the cost to the country—over 130,000 dead, 203,000 wounded, and almost forty-two billion dollars spent.[50] Within days of the armistice, the President was off to Paris to present his terms for establishing a permanent peace based on the Fourteen Points he had developed. He both astonished and dismayed his European counterparts with his evangelical fervor, leading French President Georges Clemenceau to remark, "He thinks he is another Jesus Christ come upon the earth to reform men."[51] Quite frankly, no one could hope to understand Wilson or his unquenchable passion to create a League of Nations without understanding the intensity of his religious convictions.

While his European allies agreed to most of his plan, including the creation of the League of Nations, Wilson faced serious opposition back in the United States. By setting out on a solo course for peace, continuing to believe subconsciously, if not consciously, that he was God's instrument in the process, Wilson put his political future in peril. Opponents of his league and of other aspects of his plan, headed by the powerful Senator Henry Cabot Lodge of Massachusetts, gained momentum, derailing Wilson's efforts. Ignoring the Senate's constitutional responsibility to ratify the Treaty of Versailles was to be a fatal blow to the President.

When Wilson returned to the United States, he had a storm on his hands. Physically exhausted but choosing to take his case to the people directly, he launched a national speaking-tour campaign, traveling across the country by train. With the zealotry of an itinerant evangelical preacher, Wilson was consumed with the challenge. When he reached Colorado, however, the unthinkable occurred. The President suffered a major stroke, and he and the presidential party turned around and returned to Washington. Although Wilson served out his term, he suffered from the effects of his stroke until his death in 1924.

Wilson's legacy has always been bittersweet for historians. As important as prayer and his relationship to God were to him, Wilson ignored the political instincts and advice of those around him. Nevertheless, he was a major figure in crafting America's approach to the postwar world, even though America was not present in Geneva at the League of Nations. The United States had been forced into a war not of its choosing, but once committed, it would not look back. Within the very soul of the country came the faint heartbeat of its Puritan forefathers. To men like Wilson, the people of the United States had been "the chosen elect of God," and he was their leader, standing firm as a beacon for freedom and Christian principles the world over. The experience of the Great War was a prelude to things to come.

CHAPTER 11

THE INNOVATORS

1920–1935

*You pray in your distress and in your need; would that you might pray also
in the fullness of your joy and in your days of abundance.*

—Kahlil Gibran, *The Prophet* (1923)

THE 1920S SEEMED LIKE A BLUR but in retrospect became the most identifiable decade in American history, positioned between the exuberant highs of victory after World War I and the plunging lows of the Great Depression. F. Scott Fitzgerald called it the "Jazz Age," while Ernest Hemingway and Gertrude Stein remembered those ten years as belonging to the "lost generation." Still others christened the decade the "Roaring Twenties." What was clear was that the 1920s stood as a critical period, a decade defined by its art, music, literature, and entertainment.

It was only natural that such a flourishing of the arts and humanities would have an impact on the prayer culture of the United States. While these American innovators to a person were well versed in the Bible and in Western civilization, they were of two minds. Some were spiritually devout, using their artistry to find answers to age-old questions, while others searched for more personal enlightenment in the midst of their agnosticism. Satirist Dorothy Parker, for example, wrote "Prayer for a Prayer," conveying a rare tenderness in the midst of personal loss. The Pulitzer Prize–winning novelist Willa Cather, in her nostalgic and doleful *April Twilights,* embraced the divine ideal in "Thou Art the Pearl." The poet and folklorist Carl Sandburg composed a piece as traditional as "Our Prayer of Thanks," and then wrote "Prayers of Steel" to intertwine himself permanently with his beloved Chicago through the building of its skyscrapers.

Most artists exhibited a clear agnosticism not only in their relationship to God but also in understanding their purpose in life and any anchoring they might have had to family or community. Many of these individuals, although certainly not all, fled to Paris, London, and other foreign destinations, consumed in part by intellectual and spiritual restlessness. They wanted to learn about and expand their universe, to find adventure, and to commiserate with other artists. Some found inspiration in viewing and loving their country and culture by looking from the outside in. Still, they showed a spiritual skepticism that haunted their works and permeated their personal lives.

In retrospect it is rather astounding to realize how many of the great writers of the first half of the twentieth century led torturous lives. While they had the presence of mind to manage their lives and their literary gifts in some orderly measure, in the end alcoholism, sexual addiction, gambling, drugs, and other forms of personal abuse took their toll. As they constructed their story lines, plunging themselves into the nature of the human condition, these writers employed prayer to penetrate the depths of their characters either by dismissing any connection to the supernatural, relying instead on their own senses in the here and now, or by struggling to resolve their relationship to a supreme being, an entity they could never fully grasp. Either way, prayer was a powerful vehicle for these fictional plotters as they developed their subjects and constructed their stories, always revealing a part of themselves.

The first of the great writers of the period, the first American recipient of the Nobel Prize in literature, in 1930, was Sinclair Lewis. Born in the small town of Sauk Centre, Minnesota, in 1885, Lewis was a product of the Midwest. While studying at Oberlin College in Ohio to prepare for Yale University, he became a member of the YMCA, exuding, as he said, the sentiments of "earnest muscular Christianity."[1] Excoriating his roommates and others to pray, to read the Bible, and to lead good, clean Christian lives, he was resolute in converting souls. He even gave serious thought to becoming a missionary. Despite his outward religious fervor, however, Lewis began to have serious doubts about the existence of God, and by the time he left Yale, he had become a confirmed agnostic.[2]

Biographers of Lewis have tried to determine, without much success, why he underwent such a total transformation in so little time. Clearly he became disillusioned by the hypocrisy of certain Christians he had encountered, particularly among the clergy, and he seemed to take great delight in pillorying them at the height of his career.

From *Main Street* to *Babbitt* and *Arrowsmith*, Lewis produced poignant novels that reflected the tensions he had confronted in his own life. One of his most vivid characters, Elmer Gantry, is an intoxicated, womanizing preacher who can work a crowd into religious frenzy through extemporaneous prayers and impassioned sermons. In many ways, Gantry seems to embody the musings of Lewis, trying to imagine what his own fate might have been had he entered the ministry.

No American writer epitomized the 1920s through his writings or lifestyle more than F. Scott Fitzgerald. Originally from St. Paul, Minnesota, he was named after the poet Francis Scott Key, the brother of his great-grandfather. Fitzgerald relished using his gift with words to give life and description to his era, writing, "It was an age of miracles, it was an age of art, it was an age of excess, and it was an age of satire."[3]

Central to his masterpiece, *The Great Gatsby*, is a "character" constructed in the form of a billboard advertisement for Dr. T. J. Eckleburg, who looks down on all passersby with ominous owl-rimmed glasses. Eckleburg, a local optometrist who has long been out of business due to bankruptcy, becomes Fitzgerald's metaphor for a lifeless God, creating guilt in the flawed characters of the novel. No pretense of prayer or connection to the Almighty exists, just a wary distance between God and creation.

It was Fitzgerald's state of mind before he had reached his teens, from the day his father, Edward, was fired from his job at Procter & Gamble. He had had a premonition that something was wrong before his father walked in the door that night, remembering how earnestly he had prayed, "Dear God . . . Please don't let us go to the poorhouse."[4] While family money sustained the Fitzgeralds, allowing Scott to attend Princeton, his father's firing had left Scott numb. Fitzgerald later claimed that the memory haunted him and found its way into all his writings. Ultimately alcohol and financial recklessness led to Fitzgerald's fatal heart attack at the age of forty-four.

Fitzgerald's early literary compatriot, who later turned against him, was Ernest Hemingway. When a young man, Hemingway had led a life of adventure as an ambulance driver in World War I and as a correspondent in the Greco-Turkish War of 1919–22. Although later in life he became a Catholic, albeit in name only, Hemingway was baptized into the First Congregational Church in Oak Park, Illinois. His sister later claimed that the entire family had grown up in a household in which daily morning prayer was recited in addition to grace before every meal.[5]

Although Hemingway turned his back on his religious roots, he once confided to a friend it was a "fear of death" that brought him to his knees and instilled in him some "belief in *personal* salvation or maybe just preservation through prayers." At the same time, however, he proudly described how he had survived World War II "without praying once." Given that he had led less than a virtuous life, he believed it would be "absolutely crooked" to petition God for anything, "no matter how scared" he became.[6] Hemingway clearly found spiritual closeness to God only when sitting on death's doorstep. Otherwise, he exhibited a certain agnostic awe.

From an intimate conversation about prayer between Brett and Jake in *The Sun Also Rises* to the anguish of the battle-weary soldier in the short story "Now I Lay Me," Hemingway infused a mixture of spiritual pathos and languor into his works. While he dismissed any allegorical allusions in *The Old Man and the Sea*, he realized that many readers saw the tale of the old fisherman and his young apprentice as prayer in motion.

Despite the outward appearance of a glamorous, accomplished life, which included a Nobel Prize in literature in 1954, Hemingway fought his own demons. Married four times, he took little comfort in an existence that seemed to hold little in the way of absolute truths. Like his father, a small-town family physician, and his brother and his sister before him, Hemingway, in 1961, committed suicide.

None of the major novelists of the era was more steeped in religion than the gifted southern writer William Faulkner of Oxford, Mississippi. *As I Lay Dying, Absalom, Absalom!,* and *Sanctuary* gave voice to a major literary talent. Versed in almost every passage and nuance of the Bible, the five-foot-five, mustached Faulkner turned to both the Old and the New Testament for themes and references in almost all of his novels.

In confronting race relations, class distinctions, or the powerful roots of Christianity, Faulkner developed complex, heavily laden characters exhibiting traits from base to the most endearing. By using prayer as a vehicle, he depicted personalities and devised plots that showed depth, shallowness, and duplicity. It was an effect that would profoundly influence such writers as Jean-Paul Sartre and Albert Camus.

Poring over a Faulkner novel can be a tough undertaking, the reader never quite knowing what to expect from one chapter to the next. At least a piece of these complicated, at times decaying, characters can be found in Faulkner himself. Despite being a son of the South, he could never abide by its conventions The cultural and spiritual clashes filled him with constant restlessness.

After receiving the Nobel Prize for Literature in 1949, Faulkner divided his time between writing and accepting invitations on the lecture circuit. His fame, however, only seemed to exacerbate his drinking, and by 1962, at the age of sixty-four, he suffered a major heart attack as he fell off his horse.

Another writer with a resounding impact on American letters and culture was the playwright Eugene O'Neill. A winner of the Nobel Prize in literature, he single-handedly transformed American drama from popular entertainment to serious art form. Raised in New York City, O'Neill was sent away to Catholic schools as a boy. Although he attended Mass regularly, knew his prayers forward and backward, and became intimately familiar with Church doctrine, he told his roommate, not having reached ten, "religion is so cold."[7] By the time he was a teenager, he had become fed up with religion altogether and vowed never to walk inside a church again.

The product of a seriously dysfunctional family, O'Neill was haunted by the demons of alcohol, delinquency, and womanizing, all of which led to a failed suicide attempt when he was twenty-one. The problems that haunted O'Neill arise time and again in the characters and story lines of his plays. His facile mind allowed him to write powerful dramas in a variety of styles, from realism to expressionism. *Long Day's Journey into Night, Mourning Becomes Electra, Anna Christie,* and *The Iceman Cometh* all attest to O'Neill's genius and in varying degrees show the extent to which his characters search for moral truth while pillorying traditional religion. In many of his dramas, he used some form of prayer to illustrate his writhing discomfort with the relationship between God and humanity, as well as with the established religious mores of the day.

Eugene O'Neill spent his last years as a recluse. Suffering from Parkinson's disease, he became even more depressed, finally dying at sixty-five with his third wife, Carlotta, at his side.

THERE WERE NOVELISTS of another sort as well. One of the more influential spiritual writers of his day, who achieved a cult status both inside and outside the United States, was the Arab-American Kahlil Gibran. Part philosopher, part mystic, Gibran masterfully used the English language to merge Middle Eastern spirituality with Western sensibilities.

At the core of his philosophy, Gibran promoted the notion that God is not the model of perfection, as most religions espouse. Rather, the perfection of God is an ongoing process, an evolution, much as it is for human beings. In life's journey, Gibran believed that prayer was critical for anyone to understand God while recognizing the inherent conflict in this idea. In effect, men and women would never be able to achieve complete consciousness of God, because while they searched for divine knowledge, God continued to move to newer levels. In essence, then, the act of prayer allows men and women to lift themselves to higher levels of awareness, but their understanding of the Almighty can never be complete.

A single work, *The Prophet,* published in 1923, brought Gibran unique fame and fortune. No more than twenty thousand words long, it is the poetic and metaphoric tale of Almustafa (Gibran) conferring with the people of Orphalese (New York) as to the universe and their place in it. In a chapter titled "On Prayer," Gibran asks, speaking through Almustafa, "For what is prayer but the expansion of yourself into the living ether?" He then admonishes his listeners: "I cannot teach you how to pray in words. God listens not to your words save when He Himself utters them through your lips. And I cannot teach you the prayer of the seas and the forests and the mountains. But you who are born of the mountains and the forests and the seas can find their prayers in your heart."[8]

Narcissistic and abusive at times, brilliant and charismatic at others, Kahlil Gibran died from complications of alcoholism at the age of forty-eight. His truly unique perspective on spirituality left a lasting imprint on America's prayer culture.

AS THE COUNTRY'S WRITERS were leaving their cultural mark, giving nuance to American spirituality and prayer, other artists were having just as lasting an impact. The truly brilliant but eccentric Frank Lloyd Wright, the son of an itinerant preacher and lawyer, helped to redefine architecture in the twentieth century and created spectacular new imagery in framing his vision of the relationship between God and humanity. Although an avowed Unitarian, Wright was more a latter-day transcendentalist, insisting, "I believe in God, only I spell it Nature."[9] Despite being a bit of a spiritual anomaly, he left a legacy of architectural masterpieces that have allowed people to relate to God in ways that even Wright could never have imagined. He built churches and synagogues whose translucent ceilings, filtered lighting, material symbolism, and floor plans served to join members of congregations to one another and to the Almighty. Every house of worship that he designed or built conveys some sense of effecting communal prayer.

When a young draftsman of nineteen, Wright was given his first assignment: designing the interior of the Unity Chapel in Spring Green, Wisconsin, later the site of Taliesin East, where the architect and his team designed and executed many of their projects. It was also where Wright led his young protégés and their families in Sunday services and where he would be buried in 1959.

The first major commission of a church came in the early twentieth century when Wright was asked to design a new building for the Universalist congregation in Oak Park, Illinois. The original structure had burned to the ground, and the pastor and elders fully expected Wright to show them a blueprint that envisioned a traditional white spired structure, in the tradition of New England Congregationalist churches. Wright stunned everyone when he laid out a plan focused on "God's presence . . . within the praying congregation itself."[10] As they began to bemoan his avant-garde approach, they were met by Wright's irascible glibness. "Why point to heaven?" he admonished. Relying on his transcendentalist instincts, he told them he intended to build "a temple to man, . . . in which to study man himself for his God's sake." He won the day, and Unity Temple was built.

And yet Wright, who would design everything from the highly original Guggenheim Museum in New York City to a blueprint for rebuilding Baghdad, Iraq, could never be accused of complete consistency, that hobgoblin of little minds deplored by his spiritual compatriot Ralph Waldo Emerson. In designing a Unitarian meetinghouse in Shorewood Hills, a suburb of Madison, Wisconsin, he constructed a sanctuary with a soaring copper roof, set off by low eaves, creating the feeling for its congregation of being both sheltered and uplifted. He later remarked that he had built a prow-like apse and triangular planning grid for the meetinghouse as an architectural metaphor for "the hands of a supplicant in prayer emerging from their habit."[11]

For the Beth Sholom Synagogue in Elkins Park near Philadephia, he constructed a hexagonal plan that suggested God's cupped hands protecting the congregation in prayer. In conceptualizing the Annunciation Greek Orthodox Church in Wauwatosa, Wisconsin, Wright was anything but orthodox as he envisioned a circular, domed building with an unobstructed interior. Designing the structure to be infused with natural lighting from all sides, he also minimized the distance between the parishioners and their priest during Mass.

Frank Lloyd Wright used his vision of organic architecture to help open up the individual's quest for spiritual truth. Terribly elaborate structures or interior treatments held no appeal for him whatsoever. As Wright's contemporary the groundbreaking designer and German émigré Ludwig Mies van der Rohe remarked, to understand the essence of design and true human contentment, it is critical to realize that "less is more." Only by showing restraint could one ever find that "God is in the details."[12]

THE COUNTRY WAS ALSO developing a new generation of musical artists who were breaking Old World traditions by writing music uniquely American, drawing many melodies from the country's spiritual heritage.

America's first quintessential classical composer, Charles Ives, wrote music that relied on creative intuition, much of it steeped in the spiritual traditions of his beloved New England. Hailing from Danbury, Connecticut, and a graduate of Yale, Ives built a small fortune in the insurance business while writing music on the side. What he produced in music was Americana at its finest—refreshingly cutting-edge while relying on the roots of the country's past. His use of dissonance, conflicting rhythms, and polytonal harmonies made him an original and eminently recognizable.

Greatly influenced by the transcendentalists, much like Frank Lloyd Wright, Ives wrote an extensive religious repertoire that appealed to a broad range of Christians and even Jews, pieces like "O God, My Heart

Is Fixed," "Religion," "I Think of Thee, My God," and a variety of Latin hymns and psalms. At the same time, he could create something entirely original based on traditional melodies like his Pulitzer Prize–winning Third Symphony. Subtitled "The Camp Meeting," the symphony incorporates such traditional hymns as "What a Friend We Have in Jesus" and "Oh, for a Thousand Tongues to Sing" without becoming overly sentimental or predictable. Ives once referred to "the path of God and man's spiritual part" as "a kind of spiritual causeway."[13] In finding a fresh approach to expressing prayer, he leads the listener to the climaxing, meditative "Communion" in the symphony's third, and last, movement, concluding one of his finest musical achievements. Younger contemporary composers like Virgil Thomson and William Schuman also found ways to weave American hymnody into their symphonic works.

Another composer who distinguished himself in several different musical worlds was the wildly popular George Gershwin. Born in Brooklyn to Jewish immigrant parents from Russia, Gershwin, along with his brother Ira, perhaps the most gifted lyricist of popular songs ever, became the toast of vaudeville, Broadway, and concert halls alike. In reflecting on his prodigious output of music, George Gershwin believed that his opera Porgy and Bess was by far the most difficult but most personally rewarding work he had ever written. The first American opera to be written and produced on stage, Porgy and Bess received serious, popular acclaim only after his death. A complicated story of love and betrayal between a crippled beggar and a woman in the black ghetto neighborhood of Catfish Row in Charleston, South Carolina, the opera was based on the 1925 bestselling novel Porgy, by the southern writer DuBose Heyward. It was the first major book to come out of the South that was not perceived to be condescending toward African-Americans.

In composing his elaborate, groundbreaking work, Gershwin knew he could draw from his experiences growing up in Harlem, but that was not enough. He needed to visit churches, homes, and prayer meetings in the South to gain an appreciation for African-American spirituality. Consequently, DuBose Heyward invited Gershwin to live with him at his home outside Charleston for a few months so the two men could travel throughout North and South Carolina. As they began their trek, Gershwin became fascinated by the rhythms and passions of African-American spirituals and "shouts," the roots of his beloved musical genres of jazz and blues. Haunting supplications were soon being intertwined throughout the opera, and in the end Gershwin produced a musical score that was exotic in both sound and setting, creating unique musical theater. By the time *Porgy and Bess* reached its climactic conclusion in "Oh Lawd, I'm on My Way," with its lyrics, "I'm on my way to a Heav'nly Lan' . . . but You'll be there to take my han'," Gershwin had left his audience with a profoundly American tale steeped in tragedy but holding out the great promise of hope, expressed so convincingly through prayer.

GERSHWIN HAD BEEN INFLUENCED by what Alain Locke, the first African-American Rhodes scholar, called the "Harlem Renaissance" of the 1920s. Since the turn of the century, arts, literature, science, and thought had been flourishing among a growing intellectual elite of African-Americans. Two of the group's standard-bearers were the Johnson brothers. J. Rosamond and his more famous brother, James Weldon Johnson, were passionately committed to highlighting for future generations the unique contributions of blacks to the American experience. While they understood the reluctance of former slaves and their children to share the details of their intense personal prayer life during the painful years of slavery, they nonetheless reveled in the rich heritage and took great pains to collect and publish African-American spirituals for an appreciative public. While the Fisk University Jubilee Singers had popularized many spirituals through their live performances, the Johnson brothers institutionalized these prayer songs through meticulous research, editing, and musical arrangement, writing two extensive volumes called *The Books of American Negro Spirituals*.

The story of the Johnson brothers is a remarkable saga in itself. They were born into an accomplished family that had emigrated from the Bahamas. Their father was a self-educated man who worked as headwaiter at the St. James Hotel in Jacksonville, Florida, while their mother taught at the segregated Stanton School. After James graduated from Atlanta University, he joined his mother at Stanton, where he was appointed principal.

In 1900 Johnson was set to address the school's assembly in honor of the anniversary of Abraham Lincoln's birth. Rather than deliver a traditional speech, however, he worked with his brother Rosamond, who had just graduated from the New England Conservatory of Music, to turn the speech into a musical composition. James would write the lyrics, Rosamond would compose the music, and they would assemble five hundred schoolchildren to sing it. Both brothers were convinced that the convocation would be the perfect opportunity to instill in the students a genuine sense of pride in their African-American inheritance. They called the song "Lift Ev'ry Voice and Sing":

Lift ev'ry voice and sing,
Till earth and heaven ring.
Ring with the harmony of Liberty;
Let our rejoicing rise.
High as the list'ning skies,
Let it resound loud as the rolling sea.
Sing a song full of the faith that the
dark past has taught us,
Sing a song full of the hope that the
present has brought us;
Facing the rising sun of our new day begun,
Let us march on till victory is won.

Stony the road we trod.
Bitter the chast'ning rod,
Felt in the days when hope unborn had died;
Yet with a steady beat, have not our weary feet,
Come to the place for which our fathers sighed?
We have come over a way that with tears has been watered,
We have come, treading our path through the blood
of the slaughtered,
Out from the gloomy past, till now we stand at last
Where the white gleam of our bright star is cast.

God of our weary years,
God of our silent tears,
Thou who has brought us thus far on the way;
Thou who has by Thy might led us into the light,
Keep us forever in the path, we pray.
Lest our feet stray from the places,
our God, where we met Thee,
Lest our hearts, drunk with the wine of the world,
we forget thee,

Shadowed beneath thy hand, May we forever stand,
True to our God,
True to our native land.[14]

Later, recalling how he and his brother had been inspired to write the piece, James Weldon Johnson wrote, "I paced back and forth on the front porch, repeating lines over and over to myself, going through all the agony and ecstasy of creating." By the time he had reached the third stanza, a direct appeal to God, he realized, "I could not keep back the tears and made no effort to do so."[15]

From the day of its premiere, "Lift Ev'ry Voice and Sing" hit a deep chord. By word of mouth, by being pasted to the backs of hymnals, and by being performed at school convocations, the song spread in popularity, first throughout the South and then across the rest of the country. By the 1920s the National Association for the Advancement of Colored People had adopted it as its own, and it became known affectionately as the "Negro National Hymn."

Another figure who helped define the Harlem Renaissance, and who became the driving force in launching American gospel music, was Charles Albert Tindley. Born into slavery, in 1902 he was named pastor of Philadelphia's Calvary Methodist Episcopal Church, the same church where he had worked as a janitor while attending divinity school and learning to read Greek and Hebrew through correspondence courses. Driven by a desire to provide what he referred to as a "spiritual haven" for others, he worked tirelessly to build his church into a congregation that would ultimately climb to 12,500 members.[16]

In 1916 he published a collection of hymns called *New Songs of Paradise* and became the first composer to copyright church hymns. Known to American musicologists as "the father of African-American hymnody," Tindley wrote such hymns as "We'll Understand It Better By and By" and "The Storm Is Passing Over."

Two of his works stand out as important parts of America's cultural and political heritage. The first, "Stand by Me," cries out for Divine Providence in the midst of profound faith, with the words "When the storms of life are raging . . . And my strength begins to fail . . . Stand by me." His other major work, "I'll Overcome Some Day," had such a catalyzing effect on its listeners that later leaders of the civil rights movement used it as their anthem for nonviolent protest. Writing both the words and the melody, Tindley saw his lyrics as an expression of his own remarkable odyssey:

> *This world is one great battlefield*
> *With forces all arrayed,*
> *If in my heart I do not yield*
> *I'll overcome some day . . .*
>
> *Both seen and unseen powers join*
> *To drive my soul astray,*
> *But with His Word a sword of mine,*
> *I'll overcome some day . . .*
>
> *I fail so often when I try*
> *My Savior to obey;*
> *It pains my heart and then I cry,*
> *Lord, make me strong some day . . .*
>
> *Though many a time no signs appear,*
> *Of answer when I pray;*
> *My Jesus says I need not fear,*
> *He'll make it plain some day.*[17]

Known simply as "gospel music," these spiritual works were distinctive in several ways. Not only did their lyrics originate in the Bible, but they also expressed reverence to God and to God's works, while yearning to build a stronger relationship with God through Christ.[18]

There probably was no greater tribute to the incredible spiritual force of gospel music than its effect on the great German theologian Dietrich Bonhoeffer. In 1931, while taking postgraduate courses at Union Theological Seminary in New York City, Bonhoeffer was teaching Sunday school at Harlem's Abyssinian Baptist Church, where for the first time he heard the rapturous sounds of African-American music. Listening to sacred lyrics blended with the melodies, the rhythms, and even the swaying of the church's gospel choir, he found the entire experience a spiritual epiphany.

Returning to Germany in the early 1930s as Adolf Hitler and the National Socialist Party were gaining political momentum, Bonhoeffer helped to organize a resistance movement to counter the growing influence of the Nazis. When he was finally forced underground, he found the greatest solace in listening to the recordings of the spirituals and gospel music he had brought with him from America. After being apprehended by the Gestapo and sent off to the Buchenwald concentration camp and then to Schoenberg Prison, he would hum the music he had first heard sung in that Harlem church not so many years earlier. By the time he was hanged on April 9, 1945, one week before Allied troops liberated the prisoners at Schoenberg, he had little fear in facing death. His final words would ring in the ears of seminarians and his many followers for years to come: "This is the end—but for me, the beginning—of life."

The pure sensual power of gospel music, this new form of American prayer, was given even greater meaning in the hands of Thomas Andrew Dorsey. The son of a Baptist preacher from rural Georgia, Dorsey found his inspiration in the blues, that musical idiom born out of the anguish and emotions of the spirituals. In his early days as a composer, Dorsey was more attracted to the easy money and the sexual double entendres of the blues than to anything he heard in church. In the 1920s, however, he faced a life-changing moment in Chicago. After becoming sick during a musical engagement, he went home and in the coming days grew worse. His doctor could find nothing wrong, but he continued to lose weight rapidly, and with his illness he and his wife, Nettie, soon found that their savings had dwindled to nothing. After his parson told him to shape up, that God had more work for him to do, Dorsey went home and prayed, "Lord, I am ready to do your work."[19]

Within days he began to feel better and decided that he would no longer write any of those "special double-meaning songs."[20] He and Nettie now prayed together more than ever, and their lives seemed far more stable and happy, despite his frequent absences on the road to perform his music.

In the early years of the Depression, Dorsey began to make his mark by promoting gospel music one congregation at a time. While performing in St. Louis, he learned that Nettie had died giving birth to their first child. "I slumped down in the booth, sobbing," he later wrote. He rushed home, where a nurse put his newborn son into his arms, and his eyes welled up with tears again. By nightfall, however, the baby had died, and Dorsey "came close[r] to rejecting God" than he had ever done in his life. "Was this my reward?" he cried out. Burying his family, he grieved, writing, "After putting my wife and baby away in the same casket I began to feel that God had done me an injustice. I didn't want to serve him anymore or write gospel songs . . . Then a voice spoke to me and said 'You are not alone.' "[21] He then sat down and was somehow able to write one of the most endearing gospel songs ever, "Precious Lord, Take My Hand":

> *Precious Lord, take my hand.*
> *Lead me on. Let me stand.*
> *I am tired. I am weak. I am worn.*
> *Through the storm, through the night,*
> *Lead me on to the light.*
> *Take my hand, precious Lord, lead me home.*

> *When my way grows drear,*
> *Precious Lord, linger near.*
> *When my life is almost gone,*
> *Hear my cry, hear my call,*
> *Hold my hand, lest I fall;*
> *Take my hand, precious Lord, lead me home.*[22]

The hymn somehow dispelled much of the grief, and Dorsey "knew that He had other work for me to do." Despite the song's intense spirituality, many people accused Dorsey of secularizing hymns of praise, effectively bringing "the speakeasy into houses of worship."[23] In time, however, "Precious Lord" became one of the most beloved gospel renderings ever and joined other Dorsey songs such as "Peace in the Valley" and "If You See My Savior" as standards of the gospel repertoire. Through his tireless efforts, the Thomas A. Dorsey Gospel Songs and Choruses Publishing Company became the first African-American-owned firm of its kind, dedicated solely to the publication of gospel music. Dorsey's legacy lasted long after his death in 1993, at the age of ninety-three, and influenced such diverse artists as Elvis Presley, the Beatles, Bob Dylan, and later generations of country-western and gospel musicians.

Undoubtedly, Thomas Dorsey's greatest disciple, epitomizing the performance of gospel, was the phenomenal Mahalia Jackson. "Precious Lord, Take My Hand" became her signature song after she met Dorsey in 1929, and the two toured together for the next fourteen years. With a voice that resonated strongly without amplification, she had a mesmerizing effect on her audiences.

Orphaned by the age of five and raised in New Orleans by relatives, Jackson was influenced as much by the sounds echoing from the local Holiness church as by her own Baptist church. While her obvious musical talents led people like the jazz great Louis Armstrong to offer her opportunities on the secular stage, Jackson would have none of it. Gospel was her home and her only home. Songs like "My Faith Looks up to Thee," "Prayer Changes Things," and "Jesus, Lover of My Soul" gave her life meaning. "Sometimes you feel like you're so far from God," she liked to say, "and *then* you know those deep songs have special meaning. They bring back the communication between yourself and God."[24]

In the years following World War II, gospel music entered its golden era. It not only continued to strengthen its roots within the black community but also expanded its appeal dramatically to white congregations and young audiences.

WHILE THE ARTS AND HUMANITIES were giving newer expression and dimension to prayer, challenging traditional spiritual formulas, one of the most dramatic and celebrated legal cases in American history was taking place in the heart of the country, the *Scopes* trial. It was an event that would resound even into the venues of American prayer.

For a public ready for spellbinding drama, the *Scopes* trial brought together two of the country's most famous yet polarizing personalities, the attorneys William Jennings Bryan and Clarence Darrow, locking horns in philosophical, theological, and political combat. As a titillating spectacle, it kept dozens of out-of-work reporters busy. H. L. Mencken, the iconoclastic editor and writer for *The Baltimore Sun,* referred to the trial and its various sideshows as a "religious orgy."[25]

The controversy that led to the trial arose after passage of the so-called Butler Law in Tennessee, in which the state declared it illegal for schools to teach the theory of evolution. Anyone found guilty of violating the new law would be fined one hundred dollars. The newly formed American Civil Liberties Union, based in New York City, found Dayton, Tennessee, a fundamentalist stronghold, to be an irresistible backdrop for scoring points on issues of academic freedom and the separation of church and state. Consequently, the organization convinced John Scopes,

Rhea County High School's twenty-four-year-old general science teacher and part-time football coach, to help support its cause, promising to cover all legal costs, including the expected fine.

Darwin's *Origin of Species*, with its groundbreaking thesis, had been published sixty-five years earlier but had never been central to a U.S. courtroom trial. Given the social and religious conflict that had been building in the United States between those who believed in divine creation without evolution and those who believed in evolution without divine creation, it was only a matter of time before the issue would come to a head.

The anticipated performances of Darrow and Bryan during that oppressively hot summer of 1925, however, created the greatest interest. In one corner stood Clarence Darrow, the brilliant legal showman whose courtroom tactics were legendary. Although Darrow claimed to be an agnostic, he was more than likely a full-fledged atheist, too clever to have ever been boxed into a corner. His articles for various publications with such titles as "Why I Am an Agnostic" and "Absurdities of the Bible" did not make him a popular figure in many circles. In the other corner stood the populist stump orator William Jennings Bryan, revered by his supporters as an impeccably honest, God-fearing individual. By the time the *Scopes* trial gained national attention, Bryan had run for President three times. Having served as Woodrow Wilson's Secretary of State, he abruptly resigned in 1915 when the President edged the country closer to war against Germany. Detractors found Bryan to be self-righteous and grossly naive.

While the "Monkey Trial," as Mencken first called it, was intended to address the legal issue of teaching evolution in public schools, the proceedings also put the propriety of public prayer on trial for the first time in history. Before the beginning of each day's hearings, the tradition of the court was to open with a prayer. On the first day of the trial a local fundamentalist minister delivered a seven-minute prayer, which read in part: "We beseech Thee, our Heavenly Father, that Thou wilt grant unto every individual that share of wisdom that will enable them to go out from this session of the court, with the consciousness of having under God and grace done the very best thing possible, and the wisest thing possible."[26]

Although the prayer was straightforward and held no surprises, Clarence Darrow and his legal team believed that any recitation of prayer in the courtroom was prejudicial to their case. When Judge John T. Raulston called on another fundamentalist minister the second day to open the court proceedings, Darrow stood up and objected on the grounds that clergy of other persuasions, perhaps even a rabbi, should be given the opportunity to offer the opening prayer. Without elaboration, the judge stated that he had taken note of Darrow's objections and would consider them in the future.

Not content with the judge's response, Darrow decided that he no longer cared who said the prayer and the next day argued that no invocation should be offered at all. Taking the floor, he stunned the courtroom as he articulated his case: "We object to the opening of the court with prayer, and I am going to ask the shorthand reporter to take down the prayer, and I will make specific objections again to any such parts as we think are especially obnoxious to our case."

Judge Raulston, largely fixated on his newfound fame on the national stage and clearly aware that every word was being taken down by the court press, warily responded:

This court has no purpose except to find the truth and do justice . . . I believe in prayer myself. I constantly invoke divine guidance myself, when I am on the bench and off the bench. I see no reason why I should not continue to do this. It is not the purpose of this court to bias or prejudice the mind of any individual, but to do right in all matters under investigation. Therefore, I am pledged to overrule the objection of counsel and invite Dr. Stribling to open the court with prayer.[27]

At that point, defense lawyer Dudley Malone turned to his colleague Arthur Hays and whispered, "This is to be a scrap from now on—a knock-down and drag-out—and we might as well prepare for it."[28] With camera bulbs flashing, Judge Raulston agreed to allow the official record to show that Darrow had objected to daily prayers being offered at the trial and that on every occasion he was and would be overruled.

With the trial generating so much attention, public prayer suddenly became a highly charged issue as well, second only to the trial case itself. An invocation continued to be said each day before the trial—and continued to take a battering from the Darrow defense team.

After more than ten days, the court finally ruled against John Scopes, but the outcome had never been in doubt. Knowing that Bryan could still make some important points before the court and the world media, Darrow at the last possible moment pleaded "guilty" to the charges leveled against his client, John Scopes. With that, the trial was over, and Scopes, through the coffers of the ACLU, paid his one hundred dollars. Bryan was shell-shocked at the anticlimax of the trial and the final resolution of the verdict.

In the end, the *Scopes* trial was, in the words of the historian Edward Larson, "a sign of the times rather than . . . a decisive turning point."[29] The battle between evolution and creationism, on the other hand, would continue to rage into the twenty-first century and would be joined by newer, hybrid theories such as the "big bang" and "intelligent design" to explain the origins and the eventual, natural transformation of all things.[30] Darrow's attempt to place the issue of public prayer in the legal arena, arguing that prayer should largely be confined to homes and churches, was the first of many efforts to address the matter in a judicial forum.

WHILE COURTROOM THEATRICS were taking center stage in Dayton, Tennessee, other events were erupting in regional pockets of the country, both north and south. In 1882 white supremacists had begun to organize lynchings of African-Americans and a few white sympathizers. Over the next several generations some twenty-five hundred people, mainly black men but also "errant" Catholics, Jews, and sympathetic whites, were hanged, in most instances from trees. Members of the Ku Klux Klan, whose ranks had now swelled to over eight million, would gather in their signature white-hooded costumes to launch rapid, well-targeted strikes in the still of night. Invoking in many instances God's blessing before setting out to harass, maim, or hang their victims, they sought to turn their actions into a holy cause. Once their deed had been carried out, many of the men showed up at church services the next Sunday, praising God, seeing themselves as defenders of their communities. While the Klan was responsible for many of the lynchings, they were not alone in taking matters into their own hands.

The horror of these mob executions unlocked the moral outrage of one of the most restive intellectuals of the twentieth century, W. E. B. DuBois, who constantly reminded his audiences of the parallels between "lynching as practiced by Americans and crucifixion as practiced by

Romans."[31] Educated at Fisk University, DuBois had gone on to Harvard, where he became the first African-American to receive a doctorate, in 1895. Despite drawing on the heritage of African-Americans who found strength and solace in their ability to pray, DuBois was a wandering agnostic. His constant questioning of the precepts of Christianity often found him at odds with his academic colleagues at Atlanta University, as well as with black organizations, including the NAACP, which he helped to found. Brilliant, arrogant, prophetic, stubborn, DuBois experienced a personal odyssey that led him to the forefront of the early civil rights movement to membership in the Communist Party, and to self-exile in Ghana at the age of ninety-one.

Before leaving permanently for Africa, he gave his friend and colleague Herbert Aptheker an envelope of papers, instructing him to open them upon his death. Contained in the package was a series of prayers, many beautifully written, in which DuBois showed spiritual passion. Written in his own hand, they were prayers that he had delivered early in his teaching career during chapel services. All of them were infused with messages that dealt with subjects as diverse as alcoholism and better government. One prayer he offered for the benefit of his students spoke to the sin of procrastination, words that almost jumped off the page:

> *Teach us, O God, that . . . Today is the seed time, now are the hours of work and tomorrow comes the harvest . . . May we learn in youth . . . that the man who plays and then works, rests and then studies . . . is not simply reversing nature, he is missing opportunities and . . . the touchstone of success.*[32]

Despite a capacity to write such incisive prayers and to offer them so stirringly as prescriptions to his students, DuBois could not hide his growing spiritual and political disquiet. Although he died a seemingly broken man soon after moving to Africa, he left his imprint on race relations in his native country.

THE AMERICAN PRESIDENTS who served during this period of enormous change, three Republicans and one Democrat, were as different from one another as any four men could be. Collectively they would watch the country go from boom to bust.

Warren G. Harding, the first of the post–World War I presidents, was very likely the country's worst commander in chief, allowing corruption to flourish within his administration, showing little intellect or forceful leadership, and pursuing a messy, adulterous affair with his mistress, Nan Britton, with whom he would father a child.

As a college student, Harding had flirted with atheism, but as he entered politics, he became a regular worshipper in the Baptist Church. After being elected President in 1920, he reportedly commented, "It is not time for exultation but for prayer to God to make me capable of playing my part," but his administration seemed to go downhill from there.[33]

In September 1922, Harding's wife, Florence, a dowdy, piercingly blunt woman who had worked arduously to see that her husband was elected President, came down with kidney disease, lapsing in and out of a coma for days. Although the President continued his extramarital affair with Nan Britton in various rooms of the White House, including a twenty-five-foot square closet off the Oval Office, he was shocked that he might lose his wife of over thirty years and began to feel the guilt of his adultery. Sitting outside her sickroom, he "obsessively" recited the 121st Psalm over and over again, with its appeal to Divine Providence: "I lift up my eyes to the hills. From whence does my help come? My help comes from the Lord, who made heaven and earth."[34] By the end of September, Florence had recovered considerably and begun to function normally again, although kidney failure would ultimately take her life.

Not long after his wife's recovery, Harding died in San Francisco while returning from a trip to Alaska. Whether he died of food poisoning or was the victim of a heart attack or stroke over the pressure of his administration's scandals, historians can only speculate, given that no autopsy was ever performed.

Harding's death left Calvin Coolidge, his Vice President, as the new commander in chief. Learning the news at 2:30 in the morning while vacationing on his farm in Vermont, Coolidge later recounted, "My wife and I dressed at once. Before leaving the room I knelt down and, with the prayer with which I have since approached the altar of the church, asked God to bless the American people and give me power to serve them."[35] With that, Coolidge was sworn into office by his father, a local justice of the peace.

Dubbed "Silent Cal" by journalists, Coolidge was the epitome of New England cool and puritanical piety, adhering to the same prayer discipline throughout his life. Although one of his biographers referred to Coolidge as "mystically vague," he was not as inscrutable as some had been led to believe.[36] In writing his autobiography, he became intensely philosophical, saying in one chapter that "there is a power which moves restlessly that justifies our faith," and then showing how spirituality played an important role in his own life. That faith would sustain Coolidge and his wife, Grace, after the death of their sixteen-year-old son from blood poisoning in 1924, just after he had taken office. Grief stricken, Grace Coolidge would find comfort in composing a prayer that would be reprinted in every major paper across the country, titled "The Open Door." In it she sought to reach out to her son in death as her "guide along the path" to the "glories of His grace" and the "way which leads us home."[37] It clearly struck many as the cry of an agonizing mother.

Although Coolidge was one of the country's most popular presidents, he never stood for reelection, leaving office at a time of seeming prosperity and turning over the reins of government to his Secretary of Commerce, Herbert Hoover, who won election in 1928. In assuming office, Hoover, the country's first Quaker President, asked for "the help of Almighty God in this service to my country."[38] In little more than a year, however, the stock market crashed, and Hoover's response to the impending economic depression seemed tepid at best. The pressures were enormous, and the public scrutiny intense, leading to his infamous remark: "There are only two occasions when the American people respect privacy especially in presidents. Those are prayer and fishing."[39]

Although some chroniclers viewed his cautious approach as correct and sufficient at the time, many more saw it as dangerously myopic. Whatever the truth, Hoover had effectively become the "scapegoat for cataclysm."[40]

ON OCTOBER 29, 1929, known as "Black Thursday," and during the week that followed, the world seemed upside down as Americans rushed to sell their stock portfolios at any price. The U.S. economy had been fundamentally unsound, and now the country was witnessing the consequences firsthand. As the economist John Kenneth Galbraith later wrote, "The singular feature of the great crash of 1929 was that the worst continued to worsen. What looked one day like the end proved on the next day to have only been the beginning."[41] While stories of rampant suicides were more imagined than real, the terror of economic insecurity gripped Americans everywhere whether they owned stocks or not. Within six months, over a thousand banks would close and the accounts of their depositors with them, one in four workers would be left without a job, and soup kitchens would open across the country in unprecedented numbers.

Strangely enough, the economic depression helped to precipitate a decline in Sunday worship services that did not turn around until the onset of World War II. The building of churches and synagogues, which had steadily been on the increase throughout the 1920s, slowed to a crawl. For those who walked away from traditional churches, private prayer became a refuge. For others, spirituality was kept on a low flame.

One of many individuals devastated by the Great Depression, someone who grappled with it in untold ways, was James Cash Penney. After giving up the reins of his national retail chain in 1917, when the company was growing at a record pace, he became the company's chairman and spent most of his time running the J. C. Penney Foundation. His newly formed nonprofit corporation financed numerous philanthropic causes, from supporting adoptions to caring for retired ministers and church workers. On a 120,000-acre experimental farm in northern Florida, Penney subdivided thousands of acres into small plots to provide destitute farmers with land to help rebuild their lives.

Having leveraged his fortune through bank loans to support his charitable efforts, he lost everything when the stock market crash hit. Ironically, this came at a time when the company he had founded was operating fourteen hundred stores from coast to coast. Owning just the home they lived in, he and his wife dismissed their staff and lived for the next year in just two rooms of the mansion to avoid heating the entire building. Having lost two wives to illness before marrying his third, and last, spouse, Caroline, Penney was now facing yet another profound tragedy. Yet the challanges that he confronted were in large part mitigated by the support of his faith and what he saw as the value of prayer. It was a situation that he had come to grips with long ago, remembering how after his first wife, Bertha, had died of pneumonia, he had wrestled with his lack of spiritual fortitude:

> I didn't pray during this shattering experience, for the reason that I could not. The plain fact is, I had not learned how to pray.

Loneliness and fear sometimes drive a person in desperation to prayer. But for many years now my course had been so rooted in reliance upon myself, my own powers, that there was no latent impulse toward any outside source of strength . . .

But the earth had slipped from under my feet, and insupportable loss held my mind.[42]

For years Penney had struggled spiritually until the day he admitted himself to the Kellogg Sanitarium in Battle Creek, Michigan, to be treated for a variety of health problems. Walking past the sanitarium's chapel, he heard several people singing the words "God will take care of you." He played and replayed those words over in his mind. Believing that he had experienced his own epiphany, he took every word to heart.

From that moment he decided he would never again take God or prayer for granted. By the time the Great Depression arrived, he felt more than prepared. Although he never regained the bulk of his fortune, Penney did return to a comfortable living and found far greater satisfaction in life than he had earlier, as he explained in his autobiography: "I am learning to pray, and I feel the efficacy of prayer. In a material sense I have much less now than once I had; but, and I say it most seriously, that no longer seems to matter. What matters is that in place of material possessions I believe I have been guided to a much better conception of what life really means."[43]

WHILE PRIVATE CHARITIES were trying to stanch the suffering of millions of Americans, the country looked to Washington for answers. The 1932 Democratic National Convention nominated Franklin Roosevelt for the presidency, and in the fall Roosevelt, who exuded boundless confidence, was elected in a landslide. Although Roosevelt was not overtly religious, many of his friends and associates believed after his bout with polio that "Divine Providence had intervened to save him," and that his struggles had only toughened him physically, mentally, and spiritually for the difficult days ahead.[44] Purposely kept hidden from the American people, Roosevelt instructed aides to call his designated cabinet members on the eve of his inauguration in 1933 to ask them and their spouses to join him and his family at St. John's Church for a private prayer service before the swearing in ceremony. He wanted to avoid any perception that he somehow was in panic mode now that he was about to become President.

Frances Perkins, the President-elect's choice to be Secretary of Labor and the first female cabinet member in U.S. history, remembered the desperation of the country that morning, the economic life of the country "almost at a standstill."[45] So much was at stake, the country remained on edge, and a drastic course of action had to be taken.

"If ever a man wanted to pray, that was the day," she recounted. "He did want to pray," and it was clear that he needed and wanted others to pray for him as well. Selecting the outline of the *Book of Common Prayer* as well as prayers and hymns that were particularly appropriate for the occasion, Roosevelt made sure that the service set the proper tone.[46] In the end the effect was enormous on those in attendance. It was a scene that would be repeated on the morning of each of his upcoming inaugurations.

Although Roosevelt began to attend weekly church services, he soon stopped the practice. "I can do almost everything in the 'Goldfish Bowl,' " he exclaimed, "but I'll be hanged if I can say my prayers in it." Conscious of the attention that the braces on his legs caused, not to mention the office that he held, he commented that "it bothers me to feel like something in the zoo being looked at by all the tourists in Washington when I go to church." After settling down in a pew after all of the effort and "with everybody looking at me," he had to admit that "I don't feel like saying my prayers at all."[47] Nonetheless, he kept his faith in some poignant ways, particularly when it came to prayer, as the upcoming years would show.

In adopting a defiant, controversial package to tackle the Great Depression, Roosevelt and Congress enacted dozens of federal programs, several of which helped to memorialize and influence America's prayer culture. The Works Progress Administration, created in 1935, recruited and paid thousands of scholars and specialists to record America's past by interviewing a cross section of the population. Hispanics living in remote rural areas, former slaves now living in different parts of the country, and indigenous peoples everywhere were sharing their history. This was the first time that a comprehensive and focused approach meticulously chronicled America's diverse past. The roots and traditions of the country's prayer culture came alive in rich, detailed descriptions as people shared their earliest memories of prayer in their homes, what prayer meant to them over their lifetimes, and how they verbally were passing on the traditions of their faith to their children and grandchildren. These chroniclers even uncovered melodies to prayers that had never been heard beyond families or isolated communities.

The WPA also gave unemployed artists the opportunity to work on important projects that sustained them during the lean years of the Depression. These consisted of paintings, musical compositions, and theatrical productions, many of which showcased prayer either in America's past or in its present. From murals that would grace the walls of public buildings to plays performed on small-town stages, American spirituality, particularly prayer, was being depicted in a variety of forms. There was Jacob Lawrence's tempera-on-composition-board depiction of an African-American family in prayer, *The Migration Series, Panel No. 10: "They Were Very Poor,"* as well as Rockwell Kent's *Prayer,* which gave form, much of it haunting, to the tenor of the Depression.

The Fair Labor Standards Act of 1938 also had an effect on prayer by limiting the number of hours that laborers could work. Codifying the forty-hour workweek, outlawing child labor, and establishing the two-day weekend, the new law gave Americans greater occasion to attend church services on Sunday. Clergymen across the country saw their pews fill up after years of sparsely attended church services.

IF FOR ONLY A SHORT WHILE, Americans tried to escape the desperation of the Depression by turning to baseball, the movies, and radio. All three forms of entertainment had developed considerably by the early 1930s, becoming cultural staples.

Going out to the park to watch the likes of Babe Ruth, Ty Cobb, and Lou Gehrig play ball or sitting by the family radio and imagining the plays as they were broadcast live became a national pastime. Often, even before the first pitch was thrown, "The Star-Spangled Banner" was sung, accompanied by a prayer.

The issue of prayer and religious observance became a source of great public interest in 1934, when the Detroit Tigers vied with the New York Yankees for the American League pennant and the chance to square off against the St. Louis Cardinals for the World Series title. Hank Greenberg, an Orthodox Jew who had single-handedly helped push the Tigers from fifth to first place with his .339 batting average and thirty-nine home runs, realized that the pennant championship and upcoming series were being held over Rosh Hashanah and Yom Kippur.

Jews across the country, who had taken enormous pride in one of their own, were devastated over the timing. Conferring with his rabbi, Greenberg worked out a compromise: he would play ball during the days of Rosh Hashanah but skip any games on Yom Kippur, the most important holy day of the Jewish faith, to attend synagogue services. During Rosh Hashanah, Greenberg's magic prevailed, and the Tigers won 2–1 against the Yankees as the first baseman hit two home runs. True to his promise, Greenberg then attended the Yom Kippur prayer services at his synagogue. To the applause of the congregation, he walked down the aisle to take his seat for the service while his Tiger teammates were suiting up for the game. The Tigers lost that afternoon, but Greenberg won the admiration of even the most ardent Tiger fans, who realized what his absence had cost them.[48]

No one epitomized professional sports more in the first half of the twentieth century, however, than George Herman "Babe" Ruth. Beginning as a pitcher for the Boston Red Sox in 1914 and ending as first base coach for the Brooklyn Dodgers in 1938, Ruth hit 714 home runs, batted in over 2,000 runs, and maintained a .342 batting average over the span of his career, records that would stand untouched for decades. Described by those who knew him as "incorrigible" when he was a boy, he was placed by his largely absent parents in St. Mary's Industrial Home in Baltimore, where he became a Catholic. On the road to world fame, the hard-living Ruth seemed to lose his religious roots, although he later confessed, "I never missed a night without saying my prayers."[49]

In retirement, however, Ruth began to embrace his faith. When he was diagnosed with throat cancer, his prayer life became one long, intense devotion. Admitted to the Memorial Hospital for Cancer and Allied Diseases in New York City, he surrounded himself with holy pictures, statues, medals, and relics to help him pray; one visitor remarked that his room "looked like a religious articles store."[50] Father Thomas Kaufman, a Catholic priest who remained with Ruth in his last days, remembered that "it was inspiring the way he prayed."[51] In the hours just before he died, Babe Ruth repeated over and over again, "My Jesus, mercy," his voice growing fainter and fainter. At 7:30 p.m. on August 16, 1948, baseball's great Bambino was declared dead at the age of fifty-three.

THE MOTION PICTURE INDUSTRY was also having a dramatic impact on the cultural life of the country. Cecil B. DeMille, co-founder with Samuel Goldwyn of Paramount Pictures, was with little argument the most successful director to bridge the world of silent movies and talking motion pictures. His two epic productions of *The Ten Commandments*, one in 1923 and the other in 1956, showed both his technological versatility and his enormous directorial abilities, setting a new cinematic standard for the industry. Although DeMille had made his share of "fleshpot movies," he was deeply spiritual and readily admitted it the older he became. "Let the Divine Mind flow through your own mind, and you will be happier. I have found the greatest power in the world in the power of prayer. There is no shadow of doubt of that. I speak from my own experience," he wrote in his autobiography. By his own estimation, he read the Bible and prayed every day of his life for sixty years, finding the inspiration that welled up from it "always new and marvelously in tune with the changing need of every day."[52]

Another pivotal figure at the dawn of the motion picture industry was "America's Sweetheart," Mary Pickford. In looking over her body of work and the role she played in those early days of the film industry, Kevin Brownlow, historian and photograph curator of the American Academy of Arts and Sciences, asserted that Pickford indisputably stands as "the most popular, powerful, prominent, and influential woman in the history of cinema." In becoming the world's first superstar, she had become so popular by 1915 that film statisticians concluded that well over twelve million people every day were watching her silent movie portrayals.[53]

Pickford's personal life, however, was another matter. Suffering from the effects of alcoholism and having gone through two divorces, including her ultimate estrangement from actor Douglas Fairbanks, she became a recluse until her death in 1979 at the age of eighty-seven. Having overcome the worst of her travails by 1934, and while making the transition from motion pictures to the business world, she wrote a book called *Why Not Try God?* One prayer in particular gave her comfort, a supplication that read in part, "I sincerely desire to see clearly my shortcomings, my faults, my sins. I earnestly pray to be humble, obedient and loving in order that I may inherit here and now and forever my divine sonship, to be worthy to walk with Thee."[54] Although Pickford never really crossed over into talking motion pictures, she stood as a model for actors for many years.

With the advent of "talkies" came the much-anticipated production in 1927 of *The Jazz Singer*, starring Al Jolson. Nothing like *The Jazz Singer* had been brought to the screen. This one film revolutionized the motion picture industry overnight. The story of a Jewish cantor and his family in a New York ghetto, the picture had originally been titled *The Day of Atonement*. It alternates between sound and visual cards to explain the story with the opening scene framing the heart of the film with the words "In every living soul, a spirit cries for expression—perhaps this plaintive, wailing song of Jazz is, after all, the misunderstood utterance of a prayer."[55]

As the story continues, the audience becomes absorbed in Jackie, the son of the cantor, and his desire to become a star on the Broadway stage rather than follow in the footsteps of his father and his father's father. By the close of the movie, he has suddenly substituted for his ailing father to lead services for Yom Kippur, at just the moment he is set for his big break on Broadway. In the final scene, as Jackie, now known as Jack, dressed in his prayer shawl and yarmulke, is singing prayers before the congregation, his Gentile girlfriend says, just above a whisper, "A jazz singer—singing to his God!"

Although in retrospect some critics saw the film as maudlin and overly sentimental, *The Jazz Singer* made motion picture history. America loved what it saw, and filmmakers began to produce movies with sound, putting an end to the silent-picture era forever and turning the motion picture industry into a major sector of the American economy.

With radio also having proven its impact on the American imagination and culture, it was not long before enterprising preachers found ways to reach the faithful by using these new media to full advantage. With radios now in almost every home, Americans could easily tune in to their favorite religious programs. Charles Fuller invited his audience each week to join him for his *Old Fashioned Revival Hour,* and Father Charles Coughlin, a Roman Catholic priest, mixed both spiritual and political messages with prayer. Religious radio broadcasts, local and nationwide, offered all kinds of programming, from prayer meetings and reciting the Rosary to hymn singing and sermons on the power of prayer. The country was listening in droves.

No person knew better how to exploit radio, redefining the world of the evangelical ministry forever, than the redoubtable Aimee Semple McPherson. In a word, she was mesmerizing. Overcoming childhood poverty in her native Canada and the death of her first husband, she was driven to establish some kind of religious ministry. Alone one evening she cried out, "Lord, I'll never eat or sleep again until you fill me with this promised Spirit of power." No sooner had she said the words than she looked down at the Bible in front of her open to the passage that read, "I am more willing to give than you are to receive."[56]

Early in her ministry Sister Aimee, as she was known to her followers, drove across the country in a 1912 Packard, her "gospel car," with her mother and children in tow, traveling from one revival meeting to the next. In establishing her International Church of the Foursquare Gospel, which survives to this day, she preached a gospel of spirituality and prayer that centered on the four "symbols" of Jesus Christ—the Savior, the Baptizer with the Holy Spirit, the Healer, and the Soon-Coming King.[57]

In Los Angeles, Sister Aimee built her International Church of the Foursquare Gospel, delighted by the help that Charlie Chaplin gave her in designing the props and staging for her spiritual armory. Constructed at a cost of over $1 million and able to seat 5,300 of her followers, the Angelus Temple, as she called it, was topped off by a lighted, rotating cross that could be seen some fifty miles away. On either side of the building like bookends sat two massive radio antennas powerful enough to broadcast her services across the country and overseas over the appropriate call letters of KFSG. Finally, she erected a prayer tower, the "spiritual nerve center" of her complex, where volunteers, equipped with telephones, prayed in two hour shifts for causes of all sorts.[58]

Prayer went to the heart of Sister Aimee's ministry. Combining the public's spiritual hunger with its craving for sensationalism, her special appeal was undeniable. To entice people to attend services she had members of her orchestra play hymns on the streets of Los Angeles, one that included Anthony Quinn, a fourteen-year-old saxophone player mesmerized by the evangelist who in a few short years would become an actor in Hollywood.[59] In the early days of the church's opening, she would even meet the press on airport tarmacs throughout southern California to talk about her mission and then jump into the back of a two-person cockpit, flying over local communities as she dropped prayer leaflets and information about her ministry.

Holding services seven days a week, three on Sunday, McPherson became a one-woman phenomenon. Turning away hundreds of people from a service—sometimes thousands because there was no more room—became commonplace. Los Angeles police had their work cut out for them on Sunday evenings in particular, when traffic peaked with those who wanted to attend the most sought-after service of the week.

When people walked into Angelus Temple, Sister Aimee wanted to make sure that she held their attention until the moment they walked out the door. Even before McPherson appeared onstage, the audience would be regaled with fantastic plays. The most popular of them all was a performance in which the forces of good and evil appeared as angels and devils, sparring with each other for advantage over a person's soul. A scoreboard overhead would keep tabs on who was getting the better of whom. Boos, gasps, and cheers would sweep through the audience as the faithful were urged to pray under their breath that the pure of heart would ultimately vanquish the wicked. Good would always prevail in the end. Afterwards, and at other opportune moments, ushers would take up one, two, and sometimes three collections to sustain Sister Aimee's ministry.

Hysteria would grip most of the audience as the orchestra, singers, and dancers added to the anticipation of "Sister's" entrance. With trumpets blaring a rousing rendition of John Philip Sousa's "Stars and Stripes Forever," the moment would finally come. Suddenly a hidden staircase would appear from nowhere, descending onto the rose-covered center stage like the drawbridge to a great castle. At the top of the stairs, bathed in alternating colored spotlights, Sister Aimee would be cradling a bouquet of roses, acknowledging the pandemonium of the crowd as she proceeded down the long flight of stairs. To many, she seemed to be delivered by heaven itself, so that when she finally arrived onstage, it was only natural for her to gaze back, praying to the God she had just visited. The effect was more visually spectacular than anything Metro-Goldwyn-Mayer could have produced.

Catering to the times, McPherson dramatically changed her message and her approach to prayer with the onset of the Depression. Whereas in the 1920s she had followed the lead of the Reverend Billy Sunday in stressing the wrath of an angry God on the subject of sin, after the stock market crash she emphasized a God of love. Her personal life was at times even more fascinating. From her marriages and divorces to a highly publicized incident in 1926 in which she disappeared without a trace only to reappear a few days later, her life became the stuff of tabloid fodder. Her death in 1944, reportedly due to an overdose of sleeping powders, brought to a close an American original whose approach to preaching redefined evangelization forever.[60]

★ ★ ★

EXACTLY WHEN THE Great Depression ended and what federal programs worked or did not work to revitalize the economy are open to debate. What remains clear, though, is that the onset of World War II changed the equation for America dramatically—economically, politically, militarily, and spiritually. The 1920s and 1930s leading up to that moment were arguably two of the most reflective decades in U.S. history. Not only were Americans defining themselves as global players and expressing themselves creatively, if not dynamically, through the arts and humanities, they were also experiencing the realities of economic despair and vulnerability. While there appeared at times to be a spiritual void, it would prove temporary. The country's spiritual mettle was about to be tested in even more dramatic ways.

CHAPTER 12

THE DEFENDERS

1935–1945

O God, most merciful and just . . . Make me strong in conflict, brave in adversity, and patient in suffering. Make me vigilant to defend my country against her enemies and proud to carry her cause fearlessly into battle. I do not ask to be preserved free from all bodily harm, and if death is the price I must pay for our country's freedom, I will pay it gladly, trusting in Thy infinite mercy that Thou wilt make a place for me in heaven, there to know peace and happiness in all eternity.

—Brigadier General LaVerne G. Saunders,
Twentieth Bomber Command, U.S. Army, 1942

FOR MORE THAN A DECADE, most Americans had been worn down by a wrenching economy that made even daily existence a challenge. Although Europe seemed far removed from America, many people began to wonder how much longer Germany's war machine would remain unchecked and what role the United States would be forced to take.

Of particular distress to America's Jews were the unsettling stories about the treatment of Jews in Europe. Jews and non-Jews alike began to imagine the horror and expressed their solidarity in a variety of ways.

On learning of the yellow Stars of David that German Jews were being forced to wear on their sleeves, H. Leyvik, one of the greatest Yiddish writers in American history, composed a prayer in 1940 called "Song of the Yellow Patch." In it he imagined what the victims of Hitler's methodical madness must be experiencing while he, an American Jew, sat safely in his New York City apartment. "How does it look, the yellow patch," he wrote, "against the white ground of a December snow? . . . How would it look on my own arm—the question gnaws like a gnat in my brain . . . eats at my heart like a worm."[1] What was the truth about Europe's Jews, and when would it all end?

EVEN TO THE LEAST-INFORMED AMERICAN, it became clear that the United States would enter the war. Americans' anxiousness and unvarnished patriotism were best captured in Irving Berlin's love poem for his adopted country, "God Bless America." With its opening line, "While the storm clouds gather far across the sea," it was a call of patriotic love.

Born in 1888, Israel Baline immigrated to the United States through Ellis Island at the age of five with his family from Byelorussia. Even before America entered World War I, he had enjoyed enormous success with a series of hit songs, the most popular of them being "Alexander's Ragtime Band."

Berlin originally wrote "God Bless America" in 1918 as a finale to a show he was putting together for new military recruits at Camp Upton in Yaphank on Long Island, New York. He called the show *Yip Yip Yaphank,* hoping to boost the morale of thousands of troops, most from the greater New York City area, who were about to be shipped to the front lines in Europe. He had another song, however, called "I Can Always Find a Little Sunshine in the YMCA," that closed the musical. The song was such a hit with the men that Berlin thought "God Bless America" might be overkill, and so he put the piece away—for two decades.

In September 1938, when Berlin was in London for the premiere of the movie *Alexander's Ragtime Band,* he was struck by the breakneck speed at which Europe was being pressed to war. On his way back to the United States, he began to think about his old song. Given his legendary photographic memory, the notes and words began to appear in his mind, and soon he was humming the melody and editing the song, adapting it to the theme of peace, rather than war. The question was how best to debut "God Bless America."

Within hours of his return to New York, as luck would have it, Berlin was contacted by Ted Collins, a longtime acquaintance and the agent for

Kate Smith, one of the country's most popular singers. Collins asked Berlin if he could write a song for Smith to sing on Armistice Day, November 11, 1938, commemorating the twentieth anniversary of the end to World War I. "God Bless America" was a natural. Introducing the piece on her popular weekly CBS radio show, *The Kate Smith Hour,* Smith remarked, "It's something more than a song—I feel it's one of the most beautiful compositions ever written, a song that will never die." By the time she sang it at the 1939 World's Fair in New York, the sheet music had sold over 400,000 copies.[2] The orchestra behind her then began to play while she stepped up to the microphone and said for the first time, "We raise our voices in a solemn prayer." From that day forward "God Bless America" was embedded into the country's patriotic and spiritual psyche.

BY 1939 THE PRESIDENT had grown more convinced that the United States could not remain on the sidelines in the war. With the Battle of Britain in the summer and fall of 1940, in which the German Luftwaffe relentlessly bombed targets within the United Kingdom, it became clear that the last great European bastion of democracy could not hold out indefinitely. Without support from the United States, both Roosevelt and England's Prime Minister Winston Churchill knew, the country's resources could not withstand Hitler's juggernaut for long. Responding to the threat, Roosevelt dispatched his longtime confidant Harry Hopkins to meet with Churchill and other British officials in early 1941. On the eve of Hopkins's departure from London, after several days of intense meetings, the British Prime Minister hosted a private state dinner for his guest. At the dinner Hopkins rose to address the Prime Minister, remarking, "I suppose you wish to know what I am going to say to President Roosevelt on my return. Well, I am going to quote to you one verse from that Book of Books . . . 'Wither thou goest, I will go; and where thou lodgest, I will lodge: thy people shall be my people, and thy God my God.' " And then he paused, saying just above a whisper, "Even to the end." Churchill visibly wept.[3] It was not a matter of "if" but "when" the full force of the United States would be engaged.

On his return to Washington, Hopkins wasted no time in debriefing the President. His report only reinforced the pressing need for Roosevelt to meet with Churchill in person. Preparations were soon made for the two leaders to meet that August in Placentia Bay, Newfoundland, in complete secrecy. Grasping the importance of the moment and realizing they would be meeting over the Sabbath of August 10, 1941, Churchill decided that a formal Royal Navy Sunday service should be held under the massive guns of the newly commissioned battleship HMS *Prince of Wales* to solidify the bonds between the leaders and their countries at such a crucial hour.

From the opening notes of both national anthems and the presenting of arms, the politicians and servicemen aboard ship that day realized they were experiencing one of the most emotionally charged moments of their lives. As the service began, the head chaplain offered a prayer that expressed the enormous stakes they were facing:

Let us pray for the invaded countries, in the grief and havoc of oppression; for the upholding of their courage; and the hope for the speedy restoration of their freedom. O Lord God, whose compassions fail not, support, we entreat Thee, the peoples on whom the terrors of invasion have fallen; and if their liberty be lost to the oppressor, let not this spirit and hope be broken, but stayed upon Thy strength till the day of deliverance. Through Jesus Christ our Lord. Amen.[4]

The band then played the hymn "O God, Our Help in Ages Past" as Churchill, dressed in his famous boilersuit, and the taller Roosevelt, impeccably attired in a light cream suit, seemed to sing louder than all the other men. The prayers continued with what was called an invocation for the "victory of Right and Truth":

Save us and deliver us from the hands of our enemies; abate their pride, assuage their malice, and confound their devices; that we, being armed with Thy defense, may be preserved ever more from all perils, to glorify Thee, who art the only giver of all victory.

Stablish our hearts, O God, in the light of battle, and strengthen our resolve, that we fight, not in enmity against men, but against the powers of darkness enslaving the souls of men; till all enmity and oppression be done away, and the people of the world be set free from fear to serve one another; as children of our Father, who is above all and through all and in all, God for ever and ever. Amen.[5]

At this point in the service one of the most poignant moments came as "Eternal Father, Strong to Save" was sung, a hymn of special significance to sailors, one that meant as much to Americans as to the British. It was the only personal request made by Roosevelt.

In his multivolume memoirs of World War II, Churchill wrote that the prayer service had been a "deeply moving expression of the unity of faith of our two peoples" and that "none who took part in it will ever forget the spectacle" on that quarterdeck. There they were, British and American sailors, "joining fervently together in the prayers and hymns familiar to both." The British Prime Minister would remember how "every word seemed to stir the heart" and that to all those present "it was a great hour to live." Despite the pride and warmth of that day, in retrospect it would be a bittersweet moment, Churchill recounting after the war that "nearly half those who sang were soon to die."[6]

IT WAS NOT THE WILL of the President, or of anyone else for that matter, that pushed the United States into war. It was the single act of infamy, as President Roosevelt described it, that made the difference as the Japanese bombed the Hawaiian Islands over two hours on Sunday morning, December 7, 1941. Four battleships and eighteen other warships were sunk at Pearl Harbor and nearly 188 aircraft were destroyed. Even more tragically, more than thirty-five hundred men and women, both service personnel and civilians, were either killed or injured, while the Japanese lost only fifty-five men and fewer than thirty planes.[7]

In the thick of the Pearl Harbor attack, the Reverend Howell Maurice Forgy, a naval chaplain and ordained Presbyterian minister, was part of a human chain, handing antiaircraft military shells to the gunners of the heavy cruiser USS *New Orleans*. As smoke billowed out in all directions from the strikes of Japanese bombers overhead, he realized that the men were growing tired, and finally he hollered out over all the noise, "Praise the Lord and pass the ammunition." No one ever forgot it. The next year the songwriter Frank Loesser set the words to music, with its memorable line, "Praise the Lord and pass the ammunition and we'll all stay free!"[8]

Within days of the bombing, Roosevelt and Churchill agreed to meet in Washington to discuss strategy; by Christmas the British Prime Minister had taken up temporary residence in the family quarters of the White House with President and Mrs. Roosevelt. On January 1, 1942, a day the President called for national prayer, the two leaders sat side by side, once again praying and singing hymns, at Christ Church in Alexandria, Virginia, the same Episcopal church where George Washington had worshipped.

After the experience of World War I, the country no longer had wild, idealistic illusions about war. Given the maturing of America's media and the fervor of a new, young cadre of journalists, firsthand accounts were being sent back to the United States for airing on radio and for printing in newspapers with greater speed than ever. On the home front, people crowded pews and places of worship. They lit candles, attended daily prayer services and Masses, erected small altars in their homes to pray for their sons, husbands, and fathers, and held continuous prayer vigils.

Both the U.S. government and the country's churches promoted prayer among the men and women overseas and on the home front. Over eight thousand chaplains distributed prayer books, Bibles, and prayer tracts of all kinds. Federal employees at the U.S. Government Printing Office worked around the clock to produce religious publications. Some of the editions were designed to fit into steel casings that protected them from use and damage. Small statues of Christ, Mary, and the saints were distributed. Crosses, crucifixes, and Stars of David were standard-issue to anyone who wanted them. One particularly treasured item was an American-flag pocket, in which two flags were sewn together on three sides, no longer than a grown man's thumb, containing a folded copy of the Lord's Prayer.

THE NATION'S THOUGHTS were not only on U.S. soldiers fighting in distant lands but also on the real possibility of an attack by Axis forces on America. After all, if the Japanese could bomb Pearl Harbor, it was not inconceivable that they could strike somewhere in the continental United States. The U.S. government had already made contingency plans for such a scenario, issuing air-raid instructions.

The outspoken Monsignor John Boland, chairman of the Labor Relations Board of New York, expressed alarm that the government had done little to address the spiritual needs of its citizens in the event of an air raid. In an editorial to Catholics across the country, he offered his readers suggestions, many of them involving prayer:

(1) Remember during air raids, that the privilege of praying is yours. Aids to prayer should be within easy reach or view, a crucifix, the image of the Sacred Heart, your rosary or rosary ring, spiritual books and leaflets. Holy water, which is blessed solely to invoke God's protection against dangers to soul and body, should be available. The thought of God commissioning His angels to watch over you, should give you calm and courage.

(2) Go to confession often, aware of the fact when the enemy is overhead, it may be too late. Remain in God's grace by keeping free from mortal sin. The bombs that land will not pass you by just because you are not prepared to meet your maker. If you cannot go to confession, say an act of contrition, for instance, "O my God, I am sorry for my sins because they offend Thee again."

(3) Hear Mass on weekdays, too, and receive Holy Communion.

(4) Bear in mind your Christian duties toward your neighbors, especially when they have been stricken in body or property. Be models of fearlessness and helpfulness. Your non-Catholic brethren will expect it.

(5) Obey the authorities without question, condemning, as they must, violations of the regulations and dim-out deviltry. Your air warden speaks in their name.[9]

At Christian churches and Jewish synagogues across the country, special prayer groups were formed to ask for Divine Providence for U.S. troops and for any contingency that might arise, even at home.

FOR JIMMY DOOLITTLE, the bona fide hero who led the decisive air raids on Tokyo just months after the war began, prayer had always been a "vital, personal force" to be said every day of his life. Whether in a cathedral, country church, or alone on some remote mission, "I could always talk with God," he later wrote. He also came to believe that it was important to pray early and often and not wait for a last-minute crisis, "for when the chips are down, there's often too much to do during an emergency to send out a prayer for help or guidance."[10]

In the middle of the North African campaign in 1942, when Erwin Rommel and his German troops were finally routed by Allied troops, Doolittle attributed to prayer the "wisdom and strength" that led to victory.[11] A split-second decision had to be made when, in the skies over the

Mediterranean, German supply planes unexpectedly appeared, all of which were easy targets for Doolittle and his men. The problem was that carefully devised Allied plans called for a much broader offensive a few days later. Despite the ease with which the planes could have been downed, Doolittle decided not to attack. When the day for the planned battle arrived, the air force was far better prepared and ultimately destroyed more than two hundred aircraft, cutting supply lines and effectively crippling German air superiority over North Africa once and for all.

For Jimmy Doolittle the experience only pointed to the way prayer worked in his life, preventing him from doing a "stupid and foolhardy" thing. "Not that God should remove obstacles or grant special protection or favors, but He helps give one confidence and power to overcome the difficulty and fear."[12] Doolittle would survive the war as one of the country's most decorated veterans. He went on to star in several motion pictures and became vice president and director of the Shell Oil Company, dying in 1993 at the age of ninety-seven.

A NUMBER OF EXTRAORDINARY STORIES surfaced during the war that allowed Americans to view prayer and their own faith through the eyes of others. One tale involved another decorated aviator, Eddie Rickenbacker, one of the great heroes of World War I. Beginning his career as General John J. Pershing's chauffeur in Europe in 1917, Rickenbacker transferred to the newly formed aviation service and was soon commanding the Ninety-fourth Aero Pursuit Squadron, shooting down twenty-six enemy aircraft in a series of daring dogfights. Awarded the Congressional Medal of Honor and nicknamed by the press the "Ace of Aces," Rickenbacker would retire from the military immediately after the war, founding the Rickenbacker Motor Company in 1921. He became an irresistible hire for General Motors after the war to help design automobiles and head up its new division, Eastern Airlines. In time Rickenbacker would buy Eastern from GM, building it into the first profitable commercial airline in history.

Following the attack on Pearl Harbor, no one was more qualified to inspect American air units' readiness than Rickenbacker. Having returned from a tour of bases in Great Britain, where he conferred with Churchill, Rickenbacker met with Secretary of War Henry Stimson, who lost no time in sending him out to the Pacific in the fall of 1942 to continue his government-sponsored review of Allied readiness. Taking off from Hawaii in a B-17 bomber, Rickenbacker and seven other men realized midway through the flight that their faulty navigational equipment had taken them hundreds of miles off course. With little fuel left, they ditched the massive bomber in the ocean some six hundred miles north of the Samoa Islands. From the floating wreckage the men were able to construct three makeshift rafts, holding on for dear life, hoping that somehow the Allies would find them before Japanese reconnaissance planes did—that is, if anyone would find them at all.

Rickenbacker had long believed in the enormous potential of prayer, referring to it as the "Big Radio," but always reminding himself that it was a "two-way job." In his no-nonsense approach he liked to say, "You've got to keep tuned with It, and you have to talk back."[13] From the outset Rickenbacker was the leader of the group, reminding the apprehensive men of his own past brushes with death.

For twenty-one days the men floated totally exposed to the elements as they carefully divided four oranges among themselves, the only food left from the crash. The heat, the sting of saltwater, and the hunger were relentless. "Daytimes we prayed for the coolness of the nights; nights we craved the sun," Rickenbacker remembered.[14]

Each morning and evening the men pulled their rafts together to pray "frankly and humbly" for deliverance. Before the crash Private First Class Johnny Bartek had grabbed his small New Testament that also contained the Psalms and fastened it into one of his pockets. Finding solace in those prayers of David, the men would read some of the same passages over and over again, words that had particular meaning for them:

> Therefore take no thought, saying, What shall we eat? Or, What shall we drink? Or, Wherewithal shall we be clothed? . . . For your heavenly Father knoweth that ye have need of all these things. But seek ye first the kingdom of God, and his righteousness; and all these things shall be added unto you.
>
> Take therefore no thought for the morrow: for the morrow shall take thought for the things of itself. Sufficient unto the day is the evil thereof.[15]

After a few days afloat, Rickenbacker and the men found that by singing hymns after their "prayer service," they were able to "release something" in the midst of all their anxieties, and "the talk for the first time became intensely personal." By the end of the first week, however, "one or two who had been most fervent, became backsliders. Because their prayers were unanswered within twenty-four to forty-eight hours, they condemned the Lord for His failure to save them. They wanted deliverance immediately." Nonetheless, "the rest went on praying with deep-felt hope."[16]

Rickenbacker never gave in to feelings of despair. On the eighth day, he and the men found a visible sign that all was not lost. Minutes after they had finished their morning prayers, Rickenbacker laid back on his raft, pulling his cap over his eyes to doze off for a few moments. Without warning a seagull landed on his head, and with careful, unhurried precision he grabbed the bird's legs in his bare hands. Not only did the bird provide the men with immediate food, bones and all, but Rickenbacker used the bird's intestines as bait to catch fish, later recounting in detail how "that seagull kept us alive."[17]

Given Rickenbacker's prominence as a bona fide hero from the last war, the U.S. military spent considerable resources in an all-out effort to find his plane. After a naval pilot finally sighted the wreckage and circled the rafts on the twentieth day of their ordeal, a ship was sent to pick them up the next morning.

The fifty-two-year-old Rickenbacker unfolded his latest tale to a riveted American public. From media interviews to congressional hearings, he found himself in great demand and was soon pressed by his admirers to chronicle his experience in a book, *Seven Came Through*.

He also made a number of recommendations to the U.S. armed services regarding minimum requirements for survival equipment and provisions on board military aircraft in the event of an emergency. Many of them were introduced immediately. At the same time, Rickenbacker did not forget the role Divine Providence had played in his rescue and wrote a prayer of gratitude that was widely circulated to the troops and to Americans on the home front:

> *O Lord, I thank thee for the strength and blessings thou hast given me, and even though I have walked through the valley of the shadow of death, I feared no evil, for thy rod and thy staff comforted me even unto the four corners of the world. I have sinned, O Lord, but through thy mercy thou hast shown me the light of thy saving grace.*

*In thy care we are entrusting our boys and girls in the Services scattered
throughout the entire world, and we know that in thee they are finding
their haven of hope. Be with our leaders, Lord; give them wisdom to lead us
to a spiritual victory, as well as a physical one. And until that day, be with
those at home—strengthen them for whatever may lie ahead. Be with our
enemies, O Lord, and through the light of thy divine grace, may they
reconsecrate themselves to thy service as we are reconsecrating ourselves, so
all peoples of the world will sing in unison "Glory to God in the Highest,"
as only through thee can we realize our hopes for peace everlasting. In Jesus'
name I ask it. Amen.*[18]

BEFORE THE UNITED STATES entered the war, German U-boats had
methodically patrolled the traffic lanes of the Atlantic. To support their
U-boat threat, the Germans set up a weather station in Greenland. The
outpost provided support to U-boats while radioing false weather
reports to Allied ships. Despite Allied efforts to find and destroy the station, it survived for the duration of the war.

Against this backdrop, on February 3, 1943, the *Dorchester,* a luxury ship
converted into a U.S. Army transport, was carrying nine hundred troops
from St. John, Newfoundland, to the American base on Greenland. Most
likely with the help of the weather station, the German U-233 spotted
and torpedoed the ship at 12:55 in the morning. Assigned to the *Dorchester*
were four chaplains had formed friendships with many of the men:
Rabbi Alexander Goode, the descendant of a long line of Jewish rabbis;
the Reverend George Fox, a Methodist minister and World War I veteran; Father John Washington, a Catholic priest from a large Irish immigrant family; and the Reverend Clark Poling, a Dutch Reformed minister
who had told his family when he was deployed, "Don't pray for my safe
return, pray that I do my duty."[19]

Despite the pitch darkness, the blasts of the ship's whistle and escaping steam, as well as the listing of the *Dorchester,* made it obvious that the
ship was sinking. With little hesitation the four chaplains rushed to the
deck, wearing their life jackets, and grabbed every preserver they could
find to hand out. When it became clear that there were more men than
jackets, the chaplains ripped off their preservers and handed them to
four other men, who jumped overboard, hoping to be rescued.

As the ship went down, the men floating in the icy waters of the
North Atlantic watched as the chaplains linked arms and braced them-

selves against the ship's railing while the vessel sank. A sergeant who survived the tragedy later recounted how these four men of such different faiths had always supported one another. Now, in their last moments, they stood together one more time, reciting prayers and singing hymns as though they were one.

The story of the four chaplains was told and retold. The sinking of the ship, taking almost seven hundred men with it, was the third-largest loss at sea for the United States during the war, making the heroism of the chaplains all the more striking. Almost all of the men who survived experienced some form of physical impairment for the rest of their lives.[20] Given their life-changing experience, none of the survivors ever forgot how four clergymen of different faiths had shown their ecumenism and their compassion for the men of the *Dorchester.* Stained-glass windows were etched with their likenesses and installed in military chapels from West Point, New York, to Fort Snelling, Minnesota. In 1960, Congress honored the men by striking a distinctive Congressional Medal of Honor that was awarded to them posthumously.

NO TEST OF ENDURANCE was greater than being held as a prisoner of war, and no story quite matched that of the men who endured the Death March of Bataan. On the eve of the battle that preceded the brutal march in 1942, the Reverend William Thomas Cummings, a Catholic priest, delivered a stirring field sermon. Looking into the faces of the troops, trying to reach them in a meaningful way, he uttered one of the most famous wartime lines ever: "Remember, there are no atheists in foxholes."[21] Pressing his men to face their own mortality through prayer, he helped brace many of them for what would be the greatest challenge of their lives.

This gruesome chapter of World War II began just five months after the Japanese bombed Pearl Harbor. Fortified with armaments, supplies, and a well-thought-out strategy, the Japanese unrelentingly struck U.S. and Philippine forces on the peninsula of Bataan in the Philippines. Unprepared for the onslaught and with supplies and military equipment dwindling to practically nothing, twelve thousand Americans and sixty-four thousand Filipino troops had little choice but to surrender in April 1942. With the prisoner-of-war camp some fifty-five miles away, the Japanese forced all seventy-six thousand men to march the distance on foot, providing little food or water along the way. The chronicles of that march as Japanese troops bound, tortured, and killed Allied forces at will have made for some of the most wrenching stories in modern military history.

Only fifty-six thousand men reached camp; twenty thousand soldiers died en route. For those who survived, the ordeal would continue in Japanese prison camps for another three and a half years, until General Douglas MacArthur and his troops retook the Philippines. One of the few breaks the Japanese allowed their prisoners was to pray together on occasion and observe religious ceremonies. Prison camp priests, ministers, and rabbis provided critical assistance, sustaining the men both emotionally and spiritually during some of the worst moments of their captivity. Forced to begin the workday at six in the morning, Catholics would gather at 5:00 a.m. to attend Mass, while Protestants and Jews held their own prayer services. Clinging to the regular discipline of daily prayer, most soldiers were able to stretch their limits of endurance. As Staff Sergeant William Nolan later remembered of his days in the camp, "I learned that if God wanted to take me, He'd take me, so why worry about dying."[22] By the time of liberation in 1945, two out of every three soldiers who had surrendered in 1942 would be dead.

THERE WERE, OF COURSE, the prayers of those who never escaped the war and whose last thoughts focused on what might lie in store. One of the most touching insights into a dying soldier's last moments was discovered in the pocket of a dead American soldier, a casualty of the North African campaign. Written in the form of a poem, the prayer was composed in the unvarnished language of a young man scribbling down his thoughts on the battlefield, experiencing a catharsis of monumental proportions when he realized that death might not be far behind:

> *Look, God, I have never spoken to you,*
> *And now I want to say, "How do you do?"*
> *And see, God, they told me you did not exist,*
> *And I, like a fool, believed all this.*
> *Last night, from a shell-hole, I saw your sky,*
> *I figured that they told me a lie.*
> *Had I taken time before to see things you had made,*
> *I'd sure have known they weren't calling a spade a spade.*

I wonder, God, if you would shake my poor hand?
Somehow I feel you would understand.
Strange I had to come to this hellish place
Before I had time to see your face.
Well, I guess, there isn't much more to say,
But I'm glad, God, that I met you today.
The zero hour will soon be here,
But I'm not afraid to know that you're near.

The signal has come—I shall soon have to go,
I like you lots—this I want you to know.
I am sure this will be a horrible fight;
Who knows? I may come to your house tonight,
Though I wasn't friendly to you before,
I wonder, God, if you'd wait at your door?
Look, I'm shedding tears—me shedding tears!
Oh! I wish I'd known you these long, long years.
Well, I have to go now, dear God. Good-bye,
But now that I've met you I'm not scared to die.[23]

BY THE WAR'S END, no single battle had better captured the sacrifice, the struggle, or the determination of the Allies to secure final victory than Operation Overlord. Set to commence on June 6, 1944, Operation Overlord, better known as D-day, had been in the planning for months. The ambitious plan called for an attack force of one million men supported by five thousand ships, twelve thousand aircraft, and another two million support personnel. Nothing like it had ever been executed in history.

While General Dwight D. Eisenhower was charged with overall Allied command, he was supported by British General Bernard Montgomery, who oversaw land operations. Back on their respective home fronts, President Roosevelt and Prime Minister Churchill were kept informed almost hourly. As excruciating as the wear and tear of the war years had been for both leaders, it was particularly visible on the American President. With the green light for D-day finally given, the battle begun in earnest, and the element of surprise now over, Roosevelt addressed the nation. Rather than give a summary of the war to date or any glimpse of what was to come, he chose to deliver a prayer.

Not since Abraham Lincoln's second inaugural address had a President delivered such an introspective reflection at such a crucial moment. What the President said at ten o'clock on the night of the invasion spoke volumes to what the country was facing. With the help of the Pulitzer Prize–winning playwright and presidential speechwriter, Robert Sherwood, the President made his plea to God on behalf of the nation:

> *Almighty God: Our sons, pride of our Nation, this day have set upon a mighty endeavor, a struggle to preserve our Republic, our religion, and our civilization, and to set free a suffering humanity.*
>
> *Lead them straight and true; give strength to their arms, stoutness to their hearts, steadfastness in their faith.*
>
> *They will be sore tired, by night and by day without rest—until victory is won. The darkness will be rent by noise and flame. Men's souls will be shaken with the violences of war.*
>
> *For these men are lately drawn from the ways of peace. They fight not for the lust of conquest. They fight to end conquest. They fight to liberate. They fight to let justice arise, and tolerance and good will among all Thy people. They yearn but for an end of battle, for their return to the haven of home.*
>
> *Some will never return. Embrace these, Father, and receive them, Thy heroic servants, into Thy kingdom.*
>
> *And for us at home—fathers, mothers, children, wives, sisters, and brothers of brave men overseas whose thoughts and prayers are ever with them—help us, Almighty God, to rededicate ourselves in renewed faith in Thee in this hour of great sacrifice . . .*
>
> *With Thy blessing, we shall prevail over the unholy forces of our enemy. Help us to conquer the apostles of greed and racial arrogances. Lead us to the saving of our country, and with our sister nations into a world unity that will spell a sure peace—a peace invulnerable to the schemings of unworthy men. And a peace that will let all men live in freedom, reaping the just rewards of their honest toil. Thy will be done, Almighty God. Amen.*[24]

THOUSANDS OF MILES from Washington, D-day was well under way. At the beachheads of Normandy, places named Omaha, Utah, Gold, Juno, and Sword, the Americans, British, and Canadians landed, fought, and died in the thousands as they stormed German defenses. Once onshore, and if they survived, the men had to scale cliffs one hundred feet high.

Upon reaching the summits, the first wave signaled their success by immediately radioing back to their commanders the code words "Praise the Lord."[25]

Meanwhile, back home in the United States, the sheer magnitude of the operation was just beginning to be understood. Charles E. Wilson, the president of General Electric, would remember how the word "invasion" had "hung in the air, almost touchable, just out of reach," for weeks, if not months. On the morning of the sixth, Wilson had driven to Union Station in Washington, D.C., to pick up a friend. The number of commuters at the train station at that hour was enormous, but a hush fell over the concourse as one person whispered to another and then to another, "The invasion's begun . . . they're landing in Normandy." Wilson recalled:

> While I stood watching, it began. First it was a woman who, right there in the station, dropped to her knees and folded her hands; near her a man knelt down. Then another, and another until all around me people knelt down before the hard wooden benches of Union Station.
>
> What were we praying for that morning of the Invasion? For Jim or for Franz or for Giovanni—or just for peace? Perhaps for no reason at all, except that in the hush we felt the need to pray.[26]

After a few minutes, life returned to the station as everyone got up from the floor, each in his or her own time, and continued on with their personal business. "But for those of us who witnessed the hush," Wilson later reflected, "Union Station will always have a special meaning: we were there on the day the railroad station in Washington, D.C., became a house of worship."[27]

THE INVASION OF NORMANDY was not the last great battle but only the beginning of the end to the European phase of the war. The final major German offensive in the West came in December 1944 in the Ardennes region of southern Belgium in what would become known as the Battle of the Bulge, the largest land battle involving American forces during the war.

Commanding the American troops was the indomitable General George Patton, who had been put in charge of the Third Army's half million men. Bombastic, unforgiving, and stubborn at one moment, Patton could easily commune with the divine in the next. He often referred to the definition of courage that Chaplain George Metcalf had once given him: "Courage is fear that has said its prayers."[28]

The Americans were taken by surprise by the German panzer and infantry under the command of General Karl von Rundstedt. It was critical for the Allies to reach Brussels and the strategic port of Antwerp at all costs, as quickly as possible. In addition to the stubbornness of German defenses, there was another problem in executing the strategy: the weather was creating havoc for troops on the ground and pilots in the air. Day after day a steady, drizzling rain and a low hanging fog were taking their toll. Seemingly boxed in by conditions beyond his control, Patton called in his chief Third Army chaplain, Brigadier General James O'Neill, and asked the Catholic monsignor for a special prayer to implore God for good weather and final victory. An astonished O'Neill asked Patton to give him an hour. Scouring every prayer book he had, he was unable to find anything appropriate, so he composed his own. After reading it, Patton asked him to print up 250,000 wallet-sized copies immediately and have them handed out to his men. Realizing the difficulty of the order in the middle of the war but resolute, O'Neill went even further and suggested that the prayer be sent with a personal Christmas greeting to the men with General Patton's signature attached. By December 12, the Christmas card and prayer had been distributed to every soldier in the Third Army:

> *Almighty and merciful Father, we humbly beseech Thee, of Thy great goodness, to restrain these immoderate rains with which we have had to contend. Grant us fair weather for Battle. Graciously hearken to us as soldiers who call upon Thee that, armed with Thy power, we may advance from victory to victory, and crush the oppression and wickedness of our enemies, and establish Thy justice among men and nations. Amen.*[29]

To the astonishment of Patton's men, the fog lifted, the rains stopped, and the weather cleared for a critical period from December 20 to the end of the year. When Patton saw the chaplain in early January, he stood directly in front of him, smiling, and said, "Well, Padre, our prayers worked. I knew they would."[30] He then lightly cracked his riding crop on the side of the chaplain's helmet, delighted by what he saw as the work of Divine Providence.

General Patton next asked O'Neill to draw up a training letter exclusively on the subject of prayer, believing that "there are three ways that men get what they want—by planning, by working, and by praying."[31] Traditionally, training letters had been used by the chief chaplain to relay orders and instructions to all the other chaplains on how best to minister to the soldiers. In the Third Army there were 486 chaplains representing thirty-two denominations, but Patton gave the order to have the letter sent to every commander down to the regimental level. Although the letter was to carry O'Neill's signature, Patton wanted to review it before the chaplain sent it out to some several thousand men.

Committed to having it out just as fast as the prayer card, O'Neill worked day and night to put all of the pieces together. Remembering much of his private conversations with Patton, he used some of the general's own thoughts, recounting how Divine Providence had helped the Third Army up to that moment. Part of the letter read:

> *Those who pray do more for the world than those who fight; and if the world goes from bad to worse, it is because there are more battles than prayers . . . [W]e must urge, instruct, and indoctrinate every fighting man to pray as well as fight . . .*
>
> *Urge your men to pray, not alone in church, but everywhere. Pray when driving. Pray when fighting. Pray alone. Pray with others. Pray by night and pray by day. Pray for the cessation of immoderate rains, for good weather for Battle. Pray for the defeat of our wicked enemy whose banner is injustice and whose good is oppression. Pray for Victory, Pray for our Army, and Pray for Peace . . .*
>
> *Be assured that this message on prayer has the approval, the encouragement, and the enthusiastic support of the Third United States Army Commander.*[32]

Before the end of the war, Patton personally wrote one final prayer that reinforced his image as a hardened but spiritual soldier:

> *God of our Fathers . . . strengthen my soul so that the weakening instinct of self-preservation, which besets us all in battle, shall not blind me to my*

duty to my own manhood, to the glory of my calling, and to my
responsibility to my fellow soldiers . . . Let me not mourn for the men who
have died fighting, but rather let me be glad that such heroes have lived . . .
Give us victory, Lord.[33]

By early spring Allied forces had pushed the Germans back to the Rhine River, and it was only a matter of days before the Axis powers crumbled. Benito Mussolini would soon be hanged along with his mistress over the streets of Milan by angry mobs on April 28, while Hitler would reportedly take his own life forty-eight hours later. VE day was declared on May 8, 1945. Allied victory in Europe had been won.

WITH THE WAR IN EUROPE now over, the truth about the Nazi concentration camps began to filter to the outside world. On a tour of the camps, General Eisenhower remarked, "The things I saw beggar description."[34] Experts later estimated the final toll of men, women, and children executed in the Holocaust because they were Jews, gypsies, homosexuals, or sympathizers of any outlawed group to be six million.

The future Nobel Prize winner Elie Wiesel, a child survivor of the Auschwitz and Buchenwald death camps who immigrated to the United States after the war, would chillingly write many years later, "Never shall I forget those moments which murdered my God and my soul and turned my dreams to dust . . . Never."[35] In illustrating the horror, he remembered all too well the moment he heard the haunting Kaddish being prayed in Hebrew by a man standing near him. It was the familiar Jewish prayer for the dead, with its words:

Magnified and sanctified be God's great name in the world which He has
created according to His will. May He establish His kingdom soon in our
lifetime. May we say: Amen.

May His great name be praised to all eternity.

Hallowed and honored, extolled and exalted, adored and acclaimed be
the name of the Holy One, though He is above all blessing and song. May
we say: Amen.

May God grant abundant peace and life to us and to all Israel. Let us
say: Amen.

> *May He who ordains harmony in the universe grant peace to us and to
> all Israel. Let us say: Amen.*

As everyone stood there, tears coming to their eyes, Wiesel remembered
thinking to himself, "I do not know if it has ever happened before in the
history of the Jews, that people have ever recited the prayer for the dead
for themselves."[36] The men stood together as one, weeping, as they listened to words that had suddenly taken on new meaning.

Another prayer would also come to be cherished, particularly among
America's Jews, words discovered near the body of a dead child when Allied
troops liberated Ravensbrück concentration camp in the northeast corner
of Germany. Written on a scrap of paper, it held a bittersweet message for
all people and would be enshrined in synagogues around the world:

> *O Lord, remember not only the men and women of good will, but also those
> of ill will. But do not only remember all the suffering they have inflicted on
> us. Remember the fruits we brought, thanks to this suffering: our
> comradeship, our loyalty, our humility, our courage, our generosity, the
> greatness of heart which has come out of all this; and when they come to
> judgment, let all fruits that we have borne be their forgiveness.*[37]

WHILE AMERICANS HAD GROWN accustomed to the unpredictability
of individual battles and military campaigns, the country was left numb
by the unexpected death of President Roosevelt on April 12, less than a
month before VE day.

Indeed the President had just been sworn in to office weeks earlier
after being elected to his fourth term. On that inaugural morning, members of his cabinet could not help but remember how once again he had
called them together for a prayer service. With the swearing in ceremony
being held later in the day, he was too feeble to make it to St. John's
Church, and so the service was held in the White House.[38] As the President had done on every year's anniversary of his first inauguration, he
chose the prayers that were to be recited, one of which included "Prayer
for Our Enemies."[39]

Vice President Harry Truman was now the country's commander-in-
chief. With the possible exception of Lincoln, none of his predecessors
had ever assumed the office of President with so much to confront and

achieve. The new commander-in-chief, who had been Vice President for less than three months, was following a genuinely beloved figure who had served longer as President than Truman had spent as a politician in Washington. By all accounts, Truman was ashen as he took the oath of office.

When the new President met with reporters the next day, he stared at no one and nothing in particular, transfixed by the enormity of it all. "Boys, if you ever pray, pray for me. I don't know whether you fellows ever had a load of hay fall on you, but when they told me yesterday what had happened, I felt like the moon, the stars, and all the planets had fallen on me."[40]

Collecting himself before Congress four days later, President Truman made his first joint-session address, confiding, "At this moment I have in my heart a prayer. As I have assumed my duties, I humbly pray Almighty God, in the words of King Solomon: 'Give therefore thy servant an understanding heart to judge thy people that I may discern between good and bad: for who is able to judge this thy so great a people?' I ask only to be a good and faithful servant of my Lord and my people."[41] This was not hyperbole. Truman had been stunned into office.

As Truman called for Sunday, May 13, to be observed as a national day of prayer and thanksgiving for Allied victory, the conflict in Asia continued to rage. It was also becoming clear that Soviet leader Joseph Stalin would not easily be contained in his ambitions for influence after the war. For every major success, it seemed that another problem lay just around the corner.

The President would have been even more intimidated from the outset had he known about the Manhattan Project. Committed to developing a weapon of mass destruction under orders from President Roosevelt, a group of gifted scientists was spending practically every waking hour devising the functional sequence of splitting the atom.

As uncomfortable as he was with the responsibility, Truman absorbed himself in the details of the project, assessing the situation as fully as time allowed and finally giving the order to proceed. Considering the implications of what he was about to unleash, he turned to a prayer that had been a constant source of inspiration for him. He had said the prayer every day of every year "from high school days, as a window washer, bottle duster, floor scrubber in an Independence, Missouri, drugstore, as a timekeeper on a railroad contract gang, as an employee of a newspaper, as a bank clerk, as a farmer riding a gang plow behind four horses and mules, as a fraternity official learning to say nothing at all if good could not be said of a man, as public official judging the weaknesses and shortcomings of constituents, and as President of the United States of America."[42] He had said this prayer on World War I battlefields and taught it to his fiancée, Bess, during their courtship. And now it was being invoked in perhaps the most portentous decision ever made by one man in history:

> *Oh! Almighty and Everlasting God, Creator of Heaven, Earth, and the Universe: Help me to be, to think, to act what is right, because it is right; make me truthful, honest, and honorable in all things; make me intellectually honest for the sake of right and honor without thought of reward to me. Give me the ability to be charitable, forgiving, and patient with my fellowmen—help me to understand their motives and their shortcomings—even as Thou understandest mine![43]*

The dropping of the bomb on Hiroshima and Nagasaki gave the Japanese little chance to consider anything but unconditional surrender. The nuclear age had been ushered onto the global stage, and the world would never be the same again.

The weighty reality for those involved in the development of the bomb was just as overwhelming. Robert Oppenheimer, the person in charge of the Los Alamos Laboratory in New Mexico who was considered the "Father of the Atomic Bomb," had expressed concerns from the very beginning. As the bomb grew closer to completion, his anxiety became more pronounced.

Once Oppenheimer and his colleagues witnessed for themselves the test detonation, they understood more fully what they were unleashing. While the testing range was being constructed near Los Alamos, Oppenheimer was given the choice to name the site. He decided to call it "Trinity," after a prayer written by the English poet John Donne in the early seventeenth century.[44]

The fourteenth of Donne's nineteen holy sonnets, "Trinity" shows the conflict of wanting both human love and God's love but being forced to make a choice. This is an angry prayer with a frenzied and demanding tone, every word chosen almost excruciatingly to convey anxiety. By the middle of Donne's entreaty, it has become clear that the petitioner loves God but feels he is being compromised by the perceived sin he is being forced to commit—for Oppenheimer, the unleashing of the nuclear genie. The conflict between thinking and feeling creates the most human of clashes. Donne's "Trinity" suited the dilemma of Oppenheimer and his colleagues perfectly, their own subtle, metaphoric prayer in conflict.

THE SIGNIFICANCE OF THE DETONATION of the nuclear bomb not only for the United States but for the entire globe would loom for decades.

The war in the Pacific finally ended on September 2, 1945, aboard the USS *Missouri* as General MacArthur accepted the unconditional surrender of the Japanese. With a certain amount of grace, MacArthur conducted the brief ceremony, and after the Japanese left the American battleship, he stepped forward to waiting microphones to address the nation on the historic occasion, saying, "As I look back upon the long, torturous trail from those grim days of Bataan and Corregidor, when an entire world lived in fear, when democracy was on the defensive everywhere, when modern civilization trembled in the balance, I thank a merciful God that He has given us the faith, the courage, and the power from which to mold victory."[45]

THE DECISIVE ROLE that the United States had played in ending World War II and the responsibilities that went along with it were profoundly transforming for America. More than ever the country was thrust into a role that it did not choose but that it accepted by default to fill a critical void. The tasks ahead seemed overwhelming. As the commander of the Pacific Fleet, Admiral Chester Nimitz, had said during the war, "God grant me the courage not to give up what I think is right even though I think it is hopeless."

With so much at stake for the entire country, the culture of American prayer took on added significance. For the troops who had served on the front lines, prayer had taken on a new meaning that would stay with them for the rest of their lives. When a survey was conducted at the end of the war to learn what had sustained American troops during the conflict, one answer emerged over all others. It was neither religion nor patriotism. Rather, it was the ability to pray. Reflecting on the mysteries of God and their own role in a very changed world order, many Americans adopted prayer as a means to help them thrive, if not survive, in the face of extraordinary challenges.

CHAPTER 13

THE REBUILDERS

1945–1960

Before all else, we seek, upon our common labor as a nation, the blessings of Almighty God. And the hopes in our hearts fashion the deepest prayers of our whole people.

May we pursue the right—without self-righteousness.
May we know unity—without conformity.
May we grow in strength—without pride in self.
May we, in our dealings with all people of the earth,
ever speak truth and serve justice . . .

And so the prayer of our people carries far beyond our own frontiers, to the wide world of our duty and destiny.

—President Dwight D. Eisenhower (1956)

$\mathcal{T}$HE CASUALTIES FROM World War II were staggering. Across the globe almost 59 million people had died as a direct result of the war and the ruthlessness of brutal regimes.[1] For the United States, casualties amounted to 292,000 dead and 613,611 wounded.[2] The country had escaped the worst of the carnage, not having been invaded on its mainland, yet it had still incurred serious human loss. What was most striking to the world, however, was that the United States now stood as the preeminent economic power. What the future held was far from certain. As the CBS journalist Edward R. Morrow reported from London that summer of 1945, "Seldom, if ever, has a war ended leaving the victors with such a sense of uncertainty and fear, with such a realization that the future is obscure and that survival is not assured."[3]

In the summer of 1947, U.S. and European leaders gathered in Paris to begin implementing the American offer to rebuild Europe, known as the Marshall Plan. Named after its architect, Secretary of State George Marshall, the proposed undertaking was mammoth in its proportions. After the opening statements at the conference, Soviet Foreign Minister Vyacheslav Molotov staged a dramatic walkout, calling the multibillion-dollar contribution nothing more than deceptive American imperialism. In lockstep behind him filed the representatives from the newest countries of the Soviet bloc, reinforcing the rapidly changing climate of economic, political, and military polarization that was now clearly dividing East and West, what Winston Churchill a year earlier at Westminster College in Fulton, Missouri, had framed as the drop of "an iron curtain."[4]

Against this backdrop, Peter Marshall, one of the most eloquent, spiritual voices of the day, captured the intense disquiet of the United States through his sermons, essays, and prayers. The Scottish-born Marshall first came to prominence in religious circles during the decade he served as pastor of the New York Avenue Presbyterian Church in Washington, D.C., the same church to which Abraham Lincoln had turned for comfort during some of the most difficult days of the Civil War. He so impressed Washington lawmakers that he was appointed U.S. Senate chaplain for the Eightieth Congress in January 1947, arguably becoming the most formidable and articulate chaplain ever to serve in the Senate or House of Representatives.

While he filled the traditional role of invoking God's blessing and guidance in the deliberations of the Senate, Marshall also capitalized on the opportunity to remind his listeners of the import of their decisions during such critical days. Within weeks of Marshall's taking over his new responsibilities, it became clear even to the press that senators were rearranging their daily schedules to attend his opening invocations. Soon reporters covering Capitol Hill began referring to him as "the conscience of the Senate."[5] The *Chicago Sun-Times* ran a headline that read, "A New Bite to Senate Prayers," underscoring how Marshall was avoiding the "usual platitudes" and was handing out "some tart advice" to America's elected officials.[6] The world's most exclusive club was being spiritually challenged almost every day it was in session.

What distinguished Marshall from many other clergymen was his unshakable belief in the sheer power of prayer—the "soul's tonic," he called it—and he expressed his frustration with those who would limit its use. Invoking prescribed prayers day after day was admirable, but doing so without considering the enormous advantages of more personal, spontaneous prayer, he believed, was a significant failing. He bemoaned that "prayer generally is an unexplored field," noting how even the most ardent believers had not fully "experimented with prayer, regarding it as an emergency measure or a conventional practice to be maintained, much as one's subscription to a series of cultural lectures."[7]

There was not a day that Marshall, as chaplain, did not consider the affairs of the United States and the world without taking into account the relevance of prayer in addressing both tragedy and triumph. On the morning that the Marshall Plan was unveiled at Harvard, for example, Peter Marshall stood before the Senate and entreated:

> *Our Heavenly Father, if it be Thy will that America should assume world leadership, as history demands and the hopes of so many nations desire, make us good enough to undertake it. We consider our resources in money and in men, yet forget the spiritual resources without which we dare not and cannot lead the world.*[8]

Less than a month later, as Secretary of State George Marshall and his team were about to leave for Europe to meet with their foreign counterparts on both sides of the Iron Curtain, Peter Marshall was characteristically direct, ending his invocation, "May Thy Spirit move them, that there may be concession without coercion and conciliation without compromise."[9] Early in 1949, Marshall awoke one morning with chest pains and died later that day. Despite serving as Senate chaplain for less than two years, he left a significant spiritual legacy to Congress and the country.

THE PERIOD IMMEDIATELY FOLLOWING the war became one of the most surreal moments in U.S. history. While the United States took the lead in the reconstruction of Europe and Japan, it still seemed bewildered by its place in the new world order and how best to ensure a lasting peace, particularly given the continued aggression of Stalin's forces and the decisive victory of Mao Tse-tung's Communist forces in taking over mainland China and establishing a "people's republic" in 1949. Even Theodor Geisel, better known as Dr. Seuss, would draw a memorable cartoon in *Collier's* magazine of a little boy sitting atop the earth, reaching out and asking God to tell the world "peace is good" and in the end "that's all that need be understood."[10] Unfortunately, however, life was not so simple.

Nothing seemed more pressing than to create an international organization structured to help keep the peace. Times were now considerably different from the post–World War I period, when Woodrow Wilson faced such formidable domestic opposition to his League of Nations. The term "united nations" had been coined in 1942 by President Roosevelt to describe the Allied countries that had joined together to fight the Axis powers. In the aftermath of World War II, it was being used to describe the fifty nations that joined together in San Francisco on June 26, 1945, to sign a formal accord, launching the new international organization. By year's end the UN was up and running.

Despite the extremely diverse nature of the United Nations, the UN Secretariat declared on the organization's opening day that each year's General Assembly begin and end with a prayer, a practice that has continued ever since. In fact, through the financial support of Americans like J. C. Penney, a meditation room just off the floor from the General Assembly had been built by 1957, a room that Secretary General Dag Hammarskjöld hoped would inspire "devotion to something which is greater than ourselves . . . a place where the doors may be opened to the infinite lands of thought and prayer . . . devoted to peace."[11] Hammarskjöld, a pious man who became a prolific writer of essays on Christian thought, and composed exquisite prayers of devotion, made sure the United Nations Meditation Room remained true to its purpose. He had installed on a plaque next to its entrance the words: "This is a room devoted to peace. It is a room of quiet where only thoughts should speak."[12]

From those days of the UN's founding, a story circulated about the ballot box that was installed in the chambers of the UN Security Council. The box was to be used in those rare instances when a secret vote needed to be taken among the delegates. After it had been put into place, UN officials noticed a piece of paper lodged in the box. When they opened it, they found the following message:

May I, who have the privilege of constructing this ballot box, cast the first vote? May God be with every member of the United Nations organization and through your noble efforts bring lasting peace to us all—all over the world!

    Paul Antonio, the carpenter[13]

Another figure closely associated with the launching of the United Nations and its charter was Eleanor Roosevelt, the widow of the late President. Although no longer the first lady, she took every opportunity to articulate her strong views on two subjects nearest to her heart, civil rights in America and human rights around the world, particularly as they related to the work of the United Nations.

Not one to wear religion on her sleeve, Eleanor Roosevelt nonetheless had deeply held spiritual convictions. At the age of eight, she anguished over the death of her mother, much as she did two years later, when her father, Elliott, the younger brother of Theodore Roosevelt, died. In being sent to live with her wealthy maternal grandmother, Mary Ludlow Hall, she found herself integrated into a life that included prayer twice a day. Every morning and evening her grandmother would require the entire family and the servants of the house to gather for prayer services.[14] On occasion she would invite clergymen to officiate at the ceremonies. While the strict regimen tried her patience, Eleanor nonetheless developed an appreciation for prayer that stayed with her for the rest of her life.

Reminiscing about his mother's last years, Elliott Roosevelt described how Eleanor kept a strict daily regimen, always ending her day with a prayer, one that she wrote to characterize her own spirituality:

Our Father, who has set a restlessness in our hearts and made us all seekers after that which we can never fully find, forbid us to be satisfied with what we make of life. Draw us from base content and set our eyes on far-off goals. Keep us at tasks too hard for us that we may be driven to Thee for strength. Deliver us from fretfulness and self-pitying; make us sure of the good we cannot see and of the hidden good in the world. Open our eyes to simple beauty all around us and our hearts to the loveliness men hide from us because we do not try to understand them. Save us from ourselves and show us a vision of a world made new.[15]

* * *

DESPITE THE EFFORTS of the United Nations to create an international forum to prevent wars for all time, the world had become far more fragile and certainly more dangerous by 1950 than most people could have imagined in the days just following the war. In June of that year, the peace was broken altogether when 130,000 Communist troops from the northern part of the Korean peninsula invaded the South, and the United States, under the aegis of the United Nations, became immersed in overseeing the war effort. President Harry Truman suddenly found himself in the unenviable position of being a commander-in-chief who had closed one chapter in the history of war, only to be forced into opening another. His obvious choice for leader of UN forces was the indomitable General Douglas MacArthur. Proud, condescending, and brilliant, MacArthur came from a long line of generals and believed that his call to lead U.S. troops and UN forces in Korea had been foreordained.

He also did not hesitate to convey his deep religious faith and make sure that his troops understood the personal worth of prayer. On learning that his wife, Jean, had delivered a baby boy while he was stationed in Manila before the outbreak of World War II, he went to his desk and composed a lengthy prayer, envisioning before God and himself how the MacArthur legacy might be continued. It perhaps said more about MacArthur than anything else: "Build me a son, O Lord, . . . who will be strong enough when he is weak . . . whose wishbone will not be where his backbone should be." He then went on to ask God for other strong marks of character, none more important than "to stand up in the storm" and to acquire the virtues of wisdom, humility, and "meekness of true strength." If God would only grant him these things, MacArthur prayed, "Then I, his father, will dare to whisper, 'I have not lived in vain.' "[16]

MacArthur had his own ideas on how the Korean War should be fought. Despite President Truman's visit to Wake Island in October 1950 to meet with his commander to resolve any outstanding differences, the two men became estranged, leading to MacArthur's being fired after challenging the President's direct orders.

While the firing of MacArthur echoed across the country, mainly on op-ed pages, General Matthew Ridgway was put in command of UN forces. Described by the military historian Donald Goldstein as a "Stonewall Jackson of the twentieth century—religious, eccentric, and the best tactical battlefield commander of his time"—Ridgway took great pride in keeping a small military prayer book beneath a hand grenade he had taped to the right shoulder of his field jacket.[17] During lulls in the fighting he would take out his rat-eared devotional, as much as several times a day, to read it in private or even with people around him.

For Ridgway's successor, the last of the commanders of UN forces in the Korean War, General Mark Clark, prayer had always served like a warm army blanket. He not only encouraged his men to pray but also jotted down his own prayers from the battlefield. He wrote one invocation while commanding the Fifth Army in Italy during some of the fiercest fighting of World War II. For Clark it would be as effective in Seoul, South Korea, as it had been in Salerno, Italy:

> *On this eve of battle we ask Thee, our Heavenly Father, for strength and courage. We fight, not only for our country, but for our God as well, because we battle for continuance of Christian principles among all men. Give us the strength and the courage to fight well . . . Give us Thy guidance, Dear Lord, in the hours of crisis that lie ahead. Grant us the power to face our enemies and Thine enemies without fear . . . These things we ask in your name. Amen.*[18]

As in the last two great wars, prayer books were printed by the tens of thousands and shipped off to men and to the growing number of women out in the field serving in administrative capacities and in mobile army surgical hospital (MASH) units in Korea to care for the wounded. These publications were provided not only through individual churches but through the U.S. Government Printing Office as well.

Chaplains were every bit as visible in Korea as they had been during previous wars. Chaplain John Lindvall, a Congregationalist minister from Stamford, Connecticut, prayed with the men of the Fortieth U.S. Infantry Division together and individually before each offensive, no matter how insignificant the incursion. Chaplain Harry Schreiner, a rabbi from Morristown, New Jersey, prayed with Jewish and Gentile soldiers of the First U.S. Cavalry Division as gunfire and explosives rang around them, admonishing the soldiers to don "God's armor." Chaplain Harold Prudell, a Catholic priest, would hear confessions around the clock and pray with his men next to the platoon's machine-gun emplacement.[19]

Some military units worked out prayer regimens for themselves without the benefit of chaplains before going into battle. The men of the Second Platoon, Company E of the Sixty-fifth Puerto Rican Regiment, for example, gathered daily to pray the Rosary. Although attendance was never mandatory, most of the men never missed the chance to be there. Even portable electric organs were hauled out onto the battlefield to accompany the men as they sang hymns.

Then there were those men, chaplains and soldiers alike, who, as prisoners of war, suffered in captivity as harshly as many of their fellow soldiers in World War II. Unlike the Japanese in the Pacific theater during World War II, the North Koreans would not allow prayer services of any kind to be held by captured troops. With temperatures dropping to as low as forty-five below zero, sleeping berths infested with lice and rats, warm clothing and bedding at a premium, and various forms of torture a part of daily life, the stress was beyond comprehension. Only prayer said in the silence of a soldier's heart or recited with a handful of other soldiers out of earshot from prison guards could be managed.

Sixteen hundred men died in Prison Camp No. 5 alone in the first year of the war. One of the prisoners, Private Bill Allen, was assigned to burial patrol at the camp for thirty-two months. Turning to prayer to keep his sanity, he quietly scavenged for toothpaste tubes, melting them down to make a crucifix, an artifact that he brought home to remind himself of what he and so many of his army buddies had endured.[20]

Not until the signing of an armistice splitting the Korean peninsula between north and south on July 27, 1953, did the war come to an end, with General Mark Clark signing the cease-fire agreement on behalf of the UN. Some 33,651 Americans were counted among the dead in a conflict that had lasted almost three years to the month. Another 7,140 U.S. servicemen had been captured by the North and held as prisoners of war.

DESPITE AN END TO the Korean conflict, the Cold War continued to rage. The two sides could not have been more different. In the United States a resilient corps of commercial entrepreneurs emerged, a striking contrast to the economic oligarchs of the Soviet Union. Unfettered by a central-command economy, relatively untouched by the debilitating aftermath of the war, and steeped in patriotic fervor, American business leaders cooperated with the U.S. government to support global recovery. As these industrialists showed their strong anti-Communist streak, they also openly promoted what they saw as American virtues, including religious freedom.

Few American businessmen represented this mix of ideals more than Conrad Hilton, a formidable entrepreneur whose spiritual devotion was an integral part of his daily business practices. Born and raised a Catholic in San Antonio, New Mexico, Hilton was not a regular churchgoer, but, as a close friend observed, he possessed "an active, firm belief that prayer is the wellspring of accomplishment."[21]

Influenced by a mother who had taught him that "prayer is the best investment you'll ever make," Hilton never embarked on a real-estate transaction or made a major move without the benefit of prayer. He remembered all too well the years of the Depression, when everything seemed to be collapsing around him and "men were jumping out of hotel windows—my hotel windows!" It was then that he knew the true meaning of prayer and how to pray "like a lost child."[22]

As his biographer, former executive manager, and longtime friend, Whitney Bolton, recounted at the apex of Hilton's career, "He never enters a deal without prayer, and he abandons any deal in which he feels his prayers have gone unanswered. He believes that lack of answer signals lack of rightness."[23] Bolton elaborated on how Hilton had approached his purchase of New York's Plaza Hotel:

> I knew he wanted the Plaza months before Wall Street or the banks or his own intimates knew it. I used to watch him stalking it at all hours. I once saw him leave St. Patrick's Cathedral at 6:30 one morning and walk up toward the Plaza, keeping to the opposite side of Fifth Avenue. He never crossed over for a closer look, he never made a note in a little book, he never betrayed a thing on that astonishing, mobile face. But I knew the Plaza would be his—he had just prayed for it. And over the years I have watched it work out: what Connie prays for he always gets. Maybe because he invariably goes back and gives just as fervent thanks for what he got. He's even got me doing it.[24]

Hilton would repeat this private rite time and again as he went about purchasing New York's Waldorf-Astoria, Chicago's Palmer House, San Francisco's Sir Francis Drake, Washington, D.C.'s Mayflower, and dozens of other hotels. At the time of his death in 1979, he controlled the largest hotel conglomeration in the world, becoming the stuff of legends.

In every room of his hotels Conrad Hilton instructed his managers to provide a copy of his autobiography, *Be My Guest*, as well as the Bible. He also included a prayer, which he had printed on a separate card. Written in 1951 for a speech he delivered in Chicago about the state of world affairs, the prayer had received such an overwhelming response that Hilton recited it again on national television as part of a program advocating prayer to help foster world peace. Within a year an estimated 200,000 Americans had "America on Its Knees" framed in their homes:[25]

> *Our Father in Heaven:*
> *We pray that You save us from ourselves.*
> *The world that You have made for us, to live in peace,*
>   *we have made into an armed camp.*
> *We live in fear of war to come.*
> *We are afraid of "the terror that flies by night,*
>   *and the arrow that flies by day,*
>   *the pestilence that walks in darkness*
>   *and the destruction that wastes at noon-day."*
> *We have turned from You to go our selfish way. We have broken Your*
>   *commandments and denied Your truth. We have left Your altars to*
>   *serve the false gods of money and pleasure and power.*
> *Forgive us and help us.*
> *Now, darkness gathers around us and we are confused in all our counsels.*
>   *Losing faith in You, we lose faith in ourselves.*
> *Inspire us with wisdom, all of us of every color, race, and creed,*
>   *to use our wealth, our strength to help our brother,*
>   *instead of destroying him.*
> *Help us to do Your will as it is done in heaven*
>   *and to be worthy of Your promise of peace on earth.*
> *Fill us with new faith, new strength, and new courage,*
>   *that we may win the Battle for Peace.*
> *Be swift to save us, dear God, before the darkness falls.*[26]

AT A TIME when Americans were increasingly apprehensive over the escalation of the Cold War, the country turned to Dwight D. Eisenhower, the military hero of World War II, to be its thirty-fourth President. The only general elected President in the twentieth century, Eisenhower, like MacArthur, had served in both world wars and had developed his skills and experience almost entirely on the battlefield, where he demonstrated an innate ability to manage military campaigns.

Although never considered overtly spiritual during his days in the army, he later described himself as "the most intensely religious man I ever knew," adding, "Nobody goes through six years of war without faith."[27] From the moment he was elected, he began to show his piety, convinced that he needed to set a proper example. At the first gathering of his newly nominated Cabinet, at the Commodore Hotel in New York, he turned to Ezra Taft Benson, a leader of the Mormon Church whom he would appoint Secretary of Agriculture, and asked him to offer a prayer before they started on any business. It was a practice he continued to follow as President and one emulated by his successors.

Having never been baptized in any church, not even in his parents' Church of the Brethren in Christ in Abilene, Kansas, Eisenhower decided within days of his inauguration to be christened formally into the National Presbyterian Church. This was no halfhearted conversion. Rather, Eisenhower firmly believed that he had been elected president of a country founded on basic religious principles and that he needed to show his spiritual fidelity.

On the morning of his swearing in, on January 20, 1953, he sat down at the bedroom desk of his hotel and on a yellow pad jotted down the words to a prayer he had been mulling over. Again, he realized that he would be creating yet another precedent by becoming the first President to compose and recite a personal prayer at his own inaugural.[28] On a blustery winter day, he walked up to the podium and began to set out his vision for the next four years:

My friends, before I begin the expression of those thoughts that I deem appropriate to this moment, would you permit me the privilege of uttering a little private prayer of my own? And I ask that you bow your heads.

Almighty God, as we stand here at this moment my future associates in the Executive Branch of government join me in beseeching that Thou will make full and complete our dedication to the service of the people in this throng, and their fellow citizens everywhere.

Give us, we pray, the power to discern clearly right from wrong, and allow all our words and actions to be governed thereby, and by the laws of this land. Especially we pray that our concern shall be for all the people regardless of station, race, or calling.

May cooperation be permitted and be the mutual aim of those who, under the concepts of our Constitution, hold to differing political faiths; so that all may work for the good of our beloved country and Thy glory. Amen.[29]

He ended his address with the words "This is the work that awaits us all, to be done with bravery, with charity, and with prayer to Almighty God."[30]

While Eisenhower seemed spiritually transformed as he took office, the rest of the government had been undergoing its own profound reaffirmation, publicly acknowledging American ideals and the country's belief in God. At a time when even a preeminent power like the United States felt helpless to stem the growing wave of Communism, God and prayer were being added to the country's arsenal. Even before Eisenhower was elected, President Truman had signed into law a statute that read, "The President shall issue each year a proclamation designating a National Day of Prayer on which the people of the United States may turn to God in prayer and meditation at churches, in groups, and as individuals."[31]

While the dynamics of the Cold War certainly helped to ignite the spiritual fervor of the country's leaders, instituting a national day of prayer had been part of a long American tradition. But in this case, Congress had taken the lead in putting such a declaration into effect. In the 1950s, the legislative branch was every bit as anxious to promote spiritual devotion as were the occupants of the White House. In an unprecedented move, both the House and the Senate passed legislation allowing the thirty-four-year-old Reverend Billy Graham to conduct a prayer service for the country on the steps of the Capitol, an event witnessed by thousands of people in the pouring rain on February 3, 1952.[32] Not long after, both houses of Congress passed a resolution instructing the architect of the Capitol to provide "a room, with facilities for prayer and meditation, for use of the members of the Senate and House of Representatives." When the room was finally constructed near the Rotunda, a stained-glass window of George Washington, kneeling in prayer at Valley Forge, was installed, etched with the words of the Psalm "Preserve me, O God, for in Thee do I put my trust."[33]

★ ★ ★

THE U.S. SUPREME COURT also waded into spiritual waters when the liberal Justice William Douglas, on behalf of the majority in *Zorach* v. *Clauson,* a case involving religious instruction, wrote, "We are a religious people whose institutions presuppose a Supreme Being." The court reaffirmed that "prayers" and "references to the Almighty" have always "run through our laws, our public rituals, our ceremonies."[34]

Reinforcing this latest public dynamic in promoting prayer and spirituality, Republican Senator Frank Carlson of Kansas joined forces with Abraham Vereide, a Norwegian émigré and Methodist preacher from the state of Washington, to launch an annual presidential prayer breakfast. Both houses of Congress had been holding private prayer meetings for more than a decade. Independently, Vereide had launched his own annual prayer breakfasts to bring businessmen from the Seattle area together to ask for God's blessing, reminiscent of the businessmen's lunches during the revival years before the Civil War. By having the President participate in this new initiative, tied in part to the annual national observance of prayer, the breakfasts would take on added meaning. Elevating the observance to a nationwide, nondenominational recognition of prayer as a critical force in the daily life of the country was irresistible. Although Carlson was a political ally and friend of the President's, he and Vereide decided to recruit the Reverend Billy Graham to broach the subject with Eisenhower.

Eisenhower was reluctant to participate in what was billed as the first in a series of annual prayer breakfasts. After invoking prayer in his inaugural address only weeks earlier, he was concerned that his direct involvement might be seen as sanctimonious by a skeptical public. Some critics might even perceive him to be endorsing one group of religious leaders, predominantly the Protestant evangelical minister who was taking the lead, over others or trying to break down the wall of separation between church and state.

Wrestling with the possible fallout, the President let Carlson and Graham know that he could not accept their invitation. Undeterred, Graham solicited a promise from the President to think about it a bit longer. Within days of their chat and to the surprise of his aides, Eisenhower agreed to participate. Concluding that he stood behind the purpose of the breakfast, and because friends such as Conrad Hilton had agreed to participate in and fund it, he felt he had little to lose. Still, he hedged his bets and told Carlson not to expect him to attend future breakfasts.

The guest list at the first breakfast, on April 5, 1953, was impressive. Congressmen, Chief Justice Frederick Vinson and members of the Supreme Court, the media, businessmen, and other invited guests came to hear the Reverend Billy Graham and Conrad Hilton offer special prayers, speaking to the providence of the Almighty in the affairs of the country. The President even delivered remarks to the group, making the point that "prayer today is a necessity. We know that our prayers may be imperfect . . . We are imperfect human beings. But if we can make the effort, then there is something that ties us all together."[35] The public's reaction could not have been more favorable, and Eisenhower said he would attend the prayer breakfasts as long as he was President.

The name of the annual prayer observance was later changed from the Presidential Prayer Breakfast to the National Prayer Breakfast, and the number of participants climbed from a few hundred to several thousand, complemented by regional prayer breakfasts in major cities and in small towns across the country. By the end of the 1950s, state governors had agreed to hold their own annual prayer breakfasts, and both houses of Congress had increased the frequency of private prayer gatherings, as well as the number of members attending.

In time, one of the more remarkable, unforeseen developments was how popular the nonpolitical prayer breakfasts became among foreign ambassadors. Soon presidents and prime ministers from overseas were angling for invitations to America's official annual prayer gathering. Foreign governments later introduced their own annual observances in capitals as diverse as Taipei, Bucharest, and Melbourne.

PRESIDENT EISENHOWER'S imprint could also be seen as he worked with Congress to ensure that the words of the Pledge of Allegiance were changed to include the phrase "under God." The pledge, originally written in 1892 by Francis Bellamy, a Baptist minister and a supporter of various socialist causes, had been edited slightly in 1923 and then again by the newly created National Flag Conference a year later. Finally it was passed into law as the country's official pledge during World War II. Although the Supreme Court, responding to a suit brought by the Jehovah's Witnesses, ruled in 1943 that schoolchildren could not be forced to recite any pledge except to God, the decision had little impact on the widespread adoption of the Pledge of Allegiance. It quickly became part of the daily routine of American life both in the classroom and at public functions.

When the country became immersed in the Korean War, the Roman Catholic Knights of Columbus launched an intense campaign to ensure that some reference to God was incorporated into the Pledge of Allegiance. While attending Sunday services at the New York Avenue Presbyterian Church in Washington, the church where Peter Marshall had served as pastor for a decade, Eisenhower listened to another Scottish-born minister, the Reverend George M. Docherty, deliver a sermon on the subject. Docherty argued that without "under God" in the pledge, the children of Moscow could recite the same patriotic oath as American children, and it would have the same effect. Eisenhower was sold.

In signing the bill into law, the President explained the reason for the change: "In this way we are reaffirming the transcendence of religious faith in America's heritage and future; in this way we shall constantly strengthen those spiritual weapons which forever will be our country's most powerful resource in peace and war."[36]

The Pledge of Allegiance from that day forward has remained unchanged:

BELLAMY VERSION	1954 VERSION
I pledge allegiance to my Flag	*I pledge allegiance to the Flag*
And to the Republic for which	*of the United States of America,*
* it stands:*	*and to the Republic for which it stands:*
One Nation indivisible,	*One Nation under God, indivisible,*
With Liberty and Justice for all.	*with Liberty and Justice for all.*

The government's desire to institutionalize the belief in a supreme being's authority over the affairs of the United States was further strengthened by the passage of legislation in 1956 officially designating "In God We Trust" as the national motto, using a variant of Francis Scott Key's phrase from 1814. A law was then passed to ensure that the motto was printed on all U.S. paper currency, something that had already been engraved on all coinage for almost one hundred years.

WITH BREAKTHROUGHS IN TECHNOLOGY, the growing influence of radio and the nascent television industry were also helping to bring spirituality into the living rooms of Americans. Radio stations were show-casing regional preachers, largely Protestant and evangelical, to provide prayer and inspiration to local listeners, hoping to maximize their audience market share for other programs. Soon national radio shows began to do so as well.

As World War II was winding down in 1945, Father Patrick Peyton, an Irish immigrant based in Albany, New York, persuaded the Mutual Broadcasting Company to donate a half hour each week to help him promote family prayer. Although the programming at first centered almost exclusively on reciting the Rosary, it quickly blossomed into a much more formidable production. Americans of all religious faiths tuned in to one of the most widely listened to radio programs in the country, *The Family Theater*, at ten o'clock on Thursday evenings, with its opening line, "More good is wrought by prayer than this world has ever dreamed of." Each hour program would then turn to that week's dramatization of a family problem that was faced and ultimately conquered through prayer. *Family Theater Productions* aired weekly for the next twenty-two years, making it the longest-running radio program in history.[37]

By 1951, *Family Theater* had been tailor-made for television. One of its earliest productions cast the young James Dean in his first starring role as John the Apostle, with veteran actors Ruth Hussey, Michael Ansara, and Roddy McDowall, in a teleplay called *Hill Number One*. Over the next several years Peyton brought together such stage and screen stars as Jimmy Stewart, Loretta Young, Frank Sinatra, Bob Hope, Grace Kelly, Helen Hayes, Ronald Reagan, Shirley Temple, and Gregory Peck to help him act out the spiritual messages of his films. The film director and producer George Lucas of *Star Wars* fame received his first on-screen credit as an assistant cameraman in the production of *The Soldier,* starring William Shatner, in the mid-1960s. Throughout most of these television dramas, Father Peyton ensured that the message of prayer, which had been at the heart of his original vision, remained intact.[38]

In promoting prayer, Father Peyton hired commercial writers to create sound bites that he used not only on radio and television but also on billboards. From city streets to rural highways, a national campaign communicated such messages as "God Makes House Calls" and "Troubled? Try God."[39] One of his most enduring sound bites came from a young commercial writer he hired, Al Scalpone, to help him promote his early

Family Rosary programs. They struggled to come up with a catchy phrase that would grab people's attention. Finally it came to Scalpone: "The family that prays together, stays together." Once the slogan was broadcast over the radio, it resonated overnight and was soon being repeated in churches and homes across America. Scalpone would also be responsible for coining the maxim "A world at prayer is a world at peace"[40] in the early days of the Cold War. If soap could be sold in America's living rooms through radio and television, the power of prayer had a chance as well.

THE UNITED STATES HAD PRODUCED some captivating religious personalities, but the years after the war were particularly fertile. One of the more famous healing preachers in American history, someone who would continue his ministry over the next fifty years, was Oral Roberts. Born and raised in Oklahoma, Roberts became a Pentecostal clergyman, with prayer as the centering force in dealing with every conceivable tragedy. In his revivals, for example, a prayer-card system was put into place to organize the "healing line" for those who wanted to be cured of their ailments. Colored and letter-coded, the prayer cards were handed out on a first-come, first-served basis as the sick and the maimed stood in line to have Roberts place his hands on their heads, pray for their recovery, and as a messenger of God heal them.[41]

If a person was unable to attend a meeting due either to distance or to serious illness, he or she could send for a prayer cloth, a piece of an old sheet cut into a three-by-five-inch strip imprinted with the words "I prayed over this cloth for God to deliver you—use as a point of contact" (Acts 19:11–12). By the summer of 1948, it was estimated, thousands of these handkerchiefs had been shipped out to homes across the country, each with an accompanying card assuring the recipient and any friends who might want to make a future request that Oral Roberts

> prays over each cloth separately and individually and then as our requests come into the office, even while he is away in a campaign of deliverance, the handkerchief is mailed to you. You need not send a piece of cloth or handkerchief since our cloths are of uniform size and fit nicely into a letter. Also, if you insist on using your own handkerchief it might arrive while Brother Roberts is away and there will be a delay in getting the cloth back to you.[42]

Roberts also created "prayer pacts," a controversial aspect of his fund-raising efforts. Based on the notion of "seed-faith," as interpreted from the New Testament, poverty was as much an illness in need of healing as sickness. Consequently, Roberts would promise to pray for the prosperity of the faithful, and they, in turn, would pray for his ministerial and financial success and send him a donation.

BESIDES HEALING PREACHERS, who enjoyed rather large national followings in the years after World War II, three more mainstream clergymen—a pastor, a priest, and an evangelist—stood out from the crowd, each possessing a different vocation, personal background, theology, and approach to his ministry. Norman Vincent Peale, Fulton J. Sheen, and William Franklin Graham helped to shape American culture and spirituality in unique and profound ways.

Norman Vincent Peale was ordained a Methodist Episcopal minister in 1922, following in the footsteps of his father, who had been both a minister and a physician. After three brief pastoral assignments, he took charge of the fashionable Marble Collegiate Reformed Church on New York City's Fifth Avenue in 1932 and remained its spiritual leader until 1984. A dynamic speaker, Peale merged psychiatry and religion to forge his brand of spirituality, and even went so far as to set up a psychiatric clinic called the American Foundation of Religion and Psychiatry next to his church. Like most of his successful contemporaries, Peale used radio and television to project his message. Criticized by detractors as superficial, he nevertheless became a sensation with a receptive public who found his approach to the trials of everyday life, particularly on the subject of prayer, refreshing.

Peale's first book, *The Art of Living*, became a best seller, but *The Power of Positive Thinking* firmly established him as the "Apostle of Self-Esteem." Published in 1952, *The Power of Positive Thinking* was in its nineteenth printing within three years and by the end of the decade had been translated into forty-two languages, becoming the biggest seller of its kind in the twentieth century.

At the center of his message stood the special nature of prayer. Only through prayer, Peale argued, could a person's full potential be achieved. In his chapter "Try Prayer Power" he listed ten rules for achieving "effective results from prayer," transforming the ancient art of divine invocation for modern life. He offered such prescriptions as "putting everything in God's hands" and praying "for people you do not like or who have mistreated you."[43]

Peale saw prayer as a "glorious opportunity" and wrote in his sequel, *Try Prayer Power*, of how "prayer is a sending out of vibrations from one person to another as well as to God. All the universe is in vibration." He admonished his audiences to "believe that you are receiving answers to your prayers. Belief tends to create that which is held in the mind by faith."[44] Without prayer, he argued, life would evolve into a rudderless ship.

A contemporary of Peale's who reached audiences from a more traditional footing but whose message was just as compelling was the Catholic Bishop Fulton J. Sheen. A native of El Paso, Illinois, Sheen earned philosophy degrees in Rome and Louvain, Belgium. At the age of thirty-four in 1930, the naturally gifted speaker was asked to host a weekly national radio broadcast, *The Catholic Hour*. His audiences grew so dramatically that with the advent of television he was given the opportunity in 1952 to produce and star in his own series, *Life Is Worth Living*.

Attired in his flowing crimson robe, having been elevated the year before to Bishop, Sheen cut quite a figure before the cameras. With a twinkle in his eye, armed with a piece of chalk and the "angel's blackboard" as his only props, he drew millions to the television set on Tuesday evenings. Despite his obvious showmanship, his message was heartfelt, and with his signature closing, "May God bless you," the public could hardly wait for the next week's broadcast. One young actor was so impressed by Sheen's spiritual dynamism that he asked permission to adopt his name as he began his career in Hollywood. The Bishop agreed, and Ramon Estevez changed his name to Martin Sheen.[45]

Throughout his adult life Bishop Sheen developed an intense prayer discipline, spending at least an hour every day reciting prayers and meditating, in addition to saying Mass. The "holy hour" that he carved out for himself each day was sacrosanct no matter what might be happening in his life or where he was traveling. He once remarked that the regular practice of prayer was as indispensable to him as exercise is to an athlete.

Sheen believed that meditation was the highest form of spiritual bonding with God, describing it as an even "more spiritual act than 'saying prayers.'" He went further by explaining, "It may be likened to the attitude of a child who breaks into the presence of a mother saying: 'I'll not say a word, if you will just let me stay here and watch you.'"[46]

Sheen underwent open-heart surgery at the age of eighty-three, and most individuals questioned whether he would survive his hospital stay; for a short while he did. Preparing for his 1979 Christmas Eve sermon, praying for inspiration before the tabernacle of his private chapel, he slumped and died. Having perhaps been the most watched and influential American Catholic clergyman in history, Fulton J. Sheen would later be accorded the honor of burial in New York's St. Patrick's Cathedral.

The youngest of the three clergymen, someone who enjoyed a thirty-five-year friendship with Bishop Sheen and whose influence continued into the next century, was the Reverend William Franklin Graham, known as Billy. At the age of sixteen, in the fall of 1934, in his native Charlotte, North Carolina, Graham first realized he had a religious calling. The realization struck him like lightning as he listened to the preaching of Mordecai Ham, an evangelical preacher from Louisville, Kentucky. "When my decision for Christ was made," he later recalled, "I walked slowly down and knelt in prayer. I opened my heart and knew for the first time the sweetness and joy of God, of truly being born again."[47] From the day of his ordination as a Baptist minister, Billy Graham seemed destined for great things. By the age of thirty-two, he was being introduced to America's elite, including President Harry Truman.

In what would become an important lesson for the rest of his ministry, Graham had a memorable meeting with the President in 1950. Still possessed of the innocence of youth, he visited Truman in the Oval Office. Before the meeting concluded, he put his arm around the President and asked him if they could pray together. Although a bit uncomfortable with the suggestion, Truman nevertheless fell to his knees while Graham offered a prayer for the President and the country. Walking out of the White House, Graham was surrounded by reporters looking for a debriefing on his meeting with the President. Sparing little detail, he told the journalists about how he and the President had gotten on their knees to pray. He even went so far as to demonstrate before the press corps, including photographers, how he and the President had prayed together on their knees. Predictably, Truman's reaction was swift; he directed his aides never to let Graham through the gates of the White House again. A private moment between the young minister and the President had been broadcast to the world. It was a youthful indiscretion, one that Graham discussed candidly in his later autobiography, but it was a mistake he never made again.

Throughout his ministry Graham appreciated both his God-given gifts and the center stage that he commanded. When traveling to countries where atheism and despotism were firmly established, he did not condemn his hosts. Rather, he used his celebrity to bring the Gospel and the path of prayer to people who were denied them. From North Korea's Kim Il Sung to Romania's Nicolae Ceausescu, foreign leaders wanted to gain the respectability that a visit by Billy Graham could bring.

In every one of his crusades, Graham passionately exhorted his listeners to find comfort and fortitude by turning to God through prayer. It became almost a one-note song. At the same time, he had the help of hundreds of volunteers and paid employees who were indispensable to the Billy Graham crusade. Among them, no one was more beloved than George Beverly Shea, who from the beginning of Graham's ministry led stadium crowds in song. There was more than one historian who would remark how Shea's role in the Billy Graham crusade reminded them of Ira Sankey's collaboration with Dwight Lyman Moody some seventy years earlier. Almost single-handedly, Shea helped to popularize the old Swedish hymn "How Great Thou Art," with its sweeping pronouncements, "O Lord, my God! When I in awesome wonder consider all the worlds Thy hands have made. I see the stars, I hear the rolling thunder; Thy power throughout the universe displayed. Then sings my soul, my Savior God to Thee, 'How great Thou art!' " Whenever asked about the secret of his success, Billy Graham invariably responded, "Answered prayer."[48]

AMERICANS' GREATER COMMITMENT to God through prayer was accompanied by increased personal introspection. This introspection could be seen not only in the frequency but also in the intensity and dimensions of prayer, and no philosopher, let alone theologian, reflected America's spiritual ruminations in quite the way that Reinhold Niebuhr did. Growing up in Missouri at the turn of the century and graduating from Yale Divinity School in 1914, Niebuhr was very much a product of his Lutheran roots. He became a prominent voice through his books and essays articulating his vision of Christianity, beginning with his landmark work, *Moral Man and Immoral Society.*

The cumulative effects of the Depression, World War II, and the Cold War greatly influenced Reinhold Niebuhr's thinking. His vision was "Christian realism," stressing the need to recognize that sin exists and that prayer holds a special place in confronting human maladies and limitations. In particular, he focused his intellectual and spiritual passion on writing prayers that expressed both the "indeterminate possibilities" of human beings and the need to understand their weaknesses.[49]

Of all his prayers, none had as profound an effect as "The Serenity Prayer," an ageless invocation he wrote and delivered in 1943. Far from writing some kind of traditional verse, Niebuhr put together a prayer with tight phrasing and prescriptions that his daughter Elisabeth Sifton has described as "tremendously difficult and puzzling to follow," but which in turn is the essence of its beauty.[50] The prayer has several iterations but none as powerful as Niebuhr's original words:

> God, give us grace to accept with serenity
> The things that cannot be changed,
> Courage to change the things that should be changed,
> And the wisdom to distinguish the one from the other.[51]

THE MOST SUCCESSFUL SUPPORT PROGRAM that flourished in the post–World War II years, a self-help strategy with results second to none, was Alcoholics Anonymous, known to most people as AA. Unlike the women's temperance movement several generations earlier, which looked to collective prayer to advance the cause of sobriety, AA structured its program around prayer and the individual.

Alcoholics Anonymous was the brainchild of William Griffith Wilson, a Vermonter, who in 1934 ended up for the fourth time in the rehabilitation ward of Manhattan's Towns Hospital. As he lay in bed, realizing that alcoholism was about to conquer him as it had members of his family for generations, he had a spiritual awakening. For the first time he understood that he was not alone in confronting his illness and that God was there to help. Joining forces with Dr. Robert Smith, a prominent surgeon in Akron, Ohio, who had confronted his own dependence on alcohol, Wilson started mobilizing volunteers to the cause.

As AA began to gain some organizational momentum, particularly after John D. Rockefeller contributed seed money, a 1941 article in *The Saturday Evening Post*, "Alcoholics Anonymous: Freed Slaves of Drink, Now They Free Others," made all the difference. The article provided a rare, sympathetic glimpse into the struggles of an alcoholic and the need for a revolutionary approach to overcoming the addiction. The story described how two men, both reformed alcoholics, intervened to help a young, virile adult tackle his demons.[52] Thousands of letters poured into the *Post*, and soon AA chapters were springing up across the country. Attendance at AA meetings skyrocketed. By 1950, Alcoholics Anonymous had become the most successful organization of its kind ever launched in the United States.

In their publication *Alcoholics Anonymous*, Wilson and Smith laid out a twelve-step program with prayer at its heart. Under no circumstances, AA stressed, was the program to be construed as a religious society. The sheer force of prayer, and the acknowledgment that individuals are powerless by themselves to overcome their frailties, became the key to conquering dependence. The twelve-step program evolved into AA's credo, each of the steps able to be turned into its own prayer, with such confessions as "Dear Lord, I admit that I am powerless over my addiction . . . remove me from denial."[53] The keystone prayer, however, was Reinhold Niebuhr's "Serenity Prayer," reflecting the sense of hope mixed with the hard realities of everyday life.

TRADITIONAL PRAYER was also finding voice in some unusual venues, none more vibrant than the arts during the postwar years. For many artists, prayer was the keystone for creative discovery. Martha Graham, the legendary American choreographer, believed that dance, in both its most subtle and its most accentuated movements, was a form of prayer. Reflecting on her life's passion before a live audience, she would always begin with the same simple words, "I am a dancer." It was also the way she opened her autobiography, adding that dance "is the performance of a dedicated, precise set of acts, physical or intellectual, from which comes shape of achievement, a sense of one's being, a satisfaction with spirit. One becomes in some area an athlete of God."[54] Throughout her prodigious body of work, she choreographed dance after dance that evoked expressions of prayers, from *Primitive Mysteries* to *Lamentations*.

One work, inspired and choreographed by Graham, became an American classic. Approaching her good friend Aaron Copland, the dean of American classical composers, she tried to figure out how they could collaborate on a work that would exude through dance and music the pioneering spirit of Americans, both geographic and spiritual. The two of them produced a Pulitzer Prize–winning work, *Appalachian Spring*, originally titled *Ballet for Martha*, which was renamed only hours before its premiere at the Coolidge Auditorium of the Library of Congress.

From the ballet's opening note to its closing, the work conveys the budding dreams of a newly married Quaker couple, American pioneers aspiring to their own promised land. With its memorable melody from the Shaker hymn "Simple Gifts," the piece represents the idyllic spirituality and hopes of America. Prayer comes to be equated with freedom. From encountering a revivalist preacher to building their dream house, the young couple searches for a future together in the hills of western Pennsylvania through "joy, love, and prayer."[55]

The country was also producing artists who exemplified American creativity and ideals in other ways. In capturing the country's character through his illustrations, Norman Rockwell had an effect on people from all walks of life. With the tough core of a reserved New Englander, he was unabashedly sentimental when it came to depicting American life. His illustrations were so popular in his day that working-class Americans had copies of them on display in their homes. Reproductions of his works far outnumber those of Michelangelo, Rembrandt, and Picasso combined.[56]

From his studio in Arlington, Vermont, Rockwell produced covers for *The Saturday Evening Post* that evoked American innocence and optimism as well as the country's mores and aspirations. Arguably his greatest acclaim came in 1943 with his *Four Freedoms,* individual paintings depicting freedom of speech, freedom from want, freedom from fear, and freedom of religion. The project was inspired by Roosevelt's address to Congress in which he laid out his vision of those ideals freedoms most clearly representing the essence of the American credo.

Rockwell believed that his finest work from the *Four Freedoms* project was *Freedom to Worship.*[57] Like a religious patchwork quilt, the painting depicts the profiles of men and women, young and old, black and white, praying with hands folded—the spiritual invocations of a diverse religious America. At the center of the frame is an elderly couple, each petitioning God in a different way, while off to the side a middle-aged woman holds a rosary in her hands as a man next to her clutches his copy of the Koran. In thinking over an appropriate subtitle for his painting, Rockwell chose "Each according to the dictates of his own conscience."

After completing *The Four Freedoms*, Rockwell offered the portraits to the U.S. government to help support the war effort and was surprised to be turned down. Once the illustrations were published and public approval was overwhelming, however, the government was more than delighted to use them to promote war bonds. The ad campaign was the most successful effort of its kind during the war.[58]

Another notable achievement for Rockwell came with his Thanksgiving cover for the November 1951 issue of *The Saturday Evening Post,* an illustration titled "Saying Grace." It portrayed a diner scene in which an elderly woman and a young boy pray as two rough-looking teenagers watch with some bewilderment.[59] From a technical point of view, "Saying Grace" was one of Rockwell's finest illustrations, capturing an American ideal by rendering the simple, unobtrusive act of prayer.

IN THE AFTERMATH of World War II, some writers were at the height of their literary careers, whereas others were just beginning to find a voice in depicting the spiritual restlessness of America. Few could reach the literary heights of T. S. Eliot and W. H. Auden, both of whom had a profound impact on Western humanities.

Thomas Stearns Eliot, born in 1888 to a wealthy family in St. Louis, could trace his ancestry back to the first Puritan settlers of New England. Receiving his bachelor's degree from Harvard, he was drawn irresistibly to Europe, where he studied at Oxford and at the Sorbonne in Paris. Known to most modern-day audiences for his short poems in *Old Possum's Book of Practical Cats,* the inspiration for the Broadway musical *Cats,* Eliot wrote plays, criticism, and, most notably, poetry and received the Nobel Prize in literature in 1948. No poet of the last century garnered more acclaim.

After becoming a British citizen in 1927, Eliot soon converted from Unitarianism to Anglo-Catholicism, identifying himself with the most conservative elements of the Church of England. His six-part poem *Ash-Wednesday,* written not long after his conversion, is not so much a prayer to God as a statement intended to create prayer for God. His long poem *Four Quartets,* by far his most mature work, broadly sweeps through metaphor and cosmic references to time, space, eternity, and salvation to give meaning to human existence. In the section called "Little Gidding," Eliot wrote, "Prayer is more than an order of words." At its heart it is "the conscious occupation of the praying mind, or the sound of the voice praying."[60]

With Eliot's death in 1965, Wystan Hugh Auden stood as the foremost living poet in the English language. Whereas Eliot had left the United States to settle in London and become a British citizen, Auden had left Great Britain to reside in New York and become a U.S. citizen in 1946. Like Eliot, Auden experienced a religious odyssey. Even more than Eliot, he was fascinated by the act of prayer itself—what it meant, how it was said, and why it was important. He found prayer to be a great equalizer, recognizing that each penitent was a "unique person with a unique perspective on the world, a member of a class of one." He also saw human folly in the way people approached God, believing that the "serious part of prayer" could begin only once "we have got our begging over with and listen."[61]

Other writers also made an impact. Men like Langston Hughes, Richard Wright, James Baldwin, and Ralph Ellison gave voice to their African-American heritage in new ways. Having wandered away from the traditional religion of their childhood, they returned again and again to their spiritual roots. Pain, rejection, hostility, and ultimately spiritual resilience were just some of the emotions expressed in their works, which often find even prayer to be wanting. James Baldwin's semiautobiographical *Go Tell It on the Mountain* uses the vehicle of prayer to reveal the inner recesses of a young black man's mind and each member of his family in twentieth-century America as they worship together in church. In Langston Hughes's poem "The Negro Mother," the narrator cries out from the three-hundred-year experience of slavery, "God put a song and a prayer in my mouth . . . steel in my soul."[62]

Another group of rebels, largely young white men, expressed their angst over American culture through their writings. Referred to as "Beat" by Jack Kerouac, the movement's godfather, the term had evolved from the days after World War II when jazz musicians used the word generally to mean "tired" or "rundown." Now it was being given a more positive spin. Shorthand for "beatific," Kerouac would explain that its new meaning derived in part from the beatitudes emanating from Christ's Sermon on the Mount.[63] While the term was meant to signify God's "blessed," the beatnik lifestyle was anything but selfless. Often the Beats exuded a sort of harmonic and spiritual dread at the thought of conforming to the mores of those around them.

Two major voices of the movement seemed to revel in shocking audiences and exploring the limits of sensory perception. Jack Kerouac and

Allen Ginsberg, who first met while students at Columbia University, took every opportunity to strike out against convention. Their most acclaimed works were seen by many critics as nothing less than quests for spiritual epiphany. Kerouac even went so far as to declare that his life's mission was to have God "show me his face." *Time* magazine remarked that the statement would have been "more convincing" if Kerouac's works did not preach, " 'Seek ye first the Kingdom of kicks,' e.g., drink, drugs, jazz, and kicks."[64]

Significantly, the more these writers appeared to be spiritually adrift, the more they veered back to their religious roots for psychological, if not spiritual, anchoring. For example, in his groundbreaking novel, *On the Road*, written in just three weeks, Kerouac used a spontaneous and wildly undisciplined style of prose in an attempt to find his spiritual path.

His contrarian reputation aside, Kerouac, a Roman Catholic by background, could never wander entirely from his religious roots. Indeed, when he died, he was laid out in a coffin with rosary beads dangling between his fingers as though he were in the middle of prayer. Few people realized until after his death the trove of beautiful hymns, prayers, and intensely personal spiritual essays he had written. His mystical Catholicism led him to write prayers, letters, and poems to the Holy Trinity, Mary, and the saints. His psalms cried out to God with such reverences as "Angel of the Universe," "King of Light," and "Maker of Darkness." These were pieces expressing love, adoration, and a yearning to find life's meaning through the divine. "Strike me, and I will ring like a bell," he pleaded with the Almighty. In one prayer he pleaded, "I owe You, God, for my gifts . . . Forgive me for my youth . . . oh make me a giver."[66]

Allen Ginsberg, on the other hand, came from an atheistic and rather fanatical Communist family. With his extensive poem *Kaddish*, written to honor his dead mother, he seemed to find spiritual bottom.

To fashion his own prayer in tribute to his mother, Ginsberg wrote his original draft of *Kaddish for Naomi Ginsberg, 1894–1956* in 1956. From six o'clock one Saturday morning until ten o'clock in the evening of the next day, he filled fifty-eight pages, most of which were stained by tears reflecting lost opportunities and a troubled past with his mother. *Kaddish* became catharsis, a prayer that released within Ginsberg much of the anxiety that had been built up over a lifetime. Many critics believe it to be his greatest composition. For Ginsberg, as for Kerouac and other Beat poets, prayer had the potential to serve as an escape valve.

＊ ＊ ＊

IN THE YEARS following World War II, the United States continued its love affair with amateur and professional sports. Among the crowded field, two people, Jackie Robinson and Babe Didrikson, stood out. These sports icons not only broke down cultural barriers; they did so because their outstanding athletic gifts were matched by their strong moral character and unwavering sense of self-worth. In their careers and private lives, prayer was an indispensable force, particularly when they found themselves at critical crossroads.

Born in 1919, Robinson got his big break when the legendary Brooklyn Dodger president Branch Rickey approached him about playing major-league baseball. Rickey explained to Robinson that he wanted to integrate American baseball and that Robinson was his man. When news about Robinson's contract with the Dodgers' farm team in Montreal was announced, the owners and players of other ball teams, not to mention segments of the general public, were outraged, convinced that integration was the death knell for baseball.

Facing death threats, hundreds of hate-mail letters, and even an anonymous caller threatening that if he did not resign from the game his baby boy, Jackie junior, would be kidnapped, Robinson remained undeterred. He found that he "prayed as I never prayed before." With prayer in a person's arsenal, "trouble ahead needn't bother you."[68] By 1949 he had become the National League's most valuable player while maintaining a batting average of over .300 during six consecutive seasons and spellbinding fans as he stole bases with cunning and daring. In an interview with the Brooklyn Eagle after he retired, he candidly described how he would pray on his knees: "It's the best way to get close to God and a hard-hit ground ball."[69]

Like Jackie Robinson shattering racial barriers, Babe Didrikson Zaharias shattered gender barriers and came to realize that, as the prizefighter Gene Tunney put it, "you can pray away your terrors."[70] Born in 1914 to Norwegian immigrant parents in Texas, Didrikson showed an early talent for every sport she tackled. As a member of the 1932 U.S. Olympic team in track and field, she won gold medals in every event she entered, breaking Olympic records in the javelin, hurdles, and high jump.

Although she also excelled in swimming, rifle shooting, and tennis, by the age of twenty she had realized that her real passion was golf, a sport dominated by such male figures as Bobby Jones and Walter Hagen.

Between 1946 and 1947 she won seventeen straight golf tournaments and in the process received every athletic honor that the world of sports could bestow.

Her husband, George Zaharias, became a source of strength in 1953, when at the age of thirty-nine she was diagnosed with cancer, a disease that in those days was never discussed above a whisper. Within three years she would die, but not before she stunned the world by winning the U.S. Women's Open in 1954 by twelve strokes. Through it all, she believed that the extraordinary dimensions of prayer had bolstered in her the spiritual resilience to endure to the end, and she left behind an extraordinary account:

> Once we had the doctor's diagnosis, nobody made a secret of the fact that I had cancer. I've never understood why cancer should be unmentionable. In golf, you know where the sand traps and water holes are ahead, and you try to guide your shots accordingly . . . Soon the newspapers everywhere announced that I had cancer . . .
>
> Everybody promised prayers. This was something new for me. All my life, I looked upon prayer as something very personal between God and me. I guess I've prayed for the same blessings and with the same gratitude as everyone else, but it never occurred to me that thousands of people, separated from each other, could effectively join in a barrage of prayers for the sake of one person—me.
>
> Being an athlete, I could express my feelings by saying: "Here is wonderful teamwork in faith" . . . Suddenly I looked upon prayers as muscles, and I realized that the strongest people in the world must be those who pray for each other.[71]

Although the importance of prayer to Babe Didrikson Zaharias and Jackie Robinson was largely unknown to their fans, it clearly helped both of them to mold their legacies both on and off the sports field. They learned to approach prayer much as Satchel Paige, the great Negro League pitcher who played with Robinson on the Kansas City Monarchs, did when he said, "Don't pray when it rains if you don't pray when the sun shines."[72]

THE LATE 1940S and the 1950s gave rise to some uniquely American music. While the South in particular had developed distinct forms of music, tracing its regional roots to the hymns and religious heritage of early America, wide popularity of such genres as blues, bluegrass, and country-western did not come until after World War II. The "golden age of gospel music" was ushered in, reaching audiences outside black America.

Other varieties of American music were becoming embedded in the country's cultural and spiritual psyche in the form of folk tunes. Young people in particular began to show an interest in their country's heritage after the war and gravitated toward uncomplicated folk songs.

No individual typified this trend more than the man known as "America's balladeer," Woody Guthrie. In Guthrie, American folk music found one of its greatest champions as he wrote and performed on the guitar such songs as "This Land Is Your Land," "This Train Is Bound for Glory," and "So Long, It's Been Good to Know Yuh."

From birth, Woodrow Wilson Guthrie seemed to be plagued by tragedy. Inheriting Huntington's chorea from his mother, Nora, Guthrie was traumatized after his mother's insanity caused her to kill his older sister by fire; he watched his father's physical and mental breakdown take him from political and business failures to death on skid row. By the time he was fourteen, he was facing destitution and the complete breakup of his family. Having survived his dysfunctional childhood and starting a family of his own, he again confronted tragedy when his daughter Cathy died from the devastation of a house fire.

Throughout his lifelong travails, Guthrie composed more than a thousand songs, reflecting the world as he knew it. Through it all, he believed that prayer and his bond to God, particularly to Jesus Christ, helped him survive his life and face death in 1967. He came to pray affectionately to "my deary Jesus M. Christo" and wrote unabashed songs of faith like "Jesus, My Doctor" when his health began to fail and he realized his disease would finally overtake him.[73]

While Guthrie's music influenced artists as diverse as the Beatles and Bob Dylan, it had a particularly profound effect on his friend Pete Seeger, the composer of songs like "If I Had a Hammer," co-written with Lee Hays in 1951, and "Where Have All the Flowers Gone?," released a few years later.

Pete Seeger often recounted how his father had believed that the world was trapped by an overdependence on words, that there was much more to the universe and to life than what a person's vocabulary could convey. In particular, he believed that prayer enabled a person to express the deepest human yearnings, beyond individual limitations. In time, he came to rely on a two-word prayer—"What next?"—repeated each morning when he awoke.

One of the most optimistic pieces Seeger ever composed was "Turn, Turn, Turn," the song later popularized by the Byrds and inspired by an early passage in Ecclesiastes that speaks of the value and cycles of human life. "To everything . . . there is a season . . ." Fixed on hope and faith rather than civic protest, it was a bit of a departure for Seeger, but for many Americans raised in the fifties and sixties it would become a spiritual anthem.

While simple folk tunes gained greater popularity just after World War II, country music gained even greater momentum. Bringing together their own blend of bluegrass and folk music, the Carter Family of Maces Springs, a small town cradled in the lush Clinch Mountains of southwestern Virginia, were the first commercially successful country musicians during the Depression.

Steeped in church music, they played sacred and secular songs, some borrowed, some original, using Autoharps, banjos, guitars, and fiddles. Initially, family and friends were horrified that the "devil's instruments" were being used to show God praise. Even the casual tempos were considered sacrilegious. "Keep on the Sunny Side," their signature song admonishing listeners to "trust in our Savior," and "Will the Circle Be Unbroken" speaking to the Lord as an intimate friend in mourning a mother's death, were two of their most popular songs.

If the Carters helped to integrate bluegrass and country music into the American music lexicon, no one came to represent or popularize country music more than Hank Williams. From his birth in 1923, Williams seemed destined to become a major force in the genre. "I have been singing ever since I can remember," he told Ralph Gleason of the *San Francisco Chronicle*. With his mother serving as organist at the Mount Olive West Baptist Church in Alabama, he would recall that "my earliest memory is sittin' on that organ stool by her and hollerin'."[74]

Hank Williams led a relatively happy childhood, though he was tormented by his estrangement from his father, who could not bear the responsibilities of a family. "I wish I had a dad" became an all-too-personal refrain that he would write about in an unpublished song in 1948. The circumstances of his childhood, the deep spirituality he inherited

from his mother, and the raw talent he possessed were just the right formula for spectacular success in country music.

Although Williams stopped going to church regularly before he
reached his teens, regular prayer had long been a way of life. As he
would later reflect in song, when things got tough, he would just sit back
and take comfort that "every time I close my eyes, I see Jesus coming
down the road." Prayer through song had to be pure, honest, and whole.
When he wrote songs, he would often say, "I hold the pen, and God does
the writing."[75]

Rarely did he perform a concert live or on radio in which he did not
sing at least one of his religious songs. From one of his first works, "(I'm
Praying for the Day) Peace Will Come," written in 1942, to his best-
remembered hymns, "I Saw the Light" of 1948 and "Help Me Understand" of 1950, Williams brought gospel foursquare into his country
music. By the time he died in 1953, around age twenty-nine, on the morning of New Year's Day, the "Hillbilly Shakespeare" had left behind over
one hundred classic songs.

While popular music had taken on new dimensions in the postwar
years and performing artists proliferated like never before, no one could
match the charisma of Elvis Aron Presley. Born in Tupelo, Mississippi, in
1935, Presley was raised in a poor but devout Christian family whose life
revolved around their local Assembly of God church. The Pentecostal
church condemned dancing and strictly prohibited its members from
watching most movies of the day. For Elvis Presley, the greatest problem
with the church was its emphasis on the anger rather than the love of
God. At times it seemed almost too much for him to bear. In joining the
church choir, however, he began to listen to sacred music of all kinds,
and, like Hank Williams, he quickly came to love the hymns he sang and
the African-American style of singing that was so prevalent in his little
town.

After moving with his family to Memphis and graduating from high
school, he worked as a truck driver while studying at night to be an elec-
trician. In his off-hours he would listen to the white gospel quartets that
flourished in those days in Memphis. He became a regular at Ellis Auditorium's All-Night Gospel Singings, riveted by the range of musical
styles and emotions in spiritual music.

Not content to sit on the sidelines, Presley soon tried his own hand at
performing. As a belated birthday present for his mother, Gladys, the

eighteen-year-old Presley walked into a local studio in 1953 to make a four-dollar recording of two sentimental ballads. She loved it, and he soon returned to make another recording. This time, the owner of the studio, the legendary Sam Phillips, was there, heard him, and signed the young Elvis Presley to his first contract on the road to stardom.

From *The Milton Berle Show* to *The Steve Allen Show*, America watched as Presley helped to define the new musical elements of rock and roll. What audiences did not realize until much later was how deeply spiritual Presley was. Little did they know that before each performance, he would search out a quiet corner and recite a one-line prayer. "Send me some light—I need it" was his simple invocation. He later admitted that when times of crisis brought on bouts of depression, "All I had was my prayers."[76]

Every time Presley tried to attend church services or visit a church simply to say a prayer, fans would mob him, and so he reluctantly stayed away. Although he prayed often, believing that his connection to God was central to his existence, he wanted to express himself publicly in a more spiritual way. He simply did not want to be seen solely as a hip-gyrating rock-and-roll star. Even his extremely popular love ballads such as "Love Me Tender" did not fully satisfy those needs.

Although he had recorded such gospel albums as *Peace in the Valley* in 1957 and *His Hand in Mine* in 1960, Presley became even more driven to record music that would convey his deep spiritual convictions, hoping that those feelings would resonate with his audiences. In producing *How Great Thou Art* in 1967, he intentionally set out to influence his youngest fans, remarking, "I want to feel God's love. I want to give back. I want to awaken in all these young people a closer relationship with God."[77]

When he and his entourage arrived at RCA studios in Nashville to record *How Great Thou Art*, he gathered everyone together before he sang a single note, quietly telling them what was on his mind. He let them know that he was convinced that the album had been "ordained by God himself" and that "I am his channel." Knowing that millions of people would listen to his album, he asked those around him to close their eyes and pray, making clear that he would not move from his chair until he was "guided by that still, small voice within me."[78]

Ironically, with fourteen Grammy nominations during his career, Elvis Presley would receive only three of the coveted music awards—for *How Great Thou Art, He Touched Me,* and his live Memphis concert recording in 1974 of "How Great Thou Art." All of them would become part of the large repertoire of spiritual music that he would leave behind in the midst of his unsettling death in 1977. In a career that spanned just a little more than twenty years, he would become the biggest-selling artist in history.

IN THE DECADE and a half following World War II, social and spiritual change was taking place during a period of relative prosperity. By the end of the 1950s the United States had taken center stage politically, militarily, economically, and culturally. Never before had the stakes seemed so high. In rebuilding war-torn economies and fending off the very real threat of Communism, the country realized that what it said and did truly mattered on a global scale. It is no wonder that prayer flourished during these critical years as the country and its leaders wrestled with the legacy and remnants of the recent past. More important, the American people could not help but wonder what the future would hold. As if prompted by the rise and fall of a theater curtain, one act in American history seemed to give way to the next. No one expressed this better than the next President of the United States, John F. Kennedy, when he declared in his inaugural address on January 20, 1961:

In the long history of the world, only a few generations have been granted the role of defending freedom in its hour of maximum danger. I do not shrink from this responsibility—I welcome it. I do not believe that any of us would exchange places with any other people or any other generation. The energy, the faith, the devotion which we bring to this endeavor will light our country and all who serve it—and the glow from that fire can truly light the world.[79]

CHAPTER 14

THE NEW PIONEERS

1960–1975

Heaven holds a place for those who pray.

—Paul Simon (1967)

N O DECADE IN U.S. HISTORY was more of a catalyst for enriching and deepening America's prayer culture than the 1960s. From almost every vantage point, the country's spirituality was explored, challenged, and ultimately reinforced, from church pews to city streets.

The civil rights movement, led in large part by ministers of different denominations, turned prayer into a powerful tool to inspire and coalesce the antisegregation forces. The Second Vatican Council, that historic gathering in Rome of Catholic bishops from around the world called by Pope John XXIII to "throw open the windows of the Church,"[1] allowed American Catholics to expand their visions of spirituality and to connect to the prayer traditions of other faiths. The Immigration Reform Act of 1965 raised the immigration ceiling, allowing far more émigrés from Asia, Latin America, and the Middle East to enter the country; in doing so, it multiplied exponentially the variety of religious prayer traditions in the United States. Baby boomers coming of age in the 1960s contributed to the country's spiritual diversity by borrowing from the prayer cultures of South Asia, sub-Saharan Africa, the Middle East, and indigenous peoples from around the world, finding value in adapting new approaches to their prayers. Finally, the Vietnam War brought about an intense national introspection, in which prayer became a means of exploring the national conscience and addressing the realities of an unpopular war. The sheer dynamic nature of prayer in the life of the country was only reinforced by the cultural and social transformations of the 1960s.

NO ONE SEEMED TO DEFINE the enormous promise of the decade more than John Kennedy. Born into the affluent Irish Catholic family of Joseph and Rose Kennedy in Brookline, Massachusetts, the Harvard-educated Kennedy had emerged from World War II a bona fide hero and in 1957 received the Pulitzer Prize for his nonfiction *Profiles in Courage,* all before becoming President.

Nominated for President by his party in Los Angeles in 1960, the senator from Massachusetts laid out his vision for a "new frontier," an America challenged by "uncharted areas of science and space, unsolved problems of peace and war, unconquered pockets of ignorance and prejudice, unanswered questions of poverty and surplus."[2] Throughout his campaign he discussed the spoken and unspoken biases against him because of his Catholic faith, and some detractors believed that having a Catholic run the country was the equivalent of turning the reins of government over to the Pope. The religious question became so deeply embedded in the campaign that hard-line Protestant ministers railed from the pulpit both in sermon and in prayer, trying to rally the faithful against "the papist" from New England.

In his relatively brief but electrifying inaugural address, Kennedy spoke of "the hand of God" in the rights of man and in America's affairs, stating, "With a good conscience our only sure reward, with history the final judge of our deeds, let us go forth to lead the land we love. Asking His blessing and His help, but knowing that here on earth God's work must truly be our own."[3]

The first months of the Kennedy administration were anything but tranquil. The Bay of Pigs fiasco, the space race with the Soviet Union, the Cuban missile crisis, and the growing tensions over Vietnam all placed enormous pressures on the young President. Through it all, Kennedy treasured a small, unpretentious plaque given to him by the indefatigable Admiral Hyman Rickover, father of the country's nuclear navy. Inscribed on the piece of wood were the words "O God, thy sea is so great, and my boat is so small,"[4] taken from the prayer of an unknown

Breton fisherman. The President kept the gift on his desk, within eye-sight.

While Kennedy continued to face challenges on both the domestic and foreign fronts, one of the most seminal moments in the history of American prayer was being played out in the Supreme Court. Through-out American history the propriety of public prayer had rarely risen as a topic of serious national debate. When it did, the real issue rested not so much with the act of prayer itself as with the context in which it was said and the direct involvement of the government in its exercise. By 1960, however, dissonant voices had begun to be heard over the broader issue of prayer in public places. Individuals who felt that their rights were being abrogated under the establishment clause of the Constitution, explicitly forbidding Congress to promulgate any law "respecting an establishment of religion, or prohibiting the free exercise thereof," believed that their only effective means for venting their grievances rested with the courts. In the end, their efforts would succeed beyond their wildest dreams in the landmark Supreme Court decision of *Engel* v. *Vitale.*

The case was rather simple. Since early American colonization, most schools had begun their day by reciting some combination of prayer, Bible reading, and patriotic tribute. In trying to uphold that tradition while remaining sensitive to various religious creeds, the Board of Re-gents of the State of New York had prepared a nondenominational prayer for use in New York's public schools, incorporating it into its "Statement on Moral and Spiritual Training in the Schools." The regents took great pains to compose an invocation that would be both reli-giously and politically correct. Furthermore, they explicitly stated that any student who objected to saying the prayer could be excused from doing so. Known as the "Regents' Prayer," it simply read, "Almighty God, we acknowledge our dependence upon Thee, and we beg Thy blessings upon us, our parents, our teachers, and our country."[5]

The problem arose when Steven Engel took his son to his Searing-town Elementary School one morning and watched him recite the Regents' Prayer with his classmates, hands folded and head bowed. Engel took issue with what he considered the school system's imposing a spir-itual ritual contrary to the customs of his family's Jewish faith and tradi-tions. In turn, Engel convinced the parents of nine other children to join him in challenging the local Long Island school board and its chairman,

William Vitale. After the case wound its way through the court system over many months, the New York State Court of Appeals handed down a decision in favor of the school board. At that point the petitioners decided to appeal their case one final time, taking it to the U.S. Supreme Court. By any measure, the Court's historic ruling in *Engel* v. *Vitale* on June 25, 1962, caused a tumult that few other decisions have made before or since.

Whereas lower courts had focused on the voluntary nature of reciting the prayer, the Supreme Court was more concerned about the government's even suggesting an approach to prayer in the classroom. In its six-to-one decision, with the ailing Justice Felix Frankfurter and the newly confirmed Justice Byron White abstaining, the Court found the Regents' Prayer to be unconstitutional on the grounds that "it is not part of the business of the government to compose official prayers for any group of the American people to recite as part of a religious program carried on by the government."[6]

Justice Hugo Black, speaking for the Court's majority, focused on the establishment clause of the Constitution. After working on six successive drafts, he issued an opinion that interpreted the intentions of the Founding Fathers to treat religion as "too personal, too sacred, too holy to permit its 'unhallowed perversion' by a civil magistrate."[7] In reading the opinion from the bench, he added extemporaneously, "The prayer of each man from his soul must be his and his alone."[8] The decision haunted Black like few others. By week's end hundreds of letters had poured into his office, and the telephone in his personal chambers rang without stop for days.[9]

Recognizing the historic importance of the decision, Justice William Douglas wrote a concurring opinion, arguing that government-mandated prayer was unconstitutional on grounds of misappropriation of public funds and that "if government interferes in matters spiritual, it will be a divisive force."[10] The one dissenting voice, Justice Potter Stewart, seemed mystified by the decision of his colleagues, believing that "the Court has misapplied a great constitutional principle." This was a matter not of "establishment of a state church" but of "whether children who want to begin their day by joining in prayer must be prohibited from doing so."[11]

Some constitutional scholars criticized the poor wording of the high court's decision. Others believed that the justices had taken a far broader approach to the issue of school prayer than the facts warranted. Still other legal observers felt the Court's intervention on this First Amendment issue had been long overdue. No matter where anyone stood, however, a firestorm followed. Almost every living American had been educated in an environment in which some form of prayer had played a significant part in his or her elementary- and secondary-school years. A Gallup poll taken within a month of the decision showed that 85 percent of Americans were opposed to the Court's ruling. Furthermore, the same poll showed that never in recent history had the highest court been held in such little regard.[12] The ruling on school prayer had much to do with it.

Given this backdrop, it is remarkable that within months of its ruling the Court agreed to hear two cases involving prayer and Bible readings in the classroom. The first case, *Abington Township* v. *Schempp,* involved a school district in eastern Pennsylvania where administrators required that ten verses of the Bible be read at the opening of each school day, followed by recitation of the Lord's Prayer. Although students could be excused from the classroom during the readings, Edward Lewis Schempp, his wife, and their children contended that as Unitarians they were being forced to make an unfair decision. As a matter of their faith they could not abide by the doctrine of the holy Trinity or the divinity of Christ that was part of the exercise. Although the recitation was voluntary, they argued, their children were being forced to leave the classroom, affecting their relationships with teachers and classmates.[13]

The case was potent enough; when joined with *Murray* v. *Curlett,* it became explosive. An atheist, Madalyn Murray (O'Hair) vented her outrage when her son was required by the Baltimore school system either to participate in reading the Bible and reciting prayers with his classmates or to stand out in the hall until they were finished. Although the circumstances were slightly similar to those of *Abington Township* v. *Schempp,* the protagonists could not have been more different. Whereas the Schempps tried to stay out of the limelight, Murray actively worked the media, publicizing her case, sometimes in colorful language, to show her disdain for the very existence of God. Because she was so outspoken about her atheism and the rightness of her cause, Murray was wrongly viewed for years as the catalyst in banning prayer from the classroom.

The 1963 decision in *Murray* v. *Curlett* came as no surprise to anyone, since it relied once again on the Court's earlier interpretation of the First

Amendment.[14] The eight-to-one ruling, with Justice Potter Stewart the lone dissenter, provided the country with an unambiguous legal road map to the boundaries of school prayer. The ensuing debate took on serious political drama. Recalling the fallout later in his memoirs, Chief Justice Earl Warren wrote that most of his fellow justices had been stunned at being so "heavily attacked."[15] He would further reflect on how he and his colleagues had ruminated over the explosive issue of school prayer a century earlier between Protestants and Catholics, a situation which led to fighting in city streets and senseless deaths on both sides.

Members of Congress, who had begun holding hearings to overturn *Engel* v. *Vitale,* were enraged by the Court's audacity in driving one final stake into the heart of school prayer. Taken collectively, the series of Court decisions sparked some of the harshest rhetoric ever leveled against the Court.

Republican Congressman Frank Becker, in whose Long Island district the *Engel* case had originated, called the action "the most tragic decision in the history of the United States."[16] Democratic Senator Sam J. Ervin, Jr., of North Carolina lashed out, saying that the U.S. Supreme Court "has held that God is unconstitutional."[17] His colleague Robert C. Byrd of West Virginia proclaimed from the floor of the Senate, "Somebody is tampering with America's soul, and I leave it to you as to who that somebody is."[18] Congressman Mendel Rivers of South Carolina spoke for many of his fellow southerners when he said, "The Court has now officially stated its disbelief in God."[19]

Soon more congressional hearings were held, calling for a constitutional amendment to overturn the Court's decision. Some 2,774 pages filled three volumes of hearing transcripts from the House Judiciary Committee alone.[20] Members of both parties introduced dozens of resolutions to amend the Constitution. With public opinion on their side, many legislators were convinced that the groundswell would provide overwhelming support for the amendment and easy passage. In the end, they were wrong.

Dooming the effort was the unexpected opposition from two quarters: the White House and influential voices within America's church establishment. Having faced the religious storms of the 1960 election and warming up for a tough reelection campaign in 1964, the Kennedy administration found it unthinkable to take up the gauntlet of school prayer.

Kennedy tossed off the matter at a press conference, suggesting that the remedy rested not in overturning the Court's decision but in urging Americans to pray in their homes and attend church more frequently.[21]

Several church leaders echoed the Kennedy administration line. Representing the National Council of Churches, with its membership of almost forty million Americans, Secretary General Edwin H. Tuller testified before the Senate Judiciary Committee, "It is not right for a majority to impose religious practices on the minority in public institutions."[22] He was unequivocal. The Court's decision was a proper one, and Congress should refrain from taking any actions to overturn it.

While congressional opposition was formidable, it was not fatal to passage of the legislation. What did become the bill's death knell was the inability of its sponsors to coalesce a formidable grassroots movement. There simply was no coordinated effort to demonstrate any kind of serious political muscle. Despite another Gallup survey taken in September 1964 showing that 77 percent of Americans favored passage of a constitutional amendment, the poll was incapable of turning widespread support into effective political action.

Deliberations over the amendment seemed endless, spilling over from one Congress to the next. In the end, the uphill task of managing the Senate floor vote was left to Minority Leader Everett Dirksen, the gravelly voiced and respected Republican from Illinois. While the opponents were ready for battle, the sponsors of the bill reasonably believed that victory was within reach, particularly after they had carefully crafted the necessary language:

> Nothing contained in this Constitution shall prohibit the authority administering any school, school system, educational institution or other public building supported in whole or in part through the expenditure of public funds from providing for or permitting the voluntary participation by students or others in prayer. Nothing contained in this article shall authorize any such authority to prescribe the form or content of any prayer.[23]

Helping to ensure defeat of the amendment was Indiana Senator Birch Bayh, chairman of the Senate Judiciary Subcommittee on Constitutional Amendments and a vocal opponent of the measure. Using his mastery of parliamentary procedure, he convinced the Democratic leadership to allow him, prior to consideration of the Dirksen amendment, to hold a vote on a resolution expressing the sense of the Senate that its members believed in God and in prayer. Innocuous in its wording, the resolution was a legislative masterstroke, allowing senators to show their pro-God stance for the record, and then turn around and vote against the Dirksen amendment on legal, technical grounds. The ploy worked, and the bill failed by a vote of 49 to 37, eighteen votes short of the two-thirds majority required to pass an amendment to the Constitution.

Once again, the reaction among a cross section of Americans was predictable, and letters of protest flooded Capitol Hill from across the country. In every succeeding Congress into the twenty-first century, several bills would be introduced to amend the Constitution to allow for voluntary school prayer. Most of them, although not all, would be bottled up in committee, having little chance for consideration, let alone passage.

WHILE THE COUNTRY TRIED to make sense of the Court's recent interpretation of First Amendment rights and its long-term consequences, prayer appeared more vibrant than ever in the heartland of America. The pioneer television talk-show host Phil Donahue recounted one of the most moving moments in his life involving the simple act of prayer. Five years out of the University of Notre Dame and working as a reporter for WHIO-TV and radio in Dayton, Ohio, he was assigned to cover an accident in 1962 involving thirty-six men trapped in a West Virginia coal mine.

What made the story a reporter's dream, particularly for a twenty-seven-year-old, was that CBS News had asked Donahue and the CBS affiliate he worked for to file it for the evening network news. Covering the life-and-death account over the next three days seemed interminable, but the story took on a new, more dramatic twist when a preacher in his thirties called some of the rescuers together to pray around a barrel of burning scrap wood intended to keep the men warm. Donahue and his cameraman fixed themselves on the scene as the minister spoke from his heart: "Dear God, we ask . . . at this troubled time . . ." When the minister was done with the prayer, he led the men in singing a hymn written in 1855 by the Canadian Joseph Scriven:

> *What a friend we have in Jesus,*
> *All our sins and grief to bear,*

> *What a privilege to carry*
> *Everything to God in prayer.*

With quiet petition, the minister concluded, "Bless us, Lord, hold us in your arms." The sincerity, spontaneity, and drama of the moment made the scene electric. As Donahue later wrote, "It was all there . . . rock-of-ages faith . . . fearful eyes . . . snow falling from heaven." The Protestant hymn was unfamiliar to the Catholic Donahue, but he would remember it for the rest of his life.

Just as Donahue and his cameraman began to savor their exclusive for the evening news, panic set in. They realized that the camera had broken down in the freezing temperatures. Their "magic moment" had never been captured for America's "Tiffany Network" and its huge nationwide audience. The cameraman quickly fixed the problem, and Donahue lost no time in approaching the preacher, explaining who he was, what had happened, and how he needed to have him repeat the informal prayer service for the camera.

To his amazement, the preacher calmly looked at him and said, "But I have already prayed, son." "Reverend," Donahue clearly enunciated, "I am from CEE BEE ESS NEWS." "Wouldn't be honest," the minister responded.

Donahue persisted, telling the minister that his prayer would appear on more than two hundred television stations with millions of viewers watching and petitioning God as well for the safety of the miners. "Wouldn't be right," the minister responded one final time as he walked away. Gritting his teeth, Donahue called CBS in New York, telling his assignment editor, "The son of a bitch" just will not do it. Donahue was livid that his moment of glory had blown away in the drifting snow on a mountaintop in West Virginia, despite the fact that all thirty-six miners would make it out alive.

In time Donahue realized how that one preacher had shown "more moral courage" than he had ever witnessed firsthand in his life, that repeating the prayer for others would have been "phony." On that bitterly cold day there would be "no 'take two' for Jesus." It did not matter whether it was for a young reporter, for millions of people across the country glued to their television sets, or even for "CEE BEE ESS NEWS."[24]

★　★　★

WHILE DEBATE CONTINUED among members of the scientific and intellectual community over the worth of religion, let alone prayer, in the life of the nation, certain voices helped to define the need for prayer in new ways. Igor Sikorsky, the inventor of the modern helicopter, brought to the subject a special vantage point in his book *The Message of the Lord's Prayer.* Referring to the infinite capacity of prayer, he wrote, "Modern electrical engineering knows how to send several different messages at the same time through a single wire."[25] It was the perfect metaphor, he believed, for prayer.

Margaret Mead, the most-renowned anthropologist of the twentieth century, who made her first public mark with *Coming of Age in Samoa,* a meticulously researched book that showed how the modern world could learn from the primitive world, strongly advocated the act of prayer and the traditional sacred rites surrounding it as a critical stabilizing force in society. She bemoaned what she saw as the breakdown of prayer rituals in American society, using Thanksgiving as a case in point. She believed that time-honored prayer practices *intertwined* throughout daily life and within the American calendar year could offset the tendency toward being "alienated from our own culture." In the flux of the '60s and early '70s, Mead even believed that social crisis could erupt further if such customs were neglected in the home and community.[26] She jumped at the chance to participate in reforming the *Book of Common Prayer* in the 1970s. She insisted on the need for teachers to allow schoolchildren to have a daily period of private prayer "in which each child could pray as his parents taught him to."[27] She also advocated a constitutional amendment on school prayer.

In the fields of psychology and psychiatry, there was a growing interest in the role of prayer in human development. Karl Menninger, the eminent psychiatrist and co-founder with his father, Charles, of the world-famous Menninger Clinic, strongly promoted prayer as an essential ingredient in maintaining a proper balance in a person's life. He bemoaned, for example, that prayer was not pursued more aggressively to confront human failings. "The popular leaning is away from notions of guilt and morality," Menninger wrote in *Whatever Became of Sin?* From a purely psychological standpoint, he believed that attempting to shift moral absolutes into trouble-free escapism could only have a negative effect on a person's mental stability and even physical health.[28]

In accepting personal responsibility, owning up to individual failings, and then surrendering to the healing nature of prayer, men and women could find a very real and effective means to deal with everyday life. As the country's global stature had increased, Menninger felt, pride and political correctness had superseded the examination of conscience and consequent search for forgiveness. As he wrote in his 1973 work, "So as a nation, we officially ceased 'sinning' some twenty years ago."[29]

WHILE MENNINGER WAS ADVOCATING the wider use of prayer, the individual prayer life of most Americans was essentially strong. At no time would that fact be more visible than when the country was brought to its collective knees by the unfathomable assassination of President John Kennedy.

The murder of the country's young, vibrant President by the twenty-four-year-old Lee Harvey Oswald in Dallas, Texas, on November 22, 1963, a little over three years to the day after he had been elected, created an instant, numbing void. It was a day described by presidential aide Jack Valenti as one in which "hysteria was hanging like Spanish moss."[30] Instinctively, Americans packed churches and prayed in the privacy of their homes for the slain President and his young family as well as for the country. Thousands arrived in Washington to pay their respects. As the President lay in state in a flag-draped coffin in the East Room of the White House, where other slain presidents had rested before him, a military honor guard stood at attention while both a priest and a minister knelt in prayerful vigil nearby. As the preparations for the funeral were being made, First Lady Jacqueline Kennedy asked that prayer cards be printed carrying the official photograph of the President on one side and a prayer reading, "Dear God—please take care of your servant John Fitzgerald Kennedy. Please take him straight to heaven," on the other. In the confusion of the moment, however, Bobby Kennedy, who had promised to handle the matter, misunderstood her request. Thinking that she wanted him to choose either the first or the second sentence of the prayer, he omitted the latter.[31] Nevertheless, the prayer card became a treasured remembrance for tens of thousands of people.

The whole world watched the mourners, including France's Charles De Gaulle, Canada's Lester Pearson, and Ethiopia's Haile Selassie, file into the Romanesque St. Matthew's Cathedral for solemn High Mass on a chilly fall day. Richard Cardinal Cushing, the Catholic Archbishop of Boston, officiated at the service, as he had done for the President's inau-

guration. As Kennedy was being interred at Arlington National Cemetery, the Cardinal led the country's mourners in the Lord's Prayer, followed by the Marine Band's playing the naval hymn "Eternal Father,
Strong to Save." After fifty jet fighters flew overhead in formation, with
Air Force One trailing behind, Army Sergeant Keith Clark blew "Taps"
as the final tribute. Choking with emotion, he tried to rein in his grief
but to no avail. Clark broke the haunting cadence of the twenty-four-
note bugle call in a rendition that would forever be known as "Broken
Taps." Three days of mourning had left the nation numb. A new President now took over surrounded by many of the same people who had
served his predecessor.

THE SWEARING IN of Lyndon Johnson on the plane, carrying the body
of the President back to Washington had been an excruciating experience. Although Johnson had never made any secret of his desire to
run for the presidency, the present circumstances were unimaginable.
Elected in his own right a year later, Johnson set into motion his concept
of a "Great Society," showing a unique ability to forge a national agenda,
begun in part during the Kennedy administration, by arm-twisting Congress from the Oval Office. No one could have predicted, however, the
agonizingly difficult years that lay ahead. Civil riots, other assassinations,
and the war in Vietnam would take their toll.

In addressing his first National Prayer Breakfast in March 1964, Johnson candidly admitted that prayer had played an important part in his
life: "In our home, there was always prayer—aloud, proud, and unapologetic." Having faced some of the trials of being President, however, he
also reflected: "The men who have guided the destiny of the United
States have found the strength for their tasks by going to their knees.
This private unity of public men and their God is an enduring source of
reassurance for the people of America."[32]

Despite his membership in the Disciples of Christ, Johnson kept his
religious and spiritual devotion largely out of public view. One light-
hearted moment came when he invited the White House press corps to
his Texas ranch for dinner. As they were about to eat, the President
turned to his press secretary, Bill Moyers, and asked him to say grace.
Moyers, an ordained Baptist minister, had just begun to speak when
Johnson interrupted him: "Louder, Bill, we can't hear you." With that,

Moyers turned to the President and answered, "I wasn't talking to you, Mr. President," and proceeded to finish his prayer.[33]

Whatever his spirituality, Johnson did leave behind an unanticipated legacy as President, one that spurred great religious and spiritual diversity in the United States. Specifically, he worked aggressively behind the scenes to shepherd through Congress the Immigration Reform Act of 1965, a landmark piece of legislation that dramatically changed the political, economic, and cultural makeup of America.

Politically controversial, the act removed the traditional quotas on how many immigrants could enter the United States, both as residents and as citizens. At the signing ceremony, held at the foot of the Statue of Liberty on October 3, 1965, Johnson underplayed the importance of the act, stating, "This is not a revolutionary bill. It does not affect the lives of millions. It will not restructure our daily lives."[34] Nothing could have been further from the truth.

Preferences were given to allow professionals, from physicians to scientists, to immigrate to the United States, while the bias in favor of western European immigrants was removed. With the abolition of the national-origins quota system, the Asian population of the United States quadrupled within five years, and the influx of immigrants from southern Europe, the Middle East, and Africa showed dramatic gains.[35] A little more than ten years later, preferential treatment would be given to immigrants from the Western Hemisphere again.

The diversity that evolved in the years following enactment of the Immigration Reform Act of 1965 created a far richer, far more complex prayer life in America. Indeed, no President and no Congress up to that time had ever effected by the stroke of a pen such a sweeping change in the mosaic of the country's spirituality and prayer life.

ON THE PRESIDENT'S DOMESTIC AGENDA, no issue was more critical or more explosive than civil rights, and the racial divisions they highlighted extended to the nation's prayer life. As the Reverend Martin Luther King, Jr., reminded the country, eleven o'clock on Sunday morning was the most segregated hour in America. Many Americans still remembered an incident involving the opera contralto Marian Anderson on Easter Sunday, 1939. Having made her reputation in Europe with what the legendary conductor Arturo Toscanini referred to as "a voice heard only once in a hundred years,"[36] she was booked in the spring of 1939 to perform at Washington's Constitution Hall, a concert auditorium owned by the Daughters of the American Revolution. The invitation was withdrawn when officers of the organization realized that the gifted mezzo was African-American. Overnight the furor took on momentum. When told in detail what had happened, Eleanor Roosevelt very publicly resigned her membership in the DAR and asked Secretary of the Interior Harold Ickes to find another place for Anderson to sing.

Ickes quickly secured the steps of the Lincoln Memorial, and before a crowd of seventy-five thousand Marian Anderson stood atop the white marbled steps at the feet of Lincoln and opened her program with a memorable rendition of "America," followed by such spirituals as "Gospel Train," "My Soul Is Anchored in the Lord," and the emotional "Nobody Knows the Trouble I've Seen." In the midst of thunderous applause, it had become a defining moment, not only in Washington but across the country for those listening to the broadcast live on the radio. Deeply religious, Anderson confided that her ability to persevere against racism and life's formidable odds came through prayer. "Prayer begins where human capacity ends" was the way she put it.[37]

As the civil rights movement gained momentum, one of the most potent means of unifying the activists was the chanting of freedom songs. While a minister or rally leader could inspire a crowd by calling out to God in spontaneous prayer, leading to shouts of "amen," nothing could compare to the spiritually energizing freedom songs. They served as electrical charges, with their emotive lyrics and stirring melodies. Inspired by the great spirituals and sacred songs of rural America, these uplifting, largely unrehearsed chants, using rhythm-and-blues harmonies, were sung by every protestor in attendance.

Although some of the songs were secular, most were steeped in America's spiritual roots. There were such memorable tunes as "Guide My Feet," "This Little Light of Mine," "Don't You Think It's about Time That We All Be Free?," and "I Told Jesus." There were even recent compositions like "Will the Circle Be Unbroken," made so popular by the Carter Family.

When police rounded up demonstrators and carted them off to jail, there was nothing quite like breaking out into freedom songs to link one person to another, one cell to the next. Two of the more popular ones sung at such moments were the soulful "Oh, Yes, O Lord, I'm on My

Way to Freedom Land" and "Woke Up This Morning with My Mind on Freedom," a tune with the spiritually defiant refrain "singin' and prayin' with my mind."

The movement's anthem, "We Shall Overcome," soon became instantly recognizable in living rooms across America as synonymous with the effort for civil rights, what Robert Shelton of *The New York Times* referred to at the time as "the Marseillaise of the integration movement."[38] Inspired by the words and music of "I'll Overcome Some Day" by the former slave and gospel-song composer Charles Albert Tindley, Pete Seeger and three fellow musicians adapted the piece to fit the times. With its tenacious refrain, "Oh, deep in my heart, I do believe, we shall overcome some day," the freedom song embodied the soul of the struggle and would later be used by protesters from Moscow's Red Square to Beijing's Tiananmen Square in calling for revolutionary change to forge a foundation for basic human rights.

IN THE FIGURE OF Martin Luther King, Jr., the civil rights movement took wing. The son of a Baptist minister, King entered Atlanta's Morehouse College at the age of fifteen, received his degree in 1948, and then went to Crozer Theological Seminary in Chester, Pennsylvania, where he was awarded a divinity degree three years later. After his ordination, he studied at the School of Theology at Boston University, where he received his doctorate in 1955. From there he was named pastor of the Dexter Avenue Baptist Church in Montgomery, Alabama, where his true mission in life began to unfold dramatically.

Long steeped in and moved by the teaching and example of Christ, King found that Morehouse and Crozer had opened new intellectual doors for him. During those years, he began a lifelong fascination with the writings of Walter Rauschenbusch, especially his preaching of the Social Gospel and his unfaltering belief in the efficacy of prayer to confront human strife. It was India's Mahatma Gandhi, however, who seemed to move mountains. Assassinated in 1948 for leading efforts to contain the religious and ethnic strife between Hindus and Muslims, Gandhi proved that nonviolence could be used to effect revolutionary social change. It was a powerful message for the young King. Gandhi's advocacy of prayer, both personal and communal, as a unifying force also captured his imagination. "Prayer is not an old woman's idle amusement," King remembered the great pacifist saying. "Properly applied, it is the most potent instrument of action." Furthermore, true prayer "can achieve what nothing else can in the world."[39] On a subcontinent of a billion people, speaking fifteen languages with over a thousand dialects, Gandhi had made a decided difference, and Martin Luther King intended to follow his example. Furthermore, throughout his public ministry, before speaking to any audience, King would always immerse himself in a brief prayer, asking God on each occasion for the grace to inspire.[40]

The personal toll on King and his family in taking up the cause of civil rights, however, was enormous. By some estimates, his home telephone rang thirty or forty times a day, with callers often spewing obscenities. None of them, however, was as vicious, foreboding, or catalytic as the one he received in the middle of the night just after the New Year in 1956 as the Montgomery bus strike was beginning to accelerate. "Listen, nigger, we've taken all we want from you. Before next week you'll be sorry you ever came to Montgomery. If you aren't out of this town in three days, we're gonna blow your brains out and blow up your house," threatened the caller.[41]

Quietly putting down the receiver to avoid waking up his wife, Coretta, King got out of bed and walked into the kitchen. Turning on the overhead light and making himself a cup of coffee, he sat at the kitchen table, staring blankly at the untouched cup and saucer in front of him, believing that he had finally reached his saturation point. Of all the calls he had received, this one was the last straw. While he had been consumed with his work for racial equality, he recognized, his young family had been placed in danger. Perhaps this fight should not be his fight. Perhaps he should step aside from the struggle and return to pastoral work.

He began to pray rather gently but with an unmistakable tone of despair: "Lord . . . I am at the end of my powers. I have nothing left. I can't face it alone." At that moment, he later recounted to his family and closest friends, he felt "an experience with the Divine as I had never experienced Him before." In what would become known as his "kitchen conversion," King was consumed by what he saw as a spiritual fire, confirming once and for all the road he must follow. God would help to take care of his family, he realized. The fight for human rights could not be sidelined.[42] It was a remarkable moment for someone who had just turned twenty-seven.

Not unlike early Puritan fathers such as Increase and Cotton Mather, Martin Luther King would set aside one, two, and sometimes three days a week for "silence and meditation." He used these periods to afford himself the necessary breathing room to continue his spiritual dialogue with God, seeking divine guidance, preparing for upcoming sermons, but always understanding that God expected his prayers to be joined with human invention and resolute action. In a memorable sermon he delivered to his Dexter Avenue Baptist congregation titled "The Answer to a Perplexing Question," King recoiled at the notion that individuals should sit back and let God do everything, believing that to do so was "a tragic misuse of prayer." He was repelled to see people treat God as little more than "a cosmic bellhop."[43] Prayer, he insisted, was never intended by God to be a substitute for work and applied intelligence. "No, it is not either prayer *or* human effort; it is both prayer *and* human effort" that must be joined in all of life's endeavors.[44] Great things could be accomplished through prayer, but only by those prepared to use their feet, their minds, and their other God-given talents. The Almighty never meant for it to be otherwise.

The event that catapulted Martin Luther King into national prominence was his leading the newly created Southern Christian Leadership Conference to Washington for the Prayer Pilgrimage for Freedom in 1957, the first national rally organized by the leaders of the modern civil rights movement. Not only was the demonstration intended to show public support for the Civil Rights Bill pending before Congress, but it also was scheduled to coincide with the third anniversary of the U.S. Supreme Court's landmark decision of *Brown* v. *Board of Education of Topeka,* calling for the desegregation of the public school system. Nothing could convey the idea of achieving racial equality through nonviolence better than a demonstration of solidarity through the coalescing force of prayer. No matter what one's views on civil rights, a rally billed as a "prayer pilgrimage" would be hard to deprecate.

Set for May 17, 1957, the Prayer Pilgrimage for Freedom was a milestone in the life of the civil rights movement and for Martin Luther King personally. With such seminal figures in attendance as Roy Wilkins of the NAACP, A. Philip Randolph of the Brotherhood of Sleeping Car Porters, Rosa Parks, and every other leader of the burgeoning civil rights movement, King was mesmerizing as he repeated over and over again, "Give us the ballot," to an estimated crowd of thirty thousand.

The Prayer Pilgrimage for Freedom would be eclipsed six years later, on August 28, 1963, during the March on Washington for Jobs and Freedom, when King delivered his spellbinding "I Have a Dream" speech. Breaking all attendance records for a demonstration in Washington, over 250,000 people gathered in the nation's capital to hear a series of speakers strike out against the racial injustice continuing to pervade the country.[45] Thanks to coverage by the three major television networks, several million more watched the historic moment unfold in their living rooms.

The audience listened politely, if not somewhat passively, to the speakers, but they sprang to life when Marian Anderson sang "He's Got the Whole World in His Hands" and Mahalia Jackson followed with another spiritual, "I've Been 'Buked and I've Been Scorned." The prayer songs of black America's past provided a powerful prelude to King's closing speech. Indeed, it was Mahalia Jackson who stood off to the side as King began to depart from his prepared text and audibly coaxed him to let the assembled crowd know about his "dream." In the memorable lines of his conclusion, he dreamed of the day when men and women of diversity would "join hands and sing in the words of the old Negro spiritual, 'Free at last! Free at last! Thank God Almighty, we are free at last!'"[46]

Having witnessed passage of the Civil Rights Act of 1964, which was enacted in the same year he became the youngest recipient of the Nobel Peace Prize in history, King continued to wage his campaign for social reforms. While in Memphis, Tennessee, to support the cause of sanitation workers, he was assassinated by James Earl Ray on April 4, 1968, as he stood on the balcony of his second-floor motel room.

King's death by a white racist, who had been convicted in the past of petty crimes, brought well-founded fears that cities across the country would soon be set ablaze by African-Americans venting their outrage, the very course that Martin Luther King had fought so steadfastly to avoid. President Johnson, the King family, and prominent African-American clergymen called for calm. As lawlessness erupted, one voice had a special credibility in helping to quell the violence, that of Robert F. Kennedy, the junior senator from New York. Just before landing in Indianapolis for a campaign rally to secure the Democratic Party nomination for President later that summer, he was told of what had happened in Memphis. After descending from the plane, he walked over to the throng of reporters and campaign supporters, many of whom had not yet heard what had transpired. Kennedy, recounting his own brother's death from an assassin's bullet five years earlier, spent but a few minutes delivering what became one of the most memorable speeches of his career:

For those of you who are black and are tempted to be filled with hatred and distrust at the injustice of such an act, against all white people, I can only say that I feel in my own heart the same kind of feeling. I had a member of my family killed, but he was killed by a white man. But we have to make an effort in the United States, we have to make an effort to understand, to go beyond these rather difficult times . . .

So I shall ask you tonight to return home, to say a prayer for the family of Martin Luther King, that's true, but more importantly, to say a prayer for our own country, which all of us love—a prayer for understanding and that compassion of which I spoke.[47]

Robert Kennedy personally chartered the plane that carried the slain leader from Memphis to his home in Atlanta.

JUST TWO MONTHS AFTER the assassination of Martin Luther King, Jr., having tried to soothe raw nerves particularly among young African-Americans, Robert Kennedy himself became the victim of an assassin's bullet. Minutes after winning the California Democratic Party primary for President, he was fatally shot at the Ambassador Hotel in Los Angeles by Sirhan Sirhan, a dishwasher who was incensed over Kennedy's pro-Israeli positions.

More than his brothers, Robert Kennedy had been a devout Catholic. Not only did he attend weekly Sunday Mass; he also prayed daily, went to confession, and kept a rosary in his pocket at all times. His piety was well known to his family, leading Jacqueline Kennedy to remark to the seasoned journalist Arthur Krock during the 1960 campaign, "I think it is unfair to Jack to be opposed because he is Catholic . . . now if it were Bobby: he never misses Mass and prays all the time."[48]

With his death, Robert Kennedy left behind his wife, Ethel, ten children, and another child yet to be born. As the last remaining brother, Massachusetts Senator Edward Kennedy eulogized Bobby at St. Patrick's Cathedral in New York, choking back tears as he did so:

My brother need not be idealized, or enlarged in death beyond what he was in life, to be remembered simply as a good and decent man, who saw wrong and tried to right it, saw suffering and tried to heal it, saw war and tried to stop it. Those of us who loved him

and take him to his rest today, pray that what he was to us and what
he wished for others will some day come to pass for all the world.[49]

WITH THE CIVIL RIGHTS MOVEMENT largely focusing on the racial
divisions between whites and blacks, many within the growing Latino
population in the United States found their own champion in Cesar
Chavez. Born in Yuma, Arizona, Chavez attended sixty-five elementary
schools without ever graduating from high school. Like so many sons
and daughters of migrant workers, he had wandered with his family
from farm to farm, accepting jobs whenever they were available. In 1944
he enlisted in the U.S. Navy, serving as a deck man in the Pacific theater.
Returning home after the war, he began to work on behalf of poor Lati-
nos who were facing a variety of problems ranging from immigration to
housing. Conscious of his farming roots and having learned the value of
discipline while serving in the military, Chavez knew that little could be
accomplished to redress the plight of agricultural workers without some
kind of coordinated front, and so he decided to become a labor organizer. By 1962 he had put his managerial talents to use by launching the
National Farm Workers Association, bringing together both Chicano
and Filipino workers from California and the Southwest. Anyone who
wanted to become a frontline member of his organization was required
to take a pledge of nonviolence.

Controversial at times with both farm owners and union members,
Chavez called for boycotts, strikes, and demonstrations to support the
cause of the movement. The battle became particularly tough when he
took on west-coast grape growers in the late 1960s by orchestrating a
national boycott against all of their products. Intensifying his efforts, he
fasted and prayed for almost a month in 1968 to bring attention to the
plight of farmworkers.

Viewed as the Gandhi and the Martin Luther King, Jr., of the American Hispanic community by many of his followers, Chavez turned to
both men for inspiration as well as to the examples of Saint Francis of
Assisi and Mother Teresa. Not only did he admire the way they conducted their lives, but he was also inspired by the way they placed prayer
in the center of their lives. As for his own practice, he wrote to an inquiring reporter, "I find that, if I provide time and silence for God, He will
make His presence known to me."[50]

In advancing the farmworkers' movement, Chavez would recite one prayer in particular before his supporters, an invocation that became known as "Cesar's Prayer":

Show me the suffering of the most miserable;
So I will know my people's plight.

Free me to pray for others;
For you are present in every person.

Help me to take responsibility for my own life;
So that I can be free at last.

Give me honesty and patience;
So that I can work with other workers.

Bring forth song and celebration;
So that the Spirit will be alive among us.

Let the Spirit flourish and grow;
So that we will never tire of the struggle.

Let us remember those who have died for justice;
For they have given us life.

Help us love even those who hate us;
So we can change the world.[51]

Throughout his last years Chavez often fasted and prayed to gain moral strength and raise public awareness of his cause. At the age of sixty-six, after taking on lettuce and vegetable growers, he died peacefully in his sleep on April 23, 1993. Some fifty thousand people attended his funeral, and the next year he was awarded the Presidential Medal of Freedom posthumously. To mark the anniversary of his death, many of his admirers would follow his example by fasting, praying, and reciting his special prayer.

THE COUNTERPOINT TO NONVIOLENT PROTEST, the converse of Martin Luther King, Jr., and Cesar Chavez in battling the racial inequalities of the day, came most visibly in the form of the charismatic, explosive, and highly controversial Malcolm X. Like King, Malcolm was the son of a Baptist minister. His father, the Reverend Earl Little, took every opportunity to attack and challenge white supremacists with his rhetoric from the pulpit and on the streets. Soon the family was forced to flee their home in Omaha, Nebraska, heading north to escape the threats. When Malcolm was four, arsonists burned the family's home in Lansing, Michigan, to the ground. Two years later, in 1931, his father was found dead next to the city's streetcar tracks, his skull crushed and his body mangled.

Overwhelmed by the experience and having little adult guidance after his mother was committed to a mental institution, Malcolm X spiraled downward as he hit his teenage years. Soon he was hustling drugs, gambling, and running a prostitution ring. Convicted of burglary, he was sentenced to seven years in prison, where he used the time to read voraciously and, through the influence of his brother Reginald, began to immerse himself in the teachings of Elijah Muhammad, the leader of the Nation of Islam. After his release from prison in 1952, he quickly dropped the Little family name, joined the Black Muslims, and, given his obvious speaking talents, was appointed the Nation's national spokesman.

How the Nation melded its religious and social beliefs became clear in April 1962. Inflamed over the treatment of members of a Black Muslim mosque and the killing of their fellow brother Ronald X Stokes by Los Angeles police, the leaders of the Nation of Islam took to the stump to vent their outrage and thirst for retribution. Through their prayers, Elijah Muhammad vowed, God would soon have his revenge on the white race. His answer came a few weeks later, he believed, when a Boeing 707, destined for New York from Paris, crashed on takeoff, killing all 137 people on board. Muhammad asserted that God had exacted retribution for the Los Angeles killing. Malcolm X was even more direct, admitting that he and the leaders of the Nation had been praying for a disaster of this magnitude. "I got a wire from God today," he told one reporter. "He had really answered our prayer over in France. He dropped an airplane out of the sky with over 120 white people on it."[52]

The subject of a CBS television documentary titled *The Hate That Hate Produced*, Malcolm X began to change in 1964. After traveling to Mecca to make the hajj, that annual prayer pilgrimage all devout Muslims are admonished to make at least once in their lifetime, he claimed to have had his eyes opened. Watching tens of thousands of people of all colors descend on Islam's holiest site, even "blond-haired, blue-eyed men I could call my brothers," he began to question his racist path. Their collective Arabic chants of "Labbayka! Labbayka!" (Here I come, Lord) and "I submit to no one but Thee, O Allah"[53] continued to ring in his ears.

As Malcolm X later told Alex Haley, who worked with him to write the best seller *The Autobiography of Malcolm X*, which was published posthumously, he learned that "the essence of prayer is the oneness of God."[54] For the first time in his life, he learned the proper Islamic way to crouch on his knees in prayer, a practice never taught to him by the Black Muslims. His prayer life now took on a very different tone and direction.

Returning to the United States in early 1964, Malcolm X severed his relations with the Nation and soon founded the Muslim Mosque, but his very public separation came at a price. Days after his home in East Elmhurst, New York, was destroyed by arsonists, Malcolm X was speaking before his weekly congregation of several hundred followers at Harlem's Audubon Ballroom. As he was about to finish his prepared remarks on that Sunday afternoon of February 21, 1965, three gunmen rushed him onstage, fatally shooting him at point-blank range some fifteen times. When it became known that all of the assassins were members of the Nation of Islam, Elijah Muhammad released a press statement, denying any complicity.

Certainly the legacy of Malcolm X will be debated for years to come. Both his early racial hatred and the transformation of his thinking on race relations serve as powerful examples to those who become familiar with his life. In the first instance he showed the extraordinary capacity of one human for vitriol toward innocent people; even through the act of prayer, he would wish indiscriminately for their death. It was the kind of pent-up rage cloaked in spiritual sanctimony that would lead religious terrorists almost thirty years later to kill several thousand innocent people on American soil. In the second instance, he took his first steps toward redemption, coming to understand, in the midst of prayer with his fellow Muslims, the sanctity and worth of all human life.

ONE OF THE TRANSFORMING MOMENTS in U.S. history, if not human history, came with the launching of the country's space program. Less than ten weeks after John F. Kennedy took office, he and the country were shaken by the sudden advances of the Soviet Union's space program. Not only had the cosmonaut Yuri Gagarin become the first man launched into space; he had fully orbited Earth. In less than a month, the National Aeronautics and Space Administration (NASA) sent Alan Shepard into suborbital space, but the Soviet Union continued to have an edge. For Kennedy, there was no turning back. Before a joint session of Congress on May 25, 1961, he announced his intention, "before this decade is out, of landing a man on the moon and returning him safely to earth."[55]

That single one-sentence directive drove a multibillion-dollar program, the likes of which had never been seen before. On February 12, 1962, astronaut John Glenn circled the globe three times before reentry into the earth's atmosphere. With the space race now fully engaged, the Soviet cosmonaut Gherman Titov, the second man to orbit Earth after Gagarin, visited the United States at the invitation of NASA. In a joint press conference with Glenn, a reporter asked Titov, "In communism, you don't believe there is a God. Did your space flight alter that?" The cosmonaut, echoing the official atheistic line of his country, responded, "Not at all. Only now there is proof for the communist position. I went into space and didn't see God, so that must mean that God does not exist."

John Glenn, a devout Presbyterian and future senator from Ohio, then was asked by the same reporter, "Did you see God in space, Colonel Glenn?" Having been brought up in a home where God and daily prayer had been deeply ingrained, Glenn did not miss a beat, replying, "I didn't expect to. The God I believe in isn't so small that I thought I would run into Him just a little bit above the atmosphere."[56] No one in the room that day could have imagined that American astronauts and Russian cosmonauts would be reciting prayers together as they orbited Earth in a future joint space station mission.

Thousands saw their hard work yield dramatic results with the launching of *Apollo VIII* in December 1968. Heading the mission was Frank Borman, a graduate of West Point who had served on an earlier *Gemini* mission and who would be named chairman of Eastern Airlines after his retirement from NASA. Before leaving for the Florida cape to begin final preparations for the mission, Borman took care of some unfinished business. A vestryman at St. Christopher's Episcopal Church in League City, Texas, he had long been scheduled to serve as the church's lay reader for Christmas Eve. Unable to be present physically, he came up with an idea. Why not transmit a prayer from space that could be played to the congregation during the service? With the help of a prominent engineer at mission control and fellow parishioner Rod Rose, the plan was put into action. The prayer they chose was adapted from the book *Prayers for the Church Service League* by G. F. Weld, a devotional distributed by the Episcopal Diocese of Massachusetts. Borman and Rose decided not to tell too many people of what they had in mind, simply referring to the project as "experiment P1." With the moon just ahead of the three crewmen, Borman recorded his prayer for posterity, the first ever transmitted from space:

> *Give us, O God, the vision which can see Thy love in the world in spite of human failure. Give us the faith, the trust, the goodness in spite of all our ignorance and weakness. Give us the knowledge that we may continue to pray with understanding hearts, and show us what each of us can do to set forth the day of universal peace. Amen.*[57]

Minutes after reciting the prayer, the astronauts watched in awe as Earth rose before their eyes from the other side of the moon. Capturing in full color the "earthrise," with the surface of the moon bordering the bottom of the camera's frame, Bill Anders photographed the planet in all its glory, with its iridescent blue oceans, pink-brown mountains, and wafting white clouds. Against the mysterious coal black of space, Earth looked breathtaking in the photograph. As they had planned back on Earth, the three astronauts then took turns reading the first few verses of Genesis, describing the dawn of creation as television audiences around the world watched the scene unfold before their eyes.

Like clockwork, mission control copied the recordings of the prayer as well as the Bible readings, and Rod Rose ran the tape over to St. Christopher's, where the congregation witnessed history in the making. For those gathered in church that night, the experience was deeply and uniquely spiritual beyond words as they listened to the prayer of their fellow parishioner while he viewed Earth from the distance of the moon. The significance of hearing the first prayer transmitted from space was lost on no one. Even the newly elected President Richard Nixon referred to the event in his 1969 inauguration: "In that voice so clear across the lunar distance, we heard them invoke God's blessing on its goodness."[58]

* * *

THE 1960S ALSO BROUGHT to greater light the vibrant prayer life of American Catholics, and few individuals had quite the spiritual impact through their writings and personal example as Thomas Merton, the intellectually gifted Trappist monk, and Dorothy Day, the hard-core social activist. Both of them had marched with Martin Luther King, Jr., and stood beside Cesar Chavez.

Born in Prades, France, in 1915 into an artistically cultured family, Thomas Merton had lost both of his parents by the time he was a teenager. His mother's parents, who lived on Long Island, raised him and supported his decision to enter Clare College at Cambridge University. In his first year at Cambridge, Merton took every opportunity to rebel. While the full details of what happened during those months remain hazy, Merton was clearly hell-bent on making the most of youthful temptations. Fathering a child out of wedlock, allowing himself to be crucified during a drunken fraternity party, and losing most of his scholarship because of failing grades were only some of his indiscretions.

Fortunately for Merton, he was accepted at Columbia University in New York, where he earned bachelor's and master's degrees in English. Although he continued to be emotionally rudderless, in the spring of 1937 he began to read some of the great Christian literature of Western civilization and the works of contemporary religious writers. He was instantly drawn to their spiritual, intellectual passions.

The moment of truth for Merton came one night while he was on break from Columbia, visiting Rome. After a day of touring churches and ruins in the ancient city, he was about to go to bed when suddenly he believed that his father was standing next to him. "The sense of his presence was as vivid and as real and as startling as if he had touched my arm or spoken to me," he recalled. The experience passed "in a flash," but the effect was great as he was "overwhelmed with a sudden and profound insight into the misery and corruption of my own soul." His life had changed forever. He began to pray not with his lips, intellect, or even imagination, he confessed, but "out of the very roots of my life and my being." He believed that he was praying "to the God I had never known" who was now helping him to escape "the thousand terrible things that held my will in their slavery."[59]

Although he did not yet set his course for the religious life, Merton did find that "there were a lot of tears connected with this, and they did me good." Despite his earlier agnostic, almost atheistic mind-set, he came to appreciate the force of prayer in ways that even a deeply devout person might not have understood over a lifetime. He eventually saw prayer as pure oxygen in that it enabled the individual to turn to "God, the principle of perfection."[60]

Merton soon decided not only to convert to Catholicism but to become part of a religious order. Just as the country was about to enter World War II, he joined the Abbey of Gethsemani in Trappist, Kentucky, where he professed his vows within six years as a monk of the Cistercians of the Strict Observance and was ordained a priest two years later. He took vows not only of poverty, chastity, and obedience but also of enforced silence. For the next twenty-seven years he prayed several times a day, every day. The wanderlust of a Manhattan intellectual had been traded in for a life of prayer and solitude in the hills of rural Kentucky. Almost single-handedly, he began to change American perceptions of monastic life, particularly on the fullness of prayer.

Beginning with his 1948 best-selling memoirs, *The Seven Storey Mountain,* Merton showed how he was combining the life of an ascetic monk with a serious social conscience. It seemed as though the unbridled passions of youth had been redirected to a life brimming with spirituality and new concepts of prayer. Within two weeks of arriving at the abbey, he wrote one of his most memorable prayers before attending midnight Mass at Christmas:

> *Your brightness is my darkness. I know nothing of You and, by myself, I cannot even imagine how to go about knowing You. If I imagine You, I am mistaken. If I understand You, I am deluded. If I am conscious and certain I know You, I am crazy. The darkness is enough.*[61]

Merton came to believe that "prayer is not only dialogue with God: it is the communion of our freedom with His ultimate freedom, His infinite spirit."[62] Simply put, prayer allowed men and women to understand over time that the nothingness they feared most was in fact the true "treasure" they longed for.[63]

At the height of the civil rights movement and later during the escalation of the Vietnam War, Merton unrepentantly advocated: "Prayer and sacrifice must be used as the most effective spiritual weapons in the war against war, and like all weapons, they must be used with deliberate aim: not just with a vague aspiration for peace and security, but against violence and war."[64] Merton, like Gandhi, Martin Luther King, and Cesar Chavez, believed that prayer could be a critical force for social change.

Although Merton realized that his purpose in life had been cast perfectly, he was unable to remain completely cloistered while the struggle for civil rights and the Vietnam War raged. With permission from his superiors, he became fully engaged in the issues of the day, writing books, op-ed pieces, essays, and poetry in abundance. He also explored Asian religions and Oriental mysticism, finding that they provided insights into prayer and into the human condition that Western civilization did not. He soon began to integrate their lessons into his own prayer life. After meeting Merton, the Dalai Lama came away believing that Merton understood Buddhism far better than any Christian he had ever met.[65]

Merton died in 1968 at the age of fifty-three after a tragic accident while attending a conference in Thailand. Few Americans of the twentieth century could match his sheer output of spiritual writings. Through his ever-evolving prayer life, he helped others to understand that men and women of different faiths can learn from one another in their quests for greater spirituality.

Another remarkable Catholic, whose work kept her closer to home, was the social activist Dorothy Day. Like her younger contemporary and friend Thomas Merton, Day was a Catholic convert whose early life was filled with spiritual turmoil. Flirting with the Communist Party early in her career, she eventually realized the serious inconsistencies between Communism and her growing belief in God. In the winter of 1932, during the depths of the Great Depression, Day joined street protests in Washington, D.C. People from across the country had traveled to the capital out of desperation, consumed by hunger, joblessness, and a host of other problems. Deeply affected by the experience, Day walked into the National Shrine of the Immaculate Conception and poured out her heart. "I offered up a special prayer, a prayer which came with tears and anguish, that some way would open up for me to use whatever talents I possessed for my fellow workers, for the poor."[66] It was a defining moment, captured in her 1952 autobiography, *The Long Loneliness.*

On returning to New York City, she met Peter Maurin, twenty years her senior, who would become her collaborator in publishing *The Catholic Worker,* a newspaper that took up the social and spiritual causes that meant so much to her, prayer being of prime concern. In speaking on the subject, she let people know that "there is nothing too small to pray about," and then told them how she prayed for help to pay the mortgage and find donations to provide food for the homeless in her breadlines. But she believed it was even more important to pray for the spiritual gifts to create a closer relationship with God and to understand that the Almighty could be found in the face of every human being.[67]

Like Merton, King, and Chavez, Day believed that social reform and her role in helping to effect it could never succeed without prayer. Just before her death in 1980 at the age of eighty-three, a time when she could no longer leave her home, Dorothy Day was visited by Mother Teresa of Calcutta, whose own prayer life had become legendary. In fastening to Day's dress a pin of her Missionaries of Charity, Mother Teresa made her an honorary member of the order. After Day's death, her proponents worked hard to have her proclaimed a saint of the Roman Catholic Church.

PRAYER WAS ALSO THRIVING in popular culture. Architects were designing bolder and more creative designs for houses of prayer. Eero Saarinen, heralded for such groundbreaking structures as Dulles International Airport in Washington, D.C., and the Gateway Arch in St. Louis, created the spectacular North Christian Church in Columbus, Indiana. In designing an exaggerated needlelike steeple over a structure infused with natural lighting, he erected what the architect Douglas Hoffman referred to as a "lightning rod delivering celestial messages to the gathered congregation."[68]

Philip Johnson, on the other hand, built his famous roofless church for the utopian settlement of New Harmony, Indiana, in 1960. Twenty years later, Johnson, along with John Burgee, took a very different direction in designing the country's first modern mega-church, the imposing Crystal Cathedral in Garden Grove, California, for the Reverend Robert H. Schuller and his reformed church congregation. Reveling in the idea of creating such great church architecture to enhance worship, determining everything, from proper acoustics to ethereal form and lighting, Johnson would remark, "Oh, I go mad for religious buildings. The only thing that really gives you a kick in the world is a religious building."[69]

Painters and sculptors were also using their talents to express the mystical qualities of prayer. In another building that Johnson helped design, next to the de Menil Museum in Houston, Mark Rothko, the renowned abstract expressionist, painted a series of fourteen canvases that some observers believe to be depictions of the stations of the cross. Considered the artist's finest work by many critics, the grouping of three triptychs and five panels is housed in the nondenominational Rothko Chapel. Whether standing or sitting on the few strategically positioned benches in the chapel, visitors are able to view the collection as works of art or, in the words of Rothko's patron Dominique de Menil, the heiress to the Schlumberger fortune, as a setting where, "through art, God constantly clears a path to our hearts."[70]

AS IT HAD THROUGHOUT the country's history, American music continued to evolve. The musician who left an imprint on American culture like few others was the enormously gifted Leonard Bernstein. Composer, performer, conductor, author, and teacher, Bernstein grew up in Lawrence, Massachusetts, the son of a Talmudic scholar and the grandson and great-grandson of orthodox rabbis.

Amazing everyone but his difficult and distant father, Samuel, with his musical gifts, Lenny was an emotional fireball even before he could speak. During his teens, he was asked to honor one of his early mentors, Rabbi H. H. Rubenoz, at an anniversary dinner. Remembering a prayer from the high holy days that his father liked to sing in the shower, Bernstein took the melody and played it for the rabbi and the gathered guests in the styles of Mozart, Chopin, and finally Gershwin.[71]

With his talents both as a composer and as a performer becoming clear to everyone, he soon became a protégé of the legendary Boston Symphony Orchestra conductor Serge Koussevitzky and received his first big break in 1943 when he stepped in at the last moment for the ailing Bruno Walter to conduct the New York Philharmonic. Bernstein believed that he had truly been touched by God and developed an attitude in approaching God that was both respectful and confrontational, not unlike his relationship with his father. That seeming contradiction at times spilled over into his music. In his first major work, *Jeremiah's Symphony*, Bernstein honored his father by incorporating the cants of the ancient Hebrews in their formidable struggles for survival while fostering a growing, intimate relationship with God. His second symphony, *The Age of Anxiety,* based on W. H. Auden's engaging poem bemoaning the loss of faith in the twentieth century, shows much the same kind of anguish in its passages evoking both frenzy and serenity. His third, and last, symphony, *Kaddish,* allowed Bernstein to pour out his brimming emotions over the crisis of faith among the Jewish people in the post-Holocaust era. Using the solemnity of the Jewish prayer for the dead, Bernstein wrapped together the American musical idioms of jazz, folk, and neoclassicism to express the ultimate return to God through never-ending prayer. He dedicated the piece, written in 1963, to the recently assassinated President John Kennedy, with whom he believed he shared a spiritual bond.

Having become even more famous among general audiences for his televised *Young People's Concerts* and particularly for his Broadway musical hits *West Side Story, On the Town,* and *Candide,* he took on his most ambitious work in composing his *Mass,* commissioned for premiere at the opening of the John F. Kennedy Center for the Performing Arts in Washington, D.C., in 1971. Subtitled "A Theater Piece for Singers, Players, and Dancers," *Mass* brought to the stage an enormous ensemble—a full pit orchestra, two adult choirs and a boys' choir, a huge cast of singers, a ballet company, a marching band, and a rock band. The work alternated between Latin and English, with the "officiating priest" celebrating Mass in its exact liturgical form, only to find himself buckling under the weight of sin and human misery. Controversial from its opening notes, the work radiated prayerful turmoil using every possible musical style, and to some critics the seeming chaos obscured a more distinct, personal voice. Although Bernstein's *Mass* was not a resounding success in his lifetime, it would be performed at the Vatican on June 1, 2000, ten years after his death, to far more favorable reviews than it first received almost thirty years earlier.

As it entered its own golden era, the quintessential American genre of jazz was also leaving a mark on the country's spirituality. The bass player Charles Mingus broke new ground by developing "conversational jazz," a unique style that pitted the double bass against other instruments in improvisational exchanges. This style created an exceptional musical venue for Mingus to express his deepening spirituality. Believing his talents came from God and God alone, he composed a series of "Meditations" and "Better Git It in Your Soul." His "Wednesday Night Prayer Meeting" harked back to the prayer services he had attended with his mother when a boy and the sounds he heard preachers use as they spoke in tongues, that "language that the devil can't understand," as Mingus remembered it.[72] Other compositions such as "Ecclusiastics," "Prayer for Passive Resistance," and "Oh Lord, Don't Let Them Drop That Atomic Bomb on Me" showed the progression of his musical style, his feelings about prayer, and his passionate social activism.

John Coltrane, Mingus's contemporary, was one of the most dynamic musical innovators America ever produced, particularly when it came to fusing music with prayer. Growing up in High Point, North Carolina, in the 1930s, he could play practically every brass instrument by the time he was a teenager, finally choosing the tenor saxophone. After being discharged from the navy in 1946, he began a slippery downward spiral into drugs and alcohol. With no end in sight, he underwent a "spiritual awakening" in 1957, recovered his faith, and asked God "to be given the means and privilege to make others happy through music."[73]

Soon he began to write music that personalized his faith in a free-form style, revolutionary in its approach. His early music in many ways presaged his masterpiece, *A Love Supreme.* Composed as an intimate orison to God in 1965, the four-part suite was premiered at a time when new forms of spiritual consciousness were proliferating throughout the musical world, influenced in large part by cultures outside of Europe. While *A Love Supreme,* one of the most critically acclaimed musical works of the twentieth century, captured the spiritual restiveness of the 1960s, it retained a timeless quality, embodying Coltrane's own spiritual journey. As the saxophonist and jazz composer Jesse Meman observed, "By the time 'Trane' had reached *A Love Supreme,* it became clear that his music and intense piety were no longer distinguishable from one another. At times he seemed almost to be on spiritual fire. To watch and hear him in performance was prayer in motion."[74]

Two jazz artists found the inspiration to evoke the spirit of prayer through their adopted Catholic faith. Dave Brubeck, born in 1920, was the first jazz artist ever to be featured on the cover of *Time* magazine. A pioneer in merging jazz with symphony orchestras and large choirs, he led critics to wonder at times whether he was a jazz or a classical artist. In reality he had a foot in both worlds, exuding spirituality with works like his oratorio *The Light in the Wilderness* as well as "Voice of the Holy Spirit," "Pange Lingua Variations," and "Regret," a piece he described as "sweet sadness, a longing for lost moments . . . a past that cannot be relived."[75] His "Our Father" came to him after a spiritual encounter in the middle of the night.

Likewise, Mary Lou Williams, a native of Pittsburgh, dazzled audiences with her arrangements, compositions, and interpretations of jazz classics. She became famous in the jazz world for her works "Trumpet No End" and *Zodiac Suite,* and then began to create large-scale sacred works, including *Black Christ of the Andes* and two Masses. With the help of her manager, the Reverend Peter O'Brien, a Jesuit priest, she was asked by the Pontifical Commission on Justice and Peace in Rome to compose her third, and last, Mass. In creating *Mary Lou's Mass,* a later staple of the Alvin Ailey dance troupe repertoire, she seemed to cap her life's work as one of the country's foremost jazz pioneers, blending spirituals and gospel with rhythm and blues.

Appealing even more broadly across general audiences was the great Duke Ellington, a musician who influenced his contemporaries as well as future generations of composers and performers like few others. Born in 1899 in Washington, D.C., to a father who moonlighted as a White House butler while running his own catering business and to a mother who was a housekeeper, Edward Kennedy Ellington was brought up in a loving but demanding household. By the time he reached high school, he had realized that performing and composing were in his blood. From "Mood Indigo" to "Satin Doll" to "Take the A-Train," Ellington composed works that melded various musical styles and showed incredible versatility.

While he was known for his jazz innovations almost from the outset of his career, he felt that something was missing. For all the compositions he had produced to evoke the highs and lows of human emotion, he had never written music to convey his deep spirituality. Pursuing his credo, "Every man prays in his own language, and there is no language that God does not understand," Ellington went to work, focusing almost entirely on spiritual music.[76]

In tackling what would become known as his Sacred Concerts, he borrowed from musical themes developed earlier in his career while adding fresh ideas. From arranging an unrestrained version of the Lord's Prayer to orchestrating modern-day spirituals like "Ain't but the One" and "Will You Be There?," he delighted in exuding what one critic described as the "ecumenical Ellington."[77] From there, his spiritual creativity continued to blossom. He even choreographed a piece for a tap dancer, "David Danced before the Lord with All His Might," a visual spectacle of prayer. His spiritual masterpiece, however, was "In the Beginning God," a work for choir, solo instruments, and orchestra and drummer that concentrated on the initial bonding between God and creation, beginning with Genesis.

In the fall of 1962, Ellington was ready to premiere his spiritual works at Grace Episcopal Church in San Francisco, as well as at the Fifth Avenue Presbyterian Church in New York City. These concerts of sacred music, also carried on public television and performed throughout Europe, drew mixed reviews. Ellington, however, described the concerts as "successful beyond my wildest dreams" and declared his compositions to be "the most important thing that I have ever done."[78]

By the time of his death in 1974, Duke Ellington had come to believe that God had been his life's guide, saying that he had composed his more than two thousand songs "while on his knees." He passionately believed that "the greatest thing one man can do for another man is to pray for him."[79] In the last Christmas card he designed for friends, he wrote in the shape of a cross:

L

G O D

V

E

BESIDES INFUSING CLASSICAL MUSIC and jazz, prayer entered the cultural mainstream in other ways. The arrival of the Beatles from Liverpool, England, struck a chord with young Americans, as it did for people around the world. The fascination with the Beatles, as George Harrison later confided in an interview, came from their putting music to words that tried to answer the questions "Who am I?" "What am I?" and "Where am I going?"[80] They were questions that the Beatles, individually or together, would express for a generation of Americans with such songs as "My Sweet Lord," "Awaiting on You All," and the wildly popular "Imagine."

There was light pop like Burt Bacharach and Hal David's "I Say a Little Prayer for You," a song made famous by the unmistakable voice of Dionne Warwick. Even Broadway became a spiritual outlet with such productions as *Jesus Christ Superstar,* produced by Andrew Lloyd Webber and Tim Rice. On its heels came one of the most successful musicals of all time, Stephen Schwartz's *Godspell,* with its memorable song "Day by

Day," adapted from the prayer of Saint Richard, a Bishop who lived in thirteenth-century England: "May I know Thee more clearly,/Love Thee more dearly/Follow Thee more nearly/Day by day." Running for more than twenty-seven hundred performances on and off Broadway, *Godspell* conveyed the raw sentiment of being in touch with what Alan Watts, the Episcopal priest turned Buddhist, called the "cosmic boss."[81]

Even in the world of hard rock, the theme of prayer had special appeal, and few treated the subject quite like the rock icon Jim Morrison. The son of a U.S. Navy admiral, Morrison reportedly had the I.Q. of a genius and found himself irresistibly drawn to poetry and music. While attending the University of Southern California in 1965, he launched a band with three of his classmates and called it the Doors, after Aldous Huxley's book about mescaline, *The Doors of Perception*.

By 1967 the Doors had come out with their first big hit, "Light My Fire," and Jim Morrison seemed on a frenetic quest to create while becoming consumed by alcohol, drugs, and pure exhibitionism. There seemed to be no limits on how far he would go either in his personal life or onstage. Stripping naked in Miami during a performance before a crowd of ten thousand in 1969, Morrison was arrested on the spot and sentenced to eight months of hard labor. While appealing his sentence, he immersed himself in writing poetry, culminating with the posthumous release of an album and collection of writings called *An American Prayer*. "O Great Creator of Being, grant us one more hour to perform our art and perfect our lives," he wrote. "Give us trust in the night. Give of color hundred hues a rich mandala."[82]

Sensual and self-absorbed, Morrison desperately sought a meaningful spiritual anchor to his life but in the end became more preoccupied with death. At the age of twenty-seven, he was found dead in his bathtub. The coroner ruled that a heart ailment had been the cause of death, much to the skepticism of the media and those closest to Morrison.

Country-western artists also continued to contribute to American music and spiritual expression as their songs steadily grew in popularity. The line was often blurred for many of these stars between their musical output and their spiritual lives. Johnny Cash, who would sell more than fifty million albums, receive ten Grammy awards, and, along with Elvis Presley, be the only American musician inducted into both the Country Music and the Rock and Roll Hall of Fame, faced his own "ring of fire" from an early age, mostly of his own making. In his first big hit,

"I Walk the Line," recorded in 1955, he reflected on the personal balance beam that he seemed to straddle most of his life.

In the end, Johnny Cash believed that two-way communication with God was what saved his life from self-destruction, including attempted suicide. Standing before his audiences, he would begin concerts with his signature, "Hello, I'm Johnny Cash," followed by his gratitude to God for allowing him "simply to be around." Dressed in black from head to toe, often wearing his trademark preacher's coat, he conveyed empathy for the downtrodden and the forgotten, from the inmates of Folsom Prison to the out-of-work farmers in the Midwest. Despite criticism by one critic in 1977 that "Johnny Cash and his God are a particularly tedious act,"[83] he couldn't have cared less. It was through God and prayer that he knew "I'm growing, I'm changing, I'm becoming."[84] By the time of his death in 2003, just a few months after his beloved wife, June Carter, of the famous Carter Family passed away, Johnny Cash was a household name, even to the newest generation of country-western enthusiasts.

Another legend of country-western music, Willie Nelson, also considered prayer integral to his life. Producing over two thousand songs, from "Crazy," made famous by Patsy Cline, to "Georgia on My Mind" and "On the Road Again," Nelson received every honor and distinction available to an American singer and composer. Without reservation, he credited prayer with having inspired his work as a composer and performer and with providing the spiritual ballast in his life. In his darkest days, which involved everything from substance abuse to a son who committed suicide, he came to believe "prayer has kept me from killing myself."[85] In reflecting on the power of prayer in his life and in his songs, he remarked:

> You always ask for the strength in your prayers to keep you from doing dumb things, but you have to figure out what those dumb things are . . . Prayer is more for you than it is for him.
>
> I have a crisis every few minutes, and prayer just seems like a safe place to be. I just keep saying the Lord's Prayer over and over. I don't get creative. I always seem to drift back into prayer. I'm not one to say okay, I'm going to pray now. It's just that I'm in that mode most of the time . . .
>
> Practically every song I write is a prayer in one way or another. I've always felt a spiritual element in any singing I've done, but in

the past twenty years I've been more aware and thought about it more than I used to. I think it comes with living . . .

I recall Hank Williams saying he holds the pen and God does the writing and, being a songwriter, I have to agree with that. You work the controls and God flies the airplane.[86]

A different kind of music came from the songs and performances of poet and guitarist Bob Dylan. Seen by many as the "conscience of a generation," he came to write such hits as "Mr. Tambourine Man," "The Times are A-Changin'," and his wildly popular ballad for the times, "Blowin' in the Wind." What people did not realize, however, was how very spiritual he was becoming. Having been born a Jew, he came to believe in the divinity of Christ, and although he was fiercely protective of his privacy, he made it clear that he believed he had become religiously born again. Developing a strong prayer life, he grew so committed to his newfound faith that in time he wrote an entire gospel album entitled *Slow Train Coming*. The "restless pilgrim" that he had become did not sit well with those longtime fans who longed for his earlier hits, but Dylan was obstinate in letting his music speak for itself and would in the years to come intermingle spiritual with more secular songs.

WHILE PRAYER CAPTURED the heartaches and provided the personal anchor for so many, it also pervaded American culture in some unexpected ways. Throughout history Americans had tried to close the psychological distance between them and the Almighty, to place God in the role of the all-knowing, loving parent who more than anyone understands human fallibility. It was not a huge leap for the concept of prayer to enter American humor, either subtly or overtly. As the American Yiddish novelist and 1978 Nobel Prize winner, Isaac Bashevis Singer, once wrote, "Whenever I am in trouble, I pray. And since I'm always in trouble, I pray a lot."[87]

Clergy across the country would catalog anecdotes about prayer for use in liturgical services or display pithy quotations on church marquees. The humor of the gifted cartoonist Charles Schulz was dissected by theologians for the interplay among such memorable characters as Charlie Brown, Linus, Schroeder, and Lucy. Even Snoopy, the lovable beagle, would find his prayers answered on occasion. In one comic strip, his water bowl is empty. "Dying of thirst," he runs to an outdoor spigot with the bowl in his mouth but becomes completely frustrated when he finds that, as a dog, he cannot turn it on. Finally the clouds open up, and down comes the rain. After Snoopy gets his fill and the rain stops, he climbs back to the roof of his doghouse and says to himself, "That's one I'm going to have to think about for a while."[88]

Prayer was coupled with humor in other ways as well. One story that circulated in various forms centered on a little girl who went home from school after taking a major exam. When she found out that she might have made a mistake in naming the state capitals, she prayed with all the earnestness she could muster: "Dear Lord, please let Cleveland be the capital of Ohio!" Ogden Nash, the urbane Manhattan raconteur, wrote "Prayer at the End of a Rope" to share his exasperation at the vagaries of modern social life. Comedians like Henny Youngman and Alan King regaled audiences on *The Ed Sullivan Show* with jokes showing that the human conniver could never outsmart God.

Even the versatile comedian Bill Cosby came into the public consciousness in 1963 due in large part to his hilarious but equally profound three-part routine on the conversations between Noah and God. In his continuous back and forth with God, Noah would often try to find ways to make life easier, like asking God to turn one male zebra into a female after he realized he accidentally brought two male zebras aboard the ark. "Noah, you know that I don't work like that," would come the voice of God.

Cosby would remind his audiences that God has a sense of humor and finds humans to be pretty funny. "So, go ahead and pray your heart out," he would tell audiences, "but just remember that in all of life's challenges, gray hair is nothing more than God's graffiti."[89]

Other comedians such as Lily Tomlin, who made her national debut in television's *Laugh-In*, would even give the notion of prayer a little bit of an edge. In one of her most famous lines, part of her one-woman show *The Search for Signs of Intelligent Life in the Universe*, written by Jane Wagner, she would ask, "Why is it that when we talk to God, we're praying, but when God talks to us, we're schizophrenic?"

CHILDREN HAD NEW VENUES for learning the value of prayer, moral values, and respect for racial, ethnic, and religious diversity. Harking back to *The New England Primer* and *McGuffey's Readers,* in which general and spiritual learning was intertwined, hundreds of children's books were published by church and secular sources to provide solid grounding for young people. The Public Broadcasting Service produced *Mister Rogers' Neighborhood,* a program starring the mild-mannered Fred Rogers, an ordained Presbyterian minister, and later *Sesame Street,* with its colorful puppets interacting with adults to enforce messages of tolerance and understanding. No one, however, created so elaborate an industry almost entirely around children as Walter Elias Disney. From producing live-action movies, animated films, and television programs to building theme parks and manufacturing sundry products, Walt Disney had an impact like few others.

The son of a devout church deacon, Walt Disney was born in 1901 and named after the Reverend Walter Parr, the minister of St. Paul's Congregational Church in Chicago. Barely out of his teens, he created the memorable character Mickey Mouse in the animated short *Steamboat Willie,* and from there his career took off. By 1960 he had become firmly established as one of the most successful entertainment moguls the world had ever produced. With Disneyland in operation since 1955, Disney World scheduled to open its doors in 1971, and hundreds of full-length films having been released, there seemed no end in sight for Disney and his corporation.

Despite the obvious success, few people knew of the clinical depression Disney suffered throughout his life, including a nervous breakdown in his early thirties. Through it all, exceedingly private as he was, he would admit that prayer had helped him cope with his very full, unpredictable life: "Whatever success I had had in bringing clean, informative entertainment to people of all ages, I attribute in great part to my Congregational upbringing and my lifelong habit of prayer."[90]

Not long before his death in 1966, having received many honors and accolades, Disney wrote about his thoughts on the subject of prayer and its importance in his life:

Every person has his own ideas of the act of praying for God's guidance, tolerance, and mercy to fulfill his duties and responsibilities. My own concept of prayer is not as a plea for special favors nor as a quick palliation for wrongs knowingly committed. A prayer, it seems to me, implies a promise as well as a request; at the highest level, prayer is not only supplication for strength and guidance, but also becomes an affirmation of life and thus a reverent praise of God.[91]

WHILE THE DYNAMIC CULTURE of the United States helped to define prayer in more creative and expansive ways, no single influence on the prayer life of the country was as great as the war in Vietnam, that great conflict waged to stem the tide of Communism in Southeast Asia. For the men who fought on the front lines and the women who supported them in field installations, prayer was an indispensable part of the GI survival kit.

Church organizations in the United States were printing prayer books in unprecedented numbers to send over to the troops. Prayers, hymns, and spiritual guides were being laminated to protect them from the oppressively humid weather of Southeast Asia.[92] Some chaplains even adapted well-worn prayers and hymns to the unusually rough circumstances the troops were facing. In the case of the immortal "Battle Hymn of the Republic," the words "as he died to make men holy, let us die to make men free" were changed to the more palatable "live to make men free."[93]

Nothing set the country's imagination on overdrive more than envisioning the horror of American soldiers, sailors, and airmen captured and held as prisoners of war. For many of the men, playing mind-stimulating games, finding creative ways to communicate with fellow prisoners, and exercising in their cells helped to create some sanity. Prayer, however, became their constant companion.

Admiral Jeremiah Denton, who was shot down in the summer of 1965 near a targeted North Vietnamese military installation and who later became a U.S. senator from Alabama, was a case in point. Paraded in front of television cameras in Hanoi to denounce American policy in Vietnam, Denton never fell into his captors' trap. Feigning that the lights overhead were too bright during the telecast, he blinked his eyelids, spelling T-O-R-T-U-R-E in Morse code, to let the world know what he and the other Americans were facing. "Threats, intimidation, physical brutality, deprivation of food and light, isolation, torture to unconsciousness" was how Denton described his seven years and seven months. "Prayer was the biggest weapon we had," he remembered. Every time he was about to be taken off to be tortured, he "just prayed and prayed about what was going to happen." As weeks turned into months and months stretched into years, Denton came to realize that "when you intensely petition God to help you, he answers your prayers more generously than you can imagine. When you find evidence of the limits of humanity, you go to God. You beg and you receive. I had that happen a lot."[94]

John McCain, another future senator and later presidential candidate, confronted his own trials as a prisoner of war for five years, most of them in the infamous "Hanoi Hilton" camp. With his plane shot down over North Vietnam and with two broken arms and a broken leg, he was dragged out of a lake and beaten severely by a crowd of people. As he, too, would recount later, "I prayed to live, because there was no certainty that I or the friends I was in prison with would survive. I also prayed for deliverance from prison, but there was a strong caveat to that: only if it was God's will . . . When I was being mistreated by the North Vietnamese, many times I found myself asking to just live one more minute rather than one more hour or one more day. And I know I was able to hang on longer because of the spiritual help that I received through prayer."[95] Two years before they released him, the Vietnamese relented in allowing McCain and the thirty to forty prisoners confined in one large cell with him to observe Christmas services. Using a bit of ingenuity to put together some semblance of a religious ceremony, McCain and the other Americans planned their service over four days. When the day arrived, the men could hardly have been more ready. Remembering the event, McCain described the extraordinary scene:

I looked around the room and there were tears in those men's eyes. They weren't tears of anger or fright or sorrow or bitterness or even longing for home. They were tears of joy that, for the first time in seven years for some of them, there was a celebration of Christmas together as Americans. It was the most powerful, moving, and remarkable experience I have ever had with prayer.[96]

In addition to those killed fighting in Vietnam, President Lyndon Johnson also became a casualty of the war. There was no mistaking the growing pangs of the Johnson White House as casualties mounted in Vietnam and chants of "Hey, hey, LBJ, how many kids did you kill today?" continued within earshot of the Oval Office. In one of the most poignant moments of any presidency, he addressed his last Presidential Prayer Breakfast on February 1, 1968, using imagery that was both spiritually and tragically poetic:

> At this season of the calendar, the nights are long, the winds are chill, the light of day is often dull and gray. Our minds know that the chill will pass, that spring will come, that the days will be brighter once again . . . At this season of the affairs of men, it is all much the same. The nights are very long. The winds are very chill. Our spirits grow weary and restive as springtime seems farther away. It is for such seasons as this one that man was given by his Creator the saving strength of faith—the strength we summon to sustain us when we pray . . . I can tell you that in these long nights your president prays . . . We cannot know what the morrow may bring. We can know that to meet its challenges and to withstand its assaults, America never stands taller than when her people go to their knees.[97]

Despite Johnson's departure, the war would not end until months after Richard Nixon left office, when the last U.S. troops and embassy personnel were airlifted out of Saigon, now Ho Chi Minh City, in April 1975. Although the lessons of Vietnam would be debated for decades, the nation had clearly confronted its own limitations. Soldiers returned home, most having learned more about prayer in those months in service than at any other time in their lives.

WITH THE WAR IN VIETNAM coming to a close, the United States faced yet another debacle of historic proportions: Watergate. Although the country had encountered scandals in past administrations, this one had far graver implications as it slowly became clear that it had emanated from the Oval Office itself.

For most historians and political pundits, Richard Nixon was arguably America's most complex and enigmatic President ever. Growing up in a devout Quaker home in Yorba Linda, California, he never sat down to a meal without his mother, Hannah, making sure that the family first said grace. Receiving a bachelor's degree from Whittier College and a law degree from Duke University, Nixon had a penchant for politics. After his tour of duty in the navy during World War II, he waged a successful campaign for the U.S. House of Representatives in 1946 and four years later was elected to the U.S. Senate. Partway into his first Senate term, Nixon was elected in 1952 to serve as Eisenhower's Vice President. Not yet forty, he reached a pinnacle in American politics that few could have imagined, let alone achieved.

In assuming the presidency, Nixon delivered an inaugural address filled with references to God. Within hours of his swearing in, he made it clear that he wanted to institutionalize formal prayer services at the White House, and soon he far eclipsed President Eisenhower's open embrace of religion, particularly emphasizing the bond between God and the United States. On the Sunday after the inauguration, Nixon hosted his first Sunday morning prayer service in the East Room of the White House. Although such events had been held in the White House as far back as the nineteenth century, nothing this formal or elaborate had ever been done on a continuing basis.

The President proudly rebuffed critics who believed that the separation of church and state made it either sacrilegious or inappropriate to turn the East Room into a church on Sunday mornings, saying, "It serves as an appropriate reminder that we feel God's presence here, and that we seek His guidance here—and that ours is, in the words of the Pledge of Allegiance, 'one nation under God, indivisible.' "[98] He also took considerable pride in providing a setting in which prayer could be said by those of different faiths: "We believe in the ecumenical principle, and if it turns out that a Methodist choir sings at a service conducted by a cardinal of the Catholic Church, we feel it may contribute to the broadening of religious thinking and practice in this beloved America of ours."[99]

The beginning of the end for President Nixon came with the break-in at the Democratic Party headquarters in the Watergate complex in Washington, D.C., on June 17, 1972. Men hired by the President's aides tried to gain access to Democratic Party files, and their subsequent discovery and arrest began the downward spiral of the Nixon presidency. As the weeks turned into months, the magnitude of Watergate became all the more clear—the government officials involved, the secrets, the lies, and the potential fallout. When Senate Minority Leader Hugh Scott, House Minority Leader John Rhodes, and Arizona Senator Barry Goldwater, the Republican Party's presidential nominee in 1964, met with the President to tell him that he not only would be impeached overwhelmingly by the House, but would also be convicted by the Senate, Nixon realized he had no choice but to resign—effective immediately. After the men left and he regained his composure, he told his family of his decision. He then asked Henry Kissinger to join him that evening for drinks.

On that historic evening of August 7, 1974, the two men got together in the Lincoln Sitting Room, where they had often huddled to discuss Soviet détente, the opening up of China, the Yom Kippur War of 1973, and so much more. As Kissinger walked into the small alcove, the President was clearly distraught over his decision to resign. As the Watergate chroniclers Bob Woodward and Carl Bernstein later reported, Nixon's closest advisers were concerned that he might take his own life.[100]

Tears began to flood the President's eyes as the two men recounted the successes of the Nixon years in broad strokes, trying with some desperation to counter the verdict that Watergate, and in turn history, were now imposing. As tears turned into audible sobs, the President said to Kissinger, "Henry, you are not a very orthodox Jew, and I am not an orthodox Quaker, but we need to pray." Nixon then rose from his chair and got down on his knees. Kissinger had little choice but to join him as the President began to pray aloud, asking God "for help, rest, peace, and love."[101] After he finished, Nixon beat his fist against the carpet, wailing, "What have I done? What has happened?" With that, he "curled on the carpet like a child" as Kissinger tried to console him. After leaving the Lincoln Sitting Room to return to his office around eleven o'clock that night, Kissinger remarked to Nixon's aide Lawrence Eagleburger and to Brent Scowcroft, "That was the most difficult thing I ever went through in my life."[102]

It was difficult for some Americans to reconcile the Watergate scandal with the words of the President in his second inaugural address delivered some seven months after the break-in. "We shall answer to God, to history, and our consciences for the way in which we use these years," he declared. "Today, I ask your prayers that in the years ahead I may have God's help in making decisions that are right for America, and I pray for your help so that together we may be worthy of our challenge."[103]

The exit of Richard Nixon, who had been part of the nation's political consciousness for more than a quarter century, was as surreal as it was tragic. The day after his meeting with Kissinger, the President addressed an emotionally drained yet stunned nation, stating, "Therefore, I shall resign the presidency effective at noon tomorrow. Vice President Gerald Ford will be sworn in as president at that hour in this office." He ended his remarks: "To have served in this office is to have felt a very personal sense of kinship with each and every American. In leaving it, I do so with this prayer: May God's grace be with you in all the days ahead."[104] The next day he delivered his last official remarks as president in the East Room, his staff standing before him as he ended with the words, "I can only say to each and every one of you, we come from many faiths, we pray perhaps to different gods—but really the same God in a sense—but I want to say . . . you will be in our hearts and you will be in our prayers." And with that he and his family walked out to the White House lawn and boarded a helicopter to begin the first leg of their journey home to California.[105]

FEW PERIODS IN AMERICAN HISTORY were as fraught with both tension and promise as the sixties and early seventies. Despite significant highs and lows, the prayer life of the country and of Americans generally became deeper and more vibrant than ever. Legal decisions to curtail prayer's recitation in certain public places did little to dampen the desire of the vast majority of Americans to find ways to practice their faith and to connect with God. This defining, socially explosive era was a prologue to America's spiritual dynamism in the decades to come.

CHAPTER 15

THE CONTEMPORARIES

1975–the New Millennium

Many of us have been taught to pray by people we love. In my case, it was my mother. I learned quite literally at her knee. My mother gave me a great deal, but nothing she gave me was more important than that special gift, the knowledge of the happiness and solace to be gained by talking to the Lord. The way we pray depends upon both our religious convictions and our own individual dispositions, but the light of prayer has a common core. It is our hopes and our aspirations, our sorrows and fears, our deep remorse and renewed resolve, our thanks and joyful praise, and most especially our love, all turned toward a loving God.

—Ronald Reagan, 1987

W HILE RICHARD NIXON was on his knees praying with Henry Kissinger in the family quarters of the White House, a very different scene was taking place just a few miles away. In their modest home in Alexandria, Virginia, Vice President Gerald Ford and his wife, Betty, remained behind closed doors on August 8, 1974, away from an anxious public, thinking mainly about the future. Throughout the day and into the evening, Ford would remember, the two of them "prayed for guidance and assurance for the responsibilities I was about to assume as president."[1]

The office of President was something that the former minority leader of the U.S. House of Representatives had never sought, let alone thought he would attain. Having been appointed and confirmed as Vice

President to replace Spiro Agnew, who stepped down after allegations of misconduct during his tenure as governor of Maryland, Ford was about to become the only person in U.S. history to assume the country's highest office without ever standing for national election. The situation seemed incomprehensible.

Less than a handful of presidents ever assumed the Oval Office facing such enormous, fractious problems as Gerald Ford. Mapping out and executing the last days of the Vietnam War, dealing with a faltering economy, bracing for an energy crisis over an Arab oil embargo, or confronting the ever-growing national preoccupation with the probable prosecution of former President Nixon was each daunting in its own right. Taken together, these issues were overwhelming.

As the helicopter took off from the White House lawn on the morning of August 9, beginning Nixon's somber flight back to his native California, the historic significance of the moment was lost on no one. After waving good-bye to his predecessor, shortly before noon Gerald Ford was sworn in by Chief Justice Warren Burger. "Our long national nightmare is over," Ford assured the nation. The next evening, after his first full day in office, he spoke candidly to the country in a televised address from the Oval Office: "I am acutely aware that you have not elected me as your president by your ballots, and so I ask you to confirm me as your president with your prayers. And I hope that such prayers will also be the first of many."[2] Ford later confided, "At this historic moment I was aware of kinship with my predecessors. It was almost as if all of America's past presidents were praying for me to succeed."[3]

Prayer had never seemed more important to Ford, although it had always been a major part of his life:

I definitely pray, and have most of my life. I do it because of a tradition in our family and because, at my current age, it means a great deal to me on a personal basis. I pray every night when I go to bed. It's a daily routine. I start with a prayer that is very meaningful to me and has been for many, many years: Trust in the Lord with all thine heart; and lean not unto thine own understanding. In all thy ways acknowledge him and he shall direct thy paths. I pray for my family. I pray for those friends who have health problems or other challenges.[4]

No sooner had Ford, a lifelong Episcopalian, taken office than he began to attend regular services at St. John's Church across from the White House, as so many of his predecessors had done. Realizing that he would soon be traveling aboard Air Force One, he asked the stewards to place a Bible on the desk in his stateroom.[5] That way, just as he did each day in Washington, he could take a few minutes to read a passage, and then spend some time praying. From that day forward, a Bible would always be in the presidential stateroom on Air Force One.

For Ford, prayer was a living, breathing force, a source of recurrent strength, invoked never more fervently than in thanks after he escaped two assassination attempts. Of all the problems he faced, however, none seemed more intractable than the lingering issue of Richard Nixon. Ford turned to prayer in tackling the issue, confirming in an August 28 news conference, "I've asked for prayers for guidance on this very important point."[6]

The President finally concluded that he had no choice but to pardon Richard Nixon. If the country was to confront its other major problems, the roar of the Watergate debacle had to be contained to ensure "domestic tranquillity," even if it cost him election to office in his own right.[7] In his address to the nation from the Oval Office announcing his September 8 pardon, he again asserted:

> I have asked your help and your prayers, not only when I became president but many times since. The Constitution is the supreme law of our land and it governs our actions as citizens. Only the laws of God, which govern our consciences, are superior to it.
>
> As we are a nation under God, so I am sworn to uphold our laws with the help of God. And I have sought such guidance and searched my own conscience with special diligence to determine the right thing for me to do with respect to my predecessor in this place.[8]

The consequences of this decision were felt immediately. Ford's press secretary, Jerry TerHorst, resigned in protest, and the November midterm election turned into a landslide for the Democratic Party. In the end, President Ford would never serve a full term, being defeated by Jimmy Carter in 1976. Political analysts were almost universal in their assessment that he had lost the election largely over the Nixon pardon.

Ford never regretted his decision, and would live to see it vindicated among historians and the American people.

ONE OF THE MOST UNUSUAL FALLOUTS from the Watergate debacle centered on the spiritual transformation of Charles Colson, a lawyer who had served as President Nixon's special counsel. Specifically, Colson had been responsible for organizing the "plumbers unit" that broke into Democratic Party headquarters at the Watergate complex, claiming at one point that he would run over his grandmother, if he had to, to serve Richard Nixon. Resigning from his government position in August 1973 before the scandal caught fire, he went to work for Tom Phillips, president of the Raytheon Company. One evening, when the two men got together for a quiet dinner, Phillips gave Colson a copy of C. S. Lewis's *Mere Christianity*. He explained how the book had helped turn his life around with its message of God's love and the power of prayer. Colson listened intently, and after leaving the Phillips home that evening, he got into his car and began to weep uncontrollably, convinced that he, too, had just undergone a spiritual turning point in his life.

That moment helped gird him for what came next, his conviction and imprisonment for being an accomplice in the Watergate scandal. Dumbstruck over his sentencing, he was taken away to Georgia's Maxwell federal prison, where he had to deal daily with bullying inmates, one prisoner even trying to kill him. With nowhere else to turn, Colson begged God to "get me through this, help me out of here, and, if not, take care of my family." As he related to audiences in the years after his release, "You have to know, during those months in prison I was praying consistently that God would show himself to me because I was feeling so desperate. You feel so alone."[9]

As surprised as anyone, he learned that his three-year sentence had been reduced to seven months. After leaving Maxwell federal prison, Colson decided to dedicate the rest of his professional life to forming Prison Fellowship Ministries, an organization that supports the spiritual needs of prisoners. Having sat in their cells, he knew their backgrounds, their desperation, and their questionable futures. He realized how lonely inmates were and how the prison system endemically led to more hatred and violence, becoming a breeding ground for later crimes and even terrorism. Turning to prayer and understanding its solace, if not its ultimate power to heal and sustain, Colson believed, were key to these men and women during their incarceration and after their release back into society.

Consequently, he began to organize his new ministry from his home in Virginia, a program that eventually included inmates in over eight hundred prisons in nearly sixty nations. Not unlike Alcoholics Anonymous, Prison Fellowship Ministries used prayer to confront alcoholism and drug addiction. For his work and success in implementing such a cutting-edge program, Colson was awarded the coveted Templeton Prize for Progress in Religion in 1993. The work that he began would grow into a formidable force in all fifty states.

ANOTHER CONSEQUENCE of Watergate was the public's considerable distrust for Washington insiders, a major factor in electing Governor Jimmy Carter of Georgia for President, a relatively new face on the national political scene. Carter's background appeared to be ideal for the times; he was a southern Democrat whose personal morality was beyond reproach. No President in the history of America ever wrote more about prayer, its theological roots, or its role in the life of the individual.

Born in Plains, Georgia, in 1924, Carter came from a modest, religiously devout farming family. He attended mandatory chapel services before class each day and often recalled the powerful example of his father, who would pray for dry weather but would also ask God "for strength and courage to deal with whatever came."[10] The first President to be educated at the U.S. Naval Academy, Carter went on to serve in the navy as an electronics instructor in the years immediately following World War II. Returning to Plains after his discharge, he managed the family's peanut farm and after a few years ran successfully for the Georgia state senate.

His decision to run for governor in 1966 and his ultimate defeat became a pivotal moment for Carter. Up to that time he had been, by his own admission, a lukewarm Christian. His loss forced him to put his life in better perspective, and through the help of his sister, Ruth Carter Stapleton, an evangelist preacher, he became a born-again Christian. After winning his second try for governor by a wide margin, Carter was more than ready to tackle his new responsibilities in January 1971. Days after being sworn in as governor, he spoke before a prayer breakfast in Washington, D.C., where he remarked, "I have never been disappointed when I asked in a humble and sincere way for God's help. I pray often. I think I pray more often since January 12th."[11]

While he prayed often as governor, he later admitted that, as President, "I prayed more during those four years than at any time in my life . . . The effort to maintain a partnership with God was reassuring to me and, at the same time, a humbling experience, helping me in my effort to resist the temptations of isolation and arrogance that all leaders face."[12] When he arose in the morning and went to bed at night, he would pray. When he walked past the White House Rose Garden to his office and when he was traveling, he would pray, sometimes with his wife, Rosalynn. During the day, he reserved a private area just off the Oval Office for his own personal prayer space. Retreating to the small room, particularly at difficult moments, gave him spiritual sustenance because, he said, "I wanted to benefit from God's help to have the maturity and sound judgment to make the right decision."[13]

Prayer also helped the President strike his greatest foreign policy coup, the Camp David Accords. It was a moment like few others.

Since the end of the 1967 Arab-Israeli War, Israel had occupied the Sinai peninsula in addition to the lands it gained in the Gaza Strip, the West Bank, the Golan Heights, and Jerusalem. Extracting the parties from positions staked out in the decade since the war seemed difficult, but Carter decided to try doing so.

From the outset it seemed almost unimaginable that Israel's hard-line Prime Minister Menachem Begin would agree to negotiate the return of lands with Egyptian President Anwar Sadat. Even more striking, however, was the enormous political, if not personal, risk Sadat seemed willing to take by beginning a peace process with Israel. The decision would cost him his life.

With some deft diplomacy on the part of President Carter and his team and with the tough mettle of both Sadat and Begin, the three men finally met on September 5, 1978, in the quiet setting of Camp David, the presidential retreat in the Catoctin Mountains of Maryland. While each leader was vastly different in temperament and demeanor, the one trait they held in common was their daily observance of prayer. As Carter would remember about his preparations for the summit:

> Begin, Sadat, and I all wanted to pray. But before our first talks, I spent several hours negotiating the text of the prayer. I got a pro-

posed draft from a prayer group in Washington, and I made some edits. Sadat approved it, Begin made some changes, and we issued the prayer the first day.

Conscious of the grave issues that face us, we place our trust in the God of our fathers from whom we seek wisdom and guidance. As we meet here at Camp David, we ask people of all faiths to pray with us that peace and justice may result from our deliberations.[14]

Despite the initial good intentions and the invocation of a negotiated prayer, Begin and Sadat were personally incompatible. After a bit more than a week, the talks began to unravel completely. Sadat, believing he had reached his end, asked Carter's National Security Adviser, Zbigniew Brzezinski, to provide him and his aides with a helicopter to begin the trip back to Cairo. On hearing what was unfolding, the President immediately walked over to Sadat's cabin and had what he described as a "very sharp exchange," trying to hold the Egyptian President to the promise he made not to leave the negotiations until some kind of agreement had been hammered out. Sadat said he would reconsider, and Carter walked away, finding a quiet spot in the woods to pray for God's intervention. No doubt Sadat did the same thing, and within three days Carter, Sadat, and Begin appeared on the front lawn of the White House to sign the Camp David Accords. Not only did the agreement open diplomatic relations between the two former enemies, but it put into place a timetable to return the vast Sinai territory to the Egyptians. Carter later remarked that Sadat was the most impressive leader he had ever known.[15]

The President's jubilation, however, was short-lived, because he was soon forced to confront the most difficult challenge of his presidency, the 444-day hostage crisis in Iran. With the fall of the Shah and the return of the Islamic Shiite fundamentalist Ayatollah Khomeini from exile in Paris to head up the new government in Tehran, the United States became the target of unspent rage. Khomeini rallied his people to seek retribution, arguing that Washington had propped up the Shah for decades. Prepared to take up the cause, hundreds of Iranians, mainly students, rushed the gates of the U.S. Embassy on November 4, 1979, capturing ninety employees, later reduced by the Iranian government to fifty-two hostages, and taking over the embassy compound.

When the President was asked how soon he began to pray after learning of the takeover, he responded, "I remember precisely when I prayed. It was immediate."[16] For more than a year President Carter tried every measure possible to secure the release of the Americans, all to no avail. When the U.S. military attempted a rescue mission, eight persons were killed during the aborted evacuation.

Asked whether he had ever prayed for the Ayatollah, President Carter admitted, "I asked for God's guidance or Allah's guidance or for the Supreme Being to induce the Ayatollah to live within the parameters of the Koran. I was praying he would treat the hostages humanely. I would say, in retrospect, all those prayers were answered."[17] And yet the hostage crisis was drawn out into a tortured international drama for the rest of his term, coming to an end only on the day that President Ronald Reagan, the man who defeated Carter at the polls, was sworn in to office.

The disappointment of not being reelected was devastating, and Carter again turned to prayer. In the years after his tenure as President, he has led an exceedingly productive life, from helping to fight deadly disease in sub-Saharan Africa to monitoring elections in nascent democracies around the world, all of which helped earn him the Nobel Peace Prize in 2002. He has also spent considerable time writing books, most notably *Living Faith* and *Sources of Strength,* both speaking eloquently of his private prayer life.

WHILE PRESIDENT CARTER quietly conveyed his genuine piety, he was taken aback by the growing grassroots movement of the "religious right," which took issue with his policies. With such figures as the Reverend Pat Robertson and the Reverend Jerry Falwell mobilizing large groups of followers to pray and vote their fundamentalist principles, a potent political force was emerging in the country. In reaching out to America's "moral majority," as Falwell called them, the movement was crossbreeding religion and politics. Through their radio and television programs, work on college campuses, and targeted mailings, leaders of the movement first invoked the favor of the Almighty, and then admonished their followers to turn their faith into active civic participation.

Due in part to the political support of this fundamentalist groundswell, Ronald Reagan was swept into office. Not since Franklin Roosevelt defeated Herbert Hoover had a challenger unseated an incumbent. It soon became clear that the new President's approach to government and the spiritual life of the country would be very different from that of his immediate predecessors.

If Jimmy Carter's writings on prayer were more prolific than those of any other American President, Ronald Reagan, who quickly became known as the "great communicator," spoke more frequently and eloquently on the role of prayer in American life. His solutions to the problems facing the country could be reduced to a few simple common denominators, one of which was the bond between God and the American people. It was a belief he expressed in his first presidential proclamation calling for a national day of prayer:

> Prayer is today as powerful a force in our nation as it has ever been. We as a nation should never forget this source of strength. And while recognizing that the freedom to choose a Godly path is the essence of liberty, as a nation we cannot but hope that more of our citizens would, through prayer, come into a closer relationship with their Maker.[18]

Originally from Dixon, Illinois, Ronald Reagan became a member of the Disciples of Christ as a boy and like so many others credited his mother with teaching him how to pray. Despite a relatively successful career in Hollywood, he found that his "real" professional life began after his election as governor of California. From that point on his personal faith only deepened. For someone who had never served in government before and was now heading a state with the fifth-largest economy in the world, the task was daunting. As he would remember:

> During my first months in office, when day after day there were decisions that had to be made, I had an almost irresistible urge— really a physical urge—to look over my shoulder for someone I could pass the problem on to. Then without my knowing quite how it happened, I realized I was looking in the wrong direction. I started looking up instead and have been doing so for quite a while now. My faith is unshakeable.[19]

William Clark, who served as Reagan's chief of staff, justice of the California Supreme Court, and U.S. Secretary of the Interior, was especially taken by the way Reagan often turned to prayer. Riding horses together at the Reagan ranch in southern California, overlooking the Pacific Ocean in one direction with the Santa Ynez Valley in the other, the two men often recited together the Prayer of Saint Francis, with its opening line, "Lord, make me an instrument of Your peace."

On inauguration day, Reagan had his mother's Bible used for his swearing in and had it turned to the passage in Chronicles that reads, "If my people, which are called by name, shall humble themselves, and pray, and seek my face, and turn away from their wicked ways; then will I hear from heaven, and will forgive their sin, and will heal their land."[20] It was his mother's favorite verse.

Reagan's wit surfaced continuously throughout his presidency, even on the most unusual occasions. Clark remembered joining the Reagans to pay respects at the Soviet Embassy on learning of the death of the country's president, Leonid Brezhnev. After they had signed the book of condolences, "he looked over at me with that wonderful catbird grin of his, and he asked, 'Do you think they'd mind if we just said a little prayer for the man?' "[21] With that, the Reagans and Clark bowed their heads, praying for the Soviet Union's avowedly atheist leader.

Reagan's disarming wit also came through during protracted negotiations with an unnamed senator. After intense discussions behind the closed doors of the Oval Office, the senator got up to leave, turned to the President, and said, "Mr. President, I'm going out of here and do some praying." Reagan responded, "Well, if you get a busy signal, it's me there ahead of you."[22] It was a story he would retell more than once.

Never did prayer seem so dear to Reagan, however, as when the mentally unbalanced John Hinckley tried to assassinate him a little more than two months after he had taken office. As the President was leaving the Washington Hilton on the afternoon of March 30, 1981, having delivered a speech before a labor union, Hinckley pulled out a .22 Devastator pistol, a weapon whose bullets are designed to explode on impact. In quick succession he shot six times, striking the President; the presidential press secretary, James Brady; a Secret Service agent; and a local policeman. The bullet that penetrated the President under his left arm, however, malfunctioned and never exploded. Instead, it lodged within an inch of the President's heart.

Rushed to George Washington Hospital in less than four minutes, Reagan was fast losing blood and in far worse condition than the public knew or would know for months. Although much was made of the President's humor and his trying to raise everyone's spirits under such extraordinary circumstances, there was a more serious side to that moment.

Reagan later remembered being wheeled into the hospital from the presidential limousine and overhearing a nurse whisper to someone as she lifted his arm, "Uh-oh, he's been shot." While his thoughts had been running together up to that point, he began to think about his would-be assassin. "I focused on that tiled ceiling and prayed," he later recounted. "But I realized I couldn't ask for God's help while at the same time I felt hatred for the mixed up young man who had shot me. Isn't that the meaning of the lost sheep? We are all God's children and therefore equally beloved by him. I began to pray for his soul and that he would find his way back into the fold."[23]

Returning to the White House to recover, Reagan asked to meet with Terence Cardinal Cooke of New York to pray and to put what had happened to him in some kind of spiritual perspective. As the Archbishop was about to leave, the President said to him, "I have decided that whatever time I have left is left for Him."[24]

IF REAGAN POSSESSED spiritual conviction prior to the attempt on his life, he showed even greater resolve afterward. Although he did not attend Sunday services, making clear that he did not want to create a circus atmosphere on the Sabbath, he did have an interdenominational chapel built at Camp David for his successors.

A defining moment of his presidency came, almost exactly two years after he had been shot, when he delivered one of his most famous speeches ever, reiterating his support for school prayer and other social issues, declaring, "I repeat: America is in the midst of a spiritual awakening and moral renewal." This address caused considerable controversy when he referred to the Soviet Union as the "evil empire" and immediately followed his remark by saying, "Let us pray for the salvation of all those who live in totalitarian darkness, pray they will discover the joy of knowing God."[25] American and international pundits alike were aghast at what they saw as the political incorrectness of the remarks, convinced that they served only to inflame Cold War tensions. In the weeks that followed, the President held his ground.

Reagan often combined the importance of prayer with the role of paterfamilias at crucial moments, and few occasions called for it quite like the *Challenger* disaster. Just after takeoff on January 28, 1986, the *Challenger* exploded before television cameras and a disbelieving world. Seven astronauts, including Sharon Christa McAuliffe, a civilian school-teacher from New Hampshire, lost their lives aboard the spacecraft. Americans were numb. That evening the President addressed the nation from the Oval Office in a way that touched even his most ardent detractors. People most remembered the last line of his remarks, paraphrased from a poem written in 1941 by John Gillespie Magee, Jr., an American who had joined the Royal Canadian Air Force just before World War II. The image would be adopted by ministers and air-force chaplains alike:

> Ladies and Gentlemen: I'd planned to speak to you tonight to report on the state of the Union, but the events of earlier today have led me to change those plans. Today is a day for mourning and remembering . . . Nothing ends here; our hopes and our journeys continue . . . The crew of the space shuttle *Challenger* honored us by the manner in which they lived their lives. We will never forget them, nor the last time we saw them, this morning, as they prepared for the journey and waved good-bye and "slipped the surly bonds of earth" to "touch the face of God."[26]

Coming off almost like a presidential homily, the words left hardly a dry eye in the White House newsroom.

IN THE LAST YEAR of Reagan's presidency, both houses of Congress passed into law a permanent national day of prayer. The measure, sponsored by Republican Senator Strom Thurmond of South Carolina and Democratic Representative Tony Hall of Ohio, passed overwhelmingly. In effect it amended the 1952 act, which required the President to proclaim a national day of prayer on a date of his choosing. The amended law set aside the first Thursday of each year for that purpose.

The invocation of prayer by the U.S. government in official settings, including daily sessions of the House and Senate and the Supreme Court, had continued unbroken from the country's earliest days. Over the years, all fifty states had instituted their own prayer rituals, mirroring in large part the customs in Washington. While prayer had always been offered to unify and break down partisan or personal barriers among government officials, on one occasion a minister's invocation went well beyond expectations.

Invited to open the new session of the Kansas state senate on January 23, 1996, the Reverend Joe Wright of Wichita stood before the gathered senators, invited guests, and members of the media and delivered a prayer he had composed to voice his personal views on a variety of political, social, and cultural issues:

> *Heavenly Father, we come before you today to ask your forgiveness and to seek your guidance. We know your Word says, "Woe to those who call evil good," but that is exactly what we have done.*
>
> *We have lost our spiritual equilibrium and inverted our values.*
> *We confess that we have ridiculed the absolute truth of your Word and called it moral pluralism.*
> *We have worshipped other gods and called it multiculturalism.*
> *We have endorsed perversion and called it alternative lifestyle.*
> *We have exploited the poor and called it the lottery.*
> *We have rewarded laziness and called it welfare.*
> *We have killed our unborn and called it choice.*
> *We have shot abortionists and called it justifiable.*
> *We have neglected to discipline our children and called it building self-esteem.*
> *We have abused power and called it political savvy.*
> *We have coveted our neighbor's possessions and called it ambition.*
> *We have polluted the air with profanity and pornography and called it freedom of expression.*
> *We have ridiculed the time-honored values of our forefathers and called it enlightenment.*
>
> *Search us, Oh God, and know our hearts today; try us and see if there be some wicked way in us; cleanse us from every sin and set us free. Guide and bless these men and women who have been sent here by the people of Kansas, and who have been ordained by you, to govern this great state. Grant them the wisdom to rule and may their decisions direct us to the center of your will. I ask it in the name of your Son, the living Savior, Jesus Christ. Amen.*[27]

The prayer created an immediate sensation. Some senators and their staff members walked out of the chamber, while others remained in their chairs, stunned that an ordained minister had used prayer to further his own political agenda. Still other senators cheered, believing that Wright had properly spoken from the heart on his concerns about the moral decay of the state and the country.

The moment "Amen" left the minister's lips, journalists flew out of the senate chamber to file the story. People on all sides of the controversy were sending e-mails to friends, titillated by what had taken place in the country's heartland. The veteran radio commentator Paul Harvey aired the invocation on his daily program, and listeners flooded the station with calls, both pro and con. Although Wright's prayer did not substantively sway lawmakers on the issues, his using that particular forum to share his opinions on such hot topics, and with such politically charged rhetoric, did create a furor.

The issue of prayer in public settings became even more complicated when all three branches of government entered the fray. In 1979 North Carolina Senator Jesse Helms had first introduced to a Senate bill a legislative rider forbidding the Supreme Court from reviewing any case related to voluntary prayer in public schools. The proposal was ultimately defeated, but President Reagan, who had long advocated the "freedom to restore nonsectarian prayers in a noncompulsory manner," would take up the cause of school prayer once again.[28]

In 1985 it appeared that the Supreme Court might finally rule in favor of a daily one-minute period of "meditation or voluntary prayer" in public schools as it weighed the facts in *Wallace* v. *Jaffree*. The case involved an amended Alabama statute that authorized teachers to conduct regular prayer services in the classroom and whether it violated the First Amendment. The parents of a student had taken the state to court, alleging that their child was being forced to pray and in turn subjected to state religious indoctrination.

With public sentiment continuing to favor a return to school prayer by over 75 percent, a friendly Reagan administration, a strong grassroots campaign in favor of the statute, and recent court decisions related to religious expression, Court watchers believed that the Supreme Court might well support the position of the state. It was not to be. In a six-to-three decision handed down by Justice John Paul Stevens, the Court ruled that Alabama had engaged in a thinly veiled attempt to promote "an impermissible endorsement of prayer in public schools."[29] While the original Alabama statute allowing for a moment of silence was deemed constitutional, amending the law to allow the recitation of prayer in the classroom made the act inherently religious and therefore unconstitutional under the First Amendment, in which "Congress shall make no law respecting an establishment of religion."

For supporters of voluntary school prayer the ruling came as a double blow, given that both the House and the Senate had been prepared to take up the issue of school prayer and passage appeared imminent. Even if a bill could be voted out of committee, however, the Supreme Court's ruling in *Wallace* v. *Jaffree* made it certain that the legislation would be dead on arrival before it reached either floor. The sequence of events prevented any serious efforts to force the issue.

The question of prayer in the schools arose again several years later, however, when the Supreme Court in 1992 agreed to hear *Lee* v. *Weisman*. Despite the Court's 1962 decision in *Engel* v. *Vitale*, school districts across the United States had continued to allow prayer to be said on special occasions when clergy were invited to participate and certain prayers were prescribed. The facts of *Lee* v. *Weisman* were very straightforward.

In this case, the city of Providence, Rhode Island, had traditionally allowed its principals to invite local clergy to offer both invocation and benediction prayers during graduation ceremonies. To ensure that each invited guest was aware of the nondenominational setting of the gathering, everyone was given the pamphlet "Guidelines for Civic Occasions." Daniel Weisman and his fourteen-year-old daughter, Deborah, objected to prayers being said during her 1989 graduation from the Nathan Bishop Middle School.[30] Weisman had long been involved in civil rights issues as a professor of social work at Rhode Island College. If prayer could not be said in the classroom, he reasoned, it should not be allowed in graduation exercises either.

Despite the Weismans' objections, the school decided to proceed as planned and invited Rabbi Leslie Gutterman of Temple Beth El in Providence to deliver two prayers for the occasion. Both prayers written by the rabbi showed considerable sensitivity toward the multi-faith composition of the students, parents, and faculty attending the ceremony.

When the commencement was over, however, the Weisman family decided to sue the school's principal, Robert Lee, in court, and the matter worked its way to the U.S. Supreme Court. In a five-to-four decision, the Court sided with the Weismans.

Once again the establishment clause was cited in the majority opinion handed down by Justice Anthony Kennedy, who termed the government's involvement in the matter "pervasive," writing, "The prayer exercises in this case are especially improper because the State has in every practical sense compelled attendance and participation in an explicit religious exercise at an event of singular importance to every student, one the objecting student had no real alternative to avoid."[31]

Justice Antonin Scalia, in speaking for the minority, wrote, "The Founders of our Republic . . . knew that nothing, absolutely nothing, is so inclined to foster among religious believers of various faiths a toleration—no, an affection—for one another than voluntarily joining in prayer together, to the God whom they all worship and seek . . . To deprive our society of that important unifying mechanism, in order to spare the non-believer what seems to me the minimal inconvenience of standing or even sitting in respectful nonparticipation, is as senseless in policy as it is unsupported in law."[32]

Subsequent Supreme Court decisions over the next decade reinforced the interpretation that prayer was inextricable from religion and therefore government had no business promoting its recitation. The 2000 decision in *Santa Fe Independent School District* v. *Doe*, for example, prohibited schools from holding votes on student-led prayer or allowing their public-address system to be used at sporting events for such purposes.

At the same time, however, the Court had upheld the rights of high-school students in *Board of Education of Westside Community Schools* v. *Mergens* in 1990 to meet in classrooms during noninstructional periods for prayer and religious studies. In its 2001 decision in *Good News Club* v. *Milford Central School*, the Court allowed for a community religious group to hold prayer meetings and Bible studies at school facilities if other community clubs were given the same access.

In essence, the Court took great pains in the years following the 1962 case *Engel* v. *Vitale* to protect individual rights of religious expression while prohibiting any government-sponsored prayer from being invoked in the classroom. The highest court in the land had interpreted the intentions of the Founding Fathers as confining prayer exclusively to the realm of religion under the First Amendment to the Constitution.

Legal questions regarding prayers in certain public settings would continue to loom over the country. In the case of the state-financed Virginia Military Institute, the same college where the pious Stonewall Jackson once taught and served as president, the Supreme Court would refuse to hear any appeals to overturn lower court decisions barring the practice of saying grace before meals. After more than 150 years, the courts would hold that VMI cadets were being "plainly coerced into participating" in an environment that values "obedience and conformity," setting off another heated debate.[33]

FOR ALL THE LEGAL CONSTERNATION over public prayer, every President since Dwight Eisenhower has actively encouraged the country to pray, believing that doing so remains a powerful unifying force, and is very much in keeping with the wishes of the Founding Fathers. As David J. Wolpe, the rabbi of Sinai Temple in Los Angeles, would stress, people cannot look at prayer as a monologue. Rather, prayer "speaks to God and to the community." While some people restrict prayer to the recesses of their souls, "it is what goes on in the world, between people, between us and God." To view it otherwise "undermines the true interchange of all belief."[34] This approach to prayer and the sense of the divine helped shape the presidency of Ronald Reagan's Vice President and successor, George H. W. Bush.

A lifelong Episcopalian, Bush attended Sunday services regularly from childhood but, like many Americans, was uncomfortable discussing his spirituality in public. After marrying Barbara Pierce and starting a family, he would have his faith tested when their four-year-old daughter Robin died of leukemia after months of trying to fight off the disease. Partly from that experience, the prayer life of George and Barbara Bush grew stronger, not simply mere rote.[35] "George and I pray every night together, by phone if we are in different cities," Barbara Bush once admitted in a television interview. "We have been doing this ever since we've been married. We never pray for financial gain or political victory—we have prayed for health of family and friends . . . We both believe our prayers have been answered, but then we have never prayed for the miraculous—like terminal illness being cured tomorrow. I can say I feel relieved after having said my prayers."[36]

Rabbi Wolpe's notion of prayer was reinforced when George H. W.

Bush took the oath of office, becoming only the second President, after Eisenhower, to offer a prayer to the nation in his address, stating unequivocally that prayer would be "my first act as President":

> We meet on democracy's front porch, a good place to talk as neighbors and as friends. For this is a day when our nation is made whole, when our differences for a moment are suspended. And my first act as President is a prayer—I ask you to bow your heads.
> *Heavenly Father, we bow our heads and thank You for Your love. Accept our thanks for the peace that yields this day and the shared faith that makes its continuance likely. Make us strong to do Your work, willing to heed and hear Your will, and write on our hearts these words: "Use power to help people." For we are given power not to advance our own purposes nor to make a great show in the world, nor a name. There is but one just use of power and it is to serve people. Help us remember, Lord. Amen.*[37]

The new President was forced to become more open about his spirituality, knowing that doing so would be catalytic for him and the country. In his first appearance before the National Prayer Breakfast as President, he became almost evangelical when he said, "I freely acknowledge my need to hear and to heed the voice of Almighty God."[38]

Not long into his presidency, Bush watched with awe, as did the American people and the world, as the Berlin Wall was physically and symbolically torn down. In turn, the dismantlement of the Soviet Union and its iron grip on the countries of central and eastern Europe effectively came to an end. The reality of what happened had seemed unfathomable just a few years earlier. In trying to convey the moment, President Bush addressed the National Association of Evangelicals in Chicago that following spring:

> Tonight our children and grandchildren—and I take great pride in this—tonight our children and grandchildren will go to their beds untroubled by the fears of nuclear holocaust that haunted two generations of Americans. In our prayers we asked for God's help. I know our family did, and I expect all of you did. We asked for God's help. And now in this shining outcome, in this magnificent triumph of good over evil, we should thank God.[39]

The end of the Cold War buoyed the country and the world, but the peace was short-lived. Within months of the President's speech in Chicago, the forces of Iraq's Saddam Hussein invaded Kuwait. In short order the President and his team put together what would be seen as a highly effective international coalition to force Saddam and his troops back to Baghdad. On the eve of the Gulf War, Bush wrote in his diary of the anguish he was facing: "Oh, God, give me the strength to do what is right." He also asked the Reverend Billy Graham, who reinforced the "importance of turning to God as a people of faith, turning to Him in Hope," to stay at the White House that night.[40] The next morning the two men drove to nearby Fort Myer to pray with and for the U.S. troops. Later that day the President's proclamation for a national day of prayer was issued as well.

Commenting on the response of the country to the war, *Time* magazine reported, "Last week produced a surprising portrait of the nation's faith, a tableau of people praying hard, slipping into chapels for special services during lunch breaks, joining candlelight vigils, seeking moral certainty."[41] After an overflowing crowd of more than six thousand attended a prayer service at Washington National Cathedral, Americans continued their vigil through the streets of the capital. One Quaker participant, hobbling along in crutches, remarked that "up at the cathedral they told us to fling our prayers to heaven. So I'm flinging mine—nonviolently."[42]

With over 200,000 U.S. troops on the ground and the general offensive launched on February 23, 1991, the hard fighting took less than one hundred hours, after which the President suspended military operations. Iraqi forces were driven back behind Iraq's borders, and the war effectively came to an end, with 148 American deaths and another 458 soldiers wounded in combat.[43]

Responding to the victory of coalition forces in repelling Saddam's forces, President Bush issued a rather emotive proclamation calling on the country to observe a national day of prayer on April 7, 1991. It was an official decree every bit as poignant as those offered by any of his predecessors. "Almighty God has answered the prayers of millions of people with the liberation of Kuwait," he declared. "It is fitting that we give thanks to our Heavenly Father, our help and shield, for his mercy and protection." He even went so far as to ask the Lord to "welcome all who have fallen into the glory of Heaven" and to ask Americans to pray for "the innocent men, women and children—wherever they may be—who have suffered." Liberally quoting the psalms throughout the proclamation, the President called for reconciliation with people everywhere.[44]

Although the success of Desert Storm caused the President's popularity to spike temporarily, he was defeated at the polls for reelection in a three-way race with Arkansas Governor Bill Clinton and Texas businessman H. Ross Perot. In the final tally, Clinton won 43 percent of the popular vote and became the country's first President to be elected from the baby-boom generation.

Born in Hope, Arkansas, in 1946, just months after his father, William Jefferson Blythe, died in an automobile accident, Bill Clinton had a difficult childhood. Wanting to make a decent living to give her fatherless son a good home life, his mother, Virginia, left young Bill with her parents to study nursing in New Orleans. After graduating as a nurse-anesthetist, she married Roger Clinton, whose name the future President would take, and after the wedding the Clintons moved to Hot Springs, Arkansas, where another son, Roger, was born. Becoming a member of the Southern Baptist Church at age nine, Bill Clinton always attended Sunday services, even if it meant walking to church alone.

Deeply influenced by President Kennedy, whom he had met at the White House when a teenager, Clinton decided to attend Georgetown University, where he could study in a city that he loved and at a school that offered a strenuous academic program. After graduation, he studied at Oxford University as a Rhodes scholar but returned to the United States before graduating, ultimately accepting a scholarship to study law at Yale. It was there that he met his future wife, Hillary Rodham.

With a law degree in hand, Clinton became a law professor and before the age of thirty was elected attorney general of Arkansas. Two years later he was elected the state's governor, the youngest in the nation. Throughout his stay in Little Rock, he regularly attended Immanuel Baptist Church, where he sang in the choir.

As a young man he was both spiritually and intellectually curious, and decided to visit a wide variety of churches. On one occasion he attended Morning Star Baptist Church in North Little Rock and became mesmerized as parishioners grew into a frenzy during their worship service. One man became so emotional in his prayers that he had to be taken out bodily from the sanctuary into a small nearby room. Continuing to hear the man shout and bang the walls, Clinton would later remember, "I turned around just in time to see him literally tear the door off its hinges, throw it down, and run out into the churchyard screaming."[45] He also became fascinated by the Pentecostals and, at the invitation of a friend, attended one of their services in nearby Redmond. It was a night he would not forget. One member after another spoke "in tongues" and showed such devotion and release of spiritual and physical emotion that Clinton was reduced to tears, calling the experience "breathtaking." He had never seen anything like it, and soon decided to attend their annual summer prayer camps, a practice he kept every year from 1977 until he became president in 1992. When camp organizers realized that he sang in his local church choir, they invited him to sing with a quartet of balding ministers who called themselves the Bald Knobbers. He loved it, except for the fact that he stood out with a full head of hair.[46]

Baptist by choice, with an abiding interest in Pentecostalism and other denominations, steeped in Catholicism during his four years at Georgetown, and married to a devout Methodist, few Presidents have ever come to office more ecumenically conscious than Bill Clinton.

Elected and reelected to the presidency, Clinton, like his predecessors, continued to invoke God's help, asking God in his second inaugural address to "strengthen our hands for the good work ahead and always, always bless our America."[47] Attending Sunday services each week in Washington and at Camp David, he did not hide his religious convictions. There was much for which to be grateful, including a prosperous economy at home and, even with conflicts in eastern Europe and Somalia, relative peace abroad.

What unexpectedly preoccupied the nation in the last years of Clinton's administration was the torturous Monica Lewinsky episode, a situation that the President emotionally responded to at a prayer breakfast. The story of the scandal first broke when a White House intern admitted to having sexual relations with the President over several months. To Clinton's later remorse, the situation was compounded by his continued denials that anything untoward had taken place. In a televised address on August 17, 1998, having testified before a grand jury that same day, the President finally told the nation in a live broadcast from the White House that he in fact did have "a relationship with Miss Lewinsky" and that "now, this matter is between me, the two people I love most—my wife and our daughter—and our God."[48] No sooner had he finished his remarks than commentators pounced on him for not showing proper contrition and for using an arrogant tone. What the President had hoped would be a salving moment instead exacerbated the situation.

Trying to make things right, Clinton and his advisers determined that there was no better venue to confront the issue than the National Prayer Breakfast scheduled for September 11. With his wife, Hillary, sitting just a few seats away, the President began his remarks:

> I may not be quite as easy with my words today as I have been in years past, and I was up rather late last night thinking about and praying about what I ought to say today . . . I don't think there is a fancy way to say that I have sinned . . . I believe that to be forgiven, more than sorrow is required. At least two more things: First, genuine repentance, a determination to change and to repair breaches of my own making. I have repented. Second, what my Bible calls a broken spirit. An understanding that I must have God's help to be the person that I want to be. A willingness to give the very forgiveness I seek . . .
>
> In this I ask for your prayers and for your help in healing our nation . . . It is very important that our nation move forward.

With that, the President offered a prayer from the Yom Kippur liturgy:

> *Lord, help us to turn from callousness to sensitivity, from hostility to love, from pettiness to purpose, from envy to contentment, from carelessness to discipline, from fear to faith.*
>
> *Turn us around, O Lord, and bring us back toward you. Revive our lives as at the beginning. And turn us toward each other, Lord, for in isolation, there is no life.*

He then ended his remarks by asking for empathy from those in attendance: "I ask you to share my prayer that God will search me and know my heart, try me and know my anxious thoughts, see if there is any hurtfulness in me and lead me toward a life everlasting. I ask that God give me a clean heart, let me walk by faith and not sight."[49]

The response to the President's remarks was predictably mixed, some people questioning his sincerity, others believing that he had finally shown true contrition. The crescendo of the Lewinsky affair had built up to that climactic moment, remarks from the President that lasted no more than fifteen minutes. Legally, however, the matter was far from over, and in less than two weeks the House Judiciary Committee began proceedings leading to the President's impeachment. In the end Clinton was spared conviction by the Senate. As First Lady and later Senator Hillary Rodham Clinton later wrote in her memoirs, "If I hadn't believed in prayer before 1992, life in the White House would have persuaded me."[50] As for the President, he turned to two ministers and a lay friend, asking them to visit him in the White House monthly to pray, read Scripture, and discuss life issues. The Lewinsky affair would take its toll on the President, his family, and indeed the entire country.

WHILE AMERICANS WATCHED the political drama unfold in Washington, the country was experiencing strong economic growth. Productivity was up, unemployment rates hit historic lows, and budget deficits were being converted into surpluses. That expansion, coupled with the momentum of globalization, was allowing U.S. companies to enjoy record growth and profits. At the same time, the strength of the economy obscured the realities of the high-tech boom, creating an untenable balloon effect. More ominously, however, the pressures to show record profits every quarter, the lack of transparency in corporate accountability, the deceptive bookkeeping in multibillion-dollar corporations, and the ever-present motive of greed produced a series of business scandals that sent shock waves around the world.

While the reasons behind the corruption were as old as time itself, the ripple effects were staggering, from depletion of employee pension funds to the value of shareholder portfolios plummeting to almost junk status. In the midst of the scandals, however, a number of corporate executives showed that business objectives could be compatible with spiritual values. More to the point, several successful CEOs went so far as to attribute their success to prayer.

Four chief executive officers in particular, from very different industries, found that their ability to pray was integral to their business day. They never asked for riches or even specific quantitative success. Rather, they asked for the wisdom to make the right decisions, to understand that their actions had consequences.

One of those individuals, Howard Schultz, the dynamic president and CEO of Starbucks, turned the fledgling Seattle coffee company into a multibillion-dollar enterprise. Purchasing the company in 1983 for $3.8

million, he realized that in building it up, he faced significant risks as well
as rewards:

> I prayed a great deal for the opportunity to be put in the position
> where my big dream could come true. It wasn't anything formal,
> but I found myself looking toward God for the wisdom to help me
> make it happen.
>
> I know I found comfort in it, and also things did work out. I
> remember going back to a place, spiritually, where I said "thank
> you" . . .
>
> So I prayed to God on an ongoing basis about this opportunity.
> I wanted to build a company that valued the human spirit, which
> did not leave people behind. That responsibility is not only about
> building profit but about being the kind of person who does the
> right thing.
>
> I remember praying that if I got this opportunity, if God would
> help me to make it happen, that I wouldn't abuse it. Today I thank
> God for the opportunity to have done just that.[51]

Throughout the 1990s Starbucks became one of the great business
success stories of the decade. Projecting a total of ten thousand stores in
sixty countries by 2005, Schultz would take justifiable pride in empower-
ing his employees with generous stock options and benefits packages.[52]
Consistently named over the years one of corporate America's most
admired managers, he emphasized the need to "compromise anything
but your core values" and to turn to prayer always as a means "to renew
yourself even when you are hitting home runs."[53]

J. W. Marriott, the chairman of the Fortune 500 company Marriott
International and son of the company's founder, discovered prayer to be
central to his life at an early age. Named president of the company in
1964, Marriott never forgot some words of advice from his father: "Good
timber does not grow with ease; the stronger the wind, the stronger the
trees." Prayer was critical to success, allowing a person to develop "a
clear mind, good judgment, good sense, guidance, and direction." True
to his Mormon roots, Marriott came to believe that while prayer, coupled with fasting, "requires a lot of work sometimes," it "cleanses the
body and weakens you to the point where you are more humble and
attuned with what you need to say, and it helps you listen."[54] With annual

sales of twenty billion dollars generated from twenty-five hundred hotels, almost two hundred senior living communities, and various food services by 2004, Marriott and his company would continue to expand around the world.

Another legendary business figure, Wayne Huizenga, began his career with a five-thousand-dollar loan from his father-in-law and by the age of thirty-four owned Waste Management Inc., the largest sanitation company in the world. Before he turned fifty, he purchased a small video chain in Chicago called Blockbuster Video. Within seven years, before selling the company to the media giant Viacom, Huizenga would see Blockbuster grow company assets from seven million to four billion dollars. He, too, attributed his success to prayer:

> I would say that prayer is the most important thing that I do. When you're in prayer, you're not kidding anyone. You are saying exactly the way it is, and that's the power of prayer. That alone requires faith and so the very act of prayer says you have faith. And if you didn't believe God was listening, you wouldn't pray.
>
> I've never used prayer to make a deal. But I do use prayer in business a lot . . . I have God and that's the security that gives me the strength to go out and make things happen and accomplish my goals . . . I'd have to say most of my prayers have been answered. I sometimes wonder why. My wife and I talk about it a lot. It just keeps getting better and better.[55]

Few business giants, however, made prayer such a visible part of their personal and professional life as Sir John Templeton. Born in Winchester, Tennessee, Templeton graduated from Yale in 1934 and went on to become a Rhodes scholar, turning to investment banking after studying at Oxford University's Balliol College. Forming his own investment firm and helping to pioneer international growth-fund portfolios, he ultimately amassed considerable wealth for himself and his clients. By the 1960s, however, he had turned his attention to his great passion for fostering ecumenical dialogue and in 1972 established the annual Templeton Prize, regarded as the Nobel Prize for contributions to religious life in the world.

In describing his personal life and managerial style in the boardroom and in the day-to-day management of his company, Templeton always spoke of prayer as the essence of his success. The moment he arose, he always spoke to God in words filled with gratitude and supplication, committed to "total one unity with Thee." He also explained how prayer was intertwined with his companies:

> We start all of our meetings, including shareholders meetings and directors meetings, with prayer. If you start meetings with prayer, the meetings are more fruitful and productive—you reach decisions that are more likely to help everybody concerned. There is less controversy when you begin with prayer. Or, as I like to say, "Prayer helps you to think more clearly" . . . Everything you do following such a prayer is likely to be more successful. Your mind is not twisted by conflicts. You're less likely to disagree with your associates or do something you'll regret next year. So your decision-making may be improved if you try to bring yourself into contact with the Creator, into harmony with His purposes.[56]

The common thread running through the stories of all these business leaders was that they structured their lives and actions to a far greater purpose than the quarterly bottom line, using prayer as their constant cue and companion. At a time of corporate scandal, these CEOs and many others stood out from the pack.

Prayer and business were taken to a different level with the publication of the wildly successful *Prayer of Jabez* by Bruce Wilkinson. In his compact, ninety-three-page best seller first published in 2000, Wilkinson, a grandfather and doctoral graduate from Western Conservative Baptist Seminary, shared his firm belief in the power of an ancient invocation to enrich, if not change, the material and spiritual lives of people in the modern world. By reciting the prayer of a little-known Old Testament figure, Jabez, individuals could receive "unclaimed blessings" from God, leading them to "live beyond the limits," according to Wilkinson. The prayer was simple and took just seconds to recite:

> *O that You would bless me indeed,*
> *And enlarge my territory,*
> *That Your hand would be with me,*
> *And that You would keep me from evil,*
> *That I may not cause pain!*

Wilkinson argued that God will support anyone who asks for help to reach his or her full potential. "If you don't ask for His blessing, you forfeit those that come to you only when you ask," he maintained.[57]

Some critics quickly denounced the contention that God could be swayed to enrich someone simply by the rote recitation of a verbal talisman. They argued that Wilkinson's prescription ignored God's limitless love and desire to bless good people whether they asked for help in a fixed way or not. Others claimed that God wanted to hear from the faithful, even in specific wants, but that a person must ask for a blessing before God would grant it. Wherever one came down on the Jabez debate, sales of the book initially took off by word of mouth, with testimonies as to the prayer's power helping to generate further sales. By the summer of 2002 the book had sold almost ten million copies in seventeen languages and had become the fastest-selling book of all time.[58] That success created its own industry with such sequels as *The Prayer of Jabez: Devotions for Kids, The Prayer of Jabez for Teens,* and *The Prayer of Jabez for Women* as well as other items.

TECHNOLOGY CONTINUED TO GIVE VOICE to prayer. By the end of the century, personal computers and the Internet had shown how prayer could be adapted to cutting-edge media, not unlike the effects of radio and television decades earlier. Prayers could now be cast as "OGod.com" and close with "enter" and "send" rather than "amen."

In the first survey of its kind, the Pew Foundation found in 2001 that over three million Americans turned to the Internet for spiritual support every day, and the number continues to grow substantially. One of the largest group of Internet users, these "religious surfers" look for everything from information on and inspiration from prayer to like-minded individuals, most of whom will never meet face-to-face, in chat rooms and "perpetual" prayer groups.[59] Even prayer bloggers have taken to the Internet to give their own spin on modern spirituality.

Realizing the possibilities of reaching out to congregants and potential followers well beyond traditional church pews, religious institutions have come to use the Internet to transmit specific tailored messages. Even monasteries and convents, which for centuries had devoted themselves to a life of prayer within the confines of a closed community, have come online to reach tens of thousands of Internet users.

Given the rapid advances in technology and the growing desire to make the prayer experience more meaningful for both the individual and larger community, mega-churches also began to spring up from New Jersey to California. Intended to accommodate thousands of worshippers at a time, these churches provide sacred spaces where dramatic visual displays and sound effects only enhance a person's spiritual experience. And like the weekly religious broadcasts that aired at the dawn of radio and television, these same churches have been reaching Americans in greater numbers than ever before through the electronic media, using every possible feature to convey their message. With the proliferation of cable television, twenty-four-hour channels devoted to gospel music and spiritual inspiration are now being broadcast not only throughout the United States but around the world.

WHILE MODERN TECHNOLOGY has enabled Americans to pray in new ways, science has been unlocking the effects of prayer on the human condition. More studies have been undertaken on the link between prayer and the human condition over the past decade than have been conducted in the whole of history. Some scientific researchers have even gone so far as to conjecture that a human gene exists that hardwires the brain to induce spiritual belief. It is believed that through the act of prayer, the chances for reproductive survival are increased dramatically by minimizing disease, reducing stress, and extending life itself.[60] While early findings remain controversial, this is a field that will be expanded for years to come.

One of the most remarkable, promising developments in health research during the 1990s was the increased attention to the effects of prayer on pain, loss, and life-threatening illness. Although some studies linking human biology to spiritual practices had been conducted in the past, the scientific community largely dismissed those results out of hand as heretical to sound medical practice. In time, however, enough anecdotal evidence from attending physicians emerged, and institutions like Harvard, Johns Hopkins, and the University of Pennsylvania set up control groups with men and women of different faiths to determine possible correlations. Although some findings were inconclusive, the great majority of studies showed definitive results, surprising even the most hardened skeptics. Even the U.S. government has taken an interest in the relationship between prayer and health. From reports issued by the U.S. Office of Technology Assessment to a five-year study now under way at the National Institutes of Health, American taxpayers are funding efforts to connect prayer with physical and mental health.

One Duke University study of four thousand individuals over the age of sixty-four showed that the immune systems of those who prayed were significantly more resilient, avoiding such conditions as higher blood pressure and coronary heart disease. At the University of Miami, researchers found that AIDS patients had a far greater chance to become long-term survivors if they engaged in prayer. At Dartmouth Medical Center, 232 heart patients were studied before and after surgery, and their chances for survival were directly connected to prayer.[61]

Efforts were also made to determine how the human brain might be hardwired for prayer, creating a calm that minimizes stress and promotes healing. Even personal absorption in the quiet repetitive sounds of prayer, as when Catholics say the Rosary or Buddhists recite their mantra, was found to be enormously therapeutic.

In an independent survey, 99 percent of family physicians acknowledged that "personal prayer, meditation, and other religious practices" can markedly enhance the medical treatment of patients.[62] Indeed, a person's life may even be extended on average by eight years through prayer.[63]

The link had become so strong by the late 1990s that 86 of the country's 126 medical schools instituted spirituality and health courses and programs, many of which were made prerequisites for graduation. Students were instructed to take down a patient's spiritual history, including the nature and regularity of his or her prayer life. Hospital-accreditation organizations began requiring hospitals to assess the spiritual needs of their patients and offer programs to address them. If patients refuse to respond to such questions, their wishes are to be respected. If they do open up to their physicians, however, the information garnered can provide an important key to treatment. While some doctors might be uncomfortable asking about such an intimate area of a person's life, Dr. Harold G. Koenig of Duke University, a leading researcher in the field, believes that asking patients about their prayer life or religion is no more invasive than inquiring about their sex life, a procedure that began in earnest some twenty years ago.[64]

More recently, scientific research has been conducted to determine the impact of intercessory prayer. By far this area of research has provided the greatest controversy among the medical community. Dr.

Mitchell Krucoff, also of Duke University, launched the MANTRA (Monitoring and Actualization of Noetic Training) project to assess patients at nine medical centers to ascertain if there is a causal relationship between intercessory prayer and improvement in a person's medical condition. The medical team under Dr. Krucoff asked Sufi Muslims, Buddhist monks, Carmelite nuns, evangelical Christians, and others to pray for 750 patients with potentially life-threatening ailments, a study that is ongoing. Despite the number of variables involved and the scientific certitude of confirming divine intervention, the National Institutes of Health will probe this field further given early findings and the irresistible desire to connect science with faith.

Hundreds of medical studies have now been conducted on the subject of prayer and health. While no one has suggested that saying prayers automatically alters serious health conditions, the existence of a direct link has become irrefutable, leading clinical researchers to spend more time, money, and effort to further explore the issue.

On another front, researchers and institutions have also confirmed that prayer has a stabilizing effect on the mental outlook of individuals, families, and whole communities. Extensive studies of children and adolescents broken down by age, religious upbringing, and economic background have shown that prayer often has the effect of providing a critical anchor to their lives.[65] In turn, predispositions to drugs, alcohol, depression, and other social maladies have been minimized because of increased spirituality, according to several extensive surveys, including a significant two-year study conducted by the National Center on Addiction and Substance Abuse at Columbia University in the fall of 2001.[66] Harvard psychiatrist and Pulitzer Prize winner Robert Coles approached the subject from a very different angle, probing the prayer life of children as "pilgrims," concluding how the spiritual quests of young people are every bit as dynamic and vital to them as they are to their parents.[67]

Clinical psychologists have also conducted exhaustive studies on the connection between spirituality and the aging process, determining that prayer provides a support system that is truly unique to the human condition.[68] For those restricted by physical challenges or disabilities beyond their control, prayer has been found to be a tool of psychological empowerment. Even the prayer practices of the sexes have been thoroughly explored to determine the similarities as well as the differences between females and males. In the early 1990s the Promise Keepers, with their phenomenal success in bringing husbands and fathers together in massive numbers across America to accept moral responsibility in part through the regimen of prayer, became its own laboratory for researchers.

No modern disease was more difficult to address, of course, than the scourge of AIDS. In the early days of its discovery, before effective medications were developed, its diagnosis nearly always carried with it a death sentence. One of the greatest champions of helping victims of AIDS was the formidable Mother Teresa. Becoming only one of a handful of foreign citizens in history to be named an honorary citizen of the United States, Mother Teresa was prolific in her insightful writings on the subject of prayer, once remarking that prayer was key to her helping "the poorest of the poor." In addition to her work in Calcutta, India, she developed a network for her Missionaries of Charity in eighty-seven countries. In the United States she became particularly known for her work in helping unwed mothers and AIDS patients. It was in these efforts that she used prayer in her own unique, inimitable way.

To help her finance a new multimillion-dollar AIDS facility in the District of Columbia, she decided to visit the Washington lawyer and one-time owner of the Baltimore Orioles and Washington Redskins, Edward Bennett Williams, to ask for a sizeable contribution. Knowing that she was coming to see him with that request in mind, but uncomfortable about channeling resources for such a project, he and his partner decided to offer her a substantial contribution for any other project she might like, just not that one.

When she and one of her sisters arrived in his office, she wasted no time in telling him about what she wanted to do. "Mother," said Williams, "I would love to help you on any other effort, but this one I am not sure we are interested in funding." "In that case," Mother Teresa surprisingly replied, "Let us pray." The seconds that passed while they bowed their heads in silence seemed to last forever. Finally, Mother Teresa looked up at the two men and continued, "Mr. Williams, as I was saying, Sister and I are here to ask for your support for this AIDS hospice." With that, Edward Bennett Williams took out his checkbook and asked her how much she wanted.

IN THE ARTS AND HUMANITIES, prayer took on greater form and creativity. Maya Angelou's *I Know Why the Caged Bird Sings,* the poet laureate Louise Glück's *The Wild Iris*, and Annie Dillard's *Pilgrim at Tinker Creek*, all award-winning books, showed the diversity of spiritual expression at the turn of the century. These and scores of other books by some of the country's most talented writers plumb the depths of spirituality through prose and poetry and provide many exquisite examples of prayer in the modern world.

In the world of music, traditional hymns and spirituals continued to be popular, whether in the sounds of small choirs in rural churches or the recordings of the celebrated Mormon Tabernacle Choir. Time-honored gospel music also grew in popularity with such artists as Della Reese, Shirley Caesar, and Andraé Crouch. Their music reached out to listeners confronting modern-day ills, leading Shirley Caesar, the winner of ten Grammy awards, to record her inspirational album *You Can Make It*.

One of the country's most recognizable artists was the "Queen of Soul," Aretha Franklin. Franklin began her career under the influence of her father, the charismatic Reverend C. L. Franklin. Her defining moment came with the album *Amazing Grace* in 1972, recorded with James Cleveland, the "King of Gospel," and the Southern California Community Choir. At the beginning of the new century, she was still recording and performing gospel, leading one critic to note, in a review of a 2003 concert at New York's Radio City Music Hall, "The Baptist church music that Ms. Franklin grew up singing is never far from her best performances." When she performs her musical prayers, she "turns listeners into a congregation."[70]

Contemporary Christian music, which became enormously popular in the 1990s, was a departure from the spiritual offerings of the past. Distinct from gospel, spiritual, or traditional hymn singing, it emerged in a variety of forms, whether hard core, punk, rhythm and blues, rock, hip-hop, or rap, intent on taking the message of Christ directly to mainstream and secular audiences, particularly by emphasizing worship music. Groups like the Third Day, Sonic Flood, and Delirious?, as well as artists such as Amy Grant, Kirk Franklin, and Michael W. Smith, saw their popularity soar, and were able to cross over to popular music also. Although these musicians were largely motivated by evangelization, conveying the limitless dimensions of prayer was a driving force as well. Selling almost fifty million albums a year by the turn of the century, this new kind of Christian music became a major force in the music industry, capturing almost 7 percent of the market. Songs such as "On Eagle's Wings," "Awesome God," and "Shine, Jesus, Shine" delighted performers and listeners alike. John Styll, president of the Gospel Music Association, described the phenomenon this way: "Our consumers desire a real connection to God with their music and are actively seeking music that extends their church experience into daily life."[71] Although contemporary Christian music would find a ready audience on traditional musical stages, it also would become a draw for thousands of young people, who traveled to rural settings for weekend music fests.

MORE SECULAR PERFORMERS also have composed and recorded music that has centered, sometimes controversially, on the subject of prayer and their own spiritual odysseys under the public glare. Madonna, whose devoutly Catholic mother regularly prayed by kneeling on uncooked rice during Lent as a form of special penance, was almost excommunicated by the Vatican after releasing her graphically explicit video "Like a Prayer" with its opening line, "Life is a mystery, everyone must stand alone." Following the example of her mother, who died when Madonna turned six, she would openly admit at the height of her fame that she had developed an active prayer life, borrowing from the religious traditions of the Far East. Like her protégée Britney Spears, she would become particularly influenced by the Jewish mystical practices of Kabbalah, going so far as to use some of her considerable fortune to set up schools and centers for people to learn its traditions, particularly the "Kabbalah of prayer."

While traditional American music continued to provide outlets for expressing prayer, a new song form emerged, also tapping into the desire to communicate with God, and that was rap. No one came to embody the new genre in its early years more than Tupac Shakur.

Having named her child Lesane Parish Crooks at his birth in 1971, Shakur's mother, who was serving time in prison while pregnant with "Pac," decided to change his name when he was a young boy, choosing Shakur from the Arabic word meaning "thankful of God." It was a difficult life for a child, growing up as he did with a father who was serving a sixty-year prison term for a fatal armed robbery. Living often in homeless shelters in the Bronx and Brooklyn, Tupac Shakur remembered "crying all the time" as a boy because he had no roots, no sense of a future. Through it all, however, he learned to pray.

By his early teens his family moved to Baltimore, where he attended the Baltimore School for the Performing Arts and quickly showed his musical, acting, and dancing talent. At the same time, however, he began to run afoul of the law, joining violent neighborhood gangs, living in a world of violence that led to his being killed by gunmen in the fall of 1996 at the age of twenty-five.

While the rap lyrics of Tupac Shakur contained some of the rawest language known in the English language, they also projected the basest of emotions generated through real-life experiences. One of his most revealing songs, an anguishing, private meditation, is called "God." As he boldly wrote the words out in longhand, he drew birds, hills, and a glowing sun around them. Verse after verse, he speaks to the unbearable "pain" and "sadness" he so often felt and how he always turned to God in his distress. By the end of the piece he makes clear that "when I am asked who I give my unconditional love 2," he looks "for no other name except . . . GOD!"[72]

More universal icons would also openly declare their fervent belief in the power of prayer. Muhammad Ali, who captured the imagination of the boxing world with his athletic prowess inside the ring and his charismatic self-assurance outside the ring, became a devout convert to Islam. Despite the ravages of degenerative Parkinson's disease, he openly admitted to Oprah Winfrey in an extended interview and to others how prayer had been and continued to be the critical anchor in his life.[73] To enrich his daily prayer regimen as a Muslim, he even went so far as to build small mosques on his properties whenever he built or moved into a new home.

Like Muhammad Ali, Oprah Winfrey too had become well known to her large following for her faith in a higher power and belief that prayer provided a critical life force. From her syndicated television program to her Harpo production studio and publication house, she would launch projects devoted directly or indirectly to the subject of prayer. With a television viewing audience of over twenty-two million people, she always encouraged her guests to open up and discuss their spiritual lives, including their practice of prayer as inspiration for others. Her reason for doing so was simple and embedded in her own experience. A child of unwed parents who was frequently abused and molested as a child and teenager by several male relatives, she found prayer to be her great refuge. While she would lift herself out of the despair of her humble

beginnings to become the first African-American woman to achieve bil-
lionaire status, she would always remind her audiences that prayer continued to provide answers for her and that it could unlock doors for
untold others. Consequently, she would often work her artistic projects
into subtle and not-so-subtle messages on the power of prayer and faith.

WHILE TREATING PRAYER ARTISTICALLY had largely been left to
writers, composers, choreographers, and architects in the past, American culture was now creating new ways to express the indefinable elements of spiritual thought and representation. In particular, artists of the
stage and screen were devising ways to treat the subject of prayer that
conveyed greater awe and inspiration than ever. Julie Taymor, for example, brought a totally fresh, unique approach to the fuller dimensions of
prayer in a number of her early plays, culminating with her extraordinary staging of Disney's dazzling *The Lion King*. There were such works
as *Black Elk Lives*, *Juan Darién: A Carnival Mass*, *The Haggadah*, and *Tirai*, a
play set in Bali to explore the earliest human spiritual awakenings.
Through puppetry, lighting, staging, costumes, and much more, she portrayed the act of prayer in fresh and exciting ways.

The Broadway production of *The Lion King*, of course, had originated
from Disney's wildly successful animated film, largely masterminded by
Jeffrey Katzenberg, chairman of Disney Pictures. In 1994 Katzenberg's
talents were brought together with those of Steven Spielberg and David
Geffen to form the Hollywood studio DreamWorks. As their first animated feature, the visionary trio produced *The Prince of Egypt*, the gripping tale of Moses and the deliverance of the Hebrews from the
Egyptian Pharaoh Ramses. With the lyrics of Stephen Schwartz, who
had made his mark in *Godspell* and Leonard Bernstein's *Mass*, and the
music of Hans Zimmer, who also composed for *The Lion King*, the film
underscored the relationship between God and Moses and in turn the
Hebrew people. The treatment of prayer through the imagination and
cutting-edge technology of twentieth-century animation resonated with
audiences around the world. Great pains were taken to decide how Moses
should talk to God, and to what kind of a presence and voice God should
have as well.

After its founding, the studio went to work for three and a half years
with a full-time staff of 350 artists, technicians, and managers to tell the
story of the Hebrew child, raised in the palace of the Pharaoh, who leads

his people to the promised land. Utilizing design, layout, voices, draw-ings, background, music, and special effects, DreamWorks produced an Academy Award–winning film that became one of the ten most success-ful animated films of all time.

THE END OF THE 1990s ushered in not only a new century and mil-lennium but also a new President. While the election of 2000 was his-torically significant because of the differing results between the electoral college and the popular vote, it was also notable for other reasons. In rather stark fashion, both Republican and Democratic candidates during the primary season candidly shared their faith and prayer life with reporters and audiences. In one early debate before the Iowa caucus, five of the six Republican candidates invoked the name of God some twenty times.[74]

When the presumptive Democratic nominee, Vice President Al Gore, a former theology student at Vanderbilt University, announced Con-necticut Senator Joe Lieberman as his running mate, he made history by selecting the first Jewish candidate to a national ticket. Overjoyed, Lieberman, an Orthodox Jew, stood next to Gore in their first campaign rally together and quoted Chronicles from the Old Testament: "Give thanks to God and declare His name." He then offered a prayer before the crowd: "Dear Lord, Maker of all miracles, I thank You for bringing me to this extraordinary moment in my life."[75]

While the American people seemed genuinely pleased that a religious barrier had been broken and were anxious to find out more about Lieberman's private religious life, they were less enthusiastic about his openly embracing his faith on the campaign trail. In an address after the election, as he helped to launch the new Pew Forum on Religion and Public Life in Washington, Lieberman mused, "The fact of my faith seemed happily to be cause for celebration. But once I opened my mouth and actually professed my faith, to give glory and thanks to God for the extraordinary opportunity I had been given, some of the hosan-nas quickly turned to how-dare-he's."[76]

More history was made at the inauguration of George W. Bush. In his address, the new President made the point that not only government but others must show compassion, that "some needs and hurts are so deep that they will respond only to a mentor's touch or a pastor's prayer." He then stressed that churches, synagogues, and mosques would continue to occupy "an honored place in our plans and in our laws."[77] It was the first time a President had included Islam in an inaugural address.

What created a stir, however, was the opening invocation by the Reverend Franklin Graham, stepping in for his father, the Reverend Billy Graham, and the closing benediction by the Reverend Kirbyjon Caldwell. In both instances, the Protestant ministers ended their prayers by emphasizing that their petitions were being made in the name of Jesus Christ. Their decision to emphasize Christ "above all other names"[78] became highly controversial, debated in op-ed pieces and on talk radio and television for weeks.

At the turn of the new millennium there was little question as to the heightened spirituality of the country and the continued invocation of prayer by the vast majority of Americans. What fascinated many people was the spirituality of the new President. Like most modern-day candidates for president, George Bush had published his autobiography, *A Charge to Keep*, during the campaign. The title was taken from a hymn written by Charles Wesley, which reads:

> *A charge to keep I have,*
> *a God to glorify,*
> *a never-dying soul to save,*
> *and fit it for the sky.*

> *To serve the present age,*
> *my calling to fulfill;*
> *O may it all my powers engage*
> *to do my Master's will!*

> *Arm me with jealous care,*
> *as in Thy sight to live,*
> *and O, Thy servant, Lord prepare*
> *a strict account to give!*

> *Help me to watch and pray,*
> *and on Thyself rely;*
> *assured, if I must betray,*
> *I shall forever die.*

The new president would also make sure that a painting by Texas artist W. H. D. Koerner, who was also inspired by the hymn, was hung in the Oval Office. The piece depicts cowboys on horseback galloping across rough mountain terrain, determined to reach their destination.

Much has been written about the influence of President Bush's religious faith on his decision making, given his domestic agenda on such proposals as the faith-based initiative and his approach to foreign policy, particularly his resolve to strike preemptively at Saddam Hussein's Iraq. While some pundits have simply been interested in the rhythms of the President's daily spiritual life, others have expressed concern that he has become a theocratic commander in chief.

Whereas his father, former President George H. W. Bush, was a lifelong Episcopalian, a traditionalist in every way, President George W. Bush had a very different spiritual experience. While he attended Yale and later Harvard Business School, his faith was lukewarm at best, more rote than anything. He also came to realize that he had a serious drinking problem.

In retrospect President Bush believed that the "seeds" of his change came during a weekend he spent with the Reverend Billy Graham at his family's home in Kennebunkport. Walking along the southern coastline of Maine, Bush and Graham talked about faith and placing life in perspective, and from that moment, Bush believed, Graham "led me to the path, and I began walking."[79] With the support of his wife, Laura, he joined the Methodist Church after briefly considering the Presbyterian Church.

A telling moment in Bush's life came when the President invited five leading clergymen—three Christians, one Jew, and one Muslim—to the White House in September 2002. After the men had exchanged pleasantries, Bush suddenly opened up to them as he asked for their prayers. "You know, I had a drinking problem," he told them. "Right now I should be in a bar in Texas, not the Oval Office. There is only one reason that I am in the Oval Office and not in a bar. I found faith. I found God. I am here because of the power of prayer."[80]

The unexpected came into play again when the President was hosting Crown Prince Abdullah, the de facto ruler of Saudi Arabia, at his Prairie Chapel Ranch in Crawford, Texas. The two men broke for lunch in the middle of their intense discussions over the Israeli-Palestinian crisis.

After sitting down to the table, Bush bowed his head to recite grace, reaching for his guest's hand and saying, "Let us pray." Unaccustomed to the Christian practice, the Crown Prince pulled back and turned to his bewildered aide, asking in Arabic, "What should I do?" After asking the question, however, he, too, bowed his head as the President proceeded to ask God for help with their difficult talks. In leaving the meeting, Prince Abdullah remarked that he found the President's deep religious convictions one of his most admirable qualities.[81]

On another occasion the President was returning to Washington after an official visit to Central America. It was Palm Sunday, the first day of Easter week, and White House aides realized that the President was disappointed because he was unable to attend church services. Just before boarding Air Force One in San Salvador, Chief of Staff Andy Card, Communications Director Karen Hughes, and National Security Adviser Condoleezza Rice suggested to Bush that they hold an informal service on board. Although some individuals questioned the appropriateness of the service, raising the issue of separation of church and state, everyone was reminded that prayer services have been held in official buildings and settings since the founding of the country. In what Bush would call "a touching moment," the prayer service became the first, but not the last, of its kind aboard Air Force One.

The President's unambiguous spirituality opened him to the charge that God was the marionette master and that Bush's prayer life served as proof. The merits of his decisions aside, the spiritual devotion of the President has been neither more profound nor more driving than that of many of his predecessors. Prayer simply has shaped his life in some profound ways.

AT THE OUTSET OF THE NEW MILLENNIUM, the United States looked back on a century labeled by historians the world over as "the American century." Despite the growing influence of the European Union and a more economically robust China, the United States remained the world's only superpower. The country had arrived at this point for many reasons, not the least of which was its great spiritual faith manifested so often by prayer. This same conviction would be needed in abundance for what was to come.

CHAPTER 16

THE INNOCENTS

September 11, 2001, and Beyond

Lord, make me an instrument of Your peace;
Where there is hatred, let me sow love;
Where there is injury, pardon;
Where there is doubt, faith;
Where there is despair, hope;
Where there is darkness, light;
Where there is sadness, joy.

O Divine Master, grant that I may not so much seek
To be consoled as to console;
To be understood as to understand;
To be loved as to love.

For it is in giving that we receive;
It is in pardoning that we are pardoned;
And it is in dying that we are born to eternal life.

—Prayer attributed to Saint Francis of Assisi

$\mathcal{F}$EW MOMENTS IN history are as instantly transforming as the hours of September 11, 2001. American prayer never seemed more important or more invoked. Up and down the east coast, Americans woke up to a beautifully crisp near-autumn day. Labor Day had passed, officially bringing to an end summer vacations. It was the second day of the workweek; children were being driven to school, and parents were preparing for another day of work. Delivery trucks were dropping off their supplies at local stores as sanitation workers made their morning rounds. America was going about its daily routine.

By mid-morning, however, the transformation of American life had begun to unfold, turning "9/11" into the country's exclamation point at the start of the new millennium. By nightfall, the word "evil" had taken on new meaning for many Americans, but as always the dark side was countered by an American sense of sacrifice and resilience.

It was a day when Americans found that what united them had far more resilience than what divided them. Nothing seemed to strike a more common chord on that Tuesday and in the days that followed than turning to prayer.

While some questions regarding the attacks would remain unanswered, one reality was clear from the outset. The country had been changed forever. It was not so much that America had lost its innocence, a description long given by historians to capture such seminal moments as the Civil War and World War I. No, September 11 represented a new kind of conflict; religious genocide had been unleashed on American shores.

The assault was nothing less than the execution of a plan to commit mass murder on U.S. soil in the name of God. The terrorists' objective, as the findings of the 9/11 Commission would confirm, was to eradicate once and for all the "religious and political pluralism, the plebiscite, and equal rights of women . . . Claiming that America had declared war against God and his messenger, they called for the murder of any American, anywhere on earth, as the 'individual duty' of every Muslim who can do it, and in any country in which it is possible to do it."[1] In the words of Osama Bin Laden, the leader of Al Qaeda, "We do not have to differentiate between military or civilian. As far as we are concerned, they are all targets."[2] Although Al Qaeda had already killed Americans and others at U.S. embassies in Kenya and Tanzania, as well as on the *USS Cole* while it was docked in Yemen, this was the first time their efforts were played out on such a scale in the United States itself.

The official time would be set at 8:46 a.m., when the first jet, American Airlines flight 11, carrying enough fuel to travel from Boston to Los Angeles, crashed into the first of the two World Trade Center towers. Any thoughts that the crash had been an accident were dispelled within minutes when United Airlines flight 175, scheduled to take the same route as the American flight, hit the second tower. Soon both buildings,

110 stories tall, took on the appearance of two enormous candles being snuffed out. Torrents of black smoke were soon choking the skies over Lower Manhattan.

With all eyes turned to New York, the unthinkable continued to unfold as yet another plane, American Airlines flight 77, bound from Washington's Dulles Airport for Los Angeles, struck the north side of the Pentagon at 9:39 a.m. Americans, riveted to their televisions and radios, soon learned that other planes were unaccounted for. America was under attack, and no one knew what targets were next. By 9:30 a.m. the country had been told that one hijacked aircraft had made a turn on its way from Newark to San Francisco and was heading toward Washington, D.C. Like all of the other flights, it was full of gasoline for a transcontinental trip, allowing any attack to be carried out with extreme lethal force. Where United's flight 93 would strike became a terrifying guessing game—possibly the Capitol, maybe the White House. Wherever it hit, the plane would be down within a half hour.

Beyond the wrenching horror of the attacks themselves and the lives that changed forever that day came the unsettling realization that the men who inflicted such carnage on innocent men, women, and children of every color, national origin, and religious persuasion had used prayer to validate their cause. Wanting the world to know of their deeds, even in the remaining minutes of their synchronized attacks, the terrorists allowed their victims to call their families from their cell phones. Passengers like Jeremy Glick called their spouses to tell them what was happening and said over and over again in their last seconds, "I love you." Tom Burnett, an executive from California with three little girls at home, ended the last conversation with his wife, "Just pray, Deena, just pray."[3]

No single call pulled the country's heartstrings more that day than the one Todd Beamer made to the GTE Airfone customer center near Chicago. Not able to contact his wife directly, Beamer was connected to Lisa Jefferson, an operating supervisor with more than eighteen years on the job. He calmly began to tell her what was happening on board. Finally Beamer and a few others, including Jeremy Glick, Tom Burnett, and Mark Bingham, realized they had no choice but to divert the flight from the nation's capital, even if it meant crashing the plane into the ground.

"I don't think we're going to get out of this thing," Beamer told Jefferson. "I'm going to have to go out on faith." Before jumping the hijackers with his fellow passengers, Beamer had a simple request: "Would you say the Lord's Prayer with me?" With precious little time left, they recited together the prayer they had learned in childhood. It was a prayer that included the words "as we forgive those who trespass against us." Somewhere over Pennsylvania, Todd Beamer and Lisa Jefferson began to recite:

> Our Father, which art in heaven,
> Hallowed be Thy name
> Thy Kingdom come
> Thy will be done
> In earth as it is in heaven.
>
> Give us this day our daily bread
> And forgive us our trespasses
> As we forgive those
> who trespass against us.
>
> And lead us not into temptation,
> But deliver us from evil:
> For Thine is the kingdom, and the power,
> And the glory forever. Amen.

When they finished, Lisa Jefferson heard Todd Beamer call out, "Jesus, help me," and then she heard him and the other passengers recite the Twenty-third Psalm: "Yea, though I walk through the valley of the shadow of death, I will fear no evil." The plane downed at approximately ten that morning in a field in Somerset County, Pennsylvania. In another fifteen to twenty minutes it would have been directly over the nation's capital.[4]

Back in Lower Manhattan, the horror escalated in a thousand different ways as the two 110-story towers began to collapse under the weight of the melting steel. One of the rescuers called to duty was Father Mychal Judge, a sixty-eight-year-old Franciscan priest, who by the end of the day would be counted among the dead as number 00001, officially the first identified victim of the World Trade Center attacks. A recovering alcoholic, Father Judge was a strong believer in Alcoholics Anonymous and its reliance on prayer, a program he called "America's greatest contribution to spirituality."[5]

When he learned of the first plane crashing into the north tower of the World Trade Center, he quickly changed from his friar's habit into his chaplain's uniform and drove to the scene with firefighter Michael Weinberg at the wheel. By the time Father Judge arrived, his longtime friend Mayor Rudolph Giuliani was already on the scene and quickly grabbed his arm. "Father, please pray for us," Giuliani said almost instinctually. "I always do," said Father Judge with a smile. In his pocket was a prayer he had written some time earlier, an invocation that he always carried to remind him of his duty as a priest and as a human being:

> *Lord, take me where You want me to go;*
> *Let me meet who You want me to meet;*
> *Tell me what You want me to say, and*
> *Keep me out of Your way.*[6]

On entering the rubble of the north tower, Father Judge came across the body of the sixteen-year veteran fireman Daniel Suhr, who had just been fatally struck by the body of a woman who had jumped from an upper floor of the building. The Franciscan priest quickly removed Suhr's helmet and took the clerical stole from his own pocket, kissed it, and placed it around the firefighter's neck to perform the last rites of the Catholic Church. Not long after he left for the other tower, he was struck by falling debris, suffering a fatal blow to the head.

His own firefighters found him in the darkness with their flashlights as they searched the rubble. "Oh, my God, it's Father Mike!" one of the men screamed. There was no breathing, no pulse. Grabbing one of the many broken chairs nearby, the firemen made a makeshift carriage. The Reuters photographer Shannon Stapleton would capture one of the more stunning moments of that awful day as the fallen priest was carried out on a chair, a sight one of his close friends later called "a modern-day Pietà."[7] Almost three years after Father Judge's death, people were still visiting his grave daily at the Holy Sepulchre Cemetery in Totowa, New Jersey, reciting the very simple prayer that the Franciscan priest had written many years earlier.[8]

IN THE FOLLOWING HOURS and days, Mayor Rudolph Giuliani stood as a critical bulwark in the midst of such human tragedy. He would walk among the rescue workers at Ground Zero, acknowledging each person he saw with "God bless you." When he later reflected on how he was able to hold up under the strain and provide leadership during those anxious days, he explained that he simply prayed for help in making so many split-second decisions. Not knowing what kind of impact each order might have, he would give instructions to his subordinates, and then say a prayer under his breath, hoping that his judgment had been sound.

At his last press conference on September 11, as dark fell over the city, Giuliani became particularly reflective before the media: "I would strongly urge that everyone in their own way should say a prayer and ask God for help and for assistance and ask God for strength to overcome this terrible tragedy to show the world . . . that terrorism can't stop us."[9]

When he attended one of the many funerals and memorial services in the days following, this one to remember almost three hundred employees of the financial management firm Marsh & McLennan, he tried to comfort the relatives of the victims. In remarks before a standing-room crowd at St. Patrick's Cathedral, Mayor Giuliani turned the tables in describing those who perished, saying, "They are in heaven praying for *us*."[10]

THE OUTPOURING OF AMERICAN SPIRITUAL and patriotic fervor in the months after September 11 astounded even the most cynical observers. The run on flags to fly over homes and to place as decals on automobiles far exceeded the supply. Within twenty-four hours, churches, synagogues, mosques, and temples were holding services to standing-room-only crowds. Draped across overpasses on major highways were flags and signs that read, "God Bless America," "Pray America," and "One Nation under One God." A bakery in Alexandria, Virginia, erected a massive poster, that read, "Prayer doesn't change things. Prayer changes people who change things." A Korean dry-cleaning store in Chicago hung a sign that read, "Peace is fragile, handle with prayer."

Paid advertisements, sponsored by various church groups, appeared in major newspapers across the country advocating prayer to confront the fear, anger, and sorrow that Americans were experiencing. A full-page petition titled "A Prayer by the Nation for the Nation" was sponsored by several Christian prayer groups and appeared simultaneously in a number of periodicals. It referred to God as "the Source of all Comfort and all Hope."

On the home front, prayer was as important to those who opposed

U.S. intervention as to those who approved of it. Given the infrastructure already in place, particularly among conservative Christians, "prayer warriors" organized through churches and homes, by telephone, and through dozens of Web sites. One site alone, www.prayerforourpresident.com, had over 50,000 visitors within the twenty-four hours following President Bush's address to the nation, in which he declared that the United States was about to go to war. William Martin, professor of religion and public policy at Rice University in Houston, noted that many of the fundamental Christians believed that the war against the evil of Saddam Hussein was in effect "a battle against Satan and Satan's minions," and that prayer was a keystone in the "pitched battle." Another committed group, headed by John Lind, launched its own popular website, www.presidentialprayerteam.org, signing up more than three million people committed to praying for the President and the men and women in uniform.[11] At the outset of the impasse between the White House and the Iraqi government, they had fervently prayed that Hussein would leave Iraq of his own will and prevent the war.

Bishop T. D. Jakes, the charismatic pastor of Potter's House in Dallas, one of the fastest-growing churches in the country, was interviewed on CNN. Without warning the interviewer asked, "Will you stop right now where you are and pray for America?" Recounting the story to his congregation, Jakes remarked, "I thought for a moment: I was on CNN, and nobody is arguing about separation of church and state now. America is coming home . . . we're praying for the nations of the world to live up on the side of right. Hear me good. My trust is in God."[12]

On the morning after the attacks Dr. Lloyd John Ogilvie, a Presbyterian minister and the sixty-first chaplain of the Senate, opened the session with the following prayer:

Almighty God, source of strength and hope in the darkest hours of our Nation's history, we praise You for the consistency and constancy of Your presence with us to help us confront and battle the forces of evil manifested in infamous, illusive, cowardly acts of terrorism . . . We pray for the thousands of victims who lost their lives as a result of these violent acts against our Nation. We intercede for their loved ones; comfort them and give them courage . . . Quiet our turbulent hearts. Remind us of how You have been with us in trouble and tragedies of the past and have given us victory over tyranny . . . You are our Lord and Saviour. Amen.[13]

Ogilvie's colleague the Reverend Daniel P. Coughlin, a Roman Catholic priest, likewise, offered at the same hour his own prayer:

> O God, come to our assistance. O Lord, make haste to help us. Yesterday we were stunned, angry and violated. Today, Lord, we stand strong and together. Yesterday changed our world. Today we are changed . . . We mourn our dead and reach out with prayer and acts of compassion to all those families splattered with blood and exhausted by tears . . . With clear insight which comes from You and You alone, reveal all that is unholy, and renew the desire of Your people to lives of deepening faith, unbounding commitment, and lasting freedom here where liberty has made her home. We place our trust in You now and forever. Amen.[14]

Throughout the day members of Congress tried to absorb what had just taken place on American soil. One of the most memorable scenes came on September 12, when Republicans and Democrats from both houses gathered on the steps of the Capitol in a show of unity, spontaneously singing "God Bless America."

MEANWHILE, ON THE OTHER side of Pennsylvania Avenue, the President and his Cabinet were dealing with events in their own way. On the night of September 11, President Bush addressed the nation from the Oval Office:

> Good evening. Today, our fellow citizens, our way of life, our very freedom came under attack in a series of deliberate and deadly attacks . . . Tonight I ask for your prayers for all those who grieve, for the children whose worlds have been shattered, for all whose sense of safety and security has been threatened. And I pray they will be comforted by a power greater than any of us, spoken through the ages in Psalm 23: "Even though I walk through the valley of the shadow of death, I fear no evil, for You are with me."[15]

At the President's first Cabinet meeting after the attacks, Secretary of Defense Donald Rumsfeld was asked to offer a prayer, and he summarized the feelings of many Americans:

Ever-faithful God, in death we are reminded of the precious birthrights of life and liberty you endowed in your American people. You have shown once again that these gifts must never be taken for granted.

We pledge to those whom you have called home, and ask of you—
Patience, to measure our lust for action;
Resolve, to strengthen our obligation to lead;
Wisdom, to illuminate our pursuit of justice, and
Strength, in defense of liberty.

We seek your special blessing today for those who stand as sword and shield, protecting the many from the tyranny of the few. Our enduring prayer is that you shall always guide our labors and that our battles shall always be just.

We pray this day, heavenly Father, the prayer our nation learned at another time of righteous struggle and noble cause—America's enduring prayer: Not that God will be on our side, but always, O Lord, that America will be on Your side.
Amen.[16]

On Friday, the day after the Cabinet meeting, a remarkable assembly gathered at Washington National Cathedral to remember the human losses and enormity of the tragedy. Present that morning were former presidents Ford, Carter, and Bush, their wives, members of Congress and the President's Cabinet, members of the diplomatic corps, and hundreds of other invited guests. In front of the sanctuary, each taking a part in the service, sat Theodore Cardinal McCarrick, Rabbi Joshua Haberman, Imam Muzammil Siddiqi, and other representatives of America's religious faiths. The Reverend Billy Graham, who had been unable to attend the President's inauguration earlier in the year, delivered the sermon that morning, reassuring those assembled and the millions watching on television, "My prayer today is that we will feel the loving arms of God wrapped around us, and we'll know in our hearts that He will never forsake us as we trust in Him."[17]

Three hymns were selected for the service, "The Battle Hymn of the Republic," "O God, Our Help in Ages Past," and "A Mighty Fortress Is Our God," all of which had been sung during other times of mourning in American history. When it came time for the President to speak, he turned his attention once again to the power of prayer:

We are here in the middle hour of our grief. So many have suffered so great a loss, and today we express our nation's sorrow . . . In many of our prayers this week, there is a searching, and an honesty. At St. Patrick's in New York on Tuesday, a woman said, "I prayed to God to give us a sign that He is still here." Others have prayed for the same, searching from hospital to hospital, carrying pictures of those still missing.

God's signs are not always the ones we look for. We learn in tragedy that His purposes are not always our own. Yet the prayers of private suffering, whether in our homes or in this great cathedral, are known and heard, and understood.

There are prayers that help us through the day, or endure the night. There are prayers of friends and strangers, that give us strength for the journey. And there are prayers that yield our will to a will greater than our own . . .

On this national day of prayer and remembrance, we ask almighty God to watch over our nation, and grant us patience and resolve in all that is to come. We pray that He will comfort and console those who now walk in sorrow. We thank Him for each life we now must mourn, and the promise of life to come.

As we have been assured, neither death nor life, nor angels nor principalities nor powers nor things present nor things to come, nor height nor depth, can separate us from God's love. May He bless the souls departed. May He comfort our own. And may He always guide our country.

God bless America.[18]

For the overwhelming majority of Americans, trying to comprehend the magnitude of September 11 and its aftermath became a process of what *The New York Times* would call "moral triage."[19] Expressed through spiritual invocations in churches, homes, and public forums, prayer became the one outlet that did not necessarily provide answers but allowed questions to be placed in a larger context, not clearly understood by human capacity alone.

Makeshift altars were built outside fire and police stations where some of the heroes who had died had worked. People stopped by to pay their respects and pray for someone they may never have met. Special prayer services and candlelight vigils were held in churches and public spaces across the country. Some public schools even allowed students to reflect and pray in their own way.

America's entertainers also came to the fore, reflecting on what had transpired and trying to comfort the country and the families of the victims who had been scarred forever by the attacks. Bruce Springsteen—whose record-breaking hit "Badlands" he once called a "prayer by Americans for Americans"—wrote the haunting "The Rising" in memory of September 11. Imagining one of the firemen who braved the inferno of the towers, facing imminent death that morning, he wrote, "May their precious blood bind me, Lord . . . come on up for the rising."[20]

The reaction of most members of the American Muslim community ranged from complete outrage to disbelief that the terrorists could distend the tenets of the Koran to justify killing innocent people. They felt the wrath of a small minority of Americans who used them as scapegoats to vent their frustrations, but found that many more Americans went out of their way to show their support. In the heart of industrial America, the Islamic Center of Toledo, Ohio, was vandalized in the days following September 11 when hoodlums tore open a hole in the roof of the mosque. Cherrefe Kadri, the president of the local Islamic community, was taken aback at what happened next:

That small hole in the dome created such a huge outpouring of support for our Islamic community. A Christian radio station contacted me wanting to do something. They called out on the airwaves for people to come together at our center to hold hands, to ring our mosque, to pray for our protection. We expected 300 people, and thought that would be enough to circle the mosque, but 2000 people showed up to hold hands and pray around the mosque. I was amazed.[21]

Beyond those prayers, the response from Americans representing the religious spectrum from the Baha'is to the Sikhs was immediate and equally profound. For many Americans, witnessing interfaith prayer services for the first time either in person or on television seemed to open new worlds. From colorful religious attire to the exotic sounds of chants and unusual musical instruments, the sights and sounds of other Americans sharing their prayer traditions proved an extraordinary backdrop to the events of September 11.

At the memorial service held at the Pentagon for those who had lost their lives, the hues of American religious diversity were cast in a special way by Diane Sherwood, Associate Director of the Interfaith Conference of Metropolitan Washington. It was a prayer that few who heard it have forgotten:

> *Holy One, Great Mystery,*
> *Known by a thousand names,*
> *We come today as a grieving family,*
> *A grieving nation, a grieving world,*
> *We open ourselves for deep healing,*
> *Courage and wisdom.*
> *We are Sikhs and Muslims, Christians and Jews,*
> *Mormons, Bahais, Hindus, Buddhists,*
> *And those on a hundred paths to Truth,*
> *We ask for Compassionate Hearts,*
> *Sorrowing, but rejoicing always,*
> *Dying but behold we live,*
> *With a unified and humble voice we pray . . .*
> *God Bless America!*

One discordant note came after an event at Yankee stadium with the suspension of the Reverend David Benke, New York district president of the Missouri Synod of the Lutheran Church. The complaint lodged against him by twenty-one Lutheran pastors centered on accusations of "unionism," mixing the beliefs of different Christian denominations, as well as "syncretism," mixing Christian and non-Christian views. Although Benke had received permission to participate in the service, he was told by his superiors, "You are still accountable for your own actions."

In notifying Benke of his suspension from ministerial duties within the Church, a formal statement was included:

By President Benke's joining with other pagan clerics in an interfaith service [no matter what the intent might have been], a crystal clear signal was given to others at the event and to thousands more watching C-Span. The signal was: While there may be difference as to how people worship or pray, in the end, all religions pray to the same God . . . To participate with pagans in an interfaith service and, additionally, to give the impression there might be more than one God, is an extremely serious offense against the God of the Bible.[22]

The letter went on to say, "In brotherly love and admonition I appeal to you, President Benke, please make a sincere apology to our Lord, to all members of The Lutheran Church–Missouri Synod, and to all Christians who are a part of Christ's Body. Joining in prayer with pagan clerics in Yankee Stadium was an offense to God and to all Christians."[23]

Disbelief was the common reaction to this discord, regardless of one's faith. As the Reverend J. Bryan Hehir of Catholic Charities remarked at the time:

> All of us prayed together—across religious lines—not to have this cast as a religious war. There was an effort to provide settings in which people would pray across those lines of faith. We could demonstrate that however we came to God, there was a common ground we could share. There was a real desire to pray for those [touched by the tragedy], that they would have strength.[24]

In the end the coalescing character of prayer allowed Americans to recognize more their commonality than their differences, and so come together. September 11, in the words of President Bush, "will always be a fixed point in the life of America." With the backdrop of the Statue of Liberty and the U.S. flag flapping against the winds of New York Harbor a year after the attacks, the President spoke for many Americans:

> We cannot know all that lies ahead. Yet we know that God has placed us together in this moment, to grieve together, to stand together, to serve each other and our country. And the duty we have been given—defending America and our freedom—is also a privilege we share.
>
> We are prepared for this journey. And our prayer tonight is that God will see us through, and keep us worthy.[25]

CHURCH ATTENDANCE in the United States increased appreciably after September 11, but the spike lasted for only a few months. Nonetheless, many historians and theologians believe that for at least a generation America has been experiencing its Fourth Great Awakening, a period marked by dramatic social adjustment spawned by powerful religious and political changes in the country. The Nobel Prize–winning economist Robert William Fogel has argued that the era may have begun as early as 1960, as evidenced by massive technological changes that transformed the U.S. economy and challenged the stability of the country's culture. In short, at the outset of the new millennium, the people of the United States were becoming more spiritual and religious, not less.

The first military incursions of the twentieth-first century in Iraq and Afghanistan only reinforced the culture of prayer for many Americans, reminding them once again of the fragility of life, and that included the President of the United States. Like so many of his predecessors, President George W. Bush had wrestled with the most daunting decision that any U.S. commander in chief can make in sending soldiers, sailors, and airmen into war. In the case of Iraq, the highly controversial decision to remove Saddam Hussein from power had hung over the President and White House for months. The moment had come.

In gathering the members of his national security team together in the Situation Room of the White House on the morning of March 19, 2003, linked to a secure video conference line with General Tommy Franks and nine of his commanders stationed at U.S. Central Command in Doha, Qatar, the President assured himself one more time that American troops were well prepared for what lay ahead. He then made the historic declaration, "I hereby give the order to execute Iraqi Freedom. May God bless the troops." The next voice came from Franks who instinctively rejoined, "May God bless America."[26] What came next was central to the character of George Bush.

In his now famous interview with journalist Bob Woodward, the President confided that after saluting his men and barely able to hold back the tears, he took a walk outside just beyond the glass-paned doors of the Oval Office. The heightened emotions of the moment seemed to come together all at once. It would have been difficult not to think of how his father had faced a similar decision to go to war a little more than a decade earlier. While he faced a similar enemy, the times and stakes were very different as he would come to realize.

"I prayed as I walked around the circle," he confided in Woodward. "I prayed that that our troops be safe, be protected by the Almighty, that there be a minimal loss of life." He added that he had prayed for days "going into this period," asking "for strength to do the Lord's will." At the same time, he made clear to Woodward, "I'm surely not going to justify war based upon God . . . in my case I pray that I be as good a messenger of His will as possible. And then, of course, I pray for personal strength and for forgiveness."[27] The days ahead would be excruciating ones for the President and for the country.

While the ability of U.S. forces to overthrow the Iraqi regime turned out to be swift and sure, the residual tasks of stabilizing and rebuilding both Iraq and Afghanistan simultaneously became fraught with setbacks. As in past wars, images of Americans brought together in prayer to remember the casualties of war became commonplace. Appearing on the front pages of major newspapers across the country, there was the Associated Press photograph of U.S. soldiers in Iraq huddled together with their heads down and arms around one another, praying for one of their own killed just moments earlier. There was the video footage of the memorial prayer service held for Pat Tillman, the former professional football star, who gave up a multimillion dollar contract to enlist in the Army Rangers in Afghanistan because he wanted to give something back to his country. And of course, there were the difficult, recurring scenes of gravesite ceremonies at Arlington National Cemetery, ending as they always have with "Taps" being played in the distance.

The war on terrorism and on the ground in Iraq and Afghanistan continued to gnaw. Like conflicts past, it conjured up a range of emotions. The horrors of confronting prisoner abuse at Abu Ghraib Prison, and Internet access to the individual decapitations of soldiers and noncombatants by religious extremists, did not help matters. Just as Americans at home had shown a greater spiritual consciousness in their everyday living, U.S. troops were also showing their own spiritual mettle.

As in past wars, American soldiers found mortal combat to have the effect of ridding the mind of frivolous distractions. Turning to prayer and putting life and death in proper perspective became important preoccupations. Whether fighting by shooting mortar shells or engaging in hand-to-hand combat while undergoing dangerous house searches, each man and woman confronted mortality in his or her own unique way, and prayer for many became the critical means to that end.

Standing on the front lines of the war, Chaplain Bill Devine of the 7th

Marine Regiment remarked to a reporter, "I don't know about you, but I find myself talking to God a lot more out here than I did at the rear." In describing how his troops were coming to him for advice and to pray, another chaplain, Colonel Douglas L. Carver, a Southern Baptist minister from Rome, Georgia, remarked, "Some of them have never fired weapons at a human being before. It's a place they've never been, an experience they've never had."[28] Prayer was everywhere.

On the USS *Harry S Truman*, one of the newest and largest aircraft carriers in the U.S. fleet, some twenty-six different faith traditions served on board at the outset of the carrier's deployment to the Middle East.[29] As with other military units, chaplains would officiate at services for individual religious denominations while also helping to create ecumenical environments, including prayer breakfasts, in which diverse groups and individuals could come together in prayer. Chaplains even worked with military personnel to form multifaith choirs to sing familiar hymns, with requisite rehearsals held during off-duty hours.

Adapting to the conditions of modern warfare, however, prayer took on a special twist on the *Truman*, as it did on other carriers. In the daily task of having dozens of personnel line up and walk across the 1,096-feet flight deck to search thoroughly for foreign object debris, better known as F.O.D., which could cause serious damage if pulled into powerful jet engines, the exercise was turned into a "prayer walk." Although the exercise would take only a few minutes to perform, it became an opportunity for the men and women on board to pray both privately and together in an outdoor setting at sea.[30]

Most often, of course, prayers were said for personal safety and guidance, for family and friends, and even for the country's military and civilian leaders. As one lieutenant admitted, "I pray for the President and my other leaders quite a bit because I know that their decisions directly affect me."[31] The most difficult prayers came after a fellow soldier had been killed.

How and when the United States and its allies would extract themselves from a war in which the enemy was so elusive, so hate-driven, and so defiantly brazen would be the fodder of generals, political observers, and American citizens for months. As with prior generations, images of Americans turning to prayer during times of war would remain indelible, part of the country's photographic memory. While each one is unique to the time and circumstances from which it was taken, it also reminds people of the vagaries of life and death, the continued realities of the world in which they live, and the vital presence of prayer to deal with those realities. At the same time, it is important to put prayer in proper perspective, whether in the face of war or in the midst of some other calamity. As Claude Newby, a Mormon chaplain in Vietnam, would reflect on war and prayer in the distance of time:

> This might seem strange coming from a former chaplain, but I cringe when I hear someone boastfully attribute his survival to God's recognition of his prayers and those of his family, as above the prayers of another family. I know that men fell in battle whose families, present or future, needed them as much as mine needed me. I know that men fell whose hopes were buttressed by the prayers of loved ones as faithful and righteous as mine. Yet I laid down my life on the line as a sacrificial offer and lived to pick it up again, while others laid their mortal lives down for keeps. Why them and not me?
>
> Of this I am certain: God in His loving and incomprehensible way can and sometimes does intervene to deflect bullets. He always answers prayers, and always from His higher perspective.[32]

THIS RESTLESSNESS OF the American people was plainly in evidence when, during the 2004 campaign for president, the Democratic Party chose Senator John Kerry of Massachusetts as its nominee. In addition to the war on terrorism, the continued U.S. presence and troop casualties in Iraq, the state of the economy, and social concerns from stem call research to the Constitutionality of gay marriage all helped shape the platforms of both parties. In confronting these issues, however, the American people clearly showed that they wanted to vote for a president who they believed would exemplify virtues of morality and spirituality.

While George Bush's opponents accused the President of being too direct in openly discussing his religious faith, Democratic Party operatives recognized that the American people were more religious than ever, and that the Republican Party continued to be perceived as more attuned to the religious community at large. According to a Pew survey released in early 2004, 70 percent of the electorate wanted their president to be a "man of faith."[33] This did not mean that they necessarily wanted an occupant in the Oval Office who was overtly religious, just a com-

mander-in-chief who believed in God, had humility, and felt beholden to
a power larger than himself or the country.

That was a problem for John Kerry when another poll taken by *Time* in
June showed that a mere 7 percent of Americans regarded him as "a religious man."[34] While Kerry became, after Al Smith in 1928 and John F.
Kennedy in 1960, only the third Roman Catholic to be nominated by a
major party for the presidency, he found that the most vocal opposition to
his candidacy among religious groups came from the hierarchy of his own
church. His long-held public position supporting abortion rights was only
one of several issues that spurred intense debate, leading some clergy and
laypeople to question whether Kerry and other like-minded Catholic
politicians should be denied the sacrament of Holy Communion.

For the reserved John Kerry, a uniquely American amalgam who could
trace his roots to John Winthrop on his mother's side and Jewish ancestry
on his father's, the notion that he was anything but religious was
extremely frustrating. During his school days, particularly the two years
he spent in Switzerland, he served as an altar boy and attended Mass frequently both on Sundays and weekdays. "I prayed all the time," he admitted. He even contemplated becoming a priest.[35] By the time he went off
to war in Vietnam, he carried a rosary and a prayer book with him, and
turned to them every chance he had throughout his tour of duty.

In the period after he served in public office, Kerry attended Mass less
regularly, though he was often seen reciting a short prayer and making
the sign of the Cross before addressing an audience.[36] For presidential
candidate Kerry and the Democratic Party, the dilemma of how to convey a reverential sense of the divine, without appearing to be politically
expedient or phony, had to be tackled. In trying to narrow the perceived
"religion gap" with the Republican Party, however, they wanted to avoid
the kind of problems that vice presidential candidate Senator Joe Lieberman had faced four years earlier. Memories were all too fresh of how
pundits had raked Lieberman over the editorial coals for his unabashed
public recitations of prayers, and for discussing his Orthodox Jewish faith
so openly on the campaign trail.

At the same time, leaders of the party made a conscious effort not to
cede spiritual ground to the Republicans in 2004. There were a variety of
reasons why Kerry turned to Senator John Edwards of North Carolina,
a Methodist, to fill out the ticket as his vice presidential candidate—
though it did not hurt that Edwards had served as chairman of the Sen-

ate prayer breakfast or that he had co-chaired the National Prayer Breakfast. Many of those attending the annual prayer breakfast in 2002 remembered vividly how Edwards had led several thousand people in prayer with the words, "We seek to be the leaders you would have us be, and we sorely need your unsearchable wisdom. We pray each day, O Lord, that you inform our judgments with your wisdom, your humility, your benevolence."[37] In time, voters would also come to learn how the force of prayer had played such a critical role for both John Edwards and his wife, Elizabeth, after the accidental death of their sixteen-year-old son Wade, when, as Edwards confided, "my faith came roaring back."[38]

By the time the Democratic National Convention was held in late July, the theme of prayer became interwoven throughout the proceedings. In the same way that the party wanted to diffuse Republican Party claims as the party of a strong national defense and a no-nonsense approach to the war on terrorism, it also wanted to show that the GOP did not hold a monopoly when it came to American spirituality. As in past conventions, organizers made sure that sympathetic black preachers, ministers, priests, rabbis, and imams offered invocations before the delegates. Kerry even made sure that his newly appointed director of religious outreach, an evangelical Christian who had been part of Vermont Governor Howard Dean's campaign for president, worked the crowd.[39]

The message was a simple and straightforward one. As future Illinois Senator Barack Obama declared in his electrifying keynote speech, referring to the Electoral College votes that had gone for Al Gore in 2000, "We worship an awesome God in the blue states!"[40] Delegates jumped to their feet in applause.

Prayer was also used in more pointed ways. Senator Edward Kennedy, Kerry's longtime mentor, indirectly attacked President Bush by referring to the famous prayer composed by another Massachusetts native son, John Adams. With its entreaty "May none but the honest and wise men ever rule under this roof," Kennedy tried to bolster his conviction that President Bush had misled the country in leading the country to war, arguing that the President had conjured up the existence of weapons of mass destruction in Iraq as a ruse to overthrow Saddam Hussein.

By the time Kerry delivered his much-anticipated nomination speech two nights later, he too made references to his differences with the President. "I don't wear my own faith on my sleeve," he declared. "I don't want to claim that God is on our side. As Abraham Lincoln told us, I want to humbly pray that we are on God's side."[41] Throughout the rest of the campaign, the Kerry/Edwards team would continue to work to dispel any public concern over their credentials of faith.

By the time the Republican National Convention was held in Madison Square Garden in late August, not far from Ground Zero in New York City, the public show of faith was far less evident during prime time. But behind the scenes, there was great effort to join prayer and faith together with the convention and the President. Prayer services and Masses were held in hotel ballrooms, churches accommodated special spiritual observances for the delegates, and smaller fundamentalist groups came together to discuss the upcoming campaign in terms of prayer and getting out the vote on election day. Even the President, his family, and 250 invited guests attended an ecumenical prayer service at Our Savior Catholic Church in midtown Manhattan hours before he was to deliver his acceptance speech. With a priest, rabbi, minister, and imam officiating at the service, the interfaith backdrop of the convention was made clear.

THE CAMPAIGN WOULD become one of the hardest-fought contests between an incumbent and challenger in many years. On November 2, however, the American people spoke, reelecting the president to a second term in office. In the midst of the highly divisive campaign, a major concern in the minds of the American people, particularly for Bush voters, centered on the vaguely defined issue of moral values.[42] Given the presidential team's underlining strategy to mobilize the Republican conservative base to vote in unprecedented numbers, the Kerry forces were simply unable to match the political, if not spiritual, fervor. In the postmortem of the campaign, Democratic Party leaders would carefully assess how they could trump future Republican efforts in appealing to the electorate on moral values.

THE SECOND INAUGURATION of President George Bush was every bit as laden with religious significance as his first swearing-in. Like so many of his predecessors, his day began with an intimate church service at St. John's that consisted of family, close friends, his cabinet, and staff members. It continued with more prayer as clergymen sought God's protection for the country and for the President while military bands played such hymns as "God of Our Fathers." Efforts by California plaintiff

Michael Newdow to prevent the recitation of any prayers during the inauguration on the grounds of separation of church and state were firmly rejected by the 9th U.S. Circuit Court of Appeals in San Francisco, and were turned down on appeal without comment by the United States Supreme Court.

After being sworn into office by an ailing Chief Justice William Rehnquist, the President launched his second term, addressing the nation and "the varied faiths of our people" from the west side of the Capitol. Articulating his hope that the country would promote liberty and democracy aggressively "in every nation and culture," the President spoke of the gift of freedom as "the hunger in dark places, the longing of the soul." Praised for its bold vision by some and criticized for its overambitious reach by others, it was an inaugural address of sweeping breadth interspersed with direct and indirect references to God, that "author of liberty."[43]

Providing the benediction as he had done four years earlier was the Reverend Kirbyjon H. Caldwell, pastor of Houston's Windsor Village, the largest Methodist church in the country. While his prayer for the occasion ended in the name of Jesus, it did not create the same kind of controversy that his first prayer had generated when he invited his listeners to acclaim the supremacy of Jesus Christ above all others.

One of the more remarkable moments, however, came at the close of the official inaugural ceremonies the next day. At a prayer service held at Washington's National Cathedral, Reverend Billy Graham, who had been unable to attend the President's first inauguration due to poor health, led the clergy of other faiths in asking for Divine Providence for both President Bush and Vice President Cheney. The man whom George Bush had credited with restoring his faith twenty years earlier stood before a packed cathedral as he leaned on a walker for balance. In crediting God for the President's reelection, he pronounced in a strong voice, "Their next four years are hidden from us, but they are not hidden from You." He then went on to ask God to "give them a clear mind, a warm heart, calmness in the midst of turmoil, reassurance in times of discouragement, and Your presence always."[44] The delivery of the prayer by the eighty-six-year-old preacher—who had prayed with every president since Harry Truman, and who stood before the assembled worshippers at the twilight of his ministry—provided a memorable moment.

A week later President Bush would appear for the fifth time as President at the fifty-third annual National Prayer Breakfast, asserting that "prayer has always been one of the great equalizers in American life."[45] He spoke of the devastating tsunami in the Indian Ocean and the generous response of the American people in prayer and in financial support, as well as of the miracles he had seen in office through the power of prayer. The breakfast provided a setting that included prominent figures from across the religious and political spectrum, including Senator Dianne Feinstein of California, who is Jewish; Senator Hillary Rodham Clinton of New York, who is Methodist; and even Senator John Kerry, who is Catholic. It was, as always, a nonpartisan affair and gave the several thousand who attended the chance to, in the words of the President, "thank God for his great blessings in one voice, regardless of our backgrounds."[46]

JUST HOW AMERICANS have reached out through prayer for answers in their daily lives has been captured in many different ways throughout the history of America. In April 2003, just as the war in Iraq was being launched, *The New York Times* published a series of visually stunning photographs of American men, women, and children of different faiths in prayer. The pictures were taken by the celebrated photographer Gueorgui Pinkhassov, a Bukharan Jew living in Paris, who was commissioned for his unique vantage as a foreigner and gifted artist.

In one photograph Pinkhassov framed four women in a beauty parlor in Cross City, Florida, one woman with curlers in her hair sitting under a dryer and holding hands with the others in prayer. Evoking the sentiments of Puritan America's Cotton Mather, the owner, Penny Robinson, confided to Pinkhassov how she often prays for her customers "right in the middle of a haircut, and they don't even know it," particularly when they have "something wrong with them."[47] There was also a portrait of little children in a Tallahassee Sunday-school room, each absorbed in thoughtful prayer. One child is praying for an uncle on the front lines in Iraq. Another is asking God to help her grandmother get better. Still another hopes that God will help him find his lost dog.

Summarizing the cross-cultural, cross-country photo spread, the editors of the *Times* wrote:

If other countries have similarly high numbers of believers . . . only America combines such intense religious devotion with such wide religious diversity. Amid all the nation's beliefs, one common practice stands out: whatever their religion, Americans pray a great deal. According to a Gallup poll, at least three-quarters of Americans pray every day. Stressful times have often been prayerful times, and the war in Iraq, with all its religious overtones, is not the exception: another poll indicates that 81 percent of Americans have prayed for peace in recent weeks.[48]

Americans have grown more conscious, more empathetic, but also more wary of those who do not share their religious views. In turn, the great common denominator of prayer has provided a window into the hearts, minds, and, at times, souls of others. As Librarian of Congress James H. Billington observed months before the September attacks, "If we do not learn to listen to other people when they are whispering prayers in their sanctuaries, we may have to meet them later when they are howling war cries over a battlefield."[49]

At the same time, prayer, particularly in the American context, has had the remarkable ability to open the door to two of life's most precious commodities—tolerance and understanding.

THE FUTURE OF AMERICAN PRAYER ultimately falls to the generation now coming of age. The potential of that future can be seen in several men and women, all under thirty, whose lives are inextricably linked to prayer. There are young people like Dmitriy Salita from Flatbush, New York, a Ukrainian émigré and one of the most promising boxers of his generation. Praying daily in the centuries-old traditions of his ultra-Orthodox Jewish faith, a devotion he never had before settling in the United States, he refuses to fight on Friday evenings or on Saturdays so that he can observe the Sabbath and spend significant time in prayer. "I have a personal relationship with God that I won't compromise," he has declared.[50] Amazed by Salita's relentlessness in the ring, his seventy-six-year-old African-American boxing coach, Jimmy O'Pharrow, has said of his protégé, "Kid looks Russian, prays Jewish, and fights black."[51]

There also is Devi Sridhar, who at the age of eighteen became the youngest American ever to be selected a Rhodes scholar. A practicing Hindu, she has found prayer to be an indispensable part of her life, a devotion she learned from her father. "Prayer is not an impersonal ritual. It becomes a daily lifeline that opens doors to the future. My father used to gather the family together in the living room after dinner, and we would pray in the tradition of our Hindu faith. Each child was given the name of a god or goddess as our special guardian and it was to that deity to whom we showed particular fealty in our prayers."[52] While working with autistic children and co-authoring the book *Puzzle Your Way through Indian Mythology* to teach young people about Indian culture, she continues to cling to the prayers of her ancestors.

For former Pennsylvania Representative Jeff Coleman, the son of an ordained Presbyterian minister father and a Filipino-American mother, prayer is much more than rote ritual. Defeating an entrenched incumbent fresh out of college, Coleman became one of the youngest legislators in state history. "There has not been a day since I was a young boy in which I haven't prayed," he has said. "In time it has only grown more important to me. In fact, I am not sure I would have run for office in the first place if it had not been for my ability to pray and to turn to God for guidance. I had to make sure that I was doing the right thing, and prayer allowed me to go through that critical thought process."[53] He also realized after being elected that prayer afforded him the chance to reflect on his public service and to examine his conscience every day to ensure that he represents his constituents to the best of his God-given ability. It is through prayer that he decided to leave a safe seat and take on a new career in broadcasting.

Sister Clare Matthiass of the Franciscan Sisters of the Renewal in the South Bronx first made an indelible impression on hundreds of people when she walked across the United States to show her support for the homeless and other forgotten people in American society. During each step of the journey, she prayed for endurance and for the chance to touch an important nerve in the people she encountered, making them aware of the less fortunate. "To combine prayer with the simple human expression of love for other people is a powerful drive. To join others who share that same commitment day in day out continues to be the greatest blessing in my life." Dressed in the traditional habit of a nun, the exuberant daughter of an air-force pilot never dreamed that she would be working in the South Bronx among the poor and among those largely forgotten by family, friends, and society. "When helping others, I think it is important to pray for them under your breath and to ask God to give you the patience, direction, and ultimate grace to make sure you can serve God's will to make a difference in their lives and your own."[54]

Finally, there is the story of Khadeeja Abdullah, a student at UCLA who was profoundly affected by the events of September 11, horrified by both the loss of life and the hijacking of her Muslim faith by terrorists claiming that they alone represented the true Islam. In the days after the attacks, she and her family began to organize prayer vigils in San Bernardino, California, for people of all religions in their community to instill an understanding of the true beliefs of the Muslim faith and to share in the grief of the nation. Given her public efforts to bring Americans together through prayer, organizers of a major interfaith service at the Roman Catholic cathedral Our Lady of the Angels in Los Angeles invited her to offer her own prayer.

Approaching the front of the sanctuary, wearing the head scarf and modest clothing of her faith, Abdullah introduced her prayer by first speaking of "getting through this test," realizing that "God works in mysterious ways." She then began:

> *Dear God, with your compassion, answer our prayer . . . We have seen the very worst that we are capable of—vengeance, greed, murder, senseless slaughter, scapegoating. And we have seen the very best that we are capable of—courage, compassion, service, faith, heroism, community, love . . . We are hopeful to see what we are truly made of. Strengthen and make us better people . . . Dear God, with your compassion, answer our prayer.*[55]

The prayers of many of the country's newest generation are as genuine and as devout as those of America's forebears.

In today's world American prayer continues to evolve in meeting the demands of modern living. Prayer chapels are erected in airports and urban malls while prayer groups are organized in corporate workplaces to handle the ever-increasing needs of a fast-paced society. Megachurches are growing into large spaces, utilizing the latest audio and video technology to enhance the experience of prayer. Artists of all kinds are trying to find fresh ways to project spiritual relevance, shaping prayer into creative expressions that are at the same time both expansive and intimate.

And yet, as much as new venues and approaches toward enhancing the spiritual life of individuals have been developed, American prayer at the outset of the twenty-first century is really nothing more than a manifestation of its past. Prayer revivals that first began in Cane Ridge, Kentucky, in 1801 have now expanded into stadiums and open fields to accommodate literally hundreds of thousands of prayer-seeking Americans. From gospel-rocking adolescents in one setting to adult males in another, there is an overwhelming desire to come together to find greater meaning in what has been dubbed "the purpose-driven life." The prayers that have opened daily sessions of both houses of Congress since 1774, when the Founding Fathers first met in Philadelphia, are now being offered by clergy of all faiths, including Jews, Hindus, and Muslims. Furthermore, they are being covered in real time on radio, cable television, and computer linkups to millions of homes. Even political parties seeking to expand electoral bases find that modern-day relevance can be achieved in part by underscoring the deeply held spiritual values of the American people, demonstrated so profoundly through the act of prayer. Few defining moments in political campaigns can be created without saluting the flag and invoking God's providence.

THE GREAT IRONY in the United States today is that while prayer has long played a central role in the life of America, it too often has become a subject best publicly avoided. Even though prayer has pervaded American life consciously and unconsciously throughout history, many people have difficulty discussing it. To paraphrase Nathan Pusey, the late president of Harvard University, we will know that we have become a mature nation when we can speak freely about the importance of prayer in American life without fear of adolescent embarrassment. It is reckless to view prayer solely as an appendage of religion, to see it as a divisive, polarizing force in American society. For it is prayer that has infused Americans with a sense of their spiritual identity in a world too often rocked by a lack of moral grounding.

To reduce America to pure vanilla, signifying both everything and nothing, ignores the true intentions of the Founding Fathers and flies in the face of recorded history, particularly when it comes to the subject of prayer. The argument that religious diversity should prevent the public recitation of prayer given the differences between, say, Jews and Christians becomes a fool's errand. After all, the followers of Jesus Christ have been divided among the Orthodox, Catholics, and Protestants. The children of Israel are defined as Hasidic, Orthodox, Conservative, and Reformed. The heirs to Muhammad identify themselves as Shia, Sunni, and Sufi. Even long-established faiths cannot agree on the proper road to salvation. They do agree, however, on the need and utility of prayer both spiritually and temporally in the world today. Much in the way that America's motto "E Pluribus Unum" (one out of many) symbolizes unity out of diversity, prayer affords an opportunity to recognize how Americans, despite their diversity, are unified in their spirituality with one another and with a higher being.

While each person may have a deeply held faith based on religious conviction, he or she cannot dismiss the inherent sanctity of all good people the world over. As Kahlil Gibran reflected in his "Voice of the Poet," "I love you when you bow in your mosque, kneel in your temple, pray in your church. For you and I are sons of one religion, and it is the spirit."

Like early Native Americans, who melded prayer into their public and private lives without the benefit of religion in the traditional sense, Americans today must understand prayer as a unique, unifying force. Prayer is not the exclusive preserve of any one faith. True prayer challenges individuals to elevate their sights to a higher power to whom they are accountable and reminds them of their ties to the destinies of those around them.

Every U.S. president, no matter how religious he may or may not have been personally, has always found it vital to invoke the name of God and to ask publicly for God's blessings and guidance on behalf of the country. At a time when the United States stands alone, unparalleled in its economic, political, and military strength, the nation implicitly recognizes that it is accountable for its actions to a higher power. It is not hubris to believe in a God who expects human creation to pray and to live, in the words of Abraham Lincoln, "by the better angels of our nature."[56]

INTRODUCTION

1. G. K. Chesterton, *The Collected Works of G.K. Chesterton* (San Francisco: Ignatius, 1990), 21:41–45.

2. Lionel Casson, *Libraries in the Ancient World* (New Haven: Yale University Press, 2001), 4.

3. Luther Standing Bear, *Land of the Spotted Eagle* (Omaha: University of Nebraska Press, 1978), 38.

4. J. C. Penney, *Fifty Years with the Golden Rule* (New York: Harper, 1950), 83.

1. THE INHABITANTS, EXPLORERS, AND SETTLERS

Epigraph: Kristen Marée Cleary, ed., *Native American Wisdom* (New York: Barnes & Noble Books, 1996), 22.

1. Joel Sherzer, "A Richness of Voices," in *America in 1492: The World of the Indian Peoples before the Arrival of Columbus*, ed. Alvin M. Josephy, Jr. (New York: Vintage Books, 1993), 251.

2. Nancy Wood, ed., *The Serpent's Tongue: Prose, Poetry, and Art of the New Mexico Pueblos* (New York: Dutton Books, 1997), 206.

3. Kent Nerbuen, ed. *The Soul of an Indian and Other Writings from Ohiyesa* (Novato, California: New World Library, 2001), 12–15.

4. Thomas Benton Williams, *The Soul of the Red Man* (Oklahoma City, 1937).

5. Nerbuen, *The Soul of an Indian and Other Writings from Ohiyesa*, 10.

6. Henry Rink, *Tales and Traditions of the Eskimo* (London: Private printing, 1875), 37.

7. John Hollander, ed., *American Poetry: The Nineteenth Century* (New York: Library of America, 1993), 2:661.

8. Edwin S. Gaustad, ed., *A Documentary History of Religion in America to the Civil War* (Grand Rapids: William B. Eerdmans Publishing, 1982), 9–10.

9. Ibid., 32.

10. Dinitia Smith, "Collector Assembles a Rare Quartet of Bibles," *New York Times*, June 10, 2002, A17.

11. Samuel Eliot Morison, "Admiral of the Ocean Sea," *Atlantic Monthly*, 168, no. 6 (Dec. 1941): 111.

12. Ibid., 663.

13. Samuel Eliot Morison, *Admiral of the Ocean Sea: A Life of Christopher Columbus* (Boston: Little, Brown, 1942), 172.

14. Ibid., 173.

15. Ibid., 182.

16. Morison, "Admiral of the Ocean Sea," 666.

17. The Log of Christopher Columbus, trans. Robert H. Fuson (Camden, Maine: International Marine Publishing, 1987), 72.

18. Samuel E. Morison, ed. and trans., Journals and Other Documents on the Life and Voyages of Christopher Columbus (New York: Heritage, 1963), 64.

19. Samuel Eliot Morison, The European Discovery of America: The Northern Voyages A.D. 500–1600 (New York: Oxford University Press, 1971), 142.

20. Ibid., 343.

21. Ibid., 143.

22. Philip Barbour, ed., The Complete Works of Captain John Smith (Chapel Hill: University of North Carolina Press, 1986), 3:86.

23. Ibid.

24. Samuel Bawlf, The Secret Voyage of Sir Francis Drake, 1577–1580 (New York: Walker and Company, 2003), prologue.

25. Deborah Cassidi, Favourite Prayers (New York: Cassell, 1998), 13.

26. James Dalton Morrison, ed., Masterpieces of Religious Verse (New York: Harper, 1948), 243.

27. Edwin S. Gaustad, Sworn on the Altar of God (Grand Rapids: William B. Eerdmans Publishing, 1996), 2.

28. Perry Miller, Errand in the Wilderness (Cambridge: Harvard University Press, 1956), 107.

29. TK, For the Colony of Virginie Brittania (London: Lawes, Divine, Morall & Martiall, 1612), 90–96.

30. Sydney E. Ahlstrom, A Religious History of the American People (New Haven: Yale University Press, 1972), 91.

31. George B. Cheever, The Journal of the Pilgrims at Plymouth, in New England, in 1620 (New York: John Wiley, 1848), 146.

32. Jerome B. Agel, ed., We, the People: Great Documents of the American Nation (New York: Barnes & Noble Books, 1997), 4.

33. Robert M. Bartlett, The Faith of the Pilgrims (New York: United Church Press, 1978), 269.

34. Edwin Scott Gaustad and Philip L. Barlow, New Historical Atlas of Religion in America (New York: Oxford University Press, 2001), 24.

35. Francis J. Bremer, John Winthrop: America's Forgotten Founding Father (New York: Oxford University Press, 2003), 29.

36. John Winthrop, "A Model of Christian Charity (1630)," Collections of the Massachusetts Historical Society (Boston, 1838), Third Series, 44.

37. Hill, Salem Witch Trials, 292.

38. Ibid., 196.

39. Michael Schmidt, Lives of the Poets (New York: Knopf, 1999), 244.

40. Leonard Bernstein, Songfest: A Cycle of American Poems for Six Singers and Orchestra (New York: Amberson Enterprises/Boosey & Hawkes, 1977).

41. Nancy Sullivan, ed., Treasury of American Poetry (New York: Barnes & Noble Books, 1978), 7.

42. Hambrick-Stowe, Early New England Meditative Poetry (Mahwah, New Jersey: Paulist Press, 1988), 79–80.

43. Richard Dunn, ed., *The Papers of William Penn,* 5 vols. (Philadelphia: University of Pennsylvania Press, 1981–87), 108.

44. James H. Hutson, *Religion and the Founding of the American Republic* (Washington, D.C.: Library of Congress, 1998), 12.

45. Mary Batchelor, *The Doubleday Prayer Collection* (New York: Doubleday, 1996), 451.

46. William Evans and Thomas Evans, eds., *The Friends' Library: Journals, Doctrinal Treatises, and Other Writings* (Philadelphia: Joseph Rakestraw, 1837), 219.

47. Batchelor, *The Doubleday Prayer Collection,* 3.

48. Richard S. Dunn and Mary Maples Dunn, eds., *The Papers of William Penn,* vol. ii, 1680–1684 (Philadelphia: University of Pennsylvania Press, 1982), 590–591.

49. Kenneth Scott Latourette, *A History of the Expansion of Christianity,* 7 vols. (New York: Harper & Brothers, 1937–45), 3:311.

50. Robert V. Hine and John Mack Faragher, *The American West: A New Interpretive History* (New Haven: Yale University Press, 2000), 49.

51. M. N. L. Couve de Murville, *The Man Who Founded California: The Life of Blessed Junipero Serra* (San Francisco: Ignatius Press, 2000), 58–59.

52. Nicolás Kanellos, ed., *Herencia: The Anthology of Hispanic Literature of the United States* (New York: Oxford University Press, 2002), 37.

53. Ibid.

54. Ibid., 38.

55. Juan B. Rael, *The New Mexican Alabado* (Stanford: Stanford University Press, 1951), 49–51.

56. Ibid., 128.

57. Owen Felltham, *Resolves* (London: Henry Seile, 1628).

2. THE PREACHERS: 1640–1750

Epigraph: Jonathan Edwards, *An Humble Attempt to Promote Explicit Agreement and Visible Union of God's People throughout the World in Extraordinary Prayer for the Revival of Religion and the Advancement of Christ's Kingdom on Earth, pursuant to Scripture Promises and Prophecies concerning the Last Time* (Boston, 1747), 5.

1. Michael Warner, ed., *American Sermons: The Pilgrims to Martin Luther King, Jr.* (New York: Library of America, 1999), 151.

2. Horton Davies, *The Worship of the American Puritans, 1629–1730* (New York: Peter Lang, 1990), 133.

3. Ibid.

4. Charles E. Hambrick-Stowe, *The Practice of Piety: Puritan Devotional Disciplines in Seventeenth-Century New England* (Chapel Hill: University of North Carolina Press, 1982), 103–4.

5. Ibid., 25.

6. Daniel Dorchester, *Christianity in the United States* (New York: Hunt and Eaton, 1890), 166.

7. Edmund W. Sinnott, *Meetinghouse and Church in Early New England* (New York: McGraw-Hill, 1963), 9.

8. Alice Morse Earle, *The Sabbath in Puritan New England* (New York: Scribner's Sons, 1891), 79.

9. Ibid., 66–67.

10. Ibid., 77–78.

11. Edwin S. Gaustad and Leigh Schmidt, *The Religious History of America* (San Francisco: HarperCollins, 2002), 53.

12. Ibid., 136.

13. Richard W. Clement, *The Book in America* (Golden, Colo.: Fulcrum Publications, 1996), 7–9.

14. Ibid., 24.

15. Stephen A. Marini, *Sacred Song in America: Religion, Music, and Public Culture* (Chicago: University of Chicago Press, 2001), 75.

16. Zoltán Haraszti, *The Enigma of the Bay Psalm Book* (Chicago: University of Chicago Press, 1956), 70–71.

17. William Warren Sweet, *The Story of Religion in America* (New York: Harper, 1950), 57.

18. Alan Heimert and Andrew Delbanco, *The Puritans in America: A Narrative Anthology* (Cambridge, Mass.: Harvard University Press, 1985), 294.

19. Ibid., 297–98.

20. Allen Mandelbaum and Robert D. Richardson, Jr., eds., *Three Centuries of American Poetry* (New York: Bantam Books, 1999), 34.

21. Davies, *Worship of the American Puritans*, 146–47.

22. Kenneth Ballard Murdock, *Increase Mather: The Foremost American Puritan* (Cambridge, Mass.: Harvard University Press, 1925), 303.

23. Heimert and Delbanco, *Puritans in America*, 324–26.

24. Gorton Carruth and Eugene Ehrlich, *The Giant Book of American Quotations* (New York: Portland House, 1988), 82.

25. Marilynne K. Roach, *The Salem Witch Trials: A Day-by-Day Chronicle of a Community under Siege* (New York: Cooper Square Press, 2002), 547.

26. *The New England Primer* (Boston: Massachusetts Sabbath School Society, 1813), 17.

27. Ibid.

28. Ibid., 64.

29. Warner, *American Sermons*, 900.

30. Ibid.

31. Jonathan Edwards, *Religious Affections* (Portland: Multnomah Press, 1984), 105.

32. Warner, *American Sermons*, 900.

33. Ibid.

34. Mark Water, ed., *The New Encyclopedia of Christian Quotations* (Grand Rapids: Baker Books, 2000), 781.

35. Perry Miller, *Errand into the Wilderness* (Cambridge, Mass.: Harvard University Press, 1956), 143.

36. Oswald J. Smith, ed., *David Brainerd: His Message for Today* (London: Marshall, Morgan & Scott, 1949), 77.

37. Ibid., 35–36.

38. George Marsden, *Jonathan Edwards: A Life* (New Haven: Yale University Press, 2003), 325.

39. *George Whitefield's Journals* (London: Banner of Truth Trust, 1960), 58.

40. Harry S. Stout, *The Divine Dramatist: George Whitefield and the Rise of Modern Evangelicalism* (Grand Rapids: William B. Eerdmans Publishing, 1991), 127.

41. John Wesley, *The Journal of the Rev. John Wesley*, ed. Nehemiah Curnock (London: Epworth, 1938), 1:385–86.

42. George Whitefield's Journals, 79.

43. Luke Tyerman, *The Life of the Reverend George Whitefield* (London: Hodder and Stoughton, 1876), vol. 1, 538–39.

44. Edwin S. Gaustad, *Faith of Our Fathers* (San Francisco: Harper & Row, 1987), 87.

45. Stephen Mansfield, *Forgotten Founding Father* (Nashville: Highland Books, 2001), 12.

46. *George Whitefield's Journals*, 489–90.

47. James H. Hutson, *Religion and the Founding of the American Republic* (Washington, D.C.: Library of Congress, 1998), 29–30.

48. Luke Tyerman, *The Life of the Rev. George Whitefield* (London: Hodder and Stoughton, 1877), 2:596.

49. Samuel Davies, *Miscellaneous Poems, Chiefly on Divine Subjects* (Williamsburg, Va. William Hunter, 1752), 22.

50. Ibid., 5.

51. Samuel Davies, *Sermons on Important Subjects* (Baltimore: Mason L. Weems, 1816), 209–27.

3. THE VISIONARIES: 1750–1800

Epigraph: John C. Fitzgerald, ed., *The Writings of George Washington*, vol. 5, May 1776–August 1776 (Washington, D.C.: Government Printing Office), 43.

1. Thomas Paine, *The American Crisis* (Norwich, Connecticut: John Trumbull, 1776), 3.

2. Michael Warner, ed., *American Sermons: The Pilgrims to Martin Luther King, Jr.* (New York: Library of America, 1999), 380.

3. David McCullough, *John Adams* (New York: Simon and Schuster, 2001), 78.

4. Theodore Roosevelt, *Gouverneur Morris* (Boston: Houghton, Mifflin & Co, 1898), 251.

5. Thomas Paine, *Common Sense* (Philadelphia: R. Bell, 1776), Introduction.

6. Ibid., 10.

7. Ibid., 31.

8. Henry Mayer, *A Son of Thunder: Patrick Henry and the American Republic* (New York: Grove Press, 1991), 160.

9. Jerome B. Agel, ed., *We, The People: Great Documents of the American Nation* (New York: Barnes and Noble Books, 1997), 10–13.

10. Mayer, 246.

11. Edwin S. Gaustad and Philip L. Barlow, *New Historical Atlas of Religion in America* (New York: Oxford University Press, 2001), 8.

12. L. H. Butterfield, ed., *The Adams Papers*, vol. 1, December 1761–May 1776 (Cambridge, Mass.: Belknap Press, 1963), 156.

13. *Journals of the Continental Congress*, vol. 1, 1774 (Washington, D.C.: U.S. Government Printing Office, 1904), 27.

14. L. H. Butterfield, ed., *Diary and Autobiography of John Adams*, vol 2, 1771–1781 (Cambridge, Mass.: Belknap Press, 1961), 126.

15. George L. Clark, *Silas Deane, A Connecticut Leader in the American Revolution* (New York: G.P. Putnam's Sons, 1913), 27.

16. *Journals of the Continental Congress*, vol. 1, 1774, 27.

17. L. H. Butterfield, 216.

18. Ibid., 254.

19. *Journals of the Continental Congress, vol. 5, 1776* (Washington, D.C.: U.S. Government Printing Office, 1906), 529–30.

20. Benjamin Dorr, *A Historical Account of Christ Church, Philadelphia* (Philadelphia: R.S.H. George, 1841), 180–81.

21. Deborah Mathias Gough, *Christ Church, Philadelphia: The Nation's Church in a Changing City* (Philadelphia: The University of Pennsylvania Press, 1995), 139.

22. L. H. Butterfield, ed., *Adams Family Correspondence, vol. 2, June, 1776–December, 1778,* 359.

23. Gough, 139.

24. *Journals of the Continental Convention, vol. 5, 1776,* 510–15.

25. William Abbott and Dorothy Twohig, eds., *The Papers of George Washington,* vol. 9, *March–June 1777* (Charlottesville, Va: University of Virginia Press, 1999), 553 and 644–45.

26. Derek H. Davis, *Religion and the Continental Congress 1774–1789* (New York: Oxford University Press, 2000), 83–84.

27. Ibid., 83.

28. David Jones, "Defensive War is a Just Cause Sinless," in Peter N. Carroll, ed., *Religion and the Coming of the American Revolution* (Waltham, Mass.: Gwinn-Blaidsel, 1970), 147.

29. James H. Hutson, *Religion and the Founding of the American Republic* (Washington, D.C.: Library of Congress, 1998), 46.

30. Ibid., 46.

31. Martha L. Stollman, *John Witherspoon: Parson, Politician, Patriot* (Philadelphia: Westminster Press, 1976), 172.

32. Abbott and Twohig, eds., *The Papers of George Washington,* vol. 9, *March–June, 1777,* 854–55.

33. Ibid., 855.

34. Hans Nathan, ed., *The Complete Works of William Billings* (Boston: American Historical Society and the Colonial Society of Massachusetts, 1977), 248.

35. Kenneth Cain Kinghorn, *The Heritage of American Methodism* (New York: Abingdon Press, 1999), 74.

36. Marilyn Gombosi, *A Day of Solemn Thanksgiving* (Chapel Hill, N.C.: University of North Carolina Press, 1977), 42.

37. Hans Nathan, *The Complete Works of William Billings* (Boston: American Historical Society and the Colonial Society of Massachusetts, 1977), 248.

38. David C. Humphrey, *From King's College to Columbia: 1746–1800* (New York: Columbia University Press, 1976), 158.

39. Leonard W. Labaree, ed., *The Papers of Benjamin Franklin,* vol. 4, *June 1–June 30, 1753* (New Haven, Conn: Yale University Press, 1961), 146.

40. F. B. Dexter, *Biographical Sketches of the Graduates of Yale College* vol. 2 (New York: Henry Holt & Co., 1896), 3–4.

41. Thomas Jefferson Wertenbaker, *Princeton: 1746–1896* (Princeton, N.J.: Princeton University Press, 1946), 189.

42. Ibid., 243.

43. Humphrey, 160.

44. Willard Sterne Randall, *Alexander Hamilton: A Life* (New York: HarperCollins, 2003), 73, and Hercules Mulligan and Robert Troup, "Narrative," *William and Mary Quarterly,* 3 ser., 4 (1947), 213.

45. Leonard W. Labaree, *The Papers of Benjamin Franklin*, vol 3, *January 1, 1745 through June 30, 1750* (New Haven: Yale University Press, 1961), 226–27 and Robert Troup, "Narrative," *William and Mary Quarterly*, 3 ser., 4 (1947), 213.

46. E. H. Scott, ed., *Journal of the Constitutional Convention* (Chicago: Albert, Scott & Company, 1893), 259–60.

47. Ibid., 260.

48. Albert Henry Smyth, ed., *Writings of Benjamin Franklin*, vol. 9 (New York: MacMillan, 1907), 601.

49. Leonard W. Labaree, ed., *The Papers of Benjamin Franklin*, vol. 2, *January 1, 1735–December 31, 1744* (New Haven: Yale University Press, 1960), 140, and vol. 7. *October 1, 1756—March 31, 1758* (New Haven: Yale University Press, 1963), 81.

50. Leonard W. Labaree, *The Papers of Benjamin Franklin*, vol. 1, *January 6, 1706–December 31, 1734* (New Haven: Yale University Press, 1959), 104.

51. Leonard W. Labaree, *The Papers of Benjamin Franklin*, vol. 15, *January 1–December 31, 1768* (New Haven: Yale University Press, 1959), 299–303.

52. Ibid., 301.

53. William B. Willcox, ed., *The Papers of Benjamin Franklin*, vol. 19, *January 1–December 31, 1772* (New Haven: Yale University Press, 1963), 30–31.

54. Ibid., 105.

55. William B. Willcox, ed., *The Papers of Benjamin Franklin*, vol. 20, *January 1–December 31, 1773* (New Haven: Yale University Press, 1976), 345.

56. Benjamin Franklin, *Autobiography* (New York: A. L. Burt Publishers, 1900), 105.

57. Scott, 259.

58. Jared Sparks, ed., *The Writings of George Washington*, vol. 12 (Boston: Ferdinand Andrews, 1838), 399.

59. Ibid., 399.

60. John C. Fitzpatrick, ed., *The Diaries of George Washington*, vol. 2, *1771–1785* (New York: Houghton Mifflin Co, 1925), 153.

61. John C. Fitzpatrick, ed., *The Writings of George Washington*, vol. 4, *Oct 1775–April 1776* (Washington, D.C.: U.S. Government Printing Office, 1931) 369–70, and vol. 5, *Oct 21, 1779–Feb 9, 1780*, 189–90.

62. John C. Fitzpatrick, ed. *The Writings of George Washington*, vol. 12, *June 1, 1778–September 30, 1778* (Washington, D.C.: U.S. Government Printing Office, 1931), 343.

63. Hutson, 76.

64. Sparks, *The Writings of George Washington*, vol. 8 (Boston: American Stationers Co., 1838), 452.

65. William Abbott and Dorothy Twohig, eds., *The Papers of George Washington*, vol 2., *January 1735–December 1744* (Charlottesville, Va.: University of Virginia Press, 1987), 152–53.

66. Sparks, *The Writings of George Washington*, vol. 10 (Boston: Ferdinand Andrews, 1838), 464.

67. William Abbott and Dorothy Twohig, eds., *The Papers of George Washington*, vol. 4, *September 1789–January 1790* (Charlottesville, Va.: University of Virginia Press, 1993), 131–32.

68. Correspondence between Abigail Adams and Louisa Catherine Adams, January 3, 1818, reel 442, Adams Papers, the Massachusetts Historical Society, Boston.

69. Charles Adams, ed., *Letters of John Adams Addressed to His Wife* (New York: Hurd & Houghton, 1841), 267.

70. Charles Adams, *The Works of John Adams*, vol. 9 (Boston: Little, Brown & Company, 1850–1856), 174–75.

71. McCullough, 543.

72. John A. Schutz and Douglas Adair, eds., *The Spur of Fame: Dialogues of John Adams and Benjamin Rush, 1805–1813* (San Marino, California: The Huntington Library, 1966), 224–25.

4. THE DEVELOPERS: 1800–1840

Epigraph: Alexis de Tocqueville, *Democracy in America*, eds. J. P. Mayer and Max Lerner (New York: Harper & Row, 1966), 271–72.

1. Papers of Melville Weston Fuller, manuscript, box 15, Library of Congress.

2. Ibid.

3. H. A. Washington, ed., *The Writings of Thomas Jefferson* (Washington, D.C.: Taylor and Maury, 1854), 5.

4. Ibid., 319.

5. Carl Sferrazza Anthony, *America's First Families* (New York: Touchstone, 2000), 218.

6. Thomas Jefferson to John Adams, Oct. 12, 1813; in Lester J. Cappon, *The Adams-Jefferson Letters*, vol. 11, *1812–1826* (Chapel Hill: University of North Carolina Press, 1959), 384.

7. Robert A. Rutland, *The Papers of James Madison*, vol. 1, March 1–September 30, 1809 (Charlottesville: University of Virginia, 1984), 17–18.

8. "Information," St. John's Episcopal Church, Lafayette Square, Washington, D.C., 2003.

9. James D. Richardson, ed., *A Compilation of the Messages and Papers of the Presidents 1789–1897*, vol. 1 (Washington, D.C.: Authority of Congress, 1898), 498.

10. Stanislaus M. Hamilton, ed., *The Writings of James Monroe*, vol. vi, 1817–1823 (New York: G. P. Putnam and Sons, 1893–1903), 2–6.

11. Grant Wacker, *Religion in Nineteenth Century America* (New York: Oxford University Press, 2000), 38.

12. William Henry Harding, *Finney's Life and Lectures* (London: Oliphants, 1956), 15.

13. Ibid., 14.

14. Conrad Wright and Richard C. Wade, eds., *Religion in American Life* (New York: Houghton Mifflin, 1972), 64.

15. Edwin S. Gaustad and Leigh Schmidt, *The Religious History of America* (San Francisco: HarperCollins, 2002), 147–48.

16. Ibid., 62.

17. John Rogers, *The Biography of Elder Barton Wamen Stone* (Cincinnati: J. A. and V. P. James, 1847), 3.

18. Henry Adams, *History of the United States of America during the First Administration of Thomas Jefferson* (New York: Charles Scribner's Sons, 1921), 2:191.

19. Harold C. Syrett, ed., *The Papers of Alexander Hamilton* (New York: Columbia University Press, 1961–1987), 20:545.

20. Ron Chernow, *Alexander Hamilton* (New York: Penguin Press, 2004), 660.

21. Willard Sterne Randall, *Alexander Hamilton: A Life* (New York: HarperCollins, 2003), 4–5.

22. Joseph Muller, ed., *The Star-Spangled Banner: Words and Music Issued Between 1814–1864* (New York: G. A. Baker, 1935), 50–51.

23. Irvin Molotsky, *The Flag, the Poet, and the Song: The Story of the Star-Spangled Banner* (New York: Dutton, 2001), 215–16.

24. Allen Mandelbaum and Robert D. Richardson, Jr., eds., *Three Centuries of American Poetry* (New York: Bantam Books, 1999), 80.

25. Ralph Emerson Browns, *The New Dictionary of Thoughts*, rev. ed. (New York: Standard Book Company, 1965), 505.

26. *The New England Primer Improved; or, An Easy and Pleasant Guide to the Art of Reading; to which is added, The Assembly's Shorter Catechism* (Philadelphia: Hogan & Thompson, 1847), 19.

27. *Juvenile Devotion for Use in the Schools* (New York: J. Seymour, 1815), 2.

28. Ibid., 10.

29. Ibid., 11.

30. *A New Collection of Family Prayers and Offices of Devotion for Various Circumstances in Life; Carefully Selected from Those Pious Authors Jenks, Ven, and Palmer* (Greenfield, Mass., B.&J. Russell 1817), preface.

31. Mark A. Noll, *Protestants in America* (New York: Oxford University Press, 2000), 51.

32. Jeffrey Lee, *Opening the Prayer Book* (Boston: Cowley Publications, 1999), 65.

33. Levi Silliman Ives, *New Manual of Private Devotions* (New York: T. and J. Swords, 1831), table of contents.

34. Ibid., 123.

35. Ibid., 248–49.

36. Charles I. White, *Life of Mrs. Eliza A. Seton* (London: John Murphy and Company, 1856), 184.

37. Sarah Josepha Hale, "Our National Thanksgiving," *Godey's Lady's Book,* November 1858, 463.

38. John Galt, *Life and Studies of Benjamin West* (Philadelphia: Moses Thomas, 1816), 67.

39. Ibid., 73.

40. *Memoirs of the Life and Religious Labors of Edward Hicks* (Philadelphia: Merrihew and Thompson, 1851), 337.

41. Edward Hicks, "Sermon," *Quaker,* Aug. 19, 1827, 156.

42. Marshall B. Tymn, ed., *Thomas Cole's Poetry* (York, Pa.: Liberty Cap Books, 1972), 167.

43. David W. Stowe, *How Sweet the Sound: Music in the Spiritual Lives of Americans* (Cambridge, MA: Harvard University Press), 232.

44. W. Thomas Marrocco, *Music in America: An Anthology* (New York: W. W. Norton, 1964), 84–85.

45. Stephen J. Stein, *The Shaker Experience in America* (New Haven: Yale University Press, 1992), 413.

46. Cathy Newman, "The Shakers' Brief Eternity," *National Geographic,* April 1997, 319.

47. Stein, *Shaker Experience in America,* 413.

48. Seth Y. Wells, comp., *Millennial Praises* (Hancock, Mass.: Josiah Tallcott, Jr., 1813), preface.

49. Stein, 215.

50. Stein, 215.

51. Stein, *Shaker Experience in America,* 214–16.

52. Ibid., 217.

53. Daniel W. Patterson, *The Shaker Spiritual* (Mineola, N.Y.: Dover Publications, 2000), 372.

54. John A. Hostetler, *Amish Society* (Baltimore: Johns Hopkins University Press, 1963), 167.

55. Donald B. Kraybill, *The Riddle of Amish Culture* (Baltimore: Johns Hopkins University Press, 2001), 120.

56. Tocqueville, *Democracy in America*, 3.

57. Ibid., 266.

58. Ibid., 514.

59. William A. DeGregorio, *The Complete Book of U.S. Presidents* (Fort Lee, N.J.: Barricade Books, 2001), 93.

60. Thomas Fleming, "A Rainbow of Mercy," *Guideposts*, July 1994, 30–34.

61. McPherson, *"To the Best of My Ability,"* 335.

62. Arthur M. Schlesinger, Jr., *The Age of Jackson* (Boston: Little, Brown, 1945), 354.

63. Robert Remini, *Andrew Jackson and the Course of American Freedom* (New York: Harper & Row, 1981), 264.

64. McPherson, *"To the Best of My Ability,"* 337.

65. John S. Bassett, ed., *Correspondence of Andrew Jackson* (Washington, D.C.: Carnegie Institute of Washington, 1931), 289–90.

66. McPherson, *"To the Best of My Ability,"* 341.

67. Robert J. Branham, *Sweet Freedom's Song: "My Country 'Tis of Thee" and Democracy in America* (New York: Oxford University Press, 2002), 64.

68. Ibid.

5. THE DREAMERS: THE LEGACY OF SLAVERY

Epigraph: John Lovell, Jr., *Black Song: The Forge and the Flame* (New York: Macmillan, 1972), 236.

1. Lawrence W. Levine, *The Unpredictable Past: Explorations in American Cultural History* (New York: Oxford University Press, 1993), 82.

2. Albert J. Raboteau, *Slave Religion* (New York: Oxford University Press, 1980), 4.

3. James H. Cone, *The Spirituals and the Blues: An Interpretation* (New York: Seabury Press, 1972), 69–70.

4. "Slavery in the Pulpit of the Evangelical Alliance: An Address Delivered in London, England, on September 14, 1846," *Inquirer* (London), Sept. 19, 1846.

5. Frederick Douglass, *Autobiographies* (New York: Library of America, 1994), 59.

6. Ira Berlin, Marc Favreau, and Steven F. Miller, eds., *Remembering Slavery: African Americans Talk about Their Personal Experiences of Slavery and Emancipation* (New York: New Press in conjunction with the Library of Congress, 1998), xli.

7. Ibid., 86.

8. Peter Randolph, *Sketches of Slave Life* (Boston, 1855), 26.

9. Ibid., 276.

10. Ibid., 56.

11. Christina K. Schaefer, *Genealogical Encyclopedia of the Colonial Americas* (Baltimore: Genealogical Publishing Company, 1998), 623.

12. John Newton, *Amazing Grace* (New York: Hyperion, 1991), 3.

13. Jeffrey L. Sheler, "Say a Little Prayer for You," *U.S. News & World Report*, July 8–15, 2002, 31.

14. Ibid.

15. William Wells Brown, *The Anti-Slavery Harp* (Boston: Bela Marsh, 1849), 29.

16. James Weldon Johnson and J. Rosamond Johnson, *The Book of American Negro Spirituals* (New York: Viking Press, 1925), 142–43.

17. Raboteau, *Slave Religion,* 250.

18. Douglass, *Narrative of the Life,* 184.

19. Raboteau, *Slave Religion,* 244.

20. Eileen Southern, *The Music of Black Americans: A History* (New York: W. W. Norton, 1997), 227–31.

21. Andrew Ward, *Dark Midnight When I Rise: The Story of the Fisk Jubilee Singers* (New York: HarperCollins, 2000), 155–56.

22. *The Believer's Daily Treasure; or, Texts of Scripture, Arranged for Every Day in the Year* (London: Religious Tract Society, 1852), 5.

23. Moses Hogan, ed., *The Oxford Book of Spirituals* (New York: Oxford University Press, 2001), 234–36.

24. Howard Thurman, *Deep River, and the Negro Spiritual Speats of Life and Death* (Richmond, Ind.: Friends United Press, 1999), 26.

25. Johnson and Johnson, *Book of American Negro Spirituals,* ii 34.

26. Johnson and Johnson, *Book of American Negro Spirituals,* 183–84.

27. Ibid., 63–65.

28. Ward, *Dark Midnight When I Rise,* 113.

29. Richard Newman, *Go Down Moses* (New York: Clarkson Potter, 1998), 171.

30. Johnson and Johnson, *Book of American Negro Spirituals,* iii.

31. Ibid., i 100.

32. Berlin, Favreau, and Miller, *Remembering Slavery,* 184–85.

33. Kenneth H. Greenberg, ed., *The Confessions of Nat Turner and Related Documents* (New York: St. Martin's Press, 1996), 47–48.

34. Jean Humez, *Harriet Tubman: The Life and the Life Stories* (Madison: University of Wisconsin Press, 2003), 187.

35. Sarah Bradford, *Harriet Tubman: The Moses of Her People* (Gloucester, Mass.: P. Smith, 1981), 49–50.

36. Sarah H. Bradford, *Harriet Tubman: The Moses of Her People* (New York: George R. Lockwood and Son, 1886) 59–61.

37. Sarah H. Bradford, *Scenes in the Life of Harriet Tubman* (Auburn, New York: WJ Moses, 1869), 49.

38. Ibid., 703.

39. William Craft and Ellen Craft, *Running a Thousand Miles for Freedom,* in *Slave Narratives* (New York: Library of America, 2000), 725.

40. James Melvin Washington, *Conversations with God: Two Centuries of Prayers by African Americans* (New York: HarperCollins, 1994), 3–5. Some editing has been done due to the illegibility of the original copy of the prayer and to clarify the prayer's meaning.

41. Mark A. Noll, *A History of Christianity in the United States and Canada* (Grand Rapids: William B. Eerdmans Publishing, 1992), 201.

42. Nell Irvin Painter, ed., *Narrative of Sojourner Truth* (New York: Penguin Books, 1998), 47.

43. Ibid., 41.

44. Ibid., 47.

45. Ibid., 41.

46. Richard Allen, *The Life Experience and Gospel Labors of the Rt. Rev. Richard Allen* (1793; Nashville: Abingdon Press, 1983), 24.

47. Ibid., 25–26.

48. Sydney E. Ahlstrom, *A Religious History of the American People* (New Haven: Yale University Press, 1972), 709.

49. Absalom Jones, "A Thanksgiving Sermon," in *American Sermons: The Pilgrims to Martin Luther King, Jr.*, ed. Michael Warner (New York: Library of America, 1999), 544–45.

6. THE PATHFINDERS: 1840–1860

Epigraph: Henry Wadsworth Longfellow, *The Complete Poetical Works of Henry Wadsworth Longfellow* (Cambridge, Mass.: Riverside Press, 1893), 2.

1. John L. O'Sullivan, "The Great Nation of Futurity," *United States Democratic Review* 6, no. 23 (1839): 426.

2. William A. DeGregorio, *The Complete Book of U.S. Presidents* (Fort Lee, N.J.: Barricade Books, 2001), 140.

3. Richardson, James D., ed., *Compilation of the Messages and Papers of the Presidents*, 10 vols. (Washington D.C.: Government Printing Office, 1896–99) 4:1887.

4. John Tyler, July 10, 1843.

5. Earl Irvin West, "Religion in the Life of James K. Polk," *Tennessee Historical Quarterly* 26 (1967): 357–71.

6. Martha McBride Morrel, *"Young Hickory": The Life and Times of President James K. Polk* (New York: E. P. Dutton, 1949), 49.

7. Milo M. Quaife, ed., *The Diary of James K. Polk during His Presidency, 1845–1849* (Chicago: McClurg, 1910), 4:177.

8. Carl Sferrazza Anthony, *America's First Families* (New York: Touchstone, 2000), 218.

9. K. Jack Bauer, *Zachary Taylor: Soldier, Planter, Statesman of the Old West* (Baton Rouge: Louisiana State University Press, 1985), 268.

10. James D. Richardson, ed., *A Compilation of the Messages and Papers of the Presidents, 1789–1908*, vol v. (Washington, D.C.: Bureau of National Literature and Art, 1908), 64.

11. DeGregorio, *Complete Book of U.S. Presidents*, 198.

12. B. H. Roberts, ed., *History of the Church of Jesus Christ of Latter-Day Saints* (Salt Lake City: Deseret Book Co., 2nd ed., rev., 1964), vol. 1, 4–6.

13. Robert L. Millet, ed., *Joseph Smith: Selected Sermons and Writings* (New York: Paulist Press, 1989), 50.

14. Ibid., 48.

15. Fawn M. Brodie, *No Man Knows My History: The Life of Joseph Smith, the Mormon Prophet* (New York: Knopf, 1963), 432.

16. Horace E. Scudder, ed., *The Poems of Holmes* (Cambridge, Mass.: Riverside Press, 1923), 163.

17. James Dalton Morrison, ed., *Masterpieces of Religious Verse* (New York: Harper, 1948), 515.

18. Alfred Kazin, *God and the American Writer* (New York: Vintage Books, 1997), 3.

19. Herman Melville, *Moby-Dick, or, The Whale* (New York: Modern Library, 1957), 58–59.

20. David H. Battenfield, "The Source for the Hymn in *Moby-Dick*," *American Literature* 27 (November 1955): 393–96.

21. Herman Melville, *Romances of Herman Melville* (New York: Tudor Publishing, 1931), 548.

22. James Russell Lowell, *A Fable for Critics* (New York: G. P. Putnam, 1848), 62.

23. *Complete Works of Edgar Allan Poe* (Akron: Werner Company, 1908), 248–51.

24. Hervey Allen, *Israfel: The Life and Times of Edgar Allan Poe* (New York: Farrar & Rinehart, 1934), 675.

25. Walt Whitman, *Leaves of Grass* (Philadelphia: David McKay, 1900), 472–73.

26. Walt Whitman, *Notebooks and Unpublished Prose Manuscripts*, ed. Edward F. Grier, 6 vols. (New York: New York University Press, 1984), 1:353.

27. Whitman, *Leaves of Grass*, 116.

28. Edwin S. Gaustad, ed., *A Documentary History of Religion in America to the Civil War* (Grand Rapids: William B. Eerdmans Publishing, 1982), 340.

29. Ralph Waldo Emerson, *The Complete Essays and Other Writings* (New York: Modern Library, 1950), 163.

30. Robert D. Richardson, Jr., *Emerson: The Mind on Fire* (Berkeley: University of California Press, 1995), 69.

31. Ralph Waldo Emerson, *Essays* (Philadelphia: Henry Altemus, 1895), 70.

32. Henry David Thoreau, *A Week on the Concord and Merrimack Rivers*, in *The Writings of Henry David Thoreau* (New York: Houghton Mifflin, 1906), 1:408–9.

33. Ibid.

34. Henry David Thoreau, *Collected Essays and Poems* (New York: Library of America, 2001), 568.

35. Jones Very, *Selected Poems*, ed. Nathan Lyons (New Brunswick, N.J.: Rutgers University Press, 1966), 85.

36. *Congressional Globe*, 25th Congress, 3d Session, February 7, 1839, 167.

37. *The Life and Speeches of Henry Clay* (New York: Barnes and Burr, 1860), 2:664.

38. Sarah K. Bolton, *Famous American Statesmen* (New York: Crowell, 1925), 228.

39. Harriet Beecher Stowe, *Uncle Tom's Cabin* (New York: Houghton Mifflin, 1943), 439.

40. Mark Galli and Ted Olsen, eds., *131 Christians Everyone Should Know* (Nashville: Broadman & Holman, 2000), 133.

41. Annie Adams Fields, ed., *The Life and Letters of Harriet Beecher Stowe* (Boston: Houghton Mifflin, 1897), 269.

42. Edward W. Knappman, *Great American Trials* (Detroit: Visible Ink Press, 1994), 119.

43. Louis Ruchames, ed., *John Brown: The Making of a Revolutionary* (New York: Grosset & Dunlap, 1969), 162.

44. Richard Marius, ed., *The Columbia Book of Civil War Poetry* (New York: Columbia University Press, 1994), 120–21.

7. THE SOLDIERS: 1860–1870

Epigraph: Roy Basler, ed., *The Collected Works of Abraham Lincoln*, vol. 6, *1862–1863* (New Brunswick, N.J.: Rutgers University Press, 1953), 155–57.

1. Kenneth W. Osbeck, *101 Hymn Stories* (Grand Rapids: Kregel Publications, 1982), 135–36.

2. Ian Bradley, ed., *The Book of Hymns* (New York: Testament Books, 2000), 218–19.

3. Lynda Lasswell Crist, ed., *The Papers of Jefferson Davis*, vol. 7, 1861 (Baton Rouge: Louisiana State University, 1992), 18–22.

4. Ibid., 46–50.

5. Ronald C. White, Jr., *Lincoln's Greatest Speech: The Second Inaugural* (New York: Simon & Schuster, 2002), 102.

6. Steven E. Woodworth, *While God Is Marching On: The Religious World of Civil War Soldiers* (Lawrence, Kansas: University Press of Kansas, 2001), 166.

7. *Prayers Suitable for the Times in Which We Live* (Charleston, S.C.: Evans & Cogswell, 1861), 1.

8. Bradley, *Book of Hymns*, 357.

9. Ibid., 357–58.

10. Ibid., 358.

11. Casualties of U.S. Civil War, 1861–1865, U.S. Department of Veterans Affairs, Office of Public Affairs, 2004.

12. Henry Steele Commager, ed., *The Civil War Archive* (New York: Black Dog & Leventhal, 2000), 394–95.

13. H. M. Wharton, ed., *War Songs and Poems of the Southern Confederacy* (Edison, N.J.: Castle Books, 2000), 98–101.

14. Julia Ward Howe, "The Battle Hymn of the Republic," *Atlantic Monthly*, Feb. 1, 1862, vol ix, no. lii, p. 10.

15. Florence Mason Howe Hall, *The Story of the Battle Hymn of the Republic* (New York: Harper, 1916), 56–57.

16. Richard H. Schneider, *Taps: Notes from a Nation's Heart* (New York: Harper-Collins, 2002), 7–12.

17. Ibid., 12.

18. Woodworth, *While God Is Marching On*, 126.

19. U.S. Department of Veterans Affairs, Office of Public Affairs, 2004.

20. Woodworth, *While God Is Marching On*, 275–76.

21. Harold I. Gullan, *Faith of Our Mothers* (Grand Rapids: William B. Eerdmans Publishing, 2001), 110.

22. Randall M. Miller, Harry S. Stout, and Charles Reagan Wilson, eds., *Religion and the American Civil War* (New York: Oxford University Press, 1998), 25.

23. J. William Jones, *Christ in the Camp* (Harrisonburg, Va.: Sprinkle Publications, 1986), 53.

24. Lynda L. Crist, Mary S. Dix, and Kenneth H. Williams, *The Papers of Jefferson Davis* (Baton Rouge, La: Louisiana State University Press, 1997), 305.

25. G. F. R. Henderson, *Stonewall Jackson and the American Civil War* (New York: Longmans, Green, 1899), 178.

26. Burke Davis, *They Called Him Stonewall: A Life of Lt. General T. J. Jackson, C.S.A.* (New York: Fairfax Press, 1988), 130.

27. Ibid., 89.

28. Miller, Stout, and Wilson, *Religion and the American Civil War*, 96–97.

29. Noah Brooks to James A. Reed, Dec. 31, 1872, "The Later Life and Religious Sentiments of Abraham Lincoln," *Scribner's Monthly*, July 1873, 340.

30. John G. Nicolay and John Hay, eds., *Complete Works of Abraham Lincoln* (New York: Francis B. Tandy, 1905), 293–94.

31. Basler, *The Collected Works of Abraham Lincoln*, vol. 8, 1864–1865, 116–17.

32. Allen Thorndike Rice, ed., *Reminiscences of Abraham Lincoln by Distinguished Men of His Time* (New York: North American Review, 1888), 528.

33. Ralph L. Woods, ed., *The World Treasury of Religious Quotations* (New York: Hawthorn Books, 1966), 753.

34. Basler, *Collected Works of Abraham Lincoln*, 8:332–33.

35. Frederick Douglass, *Autobiographies* (New York: Library of America, 1994), 802.

36. Noah Brooks to James A. Reed, Dec. 31, 1872, "The Later Life and Religious Sentiments of Abraham Lincoln," 340.

37. Basler, *The Collected Works of Abraham Lincoln*, vol. 6, 1862–1863, 537.

38. Carl Sandburg, ed., *Lincoln's Devotional* (Great Neck, N.Y.: Channel Press, 1957), 58.

39. Phineas D. Gurley, "Letters of His Career," Library of Congress.

40. Phineas D. Gurley, "Funeral Hymn," American Song Sheets, ser. 1, vol. 3, Library of Congress.

41. *New York Herald*, March 6, 1865.

42. Brian Lamb, ed., *Who's Buried in Grant's Tomb?* (New York: Public Affairs, 2003), 71.

43. Osbeck, *101 Hymn Stories*, 256–57.

44. Ibid., 255.

8. THE HEALERS: 1865–1885

Epigraph: R. W. Franklin, ed., *The Poems of Emily Dickinson* (Cambridge, Mass.: Belknap Press of Harvard University Press, 1998), 2:756.

1. John Y. Simon, ed., *The Papers of Ulysses S. Grant*, vol. 19, July 1, 1868–October 31, 1869 (Carbondale: Southern Illinois University Press, 1967), 4–6.

2. Ibid., 369.

3. James D. Richardson, *A Compilation of the Messages and Papers of the Presidents, 1789–1908, vol VII* (Washington, D.C.: Bureau of National Literature and Art, 1908), 18.

4. Henry L. Stoddard, *It Costs to Be President* (New York: Harper, 1938), 198.

5. William A. DeGregorio, *The Complete Book of U.S. Presidents* (Fort Lee, N.J.: Barricade Books, 2001), 281–82.

6. Ibid., 283.

7. *Diary and Letters of Rutherford Birchard Hayes* (Columbus: Ohio State Archaeological and Historical Society, 1922–26), 1:326–27.

8. Ibid., 5:143.

9. Anne C. Rose, *Victorian America and the Civil War* (New York: Cambridge University Press, 1992), 17.

10. Wilma R. Taylor and Norman T. Taylor, *This Train Is Bound for Glory: The Story of America's Chapel Cars* (Valley Forge, Pa: Judson Press, 1999), 5.

11. Nicholas Faith, *The World the Railways Made* (New York: Carroll and Graf, 1990), 269–70.

12. Wilma R. Taylor and Norman T. Taylor, *This Train Is Bound for Glory*, 5.

13. Louis Dupré and Don E. Saliers, *Christian Spirituality: Post-Reformation and Modern* (New York: Crossroad, 1989), 332.

14. Augustus T. Murray, *A Selection from the Religious Poems of John Greenleaf Whittier, with an Interpretive Essay* (Philadelphia: Friends' Bookstore, 1934), 64.

15. James Dalton Morrison, ed., *Masterpieces of Religious Verse* (New York: Harper, 1948), 237.

16. Horace E. Scudder, ed., *The Complete Poetical Works of John Greenleaf Whittier* (New York: Houghton Mifflin, 1894), 449.

17. Ibid., 234.

18. Roger Lundin, *Emily Dickinson and the Art of Belief* (Grand Rapids: William B. Eerdmans Publishing, 1998), 3.

19. Alfred Habegger, *My Wars Are Laid Away in Books: The Life of Emily Dickinson* (New York: Random House, 2001), 167–68.

20. Lundin, *Emily Dickinson and the Art of Belief,* 146.

21. Ibid., 97.

22. Franklin, *Poems of Emily Dickinson,* 1:317–18.

23. Max L. Christensen, *Heroes and Saints* (Louisville, Ky.: Westminster John Knox Press, 1997), 77.

24. Ibid., 100–1.

25. Edwin S. Gaustad, *A Documentary History of Religion in America since 1865* (Grand Rapids: William B. Eerdmans Publishing, 1993), 342.

26. Hannah Ward and Jennifer Wild, eds., *The Doubleday Christian Quotation Collection* (New York: Doubleday, 1998), 162.

27. Mark Water, ed., *The New Encyclopedia of Christian Quotations* (Grand Rapids: Baker Books, 2000), 587.

28. Dwight Lyman Moody, *Prevailing Prayer: What Hinders It?* (Chicago: F. H. Revell, 1884), 7.

29. Water, *New Encyclopedia of Christian Quotations,* 781.

30. Phillips Brooks, *Visions and Tasks and Other Sermons* (New York: E.P. Dutton & Co., 1886), 330.

31. Kenneth W. Osbeck, *101 More Hymn Stories* (Grand Rapids: Kregel Publications, 1985), 100–1.

32. Louis W. Rodenburg, "The Songbird in the Dark," *Outlook for the Blind* 26 (March 1932): 42–47.

33. Ibid., 47.

34. Ibid., 158.

35. Lisa Sergio, ed., *Prayers of Women* (New York: Harper & Row, 1965), 96.

36. Ibid., 46.

37. Badger Clark, "A Cowboy's Prayer," Badger Clark Memorial Society, 1993.

38. Fran Grace, *Carry A. Nation: Retelling the Life* (Bloomington: Indiana University Press, 2001), 11.

39. Ibid., 193.

40. Ibid., 85.

41. Ibid., 278.

42. Ibid., 161.

43. Colleen McDannell, *Religions of the United States in Practice* (Princeton, N.J.: Princeton University Press, 2001), 1:159.

44. Ibid., 1:163.

45. Willa Cather and Georgine Milmine, *The Life of Mary Baker G. Eddy and the History of Christian Science* (Lincoln: University of Nebraska Press, 1993), 196.

46. Mary Baker Eddy, *Science and Health with Key to the Scriptures* (Boston: Christian Scientist Publishing Company, 1875), 4–5.

47. Cather and Milmine, *Life of Mary Baker G. Eddy*, 196.

48. Eddy, *Science and Health*, 16–17.

49. Mary D. Pellauer, *Toward a Tradition of Feminist Theology: The Religious Social Thought of Elizabeth Cady Stanton, Susan B. Anthony, and Anna Howard Shaw* (Brooklyn: Carlson, 1991), 1991.

50. Dana Greene, ed., *Lucretia Mott: Her Complete Speeches and Sermons* (New York: Edwin Mellen Press, 1980), 299.

51. Alan Peskin, *Garfield* (Norwalk, Conn.: Easton Press, 1978), 250.

52. Ibid., 601–7.

53. Kenneth D. Ackerman, *Dark Horse: The Surprise Election and Political Murder of President James A. Garfield* (New York: Carroll & Graf, 2003), 445.

54. Ibid.

55. Paul F. Boller, Jr., *Presidential Wives* (New York: Oxford University Press, 1988), 136.

9. THE OPPORTUNISTS: 1885–1900

Epigraph: Stephen Crane, *The Black Riders*, ed. Wilson Follett (New York: Knopf, 1930), 41.

1. Arthur M. Schlesinger, Jr., ed., *The Almanac of American History* (New York: Barnes & Noble Books, 1993), 271.

2. Kathryn Teresa Long, *The Revival of 1857–58: Interpreting an American Religious Awakening* (New York: Oxford University Press, 1998), 83.

3. Kenneth W. Osbeck, *101 Hymn Stories* (Grand Rapids: Kregel Publications, 1982), 236.

4. Ibid.

5. Jean Strouse, *Morgan: American Financier* (New York: Random House, 1999), 75.

6. Ian Bradley, ed., *The Book of Hymns* (New York: Testament Books, 2000), 365–66.

7. Chernow, *Titan*, 451.

8. Ibid., 153.

9. Herbert Ershkowitz, *John Wanamaker: Philadelphia Merchant* (Conshohocken, Pa.: Combined Publishing, 1999), 13.

10. Ibid., 154.

11. Catherine Millard, *The Rewriting of America's History* (Camp Hill, Pa.: Horizon House Publishers, 1991), 277–78.

12. Herbert Satterlee, *J. Pierpont Morgan: An Intimate Portrait* (New York: Macmillan, 1939), 169.

13. Ibid., 274–75.

14. Alistair Cooke, *Alistair Cooke's America* (New York: Knopf, 1973), 165.

15. A. H. Saxon, *P. T. Barnum: The Legend and the Man* (New York: Columbia University Press, 1989), 48.

16. Joel Benton, *The Life and Times of P. T. Barnum* (New York: Century Company, 1902), 86.

17. Philip B. Kunhardt, Jr., Philip B. Kunhardt III, and Peter W. Kunhardt, *P. T. Barnum: America's Greatest Showman* (New York: Knopf, 1995), 343.

18. "Great and Only Barnum—He Wanted to Read His Obituary—Here It Is," *New York Evening Sun*, April 4, 1891, 1.

19. *New York Times*, March 14, 1898, 1.

20. Gary R. Kremer, ed., *George Washington Carver in His Own Words* (Columbia: University of Missouri Press, 1987), 128.

21. Ibid., 137.

22. Campbell Johnson and Emily Lemon, "Historical Census Statistics on the Foreign Population of the United States: 1850–1900" (Washington, D.C.: U.S. Bureau of the Census, Feb. 1999), p. 29.

23. "Statue of Liberty Dedicated," *New York Times*, Oct. 28, 1886, 1.

24. Eric J. Ziolkowski, ed., *A Museum of Faiths: Histories and Legacies of the 1893 World's Parliament of Religions* (Atlanta: Scholars Press, 1993), 5.

25. Walter R. Houghton, ed. *Parliament of Religions and Religious Congresses* (Chicago: F. T. Neely, 1893), 805.

26. Walter R. Houghton, ed., *Parliament of Religions and Religious Congresses* (Chicago: F. T. Neely, 1893), 439.

27. Ibid., 64.

28. Gerald Mygatt and Henry Darlington, eds., *Soldiers' and Sailors' Prayer Book* (New York: Knopf, 1944), 15.

29. "Queen Liliuokalani's Prayer" (Honolulu: John H. Wilson, 1895), 2–3.

30. John Farrow, *Damien the Leper: A Life of Magnificent Courage, Devotion, and Spirit* (New York: Doubleday, 1999), 157.

31. Cora Fremont Older, *William Randolph Hearst: American* (New York: D. Appleton–Century Company, 1936), 236.

32. Joyce Milton, *The Yellow Kids: Foreign Correspondents in the Heyday of Yellow Journalism* (New York: HarperPerennial, 1989), 212.

33. Hugh Hewitt, *Searching for God in America* (Dallas: Word Publishing, 1996), 471.

34. Osbeck, *101 Hymn Stories*, 96–97.

35. Hewitt, *Searching for God in America*, 472.

36. Charles S. Olcott, *The Life of William McKinley* (Boston: Houghton Mifflin, 1916), 2:110–11.

37. Geoffrey C. Ward, Dayton Duncan, and Ken Burns, *Mark Twain* (New York: Knopf, 2001), 159.

38. Jim Zwick, *Mark Twain's Weapons of Satire: Anti-Imperialist Writings on the Philippine–American War* (Syracuse, New York: Syracuse University Press, 1992), 84.

39. Mark Twain, *The War Prayer* (New York: Harper & Row, 1951).

40. John Sutherland Bonnell, *Presidential Profiles: Religion in the Life of American Presidents* (Philadelphia: Westminster Press, 1971), 147.

41. James D. Richardson, *A Compilation of the Messages and Papers of the Presidents, 1789–1908, Vol. VIII* (Washington, D.C.: Bureau of National Literature and Art, 1908), 26–27.

42. William A. DeGregorio, *The Complete Book of U.S. Presidents* (Fort Lee, N.J.: Barricade Books, 2001), 333.

43. Harold I. Gullan, *Faith of Our Mothers* (Grand Rapids: William B. Eerdmans Publishing, 2001), 143.

44. Supreme Court Compilation, Clerk of the Court, 1939.

45. Suzy Platt, ed., *Respectfully Quoted: A Dictionary of Quotations Requested from the Congressional Research Service* (Washington, D.C.: Library of Congress, 1989), 275.

46. Eric Rauchway, *Murdering McKinley* (New York: Hill and Wang, 2003), 178.

47. Ibid., 368.

10. THE IDEALISTS: 1900–1920

Epigraph: William Adams Brown, *The Life of Prayer in a World of Science* (New York: Charles Scribner, 1927), 18.

1. Katharine Rogers, *L. Frank Baum: The Royal Historian of Oz* (New York: St. Martin's Press, 2002), 32–33.

2. Theodore Caplow, Louis Hicks, and Ben J. Wattenberg, *The First Measured Century* (Washington, D.C.: American Enterprise Institute Press, 2001), 106.

3. George Coe, *The Religion of a Mature Mind* (Chicago: Fleming H. Revell, 1902), 329.

4. William James, *The Varieties of Religious Experience* (New York: Modern Library, 1994), 505.

5. William James, "The Energies of Men," in *Essays on Faith and Morals* (New York: World Publishing Company, 1972), 176.

6. Samuel H. Miller, ed., *The Harvard University Hymn Book* (Cambridge, Mass.: Harvard University Press, 1964), 345.

7. F. Austin Walter, ed., *The Rutgers Songbook* (New Brunswick, N.J., The Sengstack Group, Ltd. 1991), 10.

8. Clayton E. Wheat, "Acquit Ourselves Like Men," *Guideposts,* June 1948, 8.

9. Charles C. Hall and Sigismond Lasar, eds., *The Evangelical Hymnal with Tunes* (New York: A. S. Barnes & Company, 1880), 472.

10. Randall Balmer, *Religion in Twentieth Century America* (New York: Oxford University Press, 2001), 12–13.

11. Ibid., 15.

12. "Pentecost Has Come," *The Apostolic Faith* 1, no. 1 (Sept. 1906): 1.

13. William T. Ellis, *"Billy" Sunday: The Man and His Message* (Philadelphia: John C. Winston, 1917), 338–39.

14. Billy Sunday, "A Prayer for July," *Guideposts,* July 1985, 33.

15. Chuck Neighbors, "The Story of 'In His Steps,' " *Guideposts,* Sept. 1996, 52–55.

16. Robert R. Mathisen, *Critical Issues in American Religious History* (Waco, Tex.: Baylor University Press, 2001), 533–34.

17. Walter Rauschenbusch, *Prayers of the Social Awakening* (Boston: Pilgrim Press, 1910), 51–52.

18. Kenneth W. Osbeck, *Twenty-five Most Treasured Gospel Hymn Stories* (Grand Rapids: Kregel Publications, 1999), 95.

19. Kenneth W. Osbeck, *101 Hymn Stories* (Grand Rapids: Kregel Publications, 1982), 170.

20. Ibid., 169.

21. Jason Wilson, "Building the Dreams," *Washington Post Magazine,* Sept. 21, 2003, 19.

22. Wilma R. Taylor and Norman T. Taylor, *This Train Is Bound for Glory: The Story of America's Chapel Cars* (Valley Forge, Pa.: Judson Press, 1999), 11.

23. Ibid., 58.

24. Ibid., 110.

25. Ibid., 241.

26. Ibid., 58.

27. Jeffrey F. Meyer, *Myths in Stone: Religious Dimensions of Washington, D.C.* (Berkeley: University of California Press, 2001), 79.

28. Ibid.

29. *Guide to Washington Cathedral* (Washington, D.C.: National Cathedral Association, 1983), 8.

30. Richard T. Feller and Marshall W. Fishwick, *For Thy Great Glory* (Washington, D.C.: Community Press, 1965), 12.

31. Alfred Thayer Mahan, *The Harvest Within: Thoughts on the Life of the Christian* (Boston: Little, Brown, 1909), 145.

32. Theodore Roosevelt, *An Autobiography* (Norwalk, Conn.: Easton Press, 1996), 58, 4.

33. Kathleen Dalton, *Theodore Roosevelt: A Strenuous Life* (New York: Knopf, 2002), 19.

34. Ibid., 49.

35. Clifford Putney, *Muscular Christianity: Manhood and Sports in Protestant America, 1880–1920* (Cambridge, Mass.: Harvard University Press, 2001), 19.

36. John Haynes Holmes, *Collected Hymns* (Boston: Beacon Press, 1960), 39.

37. Robert Kimball and Linda Emmet, *The Complete Lyrics of Irving Berlin* (New York: Knopf, 2001), 153.

38. National Lutheran Council, *Army and Navy Service Book* (New York: National Lutheran Council, 1917), 26–36.

39. John J. Burke, ed., *Catholic Prayer Book for the Army and Navy* (New York: Chaplain's Aid Association, 1917), 8.

40. *A Prayer Book for Soldiers and Sailors* (Philadelphia: Bishop White Prayer Book Society, 1917).

41. "My Soldier" (New York: Matthews-Northrup Works, 1917), poster for the U.S. government.

42. Lew Schaeffer, *Let Us Say a Prayer for Daddy* (New York: Lew Schaeffer Music Company, 1917).

43. Joyce Kilmer, *Poems, Essays, and Letters* (Garden City, N.Y.: Doubleday, Doran, 1946), 180.

44. Ibid., 109.

45. Ibid., 101.

46. Sigmund Freud and William C. Bullitt, *Thomas Woodrow Wilson, Twenty-eighth President of the United States: A Psychological Study* (Boston: Houghton Mifflin, 1967), 148.

47. Harold I. Gullan, *Faith of Our Mothers* (Grand Rapids: William B. Eerdmans Publishing, 2001), 165.

48. Freud and Bullitt, 148.

49. Ibid., 66.

50. Arthur M. Schlesinger, Jr., ed., *The Almanac of American History* (New York: Barnes & Noble Books, 1993), 436.

51. McPherson, *"To the Best of My Ability,"* 202.

11. THE INNOVATORS: 1920-1935

Epigraph: Kahlil Gibran, *The Prophet* (New York: Knopf, 1942), 76.

1. Richard Lingeman, *Sinclair Lewis: Rebel from Main Street* (New York: Random House, 2002), 16.

2. Ibid., 16–17.

3. F. Scott Fitzgerald, "Echoes of the Jazz Age," *Scribners Magazine*, November 1931, 390.

4. Henry Idema III, *Freud, Religion, and the Roaring Twenties: A Psychoanalytic Theory of Secularization in Three Novelists: Anderson, Hemingway, and Fitzgerald* (Savage, Md.: Rowman & Littlefield, 1990), 190.

5. Ibid., 137.

6. Carlos Baker, ed., *Ernest Hemingway, Selected Letters, 1917–1961* (New York: Scribner, 1981), 592.

7. Arthur Gelb and Barbara Gelb, *O'Neill* (London: Jonathan Cape, 1962), 69.

8. Gibran, *Prophet*, 77–78.

9. Frederick Gutheim, ed., *Frank Lloyd Wright on Architecture* (New York: Duell, Sloan and Pearce, 1941), 256.

10. Ibid., 3.

11. Ibid., 176.

12. "Restraint in Design: An Interview with Mies van der Rohe," *New York Herald Tribune*, June 28, 1959, 18.

13. Charles Ives, *Essays Before A Sonata, and Other Writings* (New York: Norton, 1962), 22.

14. Charles Johnson, "Music: An Ever-Lifting Song of Black America," *New York Times*, Feb. 14, 1999, 34.

15. Ibid.

16. Bernice J. Reagon, *We'll Understand By and By: Pioneering African-American Composers* (Washington, D.C.: Smithsonian Institution Press, 1992), 55.

17. David W. Stowe, *How Sweet the Sound: Music in the Spiritual Lives of Americans* (Cambridge: Harvard University Press, 2004), 260.

18. Definition of Gospel Music Association at www.gospelmusic.com.

19. Thomas A. Dorsey, "From Bawdy Songs to Hymns," *Guideposts*, Dec. 1950, pp 3–5.

20. Ibid.

21. Ibid.

22. Ibid.

23. Stowe, 202.

24. Claudia Perry, "Hallelujah: The Sacred Music of Black America," in *American Roots Music*, eds. Robert Santelli, Holly George-Warren, and Jim Brown (New York: Abradale, 2001), 92.

25. Jules Schwerin, *Got to Tell It: Mahalia Jackson, Queen of Gospel* (New York: Oxford University Press, 1992), 27.

26. H. L. Mencken, "Mencken Likens Trial to a Religious Orgy with Defendant a Beelzebub," *Baltimore Evening Sun*, July 11, 1925, 9.

27. L. Sprague De Camp, *The Great Monkey Trial* (Garden City, N.Y.: Doubleday, 1968), 176.

28. Ibid., 265.

29. Ibid.

30. Edward J. Larson, *Summer for the Gods* (New York: Basic Books, 1997), 224.

31. Francis X. Clines, "Ohio Board Hears Debate on an Alternative to Darwinism," *New York Times*, March 12, 2002, A16.

32. W. E. B. DuBois, *Prayers for Dark People*, ed. Herbert Aptheker (Amherst: University of Massachusetts Press, 1980), viii.

33. Ibid., 36.

34. William Judson Hampton, *The Religion of the Presidents* (Somerville, N.J.: Unionist-Gazette Association, 1925), 93.

35. Carl Sferrazza Anthony, *Florence Harding: The First Lady, the Jazz Age, and the Death of America's Most Scandalous President* (New York: William Morrow, 1998), 377.

36. *The Autobiography of Calvin Coolidge* (New York: Cosmopolitan Book Corporation, 1929), 4.

37. Donald R. McCoy, *Calvin Coolidge, the Quiet President: A New Assessment* (Lawrence: University Press of Kansas, 1988), 396.

38. James Dalton Morrison, ed., *Masterpieces of Religious Verse* (New York: Harper, 1948), 344.

39. James M. McPherson, ed., *"To the Best of My Ability": The American Presidents* (New York: Dorling Kindersley, 2000), 415.

40. Herbert Hoover, *American Individualism* (Garden City, N.Y.: Doubleday, Page & Company, 1922), 321.

41. Eugene Lyons, *Herbert Hoover: A Biography* (Norwalk, Conn.: Easton Press, 1964), 323.

42. John Kenneth Galbraith, *The Great Crash, 1929* (Boston: Houghton Mifflin, 1955), 130.

43. J. C. Penney, *Fifty Years with the Golden Rule* (New York: Harper, 1950), 77.

44. Ibid., 191.

45. Frances Perkins, *The Roosevelt I Knew* (New York: Viking Press, 1946), 29.

46. Ibid., 139.

47. Ibid., 139.

48. Ibid., 144–45.

49. Hank Greenberg, *Hank Greenberg: The Story of My Life* (New York Times Books, 1989), 57–62.

50. Babe Ruth and Bob Considine, *The Babe Ruth Story* (New York: Dutton, 1948), 233.

51. Bernard Ruffin, *Profiles of Faith: The Religious Beliefs of Eminent Americans* (Liguori, Mo.: Liguori/Triumph, 1997), 320.

52. "Babe Ruth Is Dead," *New York World-Telegram*, Aug. 17, 1948, 1.

53. *Autobiography of Cecil B. DeMille*, ed. Donald Hayne (Englewood Cliffs, N.J.: Prentice Hall, 1959), 433.

54. Kevin Brownlow, *Mary Pickford Rediscovered* (New York: Harry N. Abrams, 1999), 14.

55. Lisa Sergio, ed., *Prayers of Women* (New York: Harper & Row, 1965), 195.

56. Arline DeHaas, *The Jazz Singer: A Story of Pathos and Laughter* (New York: Grosset and Dunlap, 1927), 238.

57. International Church of the Foursquare Gospel, official statement, Los Angeles, Calif.

58. Lewis Lord, "Chasing Aimee," *U.S. News & World Report*, Aug. 26–Sept. 2, 2002, 58.

59. Daniel Mark Epstein, *Sister Aimee* (New York: Harcourt Brace Jovanovich, 1993), 249.

60. Ibid., 378–80.

12. THE DEFENDERS: 1935–1945

Epigraph: Gerald Mygatt and Henry Darlington, eds., *Soldiers' and Sailors' Prayer Book* (New York: Knopf, 1944), 95.

1. Jules Chametzky, John Felstiner, Hilene Flanzbaum, and Kathryn Hellerstein, eds., *Jewish American Literature: A Norton Anthology* (New York: W. W. Norton, 2001), 285–87.

2. Laurence Bergreen, *As Thousands Cheer: The Life of Irving Berlin* (New York: Viking, 1990), 380.

3. Robert E. Sherwood, *The White House Papers of Harry L. Hopkins*, vol. 1, September 1939–January 1942 (London: Eyre and Spottiswoode, 1948), 246–47.

4. H. V. Morton, *Atlantic Meeting* (London: Methuen & Company, 1943), 100.

5. Ibid., 101.

6. Winston Churchill, *The Grand Alliance* (Boston: Houghton Mifflin, 1951), 431.

7. John Keegan, ed., *World War II: A Visual Encyclopedia* (London: PRC Publishing, 1999), 401.

8. Frank Loesser, "Praise the Lord and Pass the Ammunition!" (New York: Famous Music Corporation, 1942).

9. Chester Gillis, *Roman Catholicism in America* (New York: Columbia University Press, 1999), 173.

10. J. H. Doolittle, "It's Time for Decision," *Guideposts*, Jan. 1951, 19–20.

11. Ibid.

12. Ibid.

13. Eddie Rickenbacker, "I Believe in Prayer," June 1945, 1–4

14. Ibid.

15. Edward V. Rickenbacker, *Seven Came Through: Rickenbacker's Full Story* (Garden City, N.Y.: Doubleday, Doran, 1943), 33.

16. Ibid., 34.

17. Ibid.

18. Ibid.

19. Francis B. Thornton, *Sea of Glory: The Magnificent Story of the Four Chaplains* (New York: Prentice-Hall, 1953), 168.

20. Richard H. Schneider, "The Four Chaplains: 50 Years Later," *Guideposts*, Feb. 1993, 2.

21. Carlos P. Romulo, *I Saw the Fall of the Philippines* (Garden City, N.Y.: Doubleday, Doran, 1943), 243.

22. John Wukovits, "From Death March to POW Camp," *WWII History*, Sept. 2002, 39.

23. Owen Collins, ed., *2000 Years of Classic Christian Prayers* (Maryknoll, N.Y.: Orbis Books, 2000), 185–86.

24. Samuel I. Rosenman, *The Public Papers and Addresses of Franklin Roosevelt*, vol. 13, 1944–1945 (New York: Harper & Bros., 1950), 152–53.

25. Stephen Ambrose, *The Victors: Eisenhower and His Boys, The Men of World War II* (New York: Simon & Schuster, 1998), 151.

26. Charles E. Wilson, "The Invasion," *Guideposts*, June 1958, 20.

27. Ibid.

28. George R. Metcalf, "Prayer for Fair Weather," *Guideposts*, Dec. 1994, 36–37.

29. Ladislas Farago, *Patton: Ordeal and Triumph* (New York: I. Obolensky, 1963), 690.

30. Ibid.

31. Carlo D'Este, *Patton: A Genius for War* (New York: HarperCollins, 1995), 686.

32. Ibid.

33. Mygatt and Darlington, *Soldiers' and Sailors' Prayer Book*, 34.

34. Jeshajahu Weinberg and Rina Elieli, *The Holocaust Museum in Washington* (New York: Rizzoli, 1995), 76.

35. Elie Wiesel, *Night* (New York: Bantam, 1982), ix.

36. Ibid., 36.

37. United States Holocaust Memorial Council (Washington, D.C.: United States Holocaust Memorial, 1993).

38. Frances Perkins, *The Roosevelt I Knew* (New York: Viking Press, 1946), 140.

39. Ibid., 148.

40. David McCullough, *Truman* (New York: Simon & Schuster, 1992), 353.

41. *Public Papers of the Presidents of the United States: Harry S. Truman*, vol. 1, April 12–December 31, 1945 (Washington, D.C.: Government Printing Office, 1946), 3.

42. William Hillman, ed., *Mr. President: Personal Diaries, Private Letters, Papers, and Revealing Interviews of Harry S. Truman* (London: Hutchinson, 1952), 17.

43. Ibid., 17.

44. Richard Rhodes, "The Experiment of the Century," *American Heritage*, April 1999, 12.

45. Douglas MacArthur, *A Soldier Speaks: Public Papers and Speeches of General of the Army Douglas MacArthur* (New York: Frederick A. Praeger, 1965), 150–52.

13. THE REBUILDERS: 1945–1960

Epigraph: Alfred D. Chandler, Jr., ed., *The Papers of Dwight David Eisenhower*, vol. 20 (Baltimore: Johns Hopkins Press, 1970), 6–8.

1. Paul Dickson, *From Elvis to E-Mail* (Springfield, Mass.: Federal Street Press, 1999), 4.

2. U. S. Department of Veterans Affairs, "America's Wars," Office of Public Affairs, 2004.

3. Dickson, *From Elvis to E-Mail*, 6.

4. David Cannadine, ed., *Blood, Toil, Tears, and Sweat: The Speeches of Winston Churchill* (Boston: Houghton Mifflin, 1989), 296–305.

5. Catherine Marshall, *A Man Called Peter* (Chicago: People's Book Club, 1951), 2.

6. Ibid., 117.

7. Ibid., 322.

8. Proceedings of the U.S. Senate, opening prayer, 80th Cong., June 5, 1947.

9. Peter Burkhardt, "The Solons' Shepherd," *New York Times*, Jan. 11, 1948, SM14.

10. Theodor Geisel, "A Prayer for a Child," *Collier's*, Dec. 23, 1949, 35.

11. Andrew W. Cordier and William Foote, eds., *Public Papers of the Secretaries-General of the United Nations: DAG Hammarskjold, 1956–1957*, vol. III (New York: Columbia University Press, 1977), 710.

12. Ibid., 710.

13. "Peace Prayer," *Guideposts*, Dec. 1954, 18.

14. Blanche Wiesen Cook, *Eleanor Roosevelt*, vol. 1, *1884–1933* (New York: Viking, 1992), 94.

15. Ibid. 151–52.

16. Courtney Whitney, *MacArthur, His Rendezvous with History* (New York: Alfred A. Knopf, 1956), 547.

17. Jack Kelly, "Ridgway a Hero to Korean War GIs," *Pittsburgh Post–Gazette*, May 28, 2000, B12.

18. Gerald Mygatt and Henry Darlington, eds., *Soldiers' and Sailors' Prayer Book* (New York: Knopf, 1944), 23.

19. Chaplain Corps, http://www.usachcs.army.mil/Korea/Gallery2.htm.

20. David Maraniss and Anne Hull, "Combat's Bitter Revelations, *Washington Post,* March 9, 2003, A18–A19.

21. Whitney Bolton, *The Silver Spade: The Conrad Hilton Story* (New York: Farrar, Straus and Young, 1954), x.

22. Conrad N. Hilton, "The Best Investment," *Guideposts,* Nov. 1950, 12.

23. Bolton, *Silver Spade,* xii.

24. Ibid.

25. Ibid., xiii.

26. Conrad Hilton Foundation Annual Reports.

27. William A. DeGregorio, *The Complete Book of U.S. Presidents* (Fort Lee, N.J.: Barricade Books, 2001), 530.

28. Washington National Cathedral, *The Prayers and the Readings from God's Word at the Funeral Service of Dwight David Eisenhower* (Washington, D.C.: Washington National Cathedral, March 31, 1969), 6.

29. Chandler, vol. 18, 3–5.

30. Ibid.

31. U.S. Code, title 36, subtitle 1, pt. A, ch. 1, sec. 119.

32. Russ Busby, *Billy Graham, God's Ambassador* (San Diego: Tehabi Books, 1999), 62.

33. "The Prayer Room in the United States Capitol" (Washington, D.C.: U.S. Government Printing Office, 1956).

34. Justice William Douglas, majority opinion, *Zorach v. Clauson,* 343 U.S. 306, U.S. Supreme Court, April 28, 1952.

35. Conrad N. Hilton, "Uncle Sam's Prayer," *Guideposts,* July 1954, 4.

36. *Public Papers of the Presidents of the United States: Dwight Eisenhower,* January 1–December 31, 1954 (Washington, D.C.: Government Printing Office, 1960), 41.

37. Andrew Walther, "Catholic Groups Join the Battle for Hollywood's Soul," *National Catholic Register,* March 23–29, 2003, 1, 12.

38. "About Us," *Family Theater Productions* (Hollywood, Calif.: Promotional Report, 2002), 4.

39. Ibid.

40. Patrick J. Peyton, *All for Her* (Garden City, N.Y.: Doubleday, 1967), 144.

41. David Edwin Harrell, Jr., *Oral Roberts: An American Life* (San Francisco: Harper & Row, 1987), 96–97.

42. Ibid., 119.

43. Norman Vincent Peale, *The Power of Positive Thinking* (Englewood Cliffs, N.J.: Prentice-Hall, 1956), 68–69.

44. Norman Vincent Peale, *Try Prayer Power: Seven Spiritual Exercises for Strengthening Your Life* (New York: Foundation for Christian Living, 1959), 26.

45. Thomas C. Reeves, *The Life and Times of Fulton J. Sheen: America's Bishop* (San Francisco: Encounter Books, 2001), 240.

46. Gregory Joseph Ladd, *Archbishop Fulton J. Sheen: A Man for All Media* (San Francisco: Ignatius Press, 2001), 22.

47. Busby, *Billy Graham,* 32.

48. Ibid.

49. Gabriel Fackre, *The Promise of Reinhold Niebuhr* (Philadelphia: J. B. Lippincott Company, 1970), 66.

50. Elisabeth Sifton, *The Serenity Prayer: Faith and Politics in Times of Peace and War* (New York: W. W. Norton, 2003), 11.

51. Ibid., 7.

52. Jack Alexander, "Alcoholics Anonymous," *Saturday Evening Post*, March 1941, 9.

53. *Alcoholics Anonymous Comes of Age: A Brief History of A.A.* (New York: Alcoholics Anonymous Publishing, 1957), 50.

54. Martha Graham, *Blood Memory* (New York: Doubleday, 1991), 3.

55. Opening Night Program, *Appalachian Spring* (Washington, D.C.: Library of Congress, Oct. 30, 1944).

56. Robert Hughes, "The Rembrandt of Punkin Crick," *Time*, Nov. 20, 1978, 110.

57. Stuart Murray and James McCabe, *Norman Rockwell's Four Freedoms* (Stockbridge, Mass.: Berkshire House, 1993), 51.

58. Ibid.

59. Norman Rockwell, "Saying Grace," *Saturday Evening Post*, Nov. 24, 1951, cover.

60. Julia Maniates Reibetanz, *A Reading of Eliot's "Four Quartets"* (Ann Arbor, Mich.: UMI Research Press, 1983), 145.

61. Loren Eiseley, *The Star Thrower* (New York: Harcourt, 1979), vi.

62. Arnold Rampersad, ed., *The Collected Poems of Langston Hughes* (New York: Alfred A. Knopf, 1994), 155–56.

63. "Origins of the Beat Generation: An Interview with Jack Kerouac," *Playboy*, June 1959.

64. "Disorganization Man," *Time*, June 9, 1958, 102.

65. Douglas Brinkley, ed., *Jack Kerouac: Windblown World* (New York: Viking, 2004), 154–58.

66. Diana Culbertson, ed., *Invisible Light: Poems about God* (New York: Columbia University Press, 2000), 89.

67. Michael Schumacher, *Dharma Lion: A Critical Biography of Allen Ginsberg* (New York: St. Martin's Press, 1992), 300.

68. Jackie Robinson, "Trouble Ahead Needn't Bother You," *Guideposts*, Aug. 1948, 3–4.

69. Arnold Rampersand, *Jackie Robinson: A Biography* (New York: Ballantine Books, 1997), 310.

70. Gene Tunney, "Your Faith Can Knock Out Fear," *Guideposts*, June 1947, 5.

71. Babe Didrikson Zaharias, "Spiritual Muscles," *Guideposts*, Sept. 1954, 2–3.

72. Satchel Paige, interview, *New York Post*, Oct. 4, 1959, C1.

73. Dave Marsh and Harold Leventhal, eds., *Pastures of Plenty, A Self-Portrait: Woody Guthrie* (New York: HarperCollins, 1990), 158–62.

74. Colin Escott and Kira Florita, *Hank Williams: Snapshots from the Lost Highway* (Cambridge, Mass.: Da Capo Press, 2001), 26.

75. Larry King and Irwin Katsof, *Powerful Prayers* (Los Angeles: Renaissance Books, 1998), 44.

76. Larry Geller, *"If I Can Dream": Elvis' Own Story* (New York: Simon & Schuster, 1989), inside jacket.

77. Ibid., 363.

78. Ibid., 187.

79. *Public Papers of the Presidents of the United States: John F. Kennedy*, January 20–December 31, 1961 (Washington, D.C.: Government Printing Office, 1962), 5–7.

14. THE NEW PIONEERS: 1960–1975

Epigraph: Paul Simon, "Mrs. Robinson," BMI.

1. Richard P. McBrien, *Lives of the Popes* (San Francisco: HarperCollins, 1997), 373.

2. Janet Podell and Steven Anzovin, *Speeches of the American Presidents* (Norwalk, Conn.: Easton Press, 1995), 2:600–1.

3. James M. McPherson, ed., *"To the Best of My Ability": The American Presidents* (New York: Dorling Kindersley, 2000), 432.

4. Suzy Platt, ed., *Respectfully Quoted: A Dictionary of Quotations Requested from the Congressional Research Service* (Washington, D.C.: Library of Congress, 1989), 278.

5. 370 U.S. 421 (1962).

6. Ibid.

7. Ibid.

8. Anthony Lewis, "Supreme Court Outlaws Prayers in Regents Case Decision," *New York Times,* June 26, 1962, 1.

9. Roger K. Newman, *Hugo Black: A Biography* (New York: Fordham University Press, 1997), 523.

10. 370 U.S. 421 (1962).

11. Ibid.

12. George Gallup, "Religious Observances in School Survey," Gallup Organization, July 26–31, 1962.

13. 374 U.S. 203 (1963). *Abington School District* v. *Schempp.*

14. 319 U.S. 624 (1943). *West Virginia State Board of Education* v. *Barnette.*

15. *The Memoirs of Earl Warren* (Garden City, N.Y.: Doubleday, 1977), 315–16.

16. Anthony Lewis, "Both Houses Get Bills to Lift Ban on School Prayer," *New York Times,* June 27, 1962, 1.

17. Anthony Lewis, "Court Under Fire Again," *New York Times,* July 1, 1962.

18. Anthony Lewis, "Both Houses Get Bills to Lift Ban on School Prayer," *New York Times,* June 27, 1962, 20.

19. Anthony Lewis, "Opinion of the Week: Prayers in School," *New York Times,* July 1, 1962, 113.

20. *School Prayers, Parts 1–3,* House Committee on Judiciary, 88th Congress, 2nd Sess., 1964.

21. Ed Cray, *Chief Justice: A Biography of Earl Warren* (New York: Simon & Schuster, 1997), 388.

22. *School Prayer, Part 1,* Senate Committee on the Judiciary, 88th Congress, 2nd Sess., 1964, 656.

23. *Congressional Record,* U.S. Senate, 87th Cong., 2nd sess., Sept. 20, 1966.

24. Marlo Thomas, *The Right Words at the Right Time* (New York: Atria Books, 2002), 91–95.

25. Igor I. Sikorsky, *The Message of the Lord's Prayer* (New York: Charles Scribner's Sons, 1942), i.

26. James D. Shaugnessy, ed., *The Roots of Ritual,* Margaret Mead, "Ritual and Social Crisis" (Grand Rapids, Michigan: William B. *Eerdmans,* 1973), 98.

27. Robert Cassidy, *Margaret Mead: A Voice for the Century* (New York: Universe Books, 1982), 139.

28. Karl Menninger, *Whatever Became of Sin?* (New York: Hawthorn Books, 1973), 228.

29. Ibid.

30. Todd S. Purdum, "Film Industry's Promoter Fades to Black," *New York Times*, April 11, 2004, A16.

31. Adele O. Brown, *What a Way to Go* (San Francisco: Chronicle Books, 2001), 69.

32. *Public Papers of the Presidents of the United States: Lyndon Baines Johnson*, vol. 1, Nov. 22, 1963–June 30, 1964 (Washington, D.C.: Government Printing Office, 1965), 261–65.

33. Helen Thomas, "Personal Presidential Anecdotes and The Press' Function in Society" (Fourth Sondock Lecture in Legal Ethics, University of Houston Law Center, Feb. 8, 2001).

34. *Congressional Quarterly Almanac*, 89th Cong., 1st sess., 1965, 21:479.

35. *Statistical Yearbook 1971*, National Technical Information Service (Washington, D.C.: U.S. Government Printing Office, 1972).

36. Marian Anderson, *My Lord What a Morning* (Madison: University of Wisconsin Press, 1992), 158.

37. Marian Anderson, "Grace before Greatness," *Guideposts*, March 1954, 1–4.

38. Robert Shelton, "Rights Soup Have Own History of Integration," *New York Times*, July 23, 1963, L22.

39. Gandhi, prayer speech, May 26, 1946. Gandhi Papers, Gandhiserve Foundation, Berlin, Germany.

40. Mervyn A. Warren, *King Came Preaching* (Downers Grove, Ill.: InterVarsity Press, 2001), 158.

41. Ibid., 16.

42. Ibid., 12–16.

43. Ibid., 136–37.

44. Ibid., 26.

45. Douglas Brinkley, "Creative and Conflicted Witness," *American History*, Aug. 2003, 51.

46. Lucy G. Barber, *Marching on Washington: The Forging of an American Political Tradition* (Berkeley: University of California Press, 2002), 168.

47. Edwin O. Guthman and C. Richard Allen, eds., *RFK: Collected Speeches* (New York: Viking Press, 1993), 356–57.

48. Arthur Krock, *Sixty Years on the Firing Line* (New York: Funk & Wagnalls, 1968), 348.

49. Edward M. Kennedy, "Tribute to Senator Robert F. Kennedy," St. Patrick's Cathedral, New York City, June 8, 1968, John F. Kennedy Library, Boston, Massachusetts, and *New York Times*, June 9, 1968, A1.

50. Hugh Hewitt, *Searching for God in America* (Dallas: Word Publishing, 1996), 434.

51. Cesar E. Chavez Foundation.

52. *Los Angeles Herald Tribune*, June 6, 1962, 1.

53. Alex Haley, *The Autobiography of Malcolm X* (New York: Ballantine Books, 1999), 331.

54. *Los Angeles Herald Tribune*, June 6, 1962, 1.

55. *Public Papers of the Presidents of the United States: John F. Kennedy*, January 20–December 31, 1961 (Washington, D.C.: Government Printing Office, 1962), 404.

56. John Glenn, *John Glenn: A Memoir* (New York: Bantam Books, 1999), 288.

57. Frank Borman submission to author, June 18, 2004.

58. McPherson, "To the Best of My Ability," 437.

59. Thomas Merton, *The Seven Storey Mountain* (New York: Harcourt Brace, 1998), 123.

60. Ibid., 362.

61. Thomas Merton, *Dialogues with Silence,* ed. Jonathan Montaldo (San Francisco: HarperCollins, 2001), xiii–xix.

62. Thomas Merton, *Contemplation in a World of Action* (Garden City, N.Y.: Doubleday, 1971), 333.

63. James Finley, *Merton's Palace of Nowhere* (Notre Dame, Ind.: Ave Maria Press, 1978), 111.

64. James H. Forest, *Living with Wisdom: A Life of Thomas Merton* (Maryknoll, N.Y.: Orbis Books, 1991), 14.

65. Dalai Lama, *Freedom in Exile: The Autobiography of the Dalai Lama* (New York: HarperCollins, 1990), 189.

66. Dorothy Day, *The Long Loneliness* (San Francisco: Harper & Row, 1952), 166.

67. David Scott, "Dorothy Day's Subversive Doctrine," *National Catholic Register,* Nov. 10–16, 2002, 9.

68. Douglas Hoffman, "From Maybeck to Megachurches" (lecture, American Institute of Architects, Minneapolis, 1996).

69. Hilary Lewis and John O'Connor, *Philip Johnson: The Architect in His Own Words* (New York: Rizzoli, 1994), 101.

70. Judith Dupré, *Churches* (New York: HarperCollins, 2001), 121.

71. Joan Peyser, *Bernstein: A Biography* (New York: Billboard Books, 1998), 24.

72. Charles Mingus, liner notes to *Blues and Roots,* Atlantic 1305, 1960.

73. John Coltrane, liner notes to *A Love Supreme,* Impulse A-77, 1965.

74. Interview with Jesse Meman, October 24, 2003.

75. Nick Jones, liner notes to *Classical Brubeck,* Derry Music, 2003, 6.

76. Stanley Dance, liner notes to *Duke Ellington's Concert of Sacred Music,* RCA LSP-3582, 1966.

77. Duke Ellington, *Music Is My Mistress* (Garden City, N.Y.: Doubleday, 1973), 266.

78. Ibid., 263.

79. John Edward Hasse, *Beyond Category: The Life and Genius of Duke Ellington* (New York: Da Capo Press, 1995), 385.

80. Interview, *New York Times,* Sept. 27, 1986, A6.

81. Alan Watts, *In My Own Way: An Autobiography, 1915–1965* (New York: Pantheon Books, 1972), 360.

82. Jim Morrison, *Jim Morrison's An American Prayer* (Baton Rouge, La.: Zeppelin Publishing Company, 1983), 26.

83. Michael Streissguth, ed., *Ring of Fire: The Johnny Cash Reader* (New York: DaCapo Press, 2002), 236.

84. Johnny Cash, *Cash: The Autobiography* (San Francisco: Harper, 1998), 277.

85. Larry King and Irwin Katsof, *Powerful Prayers* (Los Angeles: Renaissance Books, 1998), 43–44.

86. Ibid.

87. Phyllis Malamud, "An Interview with Isaac Bashevis Singer," Oct. 5, 1978, Isaac Bashevis Singer Centennial, Library of America.

88. Charles Schulz, *Peanuts,* in Robert L. Short, *The Gospel According to Peanuts* (Louisville, Ky.: Westminster John Knox Press, 2000), 94.

89. Bill Cosby, *Bill Cosby Is a Very Funny Fellow—Right!,* audio CD (Burbank, California: Warner Brothers, 1995).

90. Walt Disney, "Deeds Rather Than Words," in *Faith Is a Star,* ed. Roland Gammon (New York: E. P. Dutton, 1963), 7.

91. Ibid., 8–9.

92. Rod Drejer, "God and Soldiers," *National Review,* March 10, 2003, 31.

93. Claude D. Newby, *It Took Heroes: A Cavalry Chaplain's Memoir of Vietnam* (New York: Ballantine Books, 2000), 81.

94. Jeremiah A. Denton Jr., *When Hell Was in Session* (New York: Reader's Digest Press, 1967), 67.

95. Ibid., 135.

96. King and Katsof, *Powerful Prayers,* 212–13.

97. *Public Papers of the Presidents of the United States: Lyndon Johnson, 1968–1969,* vol. 1, January 1–June 30, 1968 (Washington, D.C.: Government Printing Office, 1970), 121–22.

98. Ben Hibbs, ed., *White House Sermons* (New York: Harper & Row, 1972), vi.

99. Ibid., viii.

100. Bob Woodward and Carl Bernstein, *The Final Days* (New York: Simon & Schuster, 1976), 403.

101. Ibid., 423.

102. Ibid., 422–24.

103. McPherson, *"To the Best of My Ability,"* 439.

104. *Public Papers of the Presidents of the United States: Richard Nixon, 1974,* January 1–Aug. 9, 1974 (Washington, D.C.: Government Printing Office, 1975), 629.

105. Ibid., 632.

15. THE CONTEMPORARIES: 1975–THE NEW MILLENNIUM

Epigraph: Frederick J. Ryan, Jr., ed., *Ronald Reagan: The Wisdom and Humor of the Great Communicator* (San Francisco: Collins Publishers, 1995), 115.

1. Larry King and Irwin Katsof, *Powerful Prayers* (Los Angeles: Renaissance Books, 1998), 68.

2. Gerald R. Ford, *Public Papers of the Presidents of the United States: Gerald R. Ford, August 9–December 31, 1974* (Washington, D.C.: U.S. Government Printing Office, 1975), 1–2.

3. Gerald R. Ford, *A Time to Heal* (New York: Harper & Row, 1979), 40.

4. King and Katsof, *Powerful Prayers,* 67.

5. Kenneth T. Walsh, *Air Force One: A History of the Presidents and Their Planes* (New York: Hyperion, 2003), 114.

6. Richard Reeves, *A Ford, Not a Lincoln* (New York: Harcourt Brace Jovanovich, 1975), 113.

7. Ford, *A Time to Heal,* 159.

8. *Public Papers of the Presidents of the United States: Gerald R. Ford, 1974,* August 9–December 31, 1974 (Washington, D.C.: Government Printing Office, 1975), 101–3.

9. King and Katsof, *Powerful Prayers,* 99.

10. Jimmy Carter, *Sources of Strength* (New York Times Books, 1997), 192.

11. Jimmy Carter, address to Southeastern Seminar of the President's Prayer Breakfast, Washington, D.C., Feb. 2, 1971, press release, executive documents 1–10–43, box 3, Georgia Department of Archives and History, Atlanta.

12. Carter, *Personal Beliefs,* 97–98.

13. Ibid., 98.

14. King and Katsof, *Powerful Prayers,* 70.

15. Jimmy Carter, "The Second Sadat Lecture for Peace" (University of Maryland, College Park, Oct. 25, 1998).

16. King and Katsof, *Powerful Prayers*, 71.

17. Ibid., 72.

18. *Public Papers of the Presidents of the United States: Ronald Reagan*, 1981, January 20–December 31, 1981 (Washington, D.C.: Government Printing Office, 1982), 268–69.

19. Ronald Reagan, *Reagan: A Life in Letters* (New York: Free Press, 2003), 279.

20. Paul Kengor, *God and Ronald Reagan: A Spiritual Life* (New York: Regan Books, 2004), 158.

21. Peter Robinson, *How Ronald Reagan Changed My Life* (New York: Regan Books, 2003), 187.

22. *Public Papers of the Presidents of the United States: Ronald Reagan*, 1982, vol. 1, January 1–July 2, 1982 (Washington, D.C.: Government Printing Office, 1983), 108–10.

23. Kengor, *God and Ronald Reagan*, 429.

24. Ibid., 435.

25. *Public Papers of the Presidents of the United States: Ronald Reagan*, 1983, vol. 1, January 1–July 1, 1983 (Washington, D.C.: Government Printing Office, 1984), 359–64.

26. *Public Papers of the Presidents of the United States: Ronald Reagan*, 1986, January 1–June 27, 1986 (Washington, D.C.: Government Printing Office, 1988), 94–95.

27. *Journal of the Senate*, Kansas Legislature 1995–1996, Topeka, Kansas, January 23, 1996, 2.

28. Michael Deaver, *A Different Drummer* (New York: HarperCollins, 2001), 146.

29. *Wallace v. Jaffree*, 472 U.S. 38 (1985) and "Wallace v. Jaffree," in *The Oxford Companion to the Supreme Court of the United States*, ed. Kermit L. Hall (New York: Oxford University Press, 1992), 907–8.

30. Jamin B. Raskin, *We the Students: Supreme Court Cases for and about Students* (Washington, D.C.: CQ Press, 2000), 85.

31. Ibid., 91.

32. Ibid., 95.

33. Jerry Markon, "Federal Court Upholds Its Ban in VMI Prayers," *Washington Post*, Aug. 14, 2003, B1.

34. David J. Wolpe, *In Speech and in Silence: The Jewish Quest for God* (New York: H. Holt, 1992), 151.

35. George Bush, "Rhetoric and the Presidency" (lecture, Texas A&M, Dec. 2, 1996).

36. King and Katsof, *Powerful Prayers*, 73.

37. James M. McPherson, ed., *"To the Best of My Ability": The American Presidents* (New York: Dorling Kindersley, 2000), 448.

38. Jim McGrath, ed., *Heartbeat: George Bush in His Own Words* (New York: Scribner, 2001), 20.

39. Ibid., 209–10.

40. Ibid., 134.

41. Nancy Gibbs, "A First Thick Shock of War," *Time*, Jan. 28, 1991, 34–37.

42. Ibid., 34–37.

43. Statistics, U.S. Department of Defense.

44. George H. W. Bush, Proclamation 6257 of March 7, 1991, Federal Register, vol. 56, no. 47, Monday, March 11, 1991.

45. Bill Clinton, *My Life* (New York: Alfred A. Knopf, 2004), 249.

46. Ibid., 260.

47. *Public Papers of the Presidents of the United States: William Jefferson Clinton*, Book 1, January 1–June 30, 1997 (Washington, D.C.: Government Printing Office, 1998), 43–46.

48. Ibid.

49. *Public Papers of the Presidents of the United States: William J. Clinton*, 1998, vol. 2, July 1–December 31, 1998 (Washington, D.C.: Government Printing Office, 2000), 1565–66.

50. Hillary Rodham Clinton, *Living History* (New York: Simon & Schuster, 2003), 167.

51. King and Katsof, *Powerful Prayers*, 147.

52. Starbucks Coffee Company, fiscal 2002 annual report.

53. King and Katsof, *Powerful Prayers*, 147.

54. Ibid., 149.

53. Ibid., 150.

56. Robert L. Herrmann, *Sir John Templeton: From Wall Street to Humility Theology* (Philadelphia: Templeton Foundation Press, 1998), 142.

57. Bruce Wilkinson, *The Prayer of Jabez* (Sisters, Oreg.: Multnomah, 2000), 27.

58. Angie Kiesling, " 'Jabez' Enlarges Multnomah's Territory," *Publishers Weekly*, April 1, 2002, 8–16.

59. "Cyberspace: How Americans Pursue Religion Online," Pew Internet and American Life Project, Pew Research Center, Dec. 23, 2001.

60. Dean Hamer, *The God Gene: How Faith Is Hardwired into Our Genes* (New York: Doubleday, 2004).

61. Diane Halles, "Why Prayer Could Be Good Medicine," *Parade*, March 23, 2003, 4.

62. Yankelovich Partners, 1997 survey.

63. R. A. Hummer, R. G. Rogers, C. B. Nam, and C. G. Ellison, "Religious Involvement and U.S. Adult Mortality," *Demography* 36 (1999): 273–85.

64. Mary Jacobs, "Treating the Body and Spirit: Religion Gaining Role in Healing Process," *Washington Post*, Sept. 6, 2003, 89.

65. Kenneth E. Hyde, *Religion in Childhood and Adolescence* (Birmingham, Ala.: Religious Education Press, 1990).

66. "So Help Me God: Substance Abuse, Religion and Spirituality," The National Center on Addiction and Substance Abuse at Columbia University, November 2001.

67. Robert Coles, *The Spiritual Life of Children* (Boston: Houghton Mifflin, 1990), 303–35.

68. David O. Moberg, ed., *Aging and Spirituality: Spiritual Dimensions of Aging Theory, Research, Practice, and Policy* (New York: Haworth Pastoral Press, 2001), 3–18.

69. Evan Thomas, *The Man to See: Edward Bennett Williams* (New York: Simon and Schuster, 1991), 136.

70. Jon Pareles, "Reaping the Myriad Whims and Quirks of Aretha Franklin," *New York Times*, Sept. 22, 2003, B5.

71. Jon Ward, "Christian Quandary," *Washington Times*, Aug. 14, 2003, 2.

72. Tupac Shakur, *The Rose That Grew from Concrete* (New York: Pocket Books, 1999), 32–33.

73. Oprah Winfrey, "O Talks to Muhammad Ali," *O Magazine*, June 2001, 34–36.

74. Stephen Buttry, "Candidates Focus on Christian Beliefs," *Des Moines Register*, Dec. 15, 1999, 1.

75. Michael Medved, "The Left Prays, but the Right Pays," *Wall Street Journal*, Aug. 11, 2000, 36.

76. Joseph Lieberman, speech at the launching of the Pew Forum on Religion and Public Life, Washington, D.C., March 1, 2001.

77. George W. Bush, inaugural address, Jan. 20, 2001, The White House.

78. Bill Broadway, "God's Place on the Dais," *Washington Post*, Jan. 27, 2001, B9.

79. George W. Bush, *A Charge to Keep* (New York: William Morrow, 1999), 136.

80. David Frum, *The Right Man: The Surprise Presidency of George W. Bush* (New York: Random House, 2003), 283.

81. Elsa Walsh, "Profiles: The Prince," *New Yorker*, March 24, 2003, 62–63.

16. THE INNOCENTS: SEPTEMBER 11, 2001, AND BEYOND

Epigraph: Christian Rénoux, *La Priere Poor la Paix Attribuée à Saint Francois: Une Enigme à Ré Soudre* (Paris: Les Editions Franciscaines, 2001), 3.

1. National Commission on Terrorist Attacks Upon the United States, *The 9/11 Commission Report* (New York: W.W. Norton, 2004), XVI, 47.

2. Ibid., 47.

3. "Notes and Asides—Transcripts of Cell Phone Calls by Flight 93 Hero Tom Burnett," *National Review*, May 20, 2002, p. 5.

4. Lisa Beamer with Ken Abraham, *Let's Roll!* (Wheaton, Ill.: Tyndale House Publishers, 2002), 189–217.

5. www.saintmychal.com/life.01.htm.

6. "Personality Parade," *Parade*, Jan. 6, 2002, 2.

7. Jennifer Senior, "The Fireman's Friar," *New York*, Nov. 12, 2001, 36.

8. Daniel J. Wakin, "Killed on 9/11, Fire Chaplain Becomes Larger Than Life," *New York Times*, Sept. 27, 2002, A1.

9. Rudolph Giuliani, press conference, 6:00 p.m., Police Academy, New York City, Sept. 11, 2001.

10. Dean E. Murphy, "Slowly Families Accept the Ruins as Burial Grounds," *New York Times*, September 29, 2001, B1.

11. Alan Cooperman, "Across the Nation, Christian 'Prayer Warriors' Join Battle," *Washington Post*, March 21, p. A25.

12. John Farina, *Beauty for Ashes: Spiritual Reflections on the Attack on America* (New York: Crossroad, 2001), 29.

13. U.S. Senate, 107th Congress, 1st Sess., *Congressional Record*, September 12, 2001, S 9283.

14. U.S. House, 107th Congress, 1st Sess., Congressional Record, September 12, 2001, H 5493.

15. *Public Papers of the Presidents of the United States: George W. Bush*, vol. 2, July 1–December 31, 2001 (Washington, D.C.: Government Printing Office, 2003), 1108–9.

16. Donald Rumsfeld, "A Prayer and a Pledge," *Washington Times*, Sept. 15, 2001, A1.

17. Program, Washington National Cathedral, Sept. 14, 2001.

18. *Public Papers of the Presidents of the United States: George W. Bush*, vol. 2, July 1–December 31, 2001 (Washington, D.C.: Government Printing Office, 2003), 1108–9.

19. "America Enduring," *New York Times*, Sept. 11, 2002, A32.

20. Robert Coles, *Bruce Springsteen's America* (New York: Random House, 2003), 184.

21. Diana L. Eck, "A New Religious America: Managing Religious Diversity

in a Democracy" (keynote address at the MAAS International Conference on Religious Pluralism in Democratic Societies, Kuala Lumpur, Malaysia, Aug. 20–21, 2002).

22. Alan Cooperman, "New York Lutheran Leader Suspended," *Washington Post,* July 6, 2002, 2.

23. Ibid.

24. "How Did You Pray This Year?" *Christian Science Monitor,* Sept. 12, 2002, 11.

25. Address by President George W. Bush on Ellis Island, *Washington Post,* Sept. 12, 2002, A34.

26. Bob Woodward, "U.S. Aimed for Hussein as War Began," *Washington Post,* April 22, 2004, A1.

27. Ibid., A19.

28. Bernard Weinraub, "The Battlefield Mood: Rosaries and Bibles in Demand as Troops Face War," *New York Times,* March 20, 2003, A14.

29. Oliver North, ed., *A Greater Freedom: Stories of Faith from Operation Iraqi Freedom* (Nashville, Broadman and Holman, 2004), 26.

30. Ibid., 60.

31. Ibid., 48.

32. Claude D. Newby, *It Took Heroes: A Calvary Chaplain's Memoir of Vietnam* (New York: Ballantine Books, 2000), 521–22.

33. "Poll: Americans Comfortable with Politicians' Religious Rhetoric," The Pew Forum on Religion and Public Life, Jan. 6, 2004.

34. Nancy Gibbs, "Faith, God, and the Oval Office," *Time,* June 21, 2004, 29.

35. Douglas Brinkley, *Tour of Duty: John Kerry and the Vietnam War* (New York: William Morrow, 2004), 28.

36. Tom Shales, "Kerry Wins the Race—Against the Networks' Clock," *Washington Post,* July 30, 2004, C7.

37. National Prayer Breakfast.

38. "In Their Own Words: An Interview with John Edwards," Interfaith Alliance Press Release, Washington, D.C., Dec. 3, 2003.

39. Elizabeth Bernstein, "All the Candidates' Clergy," *Wall Street Journal,* Aug. 13, 2004, W1.

40. "Performances of the Week," *Time,* Aug. 9, 2004, 20.

41. John Kerry, "Acceptance Speech," *New York Times,* July 30, 2004, P7.

42. "Voters Liked Campaign 2004, But 'Too Much Mud-slinging'—Moral Values: How Important" (Washington, D.C.: Pew Research Center for the People and the Press, Nov. 11, 2004), 3.

43. George W. Bush, "The Inaugural Address," *New York Times,* Jan. 21, 2005, A16–17.

44. Bill Sammon, "Evangelist Graham Credits God for Re-election of President," *Washington Times,* Jan. 22, 2005, A1.

45. Bill Sammon, "'U.S. Should Be Open to God's Priorities,'" *Washington Times,* Feb. 4, 2005, A1.

46. Ibid., A112.

47. "Moment of Silence: From across the Spectrum of America's Religions, They Pray," *New York Times,* photographs by Gueorgui Pinkhassov, 27.

48. Ibid., 36.

49. James H. Billington, "Culture, Memory, and Technology," *Sewanee Review* 109, no. 2 (Spring 2001): 218–26.

50. Kevin Iole, "Keeping the Faith," *Las Vegas Review-Journal,* Feb. 20, 2002, B1.

51. Ibid., B5.

52. Deri Sridar, interview, Oct. 2002.

53. Jeff Coleman, interview, Oct. 2002.

54. Sister Clare, interview, Oct. 2002.

55. Jane Lampman, "How America Prays," *Christian Science Monitor,* Sept. 12, 2002, 13.

56. Roy P. Basler, ed., *The Collected Works of Abraham Lincoln, 1860–1861,* vol. IV, 271.

INDEX

Photo by Bachrach

JAMES P. MOORE, JR., resides in Washington, D.C., where he teaches at the McDonough School of Business at Georgetown University. He is a graduate of the Kiski School, Rutgers University, and the Graduate School of Public and International Affairs at the University of Pittsburgh. The former U.S. Assistant Secretary of Commerce for Trade Development, he was also an active member of such government boards as the National Air and Space Museum of the Smithsonian Institution, the U.S. Overseas Private Investment Corporation, the Export Import Bank of the United States, and the Committee on Foreign Investment of the United States. He has also sat on more than two dozen corporate and nonprofit boards, and has lectured at major universities across the country.